**SAGE** was founded in 1965 by Sara Miller McCune to support the dissemination of usable knowledge by publishing innovative and high-quality research and teaching content. Today, we publish over 900 journals, including those of more than 400 learned societies, more than 800 new books per year, and a growing range of library products including archives, data, case studies, reports, and video. SAGE remains majority-owned by our founder, and after Sara's lifetime will become owned by a charitable trust that secures our continued independence.

Los Angeles | London | New Delhi | Singapore | Washington DC | Melbourne

# A TEXTBOOK OF MICROECONOMIC THEORY

# A TEXTBOOK OF MICROECONOMIC THEORY

Pankaj Tandon

*Boston University*

SAGE | TEXTS

Los Angeles | London | New Delhi
Singapore | Washington DC | Melbourne

*First published in 2015 by*

SAGE | TEXTS

**SAGE Publications India Pvt Ltd**
B1/I-1 Mohan Cooperative Industrial Area
Mathura Road, New Delhi 110 044, India
*www.sagepub.in*

**SAGE Publications Inc**
2455 Teller Road
Thousand Oaks, California 91320, USA

**SAGE Publications Ltd**
1 Oliver's Yard, 55 City Road
London EC1Y 1SP, United Kingdom

**SAGE Publications Asia-Pacific Pte Ltd**
3 Church Street
#10-04 Samsung Hub
Singapore 049483

Published by Vivek Mehra for SAGE Publications India Pvt Ltd, typeset in 10/13 pt Humanist777-BT by PrePSol Entreprises Private Limited, New Delhi.

**Library of Congress Cataloging-in-Publication Data**

Tandon, Pankaj.
A textbook of microeconomic theory / Pankaj Tandon.
pages cm
Includes bibliographical references and index.
1. Microeconomics. I. Title.
HB172.T36 338.5—dc23 2015 2015012630

ISBN: 978-93-515-0275-3 (PB)

---

**The SAGE Team:** Amit Kumar, Indrani Dutta, Vandana Gupta, Anju Saxena and Rajinder Kaur

*To my partner in life,*
*Karen Clark,*
*and to our three beautiful daughters,*
*Olivia, Xandra and Lily*

# CONTENTS

# PREFACE

This book had its origin in a challenge thrown down to me many years ago by a colleague whose identity I have now sadly forgotten. I was expressing my dissatisfaction with all the available textbooks on Intermediate Microeconomics with Calculus and this colleague said something to the effect, 'If you don't like any of the books, why don't you write one yourself? There may be others like you who are equally dissatisfied with the available books, and you might be doing them a service.' Until that time, I had always thought that people wrote textbooks solely to make money; I had never considered the possibility that one might be serving others by doing so. It was in that moment that I began to entertain the thought of writing this book.

At the same time, it had always seemed odd to me that Indian students had to study Economics using textbooks from the West. At least in my student days, the only textbooks that Indian authors seemed to be writing were 'mug books' of little redeeming value. As I thought of writing a textbook, the idea of addressing a version of it to Indian students seemed like a logical thing to do. The book you hold in your hands is the result of these two streams of thought.

The content of the book is an expression of the style of course that I have developed over 30 plus years of teaching. Obviously, many individuals have played roles in helping me develop this style, and I would like to acknowledge my debt to them. My earliest Microeconomics teacher was N.C. Ray (Ray Sahib) at St Stephen's College, and no doubt my interest in the subject owes much to him. This interest was further inspired by my other teachers: Prasanta Pattanaik at the Delhi School of Economics and Kenneth Arrow at Harvard University. I also learned a lot about how to *teach* Microeconomics from Abram Bergson, when I served as the Teaching Assistant for his undergraduate class at Harvard.

My greatest debt, however, is to the many generations of students at Boston University whom I have had the privilege to teach. Their questions and comments constantly forced me to deepen my own understanding of Microeconomics, and many of the original graphs and derivations I offer here were developed in answer to their questions. Two students I would particularly like to mention are Emily Mechner and Kaiwen Leong. Their probing questions helped me to sharpen my exposition, and both of them generously let me photocopy their class notes from my course, which helped me to form an early skeleton of this book. A discussion with Josh Lanier was particularly helpful to me in the development of the graphical exposition of externalities presented in Chapter 12. Nikolai Skievaski actually got me going by starting to type up an early draft of Chapter 2, and I owe him a debt of gratitude. Philip Cherian typed up the first draft of Chapter 3. Vikram Vyas introduced me to and helped me learn LyX, the program I finally used to type up the whole manuscript. Finally, I owe much to Mary Fleming, whose workshop on Procrastination played a significant role in helping me overcome my tendency to put off those tasks that I did not particularly enjoy.

Over the years, I have read and prescribed different textbooks, and no doubt those books have also left their mark on this draft. These texts include P.R.G. Layard and A.A. Walters: *Microeconomic Theory*, Walter Nicholson: *Microeconomic Theory: Basic Principles and Extensions*, Hal Varian: *Intermediate Microeconomics: A Modern Approach* and *Microeconomic Analysis* and B. Douglas Bernheim and Michael D. Whinston: *Microeconomics.* I am also grateful for the valuable comments I received from the reviewers of the draft of this text: Professor P.G. Babu (Indira Gandhi Institute of Development Research [IGIDR], Mumbai), Dr Soumyanetra Munshi (IGIDR, Mumbai) and Dr Swati Raju (Department of Economics, University of Mumbai).

Many of the problems at the end of the chapters have been adapted from examinations given at Boston University. I would like to thank Randy Ellis, Haldun Evrenk, Bart Lipman, Ashley Miller, Greg Pavlov and Bjorn Persson for permission to use problems that they devised.

The first draft of this book was written during the 2011–12 academic year, when I taught the second year Microeconomics course at St Stephen's College. I spent the year there as a Fulbright–Nehru Fellow on sabbatical leave from Boston University and the financial support provided by the Fulbright–Nehru Program and Boston University is gratefully acknowledged. In addition, St Stephen's College provided me with a very congenial atmosphere in which to live and work; this support is also acknowledged with gratitude. Since that year, I have used successive drafts of this book as the required text in three cohorts of classes at Boston University, and the text has undergone much improvement as a consequence of the suggestions of students in those classes. Anonymous evaluations of the text by those students have been gratifyingly positive; my hope is that future readers will have an equally positive response to it. And I hope those readers who have suggestions for improvements to this book will email me with their ideas at ptandon@bu.edu.

# ABOUT THE AUTHOR

Pankaj Tandon is an associate professor of economics at Boston University. He received his PhD degree in economics from Harvard University in the year 1979. He is a graduate of St Stephen's College and the Delhi School of Economics, where he was the gold medalist in 1973. He has been teaching at Boston University since 1978, where he has won two teaching awards. His main areas of interest are microeconomic theory, cost-benefit analysis, economics of public enterprise, economics of technological change, mathematical methods for economists, economic statistics, economics of information, international economics and economics of less developed countries. He co-authored *The Welfare Consequences of Selling Public Enterprises: An Empirical Analysis* (1994) and *Selling Public Enterprises: A Cost-Benefit Methodology* (1990). He has served as a consultant to the World Bank and the Asian Development Bank.

CHAPTER

1

# Introduction to Microeconomic Theory

Economics is the study of those human activities that determine the production and distribution of goods and services in society. **Microeconomics** is that branch of Economics that attempts to understand economic activity by studying the behaviour of the individual decision-makers in the economy. The idea is that what happens in the economy as a whole is the result of the sum total of actions of these individual decision-makers and the interactions between them.

Much, though by no means all, of the economic activity in modern economies takes place through the medium of markets. A **market** is any mechanism by which buyers and sellers of goods and services can carry out their transactions. Traditionally, of course, a market was a physical place where sellers would set up their wares and buyers would come and make their purchases. Such markets continue to exist. But, in modern times, such markets see only a small proportion of the transactions in an economy, most of which are carried out through the various forms of modern communications technology. For example, a stock exchange was traditionally a place where buyers and sellers (mostly acting on behalf of others) could gather to make trades, but today the vast majority of stock transactions take place on computer networks. Building a factory involves no visits to a 'market' to buy the machinery, but putting out tenders and receiving bids. The same is true for most large transactions. Thus the notion of what constitutes a market has taken on quite a different cast.

The most important aspect of any market is the price at which trades take place and therefore one of the most central questions in Microeconomics is to understand how prices are determined. Some economists in fact refer to Microeconomics as 'Price Theory'. The Nobel laureate Milton Friedman's Microeconomics textbook was titled *Price Theory* and the Nobel laureate George Stigler's was called *The Theory of Price*. In fact, although Microeconomics does examine questions other than how prices are determined, the analysis of prices is certainly at its heart.

Apart from the question of how prices are determined (questions of **positive economics**), Microeconomics is also concerned with questions of what prices *should* be (questions of **normative economics**). These kinds of questions make Microeconomics far more meaningful, as we draw out the 'policy implications' of the theory. Ultimately, these questions help us ask and attempt to answer the truly 'big picture' questions regarding the best way to organise the economy in any society.

## 1.1 THE TWO CENTRAL IDEAS OF MICROECONOMICS

The two most important ideas in Microeconomics are the ones that define the basic approaches to answer the two sets of questions just outlined: questions of positive economics and questions of normative economics.

### 1.1.1 Marshall's Demand–Supply Cross

What determines the price (or 'value') of a good or service? This question was hotly debated in the eighteenth and nineteenth centuries and many different answers were offered in a highly confusing discussion. Perhaps the two most important schools of thought focused on one or the other of the two sides of the market. In modern terms, one view claimed that the price of a good depended on its cost of production; Marx's Labour Theory of Value is one of the expositions of this view. The other view focused on the demand side of the market, claiming that the price of a good was based on its 'value in use', that is, on what people were willing to pay for it.

The resolution of this debate was provided by the Cambridge economist Alfred Marshall in his book *Principles of Economics*, published in 1890. Marshall's key insight was that the price of a good or service is determined not just by what it costs to produce (the supply price), nor just by what people were willing to pay for it (the demand price), but rather by the *interaction* of the two. In retrospect, it seems obvious that this should be true, but, at the time that Marshall was writing, this was a huge breakthrough. Much of the theory of price determination in Microeconomics is based upon this insight. Basically, Marshall taught us that we need to understand the behaviour of both the buyers and the sellers in any market in order to understand the determinants of prices in that market.

Marshall organised the behaviour of buyers and sellers into *demand curves* and *supply curves*. A **market demand curve** shows how much of a good or service could be sold in a market at different prices. The most widely expected form of the demand curve is depicted in panel (a) of Figure 1.1, where the horizontal axis measures the quantity of the good and the vertical axis shows the price. In general, we expect the demand curve to be downward-sloping as in the figure, that is, that people will want to buy more of any good or service at lower prices than they would at higher prices. The basic task of Consumer Theory, discussed in Chapter 2, is to explain why this is so. A **market supply curve** shows how much of a good or service suppliers of a good would be willing and able to sell at different prices. A typical supply curve is shown in panel (b) of Figure 1.1. In general, we expect this to be upward-sloping, indicating that suppliers would like to sell more of a good at higher, rather than lower, prices. Why exactly this is so is the main subject of Chapter 5.

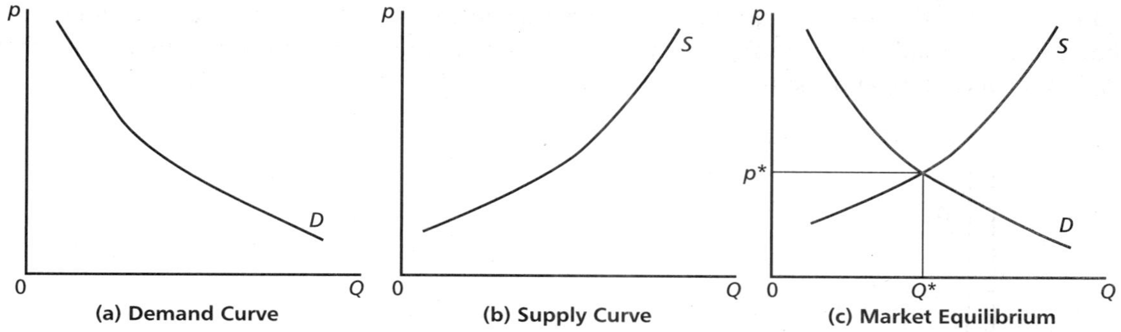


**Figure 1.1** *Marshall's Demand–Supply Cross*

Panel (c) of Figure 1.1 depicts Marshall's key insight. He argued that the relevant price in any market would be the **equilibrium price**, that is, the price at which both buyers and sellers in the market would be content with the situation. The concept of equilibrium is of great importance in Economics and one that we will use throughout this book. It denotes a state in which the forces present in any situation are in such a balance that the situation would remain unchanged until some new force was applied to it. For example, a small ball placed inside a round-bottomed bowl would settle into an equilibrium at the bottom of the bowl and would remain there until it was moved. In the same way, an equilibrium price in a market would be one which would remain unchanged until something in the market (say the level of demand or the supply conditions) changed. Marshall argued that the equilibrium price in any market would be the price at which demand and supply were equal. This is shown as the price $p^*$ in Figure 1.1. At prices above this, supply would exceed demand and competition amongst sellers would cause prices to fall. At prices below $p^*$, demand would exceed supply and sellers would find that they could raise prices without losing customers. Only when the price was at $p^*$ would demand and supply be in balance and there would be no tendency for the price to change unless the underlying conditions changed. This, therefore, should be seen as the 'price' or 'value' of the good.

Marshall's resolution of the debate on the theory of value basically settled that debate and continues to be considered valid today. For example, it neatly explained one of the examples that had been used repeatedly in the prior debate: the so-called diamond–water paradox. The paradox is this: how is it that water, which is absolutely essential to life, is so cheap, while diamonds, which are just decorative and serve no essential purpose, are so expensive? Marshall's resolution of this paradox is illustrated in Figure 1.2, where the water market is depicted in panel (a) and the diamond market in panel (b). Reflecting the life-giving importance of water, the demand curve for the precious resource might reflect a very high willingness-to-pay (the height of the demand curve in the figure) at low levels of consumption, which represent the demand for drinking water and water for cooking, but then falls rapidly as the less essential uses of water come into play. Meanwhile, the cost of producing water might be relatively low, which is reflected in a supply curve that is relatively low in the graph. The equilibrium price then, $p_w^*$, is relatively low. The diamond market, on the other hand, might reflect a demand curve that is relatively flat and a supply curve that is relatively high in the graph, reflecting a high cost of production. The equilibrium price then, $p_d^*$, is relatively high, and the paradox is resolved.

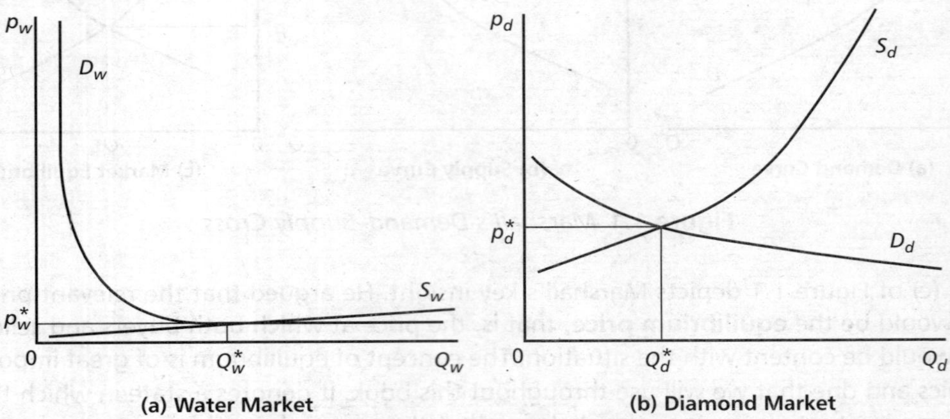


**Figure 1.2** *The Water–Diamond Paradox Resolved*

Marshall's analysis of price via demand and supply is the basic theoretical underpinning of Positive (or Descriptive) Microeconomics. Much of the first half of this book is a fleshing out of Marshall's insight. Chapters 2–4 look at the behaviour of consumers, the agents who provide the final demand for goods and services in the economy. Chapter 5 examines the basic behaviour of firms or the producers of goods and services. Chapter 6 then examines the interaction of buyers and sellers in 'perfectly competitive' individual markets and Chapter 7 extends the discussion of individual markets to the whole economy.

It is worth noting that, while the demand–supply model may have been a good model for the diamond market when Marshall was writing, it would not be a good description of the diamond market today. Demand and supply curves are drawn for and are only valid in the particular circumstance of **perfectly competitive markets**. The key aspect of such markets is that each buyer and each seller in the market is such a small part of the whole market as to have no substantive influence on the price. In other words, all buyers and sellers are **price-takers**, meaning that they believe they can buy or sell any amount within their range of possibilities without affecting the price. This is certainly not true in the diamond market today, dominated as it is by the South African company De Beers. Therefore, the description of the diamond market today would have to be modified to reflect the market position of De Beers. Other markets where individual firms (or, rarely, consumers) have market power would similarly need a revised analysis. Analysis of such markets is developed in Chapters 9–11. What we see is that the basic approach of analysing markets by clarifying the behaviour of buyers and sellers remains the same, the way to model that behaviour changes when the agents under consideration have (and exercise) their market power.

### 1.1.2 The Invisible Hand Theorem

The second central idea of Microeconomics, which forms the theoretical underpinning for Normative Microeconomics (or Welfare Economics), is the idea that has come to be called the Invisible Hand Theorem. It is associated with the Scottish economist Adam Smith, although there is a debate about whether Smith truly meant by his analysis of the so-called 'invisible hand' what it has come to mean today. In all probability, he did not. Be that as it may, this idea has nevertheless grown into one of the central tenets of Microeconomics. In his book *An Inquiry into the Nature and Causes of the Wealth of Nations*, published in 1776, Smith discussed how, under certain circumstances, individuals pursuing their own private self-interest, and having no particular goal of serving the common good, seem to be guided as if by an invisible hand to do what is in the social interest. Smith was talking about a very narrow situation, but others took up the idea and have built the edifice of modern General Equilibrium Theory, which argues that, under a certain set of conditions, a competitive market economy will, through the self-interested actions of consumers and producers, generate an 'allocation of resources' that is 'efficient'.

There are a number of technical terms in the previous sentence and much of the first half of this book is devoted to spelling out their precise meaning. For our purposes here, we could simply note that an 'allocation of resources' is a complete description of the organisation of an economy—it would specify what is being produced and in what quantity, how production is organised and how the produced goods and services are distributed amongst consumers. And when an allocation of resources is 'efficient', it is satisfying a minimal definition of desirability. Thus, what the Invisible Hand Theorem says is that, under certain conditions, a market system organises the economy in a way that is 'good', albeit in a somewhat limited sense.

The mechanism by which the market economy achieves this efficient allocation of resources is the set of prices generated in the markets. Organising the economy is a highly complex task that requires a considerable amount of information to carry out properly. Consider the problem faced in a non-market 'planned' economy such as the Soviet Union during much of the twentieth century. The planners drawing up their plans for the economy had to decide how much of each good to produce. Given the complex interrelationships between different sectors of the economy, this proved to be a very difficult task, as they needed to know the detailed input requirements for each type of production process. For example, the production of steel needs inputs of iron ore, coal, electricity, steel (for making steel-making equipment) and so on, and each of those inputs needs steel in its production process. This would be true of every good that was needed in the production processes for other goods. Further, the planners had to guess what consumers wanted. In a rather static world, this might not have been much of a problem since there might not have been much of a change in the levels of demand from year to year.

But in a world where change is rapid, where tastes are in a constant state of flux and where new products are appearing at a steady rate, it is not easy to anticipate what consumers are going to want to buy. In sum, the planning authority needed large amounts of detailed production information from all the production units in the economy and had to correctly anticipate trends in consumer demand. It would be an understatement to say the problem turned out to be extremely difficult. The inability of the Soviet planning department to set sensible production targets was one of the reasons why the Soviet Union was unable to grow or even survive as a prosperous economy.

The market economy, on the other hand, requires each consumer and producer to know only the details of their own situation. A consumer needs to know what goods satisfy her needs. A producer needs to know which inputs he needs in his own production process. What the Invisible Hand Theorem tells us is that, under certain conditions, consumers and producers seeking to pursue their own self-interest end up conveying their information to the markets through the medium of the market prices and that, as a result, the organisation of the economy that emerges is a desirable one from the social point of view. Prices are the 'invisible hand' that guides consumers and producers to act in the social interest. Since prices are determined, as we saw in the previous section, by the interaction of demand and supply, all the relevant information gets embodied into the prices that emerge in the markets. Details of how the market economy achieves an efficient allocation of resources are spelled out in Chapter 7 of this book.

The astute reader would have noticed that the Invisible Hand Theorem was said to apply only under certain conditions and that Chapter 7 is only midway through the book. The fact is that the Invisible Hand Theorem is not the culmination of Microeconomics, but rather its midway point. The conditions for a 'perfectly competitive economy' that the Invisible Hand Theorem requires are highly idealised and are seldom, if ever, satisfied in the real world. Understanding the behaviour of agents in markets that are 'imperfect' is necessary to get true insights into the world as it actually exists around us, and this is the task taken up in the second half of the book. Just as the frictionless system of Physics is an idealised model for the world as it actually exists, the perfectly competitive model of Microeconomics is a benchmark against which the behaviour of the actual market economy can be judged. The second half of this book points out many of the ways in which real market economies fall short of the ideal conditions required by the Invisible Hand Theorem. To what extent the theorem then applies to and helps us understand the real economy will be for readers to judge for themselves.

## 1.2 THINKING LIKE AN ECONOMIST

Students often ask what are the key things they need to learn in this course. Apart from the two key ideas described in the previous section, and the variations around those themes, a hoped-for important takeaway for readers of this book is to learn to think like an economist. In this section, we will look at three important ways in which economists think differently than do most people.

### 1.2.1 Think on the Margin

One of the most fundamental aspects of an economist's way of thinking is to think on the margin. Most people tend to think in terms of averages or totals rather than margins. We saw a perfect example of that in the discussion around Marshall's demand–supply model for the determination of prices. One of the sources of confusion in the discussion of 'value' prior to Marshall was the tendency of people to think in terms of averages. In the diamond–water paradox, for example, water was seen as essential and therefore it was thought its value should be high. Implicitly, that sort of thinking is based on a notion of the average value of water. What Marshall pointed out was that the price in a market is determined not by the *average* value of the good to consumers or the *average* cost of production, but by the value of the *marginal* (or 'last') unit of the good to consumers and the *marginal* cost of production for producers (the additional cost in producing the 'last' unit). Thus, we should expect the price of water to reflect the value to consumers of the last unit of water they consume (the 'marginal' unit) rather than the average unit.

To be more specific, consider the shape of the demand curve for water, which was drawn in the previous section as downward-sloping. Why is it downward-sloping? Consider the demand curve drawn in Figure 1.3. Now water has many uses. Obviously the most important use is for drinking and the value of water for this use is quite high. People would, if they had to, pay quite a lot for water when they need it for drinking. And this is reflected in the height of their demand curve. Thus the height of a demand curve at any level of consumption reflects what the consumer is willing to pay for that unit of consumption. Suppose the demand for wa-

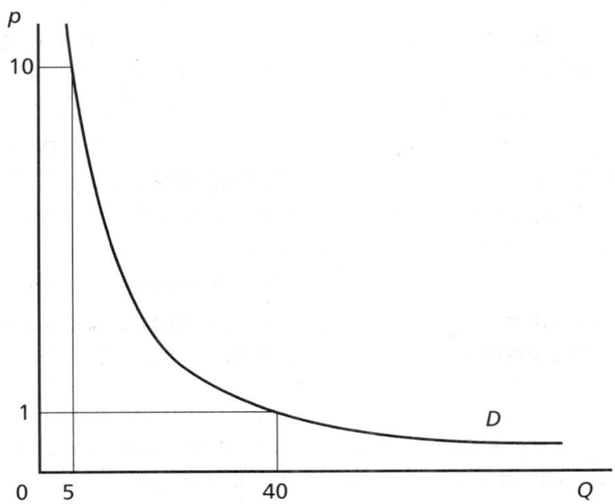


**Figure 1.3** *A Demand Curve*

ter is 5 units if the price is ₹10. That means that the fifth unit of water is worth at least ₹10, but the sixth unit of water is worth less than that. That's why the consumer would not buy a sixth unit at that price. Thus the level of demand at any price represents the value to the consumer of the *marginal* unit. ₹10 is not the average value of the first five units, but the value of the fifth unit (the marginal unit). In the same way, ₹1 is the value of the 40th unit as drawn in Figure 1.3.

A similar explanation underlies the supply curve. The 'cost' of producing a good that is relevant is the cost of the last unit produced, the *marginal* unit. The 'Marginal Revolution' that followed the publication of Marshall's book has permeated all aspects of Economics. And we will see the application of the marginal principle throughout the book. This is one of the key ways in which economists think differently from everyone else.

### 1.2.2 Think in Terms of Opportunities

Suppose Indrani decides to try her hand at starting a prepared food business. She buys a whole lot of ingredients for ₹1,000, spends all day cooking and then takes all the food she has prepared to the market where she manages to sell it for ₹1,200. Was her business a success? Many people would answer yes, because she made a profit of ₹200. But an economist would say: Before I can answer that question, I need to know what else she could have been doing with her time, what is the **opportunity cost** of the day she spent on this venture? If she could have earned ₹500 working elsewhere for the day, the economist would pronounce her business a failure, because the economic cost of producing the goods would be ₹1,500 (the out-of-pocket costs of ₹1,000 plus the opportunity cost of her time of ₹500) and so the venture would be deemed to have made a loss of ₹300.

The concept of opportunity cost is central to an economist's way of thinking. Thus the economist's notion of cost differs from that of an accountant in that the economist wants to include opportunity costs even if those costs are not explicitly paid for. Apart from the time of the owner of a business, a major type of non-monetary opportunity cost is the cost of owned capital (equity) in a firm. Suppose a firm builds a factory that costs ₹100 crore. If it finances this factory by borrowing the ₹100 crore at 10% interest, the accountant would include the ₹10 crore annual interest payment as a cost. But if the firm financed the factory with internal funds, the accountant would impute no cost to this capital. The economist, on the other hand, would want to know the opportunity cost of that ₹100 crore. If the firm could have put it in the bank and earned 9% interest on it, the economist would want to impute the ₹9 crore foregone interest as a cost.

At the same time as using the concept of opportunity costs results in the inclusion of costs that are not explicitly paid for, it also can result in the exclusion of costs that *are* explicitly paid for. This arises in the case of costs that are unavoidable or 'sunk'. For example, suppose a firm is contractually obligated to pay for certain inputs whether it uses them or not. The cost of those inputs is then unavoidable; there is no 'next best' opportunity for the funds set aside to pay for them. An economist would want such costs to be excluded from the calculation of costs or profit.

A very common example of this kind of thinking is seen in the behaviour of investors who buy and sell company shares. It is very common for investors to look at how much they paid for shares when deciding whether or not to sell them. There is a human tendency to want to not sell at a loss since it would perhaps be an acknowledgement of a poor investment decision. But to an economist, one's purchase price for a stock is a 'sunk cost' and should be excluded from the calculation of whether or not to sell. The true cost of holding a stock is the foregone opportunity of the next best investment. *That* is the relevant cost to consider when deciding whether or not to sell a stock.

### 1.2.3 Think in Terms of Equilibrium

The final key insight into the economist's way of thinking is the concept of equilibrium. This may seem like a methodological point but it speaks to something deeper. We touched upon this concept earlier when discussing the notion of equilibrium prices in markets. A system is in equilibrium if there are not present in it any forces that would cause it to change. Change would come about only when some new force is injected into the system, in other words, when the situation surrounding the system changed. By focusing on equilibrium, economists are not claiming that markets or economies are or even should be in equilibrium all the time or even ever. Because circumstances are in a constant state of flux, it is actually unlikely that any economic system would ever be in equilibrium. By focusing on equilibrium, what economists are trying to do is to focus on the most fundamental forces in the economy or in the markets, to see the forest and ignore the trees.

For example, consider the market for 'widgets', a mythical product that is a favourite of economists. It could be that there are many producers of widgets, located in different parts of the country, and, at any one point in time, they could be charging different prices for their products. Even if their products are indistinguishable from one another, they may be charging different prices and the ones charging higher prices might even be successfully holding on to their customers. An economist would look at this situation and say that it is not sustainable. Rather, she would point out that, over time, the high-priced firms would lose customers to the low-priced firms, assuming that the goods are of equal quality of course. By focusing on the equilibrium of the market, she could point to the outcome to which the market would tend over time. It might never get there, because the situation might change again, but nevertheless she could point out that the equilibrium is the situation to which the market would tend.

Once the situation changes, the economist would want to calculate a new equilibrium. Rather than trying to describe in minute detail the events that would be set in motion by the change in the situation, she would simply say that the new equilibrium was the new destination to which the fundamental forces in the market would push the market. This method of analysis of the effect of change is called 'comparative statics', in which the effect of a change is seen as the difference between the prior and the new equilibria. Sometimes the Latin phrase *ceteris paribus* is used to describe the implicit assumption that all other elements of the situation would remain unchanged, the only change allowed would be the one that is the focus of the analysis.

Using again the analogy of the ball in a bowl, suppose you have a round-bottomed bowl sitting on a table and you roll a round ball into it. Even as the ball rolls around in the bowl, we can say that its equilibrium point is at the bottom of the bowl and, left to itself, that is where it will come to rest. Now suppose that, before the ball can come to rest at the bottom of the bowl, we tilt the bowl to one side. Obviously the equilibrium point will shift to whatever is now the lowest point in the bowl. Even as the ball continues to roll around, we can identify this as the new equilibrium point for the ball. This is what economists do in comparative statics exercises. They identify the equilibrium in a market and then, in response to a change in conditions, they would simply identify the new equilibrium rather than trying to describe the movement of the market towards that equilibrium. The latter task could also be undertaken (and often is), but then the exercise is one in dynamics and is considerably more complicated. Focusing on equilibria alone allows economists to get to the essence of any situation and understand the fundamental forces in that situation in a very simple way.

## 1.3 PLAN OF THIS BOOK

This book is divided into roughly two halves. The first half (Chapters 2–7) deals with the basic building blocks of Microeconomics: the theories of Consumer and Producer Behaviour and then with the idealised world of perfectly competitive markets. This is where we will see Marshall's supply–demand cross (Theory of Partial Equilibrium) and the modern version of Smith's Invisible Hand Theorem (Theory of General Equilibrium and Welfare Economics). The first half therefore develops the main edifice of the Theory of Markets and develops the theoretical case for unfettered markets as the agents of sound economic decision-making. This is the theory that is often invoked in policy discussions where the efficiency of markets is touted and promoted. Many authors treat General Equilibrium Theory as the culmination of Microeconomics, but here it is seen only as a theoretical midway point.

The second half of the book (Chapters 8–12) points out the many ways in which the theory of efficient markets fails to apply in practice. Starting with situations involving uncertainty, we move on to consider markets where competition is not perfect but rather where the markets are dominated by powerful monopolists or oligopolists. Finally, we look at the problem of externalities and public goods, goods for which it is impossible to have normal markets. In all these cases, the free market solutions fail to be efficient and corrective government intervention in one form or another is called for.

The long list of 'market failures' discussed in the second half of the book might lead one to question the desirability of using a market-based system to organise the economy. On the other hand, it is possible that the suitable use of government interventions can be used to adequately correct imperfections in an otherwise sound system. This book emphasises the policy applications of Microeconomic Theory, and the second half of the book focuses on finding the appropriate policy responses to market failures. It is the identification of the best forms of government intervention that makes Microeconomics a subject truly worthy of study, and it is hoped that, by the end of the book, the reader will feel equipped with the basic knowledge necessary to identify these best forms of intervention.

CHAPTER

# 2 Theory of Consumer Behaviour

The starting point in the discussion of the theory of demand is the study of consumer behaviour. Consumers or households are the economic agents whose primary economic activity is consumption of goods and services. This chapter will be concerned with how microeconomists model the behaviour of households. The approach followed is essentially the one originally proposed by Sir John Hicks, an economist at Cambridge University, in his 1939 book *Value and Capital*. But before we get to that, let us briefly review Marshall's theory of demand.

## 2.1 THE MARSHALLIAN THEORY OF DEMAND

**Task for this section:**

To briefly review Marshall's theory of demand.

In studying the theory of consumer behaviour, we are trying to understand why consumers buy what they do and how they respond to changes in the market environment. The starting point for the approach is the assumption that consumers buy goods and services in order to derive utility from them. Utility is still not defined very precisely, as we do not have any natural measures for it, but it is meant to serve as a proxy for satisfaction or happiness. Somewhat tautologically, we might define utility as the object of consumption—what consumers get (and want) from their consumption of goods and services.

Marshall based his theory of demand on an assumption that seemed so reasonable to him that he called it a law: **The Law of Diminishing Marginal Utility**. This asserted that, as a consumer consumed more of a given good within a set time period, the additional utility she got from successive units (i.e., the marginal utility) would keep falling. The notion was that the first unit of consumption of any good was the most desirable one; subsequent units would be less and less so. Thus, if we plotted the marginal utility (*MU*) of a good *x* against the quantity consumed of that good, we would get a downward-sloping line, as pictured in panel (a) of Figure 2.1.

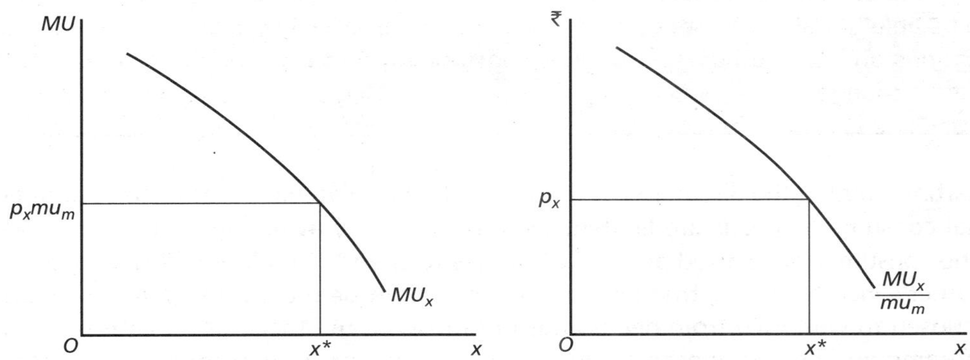


**(a) Diminishing Marginal Utility** **(b) Demand Curve**

**Figure 2.1** *Diminishing Marginal Utility and Demand*

How much of a good would a consumer buy? Marshall argued that a consumer would buy that quantity of a good such that the *MU* of the last unit she bought would equal what she would have to give up in exchange: the utility she *could have got* had she spent the money on the next best alternative. A simple way to represent this would be to calculate the utility value of what she gave up as the price of the good ($p_x$) times the *MU* of money, $mu_m$, the utility she would get per rupee of spending on the next best alternative. In panel (a) of the figure, this is $x^*$.

The consumer's demand curve could then be easily derived as the curve created by taking the *MU* curve of the good and dividing it everywhere by $mu_m$. This curve, seen in panel (b) of Figure 2.1, is the Marshallian demand curve, showing the quantity demanded of the good at different prices. Because it is a simple positive transformation of the *MU* curve, it is downward-sloping. This is the core of the Marshallian theory of demand.

One problem with Marshall's theory is that it is valid only for 'small changes'. An implicit assumption made in the theory is that the *MU* of money is constant. But this is surely not true generally. It is quite obvious that the value (i.e., the *MU*) of ₹10 is quite different to a poor person than it is to a millionaire. If the price of a basic consumption item such as food were to double or triple, the *MU* of money would almost certainly rise, particularly for someone who is relatively poor. Thus, we would like to have a theory that did not depend upon the assumption of a constant *MU* of money, and this is what Hicks's theory provides.

## 2.2 THE BUDGET CONSTRAINT

**Task for this section:**

To learn how economists model the consumer's budget limitations. After this section, you should be able to define the set of consumption bundles available to a consumer in a variety of situations and to see how the budget constraint would shift as any of the underlying parameters change.

Our starting point in the discussion of the satisfaction of material needs is the recognition that the typical consumer's means are limited. We model that by assuming that, in any given time period, the consumer has a fixed amount of money to spend, a budget $I$. This budget might be the consumer's income during that time period or it might be the income plus any amount that she has chosen to withdraw from her savings or borrow from others, or it might be the income minus the amount she has chosen to add to her savings or to lend (or repay) to others. We will consider the consumer's decisions to borrow, lend and save in the section on inter-temporal decisions. For now, we simply take as fixed the consumer's budget ($I$)— the amount of money available for consumption within the time period under consideration, after having taken into account any amounts borrowed or saved.

The consumer buys $n$ goods and services in the quantities $x_1, x_2, \ldots x_n$. The prices of these goods are, respectively, $p_1, p_2, \ldots p_n$. So the consumer's budget constraint is that her total expenditure cannot exceed the amount of money she has available to spend:

$$\sum_{i=1}^{n} p_i x_i \leq I. \tag{2.1}$$

Since we are separating out the consumer's decision to possibly save some of her current income, and assuming that the consumer has not had all of her wants satisfied, we can set this constraint as one of equality:

$$\sum_{i=1}^{n} p_i x_i = I. \tag{2.2}$$

For purposes of graphical exposition, we will often focus on a simplified case where $n = 2$. In that case, the budget constraint reduces to

$$p_1 x_1 + p_2 x_2 = I, \tag{2.3}$$

which can be represented graphically as a downward-sloping straight line as panel (a) in Figure 2.2. The intercepts of this line on the horizontal and vertical axes are $\frac{I}{p_1}$ and $\frac{I}{p_2}$, respectively; each of these points represents the total quantity of the respective good that the consumer could buy if she spent her entire income on that good. The slope of the line is $-\frac{p_1}{p_2}$, which can be seen by rearranging (2.3) as

$$x_2 = \frac{I}{p_2} - \frac{p_1}{p_2}x_1.$$

If, for purposes of illustration, we had $I = ₹100$, $p_1 = ₹2$ and $p_2 = ₹5$, the budget constraint would be the one shown in panel (b) of Figure 2.2.

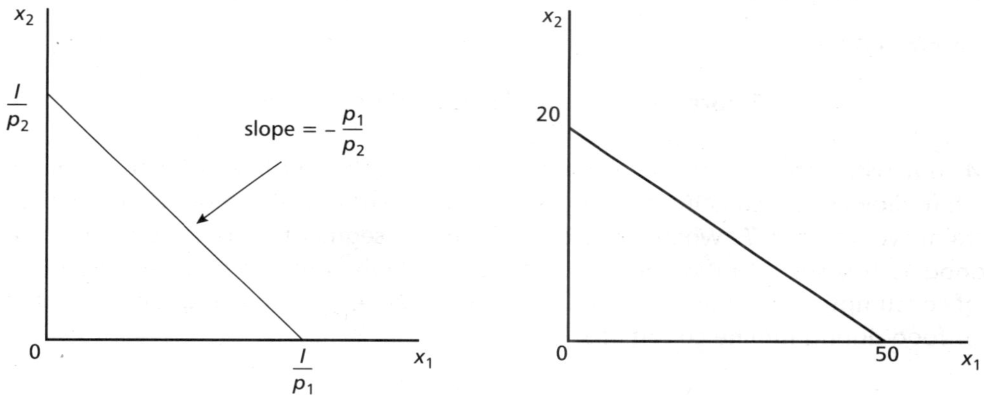


**(a) A General Budget Constraint** **(b) The Constraint When $I$=100, $p_1$=2, $p_2$=5**

**Figure 2.2** *The Budget Constraint*

We can study the effects on the budget constraint of changes in its parameters, seen in Figure 2.3. Panel (a) shows the effect of a rise in $I$, which pushes the budget constraint outward, parallel to itself (since $p_1, p_2$ have not changed, the slope has not changed). Panel (b) shows the effect of a rise in $p_1$, which rotates the budget constraint inward ($\frac{I}{p_1}$ falls if $p_1$ rises, while $\frac{I}{p_2}$ remains unchanged, i.e., the vertical intercept of the constraint remains fixed, since neither $I$ nor $p_2$ has changed). Similarly, panel (c) shows the effect of a fall in $p_1$.

### 2.2.1 Variations on the Budget Constraint

Figure 2.2 illustrated the standard budget constraint faced by the consumer. This standard version can be adapted to capture many non-standard situations as well, reflecting many situations that consumers might actually face in the market.

#### *2.2.1.1 Rationing*

Suppose one good, say good 1, is rationed: the consumer can buy it at a price $p_1$ but only to a maximum amount of $\bar{x}_1$. Without rationing, her budget constraint would have been $AB$ in

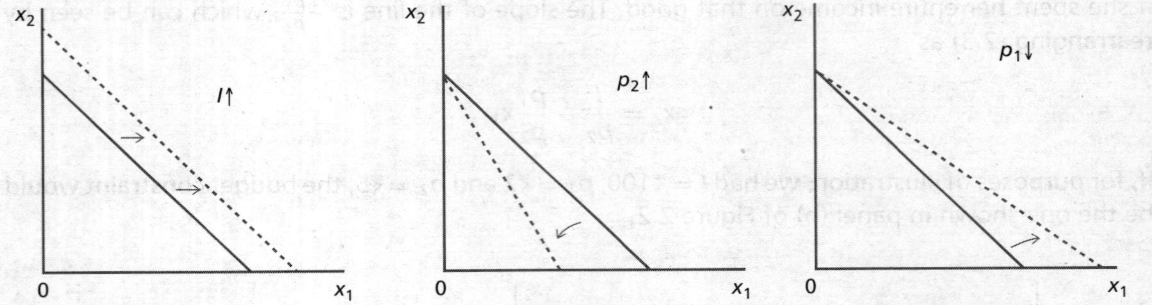


**(a) Income Rises** **(b) $p_1$ Rises** **(c) $p_1$ Falls**

**Figure 2.3** *Shifts in the Budget Constraint*

Figure 2.4, but with rationing the constraint becomes the kinked line *ACD*. If a black market emerged that allowed the consumer to buy additional quantities of the good at a higher price, the constraint would be *ACE*, where the slope of the line segment *CE* reflects the black market price of good 1. This sort of rationing is sometimes used when the government wishes to keep the level of consumption of a particular good at a low level. An example might be fuel use during wartime or food during famine conditions.

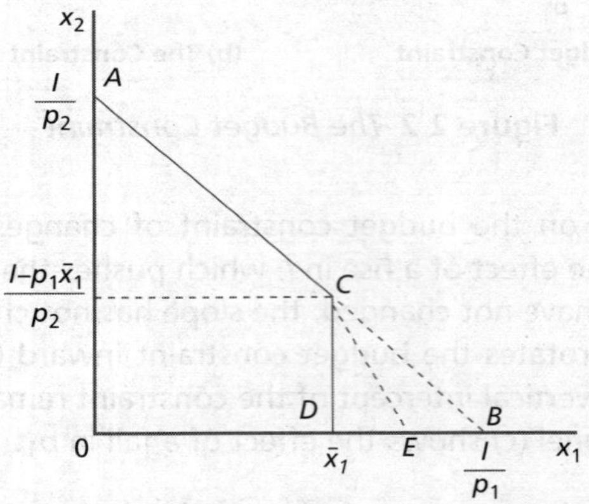


**Figure 2.4** *Budget Constraint with Rationing*

The kinked budget constraint *ACE* could also represent a case where a consumer receives an amount $\bar{x}_1$ at a subsidised price $p_1$ and can then buy more of the good at the open market price, which would be reflected in the slope of the line *CE*. This is the situation in India for qualified families in the food grains market. They receive up to a certain amount of grain at a highly subsidised price through the government's fair price shops, but of course are free to buy more grain on the open market. They therefore face a budget constraint shaped like the kinked line *ACE*.

Finally, the kinked budget constraint *ACE* could also represent a case where the price of a good rises after a certain threshold. Sometimes, power or water companies charge a relatively low price for the first so many units of consumption and then raise the price for any consumption above the threshold, as an incentive for consumers to keep their consumption levels moderate. Such pricing mechanisms would cause the budget constraint to be kinked. Sometimes, there might be two or even more thresholds, above each of which the price rises further. This would cause the budget constraint to have multiple kinks.

### *2.2.1.2 Volume Discounts*

Suppose a consumer could get a volume discount, that is, a reduced price on all purchases above a certain threshold, $\underline{x}_1$. In the absence of the volume discount, the budget constraint would have been, say, *AB* in panel (a) of Figure 2.5, but with the volume discount, it is the kinked line *ACD* if the consumer has to pay only $p_1'$ per unit for purchases above $\underline{x}_1$. Note that this constraint implies that the consumer pays the price of $p_1$ for the first $\underline{x}_1$ units of good 1 whether or not she qualifies for the volume discount, and pays the lower price $p_1'$ only on the units purchased above $\underline{x}_1$. This sort of volume discount is seen sometimes in electricity markets, where the first so many kilowatt-hours of electricity are charged at a higher price and then consumption above the threshold level is charged at a lower price.

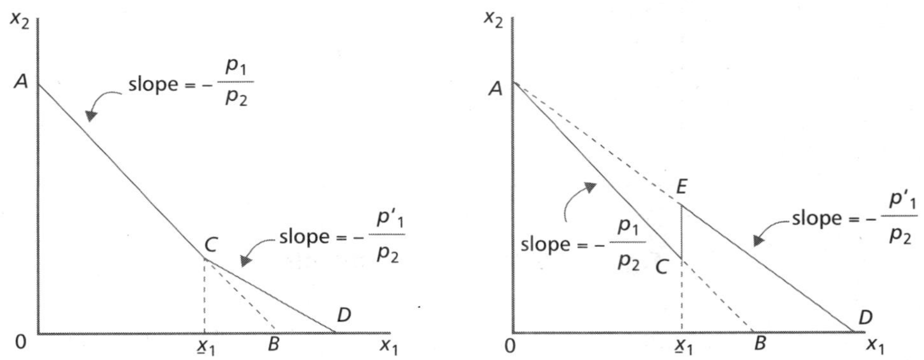


**(a) Volume Discount above Threshold** **(b) Volume Discount Throughout**

**Figure 2.5** *Budget Constraint with Volume Discount*

If, on the other hand, the volume discount applies on *all* units purchased if the total purchases exceed $\underline{x}_1$, the constraint would look like *ACED* in panel (b) of Figure 2.5. To see this, note that *AD* would have been the budget constraint if $p_1'$ had been the price throughout. But this constraint becomes operational only once the threshold level of purchases $\underline{x}_1$ is reached. For purchases less than the threshold level, the segment *AC* of the constraint *AB* applies, and then the segment *ED* of the constraint *AD* comes into play for higher levels of purchases. This sort of volume discount is quite common in situations where the seller has discretion over the price. For example, fruit and vegetable sellers will often charge a lower price if a sufficiently large quantity is chosen for purchase.

### 2.2.1.3 *Multiple Constraints*

Suppose, in addition to the usual budget constraint, a consumer faces a second constraint. A simple example might be a constraint on time; perhaps the consumer must spend time-consuming the goods, such as going to the movies or going out to dinner. Then she faces the constraints of limited resources and limited time. Each of the constraints might be a downward-sloping straight line, but if both constraints must be satisfied, a kinked line such as *ACB* in Figure 2.6 will limit the consumer's consumption possibilities and therefore acts as the constraint in this case.

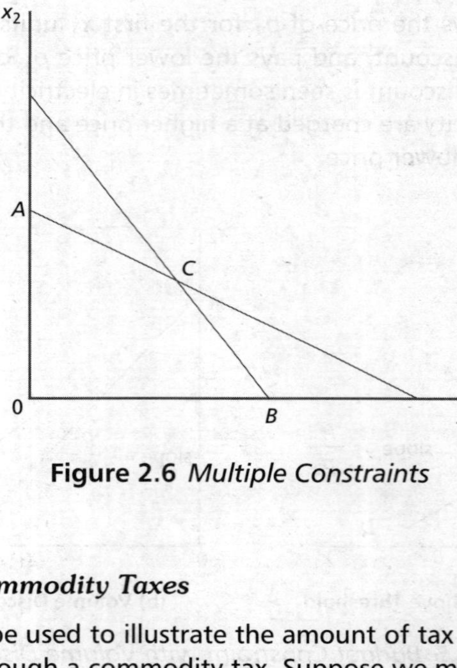


**Figure 2.6** *Multiple Constraints*

### 2.2.1.4 *The Effect of Commodity Taxes*

The budget constraint can be used to illustrate the amount of tax revenue a government would collect from a consumer through a commodity tax. Suppose we measure the quantity of a good *X* on the horizontal axis and amounts of money on the vertical axis. Then the vertical intercept of the budget constraint *AB* would represent *I*, the consumer's budget, and its slope would simply be $-p_x$, since '$p_2$' is implicitly equal to 1. Now suppose the government imposes a tax $t$ on the consumption of good *X* and, for simplicity, let us assume that the underlying price $p_x$ remains unchanged. Then the price faced by the consumer will be $p_x + t$, and the budget constraint would have rotated inward to the position represented by the line *AB′* in Figure 2.7. Now suppose the consumer chooses the bundle *C* when faced by the budget constraint *AB′*. The question is, can we see on the graph the amount of tax revenue the government will collect from this consumer?

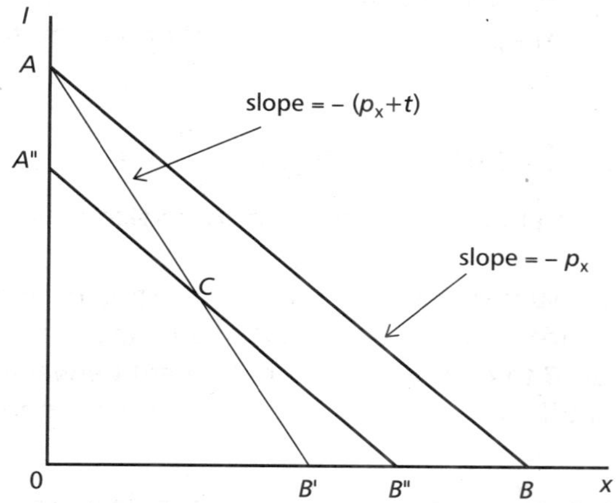


**Figure 2.7** *Effect of a Commodity Tax*

The answer is yes. If we draw a line *A"B"* through *C* parallel to the original budget constraint *AB*, the distance *AA"* will represent the tax revenue collected. Why is this? The reason is that the implicit budget, *A"*, in the line *A"B"* is the cost of the bundle *C* at the original (pre-tax) prices. Therefore the difference in budgets *A* and *A"* must be the cost of the taxes paid by the consumer, and hence the tax revenue collected by the government.

## 2.3 THE UTILITY FUNCTION

**Task for this section:**

To understand how economists model consumers' preferences. After this section, you should have a good grasp of what the utility function is, how it is represented algebraically and graphically and what exactly indifference curves (ICs) are and how they are shaped.

Having looked at the consumer's budget constraint, we turn next to consider how the consumer chooses a consumption bundle from all of the bundles available to her. The basic approach was originally proposed by John Hicks and so it is often called the Hicksian theory of demand or consumer behaviour. The starting point for the approach is the notion that consumers use their limited resources–their budget–to buy goods and services in order to satisfy their needs, wants and desires. Economists use the term 'utility' to represent whatever it is that consumers gain from consumption. This may be an over simplification; what consumers gain from consumption might be quite complex, perhaps too complex to be represented by a single variable. Nevertheless, this is what economists do. They believe that consumers have 'preferences' over the different possible bundles of goods and services they might consume and that their preferences can be represented by a utility function.

### 2.3.1 Basic Properties of Utility Functions

The preferences of the consumer are assumed to satisfy certain reasonable properties:

1. **Completeness**: The consumer is assumed to be able to rank all possible pairs of bundles. If presented with the choice between bundles *A* and *B*, she can say that she either prefers *A* to *B*, or that she prefers *B* to *A*, or that she is indifferent between the two, which means she would be equally well off with either. What she is not permitted to do is say, like Buridan's ass,[1] 'I can't decide!'
2. **Transitivity**: If the consumer prefers bundle *A* to bundle *B*, and prefers bundle *B* to bundle *C*, then she must prefer bundle *A* to bundle *C*. This is often seen as a criterion for rationality or consistency of preferences.
3. **Continuity**: If the consumer prefers bundle *A* to bundle *B*, then she must also prefer bundle *A* to all bundles *B′* that are close to *B*. This is a technical assumption meant primarily to facilitate the use of calculus in the analysis of the consumer's preferences.

Under these assumptions, it can be shown that the consumer's preferences can be represented by a utility function:

$$u = u(x_1, x_2, \ldots, x_n), \tag{2.4}$$

which provides an index value $u$ for every possible bundle of goods $(x_1, x_2, \ldots, x_n)$ that a consumer might consume. The utility index has the important property that its value is higher for bundles that the consumer prefers. In other words, if the consumer prefers bundle *A* to bundle *B*, then

$$u(A) > u(B). \tag{2.5}$$

We say a consumer is **indifferent** between two bundles if, when presented with a choice between them, she could choose either one and be just as well off. In such cases, the utility index attached

[1] Buridan's ass, named for the French philosopher Jean Buridan, refers to a paradox discussed as early as the 4th century BCE by Aristotle. In the 'ass' version, a starving ass is unable to decide which of two equally enticing piles of hay from which to eat and eventually starves to death because of his indecision! Our consumer is assumed always able to make a decision, even if it is to toss a coin and choose accordingly.

to the two bundles would be the same. In other words, if the consumer is indifferent between bundles $A$ and $B$, $u(A) = u(B)$.

The consumer's utility function is normally assumed to satisfy two more properties other than the previously listed assumptions on preferences. These properties may not hold in all cases.

4. **Non-satiety**: More of a good is always preferable to less; in other words, utility always rises as the consumer consumes more of a good, holding the quantities of all other goods constant, that is,

$$\frac{\partial u}{\partial x_i} > 0. \tag{2.6}$$

We refer to this partial derivative as the *MU* of good $i$ and may also denote it $MU_i$. Clearly, this assumption could easily be violated in that a consumer could reach a point of satiation beyond which further consumption of a good within a given period of time would not add to her well-being. A weaker form of the assumption would be

$$\frac{\partial u}{\partial x_i} \geq 0. \tag{2.7}$$

This would be true under all circumstances as long as we allow **free disposal**. If a consumer had available to her a good which she did not want to consume, free disposal simply allows her to dispose of it costlessly and therefore avoid consuming it. In that case, having more of a good can never make a consumer worse off.

5. **Diminishing Marginal Rate of Substitution:** This is a technical assumption on the derivatives of the utility function. If $x_1$ and $x_2$ represent the quantities consumed of two goods, this assumption requires

$$u_2^2 u_{11} - 2u_1 u_2 u_{12} + u_1^2 u_{22} < 0. \tag{2.8}$$

The purpose and meaning of this assumption is best explained in the context of indifference curves (ICs).

### 2.3.2 Graphical Representation of Utility Functions: Indifference Curves

Utility functions are represented graphically in the 2-good case by IC maps. An IC is a line connecting all bundles $(x_1, x_2)$ that have the same level of utility. Just as the contour lines on a topographical map connect points on the map that have the same altitude and thereby provide three-dimensional information on a two-dimensional surface, the ICs show different levels of utility on a two-dimensional graph where the quantities of the two goods are what are measured on the axes. Figure 2.8 shows a typical indifference map, where $u_3$ represents a higher level of utility than $u_2$, which in turn represents a higher level of utility than $u_1$.

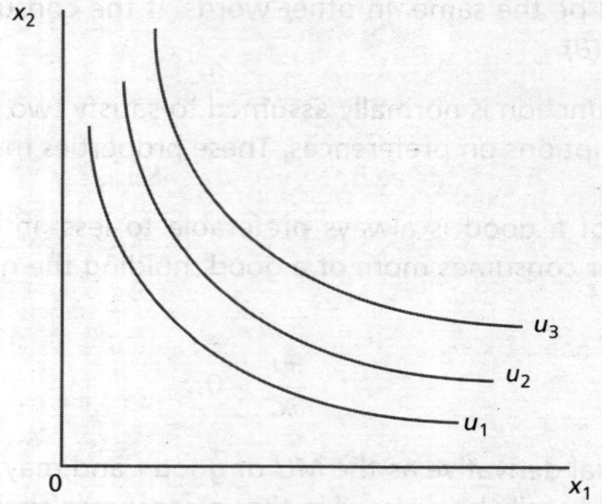


**Figure 2.8** *Indifference Map*

How might ICs be shaped? We can say several things about them:

1. ICs cannot be upward-sloping.
2. ICs cannot cross.
3. ICs are convex to the origin.

Let us consider each of these in turn.

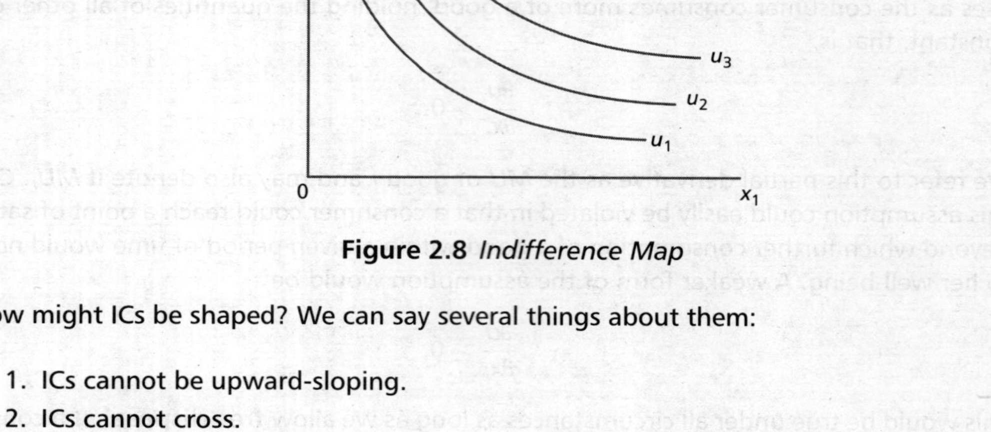


**Figure 2.9** *Indifference Curves and Satiation*

**First, ICs cannot be upward-sloping.** This is a consequence of the assumptions of non-satiety and free disposal. If a consumer reaches a point of satiation in the consumption of good $x_1$ at a level $\bar{x}_1$, her ICs would flatten out for all values of $x_1$ greater than $\bar{x}_1$, as in Figure 2.9(a). If, in addition, the consumer reached satiation at $\bar{x}_2$ for good $x_2$, her indifference map would look like the one in Figure 2.9(b). The shaded area in panel (b) of Figure 2.9 represents points that all have the same level of utility, as the consumer is fully satiated with both goods in that region.

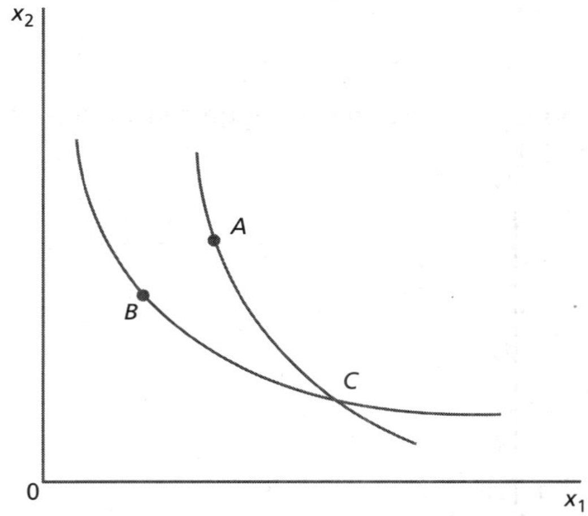


**Figure 2.10** *Indifference Curves Cannot Cross*

**Second, ICs cannot cross.** In general, because of non-satiety, a bundle such as *A* in Figure 2.10 would be preferred over bundle *B* because it contains more of both goods. But if the ICs through *A* and *B* cross at *C*, transitivity would require that the consumer must be indifferent between *A* and *B*, since she is indifferent between each of those bundles and *C*. We therefore have a contradiction, and the conclusion is that the ICs cannot cross.

**Third, ICs are convex to the origin.** This is a different way of stating the assumption of diminishing marginal rate of substitution. The **marginal rate of substitution** (*MRS*) is defined as the absolute value of the slope of the IC. Along the IC,

$$u_1 dx_1 + u_2 dx_2 = 0 \tag{2.9}$$

since utility does not change. Therefore, rearranging (2.9), we find that its slope is

$$\frac{dx_2}{dx_1} = -\frac{u_1}{u_2} \tag{2.10}$$

so that the *MRS* is

$$MRS = \left|\frac{dx_2}{dx_1}\right| = \frac{u_1}{u_2}. \tag{2.11}$$

If this is diminishing as we move along the IC to the right, the IC is becoming flatter and so is convex to the origin.

Is this assumption reasonable? It is very similar to, although not the same as, Marshall's assumption of the Law of Diminishing Marginal Utility. In the utility function context, this law states that

$$u_{ii} < 0, \text{ for all } i, \tag{2.12}$$

that is, $MU_i$ declines as $x_i$ goes up. How this is suggested by the Law of Diminishing Marginal Utility is illustrated in Figure 2.11.

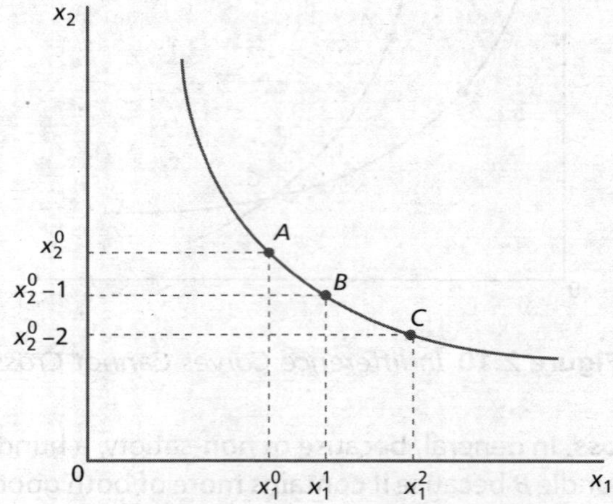


**Figure 2.11** *Diminishing Marginal Rate of Substitution*

Let us start at point $A$ where the consumer has the bundle $(x_1^0, x_2^0)$. Now suppose we took away one unit of $x_2$. The consumer would need more of $x_1$ to compensate her for this loss of $x_2$; suppose the amount $(x_1^1 - x_1^0)$ would just compensate her, so that $B$ is on the same IC as $A$. Now suppose we took away another unit of $x_2$ from the consumer so she is reduced to consuming $(x_2^0 - 2)$. How much additional $x_1$ would she need now in order to be fully compensated for the loss of $x_2$? If we just look at first-order effects, the Law of Diminishing Marginal Utility would suggest she would need more than $(x_1^1 - x_1^0)$. Why? For two reasons: (1) Since she has more $x_1$ at $B$ than at $A$, each additional unit of $x_1$ is less desirable (has lower $MU$) and therefore she would need more $x_1$ to derive the same compensation. (2) Since she has less $x_2$ at $B$ than at $A$, the loss of a unit of $x_2$ at $B$ is more 'costly' in a utility sense, hence she needs more compensation.

This exposition is not quite precise because we ignored second-order considerations. There is the possibility that $MU_1$ at $B$ is actually higher than it was at $A$ because the amount of $x_2$ at $B$ is lower. If, for example, $x_1$ and $x_2$ are close substitutes (a term we will consider and define more precisely later), it is possible that, as the quantity of $x_2$ falls from $A$ to $B$, $x_1$ becomes even more valuable to the consumer (i.e., $MU_1$ rises) and so it is possible that the consumer does not need as much $x_1$ to compensate her for the loss of $x_2$. To avoid this possibility, the assumption of diminishing *MRS* requires the technical condition (2.8) presented earlier. The proof goes as follows:

From (2.11), we know that

$$MRS = \frac{u_1}{u_2}.$$

Differentiating this with respect to $x_1$, we get

$$\frac{dMRS}{dx_1} = \frac{u_2\left[u_{11} + u_{12}\frac{dx_2}{dx_1}\right] - u_1\left[u_{21} + u_{22}\frac{dx_2}{dx_1}\right]}{u_2^2}. \tag{2.13}$$

Using (2.10), (2.13) becomes

$$\frac{dMRS}{dx_1} = \frac{u_2\left[u_{11} + u_{12}\left(-\frac{u_1}{u_2}\right)\right] - u_1\left[u_{21} + u_{22}\left(-\frac{u_1}{u_2}\right)\right]}{u_2^2},$$

which simplifies to

$$\frac{dMRS}{dx_1} = \frac{u_2 u_{11} - u_{12}u_1 - u_1 u_{21} + \frac{u_1^2 u_{22}}{u_2}}{u_2^2}. \tag{2.14}$$

From Young's Theorem, we know that $u_{12} = u_{21}$. Applying this to (2.14) and multiplying numerator and denominator by $u_2$, we get

$$\frac{dMRS}{dx_1} = \frac{u_2^2 u_{11} - 2u_1 u_2 u_{12} + u_1^2 u_{22}}{u_2^3}. \tag{2.15}$$

For *MRS* to be diminishing, this expression must be negative. And, since the denominator of (2.15) is positive, this implies that

$$\frac{dMRS}{dx_1} < 0 \quad \leftrightarrow \quad u_2^2 u_{11} - 2u_1 u_2 u_{12} + u_1^2 u_{22} < 0. \tag{2.16}$$

If $u_{12} = 0$ (i.e. if we could ignore second-order effects), (2.16) would hold if the Law of Diminishing Marginal Utility held, since that would imply that $u_{11} < 0$ and $u_{22} < 0$ (and, of course, $u_1 > 0$ and $u_2 > 0$). Further, If $u_{12} > 0$, the second-order term reinforces the negativity of the expression. So the only 'problem' arises when $u_{12} < 0$ and is sufficiently large for the second-order term to become dominant. We rule this out by condition (2.16). Essentially, the assumption of diminishing *MRS*, or convexity of the IC, amounts to assuming that consumers prefer 'balanced' bundles, with moderate amounts of many goods, over 'unbalanced' bundles dominated by just one good. This seems perfectly plausible.

### 2.3.3 Some Specific Utility Functions

Given these properties, a typical indifference map will look something like the one in Figure 2.8. Many utility functions would give rise to an indifference map similar to this one, but others may look a little different. For purposes of our discussion, we will use three specific utility functions extensively: the Cobb–Douglas, Leontief and Linear utility functions.

#### *2.3.3.1 Cobb–Douglas Utility Function*

This function has the general form

$$u(x_1, x_2, \ldots, x_n) = Ax_1^{\alpha_1} x_2^{\alpha_2} \cdots x_n^{\alpha_n}. \tag{2.17}$$

In the 2-good case, this reduces to

$$u(x_1, x_2) = Ax_1^{\alpha_1} x_2^{\alpha_2}. \tag{2.18}$$

The Cobb–Douglas function was originally proposed as a functional form to estimate production functions and it is not very realistic as a utility function, as we will see when we analyse its properties. Nevertheless, we use it a lot in expositions of consumer theory because it is easy to use and does give rise to a somewhat reasonable looking indifference map, similar to the one in Figure 2.12. One special aspect of a Cobb–Douglas utility function is that it is **homothetic**, which means that its ICs are radially parallel. Along any ray through the origin, the ICs will have the same slope.

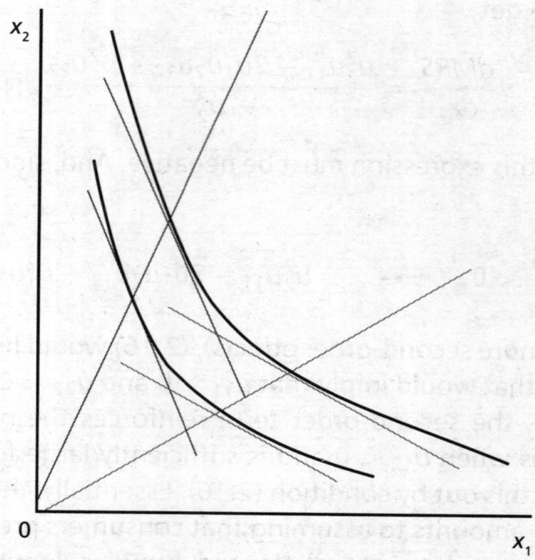


**Figure 2.12** *Cobb–Douglas Utility Function*

### *2.3.3.2 Leontief Utility Function*

This function has the property that all goods are consumed in certain fixed proportions, and may be represented as

$$u(x_1, x_2, \ldots, x_n) = \min\left[\frac{x_1}{\beta_1}, \frac{x_2}{\beta_2}, \ldots, \frac{x_n}{\beta_n}\right]. \tag{2.19}$$

The parameters $\beta_i$ may be interpreted as the per-unit-utility requirements of the $x_i'$s; when $x_i = \beta_i$ for all $i$, the utility level is 1. Again, this functional form arose in the context of the theory of production and it is not a very reasonable form for a utility function. However, it provides a limiting case for the form of the typical IC and is therefore useful for discussion purposes. In the 2-good case, this function reduces to

$$u(x_1, x_2) = \min\left[\frac{x_1}{\beta_1}, \frac{x_2}{\beta_2}\right]. \tag{2.20}$$

The indifference map for this function is illustrated in Figure 2.13. At point $A$,

$$\frac{x_1}{\beta_1} = \frac{x_2}{\beta_2} = u_1 \tag{2.21}$$

and so

$$x_1^A = \beta_1 u_1 \quad \text{and} \quad x_2^A = \beta_2 u_1. \tag{2.22}$$

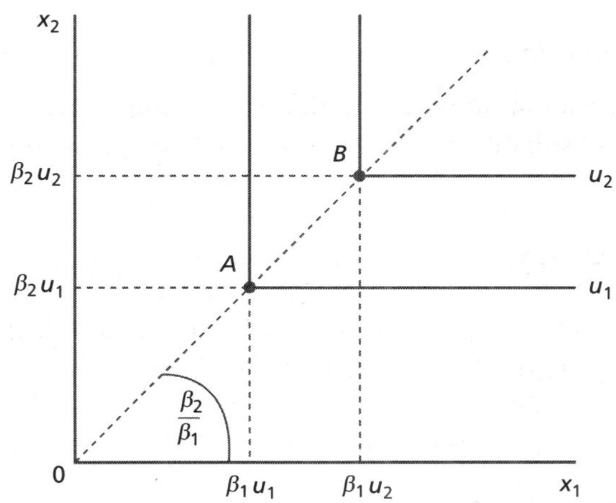


**Figure 2.13** *Indifference Map for the Leontief Utility Function*

Similarly at $B$,

$$x_1^B = \beta_1 u_2 \quad \text{and} \quad x_2^B = \beta_2 u_2. \tag{2.23}$$

We see then that the ICs are L-shaped with their corners along a ray through the origin whose slope is $\beta_2/\beta_1$. Goods with this kind of an indifference map are called perfect complements, since they are complementary to one another in an exact ratio. The curvature of normal, downward-sloping ICs reflects some substitutability between $x_1$ and $x_2$, as we saw in the discussion around Figure 2.11. Perfect complements, however, have zero substitutability and hence the curvature of the ICs completely disappears. Thus, it is a limiting case of curved ICs where substitutability has reached zero (Figure 2.13).

**Example 2.1: Utility Function for Perfect Complements**

Suppose $x_1$ and $x_2$ are the goods coffee and sugar and Anna always adds exactly 2 spoons of sugar to each cup of coffee. In this case, coffee and sugar would be perfect complements and Anna's utility function could be written as $u(x_c, x_s) = \min\left[x_c, \frac{x_s}{2}\right]$. She needs 1 cup of coffee ($x_c = 1$) and 2 teaspoons of sugar ($x_s = 2$) to yield 1 cup of prepared coffee (a composite good).

Some other examples of perfect complements that are often suggested are goods such as left shoes and right shoes or left gloves and right gloves. Goods such as these, which are perfect complements for all consumers, are naturally sold together and are properly thought of as one good, such as a pair of shoes or a pair of gloves. It is when goods are not perfect complements for everyone, or are perfect complements in different ratios for different consumers, that they are properly treated as separate products and the perfect complements case becomes more interesting.

### 2.3.3.3 *Linear Utility Function*

At the other extreme, we could imagine a situation where substitutability reaches its maximum: where goods become perfect substitutes for one another. In this case, the utility function becomes linear and takes the form

$$u(x_1, x_2, \ldots, x_n) = \gamma_1 x_1 + \gamma_2 x_2 + \ldots + \gamma_n x_n. \tag{2.24}$$

Here, each of the goods can be replaced by each of the other goods at certain fixed ratios and can leave the consumer's utility level unchanged. In the 2-good case, this becomes

$$u(x_1, x_2) = \gamma_1 x_1 + \gamma_2 x_2. \tag{2.25}$$

The indifference map for this utility function is illustrated in Figure 2.14. It is easy to see that the ICs will be straight lines parallel to one another. The slope of each ICs is $-\gamma_1/\gamma_2$.

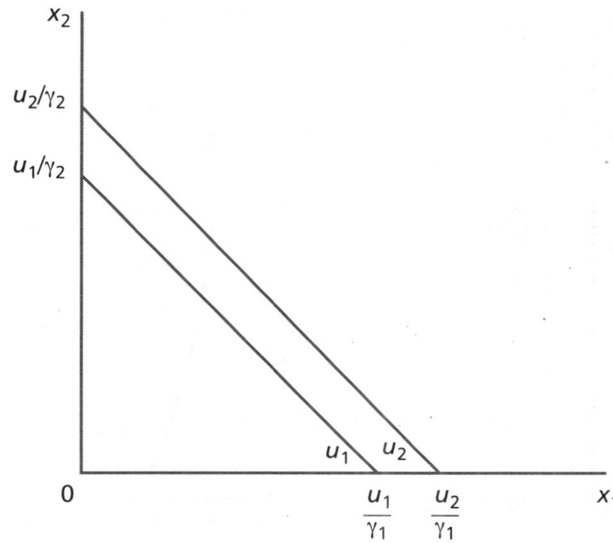


**Figure 2.14** *Indifference Map for Linear Utility Function*

**Example 2.2: Utility Function for Perfect Substitutes**

Suppose the two goods we are considering are butter and margarine and John feels $1\frac{1}{2}$ teaspoons of margarine are exactly equivalent to 1 teaspoon of butter. Then butter and margarine are perfect substitutes for John and his utility function can be written as

$$u(x_b, x_m) = x_b + \frac{2}{3}x_m$$

since it would take $x_m = \frac{3}{2}$ to yield the same utility as when $x_b = 1$.

### *2.3.3.4 Quasi-linear Utility Function*

A quasi-linear utility function has the property that all the ICs are horizontally parallel to one another (i.e. they have the same slope along any horizontal line), and the utility function has the functional form

$$u(x_1, x_2) = Bx_1 + v(x_2).$$

Figure 2.15 illustrates what the indifference map for such a function might look like. Such a function might be thought realistic for someone who is extremely poor, and the commodity $x_1$ represents food. Someone who is close to starvation may not be willing to give up much food for any amount of other goods; in the extreme case, the ICs could become vertical straight lines.

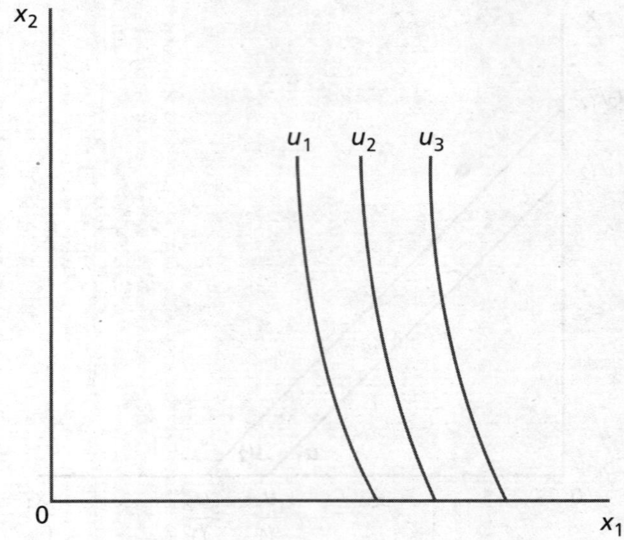


**Figure 2.15** *Quasi-linear Utility Function*

## 2.4 THE CONSUMER'S CHOICE PROBLEM

> **Task for this section:**
>
> To learn how economists model the consumer's choice problem and how to solve it. After this section, you should be able to formulate the choice problem of a consumer and be able to solve it, algebraically and geometrically. In the process, you will also learn what demand functions are and how to derive them.

The consumer would like to get to the highest utility level possible, but she is constrained by her limited budget. Her problem therefore can be represented as a constrained maximisation problem. She must choose the quantities $x_1, x_2, \ldots, x_n$ in order to

$$\text{Maximise} \quad u(x_1, x_2, \ldots, x_n) \tag{2.26}$$

$$\text{subject to} \quad \sum_{i=1}^{n} p_i x_i = I. \tag{2.27}$$

The solutions to this problem will be quantities $x_1, x_2, \ldots, x_n$ as functions of the prices of the goods and the consumer's budget:

$$\begin{aligned} x_1 &= x_1(p_1, p_2, \ldots, p_n, I) \\ x_2 &= x_2(p_1, p_2, \ldots, p_n, I) \\ &\vdots \\ x_n &= x_n(p_1, p_2, \ldots, p_n, I) \end{aligned} \tag{2.28}$$

These solutions are known as the ordinary demand functions for the goods $x_1, x_2, \ldots, x_n$.

The **ordinary demand function** for a good shows the quantity demanded of the good as a function of the good's price, the prices of all other goods and the consumer's budget. (Note that the quantities demanded of other goods do not appear as arguments of the ordinary demand function. Students often make the mistake of leaving quantities of other goods in their 'solutions' for the demand function, a mistake that should always be avoided.) The ordinary demand function is also sometimes called the **Marshallian Demand Function**. If we substitute back the ordinary demand functions (2.28) in the utility function (2.26), we get an expression showing utility as a function of prices and income:

$$u\left(x_1(p_1, p_2, \ldots, p_n, I), x_2(p_1, p_2, \ldots, p_n, I), \ldots, x_n(p_1, p_2, \ldots, p_n, I)\right) = V(p_1, p_2, \ldots, p_n, I). \tag{2.29}$$

This is called the **indirect utility function**, as it shows the level of utility not as a function of its arguments, the quantities of goods, but rather as a function of the parameters of the consumer's choice problem, the prices of the goods and the consumer's budget.

Finally, note that if we fix all prices other than the good's own-price, and fix the budget $I$, the demand function reduces to the **demand curve**, a function that shows the quantity demanded as a function of the good's own-price, holding all other prices and the consumer's budget constant. If any of these other goods prices or the consumer's budget changed, the entire demand curve would shift. We normally distinguish between shifts in the demand curve and movements along a single demand curve by calling the former a **change in demand**, while the latter is a **change in the quantity demanded**.

### 2.4.1 Solving the Consumer's Choice Problem Graphically

We can illustrate the solution to the consumer's choice problem graphically in the 2-good case. We superimpose the consumer's indifference map on her budget constraint (as in Figure 2.16) and simply try to find the highest IC, that is, the highest level of utility, that she can attain given that she cannot choose a bundle outside the budget constraint $AB$. Thus, points on the IC $u_3$ are all unattainable. It is easy to see that the solution will be at $C$ where the IC $u_2$ is tangent to the budget constraint $AB$. If the consumer considered a bundle such as $D$, where the IC was not tangent to the budget constraint, we see immediately that she could do better by choosing a

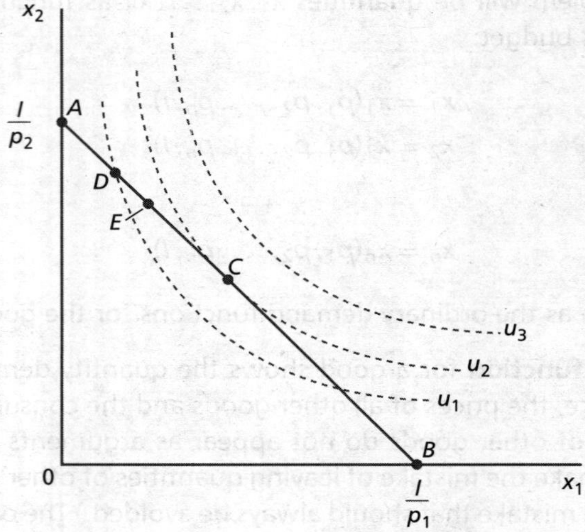


**Figure 2.16** *The Consumer's Choice Problem*

bundle such as *E* which would be on a higher IC. Thus the solution would be at *C* where the IC is tangent to the budget constraint.

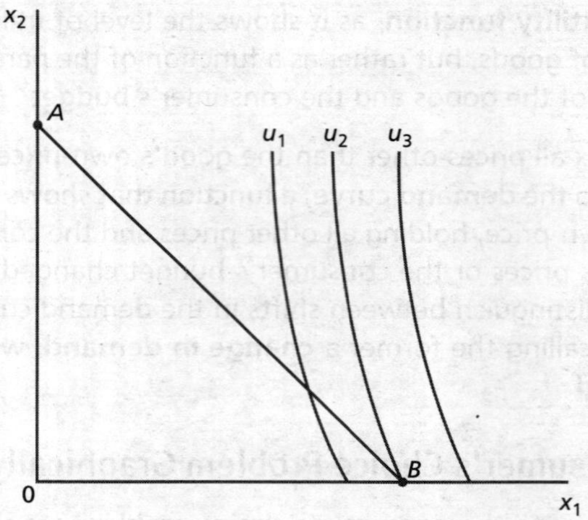


**Figure 2.17** *Corner Solution*

What if there is no point where an IC is tangent to the budget constraint? A simple example is illustrated in Figure 2.17–a situation where the ICs are all steeper than the budget constraint throughout their length. Such an indifference map might apply to someone who is extremely poor, living at a bare subsistence level, and if the good $x_1$ is food. His utility depends almost wholly on the amount of food he has, and it is difficult to compensate him for any reduction in the amount of food, accounting for the steepness in the ICs. In that case, the solution is at *B* since ICs above $u_2$ all lie completely outside the budget constraint. We have here an example of a corner solution, since the consumer's choice is not at a tangent point in the interior of the graph, but at a corner of his budget set. A particular functional form that could be used to represent the ICs pictured in Figure 2.17 is the **quasi-linear utility function**, which we saw in the previous section. This function has the property that all the ICs are horizontally parallel to one another (i.e. they have the same slope along any horizontal line), and the utility function has the form

$$u(x_1, x_2) = Bx_1 + v(x_2).$$

Two other examples where the solution is not a tangency are furnished by our polar cases of perfect complements and perfect substitutes. In the case of perfect complements (Figure 2.18), the solution is at *C*—a situation that looks very much like the solution in Figure 2.16, except that there is no tangency at *C*. The same arguments apply, however.

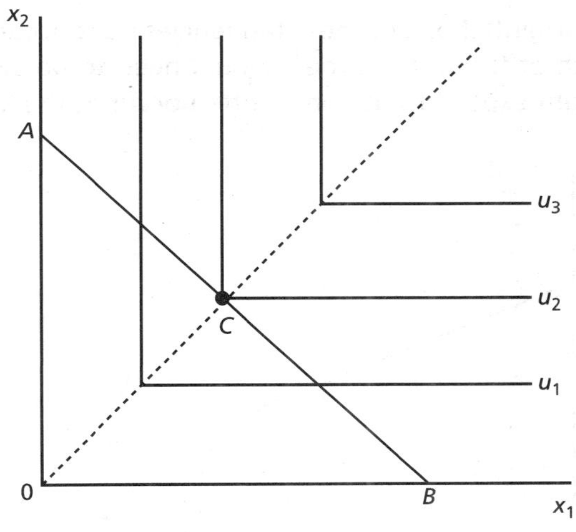


**Figure 2.18** *Perfect Complements*

In the case of perfect substitutes (Figure 2.19), the solution looks very much like Figure 2.17, with the difference being that the IC are straight lines rather than curves. But we have a similar corner solution at *B*.

Finally, we might consider cases where the budget constraint is not a simple straight line, as we saw in the section on Variations on the Budget Constraint. If the budget constraint is kinked, such as the piecewise linear line *ACE* in Figure 2.3, reproduced as Figure 2.20, there are five possibilities for the solution. It could be at any one of the corners *A*, *C* and *E*, in which case there is no tangency but a corner solution, or it could be on either of the segments *AC* or *CE* with an IC tangent to that

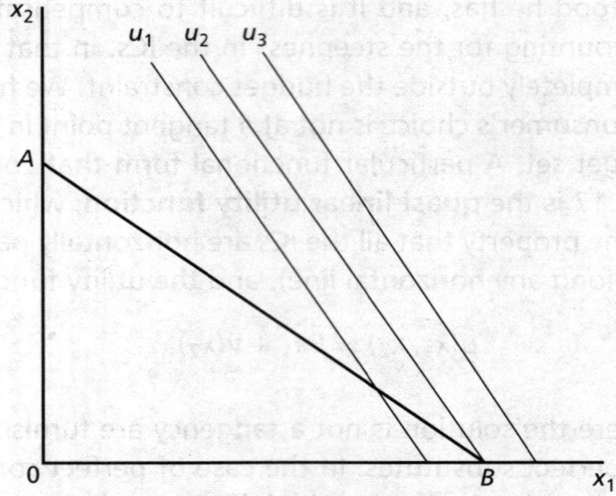


**Figure 2.19** *Perfect Substitutes*

segment of the budget constraint. If one of these tangencies does occur, it would be the solution. If there is no tangency, each of the three corners would need to be evaluated to determine the solution. In general, we might expect a solution to often occur at the kink *C*.

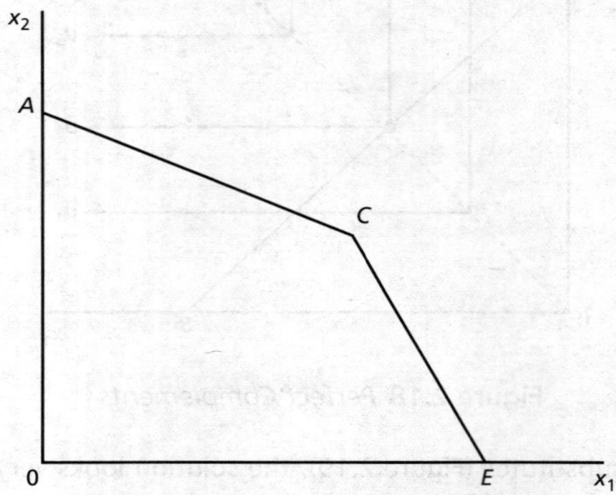


**Figure 2.20** *Choice with a Kinked Budget Constraint*

## 2.4.2 Solving the Consumer's Choice Problem Algebraically

To find the demand functions explicitly, we need to adopt an algebraic approach. We will examine each of the three cases we have looked at, using the Cobb–Douglas function as an explicit form to capture the case of convex ICs. To keep things simple, we will assume the consumer consumes just two goods; all the results are perfectly generalisable.

#### 2.4.2.1 The Cobb–Douglas Case

Suppose the utility function is Cobb–Douglas, as in (2.18):

$$u(x_1, x_2) = Ax_1^{\alpha_1}x_2^{\alpha_2} \tag{2.30}$$

and the budget constraint, as in (2.3), is

$$p_1x_1 + p_2x_2 = I, \tag{2.31}$$

so that the consumer's choice problem is to maximise (2.30) subject to the constraint (2.31). We can solve this problem by first writing down the Lagrangian function:

$$\mathcal{L} = Ax_1^{\alpha_1}x_2^{\alpha_2} + \lambda\left[I - p_1x_1 - p_2x_2\right].$$

We then find the first-order conditions by setting the partial derivatives of $\mathcal{L}$ with respect to $x_1, x_2$ and $\lambda$ equal to zero:

$$\frac{\partial \mathcal{L}}{\partial x_1} = A\alpha_1 x_1^{\alpha_1 - 1}x_2^{\alpha_2} - \lambda p_1 = 0 \tag{2.32}$$

$$\frac{\partial \mathcal{L}}{\partial x_2} = A\alpha_2 x_1^{\alpha_1}x_2^{\alpha_2 - 1} - \lambda p_2 = 0 \tag{2.33}$$

$$\frac{\partial \mathcal{L}}{\partial \lambda} = I - p_1x_1 - p_2x_2 = 0. \tag{2.34}$$

Equation (2.34) is just the budget constraint once again. Generically, (2.32) and (2.33) could be written as

$$u_1 - \lambda p_1 = 0 \tag{2.32a}$$

$$u_2 - \lambda p_2 = 0 \tag{2.33a}$$

(where $u_1$ and $u_2$ represent the first-order derivatives). Combining these equations (by dividing one by the other) we find

$$\frac{u_1}{u_2} = \frac{p_1}{p_2} \tag{2.35}$$

This is none other than the **tangency condition** since the left-hand side (LHS), the *MRS*, is the absolute value of the slope of the IC, and the right-hand side (RHS) is the absolute value of the budget constraint.

In the case of the Cobb–Douglas utility function, this equation becomes

$$\frac{\alpha_1 x_2}{\alpha_2 x_1} = \frac{p_1}{p_2} \tag{2.36}$$

which can be written as

$$p_2x_2 = \frac{\alpha_2}{\alpha_1}p_1x_1. \tag{2.37}$$

Substituting (2.37) in (2.31) or (2.34) yields

$$\left(\frac{\alpha_1+\alpha_2}{\alpha_1}\right)p_1x_1 = I$$

which can be rewritten as

$$x_1 = \left(\frac{\alpha_1}{\alpha_1+\alpha_2}\right)\frac{I}{p_1}. \tag{2.38}$$

This is the demand function for good 1 ($x_1$). Note that it also has a Cobb–Douglas form. We can similarly solve for the demand function for good 2 ($x_2$), which is

$$x_2 = \left(\frac{\alpha_2}{\alpha_1+\alpha_2}\right)\frac{I}{p_2}. \tag{2.39}$$

Looking at (2.38), the demand function for $x_1$, we see that it does not depend on $p_2$, which is not generally very reasonable. In general, we would expect the demand for a good to depend not only on its own-price and the consumer's income but also on the prices of other goods. This is a respect in which the Cobb–Douglas utility function gives rise to somewhat unrealistic behaviour. Further, we could rewrite (2.38) as

$$\frac{p_1x_1}{I} = \frac{\alpha_1}{\alpha_1+\alpha_2}.$$

This says that the budget share of $x_1$ is constant–another unreasonable property of the Cobb–Douglas utility function. We would expect that the budget share of a good changes as prices and incomes change. For example, empirical observation shows that the proportion of a typical consumer's budget spent on food declines with increasing income, an observation known as **Engel's Law**. The Cobb–Douglas utility function is not consistent with Engel's Law.

#### *2.4.2.2 The Perfect Complements (Leontief) Case*

In the case where the two goods are perfect complements, the utility function can be written (see (2.20) earlier) as

$$u(x_1, x_2) = \min\left[\frac{x_1}{\beta_1}, \frac{x_2}{\beta_2}\right]. \tag{2.40}$$

We cannot use differential calculus to solve the consumer's choice problem in this case because the utility function is not continuously differentiable. However, we know that the chosen bundle

$(x_1^*, x_2^*)$ must satisfy

$$\frac{x_1^*}{\beta_1} = \frac{x_2^*}{\beta_2} \tag{2.41}$$

since otherwise resources would be wasted. The condition (2.41) is simply saying that the consumer will choose a bundle at one of the corners of the L-shaped ICs, since choosing a bundle away from the corners would mean one of the goods would not be fully utilised. The chosen bundle must also satisfy the budget constraint (2.31). Omitting the *'s for simplicity, we can rewrite (2.41) as

$$x_2 = \frac{\beta_2}{\beta_1} x_1 \tag{2.42}$$

and substituting this in (2.31) yields

$$p_1 x_1 + p_2 \frac{\beta_2}{\beta_1} x_1 = I,$$

which simplifies to

$$x_1 = \frac{\beta_1 I}{\beta_1 p_1 + \beta_2 p_2}. \tag{2.43}$$

This is the demand function for $x_1$. By a similar process of reasoning, or by appealing to the symmetry of the problem, we can find the demand function for good 2:

$$x_2 = \frac{\beta_2 I}{\beta_1 p_1 + \beta_2 p_2}. \tag{2.44}$$

**Example 2.3: Demand Functions for Perfect Complements**

Suppose Mary consumes jam sandwiches. Each sandwich contains 2 slices of bread and 3 teaspoons of jam. So the only two goods Mary buys are bread ($x_b$) and jam ($x_j$). Her utility function then is

$$u(x_b, x_j) = \min\left[\frac{x_b}{2}, \frac{x_j}{3}\right], \tag{2.45}$$

because we need $x_b = 2$ and $x_j = 3$ to make one sandwich. So here $\beta_1 = 2$ and $\beta_2 = 3$. Then, according to (2.43), the demand function for bread will be

$$x_b = \frac{2I}{2p_b + 3p_j}. \tag{2.46}$$

A simple way to understand (2.46) is to note that the denominator $(2p_b + 3p_j)$ is the cost of a sandwich. Dividing $I$ by this cost yields the number of sandwiches Mary can buy. Finally, since

Mary needs 2 slices of bread per sandwich, we need to multiply the number of sandwiches by 2 to get the amount of bread she will buy with her budget, $I$.

### 2.4.2.3 *The Perfect Substitutes (Linear) Case*

In the case of perfect substitutes, we saw in (2.25) that the utility function is

$$u(x_1, x_2) = \gamma_1 x_1 + \gamma_2 x_2. \tag{2.47}$$

Once again, we cannot apply differential calculus to this problem because we have a corner solution. The ICs are all straight lines with slope $-\frac{\gamma_1}{\gamma_2}$ and so the solution will depend on the whether the slope of the budget constraint $-\frac{p_1}{p_2}$ is greater than or less than the slope of the ICs.

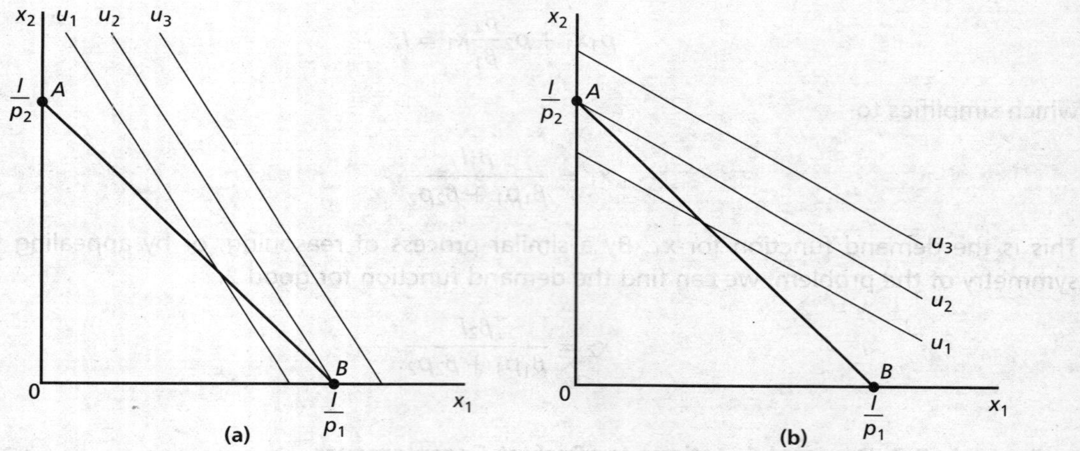


**Figure 2.21** *Choice with Perfect Substitutes*

Panel (a) in Figure 2.21 illustrates a case where the ICs are steeper than the budget constraint, that is, where

$$\frac{\gamma_1}{\gamma_2} > \frac{p_1}{p_2}. \tag{2.48}$$

In this case, the consumer would buy only good 1 so that the demands for the two goods would be

$$x_1 = \frac{I}{p_1} \quad \text{and} \tag{2.49}$$

$$x_2 = 0. \tag{2.50}$$

Panel (b) in Figure 2.21 illustrates the case where the ICs are flatter than the budget constraint, that is, where

$$\frac{\gamma_1}{\gamma_2} < \frac{p_1}{p_2}. \tag{2.51}$$

In this case, the consumer would buy only good 2 so that the demands for the two goods would be

$$x_1 = 0 \quad \text{and} \tag{2.52}$$

$$x_2 = \frac{I}{p_2}. \tag{2.53}$$

By combining (2.46) to (2.53), we can write down the demand functions in the perfect substitutes case:

$$x_1 = \begin{cases} \dfrac{I}{p_1} & \text{if} \quad \dfrac{p_1}{p_2} < \dfrac{\gamma_1}{\gamma_2} \\ 0 & \text{if} \quad \dfrac{p_1}{p_2} > \dfrac{\gamma_1}{\gamma_2} \end{cases} \tag{2.54}$$

and

$$x_2 = \begin{cases} 0 & \text{if} \quad \dfrac{p_1}{p_2} < \dfrac{\gamma_1}{\gamma_2} \\ \dfrac{I}{p_2} & \text{if} \quad \dfrac{p_1}{p_2} > \dfrac{\gamma_1}{\gamma_2}. \end{cases} \tag{2.55}$$

Note that (2.54) and (2.55) leave out the case where $\frac{p_1}{p_2} = \frac{\gamma_1}{\gamma_2}$. In this case, the quantities demanded of $x_1$ and $x_2$ are indeterminate (within the range $0 \le x_i \le \frac{I}{p_i}$) since the consumer is equally well off at any point on the budget constraint $AB$.

## 2.5 COMPARATIVE STATICS ON DEMAND FUNCTIONS

**Task for this section:**

To study the properties of the demand function, specifically, to learn how the quantity demanded changes in response to changes in each of the arguments of the demand function. After this section, you should have a good idea about the heart of the modern theory of consumer behaviour, the law of demand. You should know what substitution and income effects are and how they are used to analyse the effects of changes in prices. You should feel comfortable manipulating demand functions and working with them in different ways.

We have seen that a demand function shows the quantity demanded of a good as a function of its price, the prices of other goods and the consumer's budget. To understand the properties of demand functions, we perform comparative statics exercises. In doing so, we study the effect of changing the value of one argument of the function while keeping the values of all other arguments fixed. In this way, we gain insight into the sign of the partial derivative of demand with respect to the argument whose value is being changed. In other words, for the demand function $x_1 = x_1(p_1, p_2, \ldots, p_n, I)$, we are interested in:

- Effect of income changes: $\frac{\partial x_1}{\partial I}$
- Own-price effect: $\frac{\partial x_1}{\partial p_1}$
- Cross-price effects: $\frac{\partial x_1}{\partial p_j}$ for all $j \neq 1$.

These partial derivatives, or slopes, are not free of the units in which we measure quantities, prices and income. For example, the responsiveness of demand to a change in the price of a kilogram of a good will be different from the responsiveness to a change in the price of a pound of the good. In order to have unit-free measures of responsiveness of demand to changes in the arguments of the demand function, we often look at the elasticities. The **elasticity** of any variable $y$ with respect to a variable $x$ is a measure of the responsiveness of $y$ to changes in $x$ and is defined as

$$\epsilon_{yx} = \frac{\partial y}{\partial x} \cdot \frac{x}{y}.$$

The demand function has three classes of elasticities:

- Income elasticity of demand: $\eta = \frac{\partial x_1}{\partial I} \cdot \frac{I}{x_1}$
- Own-price elasticity: $\epsilon_1 = \frac{\partial x_1}{\partial p_1} \cdot \frac{p_1}{x_1}$
- Cross-price elasticity: $\epsilon_{1j} = \frac{\partial x_1}{\partial p_j} \cdot \frac{p_j}{x_1}$ for all $j \neq 1$.

The purpose of comparative statics exercises on the demand function is to examine what we can say about the signs of these elasticities.

We begin by looking at the effects of changing the consumer's budget.

### 2.5.1 Changes in Budget

We saw earlier that, in the 2-good case, an increase in the consumer's budget would cause the budget constraint $AB$ to shift outward parallel to itself to a position such as $A'B'$ in Figure 2.22. If

$C$ was the original chosen bundle and $C'$ is the new chosen bundle, the question is: where does $C'$ lie in comparison to $C$?

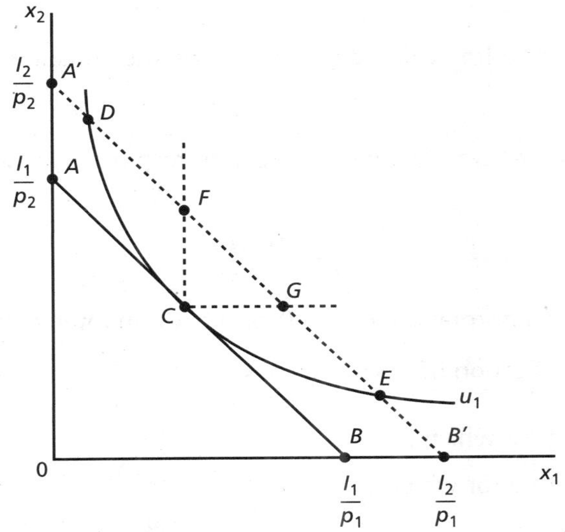


**Figure 2.22** *The Effect of Changes in the Budget*

We know that a consumer will be better-off if her budget goes up. Looking at Figure 2.22, we see that all points on the segment $DE$ of the new budget constraint $A'B'$ represent utility levels higher than $u_1$, the utility level at C. Thus, in principle, any point along $DE$ could possibly be the new chosen bundle $C'$. Draw a vertical and a horizontal line out of the point C. These lines cross $A'B'$ at $F$ and $G$ respectively, thereby dividing the line segment $DE$ into three parts: $DF$, $FG$ and $GE$. $C'$ could be on each of these segments, which are qualitatively different in what they represent in terms of the consumption pattern at $C'$ in comparison to C. If $C'$ is on the segment

- FG: consumption of both goods has gone up
- DF: $x_2$ has gone up but $x_1$ has gone down
- GE: $x_1$ has gone up but $x_2$ has gone down.

Normally, we expect that a consumer would buy more of all goods (as long as the goods are broadly defined) as her budget grows and therefore expect $C'$ to lie on the segment $FG$. For example, if goods 1 and 2 represent broad categories such as food and clothing, we would expect demand for each of these to rise as the budget rises. If, on the other hand, we had a very narrowly defined good, such as a coarse grain it is quite possible that demand for the good might fall as the consumer's budget rose because she substituted away from this good to other, superior alternatives such as wheat or rice. In that case, we call the good an inferior good.

We therefore have the following classification:

- A **normal good** is one for which demand rises as the consumer's budget increases (and vice versa).
- An **inferior good** is one for which demand falls as the consumer's budget increases (and vice versa).

The **Income Elasticity of Demand** is a measure of the responsiveness of a consumer's demand to changes in her budget:

$$\eta = \frac{\partial x}{\partial I} \cdot \frac{I}{x}. \tag{2.56}$$

We can easily see that, for a normal good, $\eta > 0$, while for an inferior good, $\eta < 0$.

We have a further classification of normal goods:

- A **luxury** good is one for which $\eta > 1$.
- A **necessity** good is one for which $0 < \eta < 1$.

Intuitively, a luxury is a good for which demand grows proportionately faster than the budget, while a necessity is one for which demand, although growing, grows proportionately more slowly than the budget. For example, as we saw with Engel's Law, the budget share of food tends to fall as consumers' incomes rise; food is a necessity. On the other hand, people tend to spend a greater proportion of their budget on vacations as their incomes rise; vacations are a luxury.

Consider the budget share of a good, the fraction of the budget spent on that particular good:

$$\theta = \frac{px}{I}. \tag{2.57}$$

Now consider how this budget share changes as $I$ changes:

$$\frac{\partial \theta}{\partial I} = \frac{I \cdot p\frac{\partial x}{\partial I} - px}{I^2}. \tag{2.58}$$

By multiplying the first term in the numerator by $\frac{x}{x}$, we can rewrite (2.58) as

$$\frac{\partial \theta}{\partial I} = \frac{px(\eta - 1)}{I^2}. \tag{2.59}$$

From (2.59) we see that

- for a luxury, $\eta > 1 \quad \rightarrow \quad \frac{\partial \theta}{\partial I} > 0$, which says that the budget share rises as $I$ rises.
- for a necessity, $\eta < 1 \quad \rightarrow \quad \frac{\partial \theta}{\partial I} < 0$, which says that the budget share falls as $I$ rises.

We have already seen Engel's Law, which says that the budget share of food falls as income rises. Thus, food would be classified as a necessity, which is intuitively reasonable, and its income elasticity of demand lies between 0 and 1. We could illustrate this relationship graphically by looking at the relationship between the quantity demanded of a good and the consumer's budget, holding all prices constant. If we plot this relationship on a graph, with the budget $I$ on the vertical axis and the amount demanded of a good on the horizontal axis, we have an **Engel Curve**, a curve showing the relationship between the quantity demanded and the consumer's budget. The Engel curve for a necessity such as food would look something like the curve in panel (a) of Figure 2.23. Note that if we draw a line from any point on the curve to the origin, the slope of that ray through the origin is $\frac{I}{x}$, and the inverse of that, $\frac{x}{I}$, is proportional to the budget share $\theta$, as long as the good's price is constant. Thus the budget share is inversely related to the slope of the ray through the origin. We see in panel (a) that, as $I$ rises, the slope of the ray rises, which means the budget share falls, as required by Engel's Law. All goods that are necessities will have Engel curves shaped like the one in panel (a).

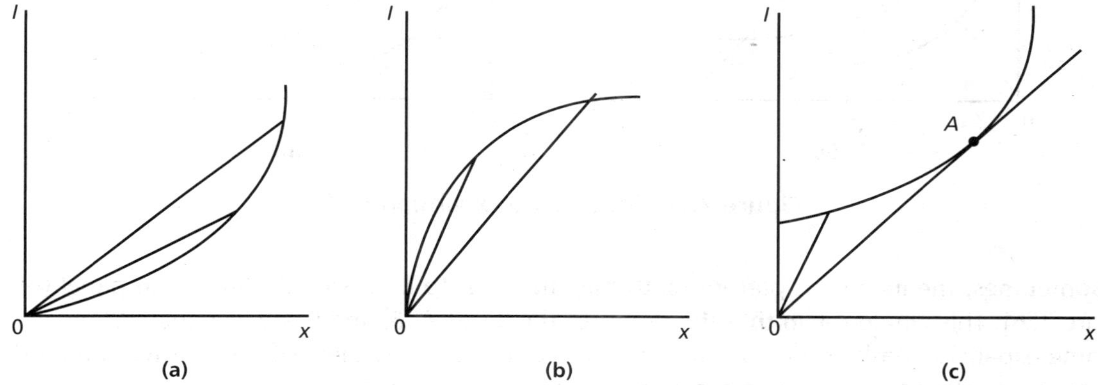


**Figure 2.23** *Engel Curves*

Panels (b) and (c) in Figure 2.23 illustrate Engel curves for goods that are luxuries. Panel (b) is clear and unambiguous, as the slope of the ray steadily falls as $I$ rises, so that the budget share rises. Panel (c) illustrates a more complicated case. Because the consumption of the good starts only at a relatively high level of $I$, the good must be a luxury, since it is starting with a budget share of zero. As we see, the slope of the ray through the origin falls as $I$ rises, indicating that the budget share rises. However, here the budget share reaches a maximum at point $A$ (the slope of the ray reaches a minimum). If $I$ rises further, the slope of the ray starts to rise, which means the budget share starts to fall. Thus this good starts out as a luxury, but becomes a necessity once the consumer's budget is large enough.

While the Engel curve presents the relationship between quantity demanded and the consumer's budget directly, the **Income Expansion Path** presents this relationship indirectly. Figure 2.22 was used to analyse the effect of a change in the consumer's budget on her consumption pattern. If, keeping commodity prices fixed, we plotted the consumer's chosen consumption bundles for all possible budget levels, the line connecting these chosen consumption bundles is called the income expansion path; see Figure 2.24, panel (a) for an example. Note that this line will always start at the origin since, if the consumer's budget is zero, the origin would have to be her consumption point.

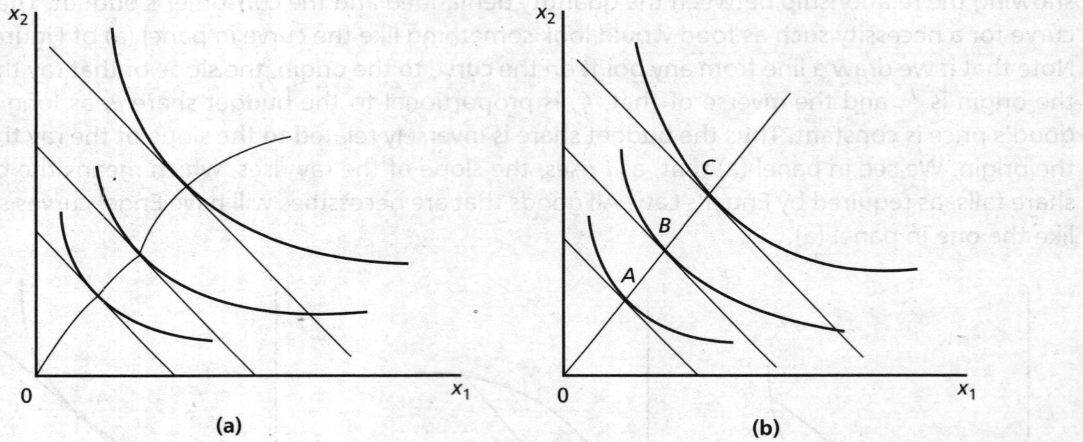


**Figure 2.24** *The Income Expansion Path*

Sometimes, the income expansion path may turn out to be a straight line, as in panel (b) of Figure 2.24. This would mean that the slopes of the ICs at $A$, $B$, and $C$ are all equal. When all the income expansion paths for a consumer are straight lines, regardless of the relative commodity prices, we say that the consumer has **homothetic preferences**. Such preferences have the property that the ICs are radially parallel to one another: the slopes are equal along every ray through the origin. Thus

$$u(x_1^0, x_2^0, \ldots, x_n^0) = u(x_1^1, x_2^1, \ldots, x_n^1) \quad \longleftrightarrow \quad u(tx_1^0, tx_2^0, \ldots, tx_n^0) = u(tx_1^1, tx_2^1, \ldots, tx_n^1) \text{ for all } t > 0.$$

All homogeneous functions are homothetic, as are all monotonic transformations of any homogeneous function. Since utility functions are unique only up to monotonic transformations, every homothetic utility function can be represented by a function that is homogeneous of degree one, that is, a function that has the property that

$$u(tx_1, tx_2, \ldots, tx_n) = tu(x_1, x_2, \ldots, x_n).$$

Each of the three specific utility functions that we have been using for illustrative examples, the Cobb–Douglas, Leontief and Linear utility function, is homothetic.

### A Restriction on the Income Elasticities of Demand

We have seen that it is possible to classify goods according to their income elasticities of demand:

- Inferior good: $0 < \eta$
- Necessity: $0 < \eta < 1$
- Luxury: $\eta > 1$.

If a consumer bought only one good, its income elasticity of demand would have to be equal to 1, since consumption of the good would always rise or fall in the same proportion as income. When a consumer buys many goods, this result generalises to say that, *on average*, income elasticities of the goods must still be equal to 1, since the consumer still spends only what she has available to spend. We can see this result as following from the budget constraint, which we saw in (2.2):

$$\sum_{i=1}^{n} p_i x_i = I. \tag{2.60}$$

Differentiating both sides of (2.60) with respect to $I$, we get

$$\sum_{i=1}^{n} p_i \frac{\partial x_i}{\partial I} = 1. \tag{2.61}$$

We can rewrite (2.61) as

$$\sum_{i=1}^{n} \frac{p_i x_i}{I} \cdot \frac{\partial x_i}{\partial I} \cdot \frac{I}{x_i} = 1, \tag{2.62}$$

which is

$$\sum_{i=1}^{n} \theta_i \eta_i = 1. \tag{2.63}$$

This says that the income elasticities must have a weighted average of 1, where the weights are the budget shares, and implies that at least one of the goods a consumer consumes must be a luxury. This restriction is known as the **Generalised Engel's Law**.

## 2.5.2 Changes in Own-Price

The next comparative statics exercise is to study the effect on demand of changes in a good's own-price–what happens to $x_i$ when $p_i$ changes, holding $I$ and all $p_j$'s constant? We will look at a 2-good example to consider this graphically before proceeding to an algebraic approach.

### 2.5.2.1 *Geometric Approach*

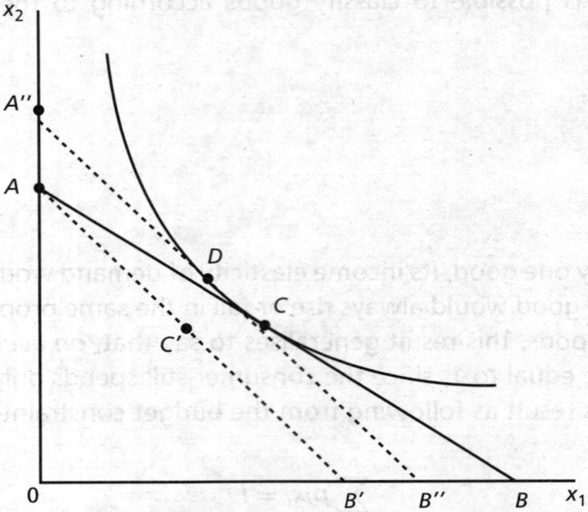


**Figure 2.25** *The Effect of Own-Price Changes*

Consider Figure 2.25. *AB* is the initial budget constraint and *C* is the chosen bundle. Suppose the price $p_1$ goes up to $p_1^{'}$, pushing the budget constraint inward to *AB′*. There will be a new chosen bundle *C′* and the question of interest is: Where will the new chosen bundle *C′* be relative to *C*?

Economists get a handle on this question by dividing up the movement from *C* to *C′* (the price effect) into two hypothetical component steps, a substitution effect and an income effect. These two steps are intended to capture two different forces that are acting on the consumer's decision. The substitution effect captures the effect of the fact that now good 1 is more expensive relative to other goods, while the income effect captures the effect of the fact that the consumer now feels worse off.

We find the substitution effect by looking for the point on the original IC $u_1$ where the slope of the IC equals the slope of the new budget constraint *AB′*. Because *AB′* is steeper than *AB* (since $p_1$ went up), this point *D* will be somewhere to the left of *C* where $u_1$ is steeper because of the convexity of $u_1$. So the substitution effect is negative:

$$\frac{\partial x_1}{\partial p_1} |_{\bar{u}} < 0. \tag{2.64}$$

If we draw a line tangent to $u_1$ at *D*, this line would represent the budget constraint which, if the consumer happened to face it, would lead to *D* being the chosen bundle. This budget constraint is labelled *A"B"*.

Now consider the actual final choice bundle $C'$, which is chosen when the budget constraint is $AB'$. Note that $AB'$ is parallel to $A''B''$, only lower. Thus, as long as good 1 is a normal good, we know that $C'$ must be to the left of $D$ since the only difference between $A''B''$ (when $D$ is chosen) and $AB'$ (when $C'$ is chosen) is that the budget is lower at $AB'$. Thus, $\frac{\partial x_1}{\partial p_1}$ is also negative on grounds of the income effect (which it already was on grounds of the substitution effect) and we are led to the conclusion that, as long as the good is normal, the quantity demanded falls in response to a rise in its price. This result is known as the law of demand.

**Law of Demand**: For a normal good, the quantity demanded and the price of the good are negatively related. In other words, as the price of a good rises, the quantity demanded falls, and as the price of a good falls, the quantity demanded rises.

Note that, for an inferior good, $C'$ would be to the right of $D$, since quantity demanded would rise in response to a fall in the budget. However, $C'$ would still be to the left of $C$ if the income effect were smaller than the substitution effect. If the income effect for an inferior good were larger than the substitution effect, then $C'$ would be to the right even of $C$ and the quantity demanded would have risen in response to a rise in the price. Such a good is called a **Giffen good**; quantity demanded and the price of the good are positively related for such a good.

The points $C$ and $C'$ in Figure 2.25 show the consumer's chosen consumption bundles at different prices of good 1, holding the size of the budget and the prices of all other goods constant. Thus, they correspond to two points on the consumer's demand curve for good 1. The points $C$ and $D$, on the other hand, show the consumer's chosen consumption bundles at different prices of good 1, holding prices of other goods constant, but with the size of the budget changing to compensate the consumer for the price increase. What is being held constant here is not the size of the budget but the level of utility, and this exercise gives rise to a different type of demand curve.

The **compensated (or Hicksian) demand curve** of a good shows the quantity demanded by the consumer as a function of the price of the good, holding the consumer's utility and the prices of all other goods constant.

The compensated demand curve could be seen as a variant of the ordinary demand curve. Starting with the ordinary demand curve, we hold prices of all other goods constant and only allow the price of the subject good to vary. What we do is that, whenever the price of the good changes, we immediately change the consumer's budget by just the right amount so as to keep her at the original utility level. In other words, we compensate her for the price change. If the price of the good goes up, we must give the consumer some extra money to compensate her, but if the price of the good goes down, we must take away some money from her in order to force her back to the original utility level. If we then look at how much of the good she consumes at different prices, having had her budget compensated each time, we trace out the compensated demand curve.

It is possible to show the derivation of the ordinary and compensated demand curves from the IC diagram in Figure 2.25, which has been reproduced as the top panel in Figure 2.26. The lower panel also has $x_1$ on the horizontal axis, but measures $p_1$ on the vertical axis and therefore is the right space in which to draw demand curves. The initial consumption choice is at $C$, when $p_1 = p^0$ (leaving out the subscript to simplify the notation), and this point is marked as the point $E$ in the lower panel. The task is to draw the ordinary and compensated demand curves through this point. Remember that the ordinary demand curve shows quantity demanded as a function of price, holding the consumer's *budget* constant, while the compensated demand curve shows quantity demanded as a function of price, holding the consumer's *utility* constant. So the ordinary demand curve through point $E$ will be the one for the initial budget $I^0$ and the compensated demand curve through $E$ will be the one for the initial utility level $u^0$.

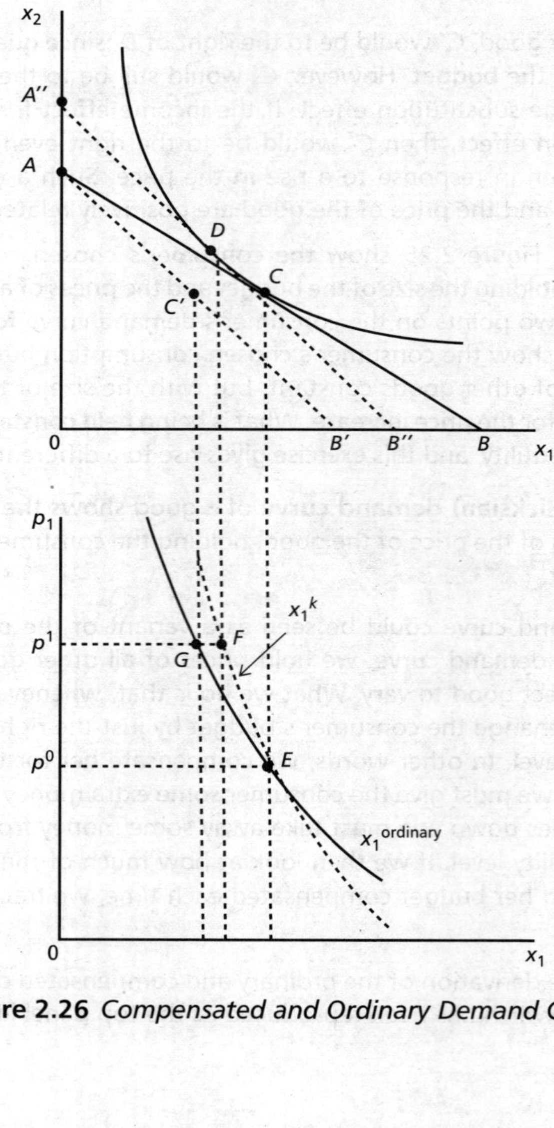


**Figure 2.26** *Compensated and Ordinary Demand Curves*

After the price of good 1 rises to $p^1$, the consumer's consumption choice shifts to $C'$. The point $G$ in the lower panel reflects this new bundle, as it shows the same quantity of good 1 as at $C'$ being consumed at the price $p^1$. Thus the point $G$ lies on the ordinary demand curve, shown as the solid line $EG$. To find the compensated demand curve, we need to compensate the consumer for the price increase, which is precisely what we did to find the substitution effect. The compensated budget is represented by the budget constraint $A''B''$ and the chosen bundle is then $D$. The corresponding point in the lower panel is point $F$, which shows the same quantity of good 1 being consumed at the price $p^1$. Since the utility level at $D$ is the same as at $C$, the point $F$ is on the compensated demand curve, shown as the dotted line $EF$ in the lower panel. We see from this analysis that, for a normal good, the compensated demand curve through any point is less elastic than the ordinary demand curve. The compensated demand curve captures only the substitution effect, while the ordinary demand curve captures both the substitution and income effects. Since these reinforce each other in the case of a normal good, the ordinary demand curve is more elastic.

Correspondingly, for an inferior good, the compensated demand curve through any point will be more elastic than the ordinary demand curve. This is left for the reader to confirm as an exercise.

#### *2.5.2.2 Algebraic Approach to the Law of Demand*

We will focus on the 2-good case to make the analysis more transparent. The first task would be to find the substitution effect, which was indicated by the bundle $D$ of Figure 2.25. In order to find this point, we need to solve the following problem, using the final prices and the initial utility level:

$$\text{Minimise} \quad E = \sum_{i=1}^{n} p_i x_i \tag{2.65}$$

$$\text{subject to} \quad u(x_1, x_2, \ldots, x_n) = u. \tag{2.66}$$

That is, we need to find the minimum expenditure needed to achieve the initial level of utility $u_1$ at the new prices $(p_1', p_2, \ldots, p_n)$.

The solutions to this problem, the quantities demanded of the goods as functions of prices and the utility level are known as the **Hicksian** or **compensated demand functions**:

$$\begin{aligned} x_1^h &= x_1^h(p_1, p_2, \ldots, p_n, u) \\ x_2^h &= x_2^h(p_1, p_2, \ldots, p_n, u) \\ &\vdots \\ x_n^h &= x_n^h(p_1, p_2, \ldots, p_n, u) \end{aligned} \tag{2.67}$$

These are in contrast to the **Marshallian** or **ordinary demand functions**, which show quantities demanded as functions of prices and the consumer's budget. Holding the prices of all other goods and the utility level constant, the compensated demand function becomes the compensated demand curve, which we saw earlier.

If we substitute (2.67) back into (2.65), we get the **expenditure function**:

$$E(p_1, p_2, \ldots, p_n, u) = \sum_{i=1}^{n} p_i x_i^h(p_1, p_2, \ldots, p_n, u), \tag{2.68}$$

which shows the minimum expenditure needed to achieve any level of utility at any given set of prices. As a consequence of the envelope theorem, if we ask how this minimum expenditure changes as $p_i$ changes, we see that

$$\frac{\partial E}{\partial p_i} = x_i^h. \tag{2.69}$$

This result is known as **Shephard's Lemma.**

We are now in a position to study the Law of Demand. Suppose we start with the consumer's ordinary demand function

$$x_1 = x_1(p_1, p_2, \ldots, p_n, I)$$

and then modify it by replacing $I$ in the function by $E(p_1, p_2, \ldots, p_n, u)$, the expenditure function. That is, whenever a price changes, we also change $I$ to 'compensate' the consumer in such a way as to make it just possible for her to achieve the initial level of utility. This will give us the compensated demand function. In other words,

$$x_1\,(p_1, p_2, \ldots, p_n, E(p_1, p_2, \ldots, p_n, u)) \equiv x_1^h(p_1, p_2, \ldots, p_n, u). \tag{2.70}$$

If we now differentiate both sides of (2.70) with respect to $p_1$, we get

$$\frac{\partial x_1}{\partial p_1} + \frac{\partial x_1}{\partial E} \cdot \frac{\partial E}{\partial p_1} = \frac{\partial x_1^h}{\partial p_1}. \tag{2.71}$$

Rearranging terms and substituting $x_1^h$ for $\frac{\partial E}{\partial p_1}$ from (2.69), we get

$$\frac{\partial x_1}{\partial p_1} = \frac{\partial x_1^h}{\partial p_1} - x_1^h \frac{\partial x_1}{\partial E}, \tag{2.72}$$

or, what is the same thing,

$$\frac{\partial x_1}{\partial p_1} = \frac{\partial x_1^h}{\partial p_1} - x_1^h \frac{\partial x_1}{\partial I}, \tag{2.73}$$

since changes in income are the same as changes in expenditure. This equation is in essence saying:

Price Effect = Substitution Effect + Income Effect.

Equation (2.73) is an important result called the **Slutsky Equation**. It proves the Law of Demand. The first term on the RHS is the substitution effect and is negative. The second term is the product of two positive terms (as long as the good is normal) preceded by negative sign. Hence the second term is also negative. Thus the RHS is the sum of two negative terms and therefore the LHS is unambiguously negative, which is what the law of demand requires: for a normal good, the price effect is negative.

The Slutsky equation can be converted to an elasticities version. Equation (2.73) can be rewritten as

$$\frac{\partial x_1}{\partial p_1} \cdot \frac{p_1}{x_1} = \frac{\partial x_1^h}{\partial p_1} \cdot \frac{p_1}{x_1^h} - \frac{p_1 x_1}{I} \cdot \frac{\partial x_1}{\partial I} \cdot \frac{I}{x_1}, \tag{2.74}$$

since $x_1 = x_1^h$ at the initial equilibrium. Equation (2.74) can be written as

$$\epsilon_1 = \epsilon_1^h - \theta_1 \eta_1, \tag{2.75}$$

where

$$\begin{aligned} \epsilon_1 &= \text{own-price elasticity of demand for } x_1 \\ \epsilon_1^h &= \text{elasticity of compensated demand for } x_1 \\ \theta_1 &= \text{budget share of } x_1 \\ \eta_1 &= \text{income elasticity of demand for } x_1. \end{aligned}$$

Equation (2.75) is called the **Slutsky equation in elasticities**. In principle, this equation is very useful. Since $\epsilon_1$, $\theta_1$ and $\eta_1$ are all estimable from market studies, (2.75) shows how $\epsilon_1^h$ can be also be estimated.

**Example 2.4: Cobb–Douglas Utility Function**

Suppose the utility function is

$$u(x_1, x_2) = x_1^3 x_2^2. \tag{2.76}$$

Using (2.38) and (2.39), we can write down the demand functions:

$$x_1 = \frac{3I}{5p_1} \quad \text{and} \quad x_2 = \frac{2I}{5p_2}. \tag{2.77}$$

Substituting (2.77) in (2.76), we get the indirect utility function:

$$V(p_1, p_2, I) = \left(\frac{3}{5}\right)^3 \left(\frac{2}{5}\right)^2 \left(\frac{I^5}{p_1^3 p_2^2}\right). \tag{2.78}$$

Now let us find the compensated demand functions and the expenditure function. For this, we need to solve the problem:

$$\text{Minimise} \quad E = p_1x_1 + p_2x_2 \tag{2.79}$$

$$\text{subject to} \quad x_1^3x_2^2 = u. \tag{2.80}$$

Write down the Lagrangian for this problem:

$$\mathcal{L} = p_1x_1 + p_2x_2 + \lambda\left[u - x_1^3x_2^2\right]. \tag{2.81}$$

Differentiating with respect to $x_1, x_2, \lambda$ and setting equal to zero:

$$\frac{\partial \mathcal{L}}{\partial x_1} = p_1 - \lambda \cdot 3x_1^2x_2^2 = 0 \tag{2.82}$$

$$\frac{\partial \mathcal{L}}{\partial x_2} = p_2 - \lambda \cdot 2x_1^3x_2 = 0 \tag{2.83}$$

$$\frac{\partial \mathcal{L}}{\partial \lambda} = u - x_1^3x_2^2 = 0. \tag{2.84}$$

Combining (2.82) and (2.83) yields the same tangency condition we had in the utility maximisation problem:

$$\frac{3x_2}{2x_1} = \frac{p_1}{p_2} \tag{2.85}$$

which can be written as

$$x_2 = \frac{2}{3} \cdot \frac{p_1x_1}{p_2} \tag{2.86}$$

Substituting (2.86) in (2.84), we get

$$u - x_1^3\left(\frac{2}{3} \cdot \frac{p_1x_1}{p_2}\right)^2 = 0. \tag{2.87}$$

Solving for $x_1$, we get the compensated or Hicksian demand function for good 1, which we denote $x_1^h$ (where the $h$ stands for 'Hicksian'):

$$x_1^h = \left(\frac{3}{2}\right)^{\frac{2}{5}} u^{\frac{1}{5}} \left(\frac{p_2}{p_1}\right)^{\frac{2}{5}} \tag{2.88}$$

By substituting (2.88) in (2.86) and solving for $x_2$, we get the compensated demand function for good 2:

$$x_2^h = \left(\frac{2}{3}\right)^{\frac{3}{5}} u^{\frac{1}{5}} \left(\frac{p_1}{p_2}\right)^{\frac{3}{5}}. \tag{2.89}$$

Notice that both of the Hicksian demand functions are also of Cobb–Douglas form.

To find the expenditure function, we substitute (2.88) and (2.89) in (2.79):

$$E(p_1, p_2, u) = p_1 \cdot \left(\frac{3}{2}\right)^{\frac{2}{5}} u^{\frac{1}{5}} \left(\frac{p_2}{p_1}\right)^{\frac{2}{5}} + p_2 \cdot \left(\frac{2}{3}\right)^{\frac{3}{5}} u^{\frac{1}{5}} \left(\frac{p_1}{p_2}\right)^{\frac{3}{5}},$$

which can be simplified to

$$E(p_1, p_2, u) = \left(\frac{3}{2}\right)^{\frac{2}{5}} \left(\frac{5}{3}\right) u^{\frac{1}{5}} p_1^{\frac{3}{5}} p_2^{\frac{2}{5}}. \tag{2.90}$$

Note that the expenditure function is also of Cobb–Douglas form.

In (2.70), we made the claim that substituting the expenditure function for the budget in the ordinary demand function would yield the compensated demand function. This can be verified for the example by substituting the expenditure function in (2.90) for $I$ in the ordinary demand function (2.77):

$$x_1^h = \frac{3}{5p_1} \cdot \left(\frac{3}{2}\right)^{\frac{2}{5}} \left(\frac{5}{3}\right) u^{\frac{1}{5}} p_1^{\frac{3}{5}} p_2^{\frac{2}{5}}$$

which simplifies to the compensated demand function we had in (2.88):

$$x_1^h = \left(\frac{3}{2}\right)^{\frac{2}{5}} u^{\frac{1}{5}} p_1^{-\frac{2}{5}} p_2^{\frac{2}{5}}.$$

We can also use this example to verify the Slutsky equation. From (2.73), the Slutsky equation is

$$\frac{\partial x_1}{\partial p_1} = \frac{\partial x_1^h}{\partial p_1} - x_1^h \frac{\partial x_1}{\partial I}. \tag{2.91}$$

Differentiating the ordinary demand function (2.77), we have

$$\frac{\partial x_1}{\partial p_1} = -\frac{3}{5} \cdot \frac{I}{p_1^2} \tag{2.92}$$

and

$$\frac{\partial x_1}{\partial I} = \frac{3}{5p_1}. \tag{2.93}$$

Differentiating the compensated demand function (2.88), we have

$$\frac{\partial x_1^h}{\partial p_1} = \left(\frac{3}{2}\right)^{\frac{2}{5}} u^{\frac{1}{5}} \left(-\frac{2}{5}\right) p_1^{-\frac{7}{5}} p_2^{\frac{2}{5}}. \tag{2.94}$$

Finally, from the indirect utility function (2.78), we can write

$$I^5 = \left(\frac{5}{3}\right)^3 \left(\frac{5}{2}\right)^2 p_1^3 p_2^2 u$$

which can be written as

$$I = \left(\frac{5}{3}\right)^{\frac{3}{5}} \left(\frac{5}{2}\right)^{\frac{2}{5}} p_1^{\frac{3}{5}} p_2^{\frac{2}{5}} u^{\frac{1}{5}}. \tag{2.95}$$

Substituting (2.95) in (2.92), we see that the LHS of (2.91) is

$$\text{LHS} = -\left(\frac{3}{2}\right)^{\frac{2}{5}} p_1^{-\frac{7}{5}} p_2^{\frac{2}{5}} u^{\frac{1}{5}}.$$

Substituting (2.94), (2.88) and (2.93) to the RHS of (2.91), we find

$$\text{RHS} = \left(\frac{3}{2}\right)^{\frac{2}{5}} u^{\frac{1}{5}} \left(-\frac{2}{5}\right) p_1^{-\frac{7}{5}} p_2^{\frac{2}{5}} - \left(\frac{3}{2}\right)^{\frac{2}{5}} u^{\frac{1}{5}} \left(\frac{p_2}{p_1}\right)^{\frac{2}{5}} \cdot \frac{3}{5p_1}$$

which simplifies to

$$\text{RHS} = -\left(\frac{3}{2}\right)^{\frac{2}{5}} p_1^{-\frac{7}{5}} p_2^{\frac{2}{5}} u^{\frac{1}{5}},$$

thereby verifying the Slutsky equation.

Finally, we may also verify the elasticities form of the equation. To do this, we can use a general property of functions that have a Cobb–Douglas form. For any function of Cobb–Douglas form, say

$$y = f(x_1, x_2) = a x_1^b x_2^c,$$

the elasticities of $y$ with respect to its arguments are simply the exponents on the respective arguments. In this example, therefore, the elasticity of $y$ with respect to $x_1$ is $b$ and the elasticity of $y$ with respect to $x_2$ is $c$. To see this, note that the elasticity of $y$ with respect to $x_1$ is

$$\epsilon_{y_1} = \frac{\partial y}{\partial x_1} \cdot \frac{x_1}{y}.$$

In this case,

$$\frac{\partial y}{\partial x_1} = ab x_1^{b-1} x_2^c$$

and therefore

$$\epsilon_{y_1} = ab x_1^{b-1} x_2^c \cdot \frac{x_1}{a x_1^b x_2^c} = b.$$

We can similarly show that $\epsilon_{y2} = c$.

Applying this result to the ordinary demand function (2.77), we have

$$\epsilon_1 = -1, \eta_1 = 1, \theta_1 = \frac{3}{5}. \tag{2.96}$$

From the compensated demand function (2.88), we have

$$\epsilon_1^h = -\frac{2}{5}. \tag{2.97}$$

From (2.96) and (2.97), it is easy to see that

$$\epsilon_1 = \epsilon_1^h - \theta_1 \eta_1,$$

which is the elasticities form of the Slutsky equation.

**Example 2.5: Leontief Utility Function**

We could perform a similar analysis for the example of the Leontief utility function we looked at in (2.45):

$$u(x_b, x_j) = \min\left[\frac{x_b}{2}, \frac{x_j}{3}\right]. \tag{2.45}$$

We saw that the ordinary demand function for bread was in (2.46):

$$x_b = \frac{2I}{2p_b + 3p_j}. \tag{2.46}$$

Similarly, we could write down the demand function for jam:

$$x_j = \frac{3I}{2p_b + 3p_j}. \tag{2.98}$$

Substituting (2.46) and (2.98) back in (2.45) gives us the indirect utility function:

$$V(p_b, p_j, I) = \min\left[\frac{I}{2p_b + 3p_j}, \frac{I}{2p_b + 3p_j}\right] = \frac{I}{2p_b + 3p_j}. \tag{2.99}$$

Note that the RHS of (2.99) is just the number of sandwiches the consumer can make, since the denominator is the cost of a full sandwich.

Now let us find the compensated demand functions. To do this, we must solve the problem of minimising the expenditure needed to achieve any given level of utility, that is:

$$\text{Minimise} \qquad E = x_b p_b + x_j p_j \tag{2.100}$$

$$\text{subject to} \qquad u = \min\left[\frac{x_b}{2}, \frac{x_j}{3}\right]. \tag{2.101}$$

At the optimum, since the consumer would not want to buy more than she exactly needs, it must clearly be the case that

$$\frac{x_b}{2} = \frac{x_j}{3} = u.$$

So the compensated demand functions are

$$x_b^h = 2u \tag{2.102}$$

$$x_j^h = 3u. \tag{2.103}$$

If we substitute these back in (2.100), we get the expenditure function:

$$E(p_b, p_j, u) = u\left[2p_b + 3p_j\right]. \tag{2.104}$$

We can draw the ordinary and compensated demand curves on a graph (see Figure 2.27). The figure is self-explanatory. We can also check the various results we checked in the Cobb–Douglas case: the transformation of the ordinary demand function to the compensated demand function

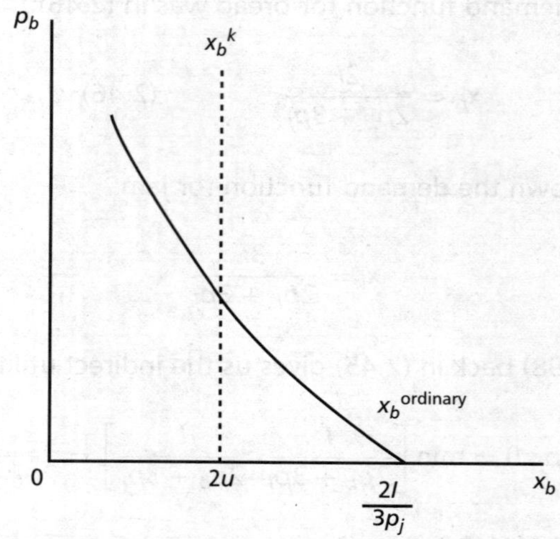


**Figure 2.27** *Ordinary and Compensated Demand Curves in the Leontief Case*

by substituting the expenditure function in the demand function, the Slutsky equation and the elasticities from the Slutsky equation. These are left to the reader as exercises.

**Example 2.6: Linear Utility**

Let us look at the same problem in the case of the linear utility function we saw in Example 2.2. In that example, $1\frac{1}{2}$ teaspoons of margarine are a perfect substitute for 1 teaspoon of butter, and the utility function is

$$u(B, M) = B + \frac{2}{3}M.$$

If we compare this to (2.47) we see that in this case $\gamma_B = 1$ and $\gamma_M = \frac{2}{3}$. Using this and (2.53) and (2.54), we can write down the demand functions for butter and margarine:

$$B = \begin{cases} \dfrac{I}{p_B} & \text{if} \quad \dfrac{p_B}{p_M} < \dfrac{3}{2} \\ 0 & \text{if} \quad \dfrac{p_B}{p_M} > \dfrac{3}{2} \end{cases} \tag{2.105}$$

$$M = \begin{cases} 0 & \text{if} \quad \dfrac{p_B}{p_M} < \dfrac{3}{2} \\ \dfrac{I}{p_M} & \text{if} \quad \dfrac{p_B}{p_M} > \dfrac{3}{2} \end{cases} \tag{2.106}$$

Substituting these back into the utility function, we get the indirect utility function:

$$V(p_B, p_M, I) = \begin{cases} \dfrac{I}{p_B} & \text{if} \quad \dfrac{p_B}{p_M} < \dfrac{3}{2} \\ \dfrac{2I}{3p_M} & \text{if} \quad \dfrac{p_B}{p_M} > \dfrac{3}{2} \end{cases} \tag{2.107}$$

To find the compensated demand functions, we need to solve the following problem:

$$\text{Minimise} \quad E = p_B B + p_M M \tag{2.108}$$

$$\text{subject to} \quad u = B + \frac{2}{3}M. \tag{2.109}$$

Once again, we know that the consumer will buy either only butter or only margarine (except for the case where $\frac{p_B}{p_M} = \frac{3}{2}$) depending on the prices. So we can write down the compensated demand functions as:

$$B^h = \begin{cases} u & \text{if} \quad \dfrac{p_B}{p_M} < \dfrac{3}{2} \\ 0 & \text{if} \quad \dfrac{p_B}{p_M} > \dfrac{3}{2} \end{cases} \tag{2.110}$$

$$M^h = \begin{cases} 0 & \text{if} \quad \dfrac{p_B}{p_M} < \dfrac{3}{2} \\ \dfrac{3}{2}u & \text{if} \quad \dfrac{p_B}{p_M} > \dfrac{3}{2} \end{cases} \tag{2.111}$$

Substituting (2.110) and (2.111) in (2.108) gives us the expenditure function:

$$E = \begin{cases} p_B u & \text{if} \quad \dfrac{p_B}{p_M} < \dfrac{3}{2} \\ \dfrac{3}{2}p_M u & \text{if} \quad \dfrac{p_B}{p_M} > \dfrac{3}{2} \end{cases} \tag{2.112}$$

Note that

$$\frac{p_B}{p_M} = \frac{3}{2} \quad \rightarrow \quad p_B u = \frac{3}{2}p_M u.$$

Substituting $E$ as in (2.112) for $I$ in (2.105) and (2.106) shows how the ordinary demand function can be converted to the compensated demand function: (2.105) becomes (2.109) and (2.106) becomes (2.110). Further, we can verify the Slutsky equation in both its original and elasticity forms. These are left as exercises to be completed by the interested reader.

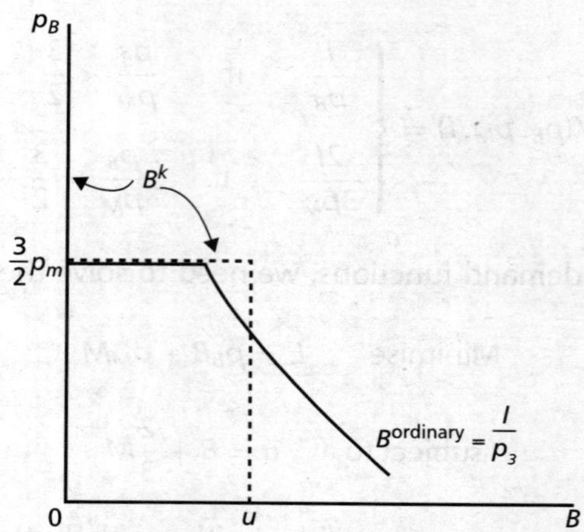


**Figure 2.28** *Compensated and Ordinary Demand Curves with Linear Utility*

Finally, it is worth illustrating the demand curves that emerge in this example. Figure 2.28 illustrates these curves.

### 2.5.3 Changes in Another Good's Price: The Cross-Price Effect

We have looked at the effect of changes in income and of the good's own-price on the quantity demanded. In this section, we look at the last comparative statics exercise on the demand function: the cross-price effect or the effect of changes in the prices of other goods.

Consider again the consumer's choice problem as illustrated in the 2-good case by the IC analysis. However, now we will change $p_2$ to look at the effect of this change on $x_1$. Suppose $p_2$ goes up. Then, in Figure (2.29), the budget constraint will rotate inward from its initial position at *AB* to a position such as *A′B*. What we are interested in is to find out where the final chosen bundle *C′* would be relative to *C*.

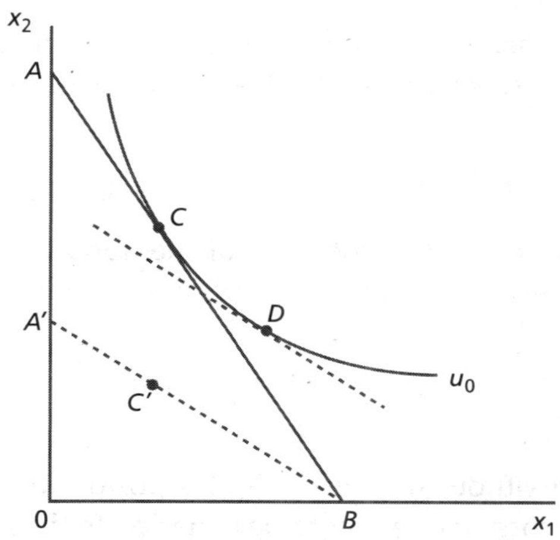


**Figure 2.29** *Cross-Price Effect*

Once again, we can analyse the effect of this price change by looking at the substitution and income effects. To find the substitution effect, we draw a line parallel to *A′B* tangent to the initial IC $u_0$. Suppose the point of tangency is *D*. *D* must be to the right of *C* in this 2-good case because the IC $u_0$ is flatter at *D* than at *C*, reflecting the higher $p_2$. From the income effect, we know that the final choice *C′* will be somewhere to the south-west of *D* if both goods are normal. More to the point, if $x_1$ is normal, *C′* will be to the left of *D*. But that gives us two possible outcomes. The final bundle *C′* could be to the right of *C* or it could be to the left of *C*, depending on how large the income effect is. Thus the cross-price effect is ambiguous.

We classify goods according to the signs of their cross-price effects. If

- $\dfrac{\partial x_1}{\partial p_2} > 0$, we say goods 1 and 2 are **gross substitutes**
- $\dfrac{\partial x_1}{\partial p_2} < 0$, we say goods 1 and 2 are **gross complements.**

Intuitively, we can see why we would expect goods that are substitutes for one another to have a positive cross-price effect. If, for example, the price of mutton goes up, we would not be surprised if people started buying more of goods that might substitute for mutton in the diet, such as chicken. So the quantity demanded of chicken might rise in response to the rise in the price of its substitute, mutton.

Similarly, it is quite intuitive that the cross-price effect of complementary goods will be negative. If the price of coffee, say, goes up, we might expect the quantity demanded of cream to fall along with the demand for coffee since cream is often used in combination with coffee.

To look at the cross-price effect in the $n$-good case, we need to adopt an algebraic approach. We can do this by deriving a Slutsky equation for the cross-price effect. Let us start with (2.70) as before:

$$x_1\left(p_1, p_2, \ldots, p_n, E(p_1, p_2, \ldots, p_n, u)\right) \equiv x_1^h(p_1, p_2, \ldots, p_n, u).$$

We differentiate this time with respect to the price of the good whose cross-price effect we are examining, say good 2. We can then derive the Slutsky equation as before for the cross-price effect:

$$\frac{\partial x_1}{\partial p_2} = \frac{\partial x_1^h}{\partial p_2} - x_2\frac{\partial x_1}{\partial I}. \tag{2.113}$$

The second term on the RHS (without the minus sign) is positive as long as $x_1$ is a normal good. Thus that term is causing the cross-price effect to be negative. In the 2-good case, the first term on the RHS is positive–on grounds of the substitution effect, a rise in $p_2$ would lead to a fall in $x_2$ and this would force an increase in $x_1$. However, this is not necessarily true in the $n$-good case. A rise in $p_2$ would lead to a fall in $x_2$ because of the substitution effect, but whether this leads to a rise or fall in $x_1$ depends on whether good 1 is a substitute or complement to good 2. If goods 1 and 2 are complementary, $\frac{\partial x_1^h}{\partial p_2}$ would be negative and then $\frac{\partial x_1}{\partial p_2}$ would be unambiguously negative. If goods 1 and 2 are substitutes, however, $\frac{\partial x_1^h}{\partial p_2}$ would be positive and so the sign of $\frac{\partial x_1}{\partial p_2}$ would be ambiguous.

We still have our definitions:

- $\dfrac{\partial x_1}{\partial p_2} > 0 \quad \rightarrow$ goods 1 and 2 are **gross substitutes**
- $\dfrac{\partial x_1}{\partial p_2} < 0 \quad \rightarrow$ goods 1 and 2 are **gross complements**.

But in the $n$-good case, we see there is a problem. We have cases where we think goods 1 and 2 are substitutes (since $\frac{\partial x_1^h}{\partial p_2} > 0$), but they may come out looking like gross complements if the negative income effect in (2.113) outweighs the positive substitution effect.

Indeed, there is a further problem. Look at the following two Slutsky equations:

$$\frac{\partial x_1}{\partial p_2} = \frac{\partial x_1^h}{\partial p_2} - x_2^h \frac{\partial x_1}{\partial I} \tag{2.114}$$

$$\frac{\partial x_2}{\partial p_1} = \frac{\partial x_2^h}{\partial p_1} - x_1^h \frac{\partial x_2}{\partial I} \tag{2.115}$$

In (2.114), we are looking at the effect of changes in $p_2$ on $x_1$, while in (2.115), we are looking at changes in $p_1$ on $x_2$. Now we know from Shephard's Lemma that

$$x_1^h = \frac{\partial E}{\partial p_1} \quad \text{and} \quad x_2^h = \frac{\partial E}{\partial p_2}.$$

Therefore

$$\frac{\partial x_1^h}{\partial p_2} = \frac{\partial^2 E}{\partial p_1 \partial p_2} \quad \text{and} \quad \frac{\partial x_2^h}{\partial p_1} = \frac{\partial^2 E}{\partial p_2 \partial p_1}.$$

But we know from Young's Theorem that

$$\frac{\partial^2 E}{\partial p_1 \partial p_2} = \frac{\partial^2 E}{\partial p_2 \partial p_1}.$$

Therefore

$$\frac{\partial x_1^h}{\partial p_2} = \frac{\partial x_2^h}{\partial p_1}. \tag{2.116}$$

Thus the first terms on the RHSs of (2.114) and (2.115) are equal. Suppose they are positive. We know that, as long as goods 1 and 2 are normal, the second terms on the RHSs of (2.114) and (2.115) are negative if we include the minus sign in them. Thus, the net signs of (2.114) and (2.115) are ambiguous. It is entirely possible that one of them, say $\frac{\partial x_1}{\partial p_2}$, turns out to be negative, perhaps because $x_2$ is quite large, while the other (in this case $\frac{\partial x_2}{\partial p_1}$) turns out to be positive (because $x_1$ is quite small). Thus the concepts of gross substitutes and gross complements are not necessarily symmetric, a property that seems unreasonable.

As an alternative, therefore, we may use the following definitions:

- $\frac{\partial x_1^h}{\partial p_2} > 0 \quad \rightarrow$ goods 1 and 2 are **net substitutes**
- $\frac{\partial x_1^h}{\partial p_2} < 0 \quad \rightarrow$ goods 1 and 2 are **net complements**.

The concepts of net substitutes and complements are symmetric, as was demonstrated in the previous analysis in (2.116). Note that, if the goods are normal, net complements will always be gross complements, since the substitution and income effects will reinforce one another. However, the inverse is not true: not all gross complements will necessarily be net complements.

# 2.6 FINAL PROPERTIES OF DEMAND FUNCTIONS

**Task for this section:**

To present two more properties of demand functions not so far considered.

We have looked at the partial effects of changes in each of the arguments of the demand function on the quantity demanded. Along the way, we have seen a few results on the elasticities:

- Generalised Engel: $\sum_{i=1}^{n} \theta_i \eta_i = 1$.
- Own-Price Slutsky: $\epsilon_i = \epsilon_i^h - \theta_i \eta_i$.
- Cross-Price Slutsky: $\epsilon_{ij} = \epsilon_{ij}^h - \theta_j \eta_i$.

We conclude with two more such results on the relationships between different elasticities of demand.

## 2.6.1 Homogeneity of the Demand Function

The first result follows from the observation that the demand function is homogeneous of degree zero. If we double all prices and income, the budget constraint would remain unchanged and so the choice would remain unchanged. Using a property of homogenous functions we can take the demand function

$$x_1(p_1, p_2, \ldots, p_n, I)$$

and write

$$p_1 \frac{\partial x_1}{\partial p_1} + p_2 \frac{\partial x_1}{\partial p_2} + \ldots + p_n \frac{\partial x_1}{\partial p_n} + I \frac{\partial x_1}{\partial I} = 0.$$

Dividing through by $x_1$ gives us

$$\frac{p_1}{x_1} \cdot \frac{\partial x_1}{\partial p_1} + \frac{p_2}{x_1} \cdot \frac{\partial x_1}{\partial p_2} + \ldots + \frac{p_n}{x_1} \cdot \frac{\partial x_1}{\partial p_n} + \frac{I}{x_1} \cdot \frac{\partial x_1}{\partial I} = 0,$$

which is

$$\epsilon_1 + \epsilon_{12} + \ldots + \epsilon_{1n} + \eta_1 = 0.$$

In other words,

$$\epsilon_1 + \sum_{j=2}^{n} \epsilon_{1j} + \eta_1 = 0. \tag{2.117}$$

The sum of the own-price elasticity the income elasticity and all the cross-price elasticities must be zero.

For example, with the demand function derived for the 2 good Cobb–Douglas case:

$$x_1 = \frac{\alpha_1}{\alpha_1 + \alpha_2} \cdot \frac{I}{p_1},$$

we have $\epsilon_1 = -1$, $\epsilon_{12} = 0$ and $\eta_1 = 1$, which confirms (2.117).

### 2.6.2 Cournot Aggregation

A final result is derived from the budget constraint

$$I = \sum_{i=1}^{n} p_i x_i.$$

Suppose $p_i$ changes and we wish to study the effects of this change. We know $I$ has not changed. So:

$$\frac{\partial I}{\partial p_i} = 0 = p_i \frac{\partial x_i}{\partial p_i} + x_i + \sum_{j \neq i} p_j \frac{\partial x_j}{\partial p_i}.$$

Multiplying through by $\frac{p_i}{I}$, and with some additional manipulation, we get

$$\frac{p_i x_i}{I} \cdot \frac{\partial x_i}{\partial p_i} \cdot \frac{p_i}{x_i} + \frac{p_i x_i}{I} + \sum_{j \neq i} \frac{p_j x_j}{I} \cdot \frac{\partial x_j}{\partial p_i} \cdot \frac{p_i}{x_j} = 0,$$

which simplifies to

$$\theta_i \epsilon_i + \theta_i + \sum_{j \neq i} \theta_j \epsilon_{ji} = 0. \tag{2.118}$$

For example, in the 2-good Cobb–Douglas case, we have

$$x_1 = \frac{\alpha_1}{\alpha_1 + \alpha_2} \cdot \frac{I}{p_1} \quad \text{and} \quad x_2 = \frac{\alpha_2}{\alpha_1 + \alpha_2} \cdot \frac{I}{p_2}$$

as the demand functions. From these, we can find

$$\theta_1 = \frac{\alpha_1}{\alpha_1 + \alpha_2}$$

$$\theta_2 = \frac{\alpha_2}{\alpha_1 + \alpha_2}$$

$$\epsilon_1 = -1, \epsilon_{21} = 0,$$

and so the LHS of (2.118) is

$$-\left(\frac{\alpha_1}{\alpha_1 + \alpha_2}\right) + \frac{\alpha_1}{\alpha_1 + \alpha_2} + 0,$$

which indeed reduces to zero.

# 2.7 INTERPRETATION OF THE LAGRANGE MULTIPLIER

**Task for this section:**

To understand the economic content of the Lagrange multipliers seen in the consumer's utility maximisation and expenditure minimisation problems.

In solving the consumer's utility maximisation problem, we use the Lagrange method as long as the utility function is continuously differentiable. This involves the creation of an artificial variable, the Lagrange multiplier, and the question arises as to whether this variable has an economic meaning. It turns out that it does: it is a measure of the *MU* of money.

## 2.7.1 The Lagrange Multiplier as the Marginal Utility of Money

To see this, consider what the *MU* of money is. It should tell us how utility changes as the amount of money at the disposal of the consumer, that is, her income or budget, changes, taking into account the changes in the consumer's optimal consumption bundle. In other words, the *MU* of money is

$$MU_m = \frac{\partial u^*}{\partial I},$$

where $u^*$ is the level of utility attained with the optimal consumption bundle. But we know from the envelope theorem that

$$\frac{\partial u^*}{\partial I} = \frac{\partial \mathcal{L}}{\partial I},$$

where $\mathcal{L}$ is the Lagrangian function corresponding to the utility maximisation problem:

$$\mathcal{L} = u(x_1, x_2, \ldots, x_n) + \lambda \left[ I - \sum_{i=1}^{n} p_i x_i \right].$$

From this, by simply taking the partial derivative, we see that

$$\frac{\partial \mathcal{L}}{\partial I} = \lambda.$$

In other words, the Lagrange multiplier is the *MU* of income or money.

This insight allows us to understand the first-order conditions of the consumer's optimisation problem more intuitively. These first-order conditions include the equations

$$u_i - \lambda p_i = 0 \qquad \text{or} \qquad u_i = \lambda p_i$$

for each *i*, which can also be written as

$$\lambda = \frac{u_i}{p_i}. \tag{2.119}$$

Here $\lambda$ becomes the factor by which price needs to be multiplied before being set equal to the *MU* of the good. Clearly, the appropriate factor is the *MU* of money, since we then multiply price (rupees per unit) by $MU_m$ ('utils' per rupee) to get the *MU* of the good ('utils' per unit of the good).

## 2.7.2 The Lagrange Multiplier in the Consumer's Expenditure Minimisation Problem

How about the Lagrange multiplier in the consumer's expenditure minimisation problem? By the same argument as before, and remembering that here we are trying to minimise the consumer's expenditure *E*, we can show that, since the Lagrangian for this problem is

$$\mathcal{L}' = \sum_{i=1}^{n} p_i x_i + \lambda' \left[ u - u(x_1, x_2, \ldots, x_n) \right].$$

the Lagrange multiplier $\lambda'$ must be $\frac{\partial E^*}{\partial u}$, the inverse of the *MU* of money! That this is so can also be seen clearly by looking at the typical first-order condition to this problem:

$$\frac{\partial \mathcal{L}'}{\partial x_i} = p_i - \lambda' u_i = 0,$$

so that

$$\lambda' = \frac{p_i}{u_i},$$

which is just the inverse of (2.119).

### 2.7.3 The Marshallian Theory Revisited

Using this interpretation of the Lagrange multiplier gives us a new way to look at the Marshallian approach to demand theory. Recall that Marshall's theory of demand was based on the assumed Law of Diminishing Marginal Utility. This stated that, as a consumer consumed more of a good in any time period, holding her consumption of other goods constant, her *MU* from successive units of the good would diminish. For most goods, this seems like a reasonable assumption. Having assumed the Law of Diminishing Marginal Utility, Marshall used it and the assumption of a constant *MU* of money as an explanation for the downward slope of the demand curve. What he was essentially doing was taking the first-order condition (2.119) and applying it to the Law of Diminishing Marginal Utility. The first-order condition tells us that the consumer would buy a good up to the point where her *MU* $u_i$ was equal to $\lambda p_i$. Looking at Figure 2.30, if the price of the good fell from $p_i^0$ to $p_i^1$, and the *MU* of money remained unchanged, the quantity demanded would rise from $x_i^0$ to $x_i^1$ because of the downward slope of the *MU* schedule.

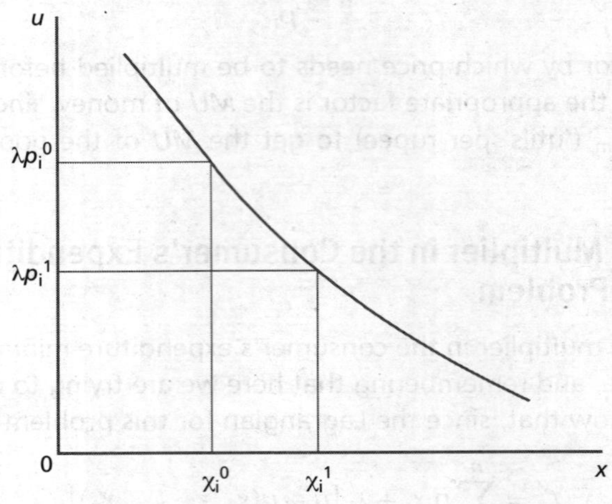


**Figure 2.30** *Marshallian Demand*

Since we can also write (2.119) as

$$p_i = \frac{u_i}{\lambda},$$

the height of the demand curve could be thought of as the *MU* divided by (or normalised by) the *MU* of money. As long as $\lambda$ can be treated as fixed, this would be a perfectly legitimate exercise. Of course, one of the main theoretical objections to the Marshallian theory is that the *MU* of money does not, or at least may not, remain fixed as prices and the consumer's income change.

## 2.8 REVEALED PREFERENCE APPROACH TO DEMAND THEORY

**Task for this section:**

To briefly examine an alternative approach to the theory of demand that succeeds in proving the demand theorem with fewer assumptions, but loses some power in the process, as we will see in the next chapter.

Some authors have criticised the Hicksian approach to the theory of the consumer as unrealistic because it implies the existence of a utility function which is arguably unknowable. Revealed Preference Theory is an attempt to derive the Law of Demand without reference to a utility function. In its place, this theory relies on the following assumption:

**Axiom of Revealed Preference:** By choosing a bundle A over a bundle B, a consumer *reveals a preference* for A over B. Therefore, the consumer can never choose B when bundle A is available.[2]

Under this assumption, we can demonstrate the demand theorem as follows. Figure 2.31 is similar to Figure 2.25 but without the indifference map. Suppose a consumer faces the budget *AB* and chooses the bundle *C*. In choosing *C*, she reveals a preference for *C* over all other bundles in the budget set *0AB*. At best, some bundles on the budget constraint *AB* could be just as good as *C* (the consumer may be indifferent between them and *C*) but all bundles in the interior of the budget set are strictly inferior to *C*.

Suppose the price of good 1 rises, shifting the budget constraint to *AB′*. Draw a line *A″B″*, parallel to *AB′*, passing through the point *C*. *A″B″* would be the consumer's budget constraint if, in response to the rise in $p_1$, we raised her budget by the change in the cost of the original bundle *C*. If she faced the budget constraint *A″B″*, she could not choose a bundle on the segment

[2] This is also called the **Weak** Axiom of Revealed Preference. The **Strong** Axiom of Revealed Preference is a more technical assumption designed to rule out circularity in a consumer's preference pattern. It says that, if a consumer reveals a preference for A over B and a preference for B over C, then that implies that she has revealed a preference for A over C. In other words, it assumes transitivity along with the weak axiom.

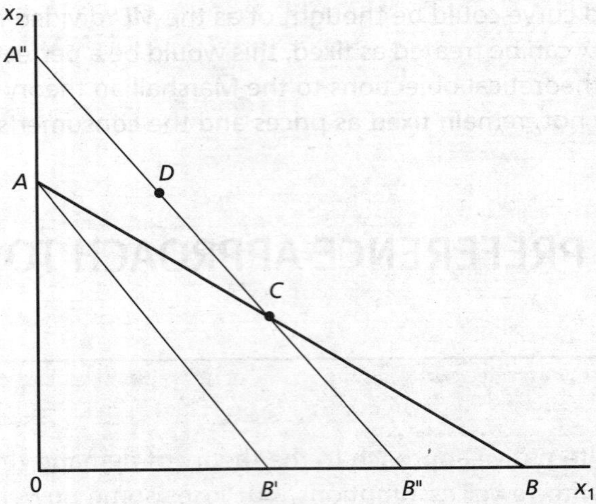


**Figure 2.31** *Revealed Preference*

*CB*" since she had already revealed that all those bundles were inferior to *C*. Therefore, she would either choose *C* or some point such as *D* to the left of *C* on the segment *A*"*C*. The movement from *C* to *D* is a kind of substitution effect.

As long as good 1 is normal, the final bundle *C′* chosen on the budget constraint *AB′* will be to the left of *D*. Since *D* is not to the right of *C*, *C′* must be to the left of *C*, thereby demonstrating the Law of Demand.

Thus the Revealed Preference approach proves the Law of Demand with a less restrictive model of consumer choice than the Hicksian approach. However, there is a downside to this. The approach does not offer as rich a model as the Hicksian approach does and, as a result, can be applied to analyse fewer problems. The Hicksian approach provides an apparatus for many applications of consumer theory, as we will see in the next chapter.

## SUMMARY

In this chapter, we have studied the standard approach to the Theory of Consumer Behaviour. The basic points were as follows:

- Consumers buy goods and services in order to derive 'utility' from them.
- Consumers want to maximise their utility, but are constrained by their limited budgets.

- The typical consumer's problem can then be formulated as a constrained utility maximisation problem.
- The solutions to the consumer's constrained utility maximisation problem are called the (ordinary) demand functions for the goods.
- A demand function shows the quantity of a good that a consumer would buy as a function of the prices of the goods and his or her budget.
- The properties of the demand function are as follows:

  1. For most goods (called 'normal' goods), demand rises as the size of the budget increases. Goods for which demand falls as the budget increases are called 'inferior' goods.
  2. For normal goods, the quantity demanded rises as the price of the good falls, an important result called the Law of Demand. For inferior goods, the law of demand may or may not hold.
  3. The effect on the demand for a good of changes in the price of another good is ambiguous; it depends upon whether the two goods are substitutes or complements for one another.
  4. The demand function is homogenous of degree zero.
  5. Some results on the elasticities of the demand function:
     a. Generalised Engel: $\sum_{i=1}^{n} \theta_i \eta_i = 1$.
     b. Slutsky Equation: $\epsilon_i = \epsilon_i^h - \theta_i \eta_i$.
     c. Cross-Price Slutsky: $\epsilon_{ij} = \epsilon_{ij}^h - \theta_j \eta_i$.
     d. Homogeneity: $\epsilon_1 + \sum_{j=2}^{n} \epsilon_{1j} + \eta = 0$.
     e. Cournot Aggregation: $\theta_i \epsilon_i + \theta_i + \sum_{j \neq i} \theta_j \epsilon_{ji} = 0$.

- The effect on quantity demanded of a change in the price of the good (the 'own-price' effect) can be divided into a 'substitution effect' and an 'income effect'.
- The substitution effect of a price change is the change in consumption pattern due purely to the change in the relative prices of goods. It is found by comparing the original consumption bundle with the cheapest bundle (at the new prices) that yields the same level of utility as did the original bundle.
- The income effect of a price change is the change in consumption pattern due purely to the change in the consumer's utility level. It is found by comparing the cheapest bundle (at the new prices) that yields the same level of utility as did the original bundle with the final bundle.

- Finding the substitution effect of a price change involves solving the consumer's 'expenditure minimisation problem', the dual to the consumer's utility maximisation problem.
- The solutions to the consumer's expenditure minimisation problem are called the consumer's compensated demand functions.
- A compensated demand function shows the quantity of a good that a consumer would buy as a function of the prices of the goods and his or her utility level.
- For a normal good, the compensated demand curve is less elastic than the ordinary demand curve at any given point.
- The Lagrange multiplier of the consumer's utility maximisation problem is the *MU* of money for that consumer. The Lagrange multiplier of the consumer's expenditure minimisation problem is the inverse of the *MU* of money.
- The Revealed Preference Approach to Demand Theory can prove the Law of Demand without recourse to any assumptions on a utility function.

## EXERCISES

1. Happy Golucki spends ₹$I$ per month on playing video games ($G$) at an arcade or going to the movies ($M$). Her utility function is:

$$U(G, M) = 0.4 \ln G + 0.6 \ln M$$

   (a) Find Happy's demand functions for $G$ and $M$.
   (b) If $I = ₹1,000$, $p_G = ₹10$ and $p_M = ₹60$, how many times will Happy go to the movies, and how many video games will she play each month? (Use your answer from part a.)
   (c) What will happen to $G$ and $M$ if $p_G$ falls to ₹5?

2. If $X$ and $Y$ are the only two goods Lily buys, and her utility function is:

$$U(X, Y) = \min[X, Y],$$

   find Lily's demand function for $X$.

3. The expenditure share of a necessity falls as a consumer's income rises. Is this statement true or false? Prove your answer.

4. (a) What is an inferior good?
   (b) Show that, if a consumer consumes only two goods, both cannot be inferior.

5. John consumes only two goods, $x$ and $y$, and his utility function is

$$U(x, y) = xy + y.$$

   (a) Find John's ordinary demand functions for $x$ and $y$.
   (b) Suppose John's income is ₹100, the price of $y$ is ₹10 per unit and the price of $x$ is ₹20 per unit. What will be John's consumption pattern?
   (c) Calculate John's elasticity of demand for $x$ at this point.

6. Karuna, who has an income of $I$, has a utility function of the form

$$U(A, B) = \ln (A - 10) + \ln B \quad \text{for} \quad A > 10.$$

   where $A$ and $B$ are the quantities of the only two goods she consumes.

   (a) Find Karuna's demand functions for $A$ and $B$, assuming that $I$ is high enough that $A > 10$ always.
   (b) Calculate the own- and cross-price elasticities of demand for $A$.
   (c) Is $A$ a necessity or a luxury?

7. Jalnidh has the utility function

$$U(F, C) = F^{\frac{1}{3}}C^{\frac{2}{3}},$$

   where $F$ and $C$ are the quantities of food and clothing, respectively, that she consumes per month. The prices of $F$ and $C$ are each ₹1. Jalnidh has a money income of ₹100 per month and, in addition, she receives an in-kind welfare allocation of 80 units of food, which cannot be resold.

   (a) How much food and clothing will Jalnidh consume per month, in order to maximise her utility? Draw a clearly labeled diagram showing Jalnidh's utility maximising choice.
   (b) If the welfare agency wished to change Jalnidh's welfare allocation from an in-kind food gift to a money allocation, how much money would they need to pay her each month in order to make her just as well off as she was under the in-kind allocation?

8. A consumer derives utility from two goods, cookies and milk. The price of a pack of cookies is ₹4 and a pint of milk costs ₹4. The consumer has a total of ₹120 to spend on the goods, and his preferences over cookies and milk are given by

$$U(x, y) = xy,$$

   where $x$ denotes packs of cookies and $y$ denotes pints of milk.

   (a) Solve the utility maximising problem.
   (b) Suppose now that the government imposes a quota on milk that allows the consumer a maximum of 8 pints. What are the optimal choices in this case?
   (c) Now suppose that the price of milk is reduced from ₹4 to ₹3 per pint. What is the consumer's optimal choice of cookies and milk without the quota? With the quota?

(d) Suppose finally that the government considers a quota $q$ in the range $0 < q \leq 15$. What quota in that range would make the consumer indifferent between the two options: (i) no quota and price ₹4, and (ii) quota $q$ and price ₹3?

CHAPTER

3

# Applications of Consumer Theory

The theory of consumer behaviour gives us a powerful tool to analyse a broad range of issues beyond the obvious one of understanding how consumers might respond to price changes, that is, estimating demand functions as a guide to companies or the government. We now consider several such applications of consumer theory to normative issues.

## 3.1 TAXES AND SUBSIDIES

**Task for this section:**

To compare the welfare effects of commodity taxes and subsidies with those of lump-sum taxes or cash subsidies. After this section, you should understand why economists are generally resistant to the imposition of taxes that distort behaviour but also be aware of some of the limitations of their analysis.

All governments need to raise revenue in order to pay for needed government services, and a pressing question in this context is: what is the best way for government to raise this revenue? However, one area in which governments often spend money is in support payments to the poor or elderly, and the question arises as to what is the best way for government to extend this assistance. This section considers the theoretical basis for thinking about such questions.

### 3.1.1 The Optimality of Lump-sum Taxation

One important insight that arises from the theory of the consumer is that lump-sum taxes are better than commodity taxes as revenue raisers. A lump-sum tax is one that cannot be avoided in any way, while a commodity tax depends on the amount of the commodity a consumer buys.

Figure 3.1 illustrates a simple way to see this. In this graph, the quantity of a good that might be taxed, $X$, is measured on the horizontal axis and all other goods are represented on the vertical axis, whose units are in money terms. Suppose the consumer faces the budget constraint *AB* and chooses the bundle *C*. We can see that *AO* is the cost of this bundle *C*.

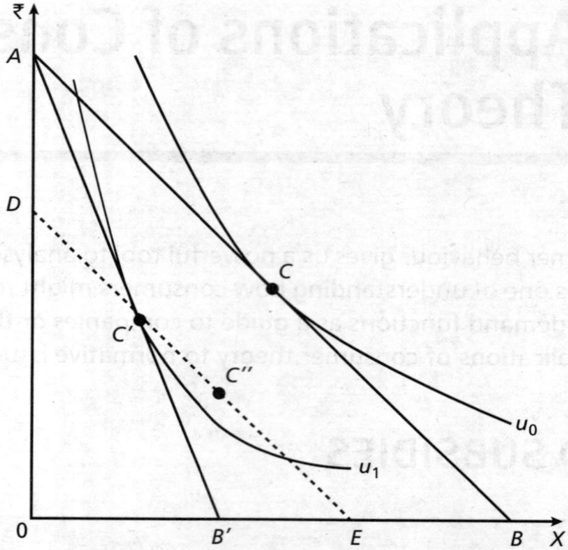


**Figure 3.1** *Effects of Lump-sum and Commodity Taxes*

Now, suppose the government decides to impose a tax on good *X*, causing the gross price of the good to the consumer to rise. For simplicity, suppose the underlying (tax-exclusive) price $p_x$ remains unchanged so that the gross price is just the previous price plus the tax. Suppose the consumer now faces the budget constraint *AB′* and chooses the bundle *C′*, where the budget constraint *AB′* is tangent to an indifference curve. The consumer is worse off because utility level has fallen from $u_0$ to $u_1$.

Let *DE* be a line passing through *C′* with the same slope as the original budget constraint *AB*. Then, *OD* is the cost of the bundle *C′* at the original prices, just as *OA* was the cost of the bundle *C* at those prices. Since the actual cost to the consumer of the bundle *C′* is *OA* and *OD* represents the cost of *C′* at the original prices, the difference *AD* must represent the amount of tax revenue collected by the government.

Now, suppose the government, instead of imposing a commodity tax on good *X*, imposed a lump-sum tax of *AD* on the consumer. This would have the effect of pushing the consumer's budget constraint down from *AB* to *DE*, since it would act just like an income decrease. But if the consumer faced the budget *DE*, she would get to a utility level higher than $u_1$, since the indifference curve $u_1$ (being tangent to *AB′* at *C′*) has a section that lies below *DE*. The consumer would choose a bundle such as *C″* where an indifference curve is tangent to the budget constraint *DE*.

This shows the superiority of the lump-sum tax. The government has collected the same amount of revenue in both scenarios, but the consumer is better-off under the lump-sum tax.

One might think that this argument provides a theoretical basis for using an income tax rather than commodity taxes as ways to raise government revenue. Unfortunately, the argument would not be quite correct. Although the use of an income tax avoids any price distortions between market commodities, it does not avoid a distortion between market commodities and leisure. An income tax alters the relative prices between goods and leisure, thereby distorting the incentives of workers to work less than optimal. Nevertheless, the essential truth of this analysis remains: that non-distorting taxes are superior to distorting commodity taxes.

Looking at the problem algebraically, we recall from Shephard's Lemma (2.69) that

$$\frac{\partial E}{\partial p_i} = x_i^h.$$

Thus, as the price of a good rises from, say, $p_0$ to $(p_0 + T)$ in response to the imposition of a tax, the expenditure needed to keep the consumer at the same level of utility will be

$$\triangle E = \int_{p_0}^{p_0+T} x^h(p)dp.$$

Now, because the function $x^h(p)$ is downward-sloping (i.e. $\frac{\partial x^h}{\partial p} < 0$), it is clear that

$$x^h(p_0 + T) < x^h(p_0)$$

and therefore

$$\triangle E > T \cdot x^h(p_0 + T).$$

Further, assuming that $x$ is a normal good, we know that

$$x^h(p_0 + T) > x(p_0 + T)$$

since $x^h(p_0 + T)$ includes only the substitution effect, while $x(p_0 + T)$ includes both the substitution and income effects of the price increase. It therefore follows that

$$\triangle E > T \cdot x(p_0 + T).$$

But the tax revenue collected from the commodity tax is $T \cdot x(p_0 + T)$ and therefore this shows that the expenditure needed to keep the consumer at the same level of utility is greater than the tax revenue collected. A lump-sum tax that raised the same amount of tax revenue would therefore leave the consumer better-off than would the commodity tax.

This analysis points to the fundamental reason for the result, that the imposition of a commodity tax distorts the consumption behaviour of the consumer, because it distorts the relative prices of goods. If the change in relative prices did not distort consumer behaviour, the effect would disappear. We can see this in the special cases where the consumer's utility function is linear or Leontief. Figure 3.2 shows these cases in graphs that correspond to Figure 3.1. In each case, $AB$ is the initial budget constraint and $AB'$ is the tax-inclusive budget constraint. The chosen bundle changes from $C$ to $C'$. In each case, a lump-sum tax that raises the same amount of tax revenue would lead to the same choice $C'$. Thus, in these cases the superiority of the lump-sum tax disappears.

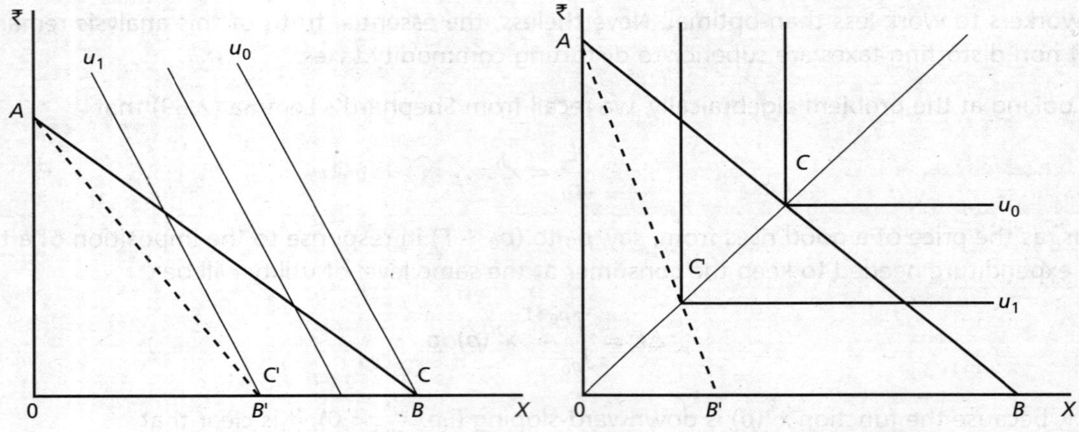


**Figure 3.2** *Effect of a Commodity Tax: Special Cases*

## 3.1.2 Cash Subsidies versus Food Subsidies

The mirror image of this argument is central to a debate with regard to food subsidies. The corollary of our result on lump-sum taxes versus commodity taxes is that a cash subsidy (which is effectively a negative lump-sum tax) is superior to a food price subsidy (a negative commodity tax). The government could provide to consumers the same welfare benefit at lower cost with a cash subsidy, or could provide a greater benefit with the same outlay on a cash subsidy rather than a food subsidy.

The essential argument goes as follows. Suppose a typical consumer's budget constraint is $AB$ in Figure 3.3. As in the previous figure, we will measure the quantity of the good (food) on the horizontal axis and the vertical axis will represent all other goods and be measured in money. Suppose the government offers a price subsidy on food, that is they buy food at the open market price and then sell it to consumers at a subsidised price lower than the market price. Let the budget constraint faced by the consumer now be $AB'$, which is flatter than $AB$ to reflect the subsidised price of food that she now faces. Suppose she chooses the bundle $C$ on this new budget constraint. Draw a line through $C$ parallel to $AB$ and label this $A''B''$. Then the cost to the government of providing the food subsidy will be $AA''$. Since the slope of $A''B''$ represented the market price of food (since it was equal to the slope of $AB$), the cost of the bundle $C$ at market

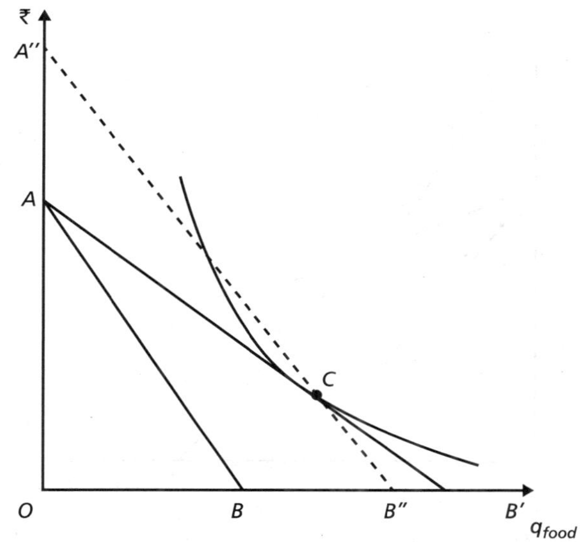


**Figure 3.3** *Comparing a Food Price Subsidy and a Cash Subsidy*

prices is *OA″*. But the consumer is able to buy it with her budget of *OA*. The difference *AA″* must then be the cost to the government.

Now suppose, instead of the food subsidy, the government gave this consumer a straight cash subsidy of *AA″*. The consumer would then face the budget constraint *A″B″* and we can see clearly from the figure that she would now be better-off, since there is a section of the constraint *A″B″* that lies above the indifference curve through *C*. There must be such a section because the slope of the indifference curve at *C* is equal to the slope of the line *AB′*, which is flatter than *A″B″*. Thus, the consumer would be able to choose a bundle that is on a higher indifference curve than the one through *C*, thereby demonstrating that a cash subsidy is superior to a food price subsidy. This is the essential theoretical underpinning for the proposal to introduce cash subsidies to replace the present food subsidy system.[1]

There are a couple of caveats to this analysis. If the government's food subsidy programme provides only a limited amount of food at the subsidised price, after which the consumer has to enter the open market, the superiority of a cash subsidy is no longer guaranteed; it depends upon whether or not the consumer does in fact buy food on the open market or not. If she does buy food in the open market, then the food price subsidy acts effectively as a cash subsidy and there is no benefit to be had from using a cash subsidy. To see this, recall Figure 2.3 which showed the budget constraint under this kind of subsidy scheme.

---

[1] See, for example, Kaushik Basu: 'India's Foodgrain Policy: An Economic Theory Perspective', *Economic and Political Weekly*, Vol. XLVI, No.5, 29 January 2011, pp. 37–45.

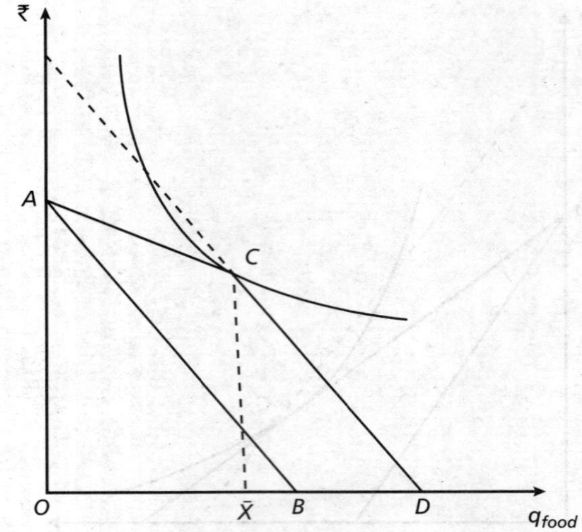


**Figure 3.4** *Cash Subsidy versus a Limited Food Subsidy*

It would look like the kinked line *ACD* in Figure 3.4, where the slope of the line segment *AC* reflects the subsidised price of food, $\bar{X}$ is the maximum quantity of food the consumer can buy at the subsidised price and the slope of the line segment *CD* (equal to the slope of the original budget constraint *AB*) reflects the price of food in the open market. If the consumer ends up choosing a bundle on the line segment *CD*, she would be using the open market price of food in her optimality calculation and so her consumption of food would not be distorted. Therefore, nothing would be gained with a cash subsidy. If the consumer chose the bundle *C*, then a cash subsidy would be beneficial, as shown in the figure, although the benefit may not be as great as in the previous case where the amount of food the consumer could purchase at the subsidised price was not limited.

The other caveat relates to the possibility that the consumer's chosen bundle may be at a corner. Recall the utility function illustrated in Figure 2.15, a quasi-linear utility function meant to represent the preferences of someone who is very poor, and drawn again here in Figure 3.5. If *AE* is the original budget constraint and *AB* is the constraint under the food price subsidy, we see that such a consumer may well be spending all of her income on food. In other words, there is no substitution effect caused by the food price change. In that case, a cash subsidy that was utility-equivalent to the food price subsidy would not be any cheaper.

Note that this discussion is quite independent of other arguments that suggest that the cash subsidy may be better for a completely different practical reason: it would reduce the ability of middlemen traders to steal subsidised food from the system. If the way the food subsidy system works is that the government provides food grain to traders at a subsidised price and they are then supposed to supply the grain to consumers at a below-market price (higher than what they paid to the government so that they are able to make a profit, but lower than the open market

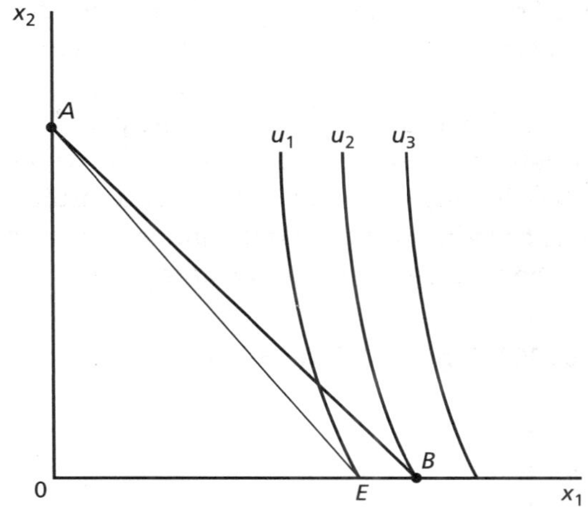


**Figure 3.5** *Cash versus Price Subsidy for a Very Poor Consumer*

price so that the poor consumers get food more cheaply), the traders have a strong incentive to divert the grain and sell it at a high price in the open market. There is evidence to suggest that about half the food grain that government supplies to the distribution system is so diverted.[2] Giving the cash subsidy directly to the consumers, enabling them to buy food at market prices, would eliminate this source of drain on the treasury.[3]

## 3.2 MEASURING THE CONSUMER'S WELFARE CHANGE

**Task for this section:**

To learn different approaches to measuring changes in a consumer's welfare as circumstances change. The goal is to be able to answer questions such as how much better-off or worse off will a consumer be. After this section, you should know the difference between consumer's surplus, the compensating variation and the equivalent variation, you should be able to measure them and you should know when to use them.

[2] See Reetika Khera: 'Trends in Diversion of Grain from the Public Distribution System', *Economic and Political Weekly*, Vol. XLVI, No. 21, 21 May 2011, pp. 106–114. Khera estimated the diversion to be 54% in 2004–05, although it came down to 43.9% in 2007–08. There were large differences in the numbers by state; in 2007–08, the worst performer was Bihar, where 89.5% of the grain was diverted.

[3] A separate argument in favour of food subsidies is that the open market price might be an oligopoly price and therefore might be significantly higher for poor people to pay.

We would frequently like to know how much better-off or worse off a consumer is as a result of changed economic circumstances, or would be as a result of certain changes that we anticipate might happen. For example, maybe the government is contemplating a policy that is going to affect consumers. Perhaps the policy is going to make some people better-off and others worse off. Before we can decide whether or not to adopt the policy, we need to be able to measure how much better-off or worse off people are going to be as a result of its adoption. Economists reduce the effects of the policies to changes in prices and incomes and use consumer theory to measure the effects of these changes on consumer welfare.

### 3.2.1 Marshall's Consumer's Surplus Change

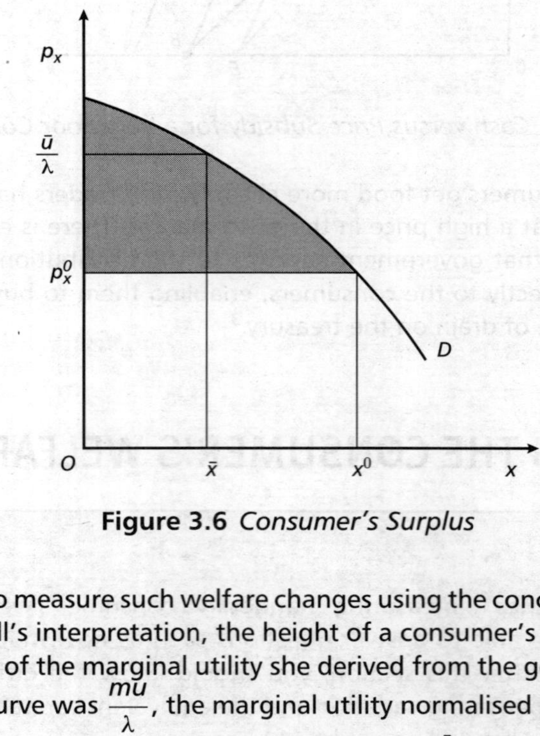


**Figure 3.6** *Consumer's Surplus*

Marshall attempted to measure such welfare changes using the concept of Consumer's Surplus. We saw how, in Marshall's interpretation, the height of a consumer's demand curve at any point showed the dollar value of the marginal utility she derived from the good at that point, since the height of the demand curve was $\frac{mu}{\lambda}$, the marginal utility normalised by $\lambda$, the marginal utility of income. Thus, in Figure 3.6, the height of the demand curve $\frac{\bar{u}}{\lambda}$ at $\bar{x}$ shows the monetary value of the marginal utility at $\bar{x}$. If the price of the good is $p_x^0$, then the consumer has to pay only $p_x^0$ for a unit of the good whose dollar 'worth' to her is $\frac{\bar{u}}{\lambda}$, thereby enjoying a 'consumer's surplus' of $\frac{\bar{u}}{\lambda} - p_x^0$. That is why, at price $p_x^0$, the consumer would buy $x^0$ units, since she will buy all units of the good from which she derives a surplus. The sum total of surplus she enjoys from this good, if the price is $p_x^0$, is given by the shaded area in Figure 3.6.

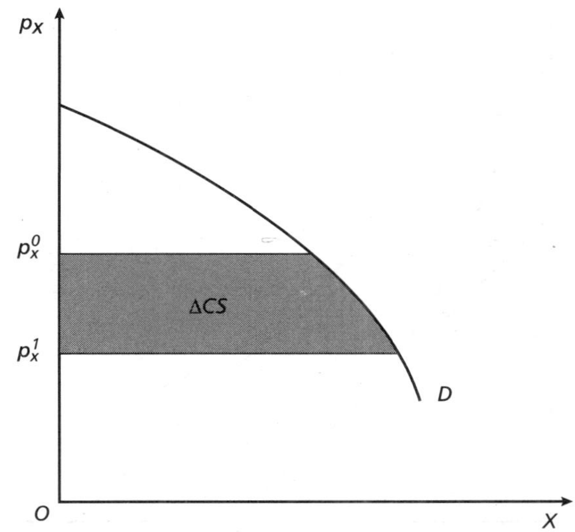


**Figure 3.7** *Change in Consumer's Surplus*

If the price of the good fell from $p_x^0$ to $p_x^1$, the consumer's surplus enjoyed by the consumer would rise by the amount given by the shaded area in Figure 3.7. This change in the consumer's surplus is Marshall's measure of how much better-off a consumer is.

This measure is a little problematic because it involves the assumption of a constant marginal utility of income, which we suspect is not a very reasonable assumption. Further, it is restricted to cases where only one price has changed; all other prices and income are assumed fixed so that the demand curve remains fixed. These problems are addressed in the Hicksian approach to consumer welfare change.

### 3.2.2 The Hicksian Approach: The Compensating and Equivalent Variations in Income

The Hicksian approach to consumer theory gives us a much more general and powerful way to address the question of consumer welfare change. In its essence, the problem is one of finding the monetary difference between two utility levels. Suppose a consumer was on utility $u_0$ initially and then, after some changes took place, ended up on utility level $u_1$ (see Figure 3.8). The changes could include price changes, income change, changes in the policy or market environment and so on. Our problem is to simply answer the question: how much better-off or worse off (in monetary terms) is the consumer after the changes than she was before?

The logical answer to this question is: the consumer is better-off by the additional amount it would cost her to attain the utility level $u_1$, as opposed to the utility level $u_0$. But that raises a further question: what prices should we use to calculate the cost of achieving the utility levels?

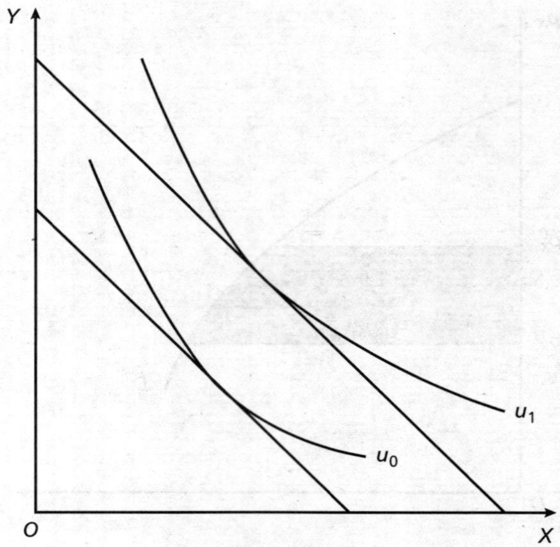


**Figure 3.8** *The Basic Welfare Measurement Problem*

There are two natural candidates for this: the original prices when $u_0$ was attained, and the final prices when $u_1$ was attained. We therefore have two natural measures of the welfare change:

$$\Delta W_{EV} = E(p_0, u_1) - E(p_0, u_0), \tag{3.1}$$

$$\Delta W_{CV} = E(p_1, u_1) - E(p_1, u_0), \tag{3.2}$$

where $E(p_i, u_j)$ is the minimum expenditure needed to attain utility level $u_j$ at prices $p_i$. Note that if $u_1 < u_0$, these same definitions would apply, only now the change in the welfare $\Delta W$ would be negative.

These alternative measures of welfare change $\Delta W$ are based on two concepts that derive from the Hicksian approach to the theory of consumer:

**The Compensating Variation in Income (*CV*)** is the change in income needed *after* an economic change has taken place that would be just sufficient to restore the consumer to the original level of utility.

$$CV = E(p_1, u_0) - E(p_1, u_1). \tag{3.3}$$

In (3.3), $E(p_1, u_0)$ is the minimum expenditure needed to achieve the original utility level $u_0$ at the new price $p_1$ and $CV$ measures the difference between this and the consumer's current income $I_1$ which is equal to $E(p_1, u_1)$. Note by comparing (3.3) and (3.2), that

$$CV = -\Delta W_{CV}$$

If $u_1 > u_0$, so that the consumer is better-off, $\Delta W_{CV} > 0$ to indicate this improvement in welfare. But the *CV* will be negative, since income has to be *reduced* in order to force the consumer back to the original utility level. Thus, *CV* and $\Delta W_{CV}$ will always be of opposite sign.

We have seen *CV* before since it is the amount by which income had to be changed to determine the substitution effect of a single price change, as in Figure 3.9. But the concept is more general and can be applied even when many prices and income have changed.

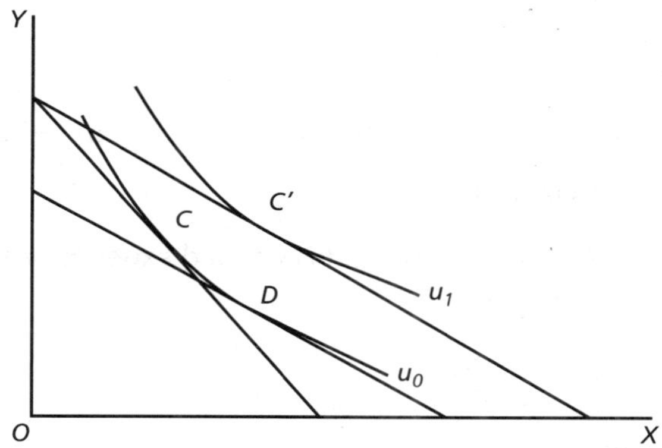


**Figure 3.9** *Compensating Variation for a Price Decrease*

**The Equivalent Variation in Income** (*EV*) is the change in income needed *before* an economic change has taken place that would be just sufficient to bring the consumer to the utility level she would enjoy if the economic change took place.

$$EV = E(p_0, u_1) - E(p_0, u_0). \tag{3.4}$$

In (3.4), $E(p_0, u_1)$ is the minimum expenditure needed at current prices $p_0$ to attain the utility level $u_1$ that the consumer would attain under the change scenario. Note by comparing (3.4) with (3.1) that

$$EV = \Delta W_{EV}.$$

## 3.2.3 An Example to Calculate *CV* and *EV*

Suppose a consumer has the utility function

$$U(x, y) = x^{0.4}y^{0.6}.$$

We know her demand functions are

$$x = \frac{2I}{5p_x} \quad \text{and} \quad y = \frac{3I}{5p_y} \tag{3.5}$$

and the indirect utility function is

$$V = \frac{2^{0.4}3^{0.6}}{5} \frac{I}{p_x^{0.4}p_y^{0.6}}. \tag{3.6}$$

Now, suppose initially our consumer's income is ₹100, and the prices she faces are $p_x^0 =$ ₹2 and $p_y^0 =$ ₹3. From (3.5) and (3.6), we find

$$x_0 = 20, \qquad y_0 = 20, \qquad u_0 = 20.$$

Finally, suppose $p_x$ falls to ₹1. Then

$$x_0 = 40, \qquad y_0 = 20, \qquad u_1 = 26.39$$

Our task is to find the *CV* and *EV* of this price change.

To find *CV*, we need to find $E(p_1, u_0)$. Suppose this needed expenditure is the income level $I'$. We can use (3.6), using $u_0$ and $p_1$, to find

$$20 = \frac{2^{0.4}3^{0.6}}{5} \frac{I'}{1^{0.4}3^{0.6}}$$

which can be solved to yield:

$$I' = 75.79.$$

Then, using (3.3), we find

$$CV = 75.79 - 100 = -24.21.$$

Note that $\Delta W_{CV} = 24.21$.

To find the *EV*, we need to find $E(p_0, u_1)$. Let this be $I''$. Again, using (3.6), $u_1$ and the prices $p_0$ we can find:

$$26.39 = \frac{2^{0.4}3^{0.6}}{5} \frac{I''}{2^{0.4}3^{0.6}}$$

which gives us

$$I'' = 131.95.$$

Thus, from (3.4), we find

$$EV = 131.95 - 100 = 31.95$$

$$\Delta W_{EV} = 31.95.$$

We have two alternative measures of the change in the consumer's welfare. Each has a sound theoretical basis, and it is not clear that one is better than the other. We will return to this issue a little later.

### 3.2.4 An Alternative Approach to Calculating *CV* and *EV*

An alternative approach to the calculation of CV and EV is to break down any economic change into individual price and income changes and to calculate the welfare impact of each of these. Any income change can be treated at face value. For each price change, we can calculate *CV* and *EV* as follows. First of all, notice that in this case we are abstracting away from any income change, so we can assume that $I_0 \equiv E(p_0, u_0) = E(p_1, u_1) \equiv I_1$.

So, in this case, (3.3) can be written as

$$CV = E(p_1, u_0) - E(p_0, u_0) \tag{3.7}$$

and (3.4) can be written as

$$EV = E(p_0, u_1) - E(p_1, u_1). \tag{3.8}$$

Note that (3.7) and (3.8), which are often presented as the definitions of *CV* and *EV*, are true only in the special case when $I_0 = I_1$.

Looking at (3.7), we see that in this case *CV* is simply the change in income needed, as price changes from $p_0$ to $p_1$, to hold the consumer's utility constant at $u_0$. Now, we know from Shephard's Lemma, (2.69), that

$$\frac{\partial E}{\partial p_x} = x^h.$$

Since the continuous version of (3.7) is

$$CV = \int_{p_0}^{p_1} \frac{\partial E}{\partial p_x} dp_x,$$

we can also write it as

$$CV = \int_{p_0}^{p_1} x^h(u_0) dp_x. \tag{3.9}$$

Thus, the *CV* is the negative of the shaded area in panel (a) of Figure 3.10, the area between the price lines and below the compensated demand curve for utility level $u_0$.

By a similar argument, it can be shown that the *EV* is given by

$$EV = \int_{p_1}^{p_0} x^h(u_1) dp_x \tag{3.10}$$

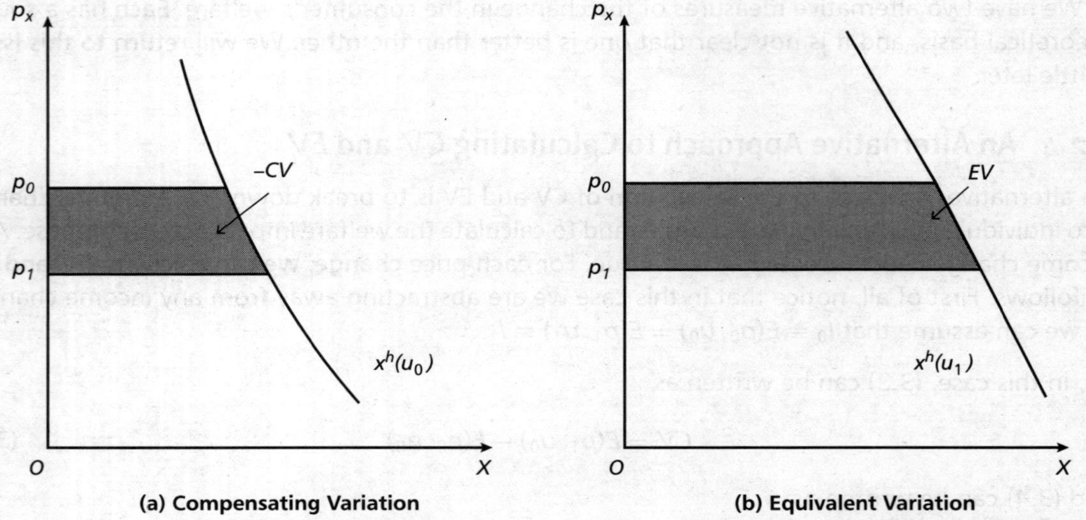


**Figure 3.10** *CV and EV Using the Compensated Demand Curve*

which is the area between the price lines and below the compensated demand curve for utility level $u_1$ in panel (b) of Figure 3.10.

### 3.2.5 Numerical Example

We can check this approach by looking at the same example we considered for the general approach. We can adapt (2.88) to write down the compensated demand function for our consumer's utility function:

$$x^h = \left(\frac{2}{3}\right)^{0.6} \left(\frac{p_y}{p_x}\right)^{0.6} u. \tag{3.11}$$

In our example, $p_y = ₹3$, $u_0 = 20$ and $p_x$ changed from ₹2 to ₹1. So applying (3.11) to (3.9), we have

$$\begin{aligned} CV &= \int_2^1 \left(\frac{2}{3}\right)^{0.6} 3^{0.6} 20 p_x^{-0.6} dp_x \\ &= 20(2)^{0.6} \frac{1}{0.4} p_x^{0.4} |_2^1 \\ &= -24.21. \end{aligned}$$

Thus, we get the same answer as before.

We can similarly calculate $EV$, using $u_1 = 26.39$:

$$\begin{aligned} EV &= \int_1^2 2^{0.6}(26.39)p_x^{-0.6}dp_x \\ &= 31.95. \end{aligned}$$

## 3.2.6 *CV*, *EV* and the Change in Consumer's Surplus

The graphs in Figure 3.10, illustrating the $CV$ and the $EV$ for the case of a single price change, are reminiscent of Figure 3.7, which showed the change in consumer's surplus for the same case. If we think of the welfare measures $\Delta W_{CV}$, $\Delta W_{EV}$ and $\Delta CS$ so that we do not have a sign difference, we see that, in panel (a) of Figure 3.11:

$$\begin{aligned} \Delta W_{CV} &: \text{area } A \\ \Delta CS &: \text{areas } A+B \\ \Delta W_{EV} &: \text{areas } A+B+C. \end{aligned}$$

For a price increase from $p_0$ to $p_1$, we have (see panel (b) in Figure 3.11):

$$\begin{aligned} -\Delta W_{CV} &: \text{areas } A+B+C \\ -\Delta CS &: \text{areas } A+B \\ -\Delta W_{EV} &: \text{area } A. \end{aligned}$$

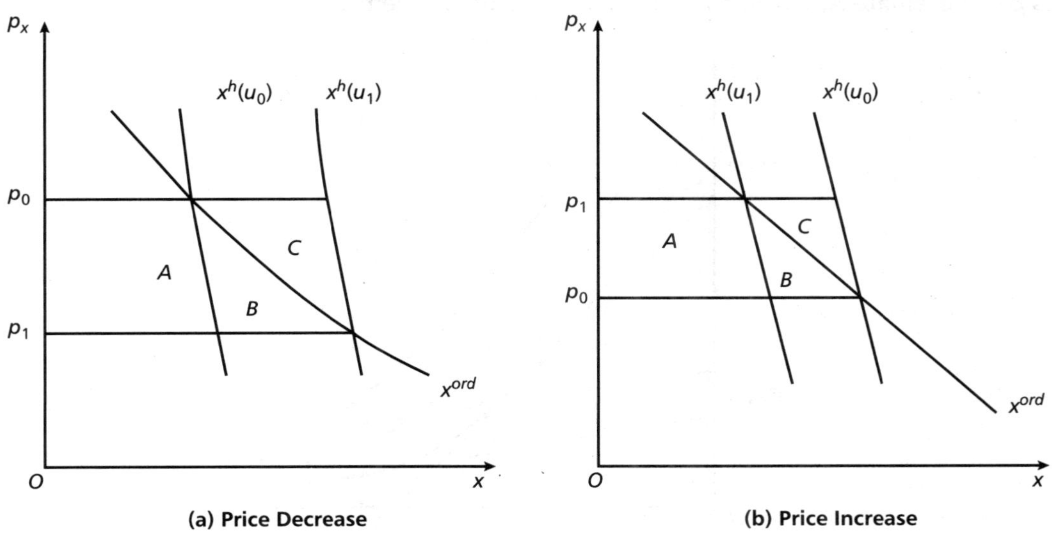


**Figure 3.11** *Comparing CV, EV and the Change in Consumer's Surplus*

So we see that the *CV* and *EV*-based measures sandwich the change in consumer's surplus, the welfare change measure proposed by Marshall. Since we do not have strong reasons to prefer either *CV* or *EV* over the other as *the* theoretically correct measure, the change in *CS* seems like a good alternative. It is simple and easy to understand, and, even though it does not have very sound theory behind it, it is sandwiched by the two theoretically sound measures that have been proposed.

It is probably worth mentioning that, if we know exactly the purpose for which we are making the welfare change calculation, we can also choose the appropriate welfare change measure. To be specific, the compensating variation measure is the appropriate one to use if we are making an *ex post* evaluation of an economic change. In other words, if a change has already taken place and we are evaluating it in order to understand what has happened, we should use the *CV* measure. For example, if we want to compensate people for a change that has made them worse off, we should use the *CV* measure. A simple case of this kind is when we want to calculate the needed cost of living adjustment to, say, social security payments or similar fixed income disbursements.

However, if the purpose of the exercise is to evaluate different policies *ex ante*, we should use the *EV* measure. Perhaps we are considering alternative ways of achieving a particular end. In such a case, we should measure welfare changes based on base period prices, so that we are using the same yardstick to measure the welfare changes. It is relatively easy to construct simple examples where using the *CV* measure in such cases might give us the wrong answer. Say we are considering either policy A or policy B. Say policy A improves the average consumer's welfare more than policy B. Using the *EV* measure will always rank A over B. But, if we use the *CV* measure, we may end up ranking B over A. This is possible because we are using prices $p_B$ to evaluate B and prices $p_A$ to evaluate A, which could obviously create problems.

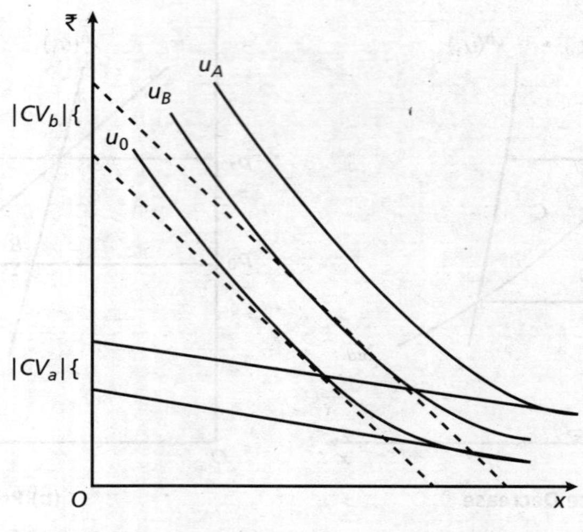


**Figure 3.12** *How the CV Can Give Incorrect Welfare Comparisons*

This can be illustrated quite easily using an indifference curve diagram. Suppose the typical consumer is currently on the utility level $u_0$. Two policies A and B are under consideration, which will lead the typical consumer to utility levels $u_A$ and $u_B$ respectively (see Figure 3.12), where $u_A > u_B$. If we were to calculate the $EV$ of each of these policies, we would clearly find $EV_A > EV_B$. Now consider what would happen if we use $CV$ as our welfare measure. For simplicity, suppose each of the policies affects only $p_x$ and $I$, leaving prices of all other goods unchanged. On the vertical axis then we can simply measure money as representative of all other goods. Suppose under $A$, $p_x$ is low but $I$ is also low, while under B, $p_x$ is high but $I$ is also high. The $CV$ measure of welfare change will be the vertical distance between $u_0$ and $u_i$ at price $p_i$ for each $i = A, B$. The way the graph is drawn, $|CV_A| < |CV_B|$. Using this measure, we would select policy B, which would be the wrong choice, since $A$ leads to a higher level of utility.

### 3.2.7 Welfare Analysis in the Revealed Preference Approach

Since the Revealed Preference theory does not admit to the existence of indifference curves (or a utility function), we can say less about the consumer's welfare. We could have welfare measures similar to those based on the compensating and equivalent variations in income; the difference would be that here the income changes needed would be computed on the basis of the bundles rather than the utility levels. If $q_0$ and $q_1$ represent the initial and final bundles of goods and $C(p_i, q_j)$ represents the cost of the bundle $q_j$ at prices $p_i$, then, similar to (3.1) and (3.2), we could have

$$\Delta W_{SE} = C(p_0, q_1) - C(p_0, q_0) \tag{3.12}$$

and

$$\Delta W_{SC} = C(p_1, q_1) - C(p_1, q_0). \tag{3.13}$$

Here the subscripts $SE$ and $SC$ stand for Slutsky-equivalent and Slutsky-compensated, respectively.

What (3.12) and (3.13) are doing is this: we are comparing the initial bundle $q_0$ and the final bundle $q_1$ and asking how different are the costs of buying these two bundles. If we use the base prices $p_0$ to calculate this difference in costs, we have the 'Slutsky-equivalent' measure of $\Delta W$, (3.12), and if we use the final prices $p_1$ to calculate the difference in costs, we have the 'Slutsky-compensated' measure of $\Delta W$, (3.13).

There is a nice symmetry of these concepts to the Hicksian measures $\Delta W_{EV}$ and $\Delta W_{CV}$ and it is tempting to think that the 'Slutsky' measures are equally valid, but unfortunately this is not so. Specifically, we would expect any reasonable welfare measure to have the property that

- $\Delta W > 0$ implies the consumer is now better-off and
- $\Delta W < 0$ implies the consumer is now worse off.

Unfortunately, neither $\Delta W_{SE}$ nor $\Delta W_{SC}$ satisfies both these properties.

Consider $\Delta W_{SE}$ first. If $\Delta W_{SE} > 0$, this means that

$$C(p_0, q_1) > C(p_0, q_0).$$

In other words, $q_1$ was not available when $q_0$ was chosen. In this case, we have no basis to judge whether the consumer is better-off with $q_1$ or $q_0$ since we do not have any information that tells us that she has revealed a preference for one over the other. It is tempting to think she is better-off with $q_1$ since that's what a positive $\Delta W$ would indicate, but a glance at Figure 3.13 should be enough to see that this is not necessarily the case. If the line represents the budget constraint when $q_0$ was chosen, the fact that $q_1$ is outside this budget constraint does not guarantee that the consumer prefers it to $q_0$.

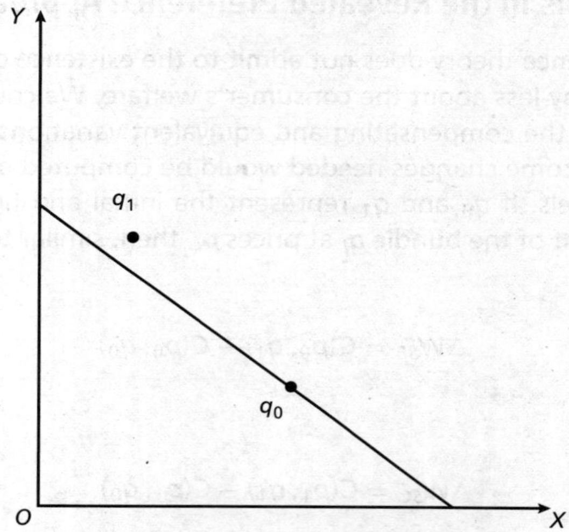


**Figure 3.13** *Bundles You Cannot Afford Are Not Necessarily Better than What You Have*

If, however, $\Delta W_{SE} < 0$, then

$$C(p_0, q_1) < C(p_0, q_0),$$

and we can be sure the consumer is now worse off since she selected $q_0$ when $q_1$ was available, thereby revealing a preference for $q_0$ over $q_1$.

Now consider $\Delta W_{SC}$. If $\Delta W_{SC} > 0$, this means that

$$C(p_1, q_1) > C(p_1, q_0).$$

In other words, $q_1$ was chosen when $q_0$ was available. Thus, the consumer has revealed she prefers $q_1$ over $q_0$, thus confirming that she is now better-off (which we would expect since $\Delta W_{SC} > 0$).

But now suppose $\Delta W_{SC} < 0$. We would expect this to indicate that the consumer's welfare has fallen, that she is now worse off. But $\Delta W_{SC} < 0$ implies that

$$C(p_1, q_1) < C(p_1, q_0).$$

Thus, $q_1$ was chosen when $q_0$ was not available: no information about preferences is revealed. While we expect the consumer to be worse off, since $\Delta W_{SC} < 0$, Figure 3.14 illustrates a simple case where this is probably not true.

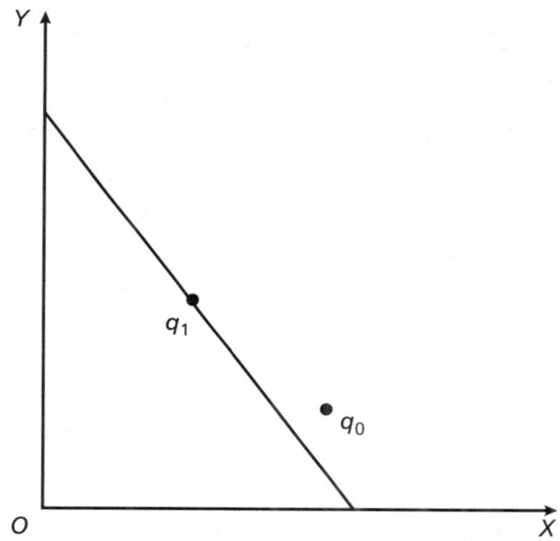


**Figure 3.14** *Bundles You Can No Longer Afford Are Not Necessarily Better than What You Have*

Thus, the welfare measures we might suggest based on the Revealed Preference approach to the theory of the consumer do not perform very well and do not have much use or standing in the theory of consumer welfare.

## 3.3 THE CONSTRUCTION OF PRICE INDICES

**Task for this section:**

To learn the theory behind the construction of price indices. After this section, you should be able to calculate the Laspeyres and Paasche price indices and should understand their limitations.

Another application of the theory of the consumer is to the construction and analysis of price index numbers. A price index is a measure of how much prices have changed over time and the broad form of such an index is

$$PI = \frac{p_1}{p_0},$$

where $PI$ is the price index, $p_1$ represents prices in the subject period and $p_0$ represents prices in the base or reference period. Normally, the ratio is multiplied by 100 so that the base price is set to 100.

### 3.3.1 Laspeyres and Paasche Price Indices

Clearly, the first issue that must be resolved in the construction of such a price index is how to aggregate the prices of all the different goods and services that a typical consumer buys. A natural approach is to take a typical 'basket' of goods and to then calculate the cost of that basket at the different prices. The next question that arises then is: what is the appropriate basket to use? Two natural candidates present themselves: the actual basket of goods consumed by the typical consumer in the base period, $q_0$, or the one consumed in the subject period, $q_1$. We thus have two possible price indices. The one using the base period quantities is called the Laspeyres Price Index:

$$PI_L = \frac{C(p_1, q_0)}{C(p_0, q_0)}, \tag{3.14}$$

where $C(p_i, q_j)$ is the cost of buying the bundle of goods $q_j$ at the prices $p_i$, and the one using the subject period quantities is called the Paasche Price Index:

$$PI_P = \frac{C(p_1, q_1)}{C(p_0, q_1)}. \tag{3.15}$$

Although these alternatives seem reasonable, they have problems in that they may not, in at least some important senses, represent an accurate picture of how much prices have changed. Indeed, the indices may not even agree whether prices have gone up or down! Consider a simple situation in which the typical consumer has a utility function

$$U(X, Y) = X^{0.4}Y^{0.6}$$

and faces the following situations:

- base situation : $I_0 = 100, p_x^0 = 2, p_y^0 = 1$
- final situation : $I_1 = 100, p_x^1 = 1, p_y^1. = 2.$

Reference to the demand functions implied by this consumer's utility function would yield the following consumption patterns:

- $q_0 : x_0 = 20, y_0 = 60$
- $q_1 : x_1 = 40, y_1 = 30.$

If we now calculate the Laspeyres and Paasche price indices, we find:

$$PI_L = \frac{(1 * 20) + (2 * 60)}{(2 * 20) + (1 * 60)} = \frac{140}{100} = 1.40$$

and

$$PI_P = \frac{(1 * 40) + (2 * 30)}{(2 * 40) + (1 * 30)} = \frac{100}{110} = 0.91.$$

Thus, the Laspeyres index says prices have gone up by 40%, while the Paasche index tells us that they have fallen by 9%.

If we wanted to see what had happened to the consumer's welfare, given that her income has not changed, we would conclude on the basis of the Laspeyres price index that she was worse off, while the Paasche price index would indicate that she was better-off.

The use of 'bundles' or 'baskets' of goods was shown to be problematic in our examination of welfare analysis under the Revealed Preference approach, and it is the same sort of problem that arises here. Suppose prices have risen and we compare the price index with an income index of the form $I_1/I_0$, indicating how much the income of the typical consumer has risen. Our price index should have the property that

- $PI > \frac{I_1}{I_0}$ implies the consumer is now worse off and
- $PI < \frac{I_1}{I_0}$ implies the consumer is now better-off.

Unfortunately, neither of those indices has both these properties.

Consider first the Laspeyres price index.

$$PI_L > \frac{I_1}{I_0} \implies \frac{C(p_1, q_0)}{C(p_0, q_0)} > \frac{I_1}{I_0}.$$

Now, $I_0 = C(p_0, q_0)$ so the denominators of the two sides of this inequality are equal. Thus, this implies that

$$C(p_1, q_0) > C(p_1, q_1).$$

Thus, $q_1$ was chosen when $q_0$ was unavailable and we cannot conclude that the consumer is now worse off. Figure 3.14 is once again illustrative of one possible scenario in this case. However,

$$PI_L < \frac{I_1}{I_0} \implies \frac{C(p_1, q_0)}{C(p_0, q_0)} < \frac{I_1}{I_0}$$

or

$$C(p_1, q_0) < C(p_1, q_1).$$

In this case, $q_0$ was available when $q_1$ was chosen, and so we can be sure the consumer is now better-off with the bundle $q_1$.

Similarly, we can look at the Paasche price index.

$$PI_P > \frac{I_1}{I_0} \Longrightarrow \frac{C(p_1, q_1)}{C(p_0, q_1)} > \frac{I_1}{I_0}$$

which yields (since the numerators are equal):

$$C(p_0, q_1) < C(p_0, q_0).$$

Thus, $q_0$ was chosen when $q_1$ was available, revealing a preference for $q_0$ over $q_1$. The price index therefore indicates that the consumer is now worse off, as we would expect.

But if

$$PI_P < \frac{I_1}{I_0},$$

then

$$C(p_0, q_1) > C(p_0, q_0),$$

showing that $q_1$ was not available when $q_0$ was chosen. We therefore cannot conclude that the consumer is better-off. The price index therefore fails us in this case.

There is a practical aspect to this problem that can be seen very easily. One important use of price indices is to make cost-of-living adjustments to income payments such as social security payments or even contracted salaries. The purpose of the cost-of-living adjustments, of course, is to hold the consumer's 'real income' or utility level constant.

Suppose we use the Laspeyres index to calculate inflation and then use it to adjust income in an attempt to hold utility constant. In other words, we set $I_1$, such that

$$\frac{C(p_1, q_0)}{C(p_0, q_0)} = \frac{I_1}{I_0}.$$

With income $I_1$ and facing prices $p_1$, suppose the typical consumer would buy the bundle $q_1$. We know then that

$$C(p_1, q_0) = C(p_1, q_1).$$

So $q_0$ is just available when $q_1$ is chosen. This suggests the consumer is better-off now; the income adjustment has been too great, as Figure 3.15 illustrates. Making sure that the consumer can buy $q_0$ guarantees that she is no worse off. But if relative prices have changed, the consumer can change her consumption pattern to take advantage of these changes and make herself better-off than before.

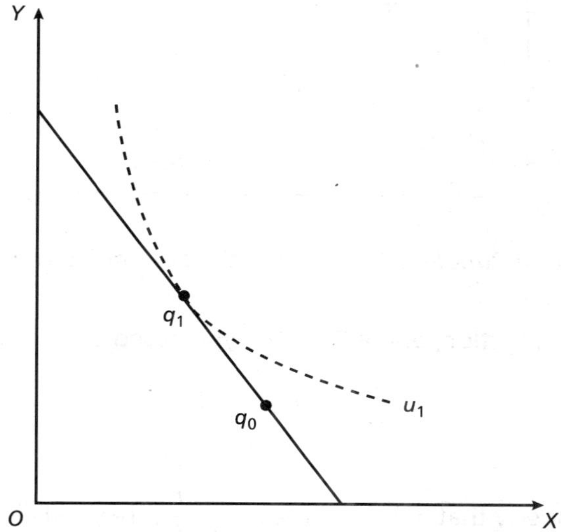


**Figure 3.15** *Compensation That Allows You to Consume the Old Bundle Makes You Better-Off*

If, however, we used the Paasche price index to make the income adjustment, we would have

$$C(p_0, q_1) = C(p_0, q_0).$$

Here, $q_1$ would be just available at the old prices and income. In this case, the income adjustment has not been sufficient and the consumer is left worse off than before (see Figure 3.16).

## 3.3.2 'True' Price Indices

The previous discussion suggests a theoretical way out of the problem; in other words, it suggests what a 'true' price index might look like. Rather than calculating the cost of buying particular bundles at different prices, we should calculate the minimum expenditure needed to obtain particular utility levels. We could have two such 'true price indices'–a Laspeyres type based on the base period utility level:

$$TPI_L = \frac{E(p_1, u_0)}{E(p_0, u_0)}, \tag{3.16}$$

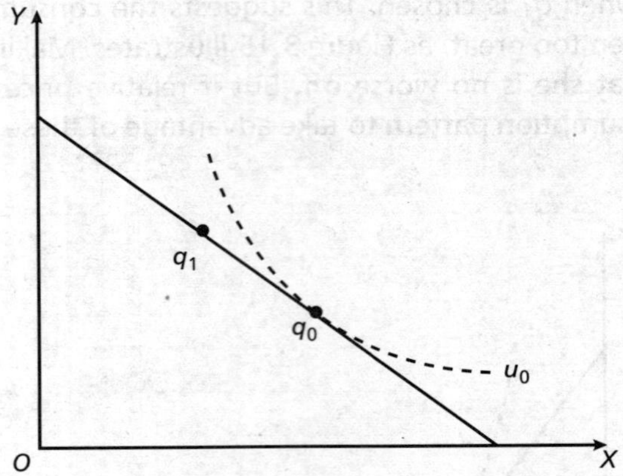


**Figure 3.16** *Chosen Bundle Is Better Than Other Bundles That Are Affordable*

where $E$ is the expenditure function, and a Paasche type based on the subject period utility level:

$$TPI_P = \frac{E(p_1, u_1)}{E(p_0, u_1)}. \tag{3.17}$$

These indices have the property that, when compared to $\frac{I_1}{I_0}$, they will always tell us correctly if the consumer is better-off or worse off. For example, for the Laspeyres type of 'true price index',

$$\frac{E(p_1, u_0)}{E(p_0, u_0)} > \frac{I_1}{I_0} \implies E(p_1, u_0) > E(p_1, u_1)$$

which means $u_0 > u_1$, the consumer is worse off as prices have risen faster than income. For the opposite case:

$$\frac{E(p_1, u_0)}{E(p_0, u_0)} < \frac{I_1}{I_0} \implies E(p_1, u_0) < E(p_1, u_1)$$

which means $u_0 < u_1$, the consumer is now better-off as prices have risen slower than income. A similar analysis can be done for the Paasche-type index.

If we wanted to make cost-of-living adjustments, the Laspeyres type of true price index would give us the appropriate adjustment factor that would lead to the correct income adjustment.

For the illustrative numerical example examined earlier (see Section 3.2.5), we can calculate the true price indices. Suppose

$$M_1 = E(p_1, u_0).$$

Then, from the indirect utility function, we have

$$20^{0.4}60^{0.6} = (0.4M_1)^{0.4}\left(\frac{0.6M_1}{2}\right)^{0.6}.$$

Solving for $M_1$, we find:

$$M_1 = 114.87.$$

Thus,

$$TPI_L = \frac{114.87}{100} = 1.1487.$$

For the Paasche type of true price index, we need $E(p_0, u_1)$. Let

$$M_2 = E(p_0, u_1).$$

Then, using the indirect utility function again, we can find

$$M_2 = 87.055$$

so that

$$TPI_P = \frac{100}{87.055} = 1.1487.$$

In this case, the Laspeyres and Paasche *TPIs* are the same, which is a property of homothetic preferences only. These two indices will not always have the same value.

## SUMMARY

In this chapter, we have looked at a few of the many applications of consumer theory. The applications, and the lessons they teach us, were as follows:

- Consumer theory can be used to study the impact of taxes and subsidies.
- Taxes and subsidies tend to cause welfare losses because they affect prices and thereby distort consumers' decisions on the quantity of goods they choose to consume.
- Lump-sum taxes do not distort the consumers' quantity decisions because they do not affect prices, and for this reason lump-sum taxes are superior to commodity taxes such as sales taxes as a way for governments to raise revenue.

- Similarly, a straight cash payment (a negative lump-sum tax) is preferable in theory to a food subsidy that subsidises food grain sales to consumers.
- Consumer theory can also be used to measure the welfare effect on consumers of changes in the price of a good.
- Marshall proposed to measure the welfare effect of a price change by the change in consumer's surplus: the area between the old and new prices below the demand curve.
- In the Hicksian approach, there are two possible measures of the welfare effect of a change in price, the compensating and equivalent variations in income. Both these measures are theoretically sound, but they yield measures that sandwich Marshall's change in consumer's surplus.
- The Compensating Variation in Income (*CV*) is the change in income needed after an economic change (such as a change in price) has taken place that would be just sufficient to restore the consumer to the original level of utility. This is equal to the difference in the cost of achieving the before and after utility levels using the final prices.
- The Equivalent Variation in Income (*EV*) is the change in income needed before an economic change has taken place that would be just sufficient to bring the consumer to the utility level she would enjoy if the economic change took place. This is equal to the difference in the cost of achieving the before and after utility levels using the initial prices.
- The *CV* is the better of the two measures when calculating needed compensation payments *ex post*.
- The *EV* is the better of the two measures when evaluating policies *ex ante*.
- Consumer theory can help in the analysis of common price indices and inform the construction of meaningful ones.
- The Laspeyres Price Index looks at the ratio of the cost of buying a 'base year' bundle of goods at the current versus the base year prices.
- The Paasche Price Index looks at the ratio of the cost of buying the 'current year' bundle of goods at the current versus the base year prices.
- Both the Laspeyres and Paasche price indices can give anomalous results.
- 'True' price indices should measure the ratio of the cost of achieving the 'base' or 'current' utility levels at the current versus the base year prices. Such indices would not yield anomalous results.

## EXERCISES

1. Over a three-year period, Joseph exhibits the following consumption behaviour:

| | $p_x$ | $p_y$ | $X$ | $Y$ |
|---|---|---|---|---|
| Year 1 | 3 | 3 | 7 | 4 |
| Year 2 | 4 | 2 | 6 | 6 |
| Year 3 | 5 | 1 | 7 | 3 |

(a) Comparing years 1 and 2, can you say in which year Joseph is better-off? Explain clearly and fully why or why not.

(b) Taking into account all three years, is Joseph's behaviour consistent with revealed preference? Again, explain clearly and fully the reasons for your answer.

(c) Construct the Paasche and Laspeyres price indices for year 2 prices with year 1 as the base year.

2. Olivia consumes only two goods, $X$ and $Y$. Her utility function is:

$$U(X, Y) = 10 + X + 2Y.$$

(a) Find Olivia's demand function for good $Y$, and draw her demand curve in a clearly labelled diagram. Comment on its shape.

(b) Find Olivia's compensated demand function for good $Y$, and draw her compensated demand curve in a clearly labelled diagram. Comment on its shape.

3. Meena consumes only two goods, $X$ and $Y$. Her utility function is

$$U(X, Y) = XY^2.$$

Initially, her income is ₹90 and the prices of both goods are ₹1. The price of X then rises to ₹2.

(a) Using consumer's surplus as your welfare measure, find how much better-off or worse off is Meena.

(b) Using the compensating variation as your welfare measure, find how much better-off or worse off is Meena.

(c) Illustrate your answers to (a) and (b) on one clearly labelled diagram.

4. Lalitha snacks every day at school on crackers ($C$) and soda ($S$). Her utility function is

$$U(C, S) = C^{\frac{1}{2}}S^{\frac{1}{2}}.$$

(a) Find Lalitha's demand functions for $C$ and $S$.

(b) If $p_C = 10$ paise and $p_S = 25$ paise, how would Lalitha spend the ₹1 her mother gives her every day to pay for her snack?

(c) If the price of crackers is raised to 40 paise, how much extra money will Lalitha's mother need to give her each day in order for her to achieve the same level of utility?

5. For the utility function

$$U(X, Y) = X^{\frac{3}{4}}Y^{\frac{1}{4}}$$

find the ordinary and compensated demand functions for $X$, and confirm from them that the elasticities form of the Slutsky equation holds.

6. A household has utility function

$$U(F, C) = F^{\frac{1}{4}}C^{\frac{3}{4}}$$

where F is the quantity of food consumed and C is a composite of all other goods. Prices of $F$ and $C$ are both ₹1 and the household's income is ₹100.

(a) How much $F$ and $C$ will the household buy?

(b) Now suppose the government wants to double the household's income by giving it an in-kind subsidy of 100 units of food, which cannot be resold. Draw a diagram showing the household's budget constraint now, in relation to its budget constraint and choice from part (a). How much $F$ and $C$ will the household buy now?

(c) Show graphically, and then calculate, a dollar measure of how much better-off the household is as a result of this subsidy. State clearly what measure you have used.

7. Lily's utility function is

$$U(X, Y) = X^2Y^3,$$

where $X$ and $Y$ represent the quantities of the only two goods Lily consumes. The prices of the two goods are $p_x$ = ₹2 and $p_y$ = ₹6. Lily's income is ₹1,000 per month.

(a) Find the quantities of $X$ and $Y$ Lily would consume in order to maximise her utility.

(b) Suppose $p_y$ goes up to ₹10. What will now be the utility maximising quantities of consumption?

(c) Find the compensating variation of this price change.

8. Ashok spends ₹1 on bottled water which he can buy in two sizes: 0.75 litre and 2 litre. The water is identical in the two sizes, and Ashok gets no utility from the containers themselves, only from the water.

(a) Write down a utility function for Ashok in terms of the number of small containers ($x$) and the large containers ($y$) that he consumes.

(b) Find Ashok's demand function for $x$ and draw it in a clearly labelled diagram.

(c) Find Ashok's compensated demand function for $x$ and draw it in a clearly labelled diagram.

9. The Subramaniam family has ₹100 available per month to buy grain. They are indifferent between wheat and rice, which they find to be perfect substitutes; they only care about the total amount of grain they are able to consume, the more the better.

   (a) Let $p_w$ and $p_r$ represent the prices per kg of wheat and rice, respectively. Write down the Subramaniam family's utility function over wheat and rice and find their demand functions.

   (b) If $p_w = ₹4$ per kg and $p_r = ₹5$ per kg, how much of each good would the Subramaniam family buy per month?

   (c) If the government decides to introduce a food subsidy programme in which they buy rice on the open market and sell it to families such as the Subramaniams at a price of ₹2 per kg, what would now be the Subramaniams' consumption pattern? Using the equivalent variation as the appropriate welfare measure, calculate how much better-off they are as a result of the food subsidy.

   (d) Assuming the market price is not affected by this programme, how much does the subsidy to the Subramaniams cost the government? Is there a cheaper way for the government to make the Subramaniams just as well off as they are under the food subsidy programme? Be as specific as you can in answering this question.

10. Olivia's utility function is

$$U(X, Y) = \sqrt{X} + \sqrt{Y},$$

where $X$ and $Y$ are the quantities consumed per month of the only two goods she buys.

   (a) Find Olivia's demand functions for $X$ and $Y$.

   (b) If Olivia's income is ₹100 per month and $p_x = ₹1$ and $p_y = ₹4$, how much of each good would Olivia buy per month?

   (c) Find Olivia's compensated demand function for $X$.

11. Lily buys only two goods, $X$ and $Y$. Here is some data on her consumption in two different years

$$\begin{aligned} \text{Year 1}: \ & p_x = ₹1, X = 50, p_y = ₹2, Y = 25, \\ \text{Year 2}: \ & p_x = ₹3, X = 30, p_y = ₹2, Y = 40. \end{aligned}$$

Can you say in which year Lily is better-off? Explain fully, and draw a diagram to illustrate your answer.

12. Rani's utility function is

$$U(X, Y) = XY^2,$$

where X and Y represent the quantities of the only two goods Rani consumes. The prices of the two goods are $p_x = ₹2$ and $p_y = ₹4$. Rani's income is ₹300 per month.

   (a) Find the quantities of $X$ and $Y$ Rani would consume in order to maximise her utility.

(b) Suppose $p_y$ goes up to ₹5. What will now be the utility maximising quantities of consumption?

(c) Find the compensating variation of this price change.

(d) Find the equivalent variation of this price change.

13. Barrack consumes only two goods, $x$ and $y$, and his utility function is:

$$U(x, y) = xy + y.$$

Let $p_x$ and $p_y$ represent the prices of $x$ and $y$ respectively.

(a) Find Barrack's ordinary demand functions for $x$ and $y$.

(b) Find Barrack's compensated demand functions for $x$ and $y$.

(c) Suppose that Barrack's income is ₹100, the price of $y$ is ₹10 per unit and the price of $x$ rises from ₹20 to ₹25 per unit. Find the minimum amount of money Barrack would have to be given after the price increase in order to make him just as well off as he was before the increase.

14. Suppose that Sam gets utility from apples and bananas. Specifically, if $A$ is the number of apples Sam consumes and $B$ is the number of bananas Sam consumes, Sam's utility can be calculated as follows:

$$U(A, B) = \ln A + 2\ln B.$$

Note that Sam can buy fractions of fruit (i.e. answers need not be whole numbers).

(a) Let income be represented by $I$, the price of apples be represented by $p_A$ and the price of bananas be represented by $p_B$. What is the Marshallian demand for apples?

(b) Suppose that apples cost ₹1/apple, bananas costs ₹0.50/banana and Sam has ₹24 to spend. How many apples and bananas will Sam consume?

(c) What is the Hicksian/compensated demand for apples?

(d) Define a normal good. Are bananas a normal good for Sam?

15. Tim's preferences over goods 1 and 2, the only goods he consumes, are represented by the utility function

$$U(x_1, x_2) = \text{Min}\,[2x_1 + x_2, x_1 + 2x_2],$$

where $x_1$ and $x_2$ denote the quantities of good 1 and good 2 that he consumes.

(a) Draw the indifference curve for utility level 24.

(b) Calculate the MRS at $(x_1, x_2) = (10, 7)$. If Tim chooses to consume the bundle (10,7) when the price of good 1 is equal to ₹4, how much is his income?

(c) Calculate the optimal consumption bundle $(x_1^*, x_2^*)$ when Tim has an income of 24, $p_1 = 1$ and $p_2 = 1$.

(d) If $p_2$ increases to 6, while his income and $p_1$ remain the same as in part (c), what will be the new optimal consumption bundle $(x_1^{**}, x_2^{**})$? Calculate how much, if any, of the change from $x_2^*$ to $x_2^{**}$ is due to the income effect and how much to the substitution effect.

(e) Now, assume that Tim's income is provided by his father who adjusts Tim's income so that, no matter what the prices are, Tim always ends up with a utility level of 24 when he consumes the optimal consumption bundle. If $p_2 = 4$, calculate Tim's (Hicksian) demand for good 1 as a function of $p_1$.

16. Ms. Smita receives a social security check of ₹100 per week and this is all she has to live on. She spends her money on food and clothing in order to maximise her utility

$$U(F, C) = FC,$$

where $F$ and $C$ are the quantities of food and clothing she consumes. The prices of food and clothing are $p_f =$ ₹2 and $p_c =$ ₹5.

(a) How many units of food and clothing would Ms. Smita buy each week?

(b) Suppose the price of food went up to ₹2.50. How much food and clothing would Ms. Smita buy each week now? Of the change in her consumption of food, how much is due to the substitution effect and how much is due to the income effect?

(c) Suppose the government wants to compensate Ms. Smita for the increase in the price of food. How much would they need to raise her weekly check in order to achieve this goal?

CHAPTER

4

# Extensions of Consumer Theory

In the theory of consumer behaviour, our starting point has been the consumer's income or budget constraint, which she then must choose how to spend in order to maximise her utility. But many decisions a consumer faces do not involve the spending of a fixed budget but rather an 'endowment' of something: time, money and so on, which then must be allocated in order to maximise utility. Typically, this situation then creates an ambiguity in the consumer's behaviour; specifically, the simple negative relationship between price and quantity demanded breaks down. In this chapter, we will look at three examples of this phenomenon: demand from producers of the good, the labour supply decision and the decision to save or borrow against one's future income.

## 4.1 DEMAND WITH HOME PRODUCTION

**Task for this section:**

To see how the theory of consumer behaviour has to be modified to allow for consumption of self-produced goods. After this section, you should understand the concept of an 'endowment' and how it alters the theory of consumer choice.

In many countries such as India or China, a large proportion of the population is engaged in agricultural production and, for many of these households, a high proportion of their consumption is of self-produced goods. This makes some differences in their consumption behaviour, and exactly what these differences are can be explained by consumer theory.

The starting point for the analysis is that the consumer's budget constraint is qualitatively different. Whereas the normal budget constraint took the consumer's income as given and was then drawn to reflect the current prices of goods, the home-producer's budget constraint starts with his 'endowment', which may be partly or fully denominated in kind. For example, suppose our consumer is a wheat farmer, let us call him Kisan, and he produces $w_0$ units of wheat per year.

Let $y$ represent the value of all other goods in his consumption basket. Then, if $p_w$ is the price of wheat, Kisan's 'income' is the value of his wheat crop $p_w w_0$ and so his budget constraint will be

$$y + p_w w = p_w w_0,$$

where $y$ and $w$ represent the quantities of goods he consumes. This is a downward-sloping straight line with a slope of $-p_w$, shown in Figure 4.1 as the line $EF$, where the point $E$ is Kisan's 'endowment'.

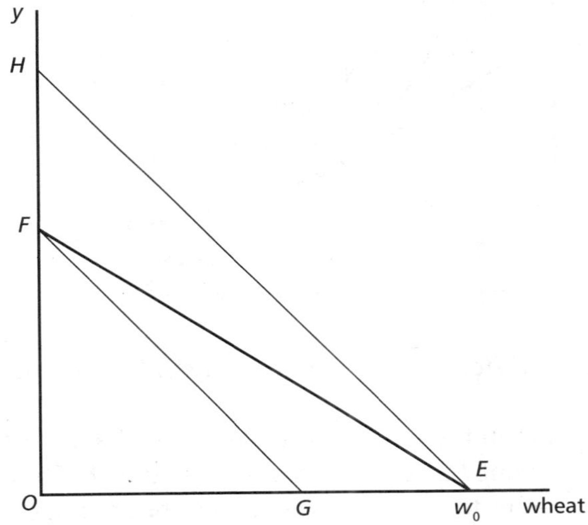


**Figure 4.1** *Budget Constraint with Home Production*

Now suppose the price of wheat goes up, while all other prices remain unchanged. The usual budget constraint would rotate *inwards* to a position such as $FG$ in the figure. But, since $E$ is Kisan's endowment, it must remain on his budget constraint. Therefore, his budget constraint rotates *outwards* to $EH$ since the rise in the price of wheat raises the value of his endowment and hence his income. And this difference in the behaviour of the budget constraint naturally creates a difference in Kisan's consumption behaviour. Whereas normal demand theory would tell us that a rise in the price of a good would lead to a fall in the quantity demanded (assuming the good is a normal good), we cannot say this in Kisan's case. The effect of the rise in the price of wheat on his demand for wheat is ambiguous.

To see why, let us look at Figure 4.2. Kisan's endowment is at $E$ and $EF$ is the original constraint he faces. He achieves the utility level $U_0$, since the indifference curve for that utility level is tangent to his budget constraint at A. When the price of wheat goes up, his constraint rotates out to $EH$. To find the substitution effect of this price change, we look for point $B$, where the slope of $U_0$ is equal to the slope of the new budget constraint (E′H′ is drawn parallel to $EH$ and tangent to $U_0$).

The substitution effect is always negative, and we confirm that here by noting that *B* is to the left of *A*, indicating a reduction in the consumption of wheat on grounds of the substitution effect.

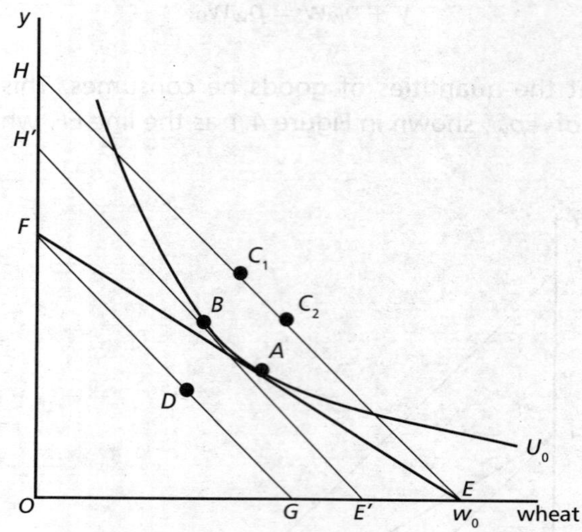


**Figure 4.2** *Effect of a Price Change with Home Production*

The final consumption point in the normal case would be at a point such as *D* on what would have been the budget constraint *FG*. But in Kisan's case, the constraint is *EH* and so the final consumption point *C* will be on that line. If wheat is a normal good (which seems reasonable to suppose), *C* must be to the north-east of *B*, that is, above it and to the right. There are two possibilities. It could be at a point such as $C_1$, which is to the left of *A*, or a point such as $C_2$, which is to the right of *A*. Thus, Kisan's consumption of wheat in response to the rise in the price of wheat could have gone down (as at $C_1$) or up (as at $C_2$). This is in sharp contrast to the normal case, where the demand for wheat would have unambiguously gone down. Notice also that the demand for other goods, represented by *y*, would here have unambiguously gone up, since *B* is above *A* and both $C_1$ and $C_2$ are above *B*. This is also in contrast to the normal case, where the demand for other goods could have gone up or down (*D* could be above or below *A*).

What is driving the difference, of course, is that Kisan is both a consumer and a producer of wheat. As a consumer, he is hurt by a rise in the price of wheat, but he is helped by it as a producer. The change in his consumption pattern from *A* to *C* (where *C* stands for either $C_1$ or $C_2$) could be thought of as consisting of three parts. The movement from *A* to *B* is the usual substitution effect. Then we could think of the movement from *B* to *D* as the normal income effect, giving us a movement from *A* to *D* as the 'normal' price effect. But then there is an additional movement from *D* to *C*. We could call this the 'endowment effect', as it reflects the effect of the change in the value of Kisan's endowment. It is the endowment effect that distinguishes the case of consumption behaviour with home production from the normal case.

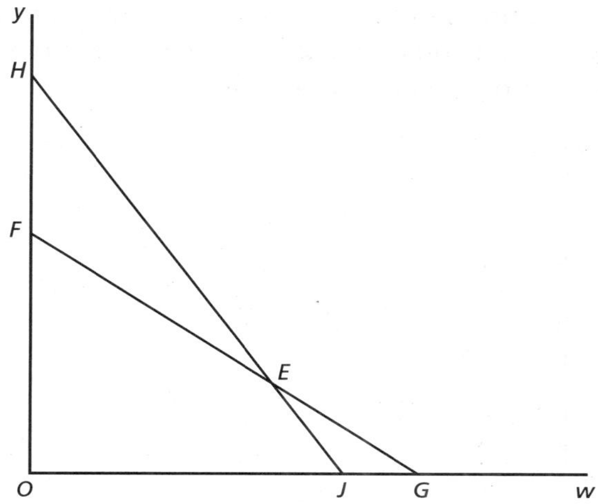


**Figure 4.3** *Budget Constraint with Multiple Endowments*

It is worth looking briefly at one more case of consumption behaviour with home production: the case where the consumer has an endowment of, say, wheat *and* some monetary income. Kisan might, for example, plant and harvest wheat and also have income from other members of his household or that he earns himself by working periodically as a casual labourer. In that case, his endowment point will not be on the axis, but in the interior of the graph, such as at point E in Figure 4.3. His budget constraint *FG* will pass through *E* and have a slope as before of $-p_w$. If the price of wheat goes up, the budget constraint will now pivot around the point *E* to a position such as *HJ* in the figure. Kisan's consumption choice and response to a change in $p_w$ can be analysed as before, and this case is not substantially different from this point of view than the previous case.

This is a good opportunity to develop a concept that we will need in later chapters: the offer curve, which is a particular way to present the consumption behaviour of a consumer who begins with some sort of endowment. Suppose Kisan starts out with *E* in Figure 4.4 and then faces the budget constraint *HJ*. Suppose he would choose bundle A if faced with that constraint, a point where one of his indifference curves is tangent to his constraint *HJ*. As the price of wheat keeps changing, we could find points such as A which would be Kisan's consumption choices for those different prices. If we then draw a line connecting all of Kisan's chosen bundles, we would get a curved line such as the dark line running from *E* to *A* to *B*. This curve is Kisan's **offer curve**, which is a summary of Kisan's consumption choices for different prices. Every point such as *A* on the offer curve has two important properties. First, the point shows the price ratio at which it would be chosen, namely the line joining it to the endowment point. For example, the line *AE* embodies the price at which *A* is the chosen bundle; this would be true of every point on the offer curve. Second, each point shows what Kisan would want to trade at that price. Consider the triangle *AXE*, the right-angled triangle with the line *AE* as its hypotenuse. The triangle *AXE* is Kisan's **trade**

**triangle**. It shows that, at the prices represented by the slope of *AE*, he wants to sell *EX* amount of wheat and buy *XA* amount of all other goods. We will see an important application of offer curves when we study the topic of general equilibrium.

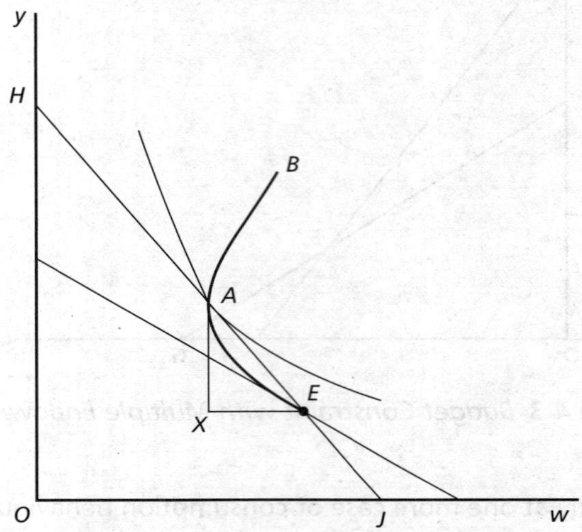


**Figure 4.4** *The Offer Curve*

# 4.2 THE LABOUR SUPPLY DECISION

**Task for this section:**

To learn the theory of labour supply and what underlies a worker's decision on how much to work. After this section, you should understand the factors underlying the labour supply decision and be able to analyse a worker's labour supply reponse to a variety of changes in his or her circumstances.

Another important application of consumer theory is to the labour supply decision. Apart from deciding how to spend their income on goods and services, consumers have to decide how much to earn, depending upon the opportunities open to them and their preferences. One might think that a lot of people have jobs with set hours, and therefore they cannot choose how much to work and therefore how much to earn, but this is not quite true. Many people work for themselves and therefore choose how hard to work and therefore how much to earn. But even people with salaried jobs can choose how hard to work in order to give themselves a greater or lesser chance on quick promotions. And even union workers are not immune to making choices. When unions negotiate labour agreements, they take into account their members' preferences on how much they want to work and earn versus how much vacation time or leisure time they want, and therefore have the option to trade off smaller pay increases against shorter working hours. Therefore, it is useful to consider the worker's labour supply decision as if he can choose his work hours.

### 4.2.1 The Basic Model

To apply the theory of consumer behaviour to the labour supply decision, we posit the existence of an ordinal utility function for the worker, let us call him Karan:

$$U = U(H, C),$$

where $H$ stands for the number of hours of leisure he enjoys per day and $C$ represents his daily consumption of goods and services. Leisure is taken to be a normal good and it is assumed that the number of hours of leisure Karan has per day is equal to $(24 - L)$, where $L$ is the number of hours he works per day. For simplicity, we will assume that $C$ is measured in value terms, so $C$ is Karan's daily expenditure on goods and services. This must equal his available income. We will assume that, in addition to his wage income, Karan has some non-wage income $N$. Therefore, we must have

$$C = wL + N,$$

where $w$ is Karan's hourly wage rate. This can be written as

$$L = \frac{1}{w} \cdot C - \frac{N}{w}. \tag{4.1}$$

Karan's true constraint in this problem is on time. Since he has only 24 hours per day, we must have

$$H + L = 24.$$

Substituting (4.1) in this and rearranging, we get

$$H + \frac{1}{w} \cdot C = 24 + \frac{N}{w}. \tag{4.2}$$

Equation (4.2) looks very much like a budget constraint, except the units of measurement here are hours. The equation shows that Karan's endowment is the equivalent of $(24 + \frac{N}{w})$ hours, since he has 24 hours per day and it is as if he has another $\frac{N}{w}$ hours, since that would be how long it would take him to earn his non-wage income $N$. Thus the right-hand side of (4.2) is Karan's endowment. The left-hand side measures his expenditure of this endowment. The 'price' of $H$ is 1, since it takes 1 hour of his time to 'buy' 1 hour of leisure. The price of $C$ is $\frac{1}{w}$ since for each unit of consumption Karan must work (and therefore 'spend') $\frac{1}{w}$ hours.

We can now write down Karan's choice problem in a form that looks very much like the traditional consumer choice problem. Karan's problem is

$$\text{Max} \quad U(H, C)$$

$$\text{subject to} \quad H + \frac{1}{w} \cdot C = 24 + \frac{N}{w}.$$

Solving this problem involves writing down the Lagrange function:

$$\mathcal{L} = U(H, C) + \lambda \left[ 24 + \frac{N}{w} - H - \frac{1}{w} \cdot C \right]$$

and the first-order conditions to find the solution are

$$\frac{\partial \mathcal{L}}{\partial H} = U_H - \lambda = 0 \qquad (4.3)$$

$$\frac{\partial \mathcal{L}}{\partial C} = U_C - \lambda \cdot \frac{1}{w} = 0 \qquad (4.4)$$

$$\text{and} \quad \frac{\partial \mathcal{L}}{\partial \lambda} = 24 + \frac{N}{w} - H - \frac{1}{w} \cdot C = 0. \qquad (4.5)$$

Equations (4.3) and (4.4) can be combined by dividing one by the other to yield

$$\frac{U_H}{U_C} = w. \qquad (4.6)$$

The condition (4.6) says that Karan will choose his work hours in such a way that his marginal rate of substitution (*MRS*) between leisure and consumption is equal to the wage rate that he faces. The similarity of this result to the standard result for utility maximisation is clear. The left-hand side of (4.6) is the MRS, the absolute value of the slope of Karan's indifference curve, and the right-hand side is the absolute value of the slope of the constraint that he faces.

The solution is illustrated in Figure 4.5. The two 'goods' in Karan's utility function are measured on the axes, leisure and consumption. Karan's 'endowment' is point *E*, where he has 24 hours of leisure and non-wage income of *N*. His constraint is the line *FE*, which could be extended to include the line segment *EG* also, although of course he will never choose a point there. The equation of the line *FE* could be written as a rearrangement of the constraint (4.2):

$$C = 24w + N - wH,$$

from which we can readily see that the slope of *FE* is $-w$. Utility is maximised at *A*, where the indifference curve $U_0$ is tangent to the constraint. At *A*, Karan 'consumes' $H_0$ hours of leisure, which means he spends $(24 - H_0)$ hours working; this is his labour supply. The income that he

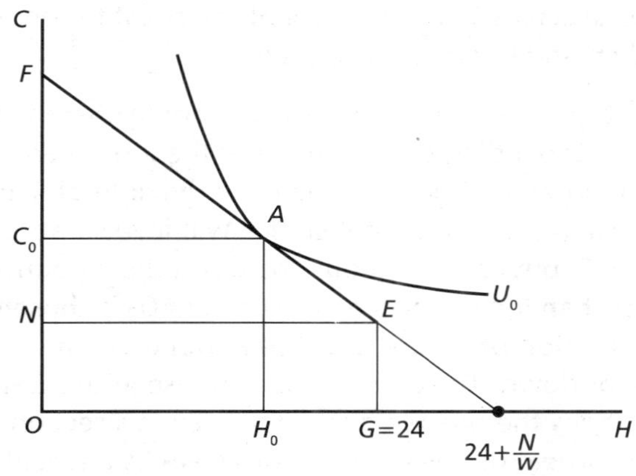


**Figure 4.5** *The Labour Supply Decision*

earns from that work plus his non-wage income *N* is just sufficient for him to be able to spend $C_0$ on goods and services.

It is possible to perform comparative statics exercises with this model, so we can ask what happens to Karan's labour supply as the wage rate goes up. We answer this question in the usual way by looking at the substitution and income effects of the wage rate change. Figure 4.6 illustrates the process. We start with the constraint at *FE* and Karan's choice at *A*. If *w* goes up, the constraint becomes steeper and pivots around the endowment point *E* to a position like *EJ*. To find the substitution effect, we draw the line E′J′ parallel to *EJ* and tangent to the original indifference curve $U_0$. This tangency will be to the left of *A*, since it is on a steeper portion of the

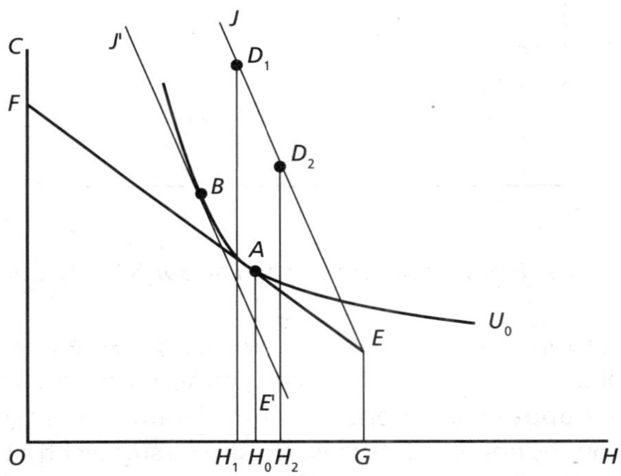


**Figure 4.6** *Effect of a Change in the Wage Rate on Labour Supply*

indifference curve, at a point such as *B*. On grounds of the substitution effect, therefore, Karan's choice of *H* would have fallen and *C* would have risen.

The income effect would then take the final choice *D* to somewhere to the north-east of *B* (that is, above it and to the right). Depending on the shape of the indifference curves, *D* could be at a point such as $D_1$, which is to the left of *A*, or $D_2$, which is to the right of *A*. Both $D_1$ and $D_2$ are above *B* and so they are both above *A*. Thus the final choice will involve an unambiguous increase in consumption of other goods *C*, but an ambiguous choice on the amount of leisure *H*, since either $H_1$ (if $D_1$ is chosen, this is less than the $H_0$ chosen at *A*) or $H_2$ (if $D_2$ is chosen, this being greater than $H_0$) is possible. Thus, consumption of leisure could have gone down or up, which means labour supply could have gone up or down. The effect of an increase in the wage rate on labour supply is ambiguous. This result echoes the one we got in the previous section, where we saw that the effect of a rise in the price of wheat on the demand for wheat by a wheat farmer was ambiguous. Analytically, the two situations are very similar. The basic reason for the result here is that there are two opposing effects of a rise in the wage rate. On the one hand, a rise in *w* is effectively a rise in the opportunity cost of leisure; for this reason, consumption of leisure should fall (labour supply should rise). On the other hand, a rise in *w* makes the worker better-off, and he would normally use this to increase his consumption of leisure (reduce his labour supply). The net effect on labour supply then depends upon which of these two effects dominates, but the result could go either way.

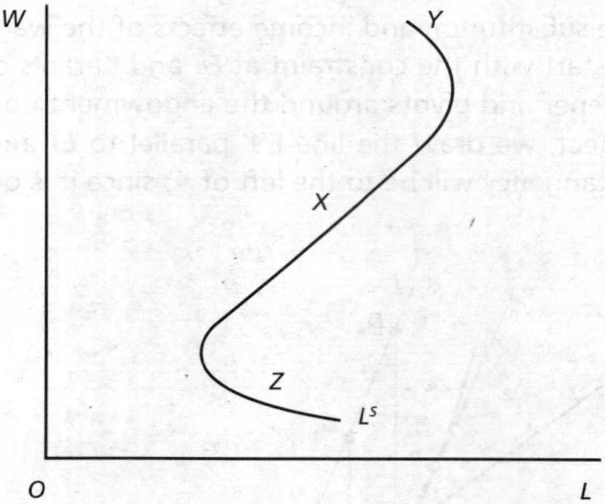


**Figure 4.7** *Possible Shape of the Labour Supply Curve*

If we draw Karan's labour supply curve, therefore, we are not sure whether to draw it upward-sloping or downward-sloping. One thing that we can surmise from the fact that the income and substitution effects work in opposite directions is that the labour supply curve will be relatively inelastic, a conclusion borne out by empirical studies. These also suggest that the labour supply curve is mostly upward-sloping, as in the segment marked *X* in Figure 4.7. However, most economists believe that, at high wage rates, the labour supply curve 'bends backwards', as in the segment marked $Y$ in the figure. The idea is that, once people become rich enough (which they do when their wage rate is high), they like to take their increased welfare in the form of increased leisure and hence reduce their labour supply as the wage rate rises further. Figure 4.7 also draws a negatively sloped section of the labour supply curve for very low wage rates (the segment marked $Z$). Here the idea is that, when people are very poor, they must actually work more as their wage rate falls in order to earn the bare minimum for survival. Hence their labour supply curve is negatively sloped. This segment has been called the 'falling forward' portion of the labour supply curve.

### 4.2.2 Numerical Example: Cobb–Douglas Utility

In this section, we will work through a numerical example and calculate a labour supply curve. We will take the simple case of a Cobb–Douglas utility function. Suppose Karan's utility function is

$$U(C, H) = AC^{\alpha}H^{\beta} \tag{4.7}$$

and suppose his non-wage income $N$ is zero. We can apply (4.6) to find the labour supply curve. Differentiating (4.7), we get

$$U_C = \frac{\partial U}{\partial C} = \alpha A C^{\alpha-1}H^{\beta}$$

$$\text{and} \qquad U_H = \frac{\partial U}{\partial H} = \beta A C^{\alpha}H^{\beta-1}$$

and therefore $\frac{U_H}{U_C}$, which we need to apply (4.6), is given by

$$\frac{U_H}{U_C} = \frac{\beta C}{\alpha H}.$$

Substituting this in (4.6), we get

$$\frac{\beta C}{\alpha H} = w \quad \rightarrow \quad C = \frac{\alpha}{\beta}wH.$$

If we substitute this in the constraint, (4.5), remembering that we have assumed $N = 0$ here, we get

$$H + \frac{1}{w}\left(\frac{\alpha}{\beta}wH\right) = 24,$$

which simplifies to

$$H = \frac{\beta}{\alpha + \beta} \cdot 24.$$

Thus the labour supply curve $L^s$, which is equal to $(24 - H)$, is

$$L^s = \frac{\alpha}{\alpha + \beta} \cdot 24.$$

This labour supply curve is perfectly inelastic (it does not depend upon the wage rate) and this is to be expected in the Cobb–Douglas case since we know that the budget shares in the Cobb–Douglas case are fixed. Thus, we see here that a fixed proportion of the 'budget' of 24 hours is spent on leisure, and therefore implicitly on labour supply.

### 4.2.3 Applications of the Labour Supply Model

The labour supply model we have developed in this section can be used to analyse a range of questions relating to the labour supply decision. Here we will look at two such applications: the analysis of salaried jobs and the effect of welfare payments on labour supply.

#### *4.2.3.1 Salaried Jobs*

Our labour supply model assumes that the worker can choose the number of hours per day that she works, but many jobs do not give workers that freedom. Rather, they require workers to work a set number of hours per day or week and they then pay a set salary per time period. We can use the labour supply model to analyse decisions around such jobs.

For example, suppose Lalita is offered a job that requires her to work 8 hours per day and would pay her a salary of ₹2,000 per day. Would she accept this job? We can use the labour supply model to find out.

Suppose Lalita's labour supply curve is the line $L^S$ in Figure 4.8. The job that she has been offered requires her to work 8 hours per day at a salary that works out to ₹250 per hour. Suppose *OC* in the figure represents 8 hours and suppose OA measures ₹250. Then the rectangle *ABCO* represents her daily salary. This is the benefit she gets if she accepts the job.

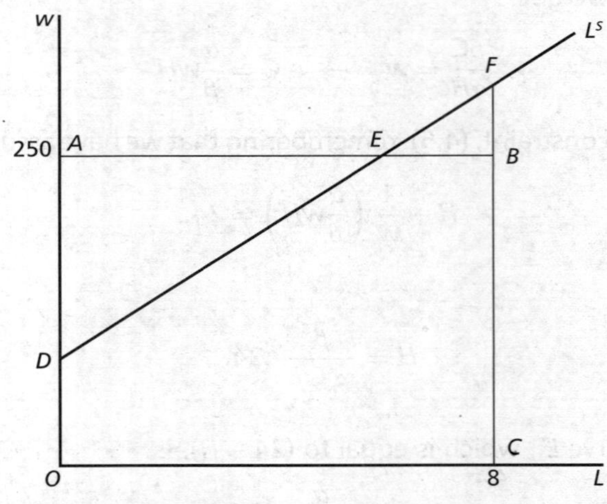


**Figure 4.8** *Analysis of a Salaried Job*

Now let us consider Lalita's cost. Just as the height of an ordinary supply curve represents the marginal cost of production, the height of a labour supply curve represents the marginal cost of labour. It is the *opportunity cost* of the worker's time, the value that she attaches to the leisure she has to give up in order to work. In that case, since Lalita must work 8 hours per day, the area *DFCO* represents the total opportunity cost of her time.

Lalita's decision on whether or not to accept this job then becomes a simple matter of comparing her benefit with her cost. She accepts the job if the benefit is greater than the cost, and rejects it if the cost is greater. In our example, the net benefit of accepting the job is the area *ABCO* minus the area *DFCO*, which is the same as the area *AED* minus the area *EFB*. As drawn in the figure, it looks like the benefit is bigger and Lalita would accept the job.

Here we just compared the net surplus from the job to the status quo of no job. If instead Lalita had to decide between competing job offers, she would calculate the net surplus from each and then pick the one with the highest net surplus.

#### *4.2.3.2 The Effect of Welfare Payments on Labour Supply*

Our second application of the labour supply model looks at how receiving welfare payments might affect a worker's labour supply. Suppose Preeti faces the constraint *EF* in the consumption–leisure space shown in Figure 4.9, and chooses point A. The simplest kind of welfare payment would be a straight grant of a fixed amount of money. Suppose Preeti is given such a grant. Her 'endowment'

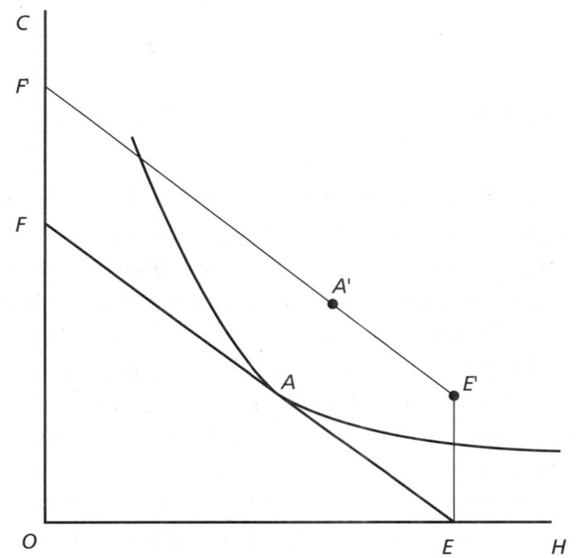


**Figure 4.9** *Effect of Welfare Payments on Labour Supply*

now, instead of being the point $E$, is the point $E'$ where the distance $EE'$ represents the amount of the fixed payment. $EE'$ is just like the non-wage income we had incorporated in our analysis of labour supply. Assuming she can still work at the old wage rate as before, Preeti now faces the constraint $E'F'$, which is parallel to $EF$. Thus her constraint has just shifted out, parallel to itself. Given that consumption and leisure are both normal goods, Preeti's new consumption bundle will be at a point such as $A'$, where her choice of level of consumption and leisure would both have gone up. Thus, she would unambiguously reduce her labour supply: the effect of the welfare payment is to reduce her incentive to work.

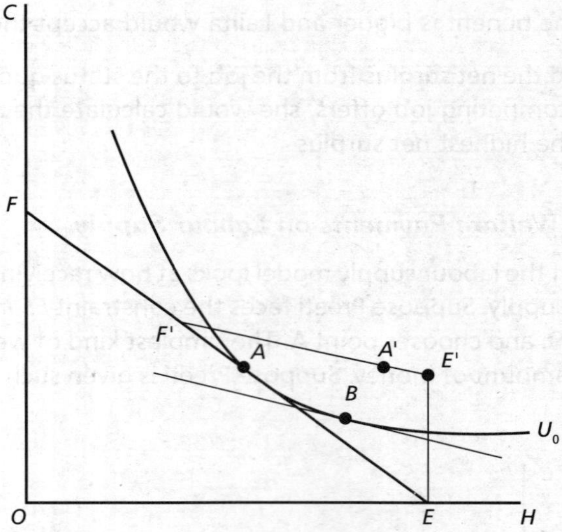


**Figure 4.10** *A More Complicated Welfare System*

The effect is exacerbated if the amount of the welfare payment depends upon the the level of other income, that is, if there is a means test. Suppose Preeti receives a payment of $EE'$ if her other income is zero, but that this amount is reduced as her other income goes up. The idea behind such a system would be that the neediest people get larger payments than ones who are not as needy. Such a system essentially amounts to a reduction in the person's wage rate, because for each hour that she works, she gets the wage $w$ but her welfare payment is reduced. Thus the new constraint she faces, $E'F'$ in Figure 4.10, will be flatter than her original constraint $EF$. We now have two effects, the substitution and income effects, both of which induce Preeti to work less. The substitution effect is found as usual by drawing a line parallel to the new constraint and tangent to the original indifference curve $U_0$. Since $E'F'$ is flatter than $EF$, the point of tangency $B$ must be to the right of $A$ where the indifference curve is also flatter. Thus on grounds of substitution effect, the consumption of leisure would have gone up, which means the labour supply would have fallen. The final choice $A'$ will be to the north-east of $B$, so there is a further increase in $H$ and fall in labour supply due to the income effect. The result that welfare payments reduce incentives to work is reinforced.

## 4.3 INTER-TEMPORAL CHOICE

**Task for this section:**

To learn the theory behind choices over time. After this section, you should understand the factors that lie behind the decisions to borrow or save, which then affect the demand for and supply of capital.

In our analysis of consumer behaviour, we have consistently assumed that the consumer spends her entire budget. This is obviously seldom true. Young people tend to borrow money and build up debt, paying their debts back as their income rises. In the process, they spend more than they earn. People later in their careers tend to save money for retirement, therefore spending less than they earn. Retired people also spend more than they earn, living off their past savings to some extent. All such behaviour can be explained by consumer theory by applying it to the question of how people decide on whether to borrow money or save. This section is devoted to analysing this question.

The basic approach to analysing this question is called the life-cycle model of consumer behaviour. The fundamental idea of this model is that consumers can borrow and lend money over their lifetimes, but that they face an overall lifetime budget constraint: they can only spend what they earn. Bequests could be included in the model, but we will ignore them to keep matters simple. To further simplify and to allow for graphical analysis, we will assume there are only two time periods: this year and next. The model can easily be extended to as many periods as desired. But for our purposes, we will assume there are just two periods and that the consumer has a lifetime utility function that is a function of the levels of consumption in the two periods.

The starting point for the analysis is the consumer's 'endowment'. In Figure 4.11, we measure the level of consumption in the first period, $C_1$, on the horizontal axis and the level of consumption in the second period, $C_2$, on the vertical axis. The levels of consumption are measured in value terms. Now suppose our consumer, let us call her Sushma, has an endowment consisting of $I_1$ in income in period 1 and $I_2$ in income in period 2. If she did not borrow or lend at all, but simply consumed in each period her income in that period, she would have the consumption bundle $E$ in Figure 4.11. This is her endowment point.

Now let us consider the possibility of borrowing and lending. Suppose Sushma can borrow or lend at an interest rate $r$. We will assume that the borrowing and lending rates are equal, which is admittedly not realistic but makes the analysis simpler without losing any of its essential features. If Sushma saves some of her year 1 income, she would have more available for consumption in the

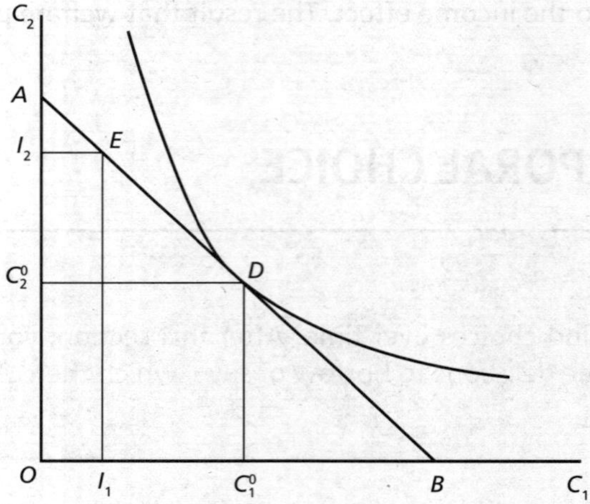


**Figure 4.11** *The Inter-temporal Choice Problem for a Young Person*

second period. She would have $(1+r)$ rupees for each rupee she saved. The maximum amount she can save, of course, is her entire income $I_1$ and, if she did, her consumption in period 2 would go up by $I_1(1+r)$. Alternatively, she could borrow against her future income so as to increase her consumption today. For each rupee she borrowed, she would have to repay $(1+r)$ rupees, so the maximum amount she could borrow would be $\frac{I_2}{1+r}$, since this would require her to pay back $I_2$ in period 2, which is her entire income.

Given these conditions, Sushma's lifetime budget constraint is the line AB in Figure 4.11. *AB* passes through *E* and has a slope of $-(1+r)$. To see why this is so, note that the distance *OA* in the figure is the maximum amount Sushma could consume in the second period, which would require her to save her entire income in year 1. Therefore

$$OA = I_1(1+r) + I_2.$$

Similarly, the distance *OB* in the figure is the maximum amount Sushma could consume in year 1, if she borrowed against her entire future income and consumed nothing in period 2. In that case,

$$OB = I_1 + \frac{I_2}{1+r}.$$

Then the slope of line *AB* is

$$slope(AB) = -\frac{OA}{OB} = -\frac{I_1(1+r)+I_2}{I_1+\frac{I_2}{1+r}} = -(1+r). \tag{4.8}$$

Another way of seeing this is to write down Sushma's inter-temporal budget constraint. It is simplest to write it in terms of future values. The future value of all consumption must equal the future value of all income:

$$C_1(1+r) + C_2 = I_1(1+r) + I_2.$$

This can be written as

$$C_2 = I_1(1+r) + I_2 - C_1(1+r), \tag{4.9}$$

which is the equation of the line *AB* and readily shows its slope to be $-(1+r)$.

Sushma is posited to have an inter-temporal utility function which shows utility as a function of the consumption levels in the two periods:

$$U = U(C_1, C_2).$$

$C_1$ and $C_2$ function just like normal goods in a Hicksian utility function and so this utility function can be analysed in the usual way. Sushma's choice problem then is

$$\text{Max} \quad U(C_1, C_2)$$

$$\text{subject to} \quad C_1(1+r) + C_2 = I_1(1+r) + I_2.$$

The Lagrange function for this problem is

$$\mathcal{L} = U(C_1, C_2) + \lambda\left[I_1(1+r) + I_2 - C_1(1+r) - C_2\right]$$

and the first-order conditions are

$$\frac{\partial \mathcal{L}}{\partial C_1} = U_1 - \lambda(1+r) = 0 \tag{4.10}$$

$$\frac{\partial \mathcal{L}}{\partial C_2} = U_2 - \lambda = 0 \tag{4.11}$$

$$\frac{\partial \mathcal{L}}{\partial \lambda} = I_1(1+r) + I_2 - C_1(1+r) - C_2. \tag{4.12}$$

Equations (4.10) and (4.11) can be combined to give the usual sort of tangency condition:

$$\frac{U_1}{U_2} = (1+r). \tag{4.13}$$

Equation (4.13) says that Sushma will maximise her utility at a point where the slope of her indifference curve is equal to the slope of her inter-temporal budget constraint. Such a point is shown as point *D* in Figure 4.11.

It is worth noting something about the equilibrium shown in Figure 4.11. The point *D* is to the south-east of E, indicating that $C_1 > I_1$ and $C_2 < I_2$. Thus, Sushma is a borrower in the first period, borrowing the amount $(C_1 - I_1)$, which she repays with interest in period 2. Including the interest, she would have to pay back $(C_1 - I_1)(1 + r)$, so that would be the reduction in her future consumption from her future income. That is,

$$I_2 - C_2 = (C_1 - I_1)(1 + r).$$

It is easy to see that this equation is just a rearrangement of the constraint (4.12), so it will hold.

This result is an artefact of where $E$ was located in the graph. In Figure 4.11, $E$ was located high on the constraint $AB$, indicating that Sushma was someone with relatively low current income $I_1$ and relatively high future income $I_2$. It is natural to expect such a person to 'smooth' her inter-temporal consumption pattern by borrowing in the first period. But had we located $E$ lower on the constraint, say in the position $E$ in Figure 4.12, representing someone with relatively high present income and low future income, we would expect such a person to save and lend in period 1 so as to have consumption in period 2 higher than $I_2$. Thus, whether a consumer is a borrower or a lender depends upon her endowment, which in turn depends upon her stage of life. The Sushma of Figure 4.11 is a student, perhaps, or someone early in her working life, while the Sushma of Figure 4.12 is someone near the end of her career, with high current income but retirement, and the attendant lower income, coming up in the near future.

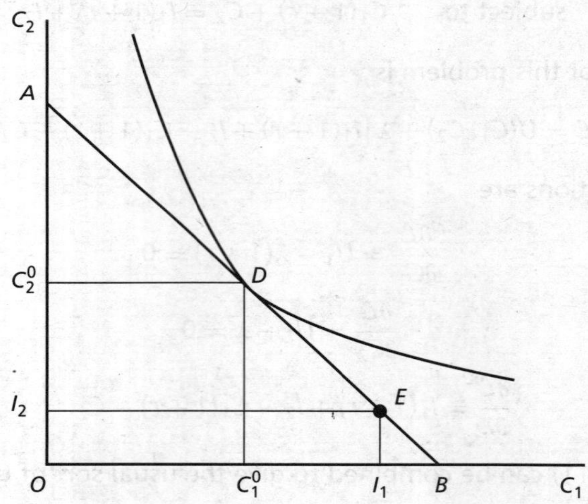


**Figure 4.12** *The Inter-temporal Choice Problem for an Older Person*

A natural question to ask of this model is the comparative statics one: what happens to Sushma's choice as the interest rate changes? This is like asking: what happens if the price of $C_2$ goes up? There are two cases, depending upon whether Sushma is initially a borrower or initially a lender.

Let us consider the borrower case first, which we had seen in Figure 4.11. If the interest rate goes up, the inter-temporal budget constraint will become steeper, pivoting on the endowment

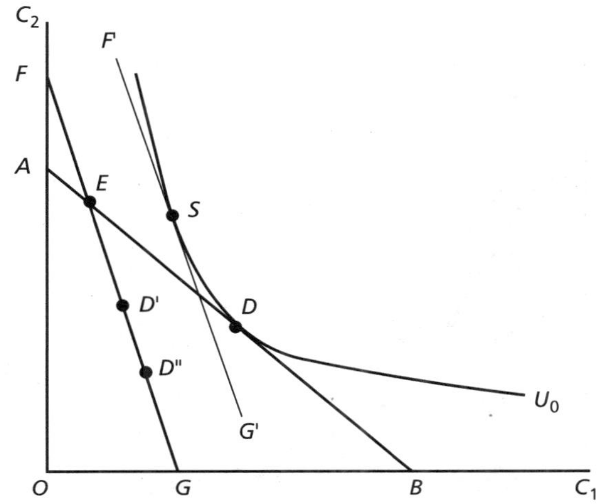


**Figure 4.13** *The Effect of a Changing Interest Rate on a Young Person*

point *E*, which remains fixed. In Figure 4.13, *AB* represents the original budget constraint and *FG* represents the new one, reflecting the higher interest rate. One thing we see immediately is that Sushma is almost certainly worse off.[1] Her new budget constraint lies below her original indifference curve $U_0$, indicating that her new choice will have to also be on a lower indifference curve. To find where her final choice will be, we look at the substitution and income effects as usual. To find the substitution effect, we draw a line $F'G'$ parallel to the new constraint *FG* and tangent to the original indifference curve $U_0$. Since the new constraint is steeper than the original one, the tangency will be to the left of *D*, at a point such as *S*, where $C_1$ has fallen and $C_2$ has risen compared to her choices at *D*. The income effect will then drive the final choice to a point somewhere south-west of *S*, thereby lowering both $C_1$ and $C_2$. We see therefore that the effect of the rise in the interest rate on $C_1$ is unambiguous; both the substitution and the income effects lead it to fall. The fall in $C_1$ means that Sushma will borrow less. This stands to reason, since her cost of borrowing, the interest rate, has gone up. The effect on $C_2$ is ambiguous, since the substitution effect is causing $C_2$ to rise, but the income effect is causing $C_2$ to fall. Thus the final choice could be either at a point like $D'$ (where $C_1$ has fallen but $C_2$ has risen) or $D''$ (where $C_1$ and $C_2$ have both fallen).

Now let us consider the case of the person who is initially a lender, as Sushma was in Figure 4.12. The effect of an increase in the interest rate is to make the inter-temporal budget constraint steeper. The new constraint is *FG* in Figure 4.14, as compared to the old constraint *AB*. Sushma the lender is better-off as a result of the interest rate increase, as she is getting a higher return on

[1] We say 'almost' because there is one circumstance in which she might be better-off: if she is initially a very small borrower and the rise in the interest rate makes her a lender. She could then be better-off as a result. Try drawing a graph for this case!

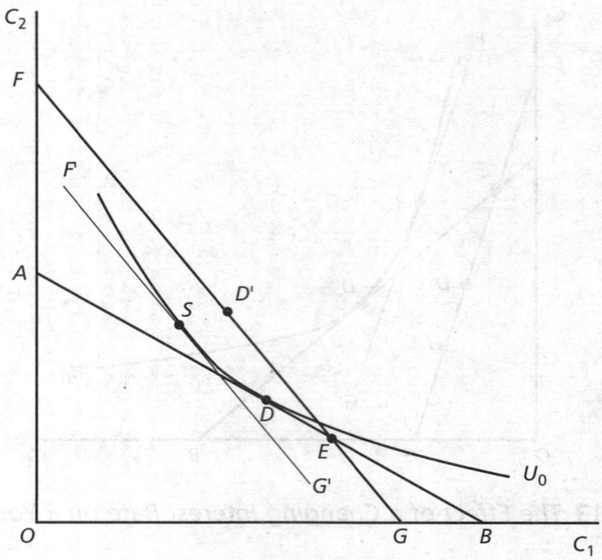


**Figure 4.14** *The Effect of a Changing Interest Rate on an Older Person*

her savings. To study the impact of this change on her saving and consumption behaviour, we look as before at the substitution and income effects of the change. The substitution effect, $D \rightarrow S$ in Figure 4.14, causes $C_1$ to fall and $C_2$ to rise. The income effect, $S \rightarrow D'$, causes both $C_1$ and $C_2$ to rise. So the net effect on $C_1$ is ambiguous, since the substitution and income effects are working in opposite directions. The rise in the interest rate implicitly raises the opportunity cost of $C_1$, and for this reason Sushma wants to reduce $C_1$. But she also feels richer, as she is getting a higher return on her savings, and for this reason she wants to increase $C_1$. Hence the ambiguity in her final choice. The effect on $C_2$, however, is unambiguous, since both effects are pushing Sushma to increase $C_2$.

## SUMMARY

In this chapter, we have looked at three extensions of consumer theory that have one thing in common: the starting point for the analysis is not a fixed income, but an endowment of some sort. We found that the effects of price changes in such situations become ambiguous. Whereas normally the increase in a price leads to a reduction in the quantity demanded, here we found that the response could go either way. The cases we looked at were:

- Demand for a good that is self-produced. The reduction in demand in response to a price increase is mitigated by the 'endowment effect', that the producer feels richer as the price of the good he produces goes up, causing him to want to increase his consumption of the good.
- Labour supply. An increase in the wage rate would normally induce a worker to work more, but he also feels richer and hence might want to work less; the net effect on labour supply therefore, is ambiguous.
- Inter-temporal choice. We studied how to analyse the decisions of a consumer to save or borrow. We found that, while a rise in the interest rate would cause a borrower to borrow less, the effect on a saver was ambiguous. Once again, while the normal effect would be for her to save more, the fact that she feels richer might cause her to consume more and therefore save less.

## EXERCISES

1. Bikram is a utility maximiser, and his utility function is $U(y, T) = yT$, where $y$ is the quantity of 'goods' consumed per day and $T$ represents the number of non-working hours per (24-hour) day. The price of 'goods' is ₹10 per unit.

   (a) Let the wage rate be ₹40 per hour. How many hours will Bikram work? How much will he earn?

   (b) Suppose a welfare system is introduced. It pays a daily benefit of ₹300, but for each ₹1 of wage income you earn, you lose 50 paise of the benefit. So if your wage income is ₹600, you get zero benefit. Draw a diagram showing Bikram's original constraint, and his constraint under the welfare system. Then use your graph and the concepts of income and substitution effects to analyse what you might predict will be the effect of the welfare system on the number of hours Bikram will choose to work. (Do not refer to Bikram's specific utility function.)

   (c) Calculate for Bikram's utility function how many hours he will choose to work under the welfare system. Also find what his total income is, including any welfare benefit.

2. Farmer Jaipal is an apple grower, whose only source of income is his apple crop of $A_0$, which he can sell at the going price of $p_a$. His utility function depends on the quantities of the only two goods he consumes, apples and bananas, according to

$$U(A, B) = AB.$$

   (a) Find Farmer Jaipal's demand functions for apples and bananas.

   (b) Find Jaipal's own- and cross-price elasticities of demand for both $A$ and $B$.

3. Ram's utility function is

$$U(c, h) = ch,$$

where $c$ is his daily consumption level (in rupees) and $h$ is the number of hours per 24-hour day that he is not working (leisure hours).

(a) Find Ram's labour supply function in terms of his hourly wage rate $w$.

(b) If the wage rate were ₹100 per hour, how many hours per day would he work?

(c) If Ram receives an inheritance which pays him ₹100 per day, what will his labour supply function be now? How many hours per day would he work, if $w = 100$?

4. Malvika can work all she wants (up to 24 hours per day!) at a wage rate of $w$ per hour. Her utility function is

$$U(I, H) = I^a H^b,$$

where $I$ is her income, $H$ is the number of hours she is not working (her leisure) and $a$ and $b$ are parameters. Find Malvika's supply curve of labour.

5. Meena has a job that pays her ₹100 per hour, and she is free to choose the number of hours she works. She chooses to work 4 hours per day.

Suppose Meena is offered a new job which would pay her ₹150 per hour for the first two hours per day that she worked, and ₹50 per hour for all subsequent hours worked. If Meena took this job, would she work more or fewer hours than before? Will she accept this new job?

CHAPTER

5

# Production, Cost and Supply

In previous chapters, we have looked at the theory of consumer behaviour, the basic model underlying the demand for goods and services in the economy. With this chapter, we begin looking at the basic model underlying the supply of goods and services – the theory of producer behaviour or of production. We will see that there are many parallels between the theory of the producer and the theory of the consumer.

## 5.1 THE PRODUCTION FUNCTION

**Task for this section:**

To introduce the central concept in production theory: the production function, which is analogous to the utility function from the theory of the consumer. After this section, you should understand what a production function is, how production functions are classified and know some of their basic properties.

### 5.1.1 Introduction to the Production Function and the Average and Marginal Products

Producers or firms are the economic agents whose primary economic activity is production of goods and services. Just as the starting point for the theory of consumer behaviour was the utility function, the starting point for the theory of producer behaviour is the production function, which summarises the technology by which the firm transforms inputs, or factors of production, into its output. The **production function** shows the maximum output that can be produced by the firm for any given combination or 'bundle' of inputs. Thus, this function shows the output as a function of the input levels:

$$q = F(K, L, E, M) . \tag{5.1}$$

Here $q$ represents the output and $K$ (capital), $L$ (labour), $E$ (energy) and $M$ (materials) represent the inputs. It is important to note that the input levels are *flows*, so many units of input per unit time. Thus, for example, $K$ would be machine-hours, $L$ would be person-hours and so on. Also, the fact that the production function shows the *maximum* output that can be produced from a given bundle of inputs means that being on the production function implies that the firm is being **technically efficient**, it is not being wasteful at all with the resources at its disposal.

To consider the basic properties of the production function, the first thing to look at would be the partial derivatives of the function with respect to each of its arguments. These partial derivatives are called the **marginal products** of the respective inputs. Thus, the marginal product of labour would be

$$MP_L \equiv \frac{\partial q}{\partial L} \tag{5.2}$$

and similarly for the other inputs. We expect that

$$MP_i > 0 \quad \text{for all } i,$$

that is, that the marginal products are positive. Adding more of an input, while holding the other input levels fixed, should allow the firm to increase its output. Further, we would expect that, in the areas of the production function where the firm might actually be operating, the second derivative

$$\frac{\partial^2 q}{\partial L^2} \equiv \frac{\partial MP_i}{\partial x_i} < 0 \quad \text{for all } i, \tag{5.3}$$

that is, that the marginal product of any product would be declining. It might be quite possible that, initially, the marginal product would be increasing as the firm enjoys the benefits of input specialisation, but (5.3) is saying that ultimately the fact that other input levels are fixed will force $MP_i$ to start falling. Thus the shape of the marginal product curve, showing $MP_i$ as a function of $x_i$, would look like the curve in Figure 5.1.

A related concept is the **average product** of an input:

$$AP_i = \frac{q(x_i)}{x_i}. \tag{5.4}$$

We can look at the relationship between $AP_i$ and $MP_i$ by differentiating (5.4):

$$\frac{\partial AP_i}{\partial x_i} = \frac{x_i \frac{\partial q}{\partial x_i} - q(x_i)}{x_i^2}$$

which simplifies to

$$\frac{\partial AP_i}{\partial x_i} = \frac{MP_i - AP_i}{x_i}. \tag{5.5}$$

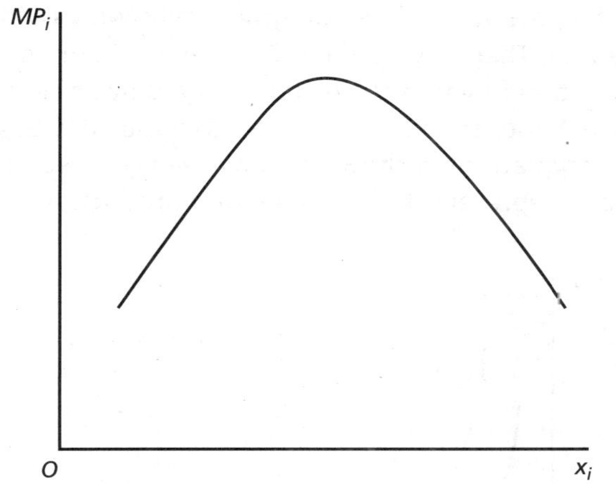


**Figure 5.1** *A Marginal Product Curve*

Equation (5.5) shows that

$$\frac{\partial AP_i}{\partial x_i} \gtreqless 0 \quad \longleftrightarrow \quad MP_i \gtreqless AP_i.$$

In other words, if $AP_i$ is rising, $MP_i > AP_i$, and if $AP_i$ is falling, $MP_i < AP_i$. The *MP* curve will therefore cut the *AP* curve at its maximum point. Figure 5.2 illustrates the relationship between the two curves.

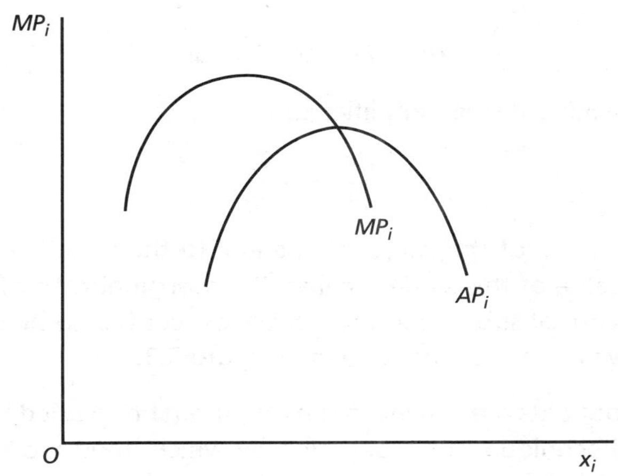


**Figure 5.2** *The Average and Marginal Product Curves*

To actually represent the production function graphically, we would need to restrict it to two inputs, say capital and labour. Then, just as the utility function can be represented by an indifference curve map, the production function can be represented by an isoquant map, as in Figure 5.3. An **isoquant**, or iso-product line, shows different combinations of the two inputs that yield the same level of output. An isoquant map shows a whole family of isoquants, one for each level of output, thereby serving as a representation of the entire production function.

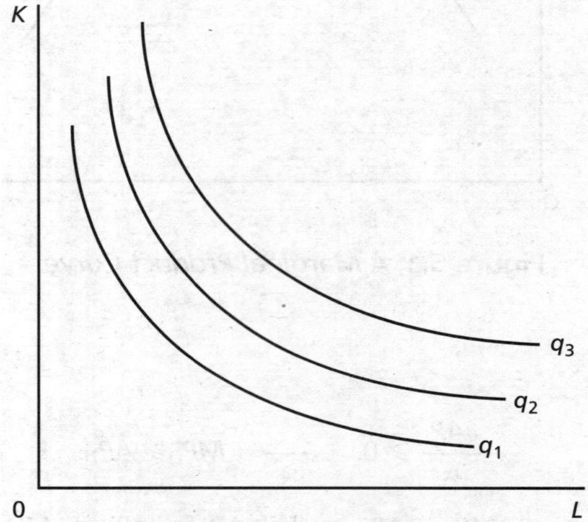


**Figure 5.3** *Isoquants or Iso-product Curves*

To find the slope of the isoquant, we totally differentiate the production function $q = F(K, L)$:

$$dq = F_K \cdot dK + F_L \cdot dL.$$

Since $dq = 0$ along any isoquant, this simplifies to

$$\frac{dK}{dL} = -\frac{F_L}{F_K}$$

along any isoquant. The slope of the isoquant is equal to the negative of the ratio of marginal products. The absolute value of this slope is called the **marginal rate of technical substitution** (*MRTS*) or the rate of technical substitution (*RTS*). We expect this to be declining as we move to the right, giving the curve its convex shape seen in Figure 5.3.

The notion that the isoquants are convex to the origin can be justified by the following analysis. Suppose there are two 'techniques' of production by which good $x$ can be produced. Suppose technique 1, represented by the line $k_1$ in Figure 5.4, is relatively capital-intensive. Using this technique, the firm needs $K_1$ units of capital and $L_1$ units of labour to produce $\bar{q}$ units of output.

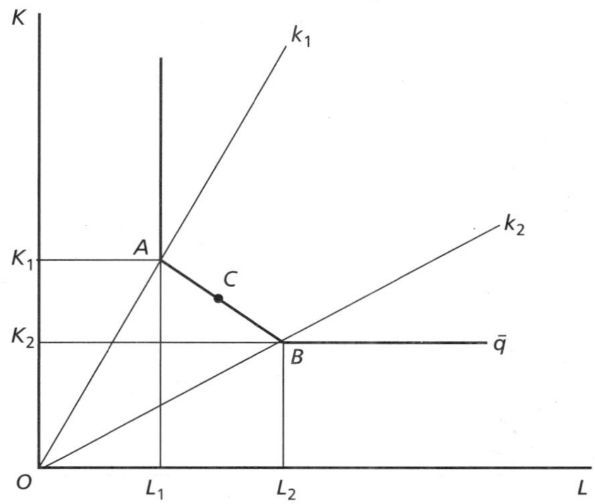


**Figure 5.4** *Construction of an Isoquant: Two Techniques*

The second technique, represented by the line $k_2$ in the figure, is less capital-intensive (which means it is more labour-intensive), requiring $K_2$ units of capital and $L_2$ units of labour to produce the same $\bar{q}$ units of output. Then the points $A$ and $B$ will be on the isoquant for $\bar{q}$ units of output. Now, if the techniques were perfectly divisible, the firm could produce $\frac{\bar{q}}{2}$ units of output using $\frac{K_1}{2}$ units of capital and $\frac{L_1}{2}$ units of labour, and another $\frac{\bar{q}}{2}$ units of output using $\frac{K_2}{2}$ units of capital and $\frac{L_2}{2}$ units of labour. Thus, the firm could produce a total of $\bar{q}$ units of output using $\frac{K_1+K_2}{2}$ units of capital and $\frac{L_1+L_2}{2}$ units of labour. By the rules of vector addition, it can be shown that this combination of inputs is at point $C$, mid way between $A$ and $B$ on the line $AB$. Thus, $C$ is another point on the isoquant for $\bar{q}$ units of output. For example, if $(K_1, L_1) = (8, 4)$ and $(K_2, L_2) = (4, 8)$, the point $C$ will be at $(6, 6)$.

At $C$, the two techniques are being used 50–50 to produce $\bar{q}$ units of output. By varying the proportions of $\bar{q}$ produced by techniques 1 and 2, all input combinations along the line $AB$ can be used to produce $\bar{q}$. Thus, the entire line segment $AB$ is on the isoquant for $\bar{q}$. We could add a vertical line up from $A$ and a horizontal line to the right from $B$ to complete the $\bar{q}$-isoquant.

If there were three techniques of production, as in Figure 5.5, the $\bar{q}$-isoquant will look even more convex. Note that, if the capital–labour combination required for $\bar{q}$ on $k_3$ were at $C$, the technique $k_3$ would never be used, since it would be dominated by a combination of techniques $k_1$ and $k_2$. But, if the combination on $k_3$ for $\bar{q}$ units of output were $D$, the isoquant would look like the line $ADB$. And as we add more techniques, the isoquant looks more and more like the smooth isoquants of Figure 5.3, which implicitly assumes that the firm has an infinite number of techniques, that is, it can use any capital–labour combination to produce each level of output.

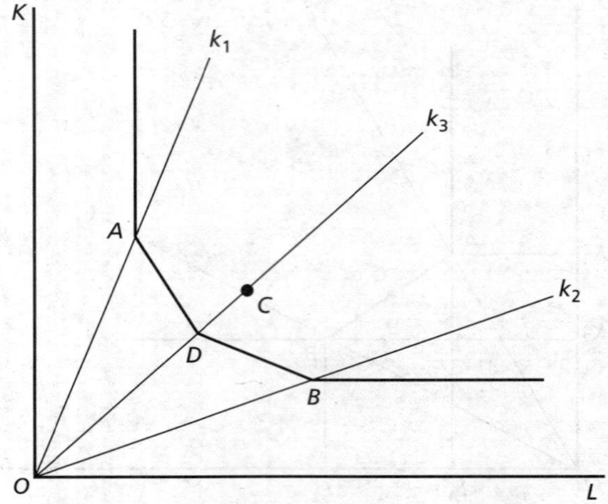


**Figure 5.5** *Construction of an Isoquant: Three Techniques*

### 5.1.2 The Elasticity of Substitution

An important property by which production functions are classified is the elasticity of substitution, a measure of how easy it is to substitute one input for another. If the two inputs are capital and labour, the elasticity of substitution $\sigma$ is defined as the elasticity of the capital-intensity (or capital–labour ratio) to the *MRTS*:

$$\sigma = \frac{\partial\left(\frac{K}{L}\right)}{\partial\left(\frac{MP_L}{MP_K}\right)} \cdot \frac{\left(\frac{MP_L}{MP_K}\right)}{\frac{K}{L}}. \tag{5.6}$$

On the face of it, the concept of the elasticity of substitution does not appear to be very appealing intuitively, but we can quickly see how well it performs its desired function. Suppose a firm's production is characterised by zero substitutability because inputs are always needed in a fixed proportion to one another (the Leontief production function). The typical isoquant looks like the one in panel (a) of Figure 5.6. At point *A*, which is where the firm would operate if it wished to produce the output $\bar{q}$, we can see that the *MRTS* varies from infinity to zero, but $\frac{K}{L}$ does not change. From (5.6) we see that therefore $\sigma = 0$, exactly what we would want our measure of substitutability to be for this production function.

At the other extreme, suppose the production function were linear, so that the inputs were perfect substitutes for each other and the typical isoquant was simply a downward-sloping straight line like $\bar{q}$ in panel (b) of Figure 5.6. Here, $\frac{K}{L}$ goes from infinity to zero as we move down the isoquant, but the *MRTS* does not change. So, from (5.6), we see that $\sigma$ goes to infinity in this

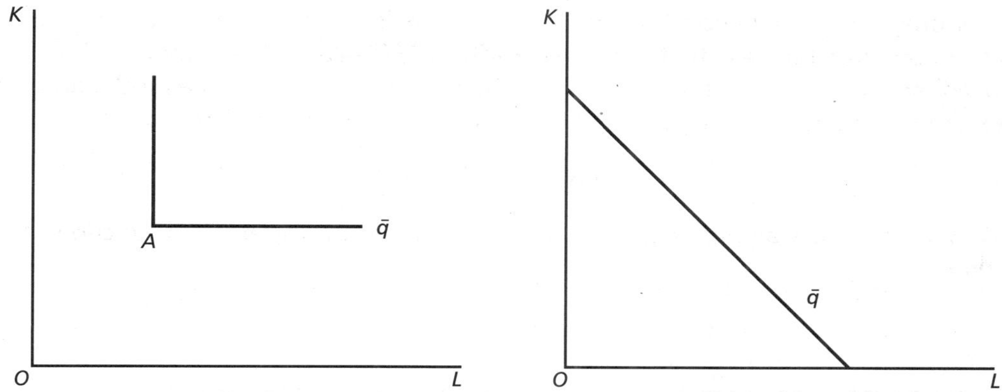


**(a) Zero Substitutability** **(b) Perfect Substitutability**

**Figure 5.6** *Isoquants for the Extreme Cases of Substitutability*

case. Again, this is just what we would like our measure of substitutability to be in the case of perfectly substitutable inputs.

Most production functions will of course have values of $\sigma$ between these two extremes. We can look at the Cobb–Douglas production function and find $\sigma$ in this case. Consider the Cobb–Douglas production function

$$q = AK^{\alpha}L^{\beta}. \tag{5.7}$$

For this production function,

$$MP_K = \frac{\partial q}{\partial K} = A\alpha K^{\alpha-1}L^{\beta} \tag{5.8}$$

and $$MP_L = \frac{\partial q}{\partial L} = AK^{\alpha}\beta L^{\beta-1}. \tag{5.9}$$

Dividing (5.9) by (5.8), we get

$$\frac{MP_L}{MP_K} = \frac{\beta K}{\alpha L}$$

or $$\frac{K}{L} = \frac{\alpha}{\beta} \cdot \left(\frac{MP_L}{MP_K}\right). \tag{5.10}$$

Equation (5.10) is itself a function of Cobb–Douglas form and so we can immediately see that the elasticity of $\frac{K}{L}$ with respect to $\frac{MP_L}{MP_K}$ is the exponent on the $\frac{MP_L}{MP_K}$ term, which is 1. Thus, $\sigma = 1$ in the case of the Cobb–Douglas production function. Note that this result did not depend in any way on the value of $(\alpha + \beta)$.

There is one more production function worth discussing in the context of the elasticity of substitution, the **constant elasticity of substitution (CES) production function**. This function was derived by asking the question: what would be the functional form of a production function that had a CES, not necessarily equal to 1? The answer is the following function:

$$q = A\left[\delta K^{-\rho} + (1-\delta)L^{-\rho}\right]^{-\frac{\nu}{\rho}}, \tag{5.11}$$

where $A$, $\delta$, $\rho$ and $\nu$ are all parameters of the function. For this production function, it can be shown that

$$\sigma = \frac{1}{1+\rho}.$$

Thus the parameter $\rho$ can vary from $-1$ to $\infty$. When $\rho = -1$, the function becomes a linear production function. When $\rho \to \infty$, the function becomes the Leontief production function. And when $\rho \to 0$, the function reduces to the Cobb–Douglas production function.

### 5.1.3 Partial Elasticity of Substitution

In our discussion of the elasticity of substitution, we have focused on the case of two inputs. However, the concept is generalisable to the $n$-input case. In this case, we have to look at the degree of substitutability between any pair of inputs $x_i$ and $x_j$ and the measure of this degree of substitutability is called the partial elasticity of substitution, $\sigma_{ij}$, defined as

$$\sigma_{ij} = \frac{\partial\left(\frac{x_i}{x_j}\right)}{\partial\left(\frac{MP_j}{MP_i}\right)} \cdot \frac{\left(\frac{MP_j}{MP_i}\right)}{\left(\frac{x_i}{x_j}\right)}.$$

### 5.1.4 Returns to Scale

A final property of the production function looks at what happens to the level of output as the scale of production is varied. In other words, we ask: what happens to the level of output if we simultaneously expand the use of all inputs by the same factor $\lambda$?

Suppose initially the firm is using $K_0$, $L_0$, $E_0$ and $M_0$ of the inputs and producing $q_0$ units of output. Thus,

$$q_0 = F(K_0, L_0, E_0, M_0).$$

Now suppose the firm changes the level of all of the inputs by the same factor $\lambda$ and suppose it now produces an output of $q_1$. In other words,

$$q_1 = F(\lambda K_0, \lambda L_0, \lambda E_0, \lambda M_0).$$

The question with returns to scale is: what is then the relationship between $q_1$ and $q_0$? The returns to scale may be one of three types or degrees, depending upon this relationship:

- if $q_1 = \lambda q_0$, we say the production function is characterised by constant returns to scale,
- if $q_1 > \lambda q_0$, we say the production function is characterised by increasing returns to scale and
- if $q_1 < \lambda q_0$, we say the production function is characterised by decreasing returns to scale.

We can examine the degree of the returns to scale in the Cobb–Douglas production function. Let

$$q_0 = AK_0^{\alpha}L_0^{\beta}E_0^{\gamma}M_0^{\delta}.$$

If we alter all the inputs by a factor $\lambda$, we get

$$q_1 = A(\lambda K_0)^{\alpha}(\lambda L_0)^{\beta}(\lambda E_0)^{\gamma}(\lambda M_0)^{\delta},$$

which can be written as

$$q_1 = \lambda^{\alpha+\beta+\gamma+\delta}AK_0^{\alpha}L_0^{\beta}E_0^{\gamma}M_0^{\delta},$$

which means

$$q_1 = \lambda^{\alpha+\beta+\gamma+\delta}q_0.$$

Therefore, for the Cobb–Douglas production function, the degree of returns to scale depends upon the sum of the exponents of the input terms:

- if $\alpha + \beta + \gamma + \delta = 1$, the production function shows constant returns to scale,
- if $\alpha + \beta + \gamma + \delta > 1$, the production function shows increasing returns to scale and
- if $\alpha + \beta + \gamma + \delta < 1$, the production function shows decreasing returns to scale.

# 5.2 COST FUNCTIONS

**Task for this section:**

To study the concept of the cost function, which introduces economic elements into the production function. After this section, you should understand what a cost function is and the principles of how to derive it from a production function.

The production function is a description of the technology of a company, and there is no economic content in it. When the firm operates on its production function, it is being *technically* efficient, but that is not enough in terms of the optimality of its behaviour. There are many input–output combinations that are technically efficient. The key for the firm is to know which of these combinations is *economically* efficient. Where does the firm need to be if it wants to maximise its profit or minimise the cost of producing any desired level of output?

In order to answer this question, we need to look at the firm's cost function. The **cost function** of a firm shows the *lowest* cost of producing every possible output level of the firm, given the factor prices. It can be written as

$$C = C(q; w, r, p_e, p_m),$$

where $C$ is the total cost of production, $q$ is the output level, $w$ is the wage rate, $r$ is the rental rate on capital, $p_e$ is the price of energy and $p_m$ is the price of materials. Note that, in order to operate on its cost function, a firm must be technically efficient (i.e. it must not waste resources), but it must also use the different inputs in the right combination in order to minimise its costs. Thus, it must also be economically efficient.

In deriving the cost functions, a distinction is made between the short run and the long run. In the **short run**, at least one input is taken to be in fixed supply to the firm and it must bear the cost of it, even if it produces nothing. Such costs are called **fixed costs**. Normally, capital is taken to be the fixed input since building a factory takes time; it cannot happen overnight. But other factors of production can also be fixed. For example, if a firm has an agreement with its labour union that it must give workers six months notice before they can be discharged or laid off, then the firm's labour cost is a fixed cost over a six-month time horizon. In the **long run**, all costs are variable and a firm can reduce its cost to zero by shutting down.

To find the long-run cost function, the firm needs to solve the following problem:

$$\text{Minimise} \quad C = wL + rK + p_eE + p_mM \tag{5.12}$$

$$\text{subject to} \quad F(K, L, E, M) = q. \tag{5.13}$$

The solution to this problem will be a set of values for the input levels:

$$K = K(q; w, r, p_e, p_m),$$

$$L = L(q; w, r, p_e, p_m),$$

$$E = E(q; w, r, p_e, p_m),$$

$$M = M(q; w, r, p_e, p_m).$$

These functions are called the **conditional input demand functions**. They are demand functions because they show the demand for inputs as functions of the input prices. They are *conditional* demand functions because they are also functions of the firm's output level $q$, which is actually an endogenous variable under the control of the firm. The (*unconditional*) input demand functions would be functions only of exogenous variables.

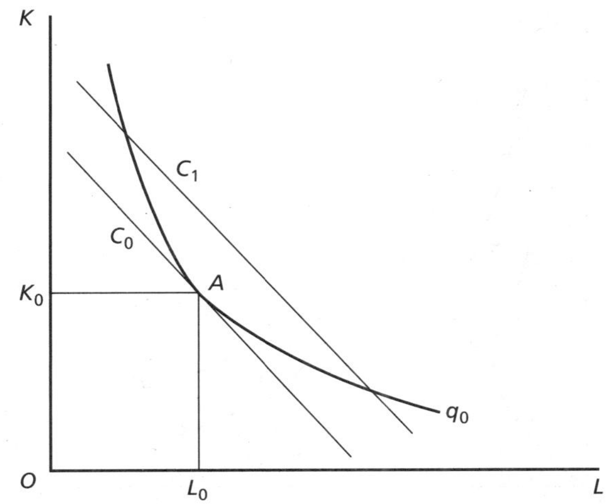


**Figure 5.7** *Cost Minimisation on an Isoquant*

We can illustrate what is happening graphically if we assume there are just two factors of production. We have already seen how we can represent the production function through isoquants that show different levels of two factors of production, say capital and labour, that yield the same level of output. Suppose the firm needs to produce $q_0$ units of output and that the curve labelled $q_0$ in Figure 5.7 represents the isoquant for that level of output. We need to find the combination of capital and labour on this isoquant that has the lowest cost.

To do this, we draw an iso-cost line such as $C_1$ in Figure 5.7, which is a line with slope $-\frac{w}{r}$, where $w$ and $r$ are the prices of labour and capital services, respectively. The **iso-cost line** is a line that shows different combinations of capital and labour that have the same total cost, just as a consumer's budget constraint shows combinations of the goods that cost the same amount. A typical iso-cost line has the equation

$$wL + rK = C$$

and the similarity to a consumer budget constraint is quite apparent. So all the points on $C_1$ in Figure 5.7 cost the same amount. To find the lowest-cost combination of inputs on the isoquant $q_0$, we need to draw an iso-cost line $C_0$ tangent to the isoquant. The point of tangency, $A$, shows the input combination we need. Thus, $K_0$ and $L_0$ are the needed amounts of capital and labour, and these are the conditional input demands for these inputs for the output level $q_0$.

We can carry this a step further and ask what happens to the choice of input combination as the firm's desired output level changes. If we hold the input prices constant and then look at the least-cost combinations of capital and labour needed to produce different levels of output, it would be analogous to looking at the changing consumption pattern as a consumer's income

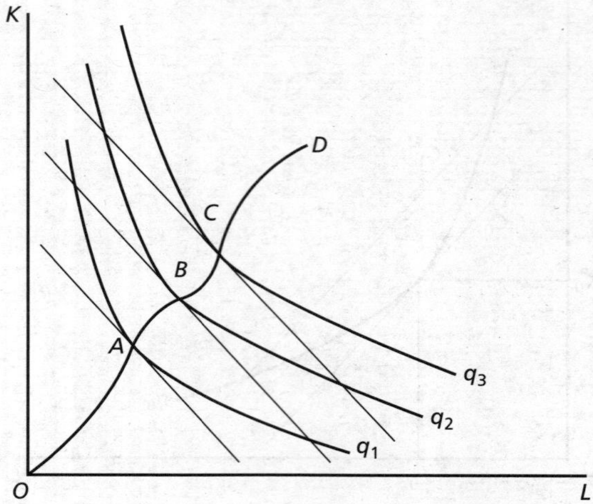


**Figure 5.8** *Cost Minimisation and the Output-Expansion Path*

goes up. Figure 5.8 shows three isoquants $q_1, q_2$ and $q_3$ and the corresponding least-cost ways of producing them, *A*, *B* and *C*. If we draw a line from the origin (which shows the least-cost way of producing zero output) connecting all these least-cost input combinations for producing different levels of output, such as the line *OABCD* in Figure 5.8, we have the **output-expansion path** of the firm.

When we substitute the conditional input demand functions derived from the problem (5.12) and (5.13) back in the expression (5.12) for total cost, we get the cost function:

$$C = wL(q; w, r, p_e, p_m) + rK(q; w, r, p_e, p_m) + p_e E(q; w, r, p_e, p_m) + p_m M(q; w, r, p_e, p_m),$$

or, in short,

$$C = C(q; w, r, p_e, p_m).$$

If we treat the input prices as constants, the cost function reduces to the **cost curve** or **total cost curve**:

$$C = C(q).$$

The cost curve could have many shapes, but one shape that economists find plausible is shown in Figure 5.9. Obviously, cost must rise as *q* rises, so

$$C'(q) > 0$$

and the curve is upward-sloping. Within this general shape, the curve in the figure is one where the cost is initially increasing at a decreasing rate (the function is concave), but then starts to increase at an increasing rate (the function turns convex) after passing some threshold level of

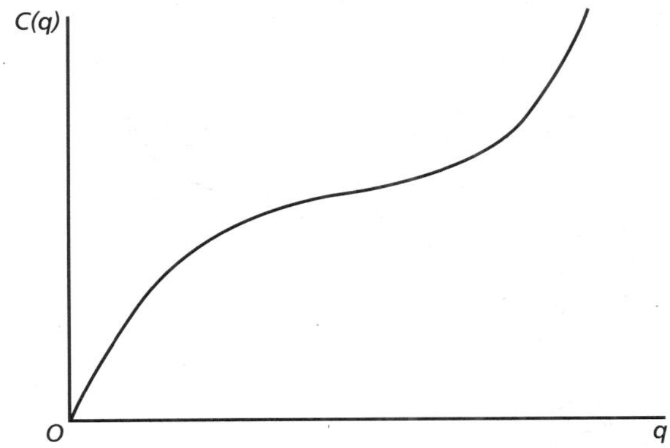


**Figure 5.9** *A Possible Shape for the Total Cost Curve*

output. The argument for such a shape is that, when it first starts to grow, the firm can allow its inputs, especially labour, to become more and more specialised as output grows, leading to higher productivity and a slower rate of cost increase. But after these opportunities to economise through specialisation have been exhausted, there is a possibility of 'diseconomies' of scale setting in. Whether or not they do is a matter to be determined by empirical observation. The shape shown in Figure 5.9 is therefore just one possible outcome. It is the one of most relevance to the discussion of perfectly competitive markets, because the convexity of the cost function puts a constraint on the expansion of individual firms. If the cost curve does not become convex, we would expect firms to become relatively large and for perfect competition to break down.

Related to the total cost function are two other functions, the marginal cost function and the average cost function. The **marginal cost function** is simply the partial derivative of the total cost function with respect to the output level, that is, it shows the rate at which total cost changes as output changes:

$$MC(q; w, r, p_e, p_m) = \frac{\partial C}{\partial q}(q; w, r, p_e, p_m).$$

The **average cost function** is defined as the total cost divided by the output level:

$$AC(q; w, r, p_e, p_m) = \frac{C(q; w, r, p_e, p_m)}{q}.$$

As in the derivation of the cost curve from the cost function, fixing all the factor prices in these two functions gives us the marginal and average cost curves, respectively. Given the total cost curve shaped as it was in Figure 5.9, we can see what the shapes of the *MC* and *AC* curves would be. The *MC* curve is just the slope of the total cost curve. For example, at $q = q_0$ in Figure 5.10, the slope of $C(q)$ is given by the slope of the line $MC_0$. We can see that, for low values of $q$, the

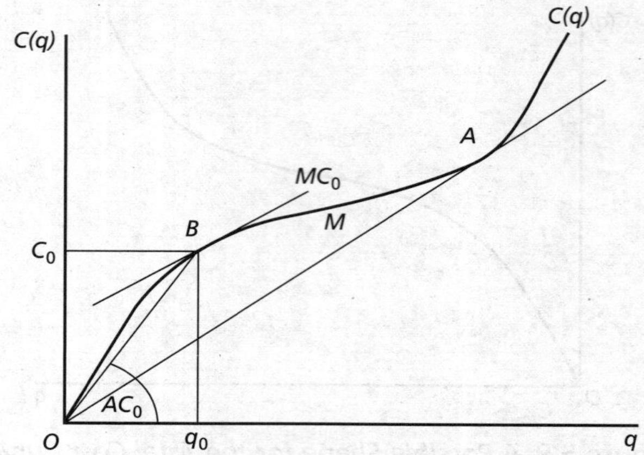


**Figure 5.10** *Finding the Average and Marginal Costs from the Total Cost Curve*

slope is high but falling until the cost curve reaches the point of inflection at $M$. Then the slope, and $MC$, start to rise. Thus the $MC$ curve is U-shaped, as shown in Figure 5.11.

Turning to the $AC$ curve, we can read the average cost from the total cost curve in Figure 5.10. At $q = q_0$, the average cost is given by the slope of the line from the point B on the cost curve to the origin. We can see that the slope of the line $OB$ is $\frac{C_0}{q_0}$, which is the $AC$ by definition. We can see that the $AC$ also starts out high when $q$ is low, and falls as $q$ rises. It keeps falling through the

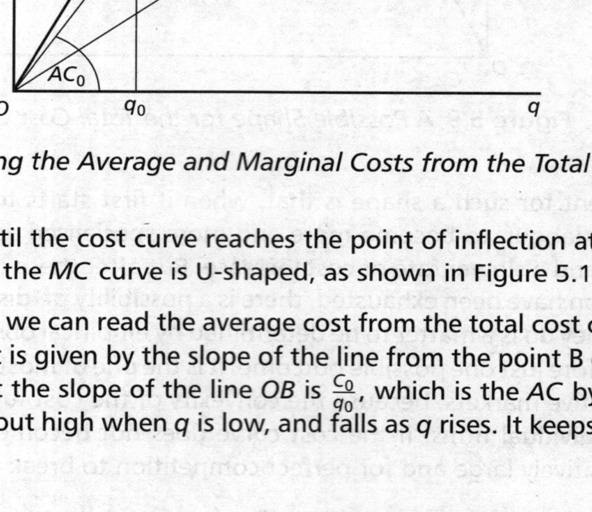


**Figure 5.11** *The Average and Marginal Cost Curves*

point $M$ where $MC$ reached a minimum, until we reach the point $A$ on the cost curve. $AC$ is at a minimum at point $A$, because the line $OA$ is tangent to the cost curve at that point. After that point, $AC$ starts to rise again. Thus, $AC$ is also U-shaped.

Figure 5.11 illustrates both the $MC$ and the $AC$ curve and shows the relationship between them. Both curves are U-shaped, and the $MC$ curve reaches a minimum at a lower level of output than the $AC$ curve. The points $M$ and $A$ in Figure 5.11 correspond to the points $M$ and $A$ in Figure 5.10. The only other thing to note about Figure 5.11 is that the $MC$ curve cuts the $AC$ curve at its minimum point, that is, $MC = AC$ when $AC$ is at a minimum. We can see this from Figure 5.10 because $AC$ reached a minimum at $A$, where the ray to the origin $OA$ (whose slope is the $AC$) is tangent to the cost curve (whose slope is the $MC$). Thus, $MC = AC$ at that point.

We can also prove this algebraically. At the minimum point of the $AC$, the derivative of the $AC$ curve with respect to $q$ must be equal to zero. Now

$$AC = \frac{C(q)}{q}.$$

Therefore, at the minimum point,

$$\frac{dAC}{dq} = \frac{q\frac{dC}{dq} - C}{q^2} = 0,$$

which means

$$\frac{\frac{dC}{dq} - \frac{C}{q}}{q} = 0,$$

and therefore

$$\frac{dC}{dq} - \frac{C}{q} = 0. \tag{5.14}$$

The first term in (5.14) is the $MC$, and the second term is the $AC$, so (5.14) shows that the two are equal at the point where $AC$ is at a minimum.

The cost curves we have drawn so far have implicitly been long-run cost curves, since no mention has been made of fixed inputs or fixed costs. We have drawn the total cost curve from the origin, indicating that cost would be zero if output were zero. This is a characteristic of long-run cost curves. Figure 5.12 shows a short-run total cost curve. It can be essentially the same shape as a long-run total cost curve, but it will have a positive intercept on the vertical axis to indicate that there is a fixed cost, which cannot be avoided and must be borne by the firm even if its output is zero.

Short-run total cost can be divided into two components, fixed cost ($FC$) and variable cost ($VC$). Similarly, average cost ($AC$) can be divided into average fixed cost ($AFC$) and average variable cost ($AVC$). We can see that

$$C = FC + VC.$$

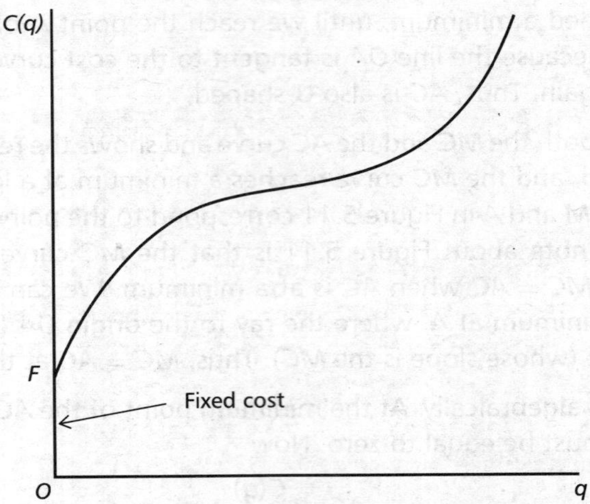


**Figure 5.12** *Total Cost Curve in the Short Run*

Dividing by $q$, we get

$$\frac{C}{q} = \frac{FC}{q} + \frac{VC}{q}$$

which gives us

$$AC = AFC + AVC.$$

Of course, since $C$ is a function of $q$, all these components are functions of $q$ and their graphs can be drawn. Figure 5.13 shows the $AFC$ and $AVC$ curves and their relationship to the $AC$ and $MC$ curves. The $AFC$ curve is downward-sloping throughout and its form is that of a rectangular hyperbola. $AVC$ can be U-shaped, but of course will everywhere be lower than the $AC$, the gap between the two being the $AFC$. The $MC$ curve will cut the $AVC$ curve at its minimum point for the same reason that it cuts the $AC$ curve at *its* minimum point.

## 5·3 RELATIONSHIP BETWEEN THE SHORT- AND LONG-RUN COST CURVES

**Task for this section:**

To learn the difference between what economists call the 'short run' and the 'long run' and how their cost functions differ.

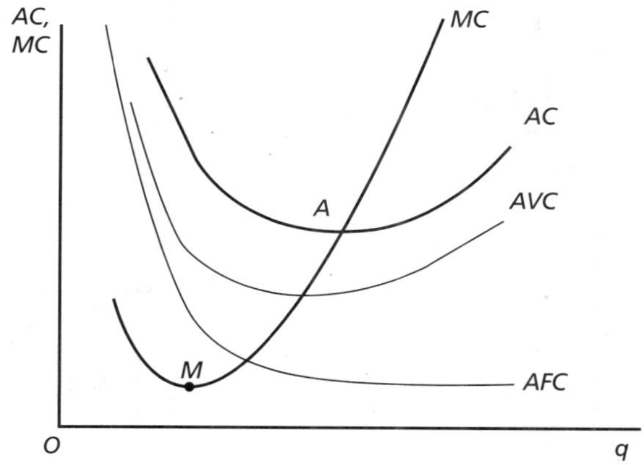


**Figure 5.13** *Various Average Cost Curves*

In this section, we will look at the relationship between the short- and long-run cost curves. We will take capital to be the only fixed factor and, for simplicity, will assume that labour is the only other factor and the only variable factor. This assumption in no way causes the discussion on the cost curves to be oversimplified or a special case; the basic ideas put forward will be perfectly general. Now, with capital fixed at, say, $\bar{K}$, and only one other factor, we can write the short-run cost function as

$$C_{SR} = C_{SR}(q, \bar{K}, w, r).$$

Since $\bar{K}$ can take on a wide range of possible values, there is a short-run cost curve for each value of $\bar{K}$. Then it must be the case that

$$C_{LR}(q, w, r) = \text{Min } C_{SR}(q, \bar{K}, w, r),$$

where the minimisation is carried out over $\bar{K}$. The long-run cost of producing any output level $q$ must be the lowest short-run cost of producing that output level. In other words, the short-run level of capital can be chosen optimally in the long run for any particular desired output level.

What this means for the cost curves is that the long-run total cost curve is the lower envelope of all the short-run total cost curves. It is not possible for a short-run total cost curve to ever lie below the long-run total cost curve. If it did, *that* short-run cost would be the long-run cost for that level of output!

Panel (a) in Figure 5.14 shows a family of short-run total cost curves (labelled $STC_1$, $STC_2$ and $STC_3$) and the long-run total cost curve ($LTC$) as their lower envelope (the thick curve). Panel (b) shows the corresponding short- and long-run $AC$ and $MC$ curves. Note that, in panel (a), each short-run total cost curve is tangent to the long-run curve at one point. For example, $STC_1$ is tangent to $LTC$ at $A$, $STC_2$ is tangent to $LTC$ at $B$, and so on. These points of tangency indicate the points (i.e. quantity levels) at which the capital stock associated with the short-run cost at

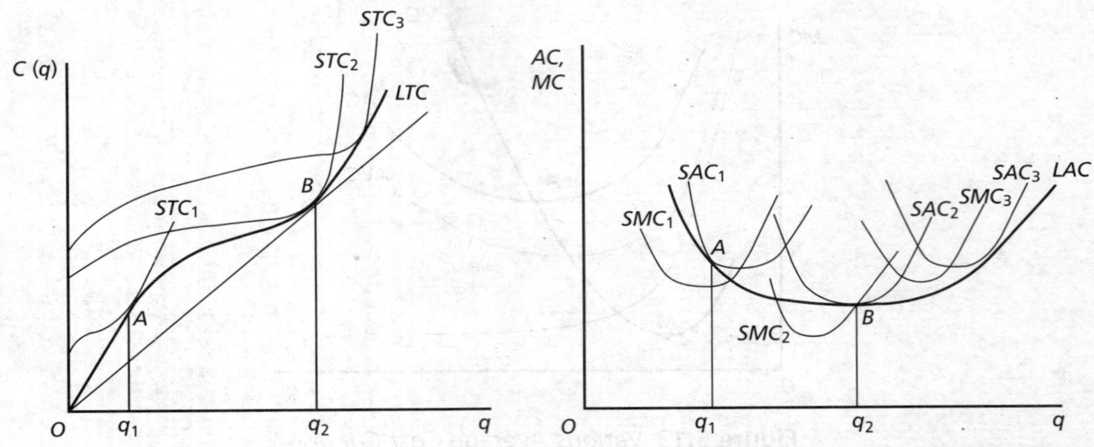


**Figure 5.14** *Relationship between Short- and Long-Run Cost Curves*

that point is the optimal capital stock for that quantity level in the long run. The capital stock underlying $STC_1$ (say $K_1$) is the optimal capital stock in the long run for the output level $q_1$, the capital stock underlying $STC_2$ (say $K_2$) is the optimal capital stock in the long run for the output level $q_2$ and so on. The short-run average and marginal costs at that point are then the long-run average and marginal costs; this is reflected in panel (b). It is worth noting that only one short-run total cost curve is tangent to the long-run total cost curve at its minimum point. In our graph, that is $STC_2$, which is tangent to the *LTC* at *B*, which is the minimum point of the *LTC*. We can see this from the ray through the origin *OB*, which is tangent to the *LTC* at *B*.

# 5.4 CALCULATING THE COST FUNCTION: EXAMPLES

**Task for this section:**

To look at some specific examples of how to calculate the cost function from different production functions.

We have discussed the general procedure for finding the cost function from the production function. In this section, we will work through examples of three specific production functions and calculate their long- and short-run cost functions. In each case, we will assume there are only two factors of production, capital and labour, in order to make the calculations simple; the procedures are perfectly general.

### 5.4.1 Cobb–Douglas Production Function

We will start with the Cobb–Douglas production function:

$$q = AK^{\alpha}L^{\beta}.$$

To find the long-run cost function for this production function, we need to solve the following problem:

$$\text{Minimize} \quad C = wL + rK$$

$$\text{subject to} \quad AK^{\alpha}L^{\beta} = q.$$

The Lagrange function for this problem is

$$\mathcal{L} = wL + rK + \lambda\left[q - AK^{\alpha}L^{\beta}\right]$$

and the first-order conditions for a minimum are

$$\frac{\partial\mathcal{L}}{\partial L} = w - \lambda AK^{\alpha}\beta L^{\beta-1} = 0 \tag{5.15}$$

$$\frac{\partial\mathcal{L}}{\partial K} = r - \lambda A\alpha K^{\alpha-1}L^{\beta} = 0 \tag{5.16}$$

$$\frac{\partial\mathcal{L}}{\partial \lambda} = q - AK^{\alpha}L^{\beta} = 0 \tag{5.17}$$

Equations (5.15) and (5.16) can be combined by dividing one by the other to get

$$\frac{\lambda AK^{\alpha}\beta L^{\beta-1}}{\lambda A\alpha K^{\alpha-1}L^{\beta}} = \frac{w}{r}.$$

This equation is nothing but the tangency condition and simplifies to

$$\frac{\beta K}{\alpha L} = \frac{w}{r}. \tag{5.18}$$

The left-hand side of (5.18) is the absolute value of the slope of the isoquant (the MRTS), while the right-hand side is the absolute value of the slope of the iso-cost line (the ratio of factor prices). Thus, (5.18) is telling us that, in order to minimise cost, the firm must find a point where the isoquant for the desired level of output has a slope equal to the iso-cost line.

From (5.18), we can write

$$K = \frac{\alpha wL}{\beta r} \tag{5.19}$$

and we can then substitute (5.19) in (5.17) to get

$$A\left(\frac{\alpha wL}{\beta r}\right)^{\alpha} L^{\beta} = q,$$

which can be written as

$$L^{\alpha+\beta} = \frac{q}{A}\left(\frac{\beta r}{\alpha w}\right)^{\alpha}.$$

This can be simplified to

$$L = \left(\frac{q}{A}\right)^{\frac{1}{\alpha+\beta}}\left(\frac{\beta r}{\alpha w}\right)^{\frac{\alpha}{\alpha+\beta}}, \tag{5.20}$$

which is the conditional demand function for labour, showing the demand for labour as a function of the output level $q$ and the input prices $w$ and $r$.

Substituting (5.20) in (5.19) and simplifying give us the conditional demand function for capital:

$$K = \left(\frac{q}{A}\right)^{\frac{1}{\alpha+\beta}}\left(\frac{\alpha w}{\beta r}\right)^{\frac{\beta}{\alpha+\beta}}. \tag{5.21}$$

Note how (5.20) and (5.21) are symmetric to one another.

The definition of total cost is

$$C = wL + rK.$$

Substituting (5.20) and (5.21) in this expression gives us the cost function:

$$C = w\left(\frac{q}{A}\right)^{\frac{1}{\alpha+\beta}}\left(\frac{\beta r}{\alpha w}\right)^{\frac{\alpha}{\alpha+\beta}} + r\left(\frac{q}{A}\right)^{\frac{1}{\alpha+\beta}}\left(\frac{\alpha w}{\beta r}\right)^{\frac{\beta}{\alpha+\beta}}$$

which can be written as

$$C = \left(\frac{1}{A}\right)^{\frac{1}{\alpha+\beta}}\left[\left(\frac{\beta}{\alpha}\right)^{\frac{\alpha}{\alpha+\beta}} + \left(\frac{\alpha}{\beta}\right)^{\frac{\beta}{\alpha+\beta}}\right] q^{\frac{1}{\alpha+\beta}} r^{\frac{\alpha}{\alpha+\beta}} w^{\frac{\beta}{\alpha+\beta}}. \tag{5.22}$$

This is the long-run cost function. Note that this long-run cost function is of the form

$$C = A' q^{a} r^{\alpha'} w^{\beta'},$$

so it is itself Cobb–Douglas in form, as are the two conditional demand functions (5.20) and (5.21).

To draw the long-run cost curve from this function, we can write the cost function as

$$C = kq^{\frac{1}{\alpha+\beta}}, \tag{5.23}$$

where $k$ includes all the terms in (5.22) other than the term in $q$. If we differentiate (5.23) twice, we get

$$\frac{dC}{dq} = k \cdot \frac{1}{\alpha+\beta} \cdot q^{\frac{1}{\alpha+\beta}-1} \tag{5.24}$$

$$\frac{d^2C}{dq^2} = k \cdot \frac{1}{\alpha+\beta} \cdot \frac{1-(\alpha+\beta)}{\alpha+\beta} \cdot q^{\frac{1}{\alpha+\beta}-2}. \tag{5.25}$$

The expression in (5.24) is positive, showing that the marginal cost is positive (the cost curve is upward-sloping). But the sign of the expression in (5.25) is ambiguous. We have

$$(\alpha+\beta) < 1 \quad \rightarrow \quad \frac{d^2C}{dq^2} > 0, \quad \text{i.e., } C \text{ is convex,}$$

$$(\alpha+\beta) > 1 \quad \rightarrow \quad \frac{d^2C}{dq^2} < 0, \quad \text{i.e., } C \text{ is concave.}$$

The three panels of Figure 5.15 show the three alternative shapes that the cost curve could take when the production function is Cobb–Douglas. If there were more than two inputs, the conditions would replace $(\alpha+\beta)$ by the sum of the exponents on all the input terms in the production function.

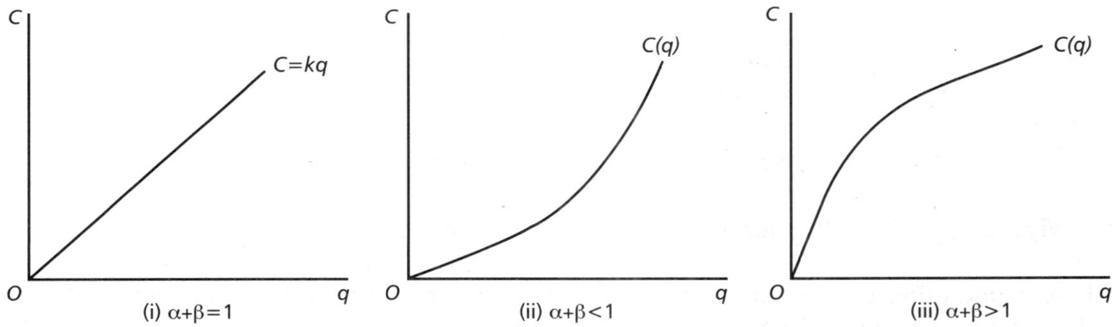


**Figure 5.15** *Cost Curves under Differing Parameter Values*

If we want to find the short-run cost function, the level of capital input must be fixed at, say, $\bar{K}$. In that case, the firm's problem is to

$$\text{Minimize} \quad C = wL + r\bar{K}$$

$$\text{subject to} \quad A\bar{K}^{\alpha}L^{\beta} = q.$$

Since the constraint has only one unknown variable, $L$, it can be solved directly and no optimisation is needed. The solution, which is the conditional demand function for labour in this case, is

$$L = \left(\frac{q}{A}\right)^{\frac{1}{\beta}} \bar{K}^{-\frac{\alpha}{\beta}}.$$

Substituting this in the definition of total cost, we get

$$C = r\bar{K} + w\left(\frac{q}{A}\right)^{\frac{1}{\beta}} \bar{K}^{-\frac{\alpha}{\beta}}. \tag{5.26}$$

This is the short-run cost function. The first term on the right-hand side of (5.26) is the fixed cost, while the second term is the variable cost. It is safe to assume that $\beta < 1$, in which case the function will be convex (since the exponent on $q$ will be greater than 1). The cost curve would therefore be shaped something like the curve in Figure 5.16. If we draw the long-run cost curve on the same graph, it would lie everywhere below the short-run cost curve, except that it would touch it at one point, at the output level for which $\bar{K}$ happens to be the optimal capital input in the long run, as in (5.21).

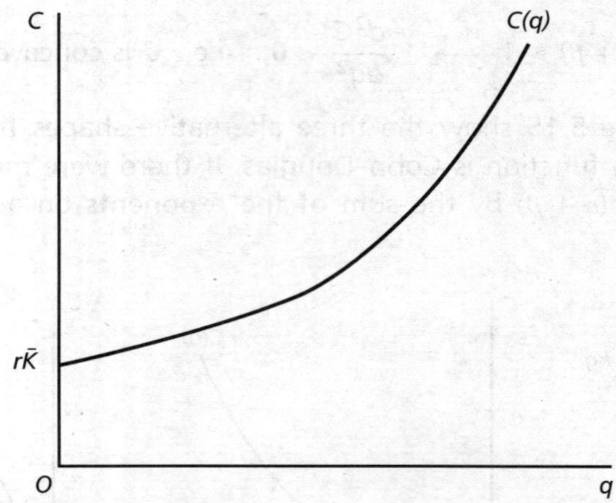


**Figure 5.16** *Short-Run Total Cost Curve for the Cobb–Douglas Production Function*

There is one other connection between the short-run and long-run cost functions, although we do not prove it or demonstrate it here. Since the long-run cost function is nothing but the short-run cost function with $\bar{K}$ optimally chosen for the particular desired value of $q$, it is possible to derive the long-run cost function from the short-run cost function. The procedure would be to minimise the short-run cost, as in the expression in (5.26), with respect to $\bar{K}$, solve for $\bar{K}$ as a function of $q$ and then substitute that back in the short-run cost function, that is, in (5.26). The result will be the long-run cost function in (5.22).

## 5.4.2 Leontief Production Function

Let us consider next the Leontief, or fixed coefficients, production function, whose functional form is

$$q = \text{Min}\left[\frac{K}{a}, \frac{L}{b}\right]. \tag{5.27}$$

The parameters $a$ and $b$ can be interpreted as the quantities of capital and labour needed per unit of output. The assumption underlying this production function is that these per unit input requirements remain constant, regardless of the level of output; there are no substitution possibilities between inputs. The isoquants for this production function are therefore L-shaped, as shown in Figure 5.17. The corners of the L-shaped isoquants will all lie along a ray through the origin, whose slope is $\frac{a}{b}$.

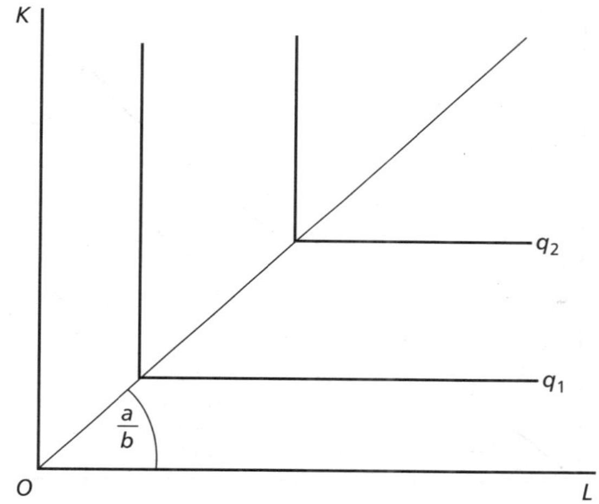


**Figure 5.17** *Isoquants for the Leontief Production Function*

Because this production function is not continuously differentiable, we cannot apply the Lagrange method to find its cost function. We must revert to first principles on how a cost function is related to a production function. We start by noting that, for any desired output level $q$, the firm would want to operate at the corner of the isoquant as the lowest iso-cost line will pass through that point regardless of the factor prices. Thus, for any given $q$, the chosen levels of $K$ and $L$ must satisfy

$$\frac{K}{a} = \frac{L}{b} = q,$$

and therefore we can write down the conditional demand functions for the two inputs as

$$K = aq \tag{5.28}$$

$$L = bq. \tag{5.29}$$

Substituting these in the definition of total cost, we get

$$C = wbq + raq,$$

so the long-run cost function is

$$C = (wb + ra)q. \tag{5.30}$$

The cost curve for this function is a straight line through the origin with slope equal to $(wb + ra)$. Figure 5.18 illustrates the function.

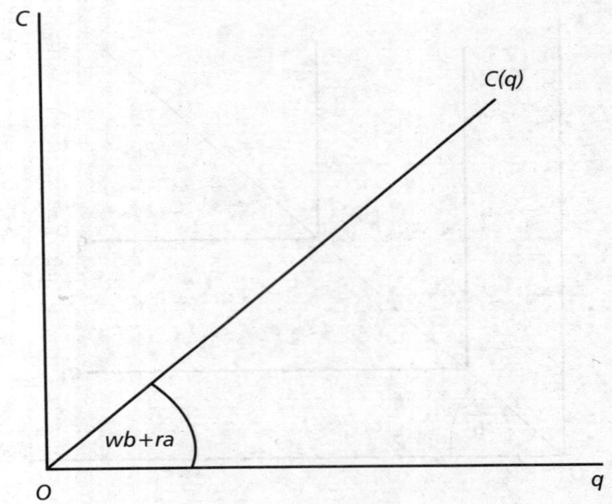


**Figure 5.18** *Long-Run Total Cost Curve for the Leontief Production Function*

Now let us look at the short-run cost function. If the firm has a fixed amount of capital available, $\bar{K}$, there is an upper limit on how much it can produce, since each unit of output requires $a$ units of capital input. Thus, in the short run,

$$q \leq \frac{\bar{K}}{a}.$$

Up until that output level, the conditional demand function for labour will be the same as the long-run function (5.29), since the same fixed amount of labour per unit output is required. Thus the short-run cost function is

$$C = wbq + r\bar{K} \quad \text{for} \quad q \leq \frac{\bar{K}}{a}. \tag{5.31}$$

Output levels of $q > \frac{\bar{K}}{a}$ are not feasible. We might present the short-run cost curve, along with the long-run cost curve, as in Figure 5.19. It starts at $r\bar{K}$ for $q = 0$ and then rises with a slope of $wb$ until it meets the long-run cost curve at $q = \frac{\bar{K}}{a}$. We then draw a vertical segment of the short-run cost curve to indicate that outputs above $\frac{\bar{K}}{a}$ are not feasible.

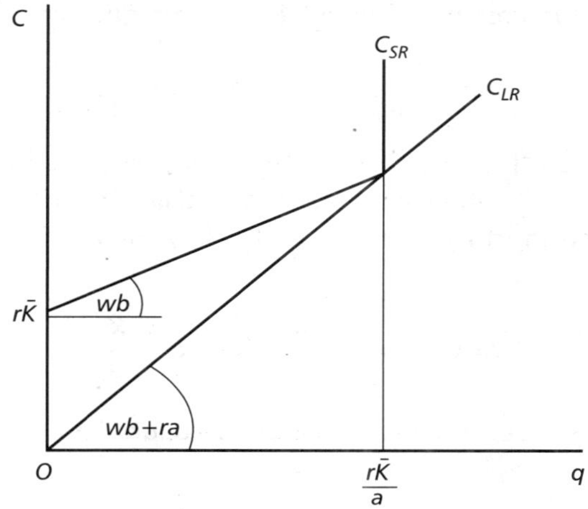


**Figure 5.19** *Short- and Long-Run Cost Curves for the Leontief Production Function*

It is interesting to also draw the average and marginal cost curves for this case. Looking at the long-run cost curve (5.30), we see that

$$AC = MC = (wb + ra).$$

Thus the long-run average and marginal cost (*LAC* and *LMC*) curves are a single flat line at a height of $(wb + ra)$, as shown in Figure 5.20.

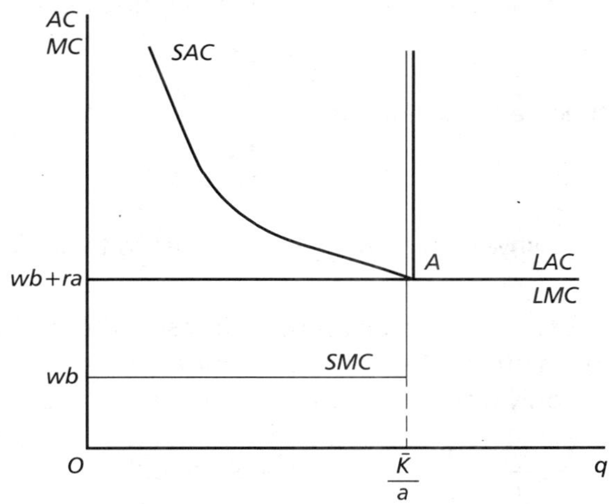


**Figure 5.20** *Short- and Long-Run AC and MC Curves for the Leontief Case*

Now consider the short-run cost function (5.31). The marginal cost is given by

$$MC = \frac{\partial C}{\partial q} = wb \quad \text{for} \quad q \leq \frac{\bar{K}}{a}.$$

Thus the short-run *MC* is also flat, but at a height of *wb*, which is lower than the long-run *MC* curve, and it terminates at $q = \frac{\bar{K}}{a}$, where we draw a vertical line to indicate that output levels higher than that are infeasible. The short-run average cost (*SAC*) curve can be obtained by dividing the cost function by *q*:

$$SAC = wb + \frac{r\bar{K}}{q} \quad \text{for} \quad q \leq \frac{\bar{K}}{a}. \tag{5.32}$$

This is a downward-sloping curve, as shown in Figure 5.20, until $q = \frac{\bar{K}}{a}$. At that point, substituting for *q* in (5.32), we get

$$SAC\Big|_{q=\frac{\bar{K}}{a}} = wb + \frac{r\bar{K}}{\frac{\bar{K}}{a}} = wb + ra,$$

which is the long-run *AC* at $q = \frac{\bar{K}}{a}$. So the *SAC* curve meets the *LAC* curve at *A* in the figure and then spikes up vertically. We see the expected pattern of the *LAC* curve being the lower envelope of the *SAC* curves; the *SAC* curve just touches the *LAC* curve at one point, but otherwise stays above it. Note also the relationship between the *SAC* curve and the *SMC* curve. As *SAC* is falling, $MC < AC$, and the *MC* curve cuts the *AC* curve at its minimum point.

## 5.4.3 Linear Production Function

For our last example, we look at the linear production function. For ease of exposition, we will take a specific numerical example. Suppose the production function is

$$q = 5L + 10K.$$

The typical isoquant will then have the equation

$$K = \frac{q}{10} - \frac{1}{2}L,$$

so the isoquants will be downward-sloping straight lines with a slope of $-\frac{1}{2}$, as shown in Figure 5.21.

We know from our study of utility functions with perfect substitutes that this kind of production function will lead to corner solutions. Capital and labour are here perfect substitutes and so the firm in the long run will use only one or the other, depending on the factor prices. Specifically,

$$\frac{w}{r} < \frac{1}{2} \quad \rightarrow \quad \text{firm will use only } L,$$

$$\frac{w}{r} > \frac{1}{2} \quad \rightarrow \quad \text{firm will use only } K.$$

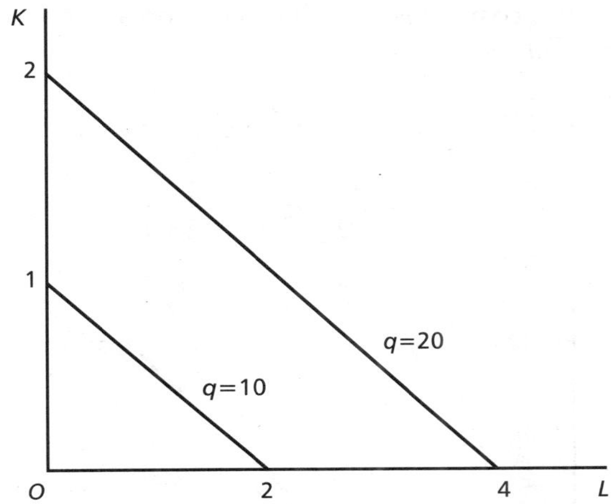


**Figure 5.21** *Isoquants for the Linear Production Function*

If $\frac{w}{r} = \frac{1}{2}$, the firm could use any combination of $K$ and $L$ that lies on the isoquant. For simplicity, we will assume that in this case it will use only $L$.

We can therefore write down the conditional demand functions, since we know that, if $\frac{w}{r} \leq \frac{1}{2}$, the firm will use only labour and therefore $q=5L$. Then the conditional demand function for labour will be

$$L = \frac{q}{5} \quad \text{if } \frac{w}{r} \leq \frac{1}{2} \tag{5.33}$$

$$= 0 \quad \text{if } \frac{w}{r} > \frac{1}{2}.$$

Correspondingly, the conditional demand function for capital will be

$$K = 0 \quad \text{if } \frac{w}{r} \leq \frac{1}{2}$$

$$= \frac{q}{10} \quad \text{if } \frac{w}{r} > \frac{1}{2}. \tag{5.34}$$

Substituting (5.33) and (5.34) in the definition of total cost ($C = wL + rK$), we get

$$C = \frac{w}{5}q \quad \text{if } \frac{w}{r} \leq \frac{1}{2} \tag{5.35}$$

$$= \frac{r}{10}q \quad \text{if } \frac{w}{r} > \frac{1}{2}.$$

Figure 5.22 shows the long-run cost curve, which will just be an upward-sloping ray through the origin, with slope equal to $s$, where

$$s = \frac{w}{5} \quad \text{if } \frac{w}{r} \le \frac{1}{2}$$
$$= \frac{r}{10} \quad \text{if } \frac{w}{r} > \frac{1}{2}.$$

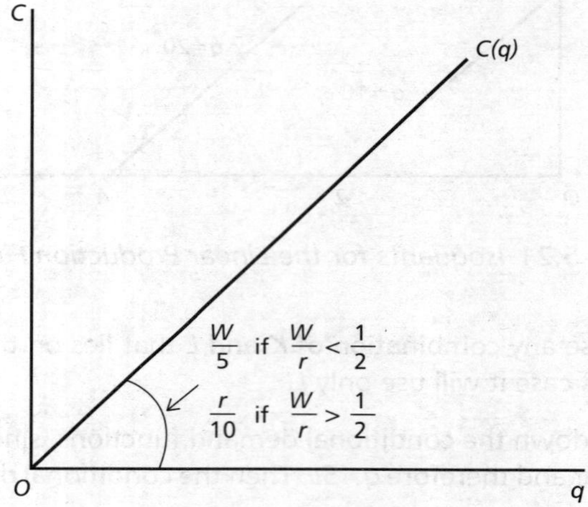


**Figure 5.22** *Long-Run Total Cost Curve for the Linear Production Function*

Now let us look at the short run. The firm's capital input is fixed in the short run at $\bar{K}$, with which the firm can make $10\bar{K}$ units of output without any need for labour. Since the firm has to pay for this capital anyway, the economic cost is zero. Therefore, regardless of what the values of $w$ and $r$ are, the firm will indeed use only capital for the first $10\bar{K}$ units of output. If it wants to produce more than that, it must use labour to produce any incremental output, that is, for all $q > 10\bar{K}$. The short-run cost function is then

$$C = r\bar{K} \quad \text{for} \quad q \le 10\bar{K} \tag{5.36}$$
$$= r\bar{K} + \frac{w}{5}(q - 10\bar{K}) \quad \text{for} \quad q > 10\bar{K}.$$

Note that the labour cost is incurred only for the units of output in excess of $10\bar{K}$. The short-run cost curve is flat at a height of $r\bar{K}$ (the fixed cost) for $0 \le q \le 10\bar{K}$ and an upward-sloping straight line with slope $\frac{w}{5}$ for $q > 10\bar{K}$.

Figure 5.23 shows the relationship between the short- and the long-run total cost curves. There are two cases. In panel (a) of the figure, we look at the case where $\frac{w}{r} > \frac{1}{2}$. Long-run production in this case would require the use of only capital, so the long-run cost curve is $C = \frac{r}{10}q$. The short-run

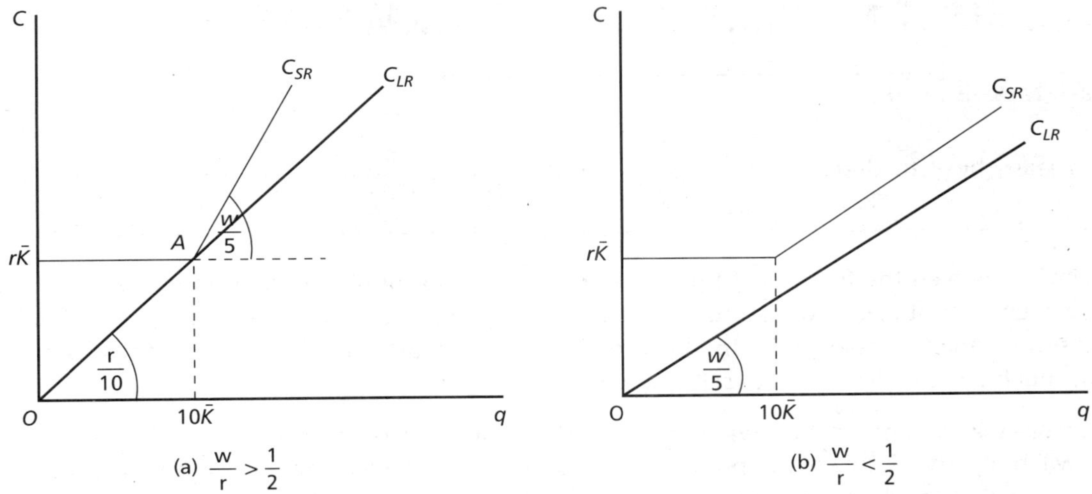


**Figure 5.23** *Short- and Long-Run Cost Curves for the Linear Production Function*

cost would be $r\bar{K}$ for all values of $q \leq 10\bar{K}$, so the short-run cost curve is initially flat. At $q = 10\bar{K}$, the long-run cost is also $r\bar{K}$, so the short-run and long-run cost curves meet at this point. This is the point $A$ in panel (a) of Figure 5.23. For higher levels of output, the firm must use labour in the short run at a cost per unit of output of $\frac{w}{5}$. Since $\frac{w}{r} > \frac{1}{2}$ in this case, $\frac{w}{5} > \frac{r}{10}$, which means the short-run cost curve will be steeper than the long-run cost curve. Panel (a) of the figure illustrates this. Note how the short-run cost curve is above the long-run cost curve except for the one point where $\bar{K}$ happens to be the optimal capital level in the long run.

The second case is where $\frac{w}{r} < \frac{1}{2}$. Now the firm would want to use only labour in the long run, as in (5.35), and so the long-run cost curve will be $C = \frac{w}{5}q$, an upward-sloping line with slope $\frac{w}{5}$. The short-run cost curve will, as in the previous case, be flat at $r\bar{K}$ for $0 \leq q \leq 10\bar{K}$. Then, for $q > 10\bar{K}$, the short-run cost curve will be upward-sloping with a slope of $\frac{w}{5}$, as we can see in the second part of (5.36). So the short-run cost curve will be parallel to the long-run cost curve. This short-run cost curve will not touch the long-run cost curve anywhere; it will be everywhere strictly above it. To see why this is the case, note that it is never optimal to use capital in the long run; the firm wants to use only labour in the long run. But the firm is stuck with $\bar{K}$ amount of capital in the short run and must use it. At $q = 10\bar{K}$, for example, its short-run cost will be $r\bar{K}$, while the long-run cost for this level of output would be $2w\bar{K}$, found from (5.35) as $\frac{w}{5} \cdot 10\bar{K}$. Since $\frac{w}{r} < \frac{1}{2}$ in this case, $2w < r$, and so the long-run cost is strictly lower than the short-run cost.

A third case would be where $\frac{w}{r} = \frac{1}{2}$. In this case, we would have a combination of panels (a) and (b) of Figure 5.23 in that the short-run cost curve will be flat at $r\bar{K}$, will meet the long-run cost curve at $q = 10\bar{K}$ and will then coincide with the long-run cost curve for all $q > 10\bar{K}$.

## 5.5 PROFIT MAXIMISATION AND FIRM SUPPLY

**Task for this section:**

To learn how to derive a firm's short-run supply curve from its short-run cost function.

Having derived the firm's cost functions, we are in a position to look at how it would choose its desired output level. We assume that the firm is in a perfectly competitive market, that is, it takes the market price as given and believes it can sell any amount at that price. The question is, how much will the firm *want* to sell at any given price?

Before we can answer this, we must know the goals of the firm. What is it trying to achieve? We will make the simple assumption that the firm is trying to maximise its profit. This will be its decision criterion when choosing its output level. We can write the firm's profit as

$$\pi = pq - C(q),$$

where $p$ is the price in the market, $q$ is the quantity it sells and $C(q)$ is its cost function. Maximisation of its profit requires

$$\frac{d\pi}{dq} = p - \frac{dC}{dq} = 0. \tag{5.37}$$

In other words,

$$p = MC. \tag{5.38}$$

This is a fundamental result and the basic decision rule of a perfectly competitive firm. It will produce an output level such that its marginal cost of production is equal to the price. The second-order condition for a maximum is

$$\frac{d^2\pi}{dq^2} = -\frac{d^2C}{dq^2} < 0. \tag{5.39}$$

Let us try to understand these results by looking at Figure 5.24. We have a U-shaped *MC* curve and the market price $p_0$ is denoted by a horizontal line which cuts the *MC* curve at two points, *A* and *B*, where the output levels are $q_a$ and $q_b$ respectively. Which of these two output levels should the firm choose?

Looking at the figure, we see that, for output levels lower than $q_a$, the marginal cost curve is above $p_0$. Thus, for each unit that the firm sells, it is losing money because it costs more to produce that unit (*MC*) than the firm receives in revenue from selling it ($p_0$). Thus, point *A* yields a profit *minimum* for the firm, not a maximum. This is what the second-order condition is telling

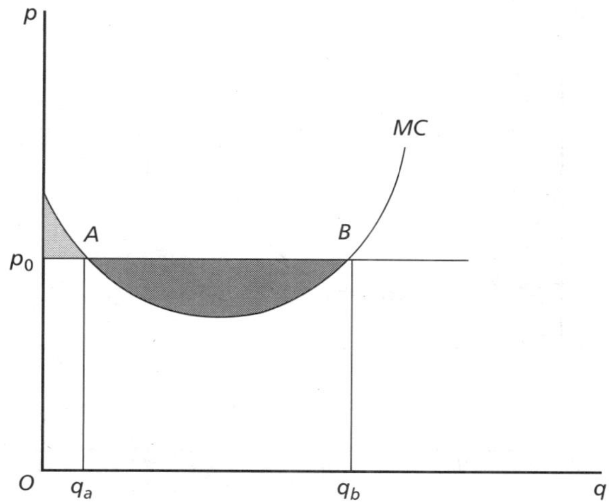


**Figure 5.24** *The Firm's Supply Decision*

us. For a maximum, we must have

$$\frac{d^2C}{dq^2} > 0,$$

which means *MC* should be rising. *MC* is falling at *A*, and we have a profit minimum. At *B*, however, *MC* is rising, and we have a profit maximum. The shaded area below $p_0$ between *A* and *B* is all profit, since this consists of the amounts by which $p_0$ exceeds *MC* for all units of output between $q_a$ and $q_b$. The firm would not want to produce any units of output above $q_b$ because here *MC* has again become higher than the price and the firm would be losing money on these marginal units. So profit is maximised at point *B*, where output is $q_b$.

What if the price lies completely below the *MC* curve, as $p_1$ does in Figure 5.25? In that case, the firm cannot cover its marginal or variable costs of production at any level of output and would elect to produce nothing, that is, to shut down. Now what if the price were a little higher, say at $p_2$? Now we see that, for $q_a < q < q_b$, the price is higher than *MC* and the firm would make a profit on those units. However, the firm loses money on the first $q_a$ units of output, where $MC > p_2$, and as we can see from the figure for this particular case, the shaded area of losses made for $0 < q < q_a$ is larger than the shaded area of profits for $q_a < q < q_b$. Thus the firm would want to shut down in this case also.

How can we tell what is the minimum price at which the firm would be willing to produce a positive level of output? The answer is given by the minimum of the *AVC*. If the price was equal to the *AVC*, the firm would be just covering its variable costs and so would be willing to stay in the market. Now the firm sets $p = MC$. So we will get $p = AVC$ only if $MC = AVC$. As we saw in our earlier discussion, this happens at the minimum point of the *AVC* curve: the *MC* curve cuts

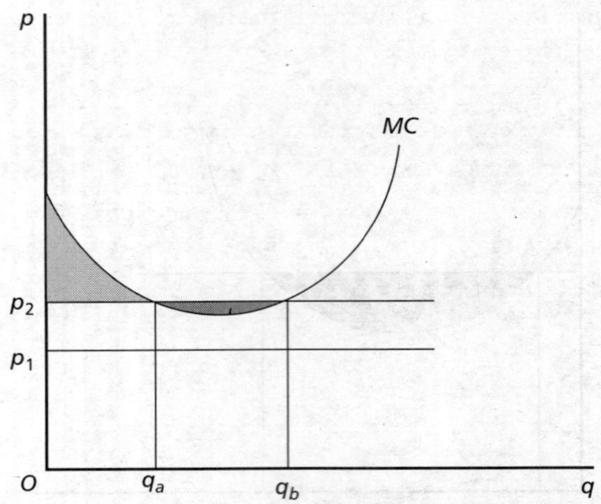


**Figure 5.25** *The Shutdown Decision*

the *AVC* curve at its minimum point (see Figure 5.13). Thus, $\underline{p}$ in Figure 5.26 is the minimum price at which the firm would stay in the market. It would produce the quantity $q_b$. At this price, the shaded area of losses *X* on the first $q_a$ units of output is exactly equal to the shaded area of profits *Y* on the units of output between $q_a$ and $q_b$. Thus the firm just breaks even.

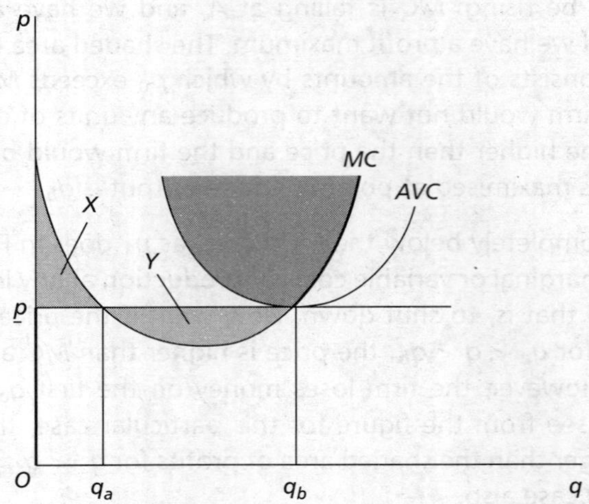


**Figure 5.26** *The Firm's Supply Curve*

For prices above $\underline{p}$, the firm will set $p = MC$ and so it will produce along its *MC* curve. This is therefore its supply curve. The **supply curve** of a firm shows the quantity of output it is willing and able to sell as a function of the price it faces, assuming it can sell any amount at the given price. We can summarise our discussion of this section as follows: **The supply curve of a firm in perfect competition is its marginal cost curve above the minimum point of its average variable cost curve, and zero for prices below that point.** The supply curve is shown as the heavy line in Figure 5.26. It hugs the vertical axis for prices below $\underline{p}$ and then jumps at that price since the quantity supplied jumps from 0 to $q_b$. Generally, we simplify the supply curve and draw it like the curve *S* in Figure 5.27.

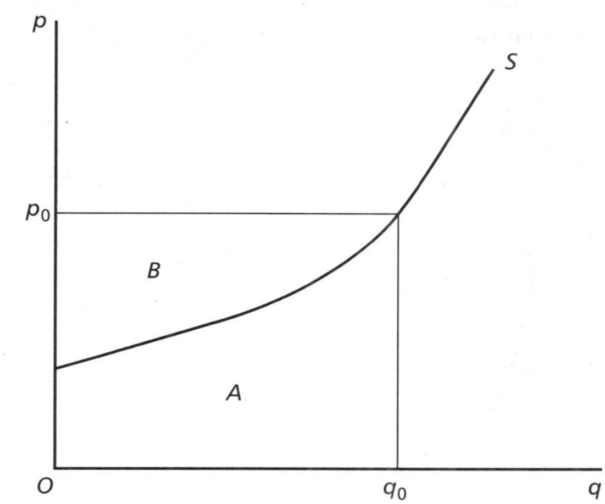


**Figure 5.27** *The Supply Curve and Producer's Surplus*

An important consequence of the supply curve being the *MC* curve is that we get a measure of the firm's profits from the supply curve. Suppose the market price is $p_0$ and the quantity sold by the firm is $q_0$ in Figure 5.27. The area *A* under the supply curve for $0 \leq q \leq q_0$ is then the total variable cost of producing the quantity $q_0$, since it adds up the *MC* of producing each unit of output. Total revenue ($= p_0 \cdot q_0$) is of course the rectangle formed by the price and quantity. Thus the area *B* above the supply curve and below the price for $0 \leq q \leq q_0$ is the firm's economic profit or **producer's surplus**. The concept is analogous to the concept of consumer's surplus from consumer theory. It gives us a simple measure of the firm's profit from the supply curve.

## 5.6 SUPPLY IN THE LONG RUN

**Task for this section:**

To study a firm's supply behaviour in the long run, and to see why a perfectly competitive firm does not have a long-run supply curve.

We have seen that the firm's supply curve in the short run is the upward-sloping portion of its *MC* curve that lies above the *AVC* curve. Now we know that the *AVC* curve lies below the *AC* curve, the difference being the average fixed cost. So there could be prices such as $p_0$ in Figure 5.28 where the price is below the *AC* but above the *AVC*. In the short run, at this price the firm would supply the quantity where the $p_0$ line cuts the *MC* curve. At this price the firm is covering its variable cost but not its fixed cost, since $p < AC$. In the short run, it has to tolerate this situation since it cannot avoid its fixed cost, but this situation would be untenable in the long run and the firm would go out of business. Therefore, a price below *AC* is not compatible with equilibrium in the long run.

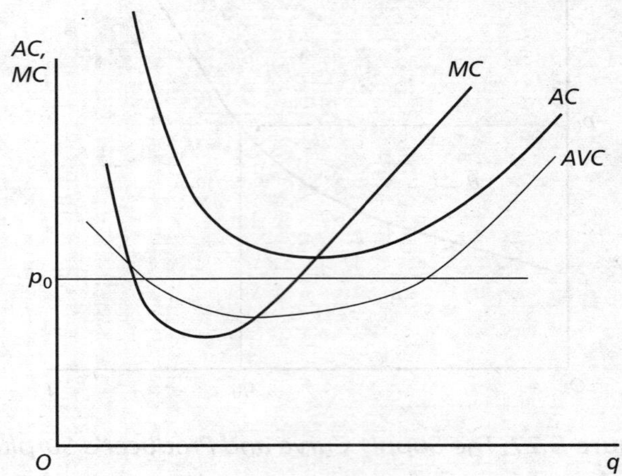


**Figure 5.28** *The Supply Decision in the Long Run*

It might be tempting then to think that the firm's supply curve in the long run is the upward-sloping portion of the *MC* curve that lies above the *AV* curve, but this would not be correct. Consider Figure 5.29 where we have a price $p_1$ that lies above the minimum point of the *AC* curve. Let us see if this could be an equilibrium price. The firm would choose to produce $q_1$, since that is the quantity at which $p = MC$. Since the *AC* is at *A*, the price is well above the average cost and the firm is making extra-normal profits. Other firms outside this market will see these high profits and will enter the market, thereby increasing the supply in the long run and therefore causing the price to fall. Thus the price $p_1$ cannot be an equilibrium price in the long run. As long as $p > AC$, extra-normal profits would be made, new firms would enter, and the price would fall. Thus, no price above *AC* can be an equilibrium price in the long run.

That leaves us with just one possibility: **in the long run, the price must equal the minimum average cost**. That is the only price at which $p = MC$, so firms are maximising their profits, and $p = AC$, so no firms are either entering or exiting the market.

This result has another important implication. Under perfect competition, all firms in the market must have the same *AC*; only the most efficient firms, with the lowest possible *AC*, will survive.

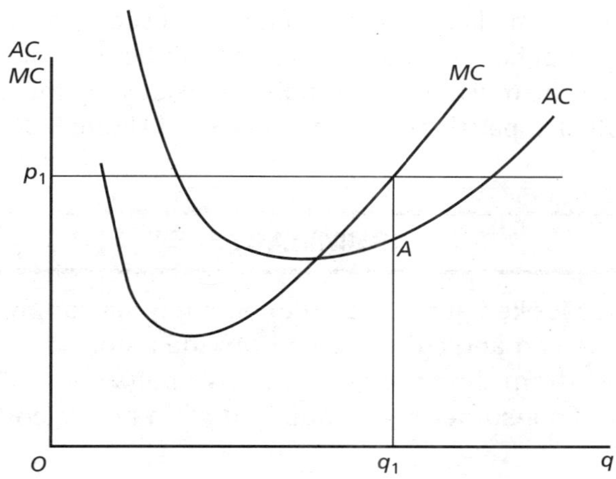


**Figure 5.29** *Price above Average Cost Is Not Possible in the Long Run*

Any firm with an *AC* higher than the lowest will be driven out of business. Only firms that are all equally efficient can co exist in the long run. Since all firms should have access to the same technology in the long run, this seems like a reasonable conclusion. Situations in which firms have different technological profiles would be characterised by forms of competition other than perfect competition.

In the short run, since entry and exit cannot take place, it is possible for firms of different efficiency levels to co exist. In Figure 5.30, we have the *MC* curves (also the supply curves) of two firms, A and B, one in each of the two panels. Firm A's *MC* curve is lower than firm B's, indicating

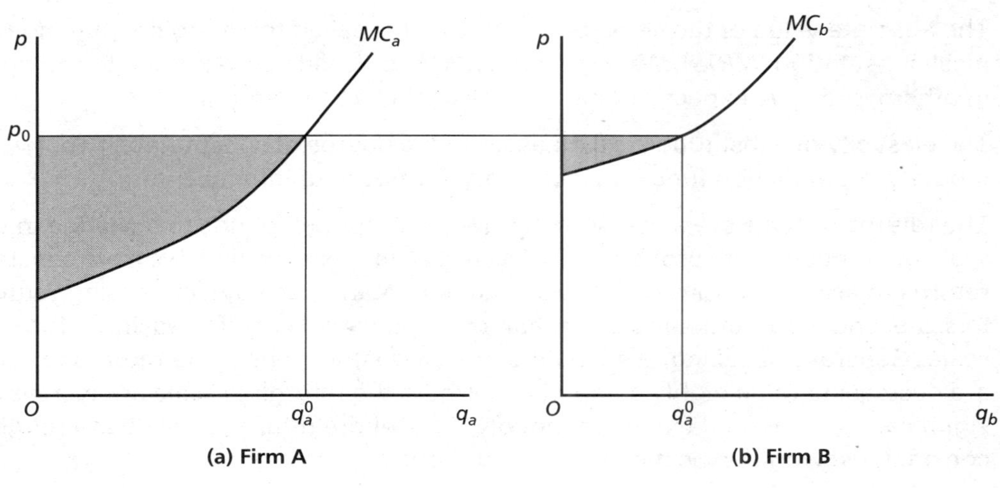


**(a) Firm A** **(b) Firm B**

**Figure 5.30** *How Firms of Differing Efficiency Can Coexist in the Short Run*

that it is more efficient. If the market price is $p_0$, firm A will supply $q_a^0$ in panel (a) of the figure, and firm B will supply $q_b^0$ in panel (b). Thus, both firms can be present in the market. The main difference is that firm A will be much more profitable, as shown by the much larger shaded area (which measures the profits) in panel (a) than in panel (b) of Figure 5.30.

## SUMMARY

In this chapter, we have looked at the theory underlying the supply curve in a competitive market. Just as the demand curve arises from the theory of consumer behaviour, the supply curve arises from the theory of producer behaviour, which has many parallels with the theory of consumer behaviour. The main points covered in the chapter were:

- The basic building block in the theory of producer behaviour is the production function, analogous to the utility function. It is a function that shows the maximum amount of its output that a firm can produce with any given 'bundle' or combination of inputs.
- The partial derivatives of the production function with respect to the input levels are called the marginal products of the inputs. After a possible segment where MP rises with the quantity of the input, we expect marginal products to decline with the level of inputs.
- The production function can be illustrated graphically by use of an isoquant map. An isoquant shows different combinations of inputs that yield the same level of output according to the production function.
- The absolute value of the slope of the isoquant is called the marginal rate of technical substitution (*MRTS*). We expect the *MRTS* to decline as we move to the right; in other words, we expect isoquants to be convex to the origin.
- The elasticity of substitution is a measure of the degree of substitutability between inputs in a production function. It can vary from zero to infinity.
- The returns to scale are a measure of how the output responds to a change in the scale of production. If output rises just as fast as inputs are rising, we have constant returns to scale. If output rises faster than the inputs, we have increasing returns to scale, and if output rises slower than the inputs, we have decreasing returns to scale. Generally speaking, we would expect industries where the returns to scale are decreasing to be highly competitive. Where the returns to scale are increasing significantly, we would expect monopoly. And where returns to scale are roughly constant, we would expect oligopoly of various degrees.

- The firm's cost function shows the lowest cost of producing different levels of output, given the input prices.
- Cost functions for the firm can be found for the short run (where at least one input is in fixed supply and no firms can enter or exit the market) and the long run (where all inputs are variable and firms may enter and exit the market freely).
- The long-run cost function of the firm is the lower envelope of all the short-run cost functions.
- The marginal cost (*MC*) function shows the rate at which cost changes as output changes. It is the derivative of the cost function with respect to the output level. With input prices fixed, the *MC* function becomes the *MC* curve.
- The average cost (*AC*) function is the cost function divided by the output level. With input prices fixed, the *AC* function becomes the *AC* curve.
- The short-run *AC* can be divided into the average fixed cost (AFC) and the average variable cost (*AVC*).
- The *MC* curve crosses the *AVC* curve and the *AC* curve from below at their minimum points.
- The supply curve of the firm in the short run is that portion of its *MC* curve that lies above the *AVC* curve.
- In the long run, the firm does not have a supply curve. Rather, each firm must produce at the minimum point of its *AC* curve.

## EXERCISES

1. Suppose a typical, perfectly competitive, widget producer's long-run cost function is given by

$$C(q) = wq^2 - 10q + 100,$$

where $q$ is the firm's output and $w$ is the wage rate it must pay its workers. Suppose the demand for widgets is given by

$$Q = 40,000 - 1,000P,$$

where $Q$ is the market demand and $P$ is the market price.

(a) Suppose the initial wage rate is ₹1. What will be the typical firm's long-run output?
(b) What will be the long-run price of widgets? How many firms will be operating?
(c) Suppose the wage rate went up to ₹4. What would be your answers to (a) and (b) now?

2. All 12 firms in the (perfectly competitive) widget industry face the following cost function:

$$C(q) = q^2 + 1,$$

where $q$ is the quantity each produces. The demand for widgets is given by

$$D(P) = 28 - P.$$

(a) Find each firm's short-run supply curve. What will be the short-run price and quantity of widgets?

(b) What would be the long-run price and quantity of widgets? How many firms would operate in the industry in the long run?

3. Widget Corp.'s production function is

$$q = \text{Min}[2L, K].$$

(a) Draw on a clearly labelled diagram some isoquants for Widget.

(b) Suppose in the short run the firm has 20 units of capital. Find the firm's short-run cost function. What will be the short-run supply curve? Draw this in a clearly labelled diagram.

(c) Find Widget Corp.'s long-run cost function. Draw this on a clearly labelled diagram. *On the same diagram*, draw the short-run cost function you found in part (b), emphasising the relationship between the two cost functions.

4. Widget Corp.'s production function is given by

$$q = \text{Min}[5K, 10L],$$

where $q$ is the quantity produced and $K$ and $L$ are the amounts of capital and labour input. Input prices are $r = 1$ and $w = 3$.

(a) Find Widget Corp's long-run cost function.

(b) Suppose, in the short run, $K$ is fixed at 10. Find Widget Corp's short-run cost function.

(c) On a clearly labelled diagram, draw both the long-run and short-run cost functions, paying attention to the relationship between the two.

5. Widget Corp's short-run total cost is given by

$$C(q, \bar{K}) = r\bar{K} + \frac{q^2}{\bar{K}},$$

where $q$ is the quantity produced, $\bar{K}$ is the level of capital input and $r$ is the rental rate on capital.

(a) Find Widget Corp's long-run cost function.

(b) Draw Widget Corp's short-run and long-run cost functions on the same diagram. For what level of output is $\bar{K}$ the optimal long-run level of capital input? Find this output level algebraically and also show it clearly on your diagram.

6. Suppose a firm has the production function

$$q(K, L) = \frac{KL}{K+L}.$$

   (a) Does this production function exhibit decreasing, constant, or increasing returns to scale? Prove your answer.
   (b) Assuming this firm is a price-taker, find its conditional input demand functions.
   (c) If labour were free to this firm, would it ever use capital in the long run? Justify your answer.

7. Widget Corp's production function is

$$q(K, L) = \sqrt{\min\left[K, \frac{L}{4}\right]},$$

where $q$ is its output level per time period and $K$ and $L$ are the levels of capital and labour, respectively, used in the same time period. Let $r$ and $w$ represent the rental rate on capital and the wage rate.

   (a) Find Widget Corp's long-run cost function.
   (b) Suppose, in the short run, Widget Corp's capital input is fixed at $K = 100$. Find Widget Corp's short-run cost function and its average and marginal cost functions.
   (c) Draw Widget Corp's short-run average cost, average variable cost and marginal cost curves in a clearly labelled diagram.
   (d) Find Widget Corp's short-run supply curve. If $w = 1$ and the price of widgets is 1,000, how many widgets would the company supply to the market?

8. Suppose a firm has the production function

$$q(K, L) = (2K + 3L)^{\frac{1}{2}}.$$

   (a) Draw the isoquant for output level 6. Calculate the marginal rate of technical substitution at (4,2).
   (b) What kind of returns to scale does this production function exhibit?
   (c) For the rest of the question, assume that the unit cost of capital is ₹3 and the unit cost of labour is ₹6. If the level of capital is fixed at $K_0$ in the short run, calculate the short-run cost function $C_S(q)$.
   (d) Calculate the long-run cost function.

CHAPTER

# 6 Markets in Partial Equilibrium

In Chapter 2, we developed the theory of consumer behaviour. The main result of that theory was the summarisation of an individual consumer's behaviour in the form of a demand curve, which would normally be downward-sloping. In the previous chapter, we have developed a theory of producer behaviour. The main result of that theory was that the behaviour of a perfectly competitive firm can be summarised in a supply curve, which would normally be upward-sloping. In the long-run, however, we saw that only the most efficient firms would survive and that they would all produce at the minimum points of their average cost (*AC*) curves.

In this chapter, we will put together these two theories and analyse the Marshallian theory of markets and price determination.

## 6.1 THE MARKET DEMAND CURVE

**Task for this section:**

To learn how to derive the market demand curve from the demand curves of all the individual consumers in the market.

A market is just the aggregation of all the individual actors who are engaged in it. On the demand side, this aggregation of all the consumers who wish to buy the good being traded in the market is the **market demand curve**. This curve aggregates, for any given price, all the individual quantities demanded at that price, to give the total market demand. Graphically, it is the horizontal summation of all the individual demand curves. For example, suppose there were 1,000 consumers in a market, each with the demand curve

$$q = a - bp,$$

then the market demand curve would be

$$Q = 1,000a - 1,000bp.$$

Figure 6.1 illustrates the situation, with panel (a) showing an individual demand curve and panel (b) showing the market demand curve. At price $p_0$, if the quantity demanded by one of the consumers is 8, the market demand will be 8,000.

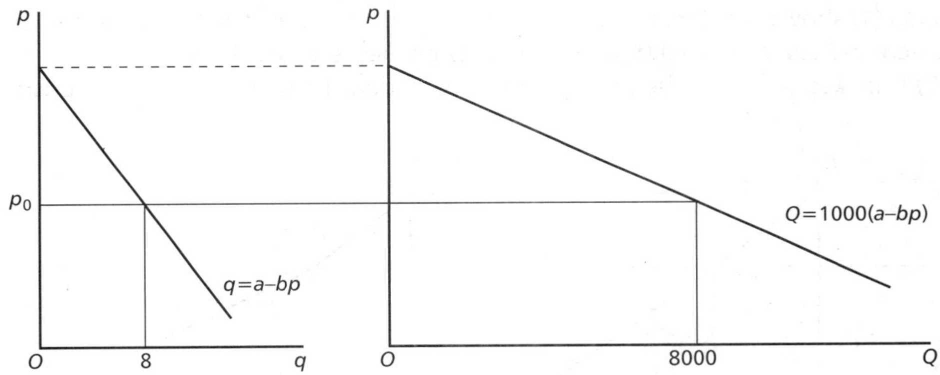


**Figure 6.1** *From the Individual to the Market Demand Curve*

To take another example, suppose there are just two consumers in a market and suppose their demand curves are

$$q_1 = 10 - 5p, \tag{6.1}$$

$$q_2 = 30 - 10p. \tag{6.2}$$

To find the market demand curve, the first thing to be aware of is that, when demand curves such as (6.1) and (6.2) are presented like this, we tend not to specify that, for prices above a certain threshold, the quantity demanded is zero. In other words, demand can never be negative. Thus, in the demand curve (6.1), note that $q_1 = 0$ for $p = 2$. Therefore, demand is zero for all prices above 2. Similarly, for demand curve (6.2), demand is zero for $p \geq 3$.

Therefore, if we take the summation of the two demand curves and write

$$Q = 40 - 15p,$$

this is the market demand curve only for $p \leq 2$, because these are the only prices for which *both* demand curves are valid. For prices where $2 < p \leq 3$, only demand curve (6.2) is valid, since $q_1 = 0$

for $p > 2$. Thus, the demand curve should be written as

$$Q_d = \begin{cases} 40 - 15p \text{ for } & p \leq 2 \\ 30 - 10p \text{ for } & 2 < p \leq 3 \\ 0 \quad \text{ for } & 3 < p \end{cases}$$

Figure 6.2 illustrates this demand curve and its derivation, showing how the market demand curve in panel (3) is the horizontal summation of the individual demand curves depicted in panels (1) and (2). Panel (1) shows the demand curve (6.1) and panel (2) draws demand curve (6.2). Because these two demand curves have different intercepts on the vertical axis, the market demand curve in panel (3) is kinked at $p = 2$, the price at which individual 1's demand becomes positive.

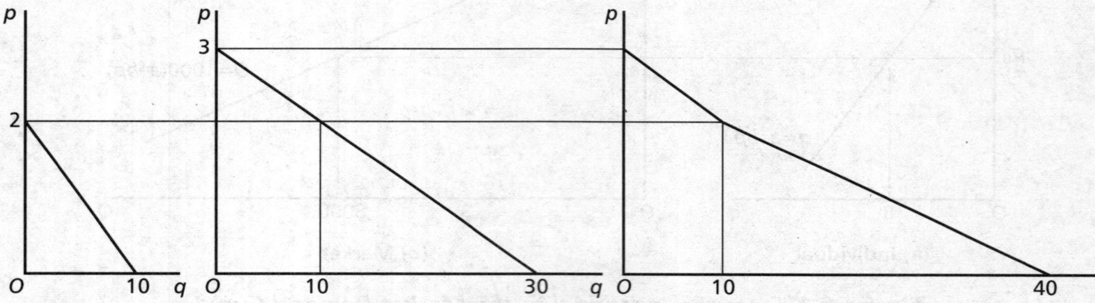


**Figure 6.2** *Summing Two Individual Demand Curves*

A word of caution. When adding individual demand curves, it is important to make sure that it is *quantities* that are being added. For example, the demand curves in (6.1) and (6.2) could sometimes be presented as the inverse demand curves:

$$p = 2 - \frac{1}{5}q_1$$

$$p = 3 - \frac{1}{10}q_2.$$

To find the market demand curve, it would be important to convert these inverse demand curves into the demand curves (6.1) and (6.2) before adding. Adding up the inverse demand curves to obtain

$$p = 5 - \frac{3}{10}Q$$

would be totally incorrect; this is the *vertical* summation of the demand curves. We will actually see a situation later, in the chapter on public goods, in which such a vertical summation is needed.

Before we move on, we look at one other property of the market demand curve. Consider Figure 6.3, which is the same aggregation of two individual demand curves to the market demand curve that we saw in Figure 6.2. Suppose the price is $p_0$. Then we know that the shaded areas in panels (1) and (2) are the amounts of consumer's surplus enjoyed by the two individuals. But it is readily seen that the shaded area in panel (3) is the sum of the shaded areas in panels (1) and (2). Thus, the area above the price and below the market demand curve is the sum of all the individual consumer surpluses and could be thought of as the aggregate consumer surplus in the market.

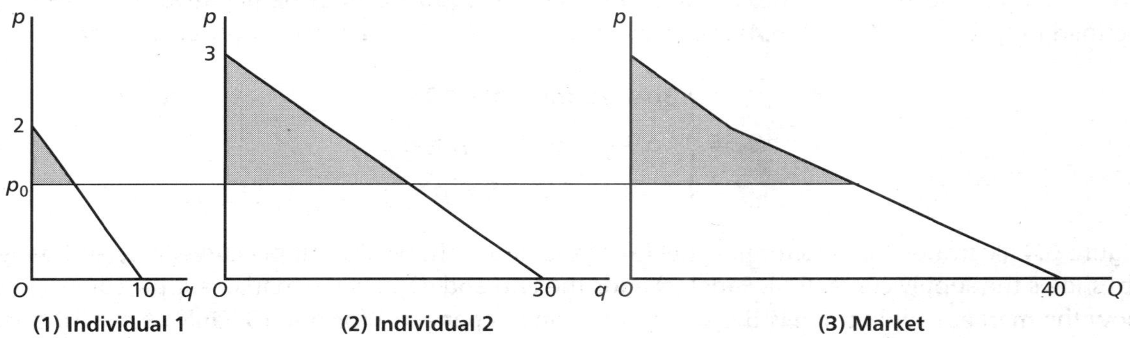


**Figure 6.3** *Aggregating Consumers' Surplus*

There is a school of thought that objects to the concept of aggregate consumer surplus on the grounds that individual utilities cannot be compared. Thus, adding up individual consumer surpluses is also equally meaningless. It is true that money has different values to different people, that the marginal utility of money may be quite different to different people. A dollar is obviously worth a lot more in a utility sense to someone who is extremely poor than to a multimillionaire. Nevertheless, the market gives equal weight to a rupee regardless of who is spending it. We may not like it, but this is the reality of the market. And so the levels of consumer surplus, which are of course measured in money terms, can be aggregated with the same level of meaningfulness that demands from different people can be added up.

## 6.2 THE MARKET SUPPLY CURVE

**Task for this section:**

To learn how to derive the market supply curve from the supply curves of all the individual firms in the market.

Like the market demand curve, the market supply curve is the aggregation of all the individual firm supply curves and is therefore the horizontal summation of the firm-level supply curves. The procedure for the summation is the same as that for the summation of demand curves. For example, suppose there are just two firms in the market, whose supply curves are

$$q_2 = 2p - 20 \tag{6.3}$$

$$q_1 = p - 5. \tag{6.4}$$

We once again need to take into account the fact that supply cannot be negative. Thus, (6.3) is defined only for $p \geq 10$, and (6.4) is defined only for $p \geq 5$. The market supply curve therefore is

$$Q_s = \begin{cases} 3p - 25 \text{ for} & p > 10 \\ p - 5 & \text{for } 10 \geq p \geq 5 \\ 0 & \text{for} \quad 5 > p \end{cases}$$

Figure 6.4 illustrates this situation. Panel (a) of the figure shows the supply curve (6.3) and panel (b) shows the supply curve (6.4). Panel (c) adds the two and depicts the market supply curve. Note how the market supply curve is the same as the one in panel (b) for $p \leq 10$. Only at $p = 10$ does supply from firm 1 kick in, rendering the market supply curve kinked at that price.

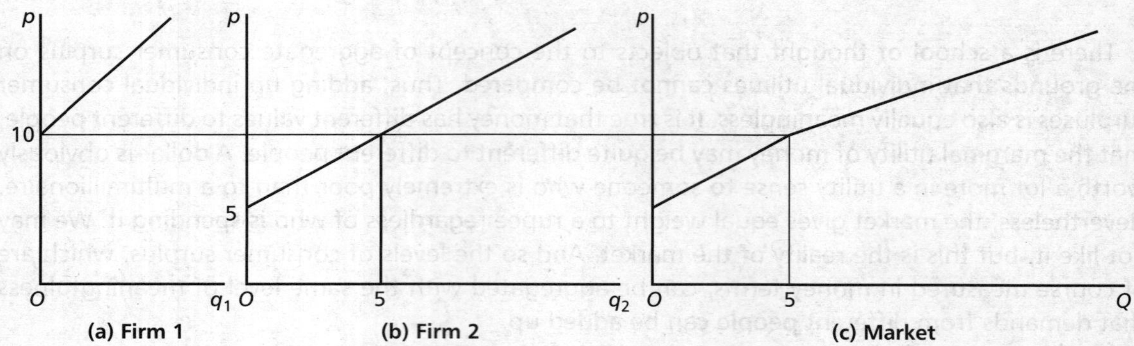


**Figure 6.4** *Aggregating Individual Supply Curves to the Market Supply Curve*

The caveat about making sure that, when adding supply curves, it is *quantities* that are being added applies here as it did for the demand curve. Also, in the same way as how the individual consumer surpluses can be aggregated as the area above the price line and below the market demand curve, the individual producer surpluses can be aggregated to yield the total producer surplus or economic profit in a market. This is simply the area below the price line and above the supply curve. There are two important ways, however, in which supply curves may differ from demand curves and these are discussed in the next two sections.

### 6.2.1 Short versus Long Run

We do not normally distinguish between short- and long-run demand curves because there are no issues of 'entry' and 'exit' for consumers and because consumers can normally adjust their demand quite quickly. One situation where consumer demand is not so flexible relates to consumer durables, goods that have a long life and are therefore a bit like 'fixed capital' for consumers. For example, consumers who already have relatively fuel-inefficient cars will not be able to adjust their demand for petrol very easily in the short-run, say if petrol prices go up, but may do so in the long-run as they could replace their cars with more fuel-efficient ones. Thus, the demand curve for petrol will be more elastic in the long-run than in the short-run. But for most goods, no meaningful distinction between demand in the short-run and long-run is necessary.

With supply curves, however, there *is* an important difference between the short-run and the long-run because firms can adjust their capital stock in the long-run and also entry and exit of firms can take place. The market supply curve that we constructed in Figure 6.4 was a short-run supply curve since the firm-level supply curves were upward-sloping. But, as we saw in the previous chapter, the perfectly competitive firm does not have a supply curve in the long-run. Rather, every firm produces at the minimum point of its long-run *AC* curve.

What is then the market supply curve in the long-run? If any number of firms can enter the market and produce the output level at which *AC* is minimised, the market supply curve will be perfectly elastic, that is, a horizontal line, at that minimum *AC*, as shown in Figure 6.5. Thus, although the perfectly competitive *firm* does not have a supply curve in the long-run, the *market* does have one, and it is perfectly elastic to reflect the fact that entry and exit can take place freely and so only the most efficient technology can survive in the long-run.

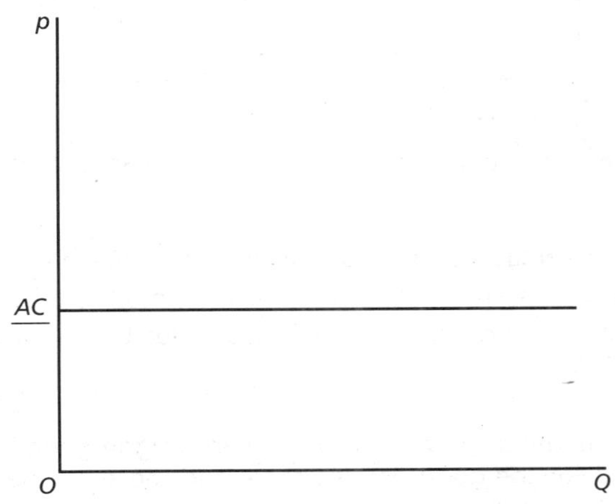


**Figure 6.5** *The Long-Run Supply Curve*

### 6.2.2 External Economies and Diseconomies

There is a caveat to the conclusion that the market supply curve is the horizontal summation of the individual firm supply curves, and this caveat marks the second important way in which the aggregation of supply curves may be conceptually different from the aggregation of demand curves. With regard to consumer demand, we generally assume that no consumer's demand depends upon the demand from any other consumer. In other words, we assume that the demands are independent. This generally seems like a reasonable assumption.[1]

With supply curves, however, the assumption of independence would not be reasonable, since all the firms in a particular market use the same inputs and are therefore affected by the same input market conditions. Thus, the firms are subject to **external economies and diseconomies,** changes in their costs caused by the actions of *other* firms. An external economy occurs when a firm's costs *fall* as a result of increased output from other firms, while an external diseconomy occurs when costs *rise* as a consequence of increased output from other firms.

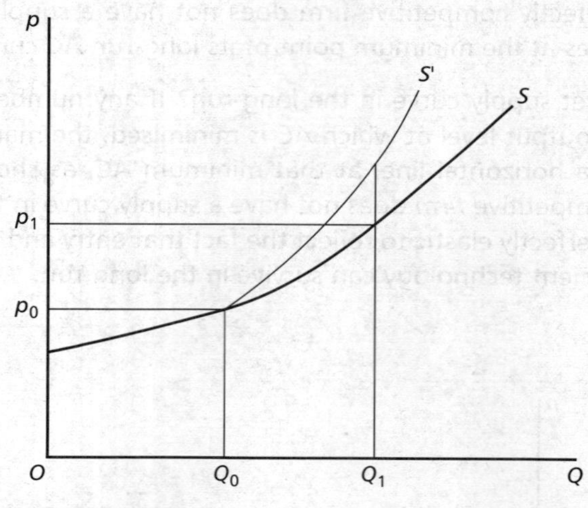


**Figure 6.6** *External Diseconomies and the Market Supply Curve*

External diseconomies are what we are more likely to see. We have drawn each firm's supply curve assuming that input prices are fixed. But it is quite possible that an input price would rise when there is a big increase in the demand for it. Consider the supply curve for, say, software

[1] One exception is goods that Thorstein Veblen called 'bandwagon goods'. With bandwagon goods, Veblen argued, the demand for the good rises as more and more people buy it, owing to what he termed a 'bandwagon effect'. Goods may become 'in fashion' and the more people buy it, the greater may be the demand.

services, $S$, shown in Figure 6.6. Suppose the price is currently $p_0$ and the quantity traded is $Q_0$. Note that the supply curve is drawn based upon the existing prices of all inputs used by the firms in the market. Remember, each firm believes all prices are fixed and will not change in response to its output decisions, so each firm's supply curve is drawn under that assumption. Now suppose the price of software services rises from $p_0$ to $p_1$. Firms would want to expand their supply to $Q_1$ as long as factor prices remain unchanged. But, as all the firms try to raise their output levels simultaneously, the demand for software engineers will naturally rise, and this may cause a rise in the salaries they must be paid. Thus, the cost of providing software services will go up, meaning that the marginal cost (*MC*) curves of all the software producing firms will shift up. The height of the supply curve at any given quantity will be higher than it was based on the old prices and therefore the supply curve might take a shape like $S'$ rather than $S$. The market supply curve is no longer the simple summation of all the individual supply curves; rather, it is less elastic because of the external diseconomy.

External *economies* would cause the supply curve to become *more* elastic than the simple summation of all the individual supply curves. It is possible that expansion of industry production levels cause some input prices to *fall*. For example, production of an input might become more efficient (and hence cheaper) as the volume of production goes up. This would be another example of a **pecuniary external effect**, an external effect (in this case an external economy) that operates through the price mechanism. But there could also be **technological external effects**, external effects that operate directly through the production process. If, for example, producers of software services become much more efficient as industry-wide experience grows, their costs could fall with expanding output without any change in input prices. In this case also, the market supply curve could then be more elastic than a simple summation of the individual supply curves.

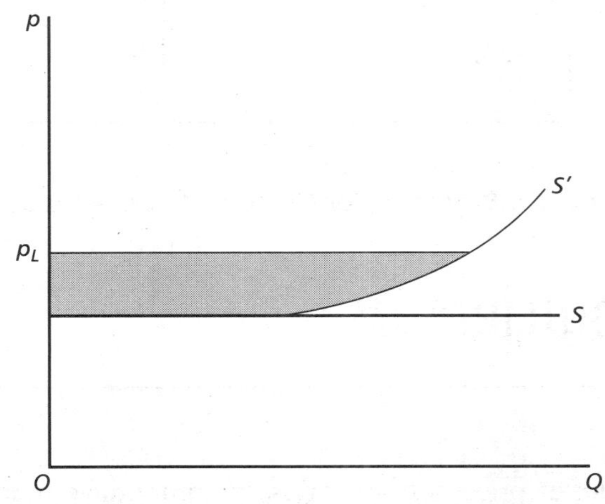


**Figure 6.7** *Long-Run Supply Curve with External Diseconomies*

External economies and diseconomies can also come into play in the long-run. For example, with external diseconomies, the supply curve would no longer be perfectly elastic like $S$ in Figure 6.7, but would acquire an upward slope, like $S'$. An upward-sloping long-run supply curve brings up a question. Suppose the price is $p_L$ in Figure 6.7. There would then be an area of producer's surplus, the shaded area in the figure. Now producer's surplus, as we have seen before, represents economic profits. Yet we know that perfectly competitive firms must make zero profits in the long-run; thus, their producer's surplus must also be zero. If that is so, what does the shaded area in Figure 6.7 represent? The answer is that it represents the surplus that accrues to the inputs whose prices went up due to the external diseconomy. To return to our example of software services and software engineers, suppose $S_L$ in Figure 6.8 represents the supply curve of software engineers and $w_0$ is the initial wage rate or salary for software engineers. If an expansion in supply of software services causes the demand for software engineers to rise and the wage rate to jump to $w_1$, a surplus of the shaded area in Figure 6.8 is created. Software engineers who were working happily at the original wage of $w_0$ now find themselves receiving a wage of $w_1$, so they enjoy a surplus. It is this surplus that is captured by the producer's surplus area in Figure 6.7

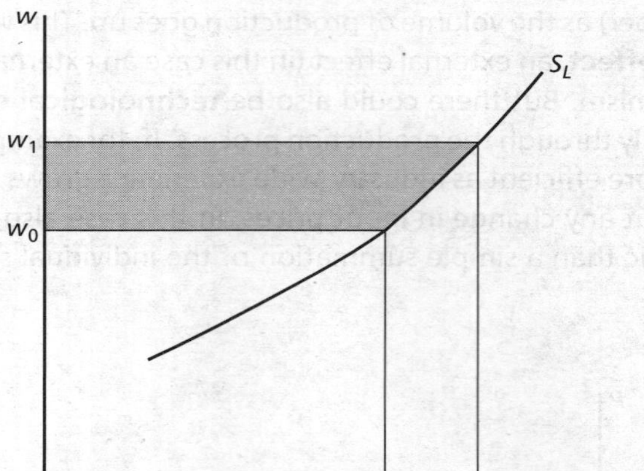


**Figure 6.8** *Surplus for Owners of Scarce Inputs*

# 6.3 MARKET EQUILIBRIUM

**Task for this section:**

To study the basic model of price determination in competitive markets as a result of the interaction between demand and supply.

Having derived the demand and supply curves, we can describe the market equilibrium, which takes place at the intersection of the two curves (see Figure 6.9). As we see from the figure, the equilibrium price and quantity are $p_c$ and $Q_c$ respectively. This is the equilibrium because, at this price, the quantity that consumers want to buy is exactly equal to the quantity that producers want to sell. Thus, the desires and expectations of all the market participants are fulfilled and no one has any incentive to change their behaviour in any way. As we can see from Figure 6.9, if the price were any higher, say at $p_H$, the quantity that sellers would want to sell would exceed the quantity that consumers would want to buy at that price. Sellers would find themselves holding too much inventory and would have to lower price in order to be able to sell their goods. Thus, the price would fall towards $p_C$. If the price were lower, say at $p_L$, the quantity demanded would be greater than the quantity supplied at that price. Sellers would be unable to keep any stock on their shelves as goods would be in great demand, and so sellers would infer that they could raise their price and earn more revenue. Thus, the price would rise towards $p_C$. Only when the price is equal to $p_c$ would the market function in an orderly way.

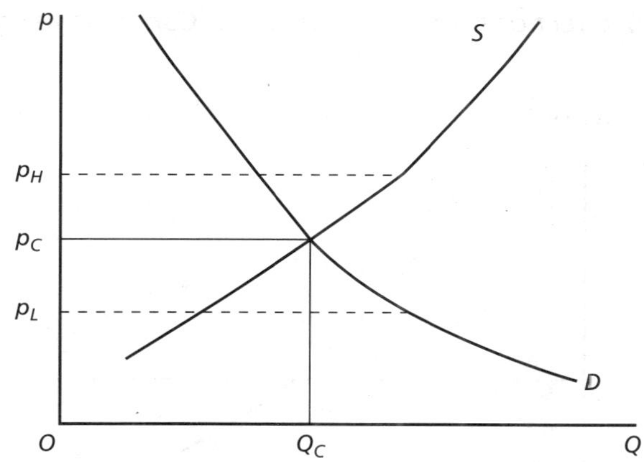


**Figure 6.9** *Market Equilibrium in Perfect Competition*

Once we have the equilibrium, we can perform comparative statics on it. Suppose *A* in Figure 6.10 represents a market equilibrium, where $p_0$ is the price and $Q_0$ is the quantity traded. Now suppose the demand for this good rises suddenly. Maybe this is the market for carrots and a new scientific study is published which shows tremendous health benefits from eating carrots. So the demand curve shifts out to $D'$. At first the price may stay at $p_0$, but at this price the quantity demanded would be $Q_d$; there is now an excess demand of $(Q_d - Q_0)$. Sellers find they cannot keep goods in stock, so they start raising the price. As the price rises, the quantity demanded falls and the quantity supplied rises. The process continues until the price reaches $p_1$, at which point the market settles into its new equilibrium at *B*.

The long-run equilibrium is shown in Figure 6.11. The price in the long-run has to be $p_c$, which is the minimum *AC* for every firm in the market. If the price were higher, new firms would enter

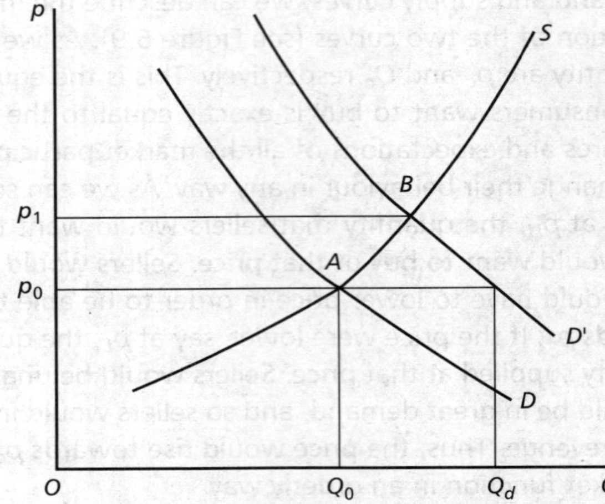


**Figure 6.10** *Effect of a Shift in Demand on Competitive Equilibrium*

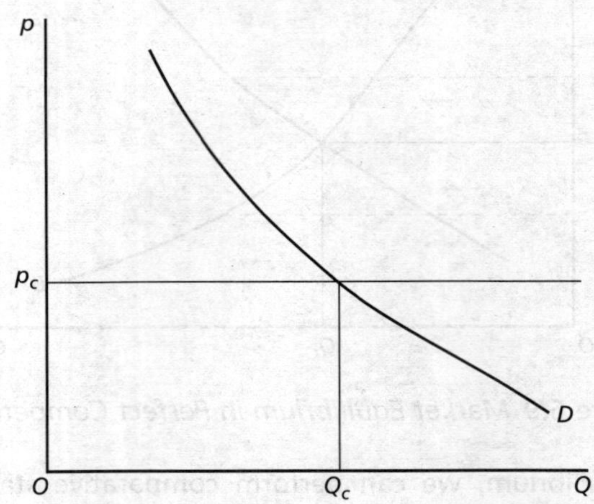


**Figure 6.11** *Long-Run Competitive Equilibrium*

and drive the price down, and if the price were lower, some firms would exit and the price would rise. Thus, the equilibrium price must be $p_c$ and the quantity traded $Q_c$ simply depends upon the level of demand at that price.

How exactly might this long-run equilibrium be maintained? Suppose the market is in long-run equilibrium at *A* in Figure 6.12. The price is the long-run equilibrium price $p_c$ and the quantity traded is $Q_0$. At any point in time, the market has to have a given number of firms and hence a short-run supply curve. Suppose $S_0$ is the short-run supply curve in this situation. Thus, $S_L$

and $D_0$ are the long-run supply and demand curves and $S_0$ and $D_0$ are the short-run supply and demand curves.

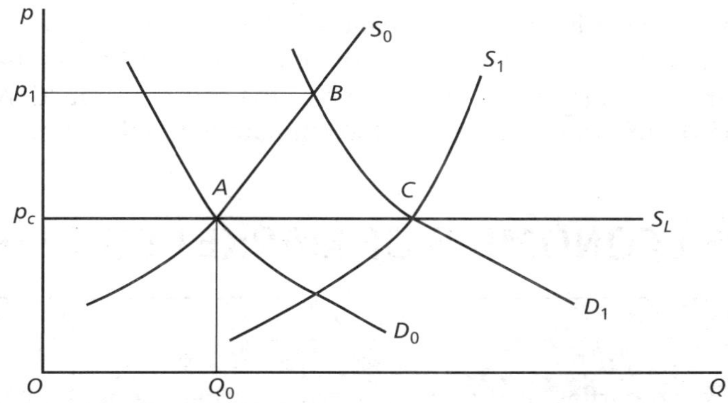


**Figure 6.12** *Market Adjustment in the Long-Run*

Now suppose the demand curve shifts to the right, to $D_1$. If the price stays at $p_c$ in the short-run, there would be excess demand, since supply would be at *A* and demand would be at *C*. This would obviously be unsustainable and so the price would rise to $p_1$; this would be the short-run equilibrium. However, this equilibrium would not be sustainable in the long-run, as firms would be making extra-normal profits. New firms would enter, pushing the (short-run) supply curve to the right. Entry would continue until the short-run supply curve is at $S_1$. At that point, a new short-run equilibrium would be established with the price at $p_c$, and this is also a long-run equilibrium as firms would be making just normal profits at this price. Thus, the long-run equilibrium is re-established.

At the same time as we discuss establishment and re-establishment of long-run equilibrium in theory, it is important to realise that the long-run equilibrium is a theoretical concept that we do not expect will ever be actually achieved, since conditions in any market are constantly changing. The importance of the long-run equilibrium is that it tells us the direction in which a competitive market would be moving. In our previous example, if we start in equilibrium at *A* and then demand shifts, causing the short-run equilibrium to move to *B*, the fact that the long-run equilibrium is at *C* tells us that, when the market is at *B*, there are long-run forces in place that would tend to lower the price and raise the quantity traded. In other words, there are forces in place that, if left unchecked and unaltered, would move the market to *C*. Of course, in reality, things will probably change before the equilibrium is reached, but at least we have an idea of the direction in which the market is headed.

At this point, it is also worth revisiting the old debate about the ultimate determinant of price, the debate about 'value in exchange' versus 'value in use'. To put it in modern terms, the two sides of the debate emphasised the two different sides of a market. One side basically argued that price was determined by the cost of production, while the other side argued that price was determined by the amount people were willing-to-pay for a good, the 'value in use'. Marshall's resolution of this debate was that price is determined by the interaction of these two forces; thus, it depends upon both. However, if we believe the model of perfect competition in the long-run, we would have to acknowledge that it is the cost of production that determines the price. Increases in demand do not shift the price in the long-run as long as the cost of production remains constant; thus, it is the long-run *AC* of production that is the ultimate determinant of price.

## 6.4 WELFARE ECONOMICS OF MARKET EQUILIBRIUM

**Task for this section:**

To study the welfare properties of the basic demand–supply model and to show that the resulting equilibrium is efficient.

A question to which economists have paid a lot of attention is whether or not the market equilibrium is in some sense 'efficient' or good. This is not an easy question to answer, mainly because what constitutes a 'good' price is open to debate. We will discuss the question in greater detail in the next chapter. But here we look at one sense in which the perfectly competitive equilibrium can be said to be good. We can show that the perfectly competitive equilibrium is efficient in the sense that it maximises at least one reasonable notion of welfare.

How does society gain from the production of a good? From the point of view taken here, the benefit to society from a good is the benefit consumers get from consuming it. We can obtain a measure of the benefit that consumers get (the 'value in use') from what they are willing-to-pay for it. From this point of view, the demand curve for a good is then also the social marginal benefit (SMB) curve, since the height of the demand curve at any point gives us the willingness-to-pay for that unit of the good. Thus, we mark the demand curve *D* in Figure 6.13 as the SMB curve also.

What does it cost to produce the good? Here the answer is straightforward: it costs the resources it takes to produce the good. Thus, the supply curve (the *MC* curve) is also the social marginal cost (SMC) of producing the good.

If we now define welfare as the surplus of benefit over cost:

$$W = B(Q) - C(Q),$$

the optimal output level from the social point of view would be the one where $W$ is maximised, that is, where

$$\frac{dW}{dQ} = B'(Q) - C'(Q) = 0.$$

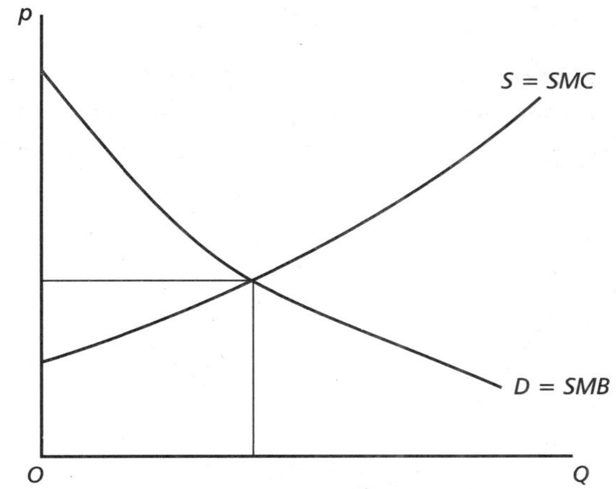


**Figure 6.13** *Optimality of Competitive Equilibrium*

That is, we would want

$$SMB = SMC.$$

This happens where the demand and supply curves cross, and therefore the social optimum occurs precisely at the competitive equilibrium. Thus, the competitive equilibrium is an optimal solution in which social welfare, defined as the surplus of benefit over cost, is maximised.

# 6.5 ANALYSING MARKET INTERVENTIONS

**Task for this section:**

To see how to use the basic demand–supply model to analyse different sorts of market conditions and interventions. After this section, you should have a good idea of how to incorporate real-life market situations into the supply–demand model to study what that model can teach us about those market situations.

The demand–supply model is a powerful tool for analysing markets. We can use the model to understand and analyse the effect of shifting demand and supply curves, caused in turn by the factors underlying these curves, such as income levels, tastes and costs of production. We can also use the model to understand the impact on markets of policy interventions of various kinds.

### 6.5.1 Price Supports and Subsidised Sales

Let us think about the impact of government policy in the food grain market. Farmers are offered a minimum support price for their grain, and many consumers are eligible to buy food at below-market prices. Let us see how we can use the market model to analyse the impact of these policies.

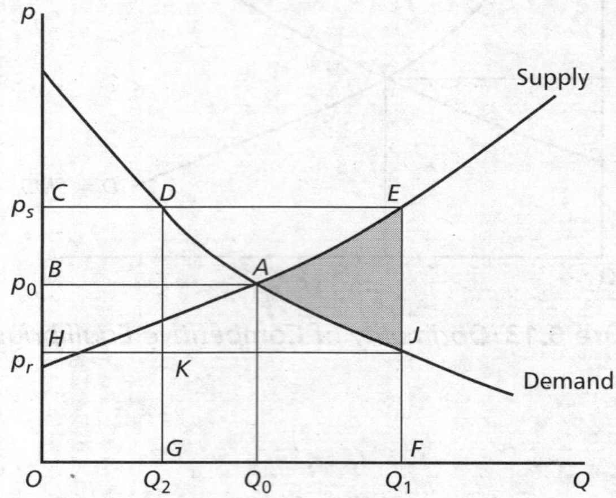


**Figure 6.14** *Analysis of a Price Support Policy*

Figure 6.14 illustrates the demand and supply curves in the food grain market. The free market equilibrium would be at the intersection *A* of the two curves and price and quantity would be $p_0$ and $Q_0$, respectively. For a support price to be effective, it must lie above $p_0$, say at a price like $p_s$. If it were below $p_0$, farmers would simply ignore it and sell their grain at the open market price. But if it is at $p_s$, it would be effective in raising the supply from $Q_0$ to $Q_1$. Thus, if the goal of the price support programme is to raise the production of food grains, the demand–supply model suggests that it should work. However, the demand at price $p_s$ is lower than $Q_0$, let alone $Q_1$, so there would be excess supply of food grains. In order to maintain the support price, government would have to step in and make purchases of food grains. If the open market is allowed to function as much as it can, $p_s$ would be the price in the market (since farmers would not sell at any price lower than that), private buyers would buy $Q_2$ units and government would have to buy $(Q_1 - Q_2)$ units. The cost to the government of these purchases would be the rectangle *DEFG*, equal to $p_s \cdot (Q_1 - Q_2)$.

We can ask normative questions such as who gains and who loses, and by how much, from this policy? Given just the price support policy, consumers face a higher price ($p_s$ instead of $p_0$) and therefore lose consumer surplus equal to the area *ABCD*. Sellers, however, gain from the higher price, to the extent of the gain in producer surplus *ABCE*. Subtracting the consumer surplus loss from the producer surplus gain leaves us a net social gain of the area *ADE*. However, government has to spend an amount given by the area *DEFG* in order to buy the 'surplus' (i.e. excess supply) food grain and support the price. How the grain they purchase is disposed of will affect the final distribution of gains and losses. For example, if the grain is stored in warehouses and basically goes bad or gets eaten by mice and rats, then the entire government expenditure on the support price will be a welfare loss since no additional benefit accrues to this spending.

Of course, the main purpose of the price support programme is to encourage food production to supply the public distribution system (PDS). If the entire government purchases (*GF* in Figure 6.14) are given to the PDS, the surplus grain could be sold through the PDS at price $p_r$ to consumers whose demand is reflected in the segment DJ of the demand curve. Much of this demand might come from poor consumers. If government sells the quantity *GF* of food grain at price $p_r$, it recovers revenue in the amount of the area *KJFG*. The net cost of the price support cum subsidised sales programme would then be *DEJK*. The 'poor' consumers buying the subsidised grain enjoy a consumer surplus of *DKJ*, since they have to pay only *KJFG* for the grain they buy. The net loss to society from all of these welfare effects would then be the shaded area *AEJ*. We can summarise all the effects to see why this is:

| | |
|---|---|
| 'Rich' consumers lose | −*ABCD* |
| Farmers gain | +*ABCE* |
| 'Poor' consumers gain | +*DKJ* |
| Government spends | −*DEJK* |
| Net welfare change | −*AEJ* |

A more direct and simple way to see that *AEJ* is the net loss to society is to note that the quantity distortion caused by this policy is from $Q_0$ to $Q_1$. The total cost of producing these additional units of output is given by the area below the supply curve, since the height of the supply curve is the *MC*. The total benefit from these additional units of consumption is the area below the demand curve, whose height is the marginal benefit from the given unit of consumption. The amount by which the total cost exceeds the total benefit is the triangle *AEJ*, which is therefore the net cost to society.

Finally, it is worth mentioning that, when we say 'net loss' or 'net cost to society', this statement and calculation is based upon the assumption that the 'value in use' or SMB from the consumption of a good is given by the height of the demand curve, what we have referred to as consumers' 'willingness-to-pay' for the good. But really the height of any consumer's demand curve is a reflection of not only 'willingness-to-pay' but also 'ability to pay'. Two consumers might have identical utility functions, so that each derives exactly the same utility from the same levels of consumption, but if one has much lower income than the other, her demand curves for all goods would everywhere be lower than her rich counterpart's demand curves. Thus, a redistributive policy such as the programme of price supports cum subsidised sale through the PDS may be justifiable, even though it seems to result in a 'net loss' to society.

## 6.5.2 Price Floors and Price Ceilings

The price supports we analysed in the previous section are an example of a general class of policy interventions that are called **price floors**, prices below which government does not wish the market price to fall. With any price floor that is effective or binding, the quantity supplied will exceed the quantity demanded, and the question arises of how the market can be sustained in such a position. In our previous example of the food grain market, the government stepped in to buy the excess supply and, in general, that is what governments would have to do in order to maintain price floors. If a government did not purchase the excess supply, the market price, whether legal or illegal, would tend to fall below the price floor. But if government was able to enforce a price floor through coercive means, say at $\underline{p}$ in Figure 6.15, the amount traded in the market would be $Q_d$, since buyers cannot be forced to buy more than their demand. Sellers would therefore be left with excess inventory.

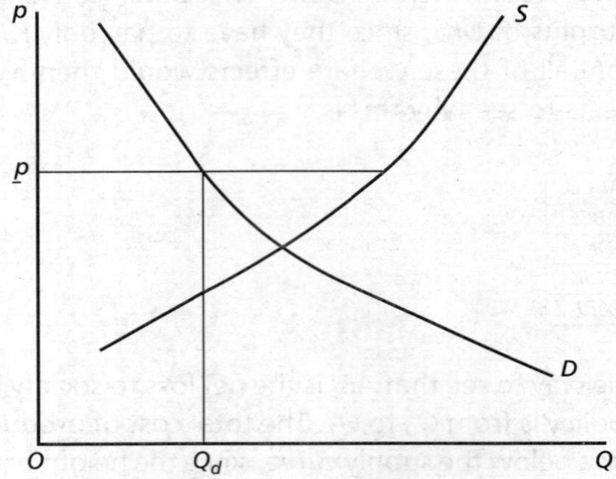


**Figure 6.15** *A Price Floor*

The subsidised sale of food grain that government made in the example of the previous section is an example of a **price ceiling**, a price above which government does not wish the market price to rise. In the example, government actually instituted a two-tier system, with an open market price and then a subsidised price targeted at certain consumers. Of course, if food grains are being offered by the government at a low price, even consumers with a high willingness-(and ability) to-pay, such as those whose demand is reflected in the segment *OG* in Figure 6.14, would like to acquire it at the low price. Government would have to institute a system such as an income test to keep out customers who do not belong to their target group, but obviously there would be strong incentives to try to circumvent such tests. This explains why there is so much 'leakage' in the PDS, since wealthy consumers would pay to have subsidised grain diverted to them. Thus, private individuals pursuing their own self-interest would tend to undermine the goals of the policy intervention.

More generally, price ceilings may not involve direct government participation in the market. A prime example of this is rent control, a declaration by the government that apartment rents cannot exceed a certain level. Normally, rent control is implemented by freezing rents at a particular point in time or by legislating that historically given rents cannot increase over time more rapidly than a target rate of increase smaller than what the free market would require for equilibrium. If *D* and *S* in Figure 6.16 represent the demand and supply curves of rental apartment units in a city, $\bar{p}$ could be an effective price ceiling as it is below the equilibrium rental level. At the rent-controlled price, there would be an excess demand for apartments, and, as usual, the 'short side of the market will rule,' meaning that the number of apartments rented will be $Q_S$, since landlords cannot be forced to rent their units. There will therefore be excess demand for apartments. Since the government does not typically intervene to bridge the demand–supply gap, some system of rationing would have to come into play in order to allocate the limited number of apartments among all the people demanding them.

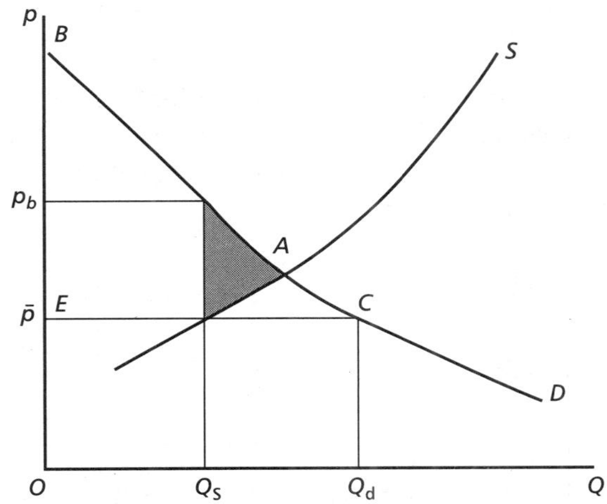


**Figure 6.16** *Rent Control as a Price Ceiling*

How might rationing of the limited number of apartment units take place? One method frequently encountered is for a 'black market' to develop, in which payments are made by tenants to landlords 'under the table'. If the number of apartments on offer remain at $Q_S$ in Figure 6.16, the limited number of apartments will then go to those with the highest willingness-to-pay. The rent will rise to $p_b$ (the gap of $(p_b - \bar{p})$ being the 'under the table' side payment) and the first $Q_S$ units of demand will be served. The deadweight loss from the rent control policy would then be the shaded area in Figure 6.16. (Can you explain why?) If the number of apartments on offer does not stay at $Q_S$, it is entirely possible that the equilibrium under the black market will revert to *A*, the competitive equilibrium. In this case, the black market essentially circumvents the rent control and restores the open market equilibrium, with the legal rent being paid 'over the table' and the difference between the equilibrium rent and the legal rent being paid 'under the table'. In this case, there is no deadweight loss from the rent control policy since it becomes completely ineffective; the market is at the competitive equilibrium and the only effect of the rent control policy is to drive some of the rent payments into the illegal black market.

If a black market does not develop, rationing of apartments must still take place and the welfare effects of a rent control policy depend very much on the mechanism by which this rationing takes place. There are several possibilities, such as rationing by willingness-to-pay, rationing by reverse willingness-to-pay and random rationing. In a way, 'first come, first served' might be the rationing mechanism and then the question would be, who gets to be first? Perhaps the order in which potential tenants arrive is randomly determined. With random rationing, the $Q_s$ apartments available would be randomly allocated among the $Q_d$ demanders. Since the potential consumer surplus from rentals at price $\bar{p}$ (assuming the entire demand is satisfied) is given by the triangle *BCE* in Figure 6.16, the actual expected consumer surplus from random rationing would be

$$CS = \frac{Q_s}{Q_d} \cdot BCE.$$

That is, the proportion $\frac{Q_s}{Q_d}$ of the potential consumer surplus *BCE* will on average be realised since it is the proportion of total demand that will be served by the limited supply. It is difficult to know if consumer welfare has now gone up or down as a result of the rent control policy without knowing all the specific details of the case.

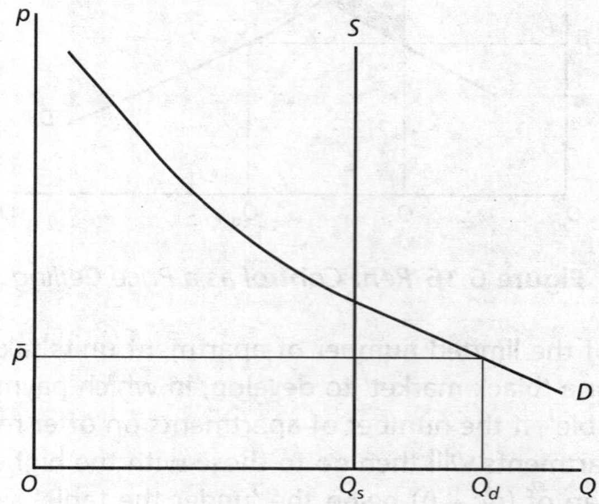


**Figure 6.17** *Inelastic Supply of Rental Units*

One might argue that, if rents are frozen at some point in time, the supply of rental units would be perfectly inelastic, as in Figure 6.17. Even in that case, if the price ceiling is effective (i.e. below the equilibrium price), rationing must occur. In any case, the situation illustrated in Figure 6.17 can only prevail in the short run, since in the long run, landlords will respond to the rent control by gradually withdrawing units from the rental market and by not building any new ones. They would also respond by reducing the quality of their apartments, by not maintaining them as well, which is a subtle form of supply reduction.

# 6.6 TAXES

**Task for this section:**

To see how to use the basic demand–supply model to analyse a very important type of market intervention: the imposition of commodity taxes. After this section, you should have a good idea of some of the different types of commodity taxes and how to calculate their effects in competitive markets.

An important application of the market model is the analysis of commodity taxes and subsidies. We looked briefly in Chapter 3 at the welfare impact on consumers of a commodity tax, but that analysis was a little simplistic as we did not have the full market model to work with at that time. Now we do, so we can do a proper analysis of the effects of commodity taxes and subsidies. Taxes are considered in this section, and subsidies in the next.

A commodity tax is a government fee or charge on certain transactions involving the production or sale of certain commodities. Commodity taxes are of two broad classes: **excise taxes** are taxes levied on the producers or sellers of a good, and **sales taxes** are taxes that are levied on buyers of a good. Each type of tax can take one of two forms: a **specific or per unit tax** is one that is a specific amount (say ₹2) for each unit of the good bought or sold, regardless of the price at which it is sold, and a **percentage or ad valorem tax** is one that is specified as a percentage of the price at which the good is sold. For example, suppose there is a specific tax of ₹20 per litre of petrol. Then the tax would be ₹20 for each litre sold, whether the price is ₹100 per litre or ₹200 per litre. However, if the tax were an ad valorem tax of 20%, the tax due would be ₹20 if the price of the petrol is ₹100, but ₹40 if the price of the petrol is ₹200 per litre.

A **subsidy** is a negative tax; the government makes subsidy payments to either buyers or sellers, depending upon the type of subsidy. Subsidies can also be specific or ad valorem.

## 6.6.1 Excise Taxes

An excise tax is levied on sellers. For example, if there is an excise tax of ₹10 per pack of cigarettes sold, sellers would have to remit to the government that amount for each pack of cigarettes that they sold. Thus, an excise tax is like an increased cost to the sellers and the result of it is to push up the $MC$ curve (and hence the supply curve) by the amount of the tax. If $S$ in Figure 6.18 is the supply curve of a good without any tax, $S'$ would represent the tax-inclusive supply curve. The vertical distance between $S$ and $S'$ is the amount of the tax.

Panel (a) of the figure shows the effect of a **specific excise tax**, in which case $S'$ will be vertically parallel to $S$, since the vertical distance between the two is the (constant) amount of the tax. The intersection of $S'$ and the demand curve $D$ will mark the new equilibrium (point B in panel (a) of

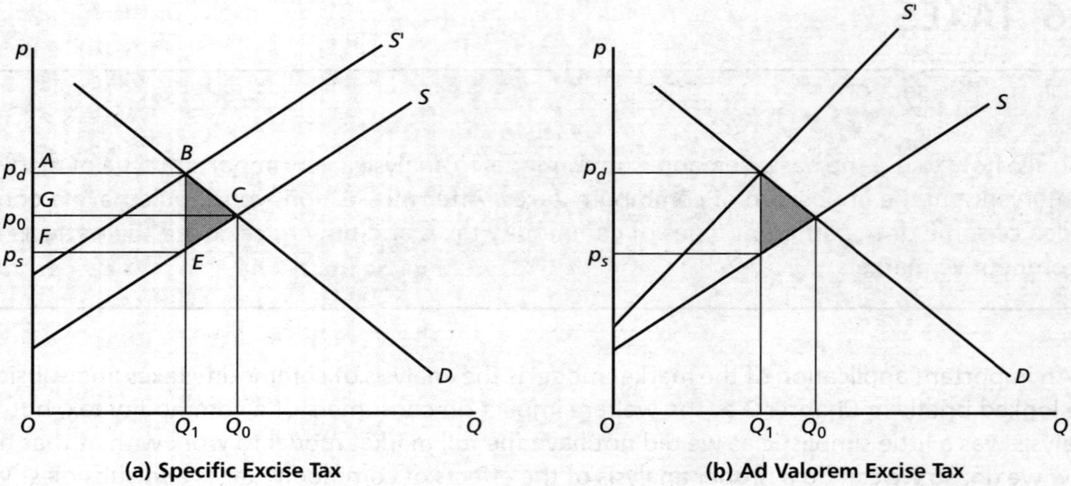


**Figure 6.18** *Two Kinds of Excise Taxes*

Figure 6.18). At this equilibrium, $Q_1$ units of output will be traded and the price to consumers will be $p_d$. Since the vertical distance between $S$ and $S'$ is the amount of the per unit tax, $p_s$ marks the amount per unit that sellers receive net of the tax payment.

What is the welfare impact of the tax? Since the price faced by buyers rises from $p_0$ to $p_d$, consumers are worse off by the loss in consumer surplus, given by the area *ABCG*. Sellers receive a net price of $p_s$ instead of $p_0$; they are therefore worse off by the loss in producer surplus, given by the area *GCEF*. Government collects tax revenue which can be measured by the rectangle *ABEF* (=$Q_1$ times the per unit tax), and this is a positive from the social point of view. However, the losses to consumers and producers exceed the gain to government by the shaded area *BCE*, and this is the deadweight loss due to the tax. Commodity taxes cause the quantity traded in the market to be distorted (here quantity traded falls from $Q_0$ to $Q_1$), and this quantity distortion causes a deadweight loss. A simple way to think of this deadweight loss, which we have already seen is equal to the area *BCE*, is to note that the units of output between $Q_1$ and $Q_0$ have a marginal benefit equal to the height of the demand curve (after all, this is what people are willing-to-pay for the good) and a *MC* equal to the height of the supply curve. The distance between the demand and supply curves is a potential surplus that is lost when the quantity traded is only $Q_1$ and the units from $Q_1$ to $Q_0$ are not traded. The sum of all these lost surpluses is the area *BCE*.

Panel (b) of Figure 6.18 shows the effect of an ad valorem or percentage excise tax. The main difference here from panel (a) is in the form of the shifted supply curve $S'$. Whereas the supply curve shifted in a parallel fashion in the case of the specific tax, here it will shift in a proportional fashion, as we see in panel (b) of the figure. The ad valorem tax is a percentage of the price. Suppose we are looking at an ad valorem tax of 10%. Then, where the height of the supply curve is ₹10, the shift will be ₹1. And where the height of the supply curve is ₹20, the shift in the supply curve will be ₹2. Thus, the size of the shift is bigger, the greater the height of the supply curve; it is the proportion of the shift that remains constant. The rest of the analysis of the tax is the same as for the specific tax, and so the shaded area in panel (b) of Figure 6.18 will represent the deadweight loss due to the tax.

## 6.6.2 Sales Taxes

A sales tax is levied on buyers of goods. When a consumer buys something subject to a sales tax, the sales tax due is added to the purchase price when totalling up the bill. The shopkeeper collects the tax on behalf of the government and sends it to them. A sales tax could in principle be set either per unit or ad valorem, although generally sales taxes are ad valorem or percentage taxes.

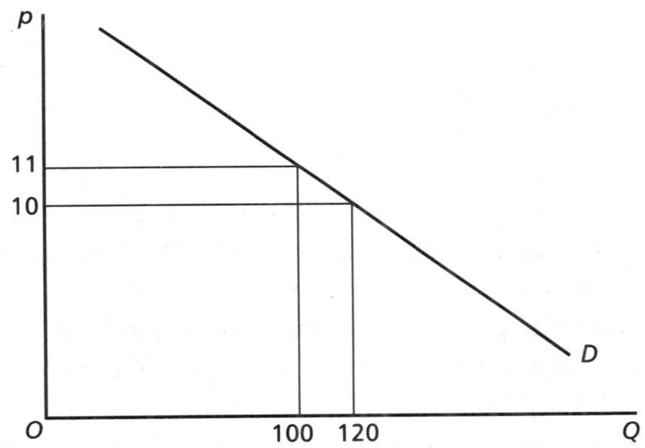


**Figure 6.19** *Demand Response to a Sales Tax*

In analysing the effect of a sales tax, we make the assumption that consumers are not myopic but are fully rational and take full account of the tax. What this means is perhaps best illustrated by an example. Suppose the curve *D* in Figure 6.19 represents the demand for soap. If there is no tax, suppose the demand at a price of ₹11 would be 100 units and at a price of ₹10 would be 120 units. Now suppose a sales tax of 10% is introduced. If the store price is ₹10, a 10% tax on top of that would make the total price to the consumer ₹11. What we assume is that the demand for soap at the store price of ₹10 will be 100 units, because the tax-inclusive price will now be ₹11. Thus, the demand curve is the consumers' willingness-to-pay curve regardless of whether all of what they pay goes to the seller or whether part of it goes to the government in the form of a tax.

Given this assumption of 'full rationality' on the part of consumers, let us see how we analyse the impact of a sales tax. Consider panel (a) in Figure 6.20. *D* and *S* are the demand and supply curves, respectively, and *C* is the equilibrium absent any tax. Price is $p_0$ and the quantity traded is $Q_0$. Note that *D* shows the quantity demanded as a function of the price. Now suppose the

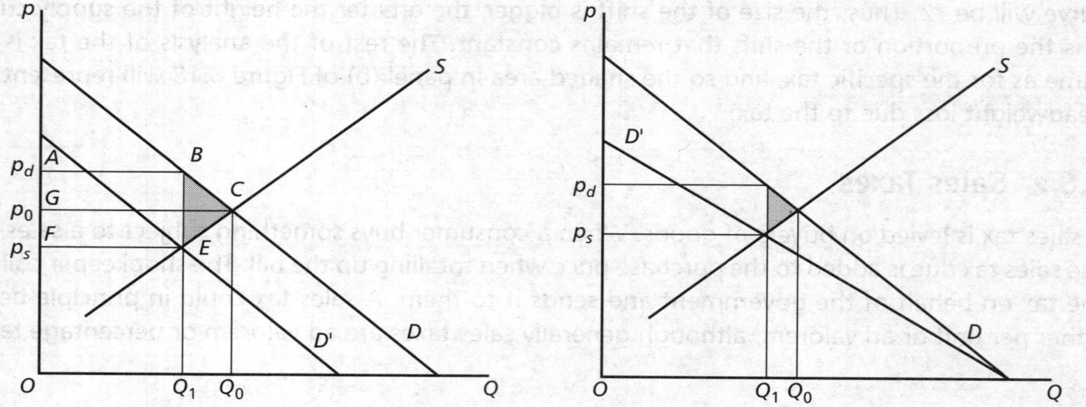


(a) Per Unit Sales Tax

(b) Percentage Sales Tax

**Figure 6.20** *The Effect of Sales Taxes*

government introduces a per unit sales tax of ₹10 per unit. Draw $D'$ everywhere ₹10 lower than $D$. $D'$ is now the demand curve as a function of the price (the 'sticker' price), because consumers know that there will be a sales tax levied on top of the price. The demand curve $D$ is still the demand as a function of the total price; it is just that now the total price is the sticker price plus the sales tax per unit. The new equilibrium is at $E$, where $D'$ cuts the supply curve $S$. $Q_1$ is the quantity traded and $p_s$ is the equilibrium price. The total price to buyers, however, will be $p_d$, which is $p_s$ plus the sales tax. A glance at the figure shows that the outcome is exactly the same as the one we saw for a per unit excise tax in panel (a) of Figure 6.18. The tax results in the same outcomes for buyers, sellers and the government, and the same deadweight loss of the triangle $BCE$.

Panel (b) of Figure 6.20 shows the situation for an ad valorem sales tax. The diagram and outcome are essentially the same as for a per unit tax; the only difference is that $D'$ is not parallel to $D$. Rather, $D'$ is proportionately lower than $D$ to reflect the tax. If $p'$ is the height of $D'$ and $p$ is the height of $D$, we must have $p = p'(1 + t)$, where $t$ is the tax rate represented as a decimal (e.g for a 10% tax, $t = 0.1$). The outcome is identical to that for an ad valorem excise tax that we saw in panel (b) of Figure 6.18.

## 6.6.3 Calculating the Effects of Commodity Taxes

In this section, we look at how we can exactly calculate the impact of a tax on a competitive market. If a competitive market is in equilibrium, with price $p_0$ and quantity $Q_0$ (see Figure 6.21), the imposition of a **specific or per unit tax** $T$ will result in a new equilibrium with quantity $Q_1 < Q_0$, and *two* prices: a demand price $p_d > p_0$ (what buyers have to pay) and a supply price $p_s < p_0$ (what sellers receive). The difference between these two prices is the amount of the tax:

$T = p_d - p_s$. This is true whether the tax is a sales tax or an excise tax, and the new equilibrium can therefore be illustrated in either case by Figure 6.21.

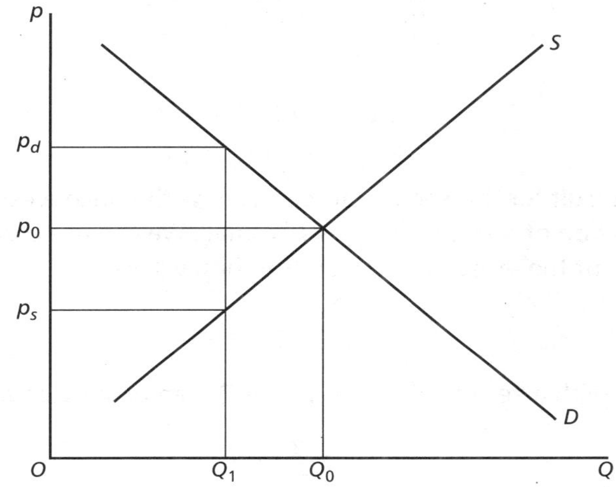


**Figure 6.21** *The Effects of a Per Unit Tax*

To find $Q_1$, $p_d$, and $p_s$, we start with the observations that

$$p_d = p_s + T$$

and

$$Q_1 = Q_d(p_d) = Q_d(p_s + T) = Q_s(p_s), \tag{6.5}$$

where $Q_d$ is the demand curve and $Q_s$ is the supply curve. Taking the last two expressions in (6.5) and differentiating both with respect to $T$, we obtain

$$\frac{dQ_d}{dp_d} \cdot \left(\frac{dp_s}{dT} + 1\right) = \frac{dQ_s}{dp_s} \cdot \frac{dp_s}{dT}$$

which can be rewritten as

$$\frac{dp_s}{dT} \cdot \left(\frac{dQ_s}{dp_s} - \frac{dQ_d}{dp_d}\right) = \frac{dQ_d}{dp_d}. \tag{6.6}$$

Multiplying both sides of (6.6) by $\frac{p_0}{Q_0}$, we have

$$\frac{dp_s}{dT} \cdot \left(\frac{dQ_s}{dp_s} \cdot \frac{p_0}{Q_0} - \frac{dQ_d}{dp_d} \cdot \frac{p_0}{Q_0}\right) = \frac{dQ_d}{dp_d} \cdot \frac{p_0}{Q_0}. \tag{6.7}$$

But $p_0 = p_d^0$ (the initial demand price), $p_0 = p_s^0$ (the initial supply price) and $Q_0 = Q_d^0 = Q_s^0$. Therefore,

$$\frac{dp_s}{dT} \cdot (\epsilon_s - \epsilon_d) = \epsilon_d,$$

or

$$\frac{dp_s}{dT} = \frac{\epsilon_d}{\epsilon_s - \epsilon_d}. \tag{6.8}$$

Equation (6.8) is a basic result for this section; it tells us how the price received by sellers changes in response to the imposition of a tax. As long as $T$ is small, we can use a discrete version of (6.8) to make actual estimates of the effect of a tax on the supply price:

$$\Delta p_s = \frac{\epsilon_d}{\epsilon_s - \epsilon_d} \cdot \Delta T,$$

which, if we are starting with a zero tax (so that $T = \Delta T$), can be written as

$$\Delta p_s = \frac{\epsilon_d}{\epsilon_s - \epsilon_d} \cdot T. \tag{6.9}$$

For the price paid by buyers, we note that $p_d = p_s + T$. Therefore,

$$\frac{dp_d}{dT} = \frac{dp_s}{dT} + 1.$$

Substituting (6.8) and simplifying, this gives us

$$\frac{dp_d}{dT} = \frac{\epsilon_s}{\epsilon_s - \epsilon_d}. \tag{6.10}$$

Once again, if $T$ is small and initially zero, we can approximate the change in demand price as

$$\Delta p_d = \frac{\epsilon_s}{\epsilon_s - \epsilon_d} \cdot T. \tag{6.11}$$

This can be used as a basic approximation formula to calculate the change in the price paid by buyers in response to a per unit tax of $T$, regardless if it is an excise or a sales tax.

Finally, to find the new quantity, we can use either of the new prices and the elasticity to find $Q_1$. We know that

$$\epsilon_d = \frac{dQ_d}{dp_d} \cdot \frac{p_d}{Q_d} \quad \text{and} \quad \epsilon_s = \frac{dQ_s}{dp_s} \cdot \frac{p_s}{Q_s}.$$

Taking discrete approximations of these formulae, and noting that $p_0 = p_d^0 = p_s^0$ and $Q_0 = Q_d^0 = Q_s^0$. we can therefore write

$$\epsilon_d = \frac{\Delta Q_d}{\Delta p_d} \cdot \frac{p_0}{Q_0} \quad \text{and} \quad \epsilon_s = \frac{\Delta Q_s}{\Delta p_s} \cdot \frac{p_0}{Q_0}.$$

Using (6.9) and (6.11), we can see that each of these reduces to

$$\Delta Q = \frac{\epsilon_s \epsilon}{\epsilon_s - \epsilon_d} \cdot \frac{TQ_0}{p_0}. \tag{6.12}$$

If the tax were a **proportional or ad valorem tax** at the rate $t$, Figure 6.21 would still illustrate the situation; the only difference now would be that the gap between the demand and supply prices would be a proportion of the supply price, rather than a fixed amount. We could calculate the effects of the proportional tax approximately by thinking of it as a specific tax, with

$$T = tp_0,$$

and then applying the formulae (6.9) and (6.11).

Alternatively, we could solve for the effects of a proportional tax by assuming that the demand and supply curves were of constant elasticity form:

$$Q_d = ap_d^{\epsilon_d} \qquad \text{and} \qquad Q_s = cp_s^{\epsilon_s}.$$

The initial equilibrium in this case would involve $Q_d = Q_s = Q_0$ and $p_d = p_s = p_0$:

$$ap_0^{\epsilon_d} = cp_0^{\epsilon_s},$$

which simplifies to

$$p_0 = \left(\frac{a}{c}\right)^{\frac{1}{\epsilon_s - \epsilon_d}}. \tag{6.13}$$

The final (post-tax) equilibrium would occur where $Q_d = Q_s$ and $p_d = p_s(1+t)$. Thus,

$$a\left[p_s(1+t)\right]^{\epsilon_d} = cp_s^{\epsilon_s}$$

$$p_s^{\epsilon_s - \epsilon_d} = \frac{a}{c}(1+t)^{\epsilon_d}$$

$$p_s = \left(\frac{a}{c}\right)^{\frac{1}{\epsilon_s - \epsilon_d}} (1+t)^{\frac{\epsilon_d}{\epsilon_s - \epsilon_d}}.$$

Using (6.13), this can be written as

$$p_s = p_0 (1+t)^{\frac{\epsilon_d}{\epsilon_s - \epsilon_d}}. \tag{6.14}$$

Equation (6.14) is a basic result on the effect of a proportional tax on the supply price; it can be used as an approximation even if the demand and supply curves are not actually of constant elasticity form.

To find the demand price, or the price paid by buyers, note that $p_d = p_s(1+t)$. Applying (6.14) to this and simplifying, we obtain

$$p_d = p_0 (1+t)^{\frac{\epsilon_s}{\epsilon_s - \epsilon_d}}. \tag{6.15}$$

Note that, if $t$ is small, we can approximate (6.14) and (6.15) by their first-order Taylor approximations:

$$p_s \simeq p_0 \left(1 + \frac{\epsilon_d}{\epsilon_s - \epsilon_d} t\right)$$

and

$$p_d \simeq p_0 \left(1 + \frac{\epsilon_s}{\epsilon_s - \epsilon_d} t\right).$$

If we take $tp_0 = T$ and differentiate, we get back the previous formulae for the specific tax:

$$\frac{dp_s}{dT} = \frac{\epsilon_d}{\epsilon_s - \epsilon_d}$$

and

$$\frac{dp_d}{dT} = \frac{\epsilon_s}{\epsilon_s - \epsilon_d}.$$

### 6.6.4 Three Basic Results on the Effects of Commodity Taxes in Competitive Markets

Developing the formulae for the changes in price and quantity in response to the imposition of a commodity tax allows us to compute these changes in any situation. They also allow us to derive some general results on the effects of taxes, the first of which we have already been using implicitly.

**Result 1: The effects of a tax are the same, whether it be levied on buyers or sellers.** In other words, excise taxes and sales taxes have the same effects. The reason is that either tax drives a wedge between the demand price $p_d$ and the supply price $p_s$, as seen in Figure 6.21. The size of the wedge is equal to the amount of the tax, but does not depend upon whether the tax is a sales tax or an excise tax.

**Result 2: The incidence of a tax on buyers is higher and on sellers is lower as demand is less elastic and supply is more elastic (the incidence on buyers is lower and on sellers is higher as demand is more elastic and supply is less elastic).**

We can see the truth of this result from our formulae for the effects of taxes. Consider (6.10):

$$\frac{dp_d}{dT} = \frac{\epsilon_s}{\epsilon_s - \epsilon_d}.$$

To see how this varies with the elasticity of demand, we can differentiate with respect to $\epsilon_d$:

$$\frac{d}{d\epsilon_d}\left(\frac{dp_d}{dT}\right) = \frac{\epsilon_s}{(\epsilon_s - \epsilon_d)^2} > 0.$$

So as $\epsilon_d$ goes up (i.e. demand becomes less elastic; remember $\epsilon_d < 0$, so $\epsilon_d$ going up means $\epsilon_d$ is getting closer to zero and falling in absolute value), the incidence on buyers is higher in that the demand price rises more.

To study the effect of the elasticity of supply, we differentiate (6.10) with respect to $\epsilon_s$:

$$\frac{d}{d\epsilon_s}\left(\frac{dp_d}{dT}\right) = \frac{-\epsilon_d}{(\epsilon_s - \epsilon_d)^2} > 0.$$

So as $\epsilon_s$ goes up (i.e. supply becomes more elastic), the burden on buyers is higher since the demand price rises more.

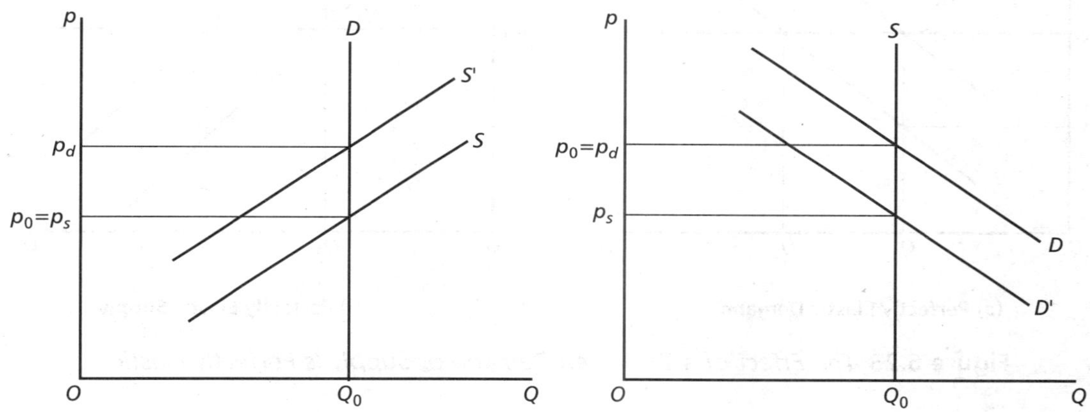


**(a) Perfectly Inelastic Demand** **(b) Perfectly Inelastic Supply**

**Figure 6.22** *The Effect of a Tax When Demand or Supply Is Perfectly Inelastic*

One way to look at this result is to take it to an extreme and look at the effect of a tax when either demand or supply is perfectly inelastic or perfectly elastic. In Figure 6.22, we look at perfectly inelastic demand in panel (a) and perfectly inelastic supply in panel (b). From panel (a) we see clearly that, when demand is perfectly inelastic, the entire burden of the tax falls on buyers. The supply price $p_s$ remains unchanged at $p_0$; the demand price adjusts by the full amount of the tax. This agrees with the basic proposition that the burden of the tax on buyers is higher, the less elastic the demand curve.

In panel (b) of Figure 6.22, we look at the case where the supply curve is perfectly inelastic. Here we see that the entire burden of the tax falls on the sellers, as the supply price falls by the full amount of the tax. Given the perfect inelasticity of the supply curve, this is not surprising, but it underscores the result that the lower the elasticity of supply, the lower the burden of the tax on buyers.

It is worth pointing out one other aspect of the equilibrium when the demand or supply curve is perfectly inelastic. In both these cases, the quantity is not distorted at all, since the inelastic side of the market absorbs the entire effect of the tax without altering the quantity. Thus, the quantity traded remains unchanged in response to the tax. We will return to this point when we discuss Result 3.

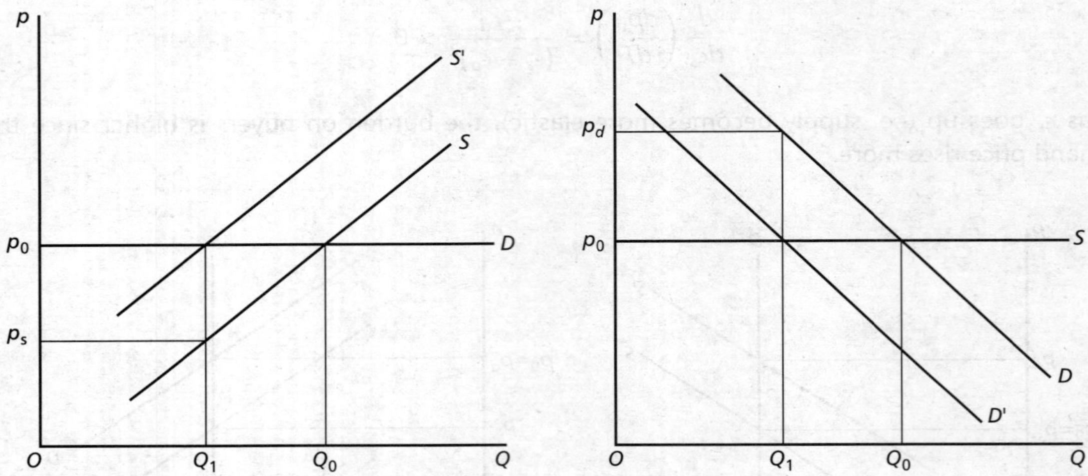


**(a) Perfectly Elastic Demand**

**(b) Perfectly Elastic Supply**

**Figure 6.23** *The Effect of a Tax When Demand or Supply Is Perfectly Elastic*

Let us look now at what happens when one of the demand or supply curves is perfectly elastic. Panel (a) in Figure 6.23 illustrates a perfectly elastic demand curve. Such a demand curve might arise if the good is traded internationally and the world price is unaffected by changes in this market. We see that the incidence or burden of a tax (here an excise tax for convenience) falls here completely on the sellers. Since demand is perfectly elastic, buyers will not tolerate any increase in price; therefore, all of the price adjustment must be made by suppliers. The supply price $p_s$ falls by the full amount of the tax. This agrees with the general result that the incidence on buyers is lower (and on sellers is higher), the more elastic the demand curve.

Panel (b) of the Figure 6.23 looks at the case where the supply curve is perfectly elastic. This might be the case in the long-run for a perfectly competitive market. Once again, since the supply is perfectly elastic, sellers will not tolerate any price change and the entire burden of the tax falls on buyers: the demand price $p_d$ rises by the full amount of the tax. So this illustrates the more general conclusion that the burden on sellers is lower (and on buyers is higher), the more elastic the supply curve.

**Result 3: The excess burden (or deadweight loss) caused by any commodity tax is greater, the more elastic the demand and supply curves.** The deadweight loss due to a tax is also called the excess burden, the amount by which the burden on buyers and sellers exceeds the amount of tax revenue collected. This result says that the size of the excess burden (in absolute value) is bigger, the more elastic the demand and supply curves. The basic reason for this result is that, the more elastic the demand and supply curves, the greater is the quantity distortion $\Delta Q$ caused by the tax. The excess burden is the shaded area in Figure 6.24, and taking the area to be roughly triangular, we can see that

$$\text{Excess Burden} \simeq \frac{1}{2} \cdot T \cdot \Delta Q.$$

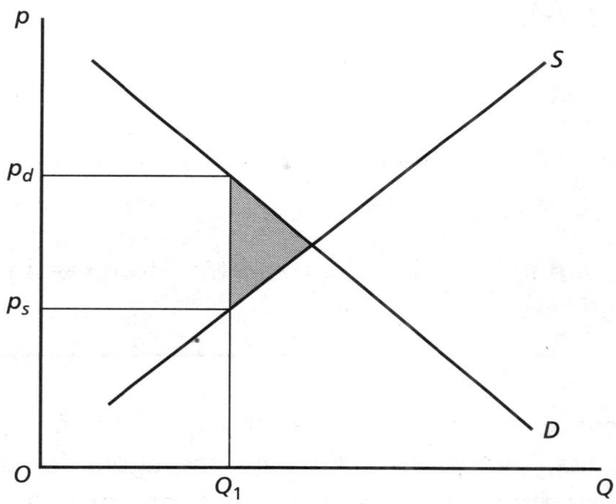


**Figure 6.24** *Excess Burden of a Tax*

In (6.12), we had seen that $\Delta Q$ is proportional to $\frac{\epsilon_s \epsilon_d}{\epsilon_s - \epsilon_d}$, and therefore so is the excess burden *EB*. We can therefore look at the effect of elasticities on *EB* by differentiating this term with respect to each of the elasticities. Note that *EB* is negative (since $\Delta Q$ is negative), and so an increase in *EB* is a *reduction* in the size of the excess burden. Now, we have

$$\frac{d}{d\epsilon_d}\left(\frac{\epsilon_s \epsilon_d}{\epsilon_s - \epsilon_d}\right) = \frac{\epsilon_s^2}{(\epsilon_s - \epsilon_d)^2} > 0.$$

Thus as $\epsilon_d$ rises (demand becomes less elastic, remember $\epsilon_d < 0$), *EB* rises in algebraic value, which means it falls in absolute value; the less elastic the demand, the smaller is the excess burden. For the elasticity of supply, we have

$$\frac{d}{d\epsilon_s}\left(\frac{\epsilon_s \epsilon_d}{\epsilon_s - \epsilon_d}\right) = \frac{-\epsilon_d^2}{(\epsilon_s - \epsilon_d)^2} < 0.$$

Thus as $\epsilon_s$ rises (supply becomes more elastic), *EB* falls in algebraic value and rises in absolute value; the more elastic the supply, the greater is the excess burden.

We actually see a reflection of this result in Figures 6.22 and 6.23. In Figure 6.22, we see that, when the demand or supply curve is perfectly inelastic, there is no quantity distortion at all and hence no excess burden. However, from Figure 6.23 we see that, if either the demand or the supply curve is perfectly elastic, the quantity distortion is at a maximum, since the relevant price adjusts by the full amount of the tax. Thus, the excess burden is also maximised in these cases.

One important implication of this result is the so-called 'inverse elasticity rule'. Since governments have to raise revenues through taxation, they would want to minimise the deadweight losses that result from the imposition of taxes. The inverse elasticity rule says that the government should tax more heavily goods for which the elasticity of demand is very low, since the deadweight losses in these markets will be low.

## 6.7 SUBSIDIES

**Task for this section:**

To see how subsidies are simply negative taxes and therefore can be analysed by a simple extension of the analysis of taxes.

A subsidy is a negative tax. Rather than charging an economic agent for a transaction (buying or selling) as in a tax, the government *pays* the agent for undertaking the transaction. Very often, subsidies are implemented by the government supplying goods (whether to consumers or producers) at prices below their MC. Subsidies could be offered to buyers or sellers, and both are reasonably common in many countries. In principle, a subsidy could be implemented as a straight payment, but it is more common for subsidies to be indirect. In India, for example, food subsidies are provided by the government buying food at higher prices, but selling it through the fair price shops at prices below what they paid for it. Farm production is subsidised by the government buying food grain at above-market support prices, but also by the subsidisation of inputs through below-market price sales of seeds, water, electricity and fertiliser.

Analysing subsidies is similar to analysing taxes. Suppose the food market is in equilibrium at $E$ in Figure 6.25, where $D$ and $S$ are the demand and supply curves, respectively. The initial price and quantity are $p_0$ and $Q_0$. Now suppose government subsidises food production. Whether this is done by a direct cash payment to farmers or by providing them with subsidised inputs makes no difference to the analysis. In either case, the MC of production for farmers effectively falls by the amount of the subsidy and so their supply curve will shift to, say, $S'$ from $S$ in Figure 6.25. The new equilibrium is at $A$, where the price has fallen to $p_d$ and the quantity produced and traded has risen to $Q_1$. Including the subsidy, producers receive a per unit revenue of $p_s$. Thus, farmers are better-off by the increase in producer surplus $CEFG$. Consumers face a lower price and are

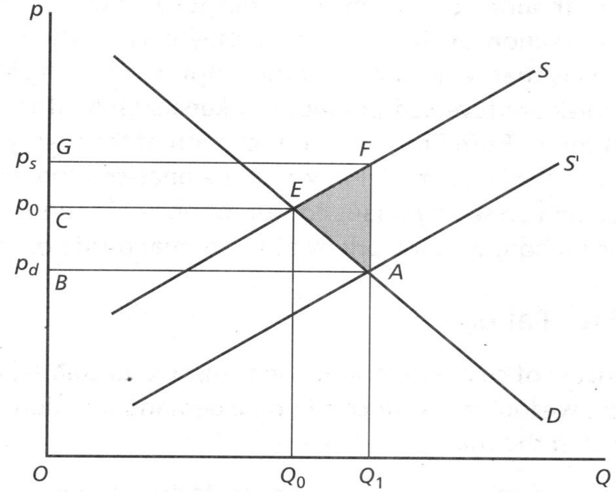


**Figure 6.25** *Analysing a Subsidy*

therefore better-off by the change in consumer surplus *CEAB*. Government, however, is worse off by the amount they have to pay out in subsidy, *ABGF*. This cost to the government is bigger than the gains to consumers and producers. The net of the three effects is the shaded area *AEF*, which is the deadweight loss due to the subsidy.

Just like taxes, subsidies therefore cause deadweight losses. The basic reason is that, like a tax, a subsidy distorts the quantity traded from the optimum quantity $Q_0$ at the competitive equilibrium to $Q_1$. The increased output ($Q_1 - Q_0$) has a higher *MC* than marginal benefit (the height of the demand curve) and so producing this output causes a loss to society. Of course, this calculation ignores the social value attached to supplying food in greater quantities to consumers who are probably poor and whose 'willingness-to-pay' is constrained by their ability to pay. Thus, the SMB of increased consumption may not be correctly reflected by the height of the demand curve. Even under conventional measurement, it could be that increased consumption may lead to better nutrition and hence to lower health care costs in the future. Thus, a fuller analysis may show the subsidy to be well justified.

## 6.8 INPUT MARKETS

**Task for this section:**

To extend the theory of price determination in output markets to markets for inputs such as labour and capital.

Input markets may be thought of as similar to output markets in that equilibrium in such markets involves the intersection of demand and supply curves. The main difference between output and input markets is that, while demand for outputs comes from consumers and supply comes from firms, the roles are reversed in input markets: supply of inputs comes largely from consumers and demand comes from firms. In our discussion of the theory of consumer behaviour, we looked at extensions of the basic model in which we analysed the individual's labour supply decision and also the decision on saving versus consumption, which underlies the supply of capital from households. In this section, we look briefly at the demand side of input markets as well.

### 6.8.1 The Demand for Labour

When looking at the process of cost minimisation in firms, we calculated the conditional demand functions for inputs. Here we look at the unconditional demand functions for inputs, using labour as our basic case to develop the theory.

Consider a firm that is perfectly competitive in both its output and its input markets. Its profit can be written as

$$\pi = p \cdot q(L) - C(L),$$

where $p$ is the price at which it sells its output, $q(L)$ is the quantity it sells, as a function of the quantity of labour $L$ that it uses, and $C(L)$ is its total cost, also a function of the amount of labour that it uses. Note that

$$C(L) = wL + rK.$$

Then, to maximise its profit, the firm will hire labour up to the point where

$$\frac{d\pi}{dL} = p \cdot \frac{\partial q}{\partial L} - w = 0,$$

or

$$p \cdot \frac{\partial q}{\partial L} = w. \tag{6.16}$$

Equation (6.16) expresses the **marginal productivity theory of input demand**. The left-hand side of the equation is called the marginal revenue product (MRP) of labour. The equation says that an input such as labour is used by the firm up to the point where its MRP is equal to its price, the wage rate. If, for example, the wage rate is $w_0$ and the MRP is as shown in Figure 6.26, the firm would use $L^*$ amount of labour. Note that, if the firm is a price-taker in its output market, the MRP is its marginal physical product (MPP, or just MP) times the price of its output.

If the wage rate changes, the quantity of labour hired will change according to the MRP curve. This shows that the MRP curve is the firm's demand curve for labour. If the MRP curve is bell-shaped, only the downward-sloping portion will be considered the demand curve. Note also that

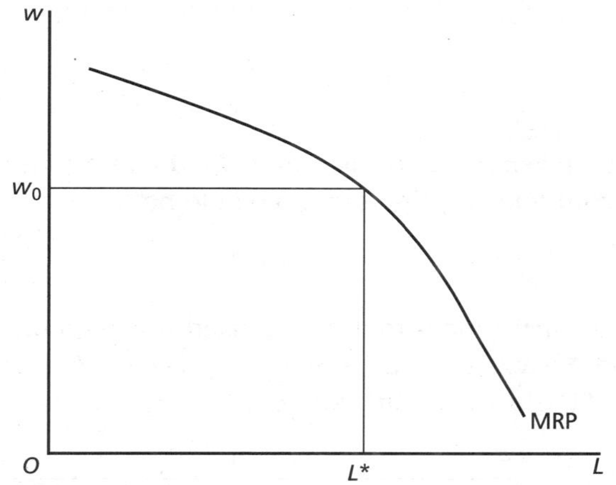


**Figure 6.26** *The Marginal Productivity Theory of Input Demand*

the position of the MRP curve depends on the amount of capital that a firm has in the short-run. Changing the level of capital would shift the MRP curve.

Once we have the demand curve for labour for each individual firm, we can sum up the individual demand curves to get the market demand curve for labour. The supply of labour is similarly found by horizontally summing the individual supply curves from workers. The market can then be analysed in the usual way by looking for the point of intersection of the demand and supply curves.

### 6.8.2 The Capital Market and the Firm's Investment Decision

Much of the demand for capital comes from firms. At one level, we could derive a demand for capital services in the same way as we derive the demand for labour. However, this would not capture the more fundamental problem the firm faces. The much larger problem is the firm's investment decision, since capital stock has to be put into place at one point of time for the purpose of delivering capital services over a long period into the future. So how does the firm make its investment decision? The key issue here is inter-temporal aggregation, how to add up monetary amounts (whether expenses or revenues) that accrue at different points in time. This is the issue taken up in the next section.

### 6.8.3 Discounting, Present Value and Inter-temporal Aggregation

It is clear that ₹100 today is more valuable than ₹100 one year from today, because ₹100 today can be invested and grow into more than ₹100 in a year's time. If it can realise a return of 10% in one year, then it could grow into ₹110 one year from today. These two amounts, ₹100 today and ₹110 one year from today, would then be equivalent to one another. The **Present Value** (PV) of a future amount is the amount of money today that would be equivalent to that future amount.

The PV of ₹$R$ delivered $t$ years from today, given that the rate of interest is $r$, is given by the formula

$$PV_d = \frac{R}{(1+r)^t} \tag{6.17}$$

if interest is compounded once per year (thus, this is the discrete formula for PV). Alternatively, if interest is compounded continuously, the formula would be

$$PV_c = Re^{-rt}. \tag{6.18}$$

An **Annuity** is a financial instrument that pays a fixed sum of money each period (say a year) for a fixed period of time. For example, an annuity might pay ₹$A$ every year for $n$ years starting one year from today. The *PV* of this annuity would be

$$PV_A = \frac{A}{1+r} + \frac{A}{(1+r)^2} + \frac{A}{(1+r)^3} + \cdots + \frac{A}{(1+r)^n}. \tag{6.19}$$

To find this sum, multiply both sides of (6.19) by $\frac{1}{1+r}$ to obtain

$$\frac{1}{1+r} \cdot PV_A = \frac{A}{(1+r)^2} + \frac{A}{(1+r)^3} + \cdots + \frac{A}{(1+r)^{n+1}}. \tag{6.20}$$

Subtracting (6.20) from (6.19), we obtain

$$PV_A \cdot \left[1 - \frac{1}{1+r}\right] = \frac{A}{1+r} - \frac{A}{(1+r)^{n+1}},$$

since all the other terms on the right-hand side cancel each other out. This simplifies to

$$PV_A = \frac{A}{r} \cdot \left[1 - \frac{1}{(1+r)^n}\right] \tag{6.21}$$

If $n$ is very large, we have

$$\lim_{n \to \infty} PV_A = \frac{A}{r}. \tag{6.22}$$

Equation (6.22) is a useful formula, because a firm's potential revenue stream from a particular investment may be somewhat like an annuity, in that it generates steady returns, and it may have a fairly long life, allowing us to apply the limit as in (6.22).

However, a firm's returns do not accrue in discrete lumps once a year. Rather, they accrue more or less continuously over time. To find the PV of such a continuous stream, we need to use a continuous time formula for PV. This is

$$PV_c = \int_0^n Ae^{-rt}dt.$$

Solving the integral, we obtain

$$PV_c = -\frac{A}{r}e^{-rt}|_0^n$$

which yields

$$PV_c = \frac{A}{r}\cdot\left[1 - \frac{1}{e^{rn}}\right]. \tag{6.23}$$

As $n$ becomes very large, this can be reduced to

$$\lim_{n\to\infty} PV_c = \frac{A}{r}. \tag{6.24}$$

Therefore, we obtain the same result for an infinitely lived annuity whether we use the discrete time or the continuous time formula.

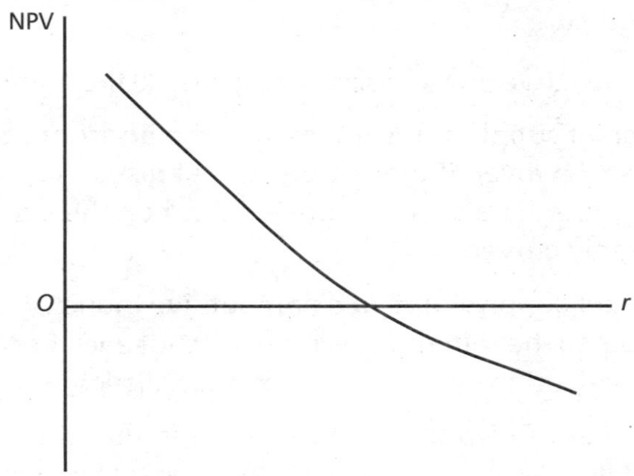


**Figure 6.27** *Net Present Value of an Investment Project*

One important consequence of this discussion is that we can see that the PV of a future revenue stream is inversely related to the rate of discount, or the rate of interest. This is generally true for more complex monetary streams as well, in which, for example, there may be negative revenues (i.e. investment expenses) in the early years, followed by many years of positive returns. The PV of such a stream is called the **Net Present Value** (NPV), since it is factoring in the costs involved in the investment. Most investment streams will have an NPV graph similar to the one in Figure 6.27, which shows the NPV as a function of the discount rate $r$. A falling NPV graph shows that the investment would have a positive NPV, and hence be a viable investment, if $r$ is sufficiently low, but a negative NPV if $r$ is too high. The intuitive reason for this is that a higher value of $r$ will reduce the relative importance of revenues that accrue further in the future. Since most investments involve incurring most of the cost early and yield most of the revenue late, a high value of $r$ reduces the importance or weight on the revenues relative to the costs and makes the investment look less attractive. Thus, more projects look attractive when the rate of interest is low and so the demand for investment capital would be high when $r$ is low. The NPV criterion for adoption of projects would say: adopt a project if NPV $> 0$, and reject it if NPV $< 0$. As the rate of interest rises, the demand for investment capital would fall, as fewer projects would seem attractive by the NPV criterion. Thus, the demand for investment capital would have the usual downward slope against its 'price,' the rate of interest.

Once we have the demand and supply curves for investment capital, the market can be analysed just like any other competitive market.

## SUMMARY

This chapter looked at the Marshallian theory of price determination in markets. The basic points were as follows:

- The market demand curve is the horizontal sum of all the individual demand curves.
- The short-run market supply curve is similarly the horizontal sum of all the individual supply curves. However, if there are external diseconomies or economies, the market supply curve will be less or more elastic than the simple horizontal sum of the individual supply curves.
- The long-run market supply curve of a competitive industry is perfectly elastic (i.e. flat) at a price equal to the minimum average cost of each firm in the market. Again, this may vary slightly in the presence of external diseconomies or economies.
- The Marshallian theory of price determination is that the equilibrium price in a competitive market is the price at which the market demand and supply curves cross. Similarly, the equilibrium quantity traded is also determined at the same point of intersection.
- The perfectly competitive equilibrium is efficient in the sense that the sum of consumer and producer surplus in the market is maximised.
- The market model can be used to analyse the impact of changes in any of the underlying causal variables on the market equilibrium.
- Similarly, the market model can be used to analyse all sorts of market interventions, such as the introduction of price floors and price ceilings. Such interventions generally lead to distortions in the market and deadweight losses (amounts by which potential surplus is lost).

- An important application of the market model is to understand the impact of commodity taxes and subsidies. These also generally lead to distortions in the market and deadweight losses.
- Commodity taxes have the same impact on the market, whether they are levied on buyers in the form of sales taxes or sellers in the form of excise taxes.
- The burden of any tax falls more on buyers, the less elastic the demand curve and the more elastic the supply curve. Similarly, the burden of a tax on sellers is greater, the more elastic the demand curve and the less elastic the supply curve.
- Input markets are different from output markets in that output markets have demand from households and supply from firms, while input markets have demand from firms and supply (largely) from households.
- The demand for inputs from firms can be explained by the marginal productivity theory which says firms use inputs up to the point where their marginal revenue product is equal to their price.
- In looking at the demand for investment capital, it is important to realise that monetary flows at different points in time need to be discounted appropriately before they can be aggregated.
- The net present value of most investment streams tends to decline as the interest rate goes up; thus, the demand for investment capital is negatively related to the interest rate.

## EXERCISES

1. Suppose the labour supply curve is

$$L_s = 160w_t - 800,$$

where $w_t$ is the hourly take-home wage rate and $L_s$ the number of millions of man-hours of work per day. Suppose also that the demand for labour is

$$L_d = 1{,}000 - 20w_c,$$

where $w_c$ is the labour cost per hour paid by the firm.

(a) What would be the equilibrium wage rate and the quantity of labour hired if $w_c = w_t$?

(b) Now suppose the government has decided to raise revenue through a payroll tax. In an attempt to spread the burden equally between workers and firms, they decide to charge workers and firms each a 10% payroll tax. That is, workers will pay 10% of their gross wage in taxes, and also firms will pay 10% of any wages they pay out. Find the new equilibrium quantity of labour hired and the (gross) wage rate.

(c) How is the burden of the tax distributed between workers and firms? What general principle does your answer illustrate? Explain clearly.

2. Current consumption of petrol is 10 million litres per day and the price is ₹100 per litre. The elasticity of demand for petrol is −0.5 and the elasticity of supply is 1.

The government decides to limit consumption by imposing rationing, with a so-called 'white market'. Under the rationing system, motorists are required to pay for petrol in the usual way, but, in addition, they must submit to the dealer a coupon for each litre purchased. The government distributes 9 million of these coupons per day, giving each motorist an equal number. Coupons not used can be bought and sold legally (and, we assume, costlessly) on the 'white market'.

(a) Draw a graph showing the original and the new market equilibria. What will be the new quantity of petrol? What price will buyers pay and what price will sellers receive?

(b) What will be the market price of the coupons?

(c) Calculate by how much consumers are better-off or worse off as a result of this change. (You can assume linearity for purposes of this calculation.)

3. The current price of widgets is ₹13.5 per unit and 75 widgets are sold per period. Econometricians have estimated that the demand curve for widgets is

$$Q_d = \frac{1{,}000}{P},$$

and the supply curve is

$$Q_s = 50P - 600.$$

These do not match the observed values of $P$ and $Q$ exactly, but are regarded as pretty good estimates.

(a) Suppose the government has found a way to reduce the marginal cost of widgets at all levels of output by ₹4. If it gave this information to the firms in the industry, what would happen to the equilibrium price and quantity?

(b) Suppose that distributing this information would cost the government ₹400. Should they distribute it? Explain clearly, drawing a diagram to show how you calculate the benefits from this information.

4. The gadget market is perfectly competitive. The demand curve for gadgets is

$$Q_d = 100 - 2P,$$

and the supply curve is

$$Q_s = 20 + 6P.$$

(a) What will be the equilibrium price and quantity of gadgets?

(b) Suppose the government imposes an excise tax of ₹4 per unit on gadgets. What will be the new (tax-inclusive) supply curve for gadgets?

(c) Using your answer to (b), find the new equilibrium quantity of gadgets. What price will buyers pay? What price will sellers receive? (*Do not use an elasticity formula to answer this question.*)

(d) How much tax revenue is collected and how is this burden divided between buyers and sellers? What is the deadweight loss due to this tax?

5. The gadget market is perfectly competitive. Currently, the price of gadgets is ₹10 and 100 gadgets are sold per period. The elasticity of demand for gadgets is −0.5 and the elasticity of supply of gadgets is 2.

(a) What will be the equilibrium price and quantity of gadgets if the government imposes a ₹1 per unit excise tax on gadgets?

(b) How much tax revenue will the government collect from this tax?

(c) Calculate the change in consumers' and producers' surplus and the excess burden of this tax. (*You may assume linearity for this part of the question.*)

6. Suppose there are 10 identical firms in an industry. The cost function for each firm is

$$C(q) = \frac{1}{2}q^2 + wq,$$

where $q$ is the firm's output of the homogenous good, and where $w$ is the wage rate of workers in the industry. Suppose further that $w = 0.9Q_s$
where $Q_s$ denotes total industry output. Suppose demand in this industry is given by

$$Q_d = 6 - p,$$

where $p$ is the price in rupees.

(a) Find the short-run industry supply curve. (*Hint: Remember that each firm takes w as fixed.*)

(b) What will be the equilibrium price and quantity in the market and how much will each firm produce?

(c) What would happen to the equilibrium price and quantity if government imposed a ₹1 per unit excise tax?

7. The monthly demand for gadgets in the country of Small is given by

$$Q_d = 5{,}000 - 100p,$$

where $Q_d$ is the market demand and $p$ is the market price. The monthly domestic supply curve of gadgets is given by

$$Q_s = 150p.$$

(a) What will be the equilibrium price of gadgets and how many will be sold each month?

(b) Suppose gadgets can be imported freely in any quantity at a price of ₹10. What will now be the equilibrium price of gadgets, how many will be consumed, how many will be produced domestically and how many will be imported?

(c) Suppose the government of Small imposes a ₹5 per unit import tax on gadgets. What will now be the equilibrium price of gadgets, how many will be consumed, how many will be produced domestically and how many will be imported?

(d) Does Small gain or lose welfare as a result of the import tax? Calculate the net welfare effect and show this in a clearly labelled diagram.

8. Because of a sharp recession, the demand for unskilled labour has fallen to

$$L_d = 80 - 10w,$$

where $w$ is the wage rate for unskilled labour. The supply of unskilled labour is

$$L_s = 10w.$$

(a) What will be the equilibrium wage rate and the level of employment if the market is free?

(b) Suppose government wants to protect labour and institutes a minimum wage of ₹5 per hour. How many workers will now be employed? What is the net welfare effect of this policy? Identify the winners and losers from this policy and find the net welfare effect on each category of economic agents. Draw a clear diagram illustrating your answer.

(c) Suppose that, instead of the minimum wage, the government offered employers a subsidy of ₹1 per hour per employee. How many workers will be employed now? Once again, identify the winners and losers from this policy and find the net welfare effect on each category of economic agents. Draw a clear diagram illustrating your answer.

9. Consider a firm which produces widgets and has the following production function:

$$q(K, L) = K^{1/4}L^{1/4},$$

where $K$ is the amount of capital used and $L$ is the amount of labour used. The unit price of each input is ₹1.

(a) Solve the firm's cost minimisation problem for a fixed level of output and find the cost function.

(b) Suppose there are 100 firms in the industry which have access to the above technology and act competitively. We are in an 'intermediate run' in which entry and exit of firms is not possible. The industry demand is

$$D(p) = \frac{1,600}{p}.$$

Find the equilibrium price $p_1$, the equilibrium firm's quantity $q_1$ and the equilibrium firm's capital $K_1$.

(c) Now consider the firm's short-run problem. In the short-run the firm is free to choose any amount of labour $L$, but cannot adjust the amount of capital $K$. Solve the short-run cost minimisation problem for a fixed level of output $q$ and a fixed level of capital $K_1$ found in part (b), and find the short-run cost function.

(d) Suppose there is an unanticipated change in the industry demand to

$$D^*(p) = 6{,}400p^{-2/3}.$$

Consider the short-run industry response to this change in demand. In the short-run, each firm can adjust the level of input $L$, but cannot adjust the level of capital which remains at the original level $K_1$. There is no entry of new firms. Find the short-run equilibrium price $p_2$ and the short-run equilibrium firm's quantity $q_2$.

(e) Consider the industry's 'intermediate-run' response to the above change in demand. In the 'intermediate-run' each firm can adjust the levels of both inputs, but there is still no entry of new firms. Find the 'intermediate-run' equilibrium price $p_3$ and the 'intermediate-run' equilibrium firm's quantity $q_3$.

CHAPTER

7

# General Equilibrium and Welfare Economics

General equilibrium analysis is the study of the whole economy as an aggregate of all the individual markets, taking into account the relationships between all the markets. We have been studying individual markets, that is, doing partial equilibrium analysis, and this is important and useful. But partial equilibrium analysis cannot properly answer two significant questions, one positive and one normative. The first question, the positive one, is: after taking into account all the market interactions, is there a set of prices, one for each market, such that each and every market is in equilibrium? This is the question of existence. The second question, the normative one, is: if there does exist a general equilibrium, is it 'good' in some sense, or would we like it to be different? This is the question of efficiency. To answer these two questions is the purpose of this chapter.

## 7.1 PARETO EFFICIENCY

**Task for this section:**

To introduce and explain the concept of Pareto efficiency, the main criterion economists use to judge whether an allocation of resources is 'efficient' or not.

Before we can begin to answer the second question, we must decide what criterion we will use to consider an equilibrium or an allocation of resources to be 'good'. There are many different proposals for what constitutes a desirable or optimal allocation of resources and proponents of each one naturally feel theirs is superior to the proposals of others. There is one criterion, however, that virtually all economists agree is a desirable property for any allocation of resources to have. This property is the Pareto criterion.

The **Pareto Criterion**, named for the Italian economist Wilfredo Pareto who first proposed it, says that an allocation of resources A is better than another allocation or economic situation B if at least one person in society prefers A to B and no one prefers B to A. In other words, A is **Pareto-superior** to B if society would choose A over B unanimously (with people who are indifferent between the two abstaining in the hypothetical vote). This criterion for ranking different allocations then gives rise to a notion for what sort of allocation is 'good': an allocation A is said to be **Pareto-efficient** if there is no other allocation that is Pareto-superior to it. Thus, if society is in the situation A, it is Pareto-efficient if no one can be made better-off without someone else being made worse off. An allocation is not Pareto-efficient if someone could be made better-off without anyone else being made worse off. If we found ourselves in a situation that was not Pareto-efficient, surely we would not want to remain there because we would like to take advantage of opportunities that are 'Pareto-improving', that is, of making everyone as well off as possible without hurting anyone else. It is these sorts of Pareto-inefficient allocations that the Pareto criterion eliminates.

It is worth looking at some examples to get a clearer picture of what exactly Pareto efficiency is. Suppose we want to divide a cake between two children, Aruna and Bala. Suppose both Aruna and Bala love cake, the more the better. In that case, every possible division of the cake is Pareto-efficient, because there is no allocation that both Aruna and Bala would agree is better than any other. Giving the entire cake to Aruna is Pareto-efficient, as is giving the entire cake to Bala, or splitting it 50-50 or in any other ratio.

Does this mean that, when people get positive marginal utility from goods (more is better), any allocation of goods is Pareto-efficient? No, not so. Suppose we want to divide between Aruna and Bala not only the cake but also a block of ice cream. And suppose both Aruna and Bala also like ice cream, the more the better. However, suppose the intensities of their preferences are different. Suppose Aruna likes cake a lot more than she likes ice cream and suppose Bala likes ice cream a lot more than he likes cake. Now not every allocation will be Pareto-efficient. For example, suppose we start with an equal division of the cake and the ice cream. Since Aruna prefers cake and Bala prefers ice cream, it should be possible to make both better-off by taking some cake from Bala and swapping it for a certain amount of ice cream from Aruna. Aruna gets better-off because the extra cake more than compensates her for the lost ice cream, and Bala gets better-off because the extra ice cream more than compensates him for the lost cake. It is this sort of welfare improvement that the use of the Pareto criterion seeks. We want to be sure that all such potential welfare improvements are actually attained.

One drawback of the Pareto criterion is that it is biased towards the status quo. The Pareto criterion requires any movement away from the existing one to be unanimous before it would endorse it. Since there are few changes that do in fact benefit everyone, or at least benefit some without adversely affecting anyone else, there are few changes that can be justified on the basis of the Pareto criterion. Nevertheless, satisfying the Pareto criterion seems to be clearly desirable and a good starting point for any discussion on the requirements of any economic allocation.

## 7.2 THE SOCIAL ALLOCATION PROBLEM

**Task for this section:**

To present a simple model that captures the essential elements of the incredibly complex problem of how resources in an economy should be allocated or used. The economy needs to decide how much of which goods should be produced, how they should be produced and then how what is produced should be distributed among consumers. The model reveals three simple criteria that should be met in order for us to be able to deem the allocation of resources 'efficient'.

We will develop a highly simplified general equilibrium model of the economy in order to illustrate the fundamental insights and ideas of this branch of micro-economics. In this model, we will assume there are just two consumers and two goods, produced by two price-taking firms. We will take the availability of resources to be fixed quantities of just two inputs, labour and capital. We will develop the algebraic version of the model first and then look at graphical interpretations of all the key results.

Suppose there are two individuals, say Aruna and Bala, who each consume two goods, $X$ and $Y$, and derive utility from them according to their utility functions

$$u^a = u^a(x^a, y^a) \tag{7.1}$$

$$u^b = u^b(x^b, y^b). \tag{7.2}$$

The goods are produced by price-taking (i.e. perfectly competitive) firms, using capital and labour according to the production functions

$$X = X(K^X, L^X) \tag{7.3}$$

$$Y = Y(K^Y, L^Y). \tag{7.4}$$

Capital and labour are traded on competitive markets and are in fixed supply, so

$$K^X + K^Y = \bar{K} \tag{7.5}$$

$$L^X + L^Y = \bar{L}. \tag{7.6}$$

The social allocation problem is to choose allocations of capital and labour $K^X, K^Y, L^X, L^Y$ which give rise to outputs $X$ and $Y$ and then to choose allocations of the goods $x^a, x^b, y^a, y^b$ among the consumers in such a way that the outcome is Pareto-efficient.

We will think of Pareto efficiency by ensuring that, whatever Bala's utility level happens to be, we must then maximise Aruna's utility level. Once we have achieved this, there would be no way to increase one person's utility level without reducing the other's and so we would have attained Pareto efficiency. Therefore, the social problem is to maximise (7.1) subject to (7.2)–(7.6) as constraints.

A note on the notation: Because of the large number of variables in this problem, it is important to be clear on the notation. The convention adopted here is that all superscripts are identifiers. For example, $x^a$ is the amount of good $X$ consumed by Aruna, and $K^Y$ is the amount of capital used in the production of $Y$. Subscripts will be used for derivatives. Thus, $u^a_x$ will be the partial derivative $\frac{\partial u^a}{\partial x^a}$ and $Y_K$ will be $\frac{\partial Y}{\partial K^Y}$.

Let us return now to the problem, to maximise Aruna's utility (7.1) subject to (7.2)–(7.6) as constraints. We will reduce all the constraints to just one by incorporating them all in the following expression:

$$u^b = u^b \left[X(K^X, L^X) - x^a, Y(\bar{K} - K^X, \bar{L} - L^X) - y^a\right]. \tag{7.7}$$

We have left four variables as unknowns: the consumption levels of Aruna, $x^a$ and $y^a$, and the input allocations to the production of X, $K^X$ and $L^X$. The fixing of the allocations $K^X$ and $L^X$ automatically implies that $(\bar{K} - K^X)$ and $(\bar{L} - L^X)$ will be the allocations for the production of Y, thanks to (7.5) and (7.6). Once the allocations of inputs to both firms are known, we know the levels of production of X and Y, thanks to (7.3) and (7.4). Then, once the consumption allocations to Aruna are fixed, $x^a$ and $y^a$, the allocations to Bala must be $x^b = X - x^a$ and $y^b = Y - y^a$ and are therefore known.

Thus, all the constraints have been accounted for in (7.7) and the problem has been simplified to

$$\textit{Maximise} \qquad u^a = u^a\left(x^a, y^a\right)$$

$$\textit{subject to} \qquad u^b = u^b \left[X(K^X, L^X) - x^a, Y(\bar{K} - K^X, \bar{L} - L^X) - y^a\right].$$

The Lagrangian for this problem is

$$\mathcal{L} = u^a\left(x^a, y^a\right) + \lambda \left\{u^b - u^b \left[X(K^X, L^X) - x^a, Y(\bar{K} - K^X, \bar{L} - L^X) - y^a\right]\right\}.$$

The first-order conditions for a maximum are

$$\frac{\partial \mathcal{L}}{\partial x^a} = u^a_x + \lambda u^b_x = 0 \tag{7.8}$$

$$\frac{\partial \mathcal{L}}{\partial y^a} = u^a_y + \lambda u^b_y = 0 \tag{7.9}$$

$$\frac{\partial \mathcal{L}}{\partial K^X} = -\lambda \left[u^b_x X_K - u^b_y Y_K\right] = 0 \tag{7.10}$$

$$\frac{\partial \mathcal{L}}{\partial L^X} = -\lambda \left[ u_x^b X_L - u_y^b Y_L \right] = 0 \tag{7.11}$$

$$\frac{\partial \mathcal{L}}{\partial \lambda} = u^b - u^b \left[ X(K^X, L^X) - x^a, Y(\bar{K} - K^X, \bar{L} - L^X) - y^a \right] = 0. \tag{7.12}$$

If we rearrange (7.8) and (7.9) and then divide (7.9) by (7.8), we obtain

$$\frac{u_x^a}{u_y^a} = \frac{u_x^b}{u_y^b}. \tag{7.13}$$

The left-hand side of (7.13) is Aruna's marginal rate of substitution (MRS), the absolute value of the slope of her indifference curve, and the right-hand side is the corresponding MRS for Bala. Equation (7.13) therefore says that, for the allocation to be Pareto-efficient, one condition that must hold is that the MRSs of the consumers must be equal. This is called the **condition for efficiency in consumption**.

Equation (7.10) can be manipulated to yield the condition

$$\frac{u_x^b}{u_y^b} = \frac{Y_K}{X_K}, \tag{7.14}$$

and (7.11) yields

$$\frac{u_x^b}{u_y^b} = \frac{Y_L}{X_L}. \tag{7.15}$$

Putting (7.14) and (7.15) together, we obtain the condition

$$\frac{Y_K}{Y_L} = \frac{X_K}{X_L}. \tag{7.16}$$

The left-hand side of (7.16) is the marginal rate of technical substitution (MRTS) in the production of $Y$, which is the absolute value of the slope of the $Y$-isoquant. The right-hand side of (7.16) is the corresponding MRTS for $X$. The condition (7.16) therefore says that, for the allocation to be Pareto-efficient, another condition that must be satisfied is that the MRTSs in the production of different goods must be equal. This is called the **condition for efficiency in production**.

Finally, (7.14) and (7.15) are important conditions that provide a bridge between the production and consumption sides of the economy. The left-hand side of (7.14) is Bala's MRS (which would be equal to Aruna's MRS if consumption is efficient) and the right-hand side can (and will) be shown to be equal to the marginal rate of transformation (MRT), a measure of the rate at which $X$ can be transformed to $Y$ in production through the reallocation of inputs. Thus, (7.14) says that, for the allocation to be Pareto-efficient, it must be the case that the rate at which consumers are willing to trade $X$ for $Y$ (the MRS) must be equal to the rate at which producers can transform $X$ to $Y$ through production (the MRT). This is called the **condition for efficiency in product-mix**.

We will now look at each of these three conditions in detail in order to better understand their meaning and why they are required for the allocation of resources to be Pareto-efficient.

# 7.3 EFFICIENCY IN CONSUMPTION

**Task for this section:**

To examine in some depth the condition that must be satisfied in order that the distribution of goods amongst consumers can be deemed 'efficient'. The section explains what it means to be efficient in consumption and looks at how perfectly competitive markets ensure that consumption efficiency is attained.

We had briefly discussed earlier the possibility that not all allocations of two goods between two people, both of whom like both goods (i.e. have positive marginal utility from each good), need be Pareto-efficient. Even though Aruna and Bala might both like cake and ice cream, only certain allocations of these goods between them will be Pareto-efficient. In fact, it will turn out that very few allocations are actually Pareto-efficient, as we have seen that the condition these Pareto-efficient allocations must satisfy is (7.13), that the slopes of the indifference curves for both consumers must be equal. To see why exactly this is the case, we will use the device of the Edgeworth box diagram.

Suppose we need to decide on the allocation of fixed quantities of two goods $X$ and $Y$ (they could be cake and ice cream) between two consumers, Aruna and Bala. Suppose also that the goods are in fixed supply, $\bar{X}$ and $\bar{Y}$. The Edgeworth box is a rectangle drawn with dimensions $\bar{X}$ and $\bar{Y}$. If, for example, $\bar{X} = 100$ and $\bar{Y} = 60$, the Edgeworth box would be drawn with the horizontal side of the rectangle measuring 100 units of $X$ and the vertical side of the rectangle measuring 60 units of $Y$ (see Figure 7.1). The great feature of the box is that, with the dimensions representing the quantities of the goods, each point in the box represents an allocation of the goods between the two consumers and any allocation can be represented by a unique point in the box. For example, suppose the allocation is $x^a = 60, y^a = 10, x^b = 40, y^b = 50$. This allocation is fully represented by the point $E$ in the box. We measure Aruna's allocation normally from the origin $O^a$, giving us the point $E$ with coordinates (60, 10). But this point also denotes Bala's allocation, *measured from the 'origin' $O^b$ at the top right-hand corner*. Think of that corner as Bala's origin. Then $E$ measures his allocation; it is just upside down! You can see this clearly if you turn this page upside down and look at $E$ relative to the origin $O^b$; it has the coordinates (40, 50) which are exactly the quantities of the two goods in Bala's allocation. Since the dimensions of the box are $\bar{X}$ and $\bar{Y}$, any point in the box then represents a division of the goods between Aruna and Bala.

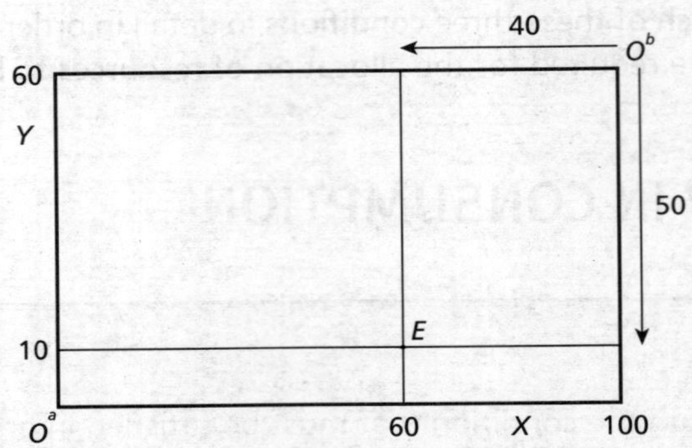


**Figure 7.1** *The Edgeworth Box*

### 7.3.1 Efficiency in Consumption and the Consumers' Contract Curve

Now suppose we want to use the box to explore the issue of Pareto efficiency. Let us start with the allocation $E$ and see if it is Pareto-efficient. $E$ is Pareto-efficient if, given Bala's utility level at $E$, Aruna's utility is maximised at $E$. How can we test if this is true? What we do is to draw Bala's indifference curve through $E$, which is the heavy curve labelled $u_0^b$ in Figure 7.2. Remember that Bala's origin is at $O^b$, so his indifference curve will look upside down in the box. If you turn this page upside down, you will see that the curve $u_0^b$ looks just like a normal indifference curve with respect to the origin at $O^b$. Now, if we hold Bala's utility constant at $u_0^b$ and ask where Aruna's utility is maximised subject to $u_0 = u_0^b$, we would need to draw Aruna's indifference map on the graph (the lightly drawn curves) and look for the highest one we can reach while staying on $u_0^b$. This will occur at the point $C$, where Aruna's indifference curve $u_1^a$ is tangent to $u_0^b$. Clearly, this is the highest utility level Aruna can attain while ensuring that Bala's utility stays at $u_0^b$.

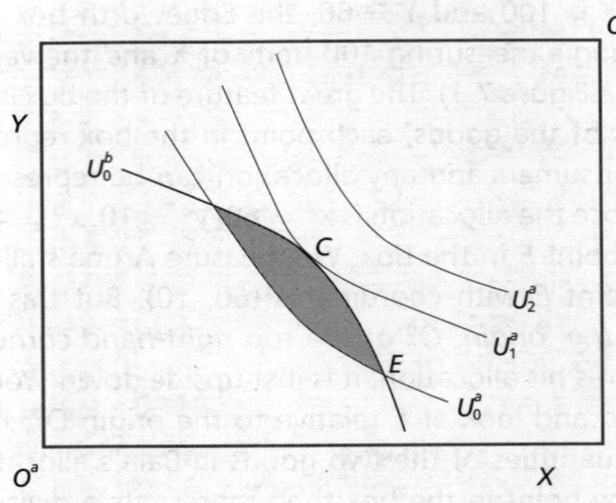


**Figure 7.2** *Efficiency in Consumption*

The allocation represented by point *C* in Figure 7.2 is Pareto-efficient since it is impossible to increase one person's utility without reducing the other's. However, we have shown that point *E* is not Pareto-efficient, since it *is* possible to increase one person's utility without reducing the other's; specifically, at *C*, Bala is no worse off and Aruna is better-off (Aruna is on utility level $u_0^a$ at E and $u_1^a$ at *C*). Thus the allocation *C* is Pareto-superior to *E*. In fact, all the allocations in the shaded area (between the indifference curves $u_0^b$ and $u_0^a$) are Pareto-superior to *E* since at all these points, one or both of the consumers is better-off than at *E* and no one is ever worse off. Whenever the indifference curves cross at a given allocation, as they do at *E*, they create an area such as the shaded one in the figure that consists of allocations that are Pareto-superior to the one at the crossing point. Only when the indifference curves are tangent to one another, as they are at *C*, is there no 'shaded' area of Pareto-superior allocations. And note that this is exactly the condition represented by (7.13), our condition for efficiency in consumption: that the MRSs (i.e. slopes of the indifference curves) had to be equal.

Of course, *C* is not the only Pareto-efficient allocation in this situation. If we draw both sets of indifference curves, we will find many points of tangency, one for each indifference curve for each consumer. The origins $O^a$ and $O^b$ will also be Pareto-efficient, as long as the marginal utilities for both goods are positive for both consumers. The line connecting all the Pareto-efficient allocations, which looks roughly like a diagonal in Figure 7.3, is called the **consumers' contract curve**. For every possible utility level for Bala, it shows where Aruna's utility would be maximised. For the allocation of consumption goods to be Pareto-efficient, it must lie somewhere on the consumers' contract curve.

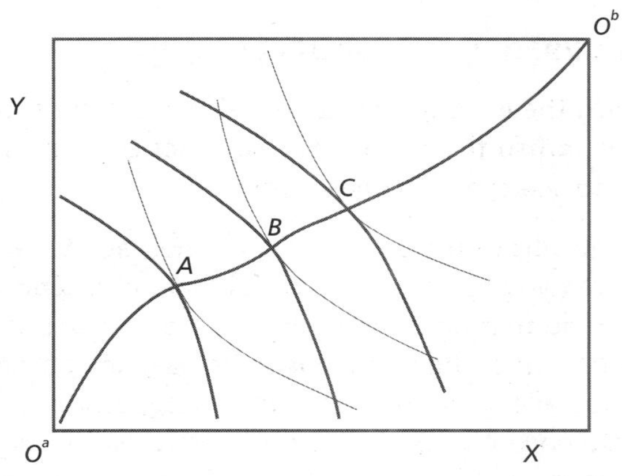


**Figure 7.3** *The Consumers' Contract Curve*

Closely related to the consumers' contract curve is the **utility possibilities frontier (UPF)** (Figure 7.4). This takes every point on the consumers' contract curve and plots the utility levels at that point on a graph where $u^a$ is measured on the horizontal axis and $u^b$ is measured on the vertical. The line joining all these points is the UPF. For every possible utility level for Bala,

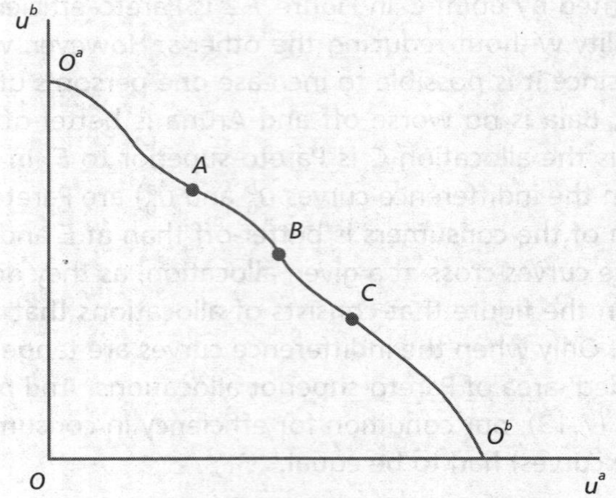


**Figure 7.4** *The Utility Possibilities Frontier*

it tells us what Aruna's maximum utility would be, and vice versa. Because the utility levels are ordinal, we cannot say much about the shape of the UPF other than that it is downward-sloping. What we can say is that, for consumption to be Pareto-efficient, the consumers should be on the UPF, which is the same as saying they must be on the consumers' contract curve. Points in the Edgeworth box that are off the consumers' contract curve correspond to points in the interior of the UPF, and these are of course not Pareto-efficient.

## 7.3.2 Other Types of Consumers' Contract Curves

There are situations in which the indifference curves of the two consumers may not have interior tangencies as in Figure 7.3 and so the consumers' contract curve may look different. It is worth looking at some examples to see the principles involved.

An extreme example comes from the old nursery rhyme: *Jack Sprat could eat no fat, his wife could eat no lean*. If there are two goods, 'lean' and 'fat', and Jack cannot consume fat and his wife cannot consume lean, their indifference maps will be quite unusual. We assume free disposal, so Jack's utility is dependent only upon how much lean he has, any fat he has will be thrown away. Thus, his indifference curves will be vertical straight lines, assuming 'lean' is measured on the horizontal axis, with indifference curves to the right representing higher levels of utility, since they have more lean (see Figure 7.5). Similarly, Jack's wife's indifference curves will be horizontal straight lines, with indifference curves closer to Jack's origin $O^j$ representing higher levels of utility. Obviously, these indifference curves never have any points of tangency. So which allocations are Pareto-efficient? For any indifference curve of Jack's wife, say $u_0^b$, Jack's utility is maximised on the right-hand side border, and for any indifference curve of Jack's, say $u_2^a$ or the right-hand side border (which is also an indifference curve for Jack), the wife's utility is maximised along the lower border. Thus, there is only one Pareto-efficient allocation, the point *A* at the lower right corner.

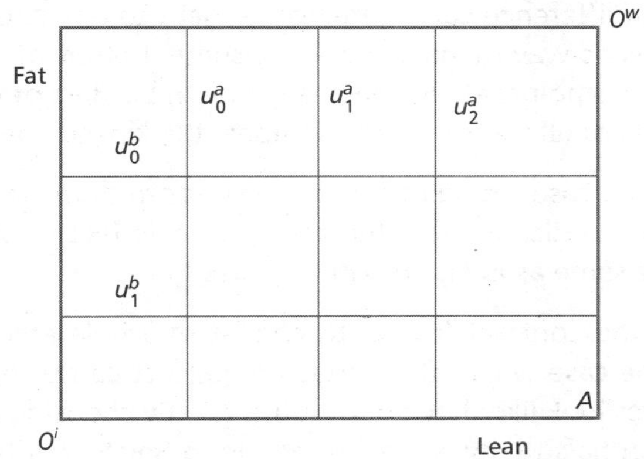


**Figure 7.5** *Contract 'Curve' for Jack Sprat and His Wife*

At this point, Jack has all the lean and his wife has all the fat, and a little reflection will confirm that that is the only efficient allocation of the goods in this case.

Consider another example, which is a slight variation of the previous one but gets quite a different result. Suppose Aruna's indifference curves are curved, but are all very steep and so almost vertical like Jack's indifference curves. They are the lightly drawn indifference curves in Figure 7.6. And suppose Bala's indifference curves are all rather flat, the heavy curves in Figure 7.6. As these curves are not very different from the straight line indifference curves of Jack Sprat and his wife, they similarly do not have any interior tangencies. So the Pareto-efficient points are going to be on the corners. To find the efficient points, we need to ask what is the highest utility level Aruna can reach for any given utility level for Bala? For example, if we fix Bala's utility level at $u_0^b$, we can see from Figure 7.6 that the highest utility level Aruna can reach is $u_2^a$, which

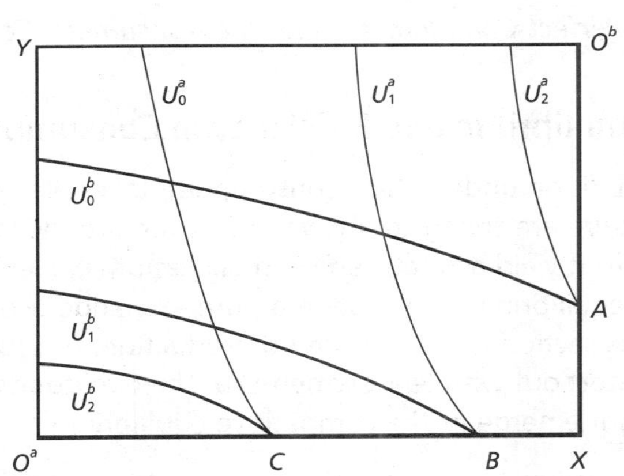


**Figure 7.6** *Corner Solutions and the Consumers' Contract Curve*

meets $u_0^b$ at $A$. Here the indifference curves are not tangent to one another, but the allocation is Pareto-efficient, as there is no way to make either consumer better-off without hurting the other. Similarly, $B$ and $C$ and all the points along the heavy-drawn borders of the box are efficient. Thus the contract curve consists of all these corner solutions, the kinked line $O^aCBAO^b$.

A simple extension of this case would be where one or both of the indifference maps consisted of linear indifference curves, indicating that the goods were perfect substitutes. The contract curve in that case would be the same as in Figure 7.6.

It is also possible for the contract 'curve' to consist of whole areas of the Edgeworth box. Consider, for example, the case where the goods are perfect complements for both consumers and the indifference curves look like they do in Figure 7.7. By choosing any indifference curve for Bala and asking where Aruna's utility is maximised along Bala's indifference curve, we see that all the allocations in the shaded area are efficient and therefore the shaded area constitutes the contract 'curve' in this case.

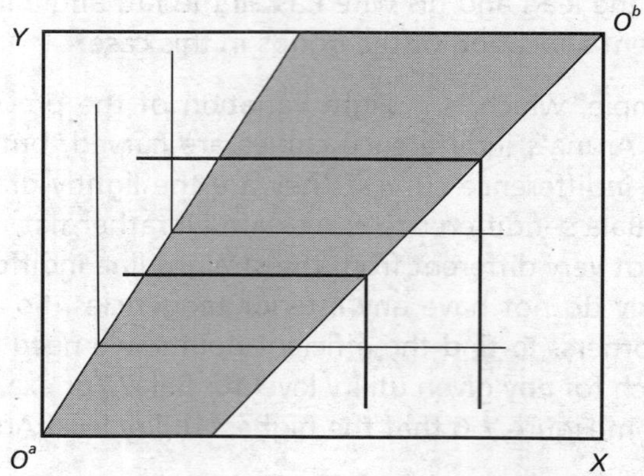


**Figure 7.7** *Perfect Complements and the Consumers' Contract Curve*

## 7.3.3 Competitive Equilibrium and Efficiency in Consumption

We have looked at the condition under which consumption takes place efficiently in an economy. The underlying questions we are trying to answer, however, are: does there exist a competitive equilibrium and, if so, does it yield a Pareto-efficient allocation? So let us turn to an examination of what the competitive equilibrium might be in a pure exchange economy such as the one we have been studying in this section (i.e. one with no production; production will be added later). Suppose Aruna and Bala start out with 'endowments' of the two goods, represented by the point $E$ in Figure 7.1. What might emerge as the competitive equilibrium in this case?

To answer this question, we resort to a fictitious process that mimics what a market might do. This fictitious process is named for Leon Walras, a French economist who first proposed it, and is called the Walrasian process of tâtonnement. Imagine a market-maker, whom we will call the Walrasian auctioneer, who announces prices of the two goods and then asks each consumer to tell him how much of each good they would like to buy or sell at those prices. The consumers' desired trades must 'balance' (i.e. be of equal value). For example, if Aruna wants to buy a certain amount of $Y$, she must sell an amount of $X$ of equal value in order to finance her purchase. The auctioneer looks at the trade 'offers' from each consumer, and if they are mirror images of one another (i.e. if the amount of $Y$ Aruna wants to buy exactly matches the amount of $Y$ Bala wants to sell), the auctioneer announces an equilibrium and trading can proceed at the equilibrium prices. If the trade offers do not match, the auctioneer looks to see for which good there is an excess demand and he raises the relative price of that good. He then asks for new trade offers at the new prices and continues the process until the trade offers match and equilibrium is reached. This process mimics a market, because in real markets, prices rise when there is excess demand and prices fall when there is excess supply. This is exactly what the Walrasian auctioneer does.

So the first question to ask of the tâtonnement process is, will there be a set of prices at which the trade offers match, that is, does there exist an equilibrium? And the second question is, if there is an equilibrium, will the allocation it results in be Pareto-efficient? Let us see how we might answer these questions.

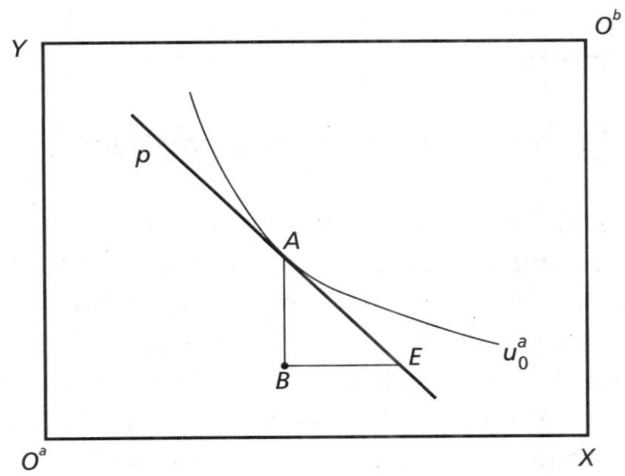


**Figure 7.8** *A Trade Offer*

Figure 7.8 shows one price ratio (the slope of the line $p$) and one trade offer by Aruna. She starts at her endowment point $E$, and the auctioneer announces prices whose ratio is the absolute value of the slope of the line marked $p$ in the figure, which is Aruna's budget constraint at the announced prices. Note that the absolute values of the prices do not matter, only the relative prices do. A doubling of all prices would leave Aruna's budget constraint exactly where it is, since her endowment doubles in value at the same time as the cost of goods doubles. We could, therefore, fix $p_y$ at 1 (we would then call $Y$ the 'numeraire' good) and just vary $p_x$ for purposes of relative price adjustment. Now, faced with the budget constraint $p$, Aruna would like to consume at point *A*, where her indifference curve $u_0^a$ is tangent to her budget constraint. Since her starting point is her endowment *E*, the triangle *ABE* could be called her "trade triangle" or 'trade offer'. *BE* is the amount of X she wants to sell, and *BA* is the amount of *Y* she wants to buy. The point *A* lies on Aruna's offer curve, a concept we had originally seen and derived in Chapter 4. The offer curve shows all of Aruna's desired consumption points at different price ratios, starting from the endowment point *E*. It has the property that every point on it, such as *A*, is the chosen bundle when the prices are given by the line (like *AE*) connecting the bundle to the endowment point *E*. The offer curve looks like the lightly drawn curve *ECA* in Figure 7.9.

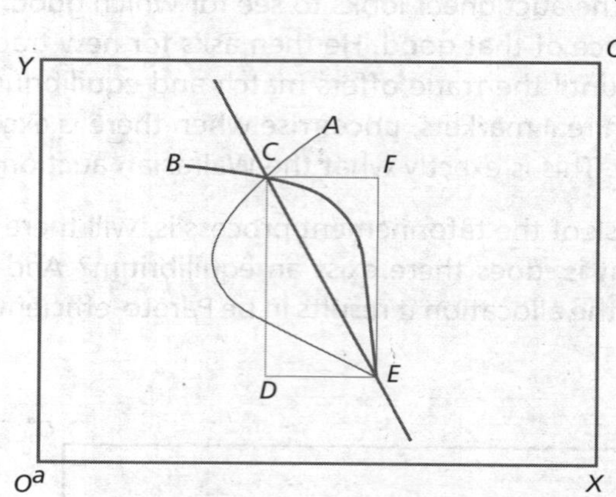


**Figure 7.9** *Competitive Equilibrium and Trade Triangles*

If we draw both Aruna's and Bala's offer curves on the same graph, we see that their point of intersection is a competitive equilibrium. The argument is illustrated in Figure 7.9. The lightly drawn curved line *ECA* is Aruna's offer curve and the heavy curved line *ECB* is Bala's offer curve. Their point of intersection *C* is a competitive equilibrium, with relative prices given by the slope of the line *CE*. We can see why this is so by looking at the trade triangles. If *C* is Aruna's chosen bundle when she faces the prices represented by the slope of the line *CE*, her trade triangle is *CDE*, meaning she wants to sell *ED* amount of *X* in exchange for *DC* amount of *Y*. Now if *C* is also Bala's chosen bundle when he faces the prices represented by the slope of the line *CE* (remember *C* is on his offer curve too), then his trade triangle is *CFE*. He wants to sell *EF* amount of *Y* in exchange for being able to buy *FC* amount of *X*. It is obvious from the geometry of the construction that those two trade triangles are mirror images of one another: $DE = CF$ and $CD = FE$. Therefore, *C* is a competitive equilibrium with the prices represented by the slope of the line *CE*. Thus, a competitive equilibrium exists as long as the offer curves intersect.

What about the efficiency of this competitive equilibrium? We can show that it is efficient. Note that *C* is Aruna's choice when she faces the budget constraint *CE*. That means she must have an indifference curve (marked $u_0^a$ in Figure 7.10) tangent to the line *CE* at the point *C*. Similarly, *C* is Bala's chosen bundle when he faces the budget constraint *CE*, which means he must have an indifference curve (marked $u_0^b$ in Figure 7.10) tangent to *CE* at *C*. But if both indifference curves are tangent to *CE* at *C*, they must have the same slope at *C* and be tangent to each other. And that means that the point *C* is a Pareto-efficient allocation. Thus the competitive equilibrium is Pareto-efficient.

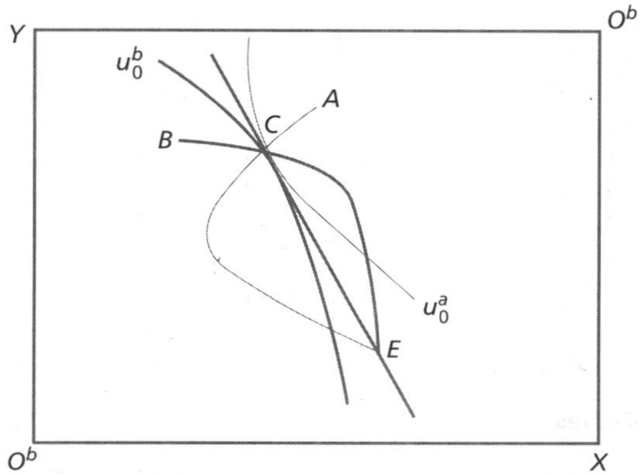


**Figure 7.10** *The Pareto Efficiency of the Competitive Equilibrium*

What if the two offer curves do not intersect at a point such as *C*? It is possible that the offer curves do not intersect in the interior of the Edgeworth box, but they would then intersect on the border somewhere. For example, suppose the situation is like the one depicted in panel (a) of Figure 7.11. Suppose the thin curved line *ECA* is Aruna's offer curve. Note that her offer curve can go outside the box as along the segment *CA*, she still has positive amounts of both goods on her offer curve. Now suppose the heavy curved line *EB* is Bala's offer curve, which does not intersect Aruna's offer curve in the interior of the box. Bala's offer curve cannot continue out of the box towards point *A* because that would involve negative amounts of good *Y* on his offer curve, which is clearly an impossibility. Rather, Bala's offer curve will continue from *B* along the border of the box along the segment *BCD*.

Panel (b) of Figure 7.11 shows what is going on in Bala's choice space. In this panel, Bala's origin $O^b$ is at bottom left as in a conventional diagram. *E* is his endowment point and his indifference curves are the heavy curved lines. They must be fairly steep in order to be consistent with the shape of his offer curve in panel (a). One indifference curve is tangent to the price line *EB* at *B* and that is why point *B* is on his offer curve. If the relative price of X falls further, the price ratio becomes too flat for an interior tangency to occur. Rather, Bala will choose at the corner, at points such as *C*, where an indifference curve is not tangent to the price line but is nevertheless the highest indifference curve he can attain. The situation is similar to the one we saw in Figure 7.6, with choices lying along the boundary of the box. Thus, Bala's offer curve also lies on the boundary of the box, along the line segment *BCD*. Thus the two offer curves intersect at *C* and *CE* will be the equilibrium price ratio. And although the two indifference curves at *C* will not be tangent to one

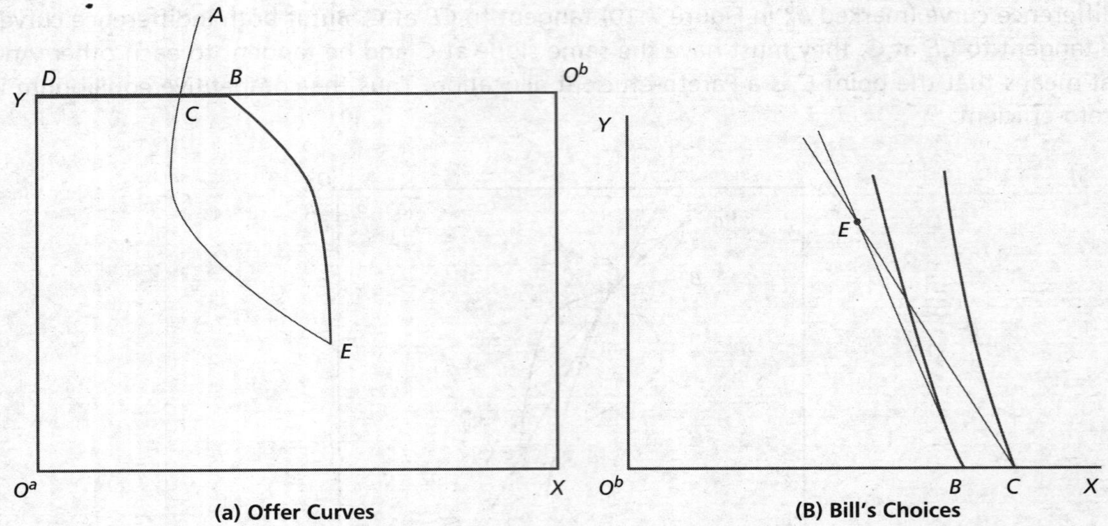


**Figure 7.11** *Offer Curves Intersecting on the Boundary of the Edgeworth Box*

another, point *C* will nevertheless be on the contract curve, which lies along the boundary of the box here, as it did in Figure 7.6. Thus, the competitive equilibrium is efficient again.

What if the offer curves intersect multiple times? This is possible, as is illustrated in Figure 7.12, where there are three points of intersection, *A*, *B* and *C*. There are therefore three equilibrium price ratios, *EA*, *EB* and *EC* (not drawn on the figure to avoid cluttering it up), and which one emerges may be a matter of history or circumstance. These three equilibria are not all alike, however. While the equilibria at *A* and *C* are **stable**, the equilibrium at *B* is **unstable**. Let us see what this means.

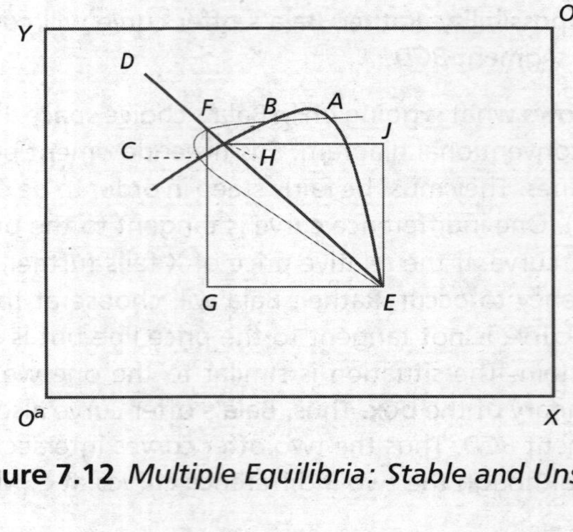


**Figure 7.12** *Multiple Equilibria: Stable and Unstable*

Suppose the price ratio were represented by the line *ED*. Here, the relative price of *X* is higher than it would be with the prices *EC* (since the line *EC* would be flatter), but lower than it would be with the prices *EB*. Now the lightly drawn offer curve *ECFBA* is Aruna's and the heavy curve *EABHC* is Bala's. So, if the prices were at *ED*, Aruna's chosen bundle would be *F* and Bala's choice would be *H*. In other words, at the prices *ED*, Aruna's trade triangle would be *FGE* and Bala's trade triangle would be *HJE*. Thus, Aruna would offer *GE* amount of *X* for sale, while Bala would want to buy HJ of *X*. Note that *GE*>*HJ*. In other words, the amount of *X* that Aruna would offer for sale is greater than the amount of *X* Bala would want to buy; there would be an excess supply of *X*. The auctioneer, or the market, would cause the relative price of *X* to fall, making the price line flatter and closer to *EC*. Eventually, the price ratio would settle at *EC*, the equilibrium price ratio. If the prices had started at *EC* and then the relative price of *X* had somehow risen (so that the prices moved slightly towards *ED*), market forces would cause the relative price of *X* to fall and therefore push the prices back to *EC*. This is the sense in which the equilibrium at *C* is stable: a small deviation away from the equilibrium brings up forces that push prices back to the equilibrium.

The situation is much like that of a marble sitting at the bottom of a hemi-spherical bowl. If you move the marble away from the bottom and then let it go, it will roll back down to the bottom. It's position there is stable. But if the bowl were upside down and you managed to perch the marble at the top of the upended bowl, it might be at rest (in equilibrium) there, but this position would be unstable. If you pushed the marble away slightly from its perch, it would roll completely off the bowl. This is the situation at *B*. The price ratio *EB* is an equilibrium, but if the relative price of *X* fell slightly towards *ED*, forces would come into play that would cause the relative price of *X* to continue to fall and for relative prices to eventually settle at *EC*. The equilibrium at *B* is unstable.

A similar argument holds for the equilibrium at *A*, which is stable and for prices between *EB* and *EA*. Note that the relative price of *X* is higher at *A* than it is at *B*. If the price ratio were between *EB* and *EA*, Aruna's trade triangle would be smaller than Bala's. Therefore, there would be excess demand for *X* and the relative price of X would rise. In other words, the prices would move towards *EA*. Once again, therefore, *B* is unstable in that even a small increase in the relative price of *X* from *EB* would engender forces that would keep raising the relative price of *X*, with prices eventually settling at *EA*. The equilibrium at *A* is stable.

## 7.4 WALRAS'S LAW

**Task for this section:**

To explain Walras's Law, an important result in general equilibrium theory that shows why a competitive equilibrium can be described only by *relative* commodity prices, the *absolute* level of prices being arbitrary.

In our discussion, we have implicitly been using an important result known as **Walras's Law**, which states that the sum of the values of excess demands for all goods must always be zero, regardless of the prices. Note that this is not a result about equilibria. Rather, it is a generalisation (or aggregation) of the fact that consumers must always satisfy their budget constraints.

In our example, if we represent desired changes in consumption (i.e. trade offers) by the symbol $\Delta$, with a positive $\Delta$ indicating a desire to buy more of the good and a negative $\Delta$ indicating a wish to sell some of the good, it follows from Aruna's budget constraint that

$$p_x \Delta x^a + p_y \Delta y^a = 0. \tag{7.17}$$

That is, if Aruna wants to sell some $X$ ($\Delta x^a < 0$) and buy some $Y$ ($\Delta y^a > 0$), (7.17) says that the value of what she wants to sell must equal the value of what she wants to buy. Otherwise, she would no longer be on her budget constraint. Similarly, for Bala, it must be the case that

$$p_x \Delta x^b + p_y \Delta y^b = 0. \tag{7.18}$$

If we now add (7.17) and (7.18), we obtain the sum of the values of the excess demands for the goods:

$$p_x(\Delta x^a + \Delta x^b) + p_y(\Delta y^a + \Delta y^b) = 0. \tag{7.19}$$

Equation (7.19) is Walras's Law. It says the sum of the values of the excess demands must be zero. Note that we did not specify anything about the prices needing to be equilibrium prices; the law holds at any prices and is really an adding up identity.

It may be helpful to work through a numerical example to see Walras's Law in action. Suppose $p_x = 2$ and $p_y = 1$ and suppose that, at these prices, Aruna wants to sell 10 units of $X$ and buy 20 units of $Y$, while Bala wants to buy 15 units of $X$ and sell 30 units of $Y$. So (7.17), Aruna's constraint, becomes

$$2(-10) + 1(20) = 0,$$

and (7.18), Bala's constraint, becomes

$$2(15) + 1(-30) = 0.$$

If we now look at the excess demands, the excess demand for $X$, say $XD^x$, is

$$XD^x = \Delta x^a + \Delta x^b = -10 + 15 = 5$$

and its value is $p_x XD^x = 2(5) = 10$. The excess demand for $Y$ will be

$$XD^y = \Delta y^a + \Delta y^b = 20 - 30 = -10$$

and its value will be $p_y XD^y = 1(-10) = -10$. Walras's Law says that the sum of the values of the excess demands must be zero, and we can confirm this:

$$p_x XD^x + p_y XD^y = 10 - 10 = 0.$$

The importance of this result is that, if there are $n$ goods and therefore $n$ excess demand equations, only $(n - 1)$ of these equations can be independent, since Walras's Law would put a restriction on the $n$-th equation once the first $(n - 1)$ are known. If we are solving for prices that will bring about equilibrium with all excess demands driven to zero, we would be able to solve only for $(n - 1)$ prices, since we would have only $(n - 1)$ independent equations. Thus, in solving for the competitive equilibrium, we can solve only for relative prices, not absolute prices. One price will have to be a **numeraire** or yardstick against which all other prices can be stated.

## 7.5 EFFICIENCY IN PRODUCTION

**Task for this section:**

To examine in some depth the condition that must be satisfied in order that the allocation of inputs among producers can be deemed 'efficient'. The section explains what it means to be efficient in production and looks at how perfectly competitive markets ensure that production efficiency is attained.

The analysis of the condition for efficiency in production follows closely the analysis of the condition for efficiency in consumption. Instead of the fixed quantities of the goods $X$ and $Y$ that need to be allocated among the consumers, we have the fixed quantities of inputs, capital and labour, that need to be allocated among the producers. The production functions replace the utility functions and the analysis then proceeds as before. Efficiency in production can then also be illustrated in two ways: through the producers' contract curve in the producers' Edgeworth box (corresponding to the consumers' contract curve in the consumers' Edgeworth box) and through the production possibilities frontier (PPF) (corresponding to the UPF).

The producers' Edgeworth box is just like the consumers' Edgeworth box, with the quantities of inputs, labour and capital, measured along its sides. The box is drawn with dimensions equal to the quantities of the two inputs available, $\bar{L}$ and $\bar{K}$, and then the isoquant maps are drawn in, with the isoquant map for $X$ right-side up (the lightly drawn curves in Figure 7.13) and the isoquant map for $Y$ drawn upside down with an orientation to the top right corner as the $Y$-origin (the heavy-drawn curves in the figure). We then look for the points of tangency of the isoquants, such as points $A$, $B$ and $C$ in Figure 7.13, in order to derive the producers' contract curve, the line connecting all the efficient points in the Edgeworth box. The tangency of the isoquants, equating of the MRTSs, is exactly what (7.16) required for efficiency in production.

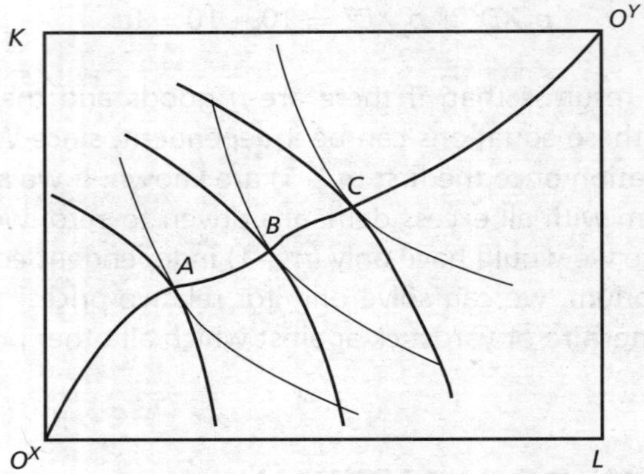


**Figure 7.13** *The Producers' Edgeworth Box*

In almost all respects then, the analysis of efficiency in production follows that for efficiency in consumption. One minor difference is that, in our pure exchange model, the consumers start out with endowments of the two goods, presumably on the basis of their ownership of productive assets, including their labour. Here there is no presumed pre-ownership of inputs by firms. Rather, inputs are in fixed supply, owned perhaps by households, and trade on competitive markets. Input prices adjust in order to ensure that all inputs are utilised. Firms take the input prices as given as they make their production decisions. Because all firms face the same input prices (because input markets are perfectly competitive), and because each firm sets its MRTS equal to the ratio of input prices in its attempt to minimise cost, the MRTS's of the different firms will be equal to one another. Thus the condition for efficiency in production, (7.16), will be satisfied by the competitive equilibrium and production will be efficient.

Turning to the PPF, this is analogous to the UPF, but is different in one important respect. While utility is ordinal, and therefore the UPF cannot have a more definite shape than being downward-sloping, production is cardinal (i.e. the level of production can be measured in an absolute sense) and therefore the PPF may have a specific shape. Finding the PPF follows the usual procedure, solving the problem to

$$\text{Maximise} \quad Y = Y(K^Y, L^Y)$$

$$\text{subject to} \quad X(K^X, L^X) = X$$

$$K^X + K^Y = \bar{K}$$

$$L^X + L^Y = \bar{L}.$$

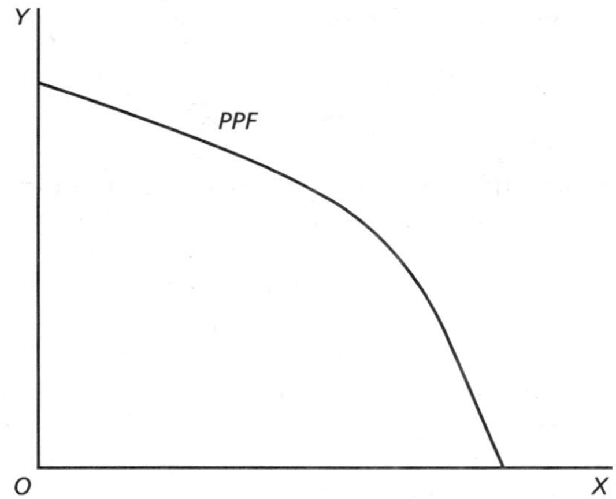


**Figure 7.14** *The Production Possibilities Frontier*

That is, for any given level of output for $X$, the output of $Y$ must be maximised, where input use is constrained to the levels of inputs available. The first-order conditions for this problem will again give rise to (7.16), the condition for efficiency in production, and the final solution will yield $Y$ in terms of $X$, the equation of the PPF, often drawn as in Figure 7.14. Efficiency in production requires the economy to be on the PPF, and this will be achieved as long as the inputs are fully employed and (7.16) is satisfied.

## 7.6 EFFICIENCY IN PRODUCT-MIX

**Task for this section:**

To study the condition that must be satisfied in order that the economy produces the right mix of goods, that is, the condition that connects producers with consumers to ensure that producers produce those goods that consumers actually want. Further, the section looks at how competitive markets lead to this required condition being satisfied.

We have looked at the conditions for efficiency in consumption and efficiency in production and have seen illustrative arguments why perfectly competitive equilibria satisfy these conditions. The remaining condition, for efficiency in product-mix, seeks to bridge the other two, to show that the system produces the 'right' mix of goods, namely the mix of goods that consumers actually want. The condition for this is (7.14), that the MRS of each of the consumers should equal the ratio of marginal products for each of the factors of production:

$$\frac{u_x^a}{u_y^a} = \frac{u_x^b}{u_y^b} = \frac{Y_K}{X_K} = \frac{Y_L}{X_L}. \tag{7.20}$$

Before we can fully understand this condition, it is useful to reinterpret the ratios of marginal products. We know that, along the PPF, the total quantities of capital and labour, $\bar{K}$ and $\bar{L}$, are fixed. That is,

$$K^X + K^Y = \bar{K},$$

and similarly for labour. That means that, as we move along the PPF and adjust the allocation of capital between the two outputs, we must have

$$dK^X + dK^Y = 0, \tag{7.21}$$

and similarly for changes in the allocation of labour. Now

$$X_K = \frac{dX}{dK^X} \quad \text{and} \quad Y_K = \frac{dY}{dK^Y}.$$

Therefore,

$$dK^X = \frac{dX}{X_K} \quad \text{and} \quad dK^Y = \frac{dY}{Y_K}.$$

Substituting in (7.21), we obtain

$$\frac{dX}{X_K} + \frac{dY}{Y_K} = 0,$$

which can be rearranged as

$$\frac{dY}{dX} = -\frac{Y_K}{X_K}. \tag{7.22}$$

This is the slope of the PPF. By a similar process of reasoning on labour, we can show that

$$\frac{dY}{dX} = -\frac{Y_L}{X_L}. \tag{7.23}$$

The MRT is defined as the absolute value of the slope of the PPF; it shows the rate at which $X$ can be transformed to Y along the PPF by the optimal reallocation of the inputs. Equations (7.22) and (7.23) show that the MRT is equal to the ratio of the marginal products of capital and labour in the two production processes. If we now look at (7.20), the condition for efficiency in product-mix, we see that it can be rewritten as

$$\frac{u_x^a}{u_y^a} = \frac{u_x^b}{u_y^b} = -\frac{dY}{dX}\Big|_{PPF} \tag{7.24}$$

which is the same as

$$MRS = MRT.$$

In other words, the condition for efficiency in product-mix is that the consumers' MRSs must equal the MRT.

Why this condition is reasonable can best be seen if we reduce the number of people in the economy to just one, to make it a so-called "Robinson Crusoe economy." Suppose Crusoe faces a PPF as shown in Figure 7.15 and needs to decide which point on the PPF he should choose to produce. If he wants to maximise his utility, it is clear he should produce that mix of goods where one of his indifference curves is tangent to the PPF. The PPF acts like a budget constraint for Crusoe in this situation, and so a tangency is the natural solution to his utility maximisation problem. Clearly, all indifference curves higher than this one are unattainable, as they lie wholly outside the PPF, so the point of tangency *C* is the best bundle for him to produce. What is notable about the bundle *C* is that Crusoe's MRS (the absolute value of the slope of his indifference curve) is equal to the MRT (the absolute value of the slope of the PPF). Thus, we can see that $MRS = MRT$ is a perfectly reasonable condition for the right product-mix in the Crusoe economy. It is a small step to extrapolate this to a more complex economy, where efficiency in consumption requires all consumers' MRSs to be equal to one another. Our condition (7.24) simply says that this common MRS must equal MRT for the product-mix to be efficient.

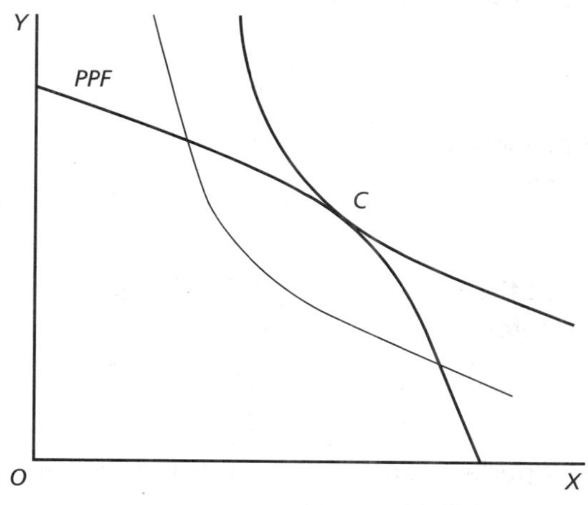


**Figure 7.15** *Efficient Product-Mix in a Robinson Crusoe Economy*

Does the perfectly competitive economy produce the right product-mix? In order to answer this, we need to look at one more way to look at the slope of the PPF. Consider the cost of producing *X*:

$$C^X = wL^X + rK^X,$$

where $w$ and $r$ are the prices of labour and capital, respectively. Then the marginal cost is

$$MC^X = \frac{dC^X}{dX} = w \cdot \frac{dL^X}{dX} + r \cdot \frac{dK^X}{dX} = \frac{w}{X_L} + \frac{r}{X_K}.$$

Gathering terms, we obtain

$$MC^X = \frac{wX_K + rX_L}{X_L X_K}$$

which can be written as

$$MC^X = \frac{w \cdot \frac{X_K}{X_L} + r}{X_K}. \tag{7.25}$$

By a similar process, we can show that

$$MC^Y = \frac{w \cdot \frac{Y_K}{Y_L} + r}{Y_K}. \tag{7.26}$$

Dividing (7.25) by (7.26), we have

$$\frac{MC^X}{MC^Y} = \frac{w \cdot \frac{X_K}{X_L} + r}{X_K} \cdot \frac{Y_K}{w \cdot \frac{Y_K}{Y_L} + r}. \tag{7.27}$$

Now, along the PPF, we know from (7.20) that

$$\frac{X_K}{X_L} = \frac{Y_K}{Y_L}.$$

Therefore, (7.27) can be simplified to

$$\frac{MC^X}{MC^Y} = \frac{Y_K}{X_K}. \tag{7.28}$$

But we know from (7.22) that the right-hand side of (7.28) is the absolute value of the slope of the PPF, that is, the MRT. Therefore, (7.28) is saying that

$$MRT = \frac{MC^X}{MC^Y}.$$

Now we know that, under perfect competition, firms produce up to the point where $p = MC$. Therefore, if $X$ and $Y$ are competitive industries,

$$MRT = \frac{p_x}{p_y}.$$

At the same time, consumers, in maximising their utility, set

$$MRS = \frac{p_x}{p_y}.$$

Therefore, in perfect competition,

$$MRS = MRT,$$

and the condition for efficiency in product-mix will be satisfied.

## 7.7 THE OPTIMALITY THEOREMS OF WELFARE ECONOMICS

**Task for this section:**

To explain the two central claims of welfare economics: that competitive equilibria are efficient, and that any desired efficient outcome can be generated by a competitive economy. The limitations of these results are also discussed.

The preceding several sections have led us to the key conclusion of welfare economics and one of the most important results in all of economics. The result is essentially an elaboration of Adam Smith's invisible hand theorem and is known as the **First Optimality Theorem of Welfare Economics**. The theorem states that, if the economy satisfies the conditions for perfect competition and there are no externalities, the competitive equilibrium is Pareto-efficient.

Whereas the First Optimality Theorem is a striking and powerful result, it is important to be clear about what it is and what it is not. It has been interpreted as proof that market forces lead to optimality and that therefore government intervention in the functioning of markets should be kept to a minimum. However, the theorem offers no such endorsement to market forces generally, only to *perfectly competitive* market forces. As we will see in subsequent chapters, markets where there is a significant amount of market power tend to be distorted and suboptimal from the welfare point of view. At best, the theorem should be regarded as a plea for governments to try to ensure that perfectly competitive conditions prevail in the economy as far as possible.

In this context, it is important to point out a limitation even to that last argument. The **theory of second best**, stated most clearly by Lipsey and Lancaster, says that, if it is not possible to satisfy *all* the conditions for Pareto efficiency, it may no longer be 'second-best' optimal to try to satisfy any of the conditions for Pareto efficiency. If, for example, one firm is not setting $p = MC$, it may no longer be optimal or desirable for other firms to be setting $p = MC$.

In light of this result, if we go back to the First Optimality Theorem and acknowledge that actual economies will never be able to satisfy *all* the conditions for Pareto efficiency, we are forced to also acknowledge that the theorem really tells us next to nothing at all about the optimality or non-optimality of market equilibrium. The theorem can at best hint that prices determined in competitive markets are helpful in allocating resources in a relatively efficient manner, but that is about all it can do.

In any case, even taking the theorem on its own terms, all it proves is that the competitive equilibrium is Pareto-efficient. That does not necessarily mean that the equilibrium is truly the best or even a good allocation. While most economists would agree that Pareto efficiency is a desirable characteristic for any allocation to have, many may find a *particular* Pareto-efficient allocation unacceptable and may be willing to sacrifice Pareto efficiency if that was necessary to achieve a more acceptable outcome. Consider Figure 7.16, which represents the UPF in a particular situation. Suppose the competitive equilibrium is at *C*. This *is* Pareto-efficient, as it is after all on the UPF, but many observers might find such an outcome highly objectionable since the distribution is so highly skewed to Aruna. Note that this is not an entirely academic discussion, as it is often observed that the distribution of income in market economies tends to be highly skewed. In our example, most thoughtful observers might say that *A*, which is also a Pareto-efficient allocation, would be a lot better outcome than *C*. Further, they might say that, if for some reason *A* was unattainable and the closest we could get to *A* was the Pareto-*inefficient* allocation *B*, they might still prefer *B* over *C*. Thus, they might sacrifice Pareto efficiency if it could lead to a more equitable distribution. To say that an allocation is Pareto-efficient, therefore, is not necessarily to say that it is highly desirable.

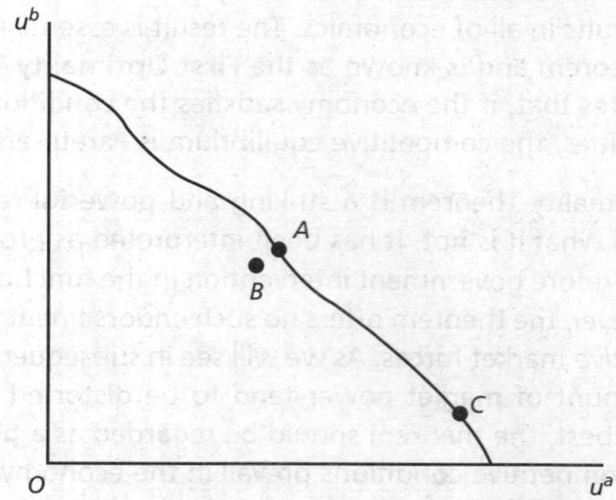


**Figure 7.16** *Doubts about Pareto Efficiency as an Optimality Criterion*

The reply of welfare economics to this last objection is the **Second Optimality Theorem of Welfare Economics**. This states that any desired Pareto-efficient allocation can be obtained as a competitive equilibrium by use of suitable taxes and transfers. Thus the theorem says that we could attain allocation *A* of Figure 7.16 as the outcome of a competitive equilibrium, simply by changing the initial endowments of the individuals through taxes and transfers.

There are two problems with reading too much into this result either. First, the taxes and transfers necessary to attain the desired initial endowment are assumed to be *lump-sum taxes and transfers*. Lump-sum taxes have the property that they are unavoidable and therefore do not affect incentives in any way. However, no one has yet designed a practical system of lump-sum taxes that would be even remotely acceptable politically; thus, they remain a purely theoretical concept. Second, implementation of a far-reaching redistributive policy tends to be vigorously opposed by those who would be adversely affected by such a policy and who, by virtue of their economic status, wield tremendous power and influence in the policy-making process. The only method by which truly far-reaching redistribution has ever occurred is political revolution.

Despite all these objections, it remains to be said that the theory of general equilibrium and the optimality theorems of welfare economics are remarkable results. They point to the powerful role that market-determined prices can play in the allocation of resources and at least suggest that the best prices to do the job of allocation well are those that emerge in highly competitive markets.

## SUMMARY

In this chapter, we have examined the theory of General Equilibrium and the optimality theorems of Welfare Economics. The main points discussed are as follows:

- Most economists agree that Pareto efficiency is a desirable characteristic of any allocation of resources.
- Pareto efficiency occurs when we achieve an allocation of resources such that no one can be made better-off without making someone else worse off. In short, all 'painless' gains have been made.
- In order to achieve Pareto efficiency, any economic system has to satisfy three broad classes of conditions, conditions for efficiency in consumption, for efficiency in production and for efficiency in the product-mix.
- For efficiency in consumption, the marginal rates of substitution of all consumers must be equalised.
- For efficiency in production, the marginal rates of technical substitution of all firms in all industries must be equalised.
- For efficiency in the product-mix, every consumer's marginal rate of substitution must also equal the marginal rate of transformation, the absolute value of the slope of the economy's production possibilities frontier.
- Perfectly competitive markets do satisfy all three sets of conditions for Pareto efficiency.
- The first optimality theorem of welfare economics says that all perfectly competitive equilibria are Pareto-efficient.

- The second optimality theorem of welfare economics says that any desired Pareto-efficient allocation can be obtained as a competitive equilibrium by use of suitable lump-sum taxes and transfers.
- The practical implications of the optimality theorems are limited because of the fact that many of the required conditions are not met by real market economies.
- Further, the theory of second best says that, if even one of the conditions for Pareto efficiency is not met, it may no longer be desirable to try to satisfy the other conditions for Pareto efficiency.

## EXERCISES

1. There are 40 people in the commune of Shangri-La. They are all identical, and each one works 10 hours per day. Two products are produced: widgets and gadgets. The daily output of these goods is given by

$$W = 5L_w \quad \text{and} \quad G = 10L_g^{\frac{1}{2}},$$

where $L_w$ and $L_g$ are respectively the total number of person-hours allocated to the production of widgets and gadgets per day.

(a) Find Shangri-La's production possibilities frontier.

(b) If each person in Shangri-La always wants to consume widgets and gadgets in the ratio 10 widgets for each gadget, how many widgets and gadgets should be produced per day? If the price of widgets is set at 1, what must be the price of gadgets to support this outcome as a competitive equilibrium?

(c) If Shangri-La can trade with the rest of the world at prices given by $p_g = 10$ and $p_w = 1$, how many widgets and how many gadgets should be produced per day? What will now be the total consumption of widgets and gadgets?

2. Shekhar and Johar each have 10 hours per day to devote to producing goods $X$ and $Y$. Shekhar's and Johar's utility functions are given respectively by

$$U_s = X_s^{0.3}Y_s^{0.7} \quad \text{and} \quad U_j = X_j^{0.5}Y_j^{0.5},$$

where $X_i$ and $Y_i$ are the quantities of $X$ and $Y$ consumed per day by person $i$. The production functions for the two goods are given by

$$X = 2L_X \quad \text{and} \quad Y = 2L_Y,$$

where $L_X$ and $L_Y$ are the total amounts of labour used in the production of each good. Suppose the wage rate is ₹1 per hour and perfect competition prevails.

(a) What would be the equilibrium price ratio $p_x/p_y$?

(b) Given this price ratio, how much $X$ and $Y$ will Shekhar and Johar demand?

(c) How much labour will be allocated to the production of each good?

3. Robinson Crusoe lives alone on a desert island. He works 9 hours per day gathering coconuts and hunting fish. His production functions for the two goods are:

$$C = 2L_c \quad \text{and} \quad F = L_f^{1/2},$$

where $C$ and $F$ are the quantities of coconuts and fish produced per day and $L_c$ and $L_f$ are the number of hours Crusoe spends producing coconuts and fish, respectively. Crusoe's utility function from consumption is

$$U(C, F) = CF.$$

(a) Find Crusoe's production possibilities frontier. Find a formula for the marginal rate of transformation.

(b) How many hours will Crusoe spend each day on each of the two production activities in order to maximise his utility? (*Allow fractional quantities of goods to be produced.*)

(c) Show that, at the optimum you found in (b), the marginal rate of transformation is equal to the marginal rate of substitution. What price ratio would support this optimum as a competitive equilibrium?

4. The economy of Edgworthia has just two individuals, Shekhar and Johar, who can each produce just two goods, $x$ and $y$. Each person's marginal product in the production of $x$ is 2 per hour and in the production of $y$ is 3 per hour, and each person works 10 hours per day. Shekhar's and Johar's utility functions are respectively:

$$U_s = x_s^3 y_s^7 \quad \text{and} \quad U_j = x_j y_j.$$

(a) In competitive equilibrium, what must be the price ratio $p_x/p_y$?

(b) In equilibrium, how much $x$ and $y$ will Shekhar and Johar demand and how much of each good will be produced?

5. Agrolia is an agrarian country with 100 workers and 400 acres of land. Only two crops are grown: beets and corn. The production functions for these two crops are:

$$B = L_b^{0.5} T_b^{0.5} \quad \text{and} \quad C = 4L_c + T_c,$$

where $L_b$ and $T_b$ are the quantities of labour and land used in the production of beets and $L_c$ and $T_c$ are the quantities of labour and land used in the production of corn.

(a) Find Agrolia's production possibilities frontier.

(b) If all the people in Agrolia have identical utility functions

$$U(X_b, X_c) = \ln X_b + \ln X_c,$$

where $X_b$ and $X_c$ are the levels of consumption of beets and corn, find the efficient levels of production of beets and corn. If the rental rate on land is normalised to 1, what must be the wage rate and the prices of beets and corn that would support the efficient production equilibrium?

6. The small country of Agrolia has a fixed labour supply of 10,000 workers, all with identical productivity, who can be used in the production of two goods: corn and bajra. The world price of corn is ₹20 per bushel and the production function for corn, in bushels, is

$$Q_c = 2{,}000 \ln L_c,$$

where $L_c$ is the number of workers engaged in corn production. The world price of bajra is ₹100 per unit and the output of bajra in Agrolia is given by

$$Q_b = 100 \ln L_b,$$

where $L_b$ is the number of workers engaged in bajra production. All markets are perfectly competitive.

What will be the equilibrium wage rate and the allocation of labour between the two production activities in Agrolia?

7. Ashok consumes only two goods, $X$ and $Y$, and his utility function is

$$U(x_A, y_A) = \min\left[x_A, \frac{y_A}{2}\right],$$

where $x_A$ and $y_A$ are the quantities of the two goods he consumes. Ashok is endowed with 20 units of $X$ and 10 units of $Y$.

Beena also consumes only $X$ and $Y$, but her utility function is

$$U(x_B, y_B) = x_B + 2y_B,$$

where $x_B$ and $y_B$ are the quantities of the two goods she consumes. Beena is endowed with 10 units of $X$ and 10 units of $Y$.

(a) Draw Ashok's offer curve in a clearly labelled diagram, explaining how you found it. Your graph should make it clear what Ashok's offers would be at all possible relative price ratios.

(b) Draw Beena's offer curve in a clearly labelled diagram, explaining how you found it.

(c) Suppose Ashok and Beena are in a pure exchange economy. Draw the Edgeworth box for this problem and draw the two offer curves in it. What would be the equilibrium price ratio if Ashok and Beena engaged in a Walrasian tâtonnement process (i.e. the perfectly equilibrium price ratio if they engaged in trade)? What would be the quantities of $X$ and $Y$ traded and by whom?

8. Jai and Benazir are the only agents who live in their village. They consume xylophones ($x$) and yogurt ($y$). Jai's utility function is

$$U_j(x_j, y_j) = \min\left[2x_j, y_j\right],$$

where $x_j$ is Jai's consumption of xylophones and $y_j$ is Jai's consumption of yogurt. Benazir's utility function is

$$U_b = x_b y_b,$$

where $x_b$ is Benazir's consumption of xylophones and $y_b$ is Benazir's consumption of yogurt. Jai is endowed with 8 xylophones and no yogurt, while Benazir is endowed with no xylophones and 12 yogurts.

   (a) Let $p_x$ be the price of xylophones and $p_y$ the price of yogurt. Write down the demand functions for $x$ and $y$ for Jai and Benazir.

   (b) Find a competitive equilibrium price ratio and the consumption of xylophones and yogurt for Jai and Benazir.

   (c) Now suppose we switch their endowments. That is, now assume Jai is endowed with no xylophones and 12 yogurts, while Benazir is endowed with 8 xylophones and no yogurt. Find the competitive equilibrium. Is Jai better-off in (a) or (b)?

   (d) Could we ever have a situation where this kind of switching of the endowments makes *both* agents strictly better-off?

9. Consider a pure exchange economy with two commodities ($x$, $y$) and total resources $(e_x, e_y) = (5, 10)$. Consumers $A$ and $B$ have identical preferences represented by the following utility function:

$$U_i(x_i, y_i) = x_i y_i,$$

for $i = A, B$. Suppose initial endowments are $(e_x^A, e_y^A) = (2, 1)$ for $A$ and $(e_x^B, e_y^B) = (3, 9)$ for $B$.

   (a) Draw an Edgeworth box and indicate the endowment point. Define the set of Pareto-efficient allocations and draw them in the diagram.

   (b) Compute the Walrasian (or perfectly competitive) equilibrium and the associated allocation. Is the equilibrium efficient?

10. Consider an exchange economy with two individuals, $A$ and $B$, and two goods, $X$ and $Y$. $A$ and $B$ each have an initial endowment of 10 units of good $X$ and 5 units of good $Y$, and their preferences are described by the utility functions:

$$u_A(x_A, y_A) = x_A + y_A \qquad \text{and} \qquad u_B(x_B, y_B) = \min\{x_B, y_B\}.$$

Answer the following questions algebraically and illustrate your answers in an appropriate graph.

(a) What is the set of efficient allocations (the Pareto set) in this economy? Describe the set of allocations that constitute a Pareto improvement over the endowment allocation. Derive the contract curve.

(b) Find a Walrasian (competitive) equilibrium. What is the price vector and allocation in equilibrium?

11. Consider an exchange economy, with two consumers, $A$ and $B$, and two commodities, $X$ and $Y$. Initially, consumer $A$ has 1 unit of $X$ and 2 units of $Y$, while consumer $B$ has 2 units of $X$ and 1 unit of $Y$. The preferences of consumers A and B are represented by the utility functions

$$u_A(x_A, y_A) = x_A y_A \quad \text{and} \quad u_B(x_B, y_B) = \min\{x_B, y_B\}.$$

(a) Construct the Edgeworth box. Label the axes. Label the endowment point with an 'E'. Sketch indifference curves for consumer $A$ and for consumer $B$. Label the set of Pareto-efficient allocations with a 'PS'.

(b) Find the set of allocations which are both Pareto-efficient and provide at least as much utility as the initial endowment. Identify both endpoints of this set.

(c) Calculate the competitive (Walrasian) equilibrium price vector and the equilibrium allocation.

CHAPTER

8

# Uncertainty and Information

Life is full of uncertainty. A student studying for an exam does not know (we hope!) what questions will be on it and how she will perform. A farmer planting his fields faces a wide range of weather outcomes and hence output levels. An investor buying company shares realises the stock price could go up or down. A homeowner confronts all sorts of risks: burglary, building damage from severe weather, burst pipes and so on. Even a consumer buying a product, especially one she has not bought before, may be quite uncertain about its quality. This chapter is concerned with situations such as these and asks the question: How do consumers make choices when faced with uncertainty?

## 8.1 BASICS

**Task for this section:**

To introduce the basic concepts economists use in their analysis of decisions under uncertainty.

Many of the earliest analyses of choice under uncertainty were motivated by the study of games of chance such as casino games and it is often useful to use the framework of such a game to think about any uncertain situation. To this end, we can think of any uncertain situation as a 'lottery' and can describe it in much the same way as we would if we were analysing a game of chance. To fully describe such a situation, we would need to have information about the following:

**Outcomes:** The first thing we must know is what all the possible outcomes are. In a simple game of coin toss, the only two possible outcomes are Heads and Tails. On a roll of a six-sided dice, there are six possible outcomes. In more complicated games, such as roulette, the number of possible outcomes is greater. In real-life situations, the outcomes will frequently be continuous variables that can take on an infinite number of values within a range. For example, the amount of rainfall that a farm might receive during a growing season could be any number between zero and the maximum conceivable level of rainfall. In considering the outcomes, what is important is that we take note of **all** possible outcomes; no possible outcome should be left out of the analysis.

**Probabilities:** It is also vital to know the probability with which each outcome could occur. The probability of an outcome tells us how likely it is, or what proportion of the time it would occur if the game were played repeatedly for a very large number of times. In the toss of a fair coin, the probabilities of Heads and Tails are each 50% or 0.5. In the roll of a fair dice, the probability of each of the numbers is 1/6 or 16.67%. Such probabilities can be calculated experimentally or by reasoning and are called **objective probabilities**, and such probabilities can be obtained for most games of chance simply by knowing the details of the game. In many real-life situations, however, a decision-maker might not be able to determine the probabilities of all the possible outcomes objectively. In that case, he or she must make estimates or best guesses on what the probabilities are; such probabilities are called **subjective probabilities**. Different people might form quite different subjective probabilities in similar situations, and this might account for differences in people's observed behaviour. For example, at any given time, there are people who are buying a particular company's stock and other people who are selling the same company's stock. Their diametrically opposite behaviour might well be due to widely differing subjective probability estimates of the future price of the stock, although other factors could also explain these different behaviours.

**Pay-offs:** For each possible outcome, the decision-maker receives a pay-off of some kind, and we would need to know the size of the pay-off under each possible outcome. For example, if Raja is playing a coin toss game, he might receive ₹100 if the coin comes out Heads and might lose ₹100 if it comes out Tails. Then ₹100 and −₹100 are his pay-offs from Heads and Tails, respectively. If Gita bets ₹10 on the number 25 on a roulette wheel, her pay-off would be ₹350 if the ball lands on the number 25 (assuming a 35-to-1 pay-off rate) and −₹10 under all other outcomes.

**Expected Pay-off:** Once we know the pay-offs and probabilities of each possible outcome, it is possible to calculate the expected pay-off, the average pay-off the decision-maker would receive if the game were repeated a large number of times. If there are $n$ possible outcomes, indexed by the variable $i$, and if $x_i$ and $p_i$ represent the pay-off in and probability of outcome $i$, the expected pay-off is

$$E(x) = \sum_{i=1}^{n} p_i x_i. \tag{8.1}$$

For example, if the two possible pay-offs in a particular game are $x_1 = ₹100$ and $x_2 = ₹36$, and the probabilities are $p_1 = 0.9$ and $p_2 = 0.1$, the expected pay-off is

$$E(x) = (0.9 \times 100) + (0.1 \times 36) = 93.6.$$

## 8.2 RISK AVERSION

**Task for this section:**

To discuss the concept of risk aversion, the desire to avoid risk, that helps explain much behaviour in the face of uncertainty.

One of the starting points for discussions about choice under uncertainty is that most individuals are not generally indifferent between two situations that have the same expected pay-off. Rather, if they are offered a choice between two 'lotteries', they will generally prefer the one that has the lower variability. For example, suppose there are two alternatives:

**A**: ₹10,000 with certainty and

**B**: ₹20,000 with probability 1/2 and ₹0 with probability 1/2,

most people will prefer **A**, even though both options have the same expected pay-off. Thus, people generally display an aversion to risk. This is very strikingly shown by a famous problem that featured prominently in the early literature on choice under uncertainty: the St. Petersburg paradox.

**St. Petersburg Paradox:** Consider the following casino game, originally proposed by the Swiss mathematician Nicolas Bernoulli. Shikha pays a fee up front to play the game and then gets a pay-off based on coin tosses. Specifically, the casino tosses a coin, and if it turns up Heads, Shikha receives ₹2. If it turns up Tails on that first toss, the casino tosses the coin again. If it turns up Heads now, Shikha receives ₹4 ($= 2^2$). If it turns up Tails again on the second toss, the casino tosses the coin a third time. In this way, the casino keeps tossing the coin until a Heads appears, at which point it pays Shikha and the game ends. How much it pays depends upon how many tosses it took to get the first Heads. If the first Heads appears on the $n$-th toss, Shikha is paid ₹$2^n$.[1] Now the probability that the first Heads appears on the $n$-th throw is $1/2^n$, since the only way for that to happen is for there to have been $(n - 1)$ Tails followed by a Heads. Therefore, the expected pay-off to Shikha is

$$E(x) = \sum_{n=1}^{\infty} \frac{1}{2^n} \cdot 2^n$$

[1] Although this is the form in which most authors today present the game, it is not in fact the form in which Nicolas Bernoulli originally proposed it. In the original form, the player receives ₹1 if a Heads appears on the first throw and $2^{(n-1)}$ if it appears on the $n$-th throw. This does not change the basic nature of the game, nor the paradox. Of course, the currency Bernoulli used was not rupees either, it was ducats. And why is the game called the St. Petersburg paradox? Because Daniel Bernoulli's paper proposing a solution was published in the journal of the Petersburg Academy of Sciences.

which is infinite, since it is the sum of an infinite number of terms, each of which is equal to 1. But most people would not be willing-to-pay much more than ₹2 to play this game, let alone a large sum of money. If, for example, a casino offered to play this game with anyone willing-to-pay an entry fee of ₹100, there would be no takers, even though the net expected pay-off from the game (net of the entry fee) is still infinite. Hence the paradox.

The Swiss mathematicians Daniel Bernoulli (a cousin of Nicolas) and Gabriel Cramer independently proposed the same solution to this paradox by suggesting that decision-makers do not maximise their expected pay-offs but rather their expected utility from wealth. Further, they argued that utility is a concave function of a person's wealth; Bernoulli proposed using the logarithmic function, while Cramer suggested the square root function. How much someone might be willing-to-pay to play the St. Petersburg game falls dramatically once the concavity of the utility function is applied; how much exactly this willingness-to-pay is depends upon the wealth of the decision-maker. For example, if we use the logarithmic function as suggested by Bernoulli, and if the player's initial wealth is ₹10,000, the maximum willingness-to-pay to play the game will be the solution for $x$ in the following equation:

$$\ln(10{,}000) = \sum_{n=1}^{\infty} \frac{1}{2^n} \cdot \ln[10{,}000 - x + 2^n].$$

The left-hand side of the equation is the player's utility if she does not play the game, while the right-hand side is her expected utility (obtained by applying the formula for expected pay-off to the utility rather than the pay-off) if she pays $x$ and then plays the game. We can use a spreadsheet to calculate an approximate solution for $x$, which turns out to be ₹14.23 in this case, still higher perhaps than most people would actually be willing-to-pay, but at least it is finite!

## 8.3 THE EXPECTED UTILITY HYPOTHESIS

**Task for this section:**

To study the basic model of behaviour under uncertainty: the expected utility hypothesis. By the end of this section, you should understand how to analyse situations according to this hypothesis, both algebraically and graphically. You should also be able to construct decision trees to analyse complex situations.

The modern theory of decision-making under uncertainty is a simple generalisation of the solutions proposed for the St. Petersburg paradox by Bernoulli and Cramer. **The Expected Utility Hypothesis states that, when faced with situations of uncertainty, individuals seek to maximise the expected utility of their wealth.** In other words, the theory assumes that people have a utility function $U(w)$, where $w$ is their wealth, and that they seek to maximise the expected value of this utility. We can think of this utility function $U(w)$ as being a reduced form of the consumer's indirect utility function that we studied in the chapter on consumer theory, where prices are not being considered explicitly and wealth has replaced income as the argument of the utility function.

To calculate expected utility, suppose Anand has a wealth of ₹100,000, but faces a 30% chance of losing ₹40,000 of this. Anand's expected utility is then

$$EU(w) = 0.7 \cdot U(100{,}000) + 0.3 \cdot U(60{,}000).$$

Now suppose an insurance company offers to insure Anand against this loss. For a premium payment of $\pi$, they guarantee to reimburse Anand the ₹40,000 if he loses it. If Anand accepts this insurance policy, his wealth will be $(100{,}000 - \pi)$ for sure, since he is reimbursed his loss if he suffers it. Then, according to the expected utility hypothesis, Anand will buy the policy if

$$U(100{,}000 - \pi) \triangleright 0.7 \cdot U(100{,}000) + 0.3 \cdot U(60{,}000)$$

and will reject it otherwise.

It is normally assumed that, for most people, the utility function is concave over wealth, although this assumption is not necessary for the hypothesis. Three possible shapes for the utility function are shown in Figure 8.1. When the utility function is concave, we say that individuals are **risk-averse**, because they prefer less risky situations to more risky situations that have the same expected pay-offs. Individuals with convex utility functions are said to be **risk-loving**, while people with linear utility functions are said to be **risk-neutral**. These concepts may perhaps be better understood in the context of a specific decision problem, and we will consider one such problem in some detail: the purchase of insurance.

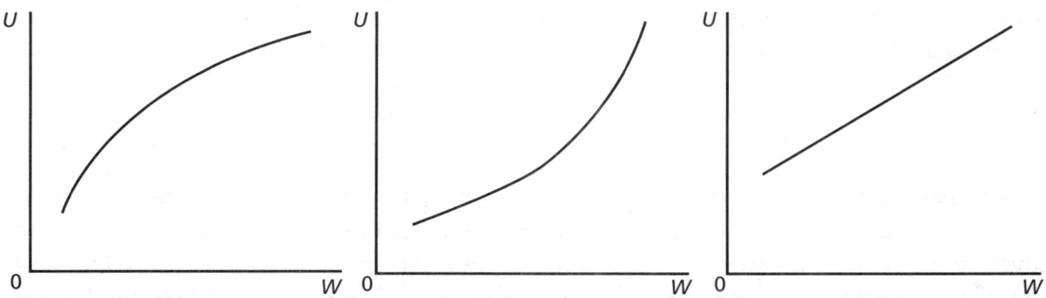


(a) Risk-averse (b) Risk-loving (c) Risk-neutral

**Figure 8.1** *Three Possible Shapes for the Utility Function*

### 8.3.1 Risk Aversion and Insurance

We will focus on the case of property insurance. We will not consider time explicitly, although it underlies the story. All the variables considered could be interpreted as the present values of the respective series. Suppose Anand has an initial wealth of $w_0$, but faces the possibility of a loss. Perhaps a good part of his wealth is concentrated in his home and the home might be damaged or burnt down in a fire. His ultimate wealth therefore will depend upon whether and how seriously he experiences an adverse event. Suppose that the extent of his loss depends upon the 'state of nature' that emerges, and let us index this state of nature by $i$. Suppose Anand's wealth after the state of nature is known is $w_i$. Then the loss he suffers is

$$L_i = w_0 - w_i.$$

Suppose the probability that the state of nature $i$ emerges is $p_i$. Then Anand's initial expected wealth is

$$E_0(w) = \bar{w} = \sum_{n=1}^{\infty} p_i w_i,$$

the expected loss becomes

$$\bar{L} = w_0 - \bar{w} \tag{8.2}$$

and his expected utility is

$$EU_0 = \bar{U}_0 = \sum_{n=1}^{\infty} p_i U(w_i).$$

Now suppose an insurance company offers to sell Anand an insurance policy to cover him against the potential losses he might suffer. In exchange for an upfront payment, known as the **insurance premium**, which we will denote $\pi$, the company promises to pay Anand $L_i$ once the state of nature is revealed. In other words, the company will reimburse Anand for any loss he suffers. Anand no longer faces any uncertainty about his wealth, which will be $(w_0 - \pi)$ with certainty, and therefore his expected utility will simply be $U(w_0 - \pi)$. He will buy this insurance policy if his expected utility with the policy is higher than his expected utility without it, that is, if

$$U(w_0 - \pi) > \sum_{n=1}^{\infty} p_i U(w_i). \tag{8.3}$$

Now an insurance company sells many policies similar to Anand's and so can predict with a fair degree of accuracy how much they will have to pay out in loss claims on all of their policies collectively, which will be the sum of all the expected losses. Thus, on average, they would expect to pay Anand his expected loss $\bar{L}$, and therefore this is the minimum they would charge for Anand's policy. If they set the premium at this level, it is called the **actuarially fair premium**, because on average the company would just be breaking even on the policy, and the policy is called an

**actuarially fair insurance policy**. Denote this actuarially fair premium $\pi_a$. Since $\pi_a = \bar{L}$, we know from (8.2) that

$$\pi_a = w_0 - \bar{w}. \tag{8.4}$$

If Anand has to pay this premium and his utility function is linear, of the form

$$U(w) = a - bw,$$

then the inequality (8.3) will become an equality, since the left-hand side becomes

$$LHS = a - b(w_0 - \pi_a)$$

and the right-hand side becomes

$$RHS = \sum_{n=1}^{\infty} p_i(a - bw_i) = a - b\bar{w},$$

proving, by application of (8.4), that the two sides are equal.

**A person with a linear utility function is said to be risk-neutral**, and we see that a risk-neutral person will be just indifferent between buying or not buying an actuarially fair insurance policy. He would reject any policy which charges a premium greater than the expected loss, and, of course, no insurance company could stay in business if it offered policies with premiums lower than the expected loss. Thus, there is not much scope for an insurance market if people are risk-neutral.

**Underwriting losses in insurance companies:**

The text says that insurance companies would never charge premiums lower than the expected losses, but this may appear to be contradicted by the observation that most insurance companies make 'underwriting losses', that is, their accounts show that they take in less revenue in the form of insurance premiums than they pay out in loss claims. How can this be? And how can insurance companies sustain this? It is all a matter of timing. Typically, insurance premiums are paid in at the *start* of the policy period, say on January 1 for an annual policy, while the loss claims are paid later, often even after the policy period is over (e.g. if a loss occurred late in a year). So the company has the use of the money in the meantime and can invest it. The investment returns, then, need to be sufficient to compensate for any underwriting losses.

However, **a person with a concave utility function is said to be risk-averse**, and such a person would strongly prefer an actuarially fair insurance policy to no insurance and would in fact be willing-to-pay more than the actuarially fair premium for an insurance policy. How much more he would be willing-to-pay depends upon his utility function. These ideas are more easily developed with a simple example.

Suppose Anand's initial wealth is $w_0 = 100$ (perhaps thousands of rupees, but we will ignore units), and there are only two potential states of nature. In one, nothing happens and Anand's wealth remains at 100. In the other, Anand suffers a major catastrophe (perhaps his house burns down) and his wealth falls to 36. Thus, his loss is $L = 100 - 36 = 64$. Suppose the probability that Anand suffers this loss is $p = 0.1$ or 10%. Then Anand's initial expected wealth is

$$E_0(w) = \bar{w} = 0.9(100) + 0.1(36) = 93.6.$$

Anand's expected loss is

$$E(L) = \bar{L} = 0.1(64) = 6.4$$

and this is also the actuarially fair premium. If Anand were able to buy actuarially fair insurance, his wealth would be 93.6 with certainty.

Now suppose Anand is risk-averse and has a concave utility function; specifically, suppose his utility function is

$$U(w) = \sqrt{w}.$$

His expected utility without insurance will be

$$EU_0 = 0.9\sqrt{100} + 0.1\sqrt{36} = 9.6.$$

With actuarially fair insurance, since he would have 93.6 with certainty, his utility would be

$$EU_a = \sqrt{93.6} = 9.6747,$$

which is clearly higher. Thus, he would unambiguously prefer actuarially fair insurance to no insurance, and would be prepared to pay more for insurance than the actuarially fair premium.

How much more? Suppose $\pi_m$ represents the maximum premium Anand would be willing-to-pay for insurance. This must be high enough so that Anand becomes just indifferent between buying insurance and not buying it. Thus, $\pi_m$ will satisfy the equation

$$\sqrt{100 - \pi_m} = 9.6. \tag{8.5}$$

Solving (8.5) yields $\pi_m = 7.84$, which is higher than the actuarially fair premium of 6.4. This is Anand's maximum willingness-to-pay for insurance.

Since the actuarially fair premium is equal to the expected loss $\bar{L}$, the amount by which $\pi_m$ exceeds $\bar{L}$ is a measure of what Anand is willing-to-pay just to avoid the risk that he faces in the uncertain situation. Think of $\pi_m$ as consisting of two parts: the actuarially fair cost of providing the insurance (the **'loss premium'** or the part of the insurance premium accounted for by the potential loss), and a **'risk premium'** that Anand is willing-to-pay just to avoid the risk. This risk premium is also called the **cost of risk** and can be represented by the symbol $C$. Thus, $C$ is the difference between the maximum willingness-to-pay and the actuarially fair premium:

$$C = \pi_m - \pi_a.$$

In this example, this risk premium or cost of risk is

$$C = 7.84 - 6.4 = 1.44.$$

Note that 9.6 in (8.5) would be the utility that Anand would enjoy if he had a wealth of 92.16 with certainty (since $\sqrt{92.16} = 9.6$). Thus, Anand *feels* like his wealth is 92.16, even though his expected wealth is 93.6; the uncertainty of this expected wealth makes him feel like his wealth is lower than it really is on average. This figure of 92.16 is called Anand's **certainty equivalent wealth**, which is the wealth level that, when enjoyed with certainty, yields the same level of expected utility as the uncertain situation. We could denote the certainty equivalent wealth by $w_{CE}$. And we now get a different way of looking at the cost of risk: **the cost of risk faced by an individual in an uncertain situation is the difference between his expected wealth and his certainty equivalent wealth**:

$$C = \bar{w} - w_{CE}, \tag{8.6}$$

which, in our example, is equal to (93.6 − 92.16) = 1.44, the same result as we got before.

### 8.3.2 Graphical Representation Using the Utility Function

The preceding analysis can be represented graphically in two ways. The first looks at the problem from the point of view of the utility function itself. We start with a graph showing the utility function $U(w)$. The level of wealth is measured on the horizontal axis and the utility on the vertical. In Figure (8.2), the utility function is shown as concave, indicating that it is the function of a risk-averse person. Alternatively, it could be linear (if the person is risk-neutral) or convex (if the person is risk-loving), and we will consider these cases later. Now let us start by marking $w_0$ and $w_L(= w_0 - L)$, and the corresponding utility levels, $U_0$ and $U_L$, noting the points $A$ and $B$ on the utility function corresponding to these wealth and utility levels. Draw the straight line $AB$ connecting these two points. Now mark $\bar{w}$, the expected wealth, and draw a vertical line from this to meet the line $AB$ at $D$. The height of the point $D$ will equal $\bar{U}$, the expected utility, because $\bar{U}$ is the same convex combination of $U_0$ and $U_L$ as $\bar{w}$ is of $w_0$ and $w_L$.

Observe:

$$\bar{U} = (1 - p)U_0 + pU_L,$$

and

$$\bar{w} = (1 - p)w_0 + pw_L,$$

where $p$ is the probability of the loss $L$ occurring. Mark as $E$ the point where the horizontal line from $D$ at $\bar{U}$ cuts the utility function, and drop a perpendicular from $E$ to the horizontal axis.

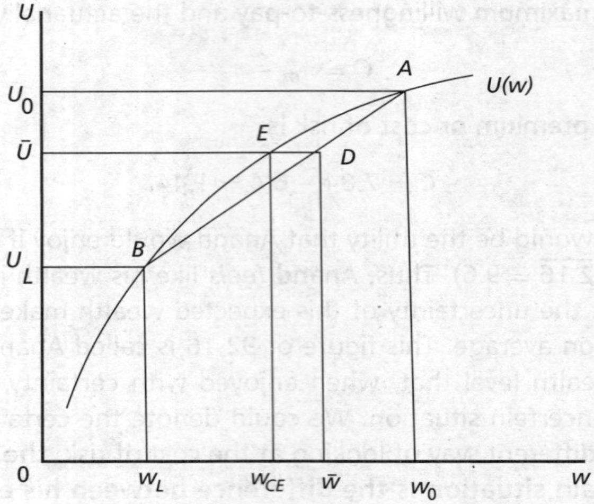


**Figure 8.2** *Utility Function and Choice under Uncertainty*

This level of wealth is $w_{CE}$, since it is the level of wealth that yields the same expected utility as the uncertain situation faced by Anand. The variables we calculated can then be seen on the graph:

$$\pi_a = E(L) = w_0 - \bar{w},$$

$$\pi_m = w_0 - w_{CE},$$

$$C = \bar{w} - w_{CE}.$$

One point worth noting about this graph is that the expected utility is not the same as the utility of the expected wealth. The expected utility is shown in the graph as $\bar{U}$. The utility of the expected value, $U(\bar{w})$, is not shown explicitly, but could be obtained by extending the vertical line at $\bar{w}$ from $D$ to the utility function. The point where that vertical line meets the utility function would be $U(\bar{w})$, which is clearly greater than $\bar{U}$. In fact, $U(\bar{w})$ is the utility Anand would enjoy if he had an actuarially fair insurance policy.

Looking at the problem in the cases where Anand is risk-neutral or risk-loving, we see there is no scope for insurance in these cases. Figure 8.3 shows how the choices considered in Figure 8.2 would look if the utility function was linear or convex. We see that, in the risk-neutral case, points D and E would coincide, indicating that $w_{CE} = \bar{w}$. The presence of risk does not make a risk-neutral person any worse off and he would not pay more for insurance than the actuarially fair premium; indeed, actuarially fair insurance makes him no better or worse off. In the risk-loving case, actuarially fair insurance would actually make Anand *worse* off. In other words, $w_{CE} > \bar{w}$! With this sort of utility function, Anand would have to be *paid* to accept insurance!

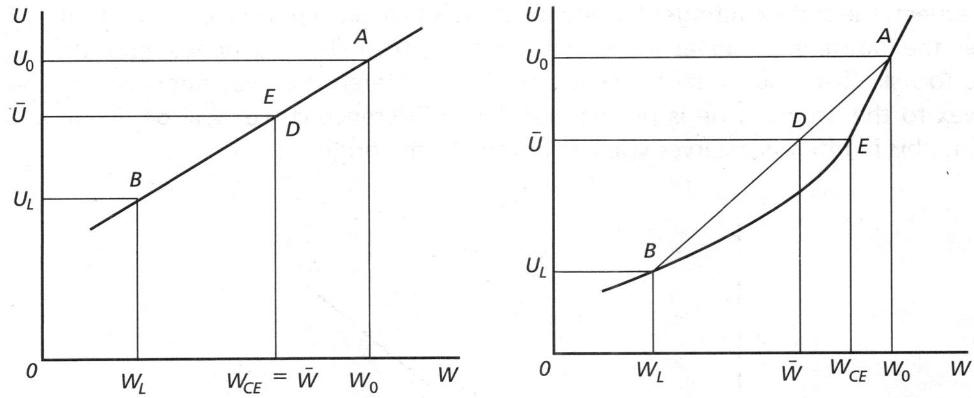


**Figure 8.3** *Choice for Risk-Neutral and Risk-Loving Persons*

## 8.3.3 Graphical Representation Using State-Contingent Utility

The second way to illustrate decision-making under uncertainty is to use indifference curve analysis. Rather than modelling utility as a function of wealth, we posit the existence of a state-contingent utility function, in which we treat as separate arguments the levels of wealth in different states of nature:

$$u(w_g, w_b),$$

where $w_g$ and $w_b$ are the levels of wealth in the 'good' state and the 'bad' state. In our example of Anand buying insurance, the good state is the one where he suffers no loss and the bad state is the one where he does suffer the loss of 64. Thus, $w_g$ is what we previously called $w_0$, and $w_b$ is what we previously called $w_L = (w_0 - L)$. The concept can be generalised to $n$ states of nature, but of course such a case would be difficult to show graphically, just as we cannot graphically represent a normal $n$-good consumer utility function. $u(w_g, w_b)$ is nothing but the individual's expected utility:

$$u(w_g, w_b) = p_g U(w_g) + p_b U(w_b), \tag{8.7}$$

where $p_g$ and $p_b$ are the probabilities of the respective states, with $p_g = (1 - p_b)$, and $U(w_i)$ could be thought of as the normal utility from wealth.

What will be the shape of this state-contingent utility function? Clearly, all other things equal, any individual would prefer to have a higher wealth in each state of nature; thus,

$$\frac{\partial u}{\partial w_i} = p_i U'(w_i) \geq 0 \qquad \text{for all } i.$$

In this respect, the state-contingent utility function is just like a normal consumer utility function. However, the indifference curves are a different story; their shape depends upon the individual's attitude to risk. If an individual is risk-averse, his indifference curves between $w_g$ and $w_b$ will be convex to the origin. If he is risk-neutral, his indifference curves will be linear, and if he is risk-loving, his indifference curves will be concave to the origin.

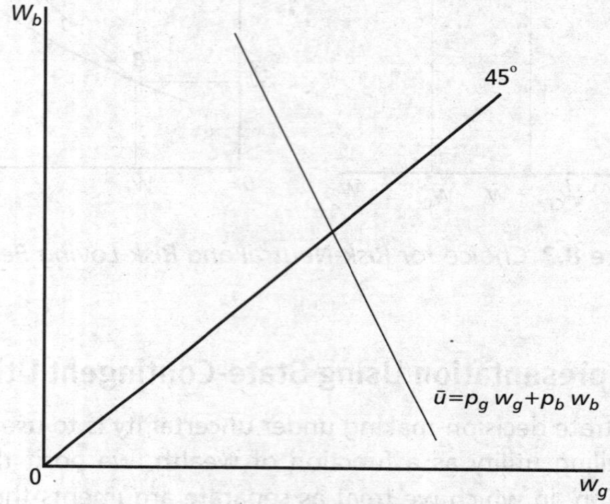


**Figure 8.4** *State-contingent Utility for a Risk-Neutral Consumer*

To see this, it is easiest to start with a risk-neutral individual. Figure (8.4) measures $w_g$ on the horizontal axis and $w_b$ on the vertical axis. The 45° line represents all those points where $w_g = w_b$, that is, where Anand does not face any uncertainty since his wealth is the same regardless of whether the state of nature is good or bad. We can call this line the **certainty line**. Now consider a typical indifference curve if Anand is risk-neutral. In this case, his underlying wealth-utility function is linear, say of the form

$$U(w) = a + bw,$$

so (8.7) becomes

$$u(w_g, w_b) = p_g(a + bw_g) + p_b(a + bw_b)$$

which simplifies to

$$u(w_g, w_b) = a + bp_g w_g + bp_b w_b,$$

since $p_g + p_b = 1$. So, since $u$ must be constant at, say, $\bar{u}$, along an indifference curve, this means the equation of a typical indifference curve is

$$\bar{u} = a + bp_g w_g + bp_b w_b,$$

which can be rewritten as

$$w_b = \frac{\bar{u} - a}{bp_b} - \frac{p_g}{p_b} w_g. \tag{8.8}$$

Clearly, (8.8) is the equation of a straight line with slope equal to $-p_g/p_b$. This is reflected in Figure (8.4), where the constants $a$ and $b$ of the wealth-utility function have each been arbitrarily, and without loss of generality, set equal to one. Thus, the state-contingent indifference curves for a risk-neutral individual are downward-sloping straight lines, with slope equal to $-p_g/p_b$.

Now consider the case of a risk-averse individual. From (8.7), we know that this individual's typical indifference curve will have the equation

$$\bar{u} = p_g U(w_g) + p_b U(w_b).$$

Differentiating this totally, we get

$$0 = p_g U'(w_g) dw_g + p_b U'(w_b) dw_b,$$

which can be simplified to

$$\frac{dw_b}{dw_g} = -\frac{p_g U'(w_g)}{p_b U'(w_b)}. \tag{8.9}$$

Equation (8.9) is the formula for the slope of the indifference curve at any point. First note that, along the certainty line, since $w_g = w_b$, $U'(w_g) = U'(w_b)$, and so the slope of the indifference curve will reduce to $-p_g/p_b$. This will be the slope of any state-contingent indifference curve along the certainty line.

The next question is, if we start at the certainty line and move down and to the right along the indifference curve, what is happening to its slope? It must be becoming flatter! Why? Because, as we move to the right along the indifference curve from a point on the certainty line where $w_g = w_b$, $w_g$ is becoming greater than $w_b$. Looking at Figure (8.5), which shows the risk-averse individual's concave utility function, we see that this implies $U'(w_g) < U'(w_b)$. And so, looking at (8.9), and noting that $p_g$and $p_b$ are constants, we conclude that the absolute value of the slope is now lower: the curve has become flatter. As we move further down and to the right of the indifference curve, $w_g$ and $w_b$ keep diverging and the slope of the indifference curve gets flatter and flatter. A similar analysis could be done for a movement to the left and up along the indifference curve, in which case $w_b > w_g$ and the indifference curve must therefore be becoming steeper. Thus, the indifference curve for the risk-averse person will be convex to the origin.

A similar analysis for a risk-loving person, whose wealth-utility function would be convex, would show that the state-contingent utility indifference curve would be concave to the origin. As we move down and to the right of the certainty line, $w_g > w_b$ and so $U'(w_g) > U'(w_b)$ since $U(w)$ is now convex. Thus, the absolute value of the slope of the indifference curve from (8.9) will be rising and the indifference curve will be concave to the origin.

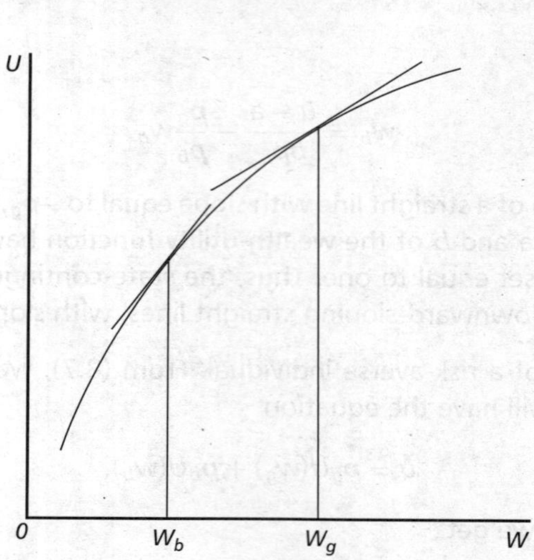


**Figure 8.5** *Utility Function for a Risk-averse Consumer*

Having established the shape of the indifference curve and the fact that its slope at the certainty line is always $-p_g/p_b$, we turn to see how we can represent an individual's choice under uncertainty using this sort of graph. Referring to our previous example, Figure 8.6 shows Anand's starting point, his 'endowment', as point *E*. In the absence of any insurance, Anand would have to 'consume' the bundle *E*. That is, he would have a wealth in the good state of $w_g = w_0 = 100$ and a wealth in the bad state of $w_b = w_0 - L = 36$. His expected utility would be $U_0$ and the indifference curve for this expected utility level is the one that passes through *E*. This indifference curve cuts the certainty line at *B*. Since $w_g = w_b$ at *B*, the wealth there is certain and therefore *B* must represent the certainty equivalent wealth, $w_{CE}$.

Note that the slope of the indifference curve at *B* must be equal to $-p_g/p_b$ (which in this case is equal to $-0.9/0.1$, or $-9$) since we have shown that that must be the slope of every indifference curve at the certainty line, regardless of the form of the utility function. If we now draw a line with this same slope through *E*, the point *A* where this line cuts the certainty line must represent the expected wealth $E(w) = \bar{w}$. Why? Because along the line *AE*, we know that $p_g w_g + p_b w_b$ is constant; evaluating this at *E*, we get $p_g w_0 + p_b(w_0 - L)$, and evaluating it at *A*, we obtain the wealth level $w_A$. Therefore,

$$w_A = p_g w_0 + p_b(w_0 - L),$$

which is $\bar{w}$. Thus, point *A* represents Anand's situation if he obtains actuarially fair insurance, since in that scenario he gets $\bar{w}$ in either state. The line *AE* can be interpreted then as the actuarially fair insurance line.

Note that the horizontal distance between *A* and *E*, the distance *DE* in Figure 8.6, is the actuarially fair premium ($= w_0 - \bar{w}$). And since $w_g$ at *B* is the certainty equivalent wealth, Anand's

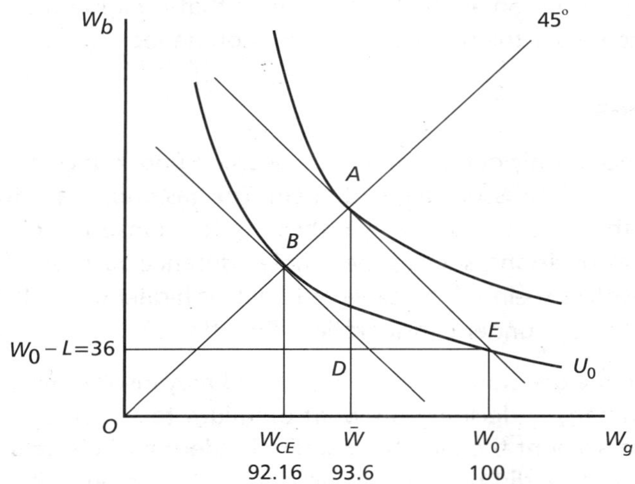


**Figure 8.6** *State-contingent Utility for a Risk-averse Consumer*

maximum willingness-to-pay for insurance would be the horizontal distance between $E$ and $B$ ($= w_0 - w_{CE}$). Finally, as a consequence, we can see that the horizontal distance between $D$ and $B$ ($= \bar{w} - w_{CE}$) is the cost of risk, $C$.

We can easily see with this approach that the risk-averse consumer would accept any insurance policy with a premium between the actuarially fair premium and the maximum willingness-to-pay. For example, in Figure 8.7, $(w_0 - F)$ represents one such premium. With this policy, Anand would

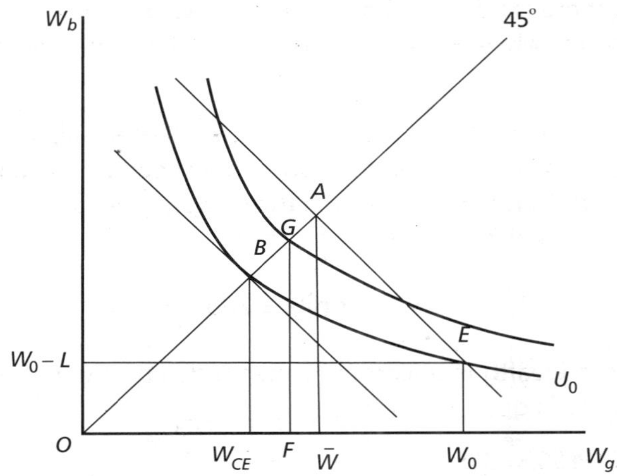


**Figure 8.7** *Alternative Insurance Policies*

be at point $G$, which clearly lies on an indifference curve that is higher than $U_0$ and hence would be a welfare improvement over the no-insurance situation he faces at $E$.

### 8.3.4 Decision Trees

The purchase of insurance is only one example of a decision under uncertainty. In fact, almost all decisions have some uncertainty associated with them. The basic approach to making or analysing these decisions under the expected utility hypothesis is to choose the decision that maximises expected utility. For many decisions, such as the simple insurance purchase decision we have been considering, this just involves seeing if the expected utility is higher under the status quo or under the scenario adopts the action under consideration. Equation (8.3) was an example of this.

Sometimes, however, the decision is not so simple, and may involve several steps. For example, when an insurance company is deciding on what premium to set on an insurance policy, they would want to take into account the fact that a policy holder may behave differently once he has insurance than he would if he did not have insurance (a phenomenon known as *moral hazard*, which we will discuss in some detail later in this chapter). An oil company trying to decide whether to undertake some exploratory surveys would want to take into consideration the fact that their subsequent decisions on drilling will be affected by the survey findings. For such situations, it is useful to analyse the situation through a **decision tree**, a device to organise a complicated decision process. The basic principle behind a decision tree is that it is important to be clear about the order in which the decisions are made and to understand what the decision-maker's optimal behaviour would be at each decision point. We will illustrate the use of a decision tree with a simple oil drilling example.

Let us start with a simple version of the problem. Suppose a risk-neutral oil company, Prospector Ltd., with a wealth of ₹200 crore, is trying to decide whether or not to drill an oil well. Drilling the well costs ₹50 crore, and there is a 50% chance that they will strike oil. If they strike oil, they will realise revenue of ₹150 crore, while if the well turns out to be 'dry' they get no revenue. Should they drill or not?

This problem is straightforward. Since the company is risk-neutral, we just need to maximise expected wealth. To solve the problem, therefore, we simply need to calculate the expected wealth under the two alternatives: drill and no-drill. Now if the company does not drill (the no-drill option), it is just left with its original wealth of ₹200 crore. Thus,

$$E(w|\text{no-drill}) = 200.$$

If it does drill, however, the wealth is uncertain: it depends upon whether the well turns out to be 'wet' or 'dry' (or the state is good or bad):

if wet: $w_g = 200 - 50 + 150 = 300.$

if dry: $w_b = 200 - 50 = 150.$

Since the probabilities of the good and bad state are each 0.5, the expected wealth is

$$E(w|\text{drill}) = \frac{1}{2} \cdot 300 + \frac{1}{2} \cdot 150 = 225. \tag{8.10}$$

Since 225 > 200, the company should drill.

Although we did not need the help of a decision tree to solve this problem, we can draw the tree to illustrate the approach. Figure 8.8 shows the tree needed to analyse this problem. The tree consists of nodes and branches, and we read from left to right to represent the sequence of events. Square nodes represent choice points for the decision-maker, with the branches radiating from them representing the different choices. Circular nodes represent points where the state of nature is revealed or uncertainties get resolved. Branches radiating from these nodes represent the different possible states of nature. At the extreme right of every sequence of branches, we write down the outcome or pay-off for the decision-maker.

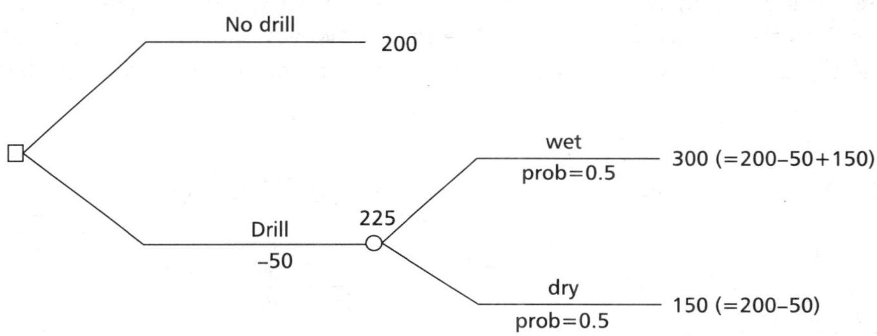


**Figure 8.8** *Decision Tree for the Simple Drilling Problem*

Turning now to Figure 8.8, we start at the left with a square node representing the firm's choice of whether or not to drill. If it does not drill, it experiences no further change in its situation and is left with its initial wealth of 200 (crore). If it does drill, which entails a cost of 50, written along that branch, it then has to see which state of nature is revealed. The round node has two branches leading away from it, reflecting the two possibilities: that the well is 'wet' or that the well is 'dry'. The pay-offs associated with each of these possibilities are written at the ends of the respective branches: 300 if the well is wet and 150 if the well is dry. Using the probabilities of each of these possibilities, we can calculate the expected pay-off if the firm drills, which we did in (8.10). We then write this expected pay-off (225) above the round node. If we now go back to the decision node, we see that the no-drill option leads to an expected pay-off of 200 and the drill option yields 225; the choice becomes very clear.

As was said earlier, we did not really need a decision tree to analyse this particular decision because it was so simple and straightforward. But now consider a slightly more complicated problem. Suppose Prospector Ltd. is trying to decide whether or not to drill the same well as before, but now has another alternative: to conduct a geological survey at a cost of ₹40 crore which would reveal to it with certainty whether the oilfield is wet or dry. Should it undertake the survey?

The tree to analyse this decision is drawn in Figure 8.9. The first decision the firm must make is whether or not to undertake the survey. If it does not undertake the survey, it finds itself at another decision node just like the one in Figure 8.8 and the rest of the tree from Figure 8.8 branches out from there. But if it does undertake the survey, it finds itself on the upper main branch of the tree in Figure 8.9. The tree is self-explanatory, so we do not need to go into the details here. But a glance at the tree shows that this is a more complicated problem than the one from Figure 8.8. Note that the four rightmost branches of the tree could perhaps have been left out because the probabilities here are all 1 or 0; they are included for completeness. In particular, if the survey did not reveal the state of the oilfield with certainty, these four branches would become essential parts of the tree. In terms of the firm's decision, we see that Prospector Ltd. is better-off not undertaking the survey, even though the survey does have a positive pay-off (210 is greater than the status quo of 200). The firm, however, maximises its pay-off by simply drilling the well directly without undertaking the survey, and ending up with the expected pay-off of 225.

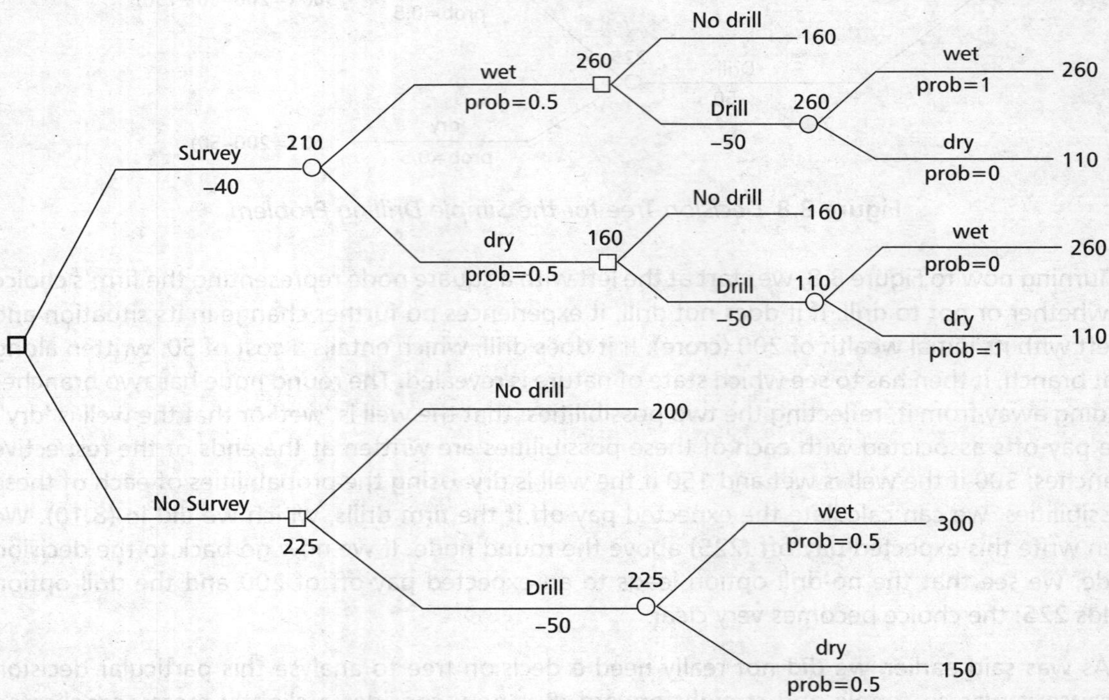


**Figure 8.9** *Decision Tree for the More Complex Drilling Problem*

Note that, in our example, the firm is risk-neutral and so the pay-offs entered were simply the expected values of the firm's wealth. But if the decision-maker were risk-averse, the pay-offs would have to be his or her utility levels or expected utility levels.

# 8.4 MARKET SOLUTIONS TO THE PROBLEMS OF UNCERTAINTY

**Task for this section:**

To understand the two basic types of market approaches to solving the problem of uncertainty: risk-pooling and risk-spreading.

In the previous section, we saw that risk-averse individuals suffer a 'cost of risk' when faced with uncertainty; they feel worse than their situation really is. The provision of insurance is a simple example of a market response to this problem of 'cost of risk'. With actuarially fair insurance, an insurance company can break even while completely eliminating the cost of risk faced by their policy holders.

In this section, we delve a little deeper into what exactly underlies this ability of the market to eliminate the cost of risk and examine two broad classes of market solutions to the problems of uncertainty: risk-pooling and risk-spreading. First, however, we need to develop an important result about the cost of risk.

## 8.4.1 A Formula for the Cost of Risk

As we saw in (8.6), the cost of risk is the difference between the expected wealth and the certainty equivalent wealth:

$$C = \bar{w} - w_{CE}.$$

This can be rewritten as

$$w_{CE} = \bar{w} - C,$$

which implies that

$$U(w_{CE}) = U(\bar{w} - C). \tag{8.11}$$

In our examples, $w$ was assumed to take on one of only two possible values, but more generally, $w$ should be treated as a random variable that can take on the values $w_i$ with probabilities $p_i$, where $\sum_{i=1}^{n} p_i = 1$.[2] Then

$$\bar{w} = \sum_{i=1}^{n} p_i w_i \tag{8.12}$$

and the expected utility is

$$\bar{U} = \sum_{i=1}^{n} p_i U(w_i).$$

Now recall that the certainty equivalent wealth yields utility equal to the expected utility under the status quo. Therefore,

$$U(w_{CE}) = \bar{U} = \sum_{i=1}^{n} p_i U(w_i).$$

Note that this is the left-hand side of (8.11).

Taking a second-order Taylor expansion of $U(w_i)$ around $\bar{w}$, we can write

$$U(w_i) \approx U(\bar{w}) + U'(\bar{w}) \cdot (w_i - \bar{w}) + \frac{1}{2} U''(\bar{w}) \cdot (w_i - \bar{w})^2.$$

Then the left-hand side of (8.11) can be written as

$$U(w_{CE}) \approx U(\bar{w}) \cdot \sum_{i=1}^{n} p_i + U'(\bar{w}) \cdot \sum_{i=1}^{n} p_i (w_i - \bar{w}) + \frac{1}{2} U''(\bar{w}) \cdot \sum_{i=1}^{n} p_i (w_i - \bar{w})^2. \tag{8.13}$$

Since $\sum_{i=1}^{n} p_i = 1$ and $\sum_{i=1}^{n} p_i (w_i - \bar{w}) = 0$, as a consequence of the definition of expected wealth seen in (8.12), (8.13) reduces to

$$U(w_{CE}) \approx U(\bar{w}) + \frac{1}{2} U''(\bar{w}) \cdot V(w), \tag{8.14}$$

since the expression

$$\sum_{i=1}^{n} p_i (w_i - \bar{w})^2$$

is by definition the variance of $w$.

Now consider the right-hand side of (8.11). Since there is not much dispersion in this expression, we can approximate it with a first-order Taylor expansion:

$$U(\bar{w} - C) \approx U(\bar{w}) - U'(\bar{w}) \cdot C. \tag{8.15}$$

---

[2] We could also treat $w$ as a continuous variable without changing this result.

We have, in (8.14) and (8.15), found expressions for the two sides of (8.11). Putting these together, we have

$$U(\bar{w}) + \frac{1}{2}U''(\bar{w}) \cdot V(w) = U(\bar{w}) - U'(\bar{w}) \cdot C,$$

which implies that

$$C = -\frac{1}{2} \cdot \frac{U''(\bar{w})}{U'(\bar{w})} \cdot V(w). \tag{8.16}$$

If we let

$$k = -\frac{1}{2} \cdot \frac{U''(\bar{w})}{U'(\bar{w})}$$

(8.16) can be written as

$$C = k \cdot V(w).$$

Now, since for a risk-averse individual $U''(\bar{w}) < 0$ and $U'(\bar{w}) > 0$, $k > 0$, and therefore we have shown that, for a risk-averse individual, the cost of risk is directly proportional to the variance of his or her wealth.

As an aside, it is worth noting that the expression for $k$ includes the ratio $-U''(\bar{w})/U'(\bar{w})$, which has been called the coefficient of absolute risk aversion and is regarded as a measure of how risk-averse an individual is. If we denote this coefficient of absolute risk aversion $A(\bar{w})$, we could write the cost of risk as

$$C = \frac{1}{2} \cdot A(\bar{w}) \cdot V(w). \tag{8.17}$$

This implies that, for any given uncertain probability distribution on wealth, the more risk-averse a person is, the higher is her cost of risk, which seems perfectly intuitive.

Equation (8.17) is an important result to help us understand market responses to uncertainty, the topic we turn to next.

### 8.4.2 Risk-Pooling

**Risk-pooling** is the process by which the cost of risk can be reduced or eliminated when there are a large number of relatively small, independent risks. Examples of risk-pooling include most kinds of insurance: life, health, disability and property insurance, and stock mutual funds.

To illustrate the principle behind risk-pooling, we will consider an idealised example. Suppose there are $n$ identical individuals, indexed by $i$, each of whose wealth, $w_i$, is drawn randomly and independently from the same distribution $f(w)$. Thus, the levels of wealth are independent and identically distributed random variables. In such a situation, the variance of the total wealth will be

$$V(w_1 + w_2 + \cdots + w_n) = V(w_1) + V(w_2) + \cdots + V(w_n).$$

That is, using the fact that all the $w_i'$s are identically distributed,

$$V\left(\sum_{i=1}^{n} w_i\right) = n \cdot V(w). \tag{8.18}$$

Letting $k = \frac{1}{2}A(\bar{w})$, we know from (8.17) that the cost of risk for each individual is

$$C_i = k \cdot V(w)$$

and so the total cost of risk among all individuals is

$$C = \sum_{i=1}^{n} C_i = n \cdot k \cdot V(w). \tag{8.19}$$

Now consider a type of insurance. The individuals all get together and decide to pool their wealth. Once they have received their wealth draws, they pool their wealth and divide it equally. Thus, each individual will get the average wealth:

$$\bar{w} = \frac{\sum_{i=1}^{n} w_i}{n}.$$

The variance of the mean $\bar{w}$ is given by

$$V(\bar{w}) = \frac{1}{n^2} \cdot V\left(\sum_{i=1}^{n} w_i\right).$$

Applying (8.18), this becomes

$$V(\bar{w}) = \frac{1}{n^2} \cdot n \cdot V(w) = \frac{1}{n} \cdot V(w).$$

The cost of risk for each individual will now be

$$C_i = k \cdot V(\bar{w}) = \frac{k}{n} \cdot V(w) \tag{8.20}$$

and, if the number of individuals in the pool is large, this cost of risk tends to zero:

$$\lim_{n \to \infty} C_i = 0.$$

The use of pooling has driven down dramatically the cost of risk for each individual. Also, even the total cost of risk has become very small relative to the pre-insurance level we saw in (8.19).

Using (8.20), we can write the total cost of risk now as

$$C = \sum_{i=1}^{n} C_i = k \cdot V(w).$$

Thus, it is at $\frac{1}{n}$th the original level.

Of course, in reality, people's wealth is not a draw from the same distribution as everyone else's. Nevertheless, insurance operates on this principle of risk-pooling. An insurance company takes the individual risks that people face, which are largely independent of each other, and pools them, reimbursing the ones who have unfortunate draws and collecting net revenues from those who do not suffer any losses. Stock mutual funds operate on the same principle also. By buying shares in many different companies, they essentially pool all the individual risks that companies face and end up getting a return that is the average of the returns of all the individual companies in their portfolio. In this way, they insulate their investors from the possibility of a large loss if a company goes out of business, say. What mutual funds cannot do is insulate their investors from the risks that all companies face together, such as the risk of an overall economic slowdown. We will return later to discuss this 'systemic' or 'market' risk.

### 8.4.3 Risk-Spreading

Another important market response to the problem of risk is **risk-spreading**, the process by which the cost of risk associated with large risks can be reduced or eliminated. This is the principle underlying the joint-stock corporation.

Say Meenakshi faces a very large risk. Perhaps she is undertaking a large, risky investment, the results of which are spread over a wide distribution. Let the net pay-off from this investment be represented by the random variable $y$, and disregard other sources of income or wealth. Then the cost of risk associated with this investment, as in (8.15), is

$$C = k \cdot V(y).$$

If $V(y)$ is large, this might be quite large also.

Now suppose Meenakshi breaks up her investment into $n$ 'shares', each of which gets $\frac{1}{n}$th of the net pay-off, and distributes (or sells) these $n$ shares to $n$ investors just like herself. Then each investor's cost of risk will be

$$C_i = k \cdot V\left(\frac{y}{n}\right) \tag{8.21}$$

$$= \frac{k}{n^2} \cdot V(y).$$

If $n$ is sufficiently large, $C_i$ can be made as small as desired, since

$$\lim_{n\to\infty} C_i = 0. \tag{8.22}$$

Even the total cost of risk has now been driven down dramatically since

$$\sum_{i=1}^{n} C_i = nC_i$$

$$= \frac{k}{n} \cdot V(y)$$

and so

$$\lim_{n\to\infty} \sum_{i=1}^{n} C_i = 0.$$

Thus, by splitting up her project into relatively small shares, that is, spreading the risk, Meenakshi can essentially eliminate the cost of risk. This is exactly what joint-stock companies do. By dividing the ownership of the company into millions of shares, they allow investors to decide what proportion of any risky investment they can handle in their portfolios.

Another example of risk-spreading is the phenomenon of reinsurance. When insurance companies write (i.e. sell) homeowner insurance policies, most of the risk they face is idiosyncratic, that is, it is specific to the individual policy. The house might burn down, or it might be burglarised, or the roof might develop a leak. These small risks in each individual home are independent from similar risks in other homes, and the insurance company can safely insure them through the pooling of risks. But there are several other risks that homeowners in any one area might face simultaneously, notably the risk from natural catastrophes such as earthquakes, cyclones and tsunamis. If, for example, a major earthquake were to hit a large city such as Delhi, or a large cyclone hit a city such as Kolkata, insurance companies which had sold homeowner policies to many individuals in these cities would suddenly face very large losses and would need to pay out large sums of money in insurance claims. This is the kind of 'large risk' we have been talking about in this section. To protect themselves from the cost of risk and the liquidity problems they may face from the need to pay out large sums of money in insurance claims, insurance companies themselves buy insurance, which is called reinsurance. There are companies that specialise in this business and they are called reinsurance companies. The way the reinsurance market works is on the principle of risk-spreading. Every large property insurance company divides their catastrophe risk into many shares, perhaps 100 or 200 shares, and sells these shares individually to many different reinsurance companies. In this way, the large risk faced by our insurance company is spread over a large number of reinsurance companies.

# 8.5 BARRIERS TO EFFICIENCY IN RISK MARKETS

**Task for this section:**

To study three types of problems that may arise in using market approaches to solving the problem of uncertainty: correlated risks, adverse selection and moral hazard. The presence of any of these problems prevents the full realisation of the potential gains from risk-pooling and risk-spreading.

In the previous section, we have seen how risk-pooling and risk-spreading allow markets to lessen or even eliminate the negative welfare effects of uncertainty. Under simplified assumptions, the cost of risk can be driven down to zero. In actual practice, however, there are barriers to markets achieving perfect efficiency, and we will discuss three broad classes of such barriers in this section.

## 8.5.1 Correlated Risks

In all of the examples discussed in the previous section, it was assumed that the risks were all independent of each other. For example, in the section on risk-pooling, it was assumed that each person's risk or wealth was independent from everyone else's. In the discussion of risk-spreading, no attention was paid to the possibility that the returns to the project under consideration might be correlated with the other sources of income or wealth of the investors. When this independence assumption is not satisfied, the ability of these market mechanisms to handle the problem of uncertainty is diminished.

For example, in the analysis of risk-spreading, we took the cost of risk to the individual shareholder in (8.21) to be

$$C_i = k \cdot V(y_i)$$

which assumes that $y_i$ is independent from the shareholder's other income. But suppose that $y_i$ is not independent from the shareholder's other income $x_i$. In that case, the cost of risk is

$$C_i = k \cdot \left[V(y_i) + 2Cov(y_i, x_i)\right],$$

where $Cov(y_i, x_i)$ is the covariance between $y_i$ and $x_i$. Contrary to our result in (8.22), the sum of these $C_i'$s may not go to zero as the number of investors becomes large. Thus, risk-spreading will not work as well as we might have hoped. It is important to note that some reduction in the cost of risk does take place through risk-spreading. It is just not eliminated completely.

Covariance between a risk and the rest of an investor's income may not be a bad thing. If

$$Cov(y_i, x_i) < 0,$$

that is, if the risk is *negatively* correlated with the investor's other income, it can serve as a hedge and may therefore be quite desirable as an investment. A **hedge** is any investment that performs well when the rest of the investor's portfolio is performing poorly and therefore tends to 'smooth' the returns. A risk-averse person may actually like actuarially unfair investments if they serve as hedges.

For example, consider a farmer (let us call him Karan) who is risk-averse with the utility function

$$U(y) = \sqrt{y}.$$

He farms without irrigation and his income is ₹10,000 if the rains are good and ₹3,600 if the rains are poor. Suppose the probability that the rains are good is $\frac{1}{2}$. Karan is thinking of buying a share in a tube well. The annual cost will be ₹1,900 and, although it will not help at all in seasons when the rains are good, it will boost the value of his harvest by ₹3,484 if the rains are poor. Now the expected value of this investment is

$$E(\Delta y) = -1900 + \frac{1}{2} \cdot 3{,}484 = -158.$$

Thus, it is actuarially unfair and this looks like a poor investment.

But consider Karan's expected utility. With the well, his income would now be ₹8,100 if the rains are good (10,000 minus the cost of the well 1,900) and ₹5,184 if the rains are poor (= 3,600 − 1,900 + 3,484). So his expected utility in the two scenarios is

$$EU|\text{no well} = \frac{1}{2} \cdot \sqrt{10{,}000} + \frac{1}{2} \cdot \sqrt{3{,}600} = 80.$$

$$EU|\text{well} = \frac{1}{2} \cdot \sqrt{8{,}100} + \frac{1}{2} \cdot \sqrt{5{,}184} = 81.$$

So Karan is actually better-off with the well than without it. Even though the well looks like a poor investment when evaluated in isolation, it is desirable since it serves as a hedge against the times when the rains are poor.

Nevertheless, the fact remains that investments that are positively correlated with investors' other sources of income are problematic in the cost of these risks cannot be driven down to zero through risk-spreading. The 'undiversifiable' or 'systemic market' risk is something all investors have to deal with.

### 8.5.2 Asymmetric Information

When two economic agents undertake a transaction under uncertainty, it is quite possible, indeed likely, that they will possess different information about it. One is likely to be better informed than the other about things that bear directly upon the transaction. For example, the seller of a product probably has a much better idea about its quality than the customer, especially when the product is used or second-hand. Someone looking to buy life or health insurance probably has a much better idea about their health status and lifestyle habits than the insurer. A person buying car insurance knows their driving style and their plans for how well they plan to maintain their car better than does the insurer. An employee will know much better than an employer, especially a potential employer, if he or she is honest, hard-working and able. These are all situations of **asymmetric information**, where the two sides to a transaction have different amounts of information that bears on the transaction, and this asymmetry makes it more difficult and perhaps even impossible to complete the transaction. In this section, we will consider two broad classes of problems that arise in situations of asymmetric information: adverse selection and moral hazard.

#### *8.5.2.1 Adverse Selection*

One particular problem that can arise in such situations of asymmetric information is **adverse selection**. This is the tendency that, at any given price, the owner of the lowest quality or least suitable product will have the greatest incentive to undertake the transaction. As a result, the less-informed other side of the transaction will be wary and might even choose to leave the market because of the uncertainty and the potential for welfare loss. In extreme cases, the market may completely unravel and cease to function.

The classic example of adverse selection was offered by George Akerlof in his seminal paper on this topic: the used car market.[3] Owners of used cars have a much better idea of their quality than do potential buyers, who perhaps assume that any car offered to them is of average quality. They are therefore willing-to-pay an 'average' price. Say there is a universe of potential used cars. In a world of perfect information, each car's quality would be known perfectly to both parties, and a transaction can be completed if the buyer's willingness-to-pay is greater than or equal to the seller's reservation value. Each car would have a price based on its quality. But, in a world of asymmetric information, if the buyer cannot distinguish between good and bad cars, he will probably base his decision on the average quality $\bar{x}$ and therefore pay an average price $\bar{p}$. If all the sellers are willing to accept this average price, all cars can be sold. The problem of adverse selection arises, however, if owners of high-quality cars feel that $\bar{p}$ is an inadequate price for their car and therefore decide not to sell their cars. If they withdraw their cars from the market, the average quality of cars on offer falls, and so will the average price buyers are willing-to-pay. Thus, the price of used cars will fall. This may cause some more sellers of relatively high-quality cars to withdraw from the market, leading to another drop in the average quality and hence in the price. This process, Akerlof argued, could continue to the point where the market completely unravels and only cars of the lowest quality are offered for sale. Even if we do not have this extreme result, we will see a tendency for owners to hold on to their cars for longer than they might in a world of perfect information; if they could get 'full price' for their used cars, they would probably sell

---

[3] George Akerlof: 'The Market for "Lemons": Quality Uncertainty and the Market Mechanism', *The Quarterly Journal of Economics*, Vol. 84, No. 3. (Aug. 1970), pp. 488–500.

earlier. The used car market will be populated disproportionately with 'lemons', cars of low quality. Thus, there has been an 'adverse selection' in terms of the quality of cars offered for sale.

The same sort of problem can arise in insurance markets. People buying insurance know more about themselves and their habits than do insurance companies. If insurance companies offer policies based on the 'average' risk, people of high quality (i.e. low risk of loss) may find the policy too expensive for their risk profile and may therefore drop out of the market. The insurance company will find that the average risk of their policyholders is higher than they had anticipated, causing them to raise prices, and resulting in a further round of relatively high-quality risks dropping out of the market. As in the used car case, the process could cause the whole market to unravel, or to result in an equilibrium in which some of the high-quality risks are unserved.

Let us see a little more specifically how this happens and what the equilibrium looks like. In order to do this, we will use the state-contingent utility model developed in section 3.3. We will take again the example of the man we called Anand whose wealth is 100, but who faces a risk that the wealth could fall to 36 if he suffers a catastrophic loss. If the probability of this loss is 0.10 or 10%, the actuarially fair insurance premium is 6.4, and if Anand's utility function is $U(w) = \sqrt{w}$, his willingness-to-pay for insurance is 7.84. We saw in Figure 8.6 how his 'endowment' could be represented as point $E$ in the state-contingent space, and that, if he obtained acuarially fair insurance, he would end up at $A$, on a higher indifference curve than he would be on at $E$. The equilibrium is shown again in Figure 8.10.

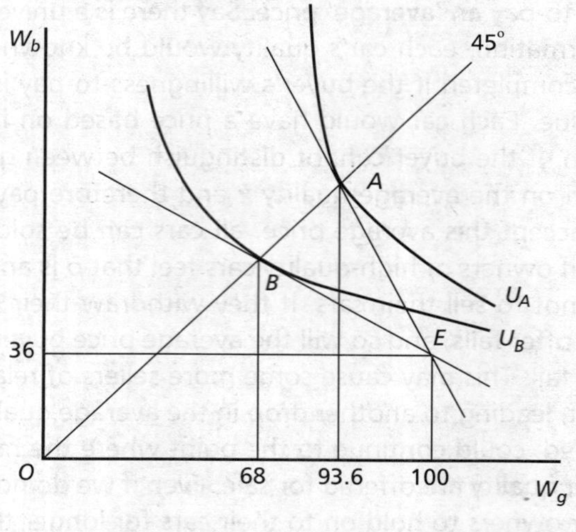


**Figure 8.10** *Adverse Selection in an Insurance Market*

Remember that $U_A$ and $U_B$ are indifference curves belonging to different people, so they can cross!

Now suppose there is another individual, let us call her Bhavana, whose situation is identical to Anand's except that, whereas his probability of loss was 10%, Bhavana's probability of loss is 50%. Thus, Bhavana is a low-quality risk compared to Anand. The actuarially fair insurance premium for her would be her potential loss (64) times the probability of loss ($\frac{1}{2}$); thus, it would be 32. If the insurance company could identify Bhavana as a low-quality risk, they could offer her a policy with a premium of 32, and she would accept this gladly, as it would get her to point *B* in Figure 8.10 as opposed to *E*.

But what if the insurance company cannot distinguish between Anand and Bhavana (in terms of their riskiness)? In that case, they have to charge them the same premium. Now, assuming Anand's and Bhavana's risks are independent of one another, the insurance company's expected loss if they insure both is the sum of the two expected losses: $32 + 6.4 = 38.4$. They would have to charge them each 19.2 in order to break even. This would be the 'average' policy they would have to offer if they cannot distinguish the good risks such as Anand from the bad risks such as Bhavana. The trouble is, while Bhavana would be quite happy with this insurance contract, Anand's willingness-to-pay for it is only 7.84, as we saw before. He would therefore drop out of the market. The insurance company would realise through their loss experience that they have only bad risks left and would raise their price to 32. Thus, adverse selection would be complete. The high-quality (low-risk) type would have been eliminated from the market and only the low-quality (high-risk) type would remain. This is the equivalent of only lemons selling in the used car market.

The best that could happen for the low-risk types such as Anand is for them to be offered partial insurance. A partial insurance policy is one which paid only part of the loss and charged only part (the same proportionate part) of the full premium. For example, a full actuarially fair insurance policy for Anand would cost 6.40 and would pay 64 if he suffered the loss. A half policy would cost 3.20 and would pay 32 in the event of a loss.

Anand cannot get full insurance because, if the insurance company offered policies that paid 64 for a 6.40 premium, low-risk types such as Bhavana would buy those policies. So the partial policy Anand would have to be offered would have to be one that was not more attractive to Bhavana than the policy at *B*, a full insurance policy for a premium of 32. Figure 8.11 illustrates the situation. The lines *a* and *b* represent the actuarially fair insurance policies for the two types, as in Figure 8.10. *B* is the point where Bhavana ends up after she takes full insurance and $U_B$ represents the utility level she attains as a result. The point *P* represents the best partial policy that Anand can get, since any policy on the line segment *PA* would be on a higher indifference curve for Bhavana and she would want to switch to it. Therefore, *P* is the largest policy Anand can be given without inducing a change in Bhavana's behaviour, since *P* is on the same indifference curve for her as *B*. The policy at *P* will be a fraction of Anand's full insurance policy, the fraction being equal to the ratio of *EP* to *EA*. If the line segment *EP* is 40% of the length of *EA*, the policy at *P* would involve a premium of $2.56 (= 6.4 \times 0.4)$ and a payout of $25.60 (= 64 \times 0.4)$ if Anand suffers the loss.

#### 8.5.2.2 Moral Hazard

Another broad class of problems caused by asymmetric information fall under the general classification known as **moral hazard**. This occurs when one party to the transaction can alter their

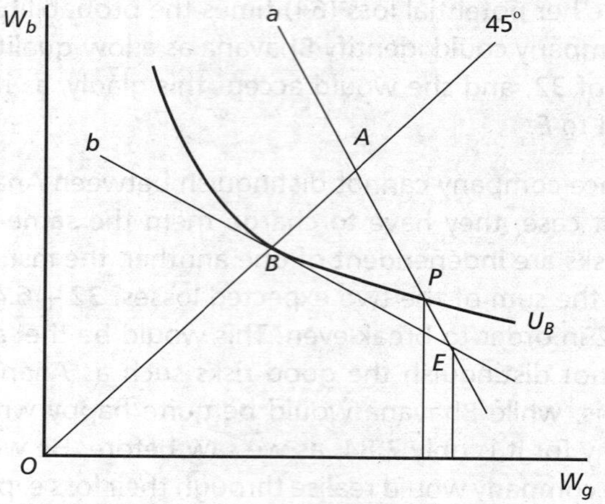


**Figure 8.11** *Separating Equilibrium with Adverse Selection*

behaviour as a result of the transaction in a way that adversely affects the other party's interests and yet cannot be observed or disentangled from the effects of uncertainty. The term originated in the insurance industry. When trade between Europe and the Americas first began, it was a highly risky activity since ships were subject to severe storms and piracy. Shipowners naturally sought insurance against these risks and the market responded by providing insurance to them. Unscrupulous shipowners realised that they could claim their ships were lost at sea even if they were not. They could, for example, be repainted, given new names and put to work sailing between America and the Caribbean, say, thereby escaping detection by the insurers in London. The fraudulent nature of this activity earned it the title 'moral hazard', which distinguished it from the true hazards of stormy weather and pirates.

Fraudulent insurance claims are, of course, still very much a bane of the insurance industry, but these are not the only examples of what we call moral hazard today. Employees, for example, can steal from their employers, both explicitly and implicitly, by not working hard or shirking their responsibilities. Contractors can use shoddy materials or take shortcuts in construction. Patients who have health insurance can go to the doctor more often than they would if they did not have insurance and so on.

Let us take the **medical insurance** case as an example, since there seems to be nothing morally wrong in what is going on and yet we have a fundamental problem caused by uncertainty and incentives to which there is no known solution. Suppose in an average year Sheila's marginal benefit curve from doctor's appointments is given by the curve $n(p)$ in Figure 8.12. This can be thought of as a demand curve; it shows that some visits have a high value for her and some have low marginal benefits. If the cost of a doctor's visit is $c$ and Sheila, not having any health insurance, is charged that much per visit, she would visit the doctor $n_c$ times in an average year, where $n_c$ is the quantity at which the height of Sheila's marginal benefit curve is $c$. Of course, this

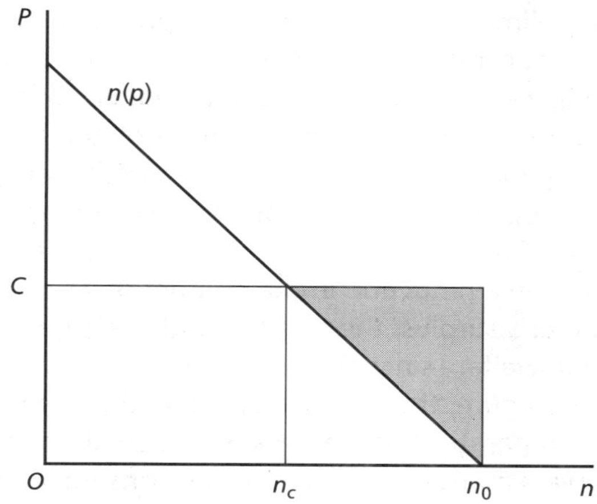


**Figure 8.12** *Moral Hazard under Medical Insurance*

'demand' curve would shift up and down depending upon whether or not Sheila got sick, and how seriously, but Figure 8.12 represents the average.

Now suppose Sheila got health insurance, precisely because there is a chance she could get sick or injured and need lots of medical care. For simplicity, let us assume she pays her health insurance premium and her policy then entitles her to visit the doctor as often as she 'needs' to at no additional cost to her. In that case, the 'price' she faces for doctor's visits is now zero and, as a result, she would visit the doctor $n_0$ times in an average year, where $n_0$ is the quantity at which her marginal benefit falls to zero. Having insurance has caused Sheila to alter her behaviour, and this is the crux of the moral hazard problem.

Note that, for the insurance company to break even, the premium they must charge for health insurance is given by the rectangle $c \cdot n_0$, which is the total cost of Sheila's visits. This is the average price they charge everyone. And everyone could be better-off if they could be persuaded to go to the doctor only if their marginal benefit exceeded $c$. Why? Because their health premiums would be lower. If the average consumer such as Sheila went to the doctor only $n_c$ times a year, their health insurance premium would be only $c \cdot n_c$, assuming a competitive insurance market. Sheila's surplus would be the consumer's surplus triangle above $c$. But, with health insurance, if the average consumer goes to the doctor $n_0$ times a year and pays a health insurance premium of $c \cdot n_0$, her surplus will be lower by the shaded area. The extra visits from $n_c$ to $n_0$ have an aggregate benefit equal to the area below the demand curve between those visits, but they cost the consumer the rectangle $c \cdot (n_0 - n_c)$. The shaded area is a deadweight loss due to moral hazard. The idea behind health insurance is to pool a large number of independent risks and thereby reduce the cost of risk to zero. Although that goal may be achieved, the presence of moral hazard creates an inefficiency and resultant deadweight loss.

The only way to completely eliminate this moral hazard problem is to force patients to pay the full cost of their doctor visits, but this would then destroy the insurance aspect of the solution. Short of this, other techniques can be used to reduce the extent of the moral hazard, but they cannot eliminate it. For example, one simple modification of the insurance contract is to add a copayment, a small amount that the patient must pay each time she visits the doctor.[4] In Figure 8.13, $m$ represents the copayment, set intentionally smaller than the cost of the visit $c$ in order to preserve the insurance function of the contract. Forcing the patient to pay $m$ each time she has an appointment results in a reduction in the number of visits from $n_0$ to $n_m$ and causes a small apparent loss in consumer's surplus, the small triangle below $n(p)$ between $n_m$ and $n_0$. But there is a large improvement in welfare since the deadweight loss is reduced by the comparatively much larger shaded area in the figure, the area below $c$ and above $n(p)$ between the same limits. The welfare improvement is comparatively great because the small copayment eliminates precisely those visits that have the lowest marginal benefit for the consumer, and the highest associated deadweight loss. In a competitive insurance market, these savings result in a reduction in the health insurance premium Sheila has to pay, so the benefit ultimately accrues to the patient.

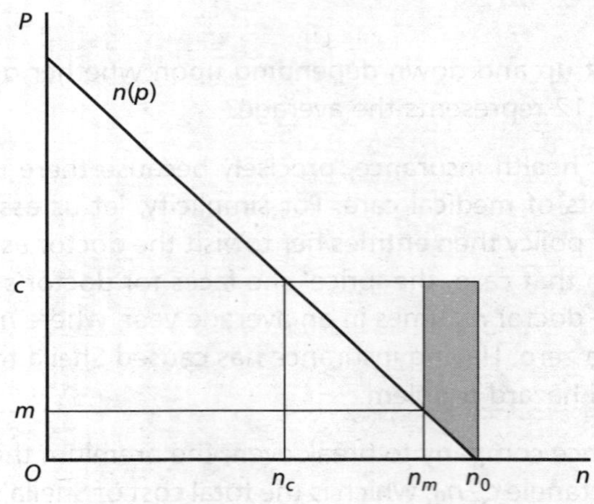


**Figure 8.13** *The Effect of a Copay under Medical Insurance*

There is a broad and important class of moral hazard problems that are classified as examples of what is called the **principal–agent problem**. These are all situations where one agent (the principal) is trying to set up a contract that will govern the behaviour and compensation of the other (the agent). The agent's actions affect the final outcome for the principal and the moral hazard problem is that the agent, in pursuing his own self-interest, will not do what he is supposed to do, at least not to the extent that the principal would like him to do it (and that he is contractually

[4] The equivalent of this in property insurance is the deductible, a small amount that is deducted from the amount of the claim before it is paid by the insurance company.

obliged to do). There are many examples of such relationships. Some prominent ones are the relationship between the shareholders of a firm (the principals) and the corporate managers (the agents), homeowners and contractors, landowners and their sharecropping tenants and so on. In all these situations, it has proved impossible to design contracts that can lead the parties to the first-best solution.

Let us take the example of the landholder and his sharecropping tenant to illustrate the problem. This particular example also has some other insurance-like aspects to it that make it particularly interesting. So consider the problem faced by the owner of agricultural land who does not plan to cultivate it himself, but needs to find someone else to do so. He needs to structure a contract with the cultivator in order to maximise his returns. There are several aspects of this problem that need to be examined.

The first thing to note is that agricultural output is inherently uncertain. Inputs such as labour applied early in the growing season bear fruit only at harvest time and a host of factors such as weather, intrusion of pests, availability of water and so on, in addition to the inputs over which the cultivator has control, affect the size of the final harvest. Thus, it is virtually impossible to disentangle the effects of reduced application of labour and effort from adverse external circumstances.

The second thing to note is that the landowner and cultivator are likely to have quite different attitudes to risk. At least in a country such as India, the landowner is likely to be considerably wealthier than the farmer. As a result, the landowner is probably much less risk-averse than the cultivator; it might even be reasonable for purposes of this analysis to assume that the landlord is risk-neutral while the cultivator is risk-averse. There are two important implications of this difference. First, while the landowner would like to maximise the expected value of the harvest, the cultivator would want to 'play it safe' and protect himself against significant adversity; thus, their choice of actions would be different. Second, because of the risk neutrality (or lower degree of risk aversion) of the landlord, he is better able to shoulder risk. The ideal contract therefore from this point of view would allocate all the risk-bearing to him, freeing the risk-averse cultivator from having to bear any risk at all.

A third thing worth noting is that, in principle, the landowner could choose from three different types of contracts: fixed rent, hired labour and sharecropping. In a fixed rent contract, the landowner would charge a fixed rent to the farmer, who would then be the residual claimant on the harvest (i.e. he would get to keep all the surplus after paying the rent). This sort of contract maximises the incentive for the cultivator to put in effort, but it also exposes him to a lot of uncertainty. It is the best contract in terms of incentives, but the worst contract in terms of the allocation of risk-bearing.

In a hired labour contract, the landlord simply hires the farmer and pays him a fixed wage. In this case, the landlord becomes the residual claimant on the harvest. This contract is ideal from the point of view of risk-bearing, since it allocates all the risk to the landlord and none to the cultivator. But it is the worst contract in terms of incentives, since the worker has little incentive to put in the requisite effort. Since his lack of effort could easily be 'hidden' behind claimed adverse circumstances, the farmer has a high incentive to shirk at his job, making it necessary to monitor him and thereby adding another layer of cost to the production process. For this reason, we tend not to see this sort of contract unless the landowner himself is on the scene and able to monitor the cultivator.

The sharecropping contract strikes a balance between the other two types of contract. In this contract, the landowner and cultivator agree to share the harvest; sharing equally is overwhelmingly the most common sharing ratio seen all over the world, although others are known. With this, neither the sharing of risk nor the incentives are ideal, but there is a balance in both. Because we want to focus on the moral hazard problem, we will abstract away from all the other issues surrounding the relationship and concentrate on the incentives aspect.

Suppose $F(L)$ represents the value of the harvest as a function of the amount of labour input $L$. $F(L)$ would be increasing and concave to indicate that, as the amount of labour input rises, output rises, but at a decreasing rate. Suppose the opportunity cost of labour can be represented by a market wage rate $w$. In that case, the surplus of the farm, $W$, can be written as

$$W = F(L) - wL$$

and maximisation of that surplus would require

$$\frac{dW}{dL} = F'(L) - w = 0. \tag{8.23}$$

In other words, labour should be input up to the point where the marginal revenue product of labour, $F'(L)$, is equal to $w$. In panel (a) of Figure 8.14, this optimum is shown as $L^*$, and this represents the first-best level of labour input. The landlord would like to design a contract that induces the cultivator to input this much labour in the farm.

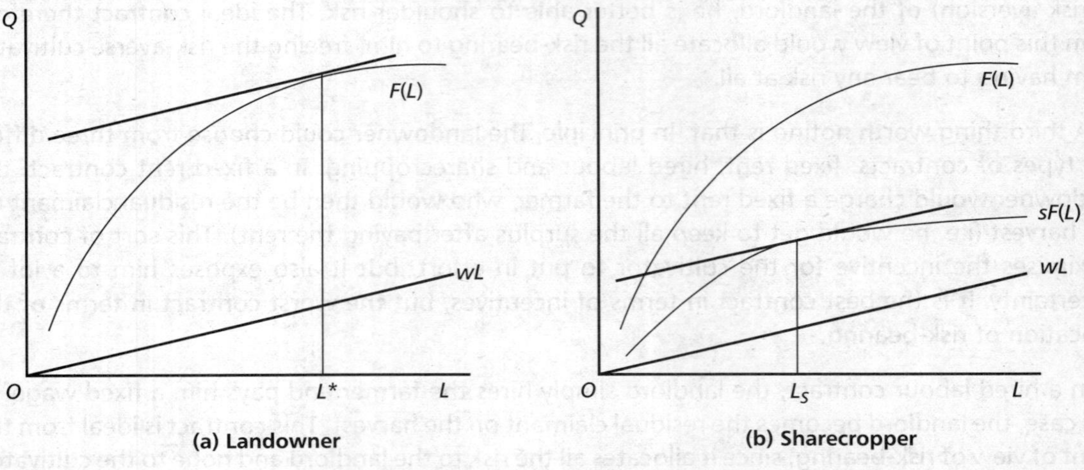


**Figure 8.14** *Moral Hazard under Sharecropping*

Let us see what the farmer's incentives are under a sharecropping contract. Suppose the contract gives him half the harvest. In that case, his pay-off is the function $sF(L)$ in panel (b) of Figure 8.14, which is everywhere half as high as $F(L)$. If the opportunity cost to him of his time is still $w$, perhaps because the alternative to working on the farm is to hire himself out as a casual labourer at that wage rate, his individual surplus is given by

$$S = \frac{1}{2}F(L) - wL$$

and maximisation of this surplus would require

$$\frac{dS}{dL} = \frac{1}{2}F'(L) - w = 0. \tag{8.24}$$

Thus, the cultivator has the incentive to input his labour only up to the point where *half* the marginal revenue product of labour is equal to the wage rate. This is shown as $L_s$ in panel (b) of Figure 8.14. We see clearly that $L_s < L^*$, and this is the crux of the moral hazard problem here. If the sharecropper were working on a fixed rent contract, he would have the incentive to put in $L^*$ amount of labour, but this contract involves a suboptimal allocation of risk-bearing. Alternatively, if the landlord could observe the worker's level of labour input, he could structure a contract that rewarded the cultivator for his labour. But this would require an expensive system of monitoring; in the extreme, the landlord would have to be physically present himself to observe the cultivator's labour input. Thus, there is no way to achieve the first-best allocation.

In India today, perhaps the biggest problem that exemplifies moral hazard is the problem of corruption at all levels of government. The government's employees, including civil servants and elected officials, are agents of the citizens of the country, who are the principals in this version of the principal–agent problem. Obviously, the electoral system is an insufficient tool to monitor the agents in this case in order to ensure their compliance with the wishes of the principals.

# 8.6 METHODS TO OVERCOME INEFFICIENCIES IN RISK MARKETS

**Task for this section:**

To look at two types of responses to the problems of adverse selection and moral hazard: screening and signalling.

In the previous section, we looked at some factors that cause inefficiències in markets characterised by uncertainty, particularly the problems that arise when the parties to transactions have informational asymmetries. As economists have become more aware of these problems, they have also become more aware of various ways in which economic agents attempt to lessen the impact of asymmetric information. We discuss a few of these in this section.

### 8.6.1 Screening

In any situation of asymmetric information, the economic actor who has less information has an incentive to acquire more. Activities by which this agent can acquire more information about the other are known as **screening**. Screening is particularly important in situations involving adverse selection, when one side of the transaction does not know the other's 'type'. The basic approach is to try to observe characteristics that are observable and are correlated with the type in order to learn more about the type. A more sophisticated approach is to screen through tests or other such methods that induce the different types to choose differently, thereby self-sorting themselves and revealing their types.

Consider the insurance example. Someone seeking life or health insurance probably knows more about their type than an insurance company would. The most direct form of screening would be for the insurance company to require that a questionnaire be filled out, in which they ask questions about the person's health history and lifestyle habits such as smoking and drug use. Perhaps they might ask also about their parents' and grandparents' health history in order to learn about any genetic predispositions. To the extent that there may be information that could be damaging to the respondent's interests, the answers on such a questionnaire may not always be truthful. The insurance company therefore has an incentive to gather information independently. They may, for example, require a medical examination. For car insurance, they may look to see if the applicant has a clean driving record or has been involved in accidents or been cited for traffic violations. For property insurance, they may inspect the property to learn the construction quality and whether or not safety equipment has been installed. All these are forms of screening to learn more about the applicant's type or risk of loss.

The more sophisticated form of screening would involve offering those seeking insurance a menu of choices in such a way that they would self-select into groups according to their different types. We saw an example of this in Figure 8.11 where, by offering two types of policies, *B* and *P*, the insurance company was able to induce the types to sort themselves. Only the high-risk types would select the policy *B* and the low-risk types would choose *P*.

Employers similarly screen potential or actual employees. They look at resumes, subject them to tests, call them to interviews and so on. All these are attempts to learn more about the job seeker so as to make a better estimate of their ability and their work habits. More sophisticated methods of screening would involve offering employees a menu of job options such that they would self-select into different groups. For example, a firm could offer their employees a choice between two types of jobs: one with low pay and low hourly requirements and the other with high pay and high hourly requirements. If designed correctly, the high-pay jobs would be infeasible for workers with low ability, as they would not be able to put in the hours *they* would need to expend (which would be more than the number of hours needed by a high-ability worker). In this way, the employees could be induced to self-select into different jobs and therefore reveal their types.

### 8.6.2 Signalling

We have seen that the problem of adverse selection creates a situation where the high-quality types (good cars, low-risk insurance customers, high-ability workers) end up being underserved or undercompensated by the market because the market is unable to distinguish them directly from the low-quality types. They therefore have the incentive to reveal their type so that the market can give them their due. Activities that credibly reveal the agent's type are called **signalling**.

For example, the owner of a good-quality car might try to reveal the quality of the car by providing to potential buyers a detailed chronology, documented by receipts, of all the servicing the car has received over its lifetime. Showing that the car was serviced regularly, had its oil changed every 5,000 km and has not been in an accident are all fairly good signals of the car's quality. The owner of a well-maintained car would therefore have an incentive to reveal this information to potential buyers.

The classic example of signalling is education, suggested originally by Michael Spence in his seminal work on the subject.[5] Spence showed that, under certain conditions, acquiring a higher education may signal a worker's ability. In such situations, potential employees would have an incentive to acquire an education even if the education itself contributed nothing to raising their ability or productivity. The key condition driving Spence's result is that education should be less costly psychically for high-ability workers than it is for low-ability workers. Low-ability workers could acquire a higher education, but it would be a struggle for them, causing them enough psychic disutility that they would find their utility would be higher if they did not acquire the education. In this case, acquiring a higher education would be optimal or rational only for high-ability workers and therefore the act of acquiring the education would signal their quality.

The basic argument is illustrated in Figure 8.15. Suppose there are two types of jobs, jobs that require a low level of skill and others that require a high level of skill. If firms can match high-ability workers with the high-skill jobs, they can pay a wage of $w_H$ and break even. Low-skill jobs can use workers of either ability and pay $w_L$. If firms cannot distinguish between the two types of workers, there would be a difficult adverse selection problem, because low-ability workers are unable to perform the high-skill jobs.

Now consider the situation created if the cost of acquiring an education is negatively correlated with ability. In the figure, the level of education is measured along the horizontal axis. Suppose $e^*$ represents a college degree, and suppose the costs of acquiring an education for the two types of workers are represented by the lines $c_L$ (for the low-ability type) and $c_H$ (for the high-ability type).

---

[5] Michael Spence: 'Job Market Signaling', *Quarterly Journal of Economics*, Vol. 87, No. 3 (Aug. 1973), pp. 355–374.

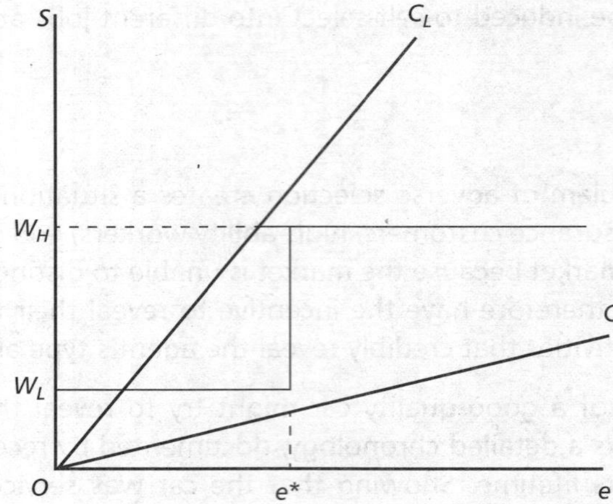


**Figure 8.15** *Education as a Signal*

Given the configuration in the figure, the low-ability types will not find it profitable to acquire the education level e*, because the cost of acquiring it is higher than the benefit from it. They are better-off with no education at all. The high-ability types could get the same surplus from no education, but they could get more surplus by acquiring the education e* and hence the wage $w_H$. Thus, they could signal their quality to employers. Note that, while education serves as a *signal* from the point of view of the workers, and they can use this signal by acquiring an education, it is a *screen* from the point of view of the firm. If they consciously set e* as the threshold for awarding the higher wage, knowing that workers will then self-sort, they are engaging in screening. To the extent that high-ability workers are consciously acquiring an education because they know firms correlate education with ability, they are engaging in signalling.

There are many other examples of signalling. An important and prominent one is brand advertising. Suppose there is a good about which consumers can acquire information only by actually consuming it. Once they try it, they would become regular customers for the good if they like it but would never consume it again if they do not like it. Now consider the problem of the firm producing the good. They know the quality of the good, which consumers do not, establishing a situation of asymmetric information. Suppose the firm could induce a lot of consumers to try the good by engaging in a major advertising campaign. The question is: would such a campaign be worth it? The answer depends upon the cost of the campaign and the quality of the good. If the quality of the good is low, not many consumers will like the good and therefore not many will become regular customers. In that case, the advertising campaign may not be worth it. However, if the quality of the good is high, many consumers will like the good and will become regular customers. In that case, the campaign would be well worth it. Under these circumstances, the advertising campaign would be a credible signal of the good's quality, because producers of low-quality goods will not find it profitable to advertise, while producers of high-quality products will.

Note that advertising by itself is not always a credible signal of quality. For example, if the good in question would be consumed by almost all customers just once, such as a movie, heavy advertising does not convey any credible information about the quality of the product. Anyone can indulge in what economists call 'cheap talk' and claim they have a fabulous product. It is only when it is unprofitable for them to do so, if the product is not really fabulous, that advertising becomes a credible signal of quality.

## SUMMARY

In this chapter, we have studied the theory of decision-making under uncertainty. The main points were as follows:

- Most people seem to be averse to risk in most situations.
- The expected utility hypothesis, that decision-makers tend to maximise their expected utility, combined with the assumption that the utility function is concave, can explain risk aversion, and is the dominant theory of decision-making under uncertainty. It explains people's risk-averse behaviour and gives rise to a central measure of the negative effect of uncertainty: the cost of risk.
- The cost of risk is the difference between an individual's expected wealth and his certainty equivalent wealth, and is a measure of how much he is willing-to-pay just to avoid uncertainty.
- Decisions under uncertainty can be analysed in three different ways: through the utility function, via indifference curves in the state-contingent utility space and using decision trees.
- Markets try to reduce the negative effects of uncertainty through two broad classes of solutions: risk-pooling and risk-spreading.
- Barriers to markets using risk-pooling and risk-spreading include the problem of correlated risks and that of asymmetric information.
- The problem of asymmetric information leads to two broad classes of market failure: adverse selection and moral hazard.
- Adverse selection is caused by the tendency that, in any transaction at any given price, the owner of the lowest-quality or least suitable product will have the greatest incentive to undertake the transaction and this makes it difficult for the owners of high-quality products to trade.
- Moral hazard occurs when one party to a transaction can alter their behaviour as a result of the transaction in a way that adversely affects the other party's interests

and yet cannot be observed or disentangled from the effects of uncertainty. In this way, efficiency is impaired.

- Markets respond to the barriers created by asymmetric information through screening and signalling.
- Screening is when a poorly informed agent attempts to evaluate well-informed agents by filtering them through various screens, particularly ones that cause the well-informed agents to reveal their type by their behaviour.
- Signalling is when well-informed agents credibly reveal information about themselves so that they can be better served by the market.

## EXERCISES

1. Jeevandeep has wealth of ₹60 and derives utility from this according to the utility function

$$U(w) = 1 - \frac{1}{w},$$

where $w$ is his wealth. Jeevandeep now finds a lottery ticket (whose drawing is tomorrow) that offers a 50% chance of winning ₹5.

(a) What is the expected value of the lottery ticket?

(b) What is the minimum amount for which Jeevandeep would be willing-to-sell the ticket?

(c) Which is bigger, your answer to (a) or (b)? Use a clearly labelled diagram to explain why.

(d) If he does not sell the ticket, what is Jeevandeep's cost of risk?

2. Mr. Will Travel is going on a major vacation, on which he is planning to spend ₹10,000. The utility he will get from the trip is a function of how much he actually spends, $Y$, according to the function

$$U(Y) = \ln Y.$$

(a) If there is a 25% chance that Mr. Travel will lose ₹1,000 of his spending money, what is the expected utility of the trip?

(b) Suppose an insurance company offers Will Travel full insurance against this loss at an actuarially fair premium. What is the amount of this premium? Would Will buy this insurance? Explain fully.

(c) What is the maximum amount Will Travel would be willing-to-pay for this insurance?

(d) Suppose that, once Will has the insurance, he would become more careless with his money, as a result of which the probability of the ₹1,000 loss goes up to 30%. What is the actuarially fair premium now? Would Will buy the insurance at this price? Explain.

3. Banmali's wealth is ₹2,500. However, he faces a 50% chance of suffering a ₹900 loss. He is an expected utility maximiser and his utility function is

$$U(w) = \sqrt{w},$$

where $w$ is his wealth.

(a) What is Banmali's cost of risk?
(b) If Banmali can buy insurance against his loss for a price of ₹500, will he buy it?
(c) What is the maximum amount Banmali would be willing-to-pay for insurance?

4. National Widget Co. has an income of ₹100. Its research department has invented a new widget, but developing this widget into a commercial product requires an expenditure of ₹36. The marketing department has estimated that with probability 0.8 the widget will have no market at all, while with probability 0.2, it would generate additional profit of ₹192.

(a) Should the company fund the development of the new widget if it wants to maximise its expected utility and its utility function is $U(y) = y$, where $y$ is its net income?
(b) What if its utility function is $U(y) = \sqrt{y}$?
(c) Now suppose the marketing department says that, by running a survey costing ₹20, it can determine for sure whether the new widget will have a market or not. Should the company run this survey? Note that the company does not have to undertake the ₹36 development expense until after it knows the results of the survey. Answer for each of the utility functions in (a) and (b).
(d) Suppose Widget's utility function is $U(y) = \sqrt{y}$ as in part (b) and $x$ is the amount it has to pay for the survey described in part (c). Write down an equation in $x$ whose solution would yield the maximum amount Widget would be willing-to-pay for the survey. Then solve for $x$.

5. A farmer believes there is a 50% chance that the coming crop year will have normal rainfall and a 50% chance that there will be a drought. He can plant two crops, wheat and corn. His income at the end of the year from each of these crops, assuming he plants all of his land with just one crop, depends upon the level of rainfall according to the following table:

| Crop | Normal | Drought |
|---|---|---|
| Wheat | 30,000 | 10,000 |
| Corn | 23,000 | 15,000 |

The farmer's utility function is

$$U(I) = I^{1/2},$$

where $I$ is his end-of-year income.

(a) If the farmer can plant only one crop on his field, which one will it be? Explain fully.

(b) Suppose he could plant half his land with one crop and half with the other, would he do so? Explain fully.

(c) If he could plant any fraction of his land with each of the crops, what would be the optimal cropping pattern? Explain.

6. Praveen is a farmer with a utility function

$$U(y) = \ln y,$$

where $y$ is his end-of-year wealth.

With normal rainfall, Praveen's crop would be worth ₹1,000 at the end of the year. But Praveen faces a 0.3 probability of drought. If there is a drought, his crop would be worth only ₹200. Praveen is thinking of digging a deep well. The well would cost ₹200, would last only one year, and would be paid for at the end of the year (with zero interest). The well would not increase the value of Praveen's crop if there is normal rainfall, but if there is a drought, the crop would be worth ₹800 if he had the well.

(a) What is the net expected value of the well 'project'?

(b) Would Praveen dig the well? Explain fully.

7. Liaqat is a farmer trying to decide whether to plant wheat or rice. His income with the different crops depends upon whether the season is dry or wet according to the following schedule:

| | Wet | Dry |
|---|---|---|
| Wheat | 64 | 81 |
| Rice | 100 | 49 |

There is a 50% probability that the weather will be dry and a 50% probability that it will be wet. Liaqat's utility function is

$$U(Y) = \sqrt{Y},$$

where $Y$ is his income.

(a) Calculate Liaqat's expected income under the two scenarios, wet and dry.

(b) Which crop will Liaqat plant, assuming he wishes to maximise his expected utility?

(c) Suppose Liaqat could plant a fraction $\theta$ of his land with wheat and the remainder with rice, and that his income from each crop would then be proportional to the levels in the table above. What is the optimal value of $\theta$?

(d) Suppose that Liaqat could buy actuarially fair insurance for each crop if he planted only one crop. For example, if he planted wheat, he could pay a premium of 8.5 and he would then receive a payment of 17 if the weather turned out to be wet. If he planted rice, he would pay 25.5 and receive a payment of 51 if the weather turned out out dry. Now

Liaqat has the option of mixed cropping (as in part (c) of the question) without any insurance, or of planting a single crop but with actuarially fair insurance. Which option would Liaqat choose, and if he chooses a single crop, which crop would he plant? Justify your answer clearly.

8. Manmohan Singh is a family farmer. He has set aside enough money to look after his family for the next 6 months and finds he has ₹250,000 available to invest. He has three options:

   (i) Put the money in a 6-month bank deposit that will pay interest of 5% at the end of 6 months.

   (ii) Buy regular seed for ₹200,000 and put the remainder of the money in a 6-month bank deposit like the one in (i). He would then plant the seed and harvest a crop in 6 months' time. The crop would be valued at ₹500,000 if the rains are good, but only ₹50,000 if there is a drought. The probability of a good rainy season is 0.7 and the probability of a drought is 0.3.

   (iii) Buy drought-resistant seed for ₹250,000 and plant that instead. The harvest would again be in 6 months, but the yields with the drought-resistant seed will be worth ₹400,000 if the rains are good and ₹350,000 if there is a drought.
   Singh wants to maximise his expected utility of wealth, which is

   $$U(W) = \sqrt{W},$$

   where $W$ is the family's wealth in 6 months' time.

   (a) Which of the three options will Singh choose? Explain fully.

   (b) Suppose Singh could buy crop insurance if he plants regular seed. The premium would be due at the time of the harvest and the insurance would pay him ₹450,000 if there had been a drought. What is the actuarially fair premium for this insurance? What is Singh's maximum willingness-to-pay for it? Explain fully.

9. Ali's total wealth is ₹100,000, half of which is the value of his house. In case there is a fire, his house will be damaged and be worth only ₹10,000. The probability of a fire occurring is estimated at $p = 10\%$. Ali can buy insurance against fire damages in a market where firms offer identical insurance contracts at a premium $\pi$ per insured dollar.

   (a) Suppose Ali purchases $x$ units of insurance. What is his state-dependent wealth?

   (b) Calculate the equilibrium premium $\pi$ assuming insurance companies make zero expected profits.

   (c) Suppose his preferences over wealth can be represented by the utility function $U(w) = \ln(w)$. Under the premium in (b), how much insurance would Ali purchase assuming he is an expected utility maximiser? What is his expected utility with this insurance contract?

   (d) Now suppose that the premium is twice that of in (b). How much insurance would Ali buy in that case? What is his expected utility?

CHAPTER

9

# Monopoly and Market Power

The optimality theorems of welfare economics require some stringent conditions in order to hold, conditions that do not always hold in practice. Starting with this chapter, we will be looking at various ways in which the conditions for Pareto optimality in an economy might not hold, and what this implies for the efficiency results we obtained for competitive markets. In this chapter, we look at the effects of market power, situations in which markets may not be characterised by large numbers of sellers or buyers, but rather where a firm may hold market power, either as a monopoly or as a monopsony. We discuss monopoly first and monopsony in section 5 of the chapter.

A market is aid to be characterised by **monopoly** if there is only one seller. In a sense, *every* seller is a monopolist if you define the 'market' in which they operate narrowly enough, and *no* firm is a monopolist if you define the 'market' broadly enough. For example, if there is a restaurant located at the intersection of Mahatma Gandhi Marg and Pandit Nehru Road, and there are no other restaurants at that intersection, the restaurant has a monopoly in 'the market for restaurants at the intersection of Gandhi Marg and Nehru Road'. This 'monopoly' may not be very effective if there are many other restaurants within a short distance of that intersection. However, it may be quite effective if there are no other restaurants within miles. By contrast, Indian Railways may have a monopoly on train service between Mumbai and New Delhi, say, and we might logically think of it as a true monopoly, but it does not have a monopoly in the market for transportation services between Mumbai and New Delhi. Rather, it must compete with the airlines, with bus services and with rental car companies. Even such an obvious 'monopoly' as the only supplier of electricity in a city faces competition from own production (by diesel generators, solar panels, etc.) and, more generally, from all the other goods and services that consumers buy in the overall 'market'. So the concept of monopoly is not as absolute as one might think; rather, it is a matter of degree. We will see later how the elasticity of demand faced by a firm can be used to measure the 'degree' of monopoly. Nevertheless, it is useful to consider a situation of a single seller, facing no competition in a particular market, however defined.

Monopoly firms can acquire their monopoly positions in one of the two ways: by their own actions, or by government sanction or directive. Firms that acquire their monopoly positions by their own actions can do so in a number of different ways:

- They could have been the first to have offered a new product or service, and no rival has as yet entered into competition with them.
- They may have control over the sole source of supply of a particular commodity, such as a rare mineral, or water from a particular spring, or even over a brand name such as 'Coca-Cola'.
- They may have, through a big cost or quality advantage or through other competitive measures, driven all competitors from the market.
- They may have created conditions under which entry of competitors is very difficult, expensive or impossible.

Firms that attain their monopoly positions by government sanction may receive such a sanction for two broad classes of reasons:

- Government may have decided they wish to control the market for some reason and grant only a single license for production in it. The East India Company, for example, was given an exclusive charter to be the sole conduit for trade between Britain and India. Normally, the reason for government to regulate entry into a market is that it is a 'natural monopoly', that is, an industry where production can be carried out most efficiently by just one firm. (We will consider this case in detail in section 4 of this chapter.) But it could also be a way for the government to maximise its tax revenue from a particular market. This may be why the China National Tobacco Corporation has a virtual (government-sanctioned) monopoly on the distribution of cigarettes in China.
- Government might grant the company a monopoly in order to give it an incentive to do something socially desirable that it might otherwise not do. The most common example of this is the monopoly granted under a patent. Patents are granted in order to give firms the incentive to undertake the investments or expenditures needed to find or develop new innovations. Discovering new drugs, for example, is a very expensive process. If newly discovered drugs could be freely copied and sold by other companies, the original discoverer would not be able to recover its investment. As a consequence, these investments would not be undertaken. By granting firms monopoly rights for a limited time (patents typically last 17 or 21 years), government gives them a chance to recover their investment and hence to undertake research in the first place. Other examples of government-granted monopolies in order to generate incentives for firms include copyright protection (very similar to patents) and the granting of exclusive development rights on real estate adjacent to roads and airports in order to induce firms to build these roads and airports at their expense. This becomes a way for government to finance infrastructure projects without having the accompanying burden of taxation and expenditure.

# 9.1 BASIC MONOPOLY MODEL

**Task for this section:**

To study the basic model of monopoly behaviour, including a study of how to construct a monopolist's cost function when it has multiple plants. This leads to a natural extension to the study of cartels. The welfare properties of a monopoly market as compared to a competitive one are also examined.

How do monopolies behave? In this section, we will look at the basic model for the behaviour of an unregulated monopolist. The basic monopoly model should be familiar from introductory microeconomics courses, so this should constitute a review. The model actually applies to any firm that seeks to maximise its profits. Profits, $\pi$, are simply Revenue ($R$) minus Cost ($C$), where both $R$ and $C$ are functions of the firm's output, $q$. Thus, the firm's profit is

$$\pi = R(q) - C(q).$$

In order to maximise profit, the firm will want to set

$$\frac{d\pi}{dq} = \frac{dR}{dq} - \frac{dC}{dq} = 0. \tag{9.1}$$

In other words, it will want to set marginal revenue equal to marginal cost:

$$MR = MC.$$

The basic monopoly model can be illustrated graphically as in Figure 9.1. In the upper panel, the line $D$ represents the demand curve and $MR$ the marginal revenue curve. $MC$ is the marginal cost curve. The intersection of the $MR$ and $MC$ curves yields the profit-maximising quantity $q^m$ and the price would then be determined by the demand curve to be $p^m$, which is the highest price consistent with sales of $q^m$. The shaded area represents the firm's economic profit, the excess of price over marginal cost for each unit sold. Fixed costs, which are not economic costs, are not accounted for in this calculation. The lower panel shows the equilibrium in terms of total revenue, $R(q)$, and total cost, $C(q)$. Profit is maximised when the gap between those two curves is at a maximum, and that hapens when their slopes ($MR$ and $MC$) are equal.

If we consider the condition $MR = MC$ again, it might seem different from the condition $p = MC$ we obtained for the perfectly competitive firm. In fact the condition $MR = MC$ applies to the perfectly competitive firm also. However, since it accepts the market price as given and believes it can sell any amount at that price, its $MR$ is simply the market price $p$ and so the condition $MR = MC$ reduces to $p = MC$.

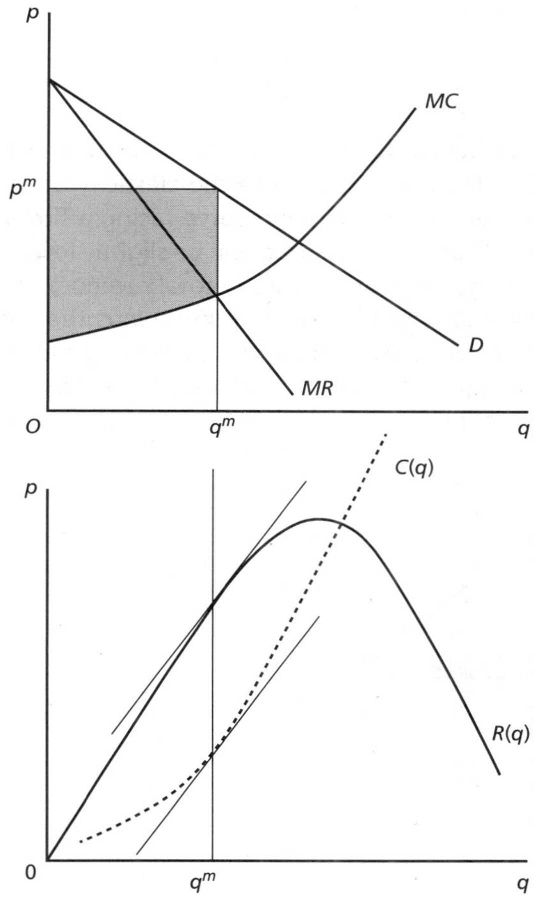


**Figure 9.1** *Profit Maximisation in the Simple Monopoly Model*

A monopoly, however, does not take the market price as fixed. Instead, it believes it can *choose* a price by choosing its quantity, since the price–quantity combination it chooses must lie on the demand curve. Thus, the monopolist's revenue is

$$R(q) = p(q) \cdot q$$

and so

$$R'(q) = q \cdot \frac{dp}{dq} + p.$$

Multiplying and dividing the first term on the right-hand side by $p$, we obtain

$$R'(q) = p \cdot \left(\frac{dp}{dq} \cdot \frac{q}{p}\right) + p$$

which can be written as

$$MR = p\left\{1 + \frac{1}{\varepsilon_d}\right\}. \tag{9.2}$$

Equation (9.2) is an important result. It shows that, for any downward-sloping demand curve, the marginal revenue is *lower* than the price, since the elasticity of demand, $\varepsilon_d < 0$. Intuitively, the reason for this is that, as long as the demand curve facing a firm is downward-sloping, the price at which it can sell $(q^0 + 1)$ units of the good will be slightly lower than the price at which it can sell $q^0$ units. The marginal revenue (or increase in total revenue) that it gains from selling the $(q^0 + 1)^{\text{th}}$ unit then is the price at which it sells that unit *minus* the lost revenue from the lower price realisation on the first $q^0$ units (known as the **infra-marginal units**). This lost revenue is shown as the shaded area in Figure 9.2, which simply shows a demand curve and the effect on price of increasing sales by one unit.

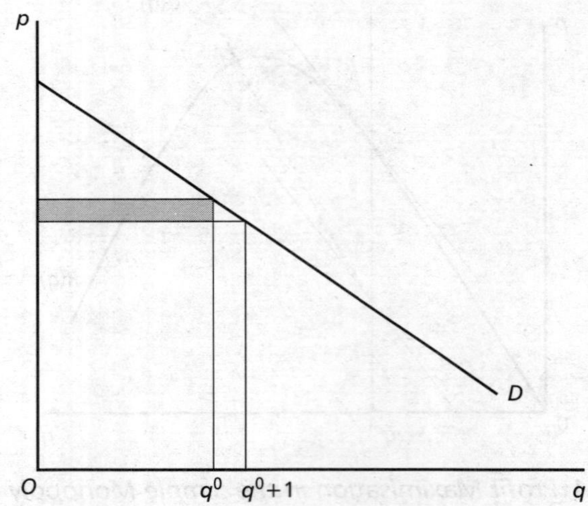


**Figure 9.2** *Revenue Loss over Infra-marginal Units as Sales Increase*

If the demand curve were linear, of the form

$$p(q) = a - bq,$$

the revenue would be

$$R(q) = q \cdot p(q) = aq - bq^2,$$

and the marginal revenue would be

$$MR \equiv R'(q) = a - 2bq.$$

In other words, the *MR* curve would also be linear, would have the same intercept *a* on the vertical axis (for $q = 0$) and would be twice as steep as the demand curve. The upper panel in Figure 9.3 illustrates this. It shows a demand curve, D, which is nothing but the firm's average revenue curve, along with the *MR* curve, which is twice as steep. The *MR* curve is drawn intentionally with a segment below the horizontal axis, to emphasise the possibility that *MR* could be negative. Indeed, *MR* turns negative once the elasticity of demand goes above $-1$ (becomes inelastic), as we will see.

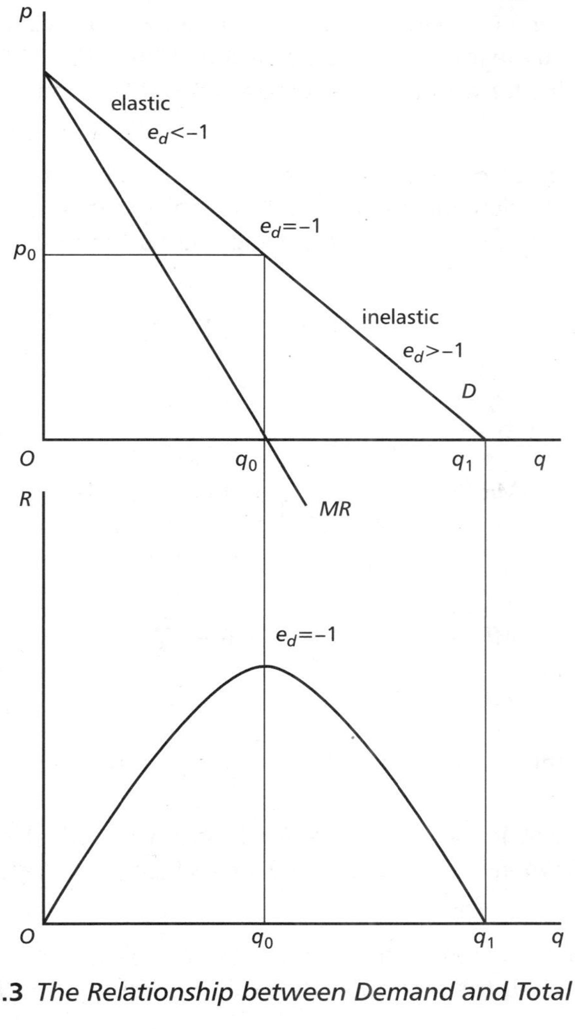


**Figure 9.3** *The Relationship between Demand and Total Revenue*

The lower panel of Figure 9.3 illustrates what is happening to *total* revenue $R(q)$ as $q$ changes. The general shape of the $R(q)$ curve shown in the lower panel of the figure is actually valid for all demand curves, not just linear ones. Starting at the origin, clearly $R(q) = 0$ if $q = 0$ since a firm cannot have any revenue if it is not selling anything. Revenue is also zero at $q = q_1$, where the demand curve meets the horizontal axis, since the price at which that many units can be 'sold' would have to be zero. In between $q = 0$ and $q = q_1$, revenue must be positive, so $R(q)$ must be rising and then falling. Note that the revenue $R$ at any intervening quantity level is given by the rectangle formed under the demand curve at that quantity. For example, the revenue at $q = q_0$ is the rectangle formed with sides $p_0$ and $q_0$. Now since $R(q)$ is rising and then falling between $q = 0$ and $q = q_1$, it must reach a maximum somewhere in that region. The point where that happens, at $q = q_0$, is the quantity where the $MR$ curve cuts the horizontal axis. As long as $MR > 0$, $R(q)$ must be rising, since $MR > 0$ means revenue is increasing. When $MR < 0$ $R(q)$ must be decreasing. Therefore, the turning point for $R(q)$ must be where $MR = 0$. This must be true for all demand curves, not just linear ones.

We can look at this result also from the point of view of the elasticity of demand. We know from consumer theory that a demand curve is said to be elastic when $\varepsilon_d < -1$ (i.e $|\varepsilon_d| > 1$) and inelastic when $\varepsilon_d > -1$ (i.e $|\varepsilon_d| < 1$) . Now (9.2) showed us the relationship between $MR$ and elasticity of demand:

$$MR = p\left\{1 + \frac{1}{\varepsilon_d}\right\}.$$

This implies that

$$MR = 0 \rightarrow \left\{1 + \frac{1}{\varepsilon_d}\right\} = 0 \rightarrow \varepsilon_d = -1.$$

Similarly,

$$MR > 0 \rightarrow \left\{1 + \frac{1}{\varepsilon_d}\right\} > 0 \rightarrow \varepsilon_d < -1 \tag{9.3}$$

and $$MR < 0 \rightarrow \left\{1 + \frac{1}{\varepsilon_d}\right\} < 0 \rightarrow \varepsilon_d > -1.$$

Thus, the demand curve is elastic ($\varepsilon_d < -1$) when $MR$ is positive and $R(q)$ is rising, and the demand curve is inelastic ($\varepsilon_d > -1$) when $MR$ is negative and $R(q)$ is falling. This result is true for all demand curves.

All of this discussion has an important implication for the monopoly model. Putting (9.1) and (9.2) together, we see that the monopolist's profit-maximising condition, $MC = MR$, can be written as

$$MC = p\left\{1 + \frac{1}{\varepsilon_d}\right\}. \tag{9.4}$$

Now, since $MC > 0$ and $p > 0$, (9.4) implies that, at the profit-maximising point,

$$\left\{1 + \frac{1}{\varepsilon_d}\right\} > 0.$$

But, from (9.3), we see that this happens when $\varepsilon_d < -1$, that is, when the demand curve is elastic. So the important implication is that **a monopolist will never operate on the inelastic part of the demand curve**, since in that part of the demand curve $R(q)$ is falling and he can always raise his revenue by lowering output. Since lowering output will also lower cost, profits would unambiguously rise. This would be true whenever demand is inelastic and so the equilibrium can only be where demand is elastic.

We can manipulate (9.4) a little further to get another interesting result. Let $c$ represent the $MC$ at the equilibrium. Then (9.4) can be written as

$$c = p + \frac{p}{\varepsilon_d},$$

which can be rearranged to yield

$$\frac{p - c}{p} = -\frac{1}{\varepsilon_d} = \frac{1}{|\varepsilon_d|}. \tag{9.5}$$

The numerator of the left-hand side of (9.5) could be called the **mark-up**, the excess of price over $MC$, and could be seen as an indicator of the extent of the monopolist's power in the market. If $(p - c)$ is small, the solution is in some sense 'close' to the competitive one. Of course, whether or not $(p - c)$ is 'small' depends in part on the units of measurement. So the whole of the left-hand side of (9.5) can be used instead as a units-free measure of monopoly power: the fraction of price that consists of the mark-up. This ratio is called the **degree of monopoly** or the **Lerner index of monopoly** and (9.5) shows that it is equal to the inverse of the absolute value of the elasticity of demand. In other words, the less elastic the demand, the greater is the degree of monopoly or the extent to which the monopoly can exercise its market power. This demonstrates the assertion made in the first paragraph of this chapter, that the elasticity of demand could be used to measure the extent or degree of monopoly. A highly elastic demand curve indicates that a product has relatively close substitutes, and so a monopoly would not have much power in such a market. A low elasticity of demand would indicate that consumers have few alternatives to the good in question, and here is where a monopoly would be able to exercise considerable power.

### 9.1.1 Multi-Plant Monopoly

In the basic model, we took the monopoly's cost function to be simply $C(q)$. If all production takes place in one plant or factory, we can derive $C(q)$ the same way we did for a competitive firm in Chapter 5. But what if production takes place in several plants? How does the monopolist decide on the levels of production in the different plants? In this section, we will answer this question for the case where the monopoly has two plants, generating a basic result that can be generalised to any number of plants. The basic result actually holds for any firm with multiple plants, not just a monopoly.

We will assume the firm has two plants which produce the identical product, which is then sold in one market. Let $q$ be the total output of the firm and $q_1$ and $q_2$ be the output levels of the two plants. Obviously,

$$q = q_1 + q_2.$$

Let $C_1(q_1)$ and $C_2(q_2)$ be the cost functions of the two plants. Then the firm's profit is

$$\pi = R(q_1 + q_2) - C_1(q_1) - C_2(q_2).$$

In order to maximise its profit, the firm will want to set the partial derivatives of $\pi$ with respect to $q_1$ and $q_2$ equal to zero. Since

$$\frac{dq}{dq_1} = \frac{dq}{dq_2} = 1,$$

we can write the first-order conditions as

$$\frac{\partial \pi}{\partial q_1} = R'(q) - C_1'(q_1) = 0 \tag{9.6}$$

$$\text{and} \quad \frac{\partial \pi}{\partial q_2} = R'(q) - C_2'(q_2) = 0. \tag{9.7}$$

Equation (9.6) and (9.7) can be combined to yield

$$C_1'(q_1) = C_2'(q_2) = R'(q). \tag{9.8}$$

The profit-maximising condition (9.8) requires that the marginal costs of production in the two plants must be set equal to each other and to the common marginal revenue.

The intuition behind this result is quite clear. The marginal costs of production have to be equal across all plants (the result generalises to any number of plants) because the total cost of producing the given output is thereby minimised. Let us look at it this way. Suppose the *MCs* in two plants were not equal; let us say $MC_1 > MC_2$. Then the firm could unambiguously raise its profit by reducing output by one unit in plant 1 and raising output by one unit in plant 2. Since its total output is unchanged, its revenue is unchanged. But it has reduced its cost by $MC_1$ in plant 1 and raised its cost by $MC_2$ in plant 2. Since $MC_1 > MC_2$, the saving in cost from plant 1 outweighs the increased cost in plant 2, and so costs would have gone down. Since revenue is unchanged, this means profits have gone up. As long as the *MC*s in two plants are different, a firm can increase its profit by reallocating production between plants. Therefore, for profit to be maximised, the *MC*s in all plants must be equal. And since the overall condition for a profit maximum is $MC = MR$, the *MCs* must also equal the *MR* of the firm.

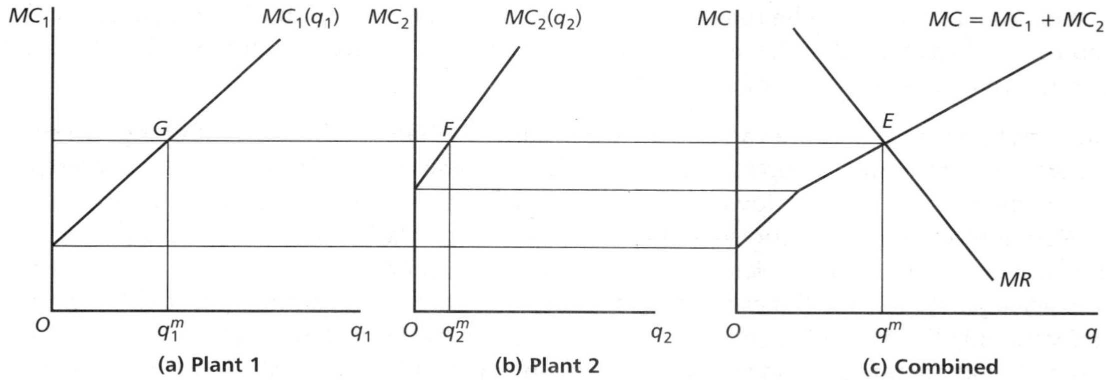


**Figure 9.4** *Optimal Production Pattern with Two Plants*

We can illustrate this result graphically. The key insight is that we can guarantee the equalisation of *MCs* across plants by constructing the firm-level *MC* as the horizontal sum of the individual plant-level *MCs*. In Figure 9.4, panel (a) shows the *MC* of plant 1 and panel (b) shows the *MC* of plant 2. In panel (c), we have constructed the combined firm-level *MC* curve by horizontally summing $MC_1$ and $MC_2$, much like we constructed the industry supply curve under perfect competition by horizontally summing the individual firm supply curves. The combined marginal cost curve, labelled *MC* in panel (c) of the figure, can then be plotted against the *MR* curve to determine the profit-maximising output level $q^m$. If we then draw a line from the point of intersection *E* of *MC* and *MR* to $MC_1$ (at *G*) and $MC_2$ (at *F*), we can read in panels (a) and (b) the output levels in the two plants, which will be $q_1^m$ and $q_2^m$, respectively. If $q_1 = q_1^m$ and $q_2 = q_2^m$, clearly $MC_1 = MC_2$. Further, each of these *MCs* is equal to *MR*. And, finally, since we constructed *MC* by horizontally summing $MC_1$ and $MC_2$, it must be the case that

$$q_1^m + q_2^m = q^m.$$

Thus, we have completely captured the conditions for profit maximisation.

It is worth reiterating that this analysis applies to any firm with multiple plants, not just monopolies. Even a perfectly competitive firm that happened to operate two or more plants would want to set their *MCs* equal and to then set each *MC* equal to the price.

## 9.1.2 Multiple Plants in the Long Run

So far, we have made no distinction between the short run and long run in the case of monopoly. As long as the monopoly can persist due to barriers to entry or patent protection, and so on, we do not have to worry about entry and exit of other firms. However, even if entry is not an issue, the monopoly would be free to build and scrap plants in the long run. If, for example, it has two plants, one of which is very much less efficient than the other, it might operate them in the short run according to the rule developed in the previous section, but we would expect it to scrap the inefficient plant in the long run and replace it with a more efficient one. So what might the long-run cost curve of the monopolist look like?

To answer this question, we can borrow the insights we had in thinking about long-run supply in a perfectly competitive industry. In such an industry, it was argued, only firms that operated the most efficient plants, with the lowest minimum average cost, would be able to survive in the long run. Now a monopolist can survive longer with inefficient plants, because it does not face any competitive pressure. Nevertheless, plants do wear out and at some point it becomes economic to replace ageing plants with new ones. We would therefore expect a monopolist in the long run to operate only the most efficient plants. Of course, if there were plant-level economies of scale, the firm would operate only one plant. But, if the plant-level average cost curve is U-shaped, and the level of demand is sufficiently high, the firm would want to build multiple plants and operate each at the minimum point of its *AC* curve. The long-run average and marginal cost curves of the firm could then be taken to be a horizontal line at the level of the minimum *AC*, much like the long-run supply curve of a competitive industry.

Because the number of plants must take an integer value, the *AC* curve is not strictly a horizontal line, but rather a wavy line consisting of a series of increasingly shallow U-shaped curves. To see why, consider the case of a firm for which the plant-level *AC* curve is U-shaped with a minimum at $q = 100$ and a minimum *AC* of ₹10. If the firm's desired level of total output is 200, it would build two plants, operate each at its minimum *AC* and would therefore have a firm-level *AC* also of ₹10. But what if the desired level of output is 150? The firm would operate only one plant if

$$C_i(150) < 2C_i(75),$$

where $C_i$ is the plant-level cost function, and two plants if that inequality were reversed. In other words, if it is cheaper to produce 150 units of output in one plant than to produce 75 units of output each in two plants, the firm would operate only one plant, and it would operate two if the opposite were true. If $Q$ represents the total desired output of the firm, and $C_i$ the plant-level cost function, there will be a critical value of $Q$, say $\overline{Q}_1$, where

$$C_i(\overline{Q}_1) = 2C_i\left(\frac{\overline{Q}_1}{2}\right).$$

When the desired level of output, $Q$, is less than $\overline{Q}_1$, the firm will operate only one plant and the firm-level *AC* curve will follow the single-plant *AC* curve. For desired levels of output above $\overline{Q}_1$, however, the firm *AC* curve will start to decline, because it will find it economical to operate two plants. Eventually, at $Q = 200$, the firm-level *AC* will be ₹10 again, since at this point each of the two plants will be producing 100 units at an *AC* of ₹10.

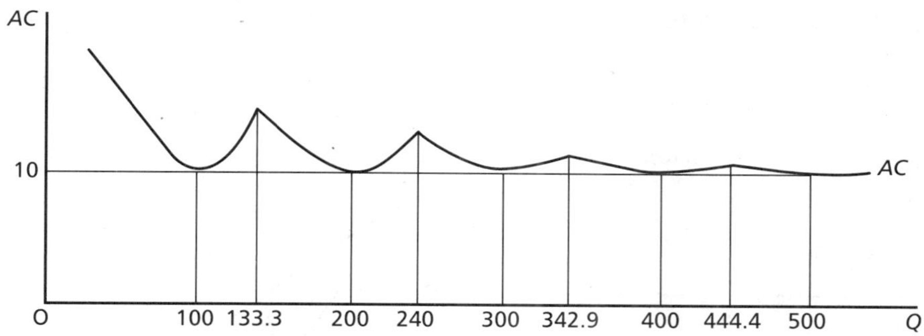


**Figure 9.5** *Multi-plant Average Cost Curve*

Similarly, there will be a critical level of output, $\overline{Q}_2$, such that

$$2C_i\left(\frac{\overline{Q}_2}{2}\right) = 3C_i\left(\frac{\overline{Q}_2}{3}\right),$$

in other words, where it would cost the same to produce $\overline{Q}_2$ in two plants, each producing $\frac{\overline{Q}_2}{2}$, or in three plants, each producing $\frac{\overline{Q}_2}{3}$. When $\overline{Q}_1 < Q < \overline{Q}_2$, the firm would operate two plants, while it would start operating a third once the desired level of output $Q$ rose above $\overline{Q}_2$. Clearly, $\frac{\overline{Q}_2}{3} > \frac{\overline{Q}_1}{2}$, that is, the output per plant at the critical output when the third plant becomes economic will be greater than the output per plant when the second plant becomes economic. For example, if the per plant *AC* curve is symmetric around its minimum point at $q = 100$, $\overline{Q}_1$ will be $133\frac{1}{3}$, so that $\frac{\overline{Q}_1}{2} = 66\frac{2}{3}$ ($133\frac{1}{3}$ and $66\frac{2}{3}$ are symmetric around 100 and will therefore have the same AC), and $\overline{Q}_2$ will be 240, so that $\frac{\overline{Q}_2}{2} = 120$ and $\frac{\overline{Q}_2}{3} = 80$ (120 and 80 are symmetric around 100 and will have the same AC). The firm's long-run *AC* can then be drawn as in Figure 9.5. It will consist of a series of U-shaped segments, each with its minimum at a multiple of the per plant output where *AC* is minimised (100 in our example), with the segments becoming shallower and shallower as *Q* rises. If the desired level of output is large relative to the plant-level *AC*-minimising output level, we can treat the long-run firm-level *AC* curve to be flat at the minimum plant-level *AC*.

## 9.1.3 Comparing Monopoly to Perfect Competition

Under perfect competition, the firm's *MC* curve is its supply curve, and the industry supply curve is the horizontal sum of all the individual firm supply curves. In the long run, the industry supply curve is taken to be perfectly elastic (ignoring externalities) at each firm's minimum *AC*. In like manner, we have seen that the monopolist may have a single *MC* curve; if it has multiple plants, the firm *MC* curve is the horizontal sum of its individual plant *MC* curves, and in the long run, its firm *MC* curve could be taken to be flat at the minimum of its plant-level *AC* curves. How do the market outcomes differ between the two forms?

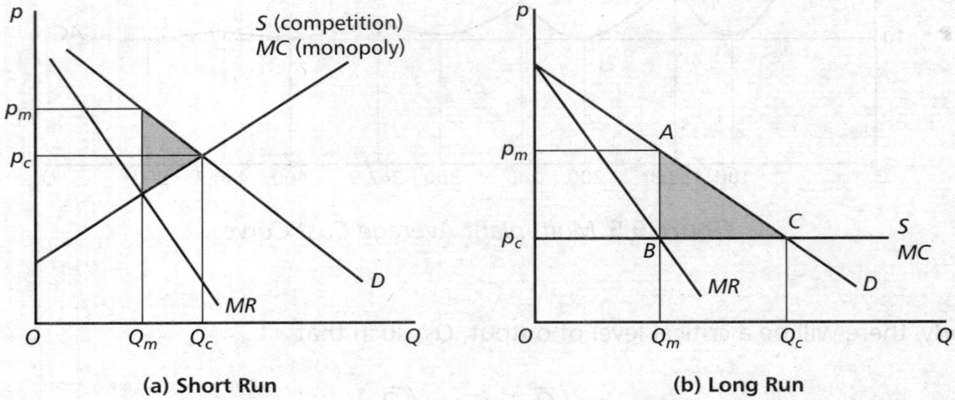


**Figure 9.6** *Monopoly versus Perfect Competition*

Figure 9.6 illustrates the outcomes, panel (a) for the short run and panel (b) for the long run. In both cases, the *MC* curve of the monopolist would have functioned as the supply curve if the market had been perfectly competitive. And in both cases, while the competitive equilibrium $(Q_c, p_c)$ occurs where the supply and demand curves cross, the monopoly equilibrium occurs where the *MC* curve crosses the *MR* curve, yielding the quantity $Q_m$, and $p_m$ is then determined from the demand curve. In both cases, as we see, $Q_m < Q_c$ and $p_m > p_c$. In other words, monopolies tend to restrict output to below the competitive level and, as a result, are able to charge prices higher than the competitive ones. The bottom line of course is that they make higher profits. The monopolist's profits are shown in Figure 9.6 by the area above *MC* and below $p_m$, between *O* and $Q_m$. This is easy to see in panel (b) and is particularly telling there: while firms under perfect competition make zero economic profits in the long run, the monopolist makes extra-normal profits represented by the area $p_mABp_c$.

This is not good from the social point of view. As we have seen, the perfectly competitive output level is efficient from the society's viewpoint, as production is carried out up to the point where the marginal social benefit (given by the height of the demand curve which reflects the value of the marginal unit to consumers) is equal to the marginal social cost (simply the *MC*, the private marginal cost of producing the good). But the monopoly output level, $Q_m$, is lower than this efficient output level. The deadweight loss created by this misallocation from the social point of view is given by the shaded area in each of the panels of Figure 9.6. For each unit of output between $Q_m$ and $Q_c$, society is losing the potential benefit given by the vertical distance between the demand curve (the social marginal benefit curve) and the *MC* (the social marginal cost curve). It is to avoid this deadweight loss, also called 'the social cost of monopoly,' that most modern governments try to keep monopoly in check. Most countries have anti-monopoly laws and require large firms that wish to merge with or acquire others to receive regulatory approval before they can do so. The idea is to make sure the level of competition does not fall too low as a result of the merger.

This analysis has been a partial equilibrium one. Let us see how monopoly affects the economy's general equilibrium and what impact this has on the optimality theorem of welfare economics. Let us suppose there are two industries in the economy and that industry $x$ is monopolised while industry $y$ is perfectly competitive. If we think about the conditions for efficiency, there is nothing in this scenario that would affect the attainment of efficiency in consumption since all consumers would still be free to maximise their utility and set their marginal rates of substitution equal to the price ratio. Nor is there any reason why efficiency in production would not be attained, since this depends upon producing firms facing competitive *input* markets and simply trying to minimise their costs, which monopolies as well as competitive firms would want to do. However, the condition for the right mix of goods requires that $MRS = MRT$, where $MRT$ is the marginal rate of transformation, the slope of the economy's production possibilities frontier (PPF). Recall that

$$MRT = \frac{MC_x}{MC_y},$$

and this gets equated to the MRS in perfect competition because consumers are setting

$$MRS = \frac{p_x}{p_y}$$

and firms are setting $p_x = MC_x$ and $p_y = MC_y$. If industry $x$ is under monopoly, however, $p_x > MC_x$ and the equality fails to hold. Instead, we will have

$$MRS = \frac{p_x}{p_y} > MRT = \frac{MC_x}{MC_y}.$$

Thus, the economy will not be producing the right mix of goods.

Figure 9.7 provides a graphical illustration of the outcome. AB is the economy's PPF. Under competition, C would be the equilibrium, where a social indifference curve $U_c$ is tangent to the PPF; the competitive prices are represented by the line $p_c$. Under monopoly, however, the output of $x$ will be curtailed to, say, $x_m < x_c$, and the relative price of $x$ will be higher at, say, the prices $p_m$ rather than $p_c$. The equilibrium will be at a point such as $M$. Although the economy is on the PPF (production efficiency occurs), it is producing the wrong mix of goods ($M$ rather than $C$) and the result is that the economy is on a lower social indifference curve $U_m$ rather than $U_c$.

Finally, mention should be made of an alternative view of monopoly that criticises the foregoing discussion as too limited because it is focused on static allocation only and ignores the dynamic aspects of the economy. In this view, associated with the name of Joseph Schumpeter, a Harvard economist who was a prime propounder of it, monopoly is far preferable to competition from a

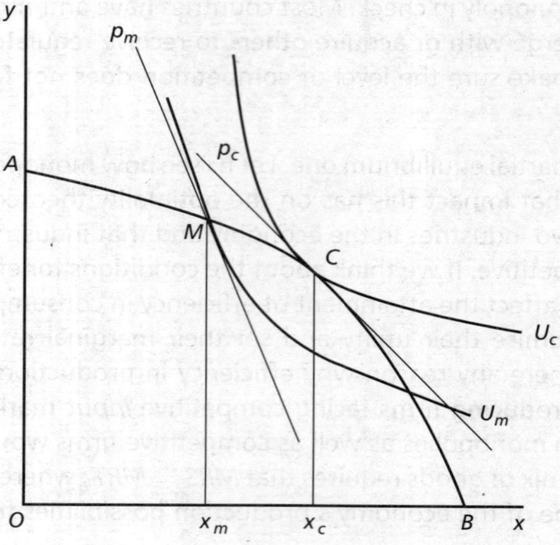


**Figure 9.7** *General Equilibrium with Monopoly*

dynamic perspective because competitive firms will be too small to be able to undertake the major investments needed to innovate successfully. Monopolies, however, will develop deep pockets and hence the ability to finance large and risky research and development efforts. There is a large literature on this subject and there is no firm conclusion to it. Whereas the basic truth of the Schumpeterian view cannot be denied, it is mitigated by two factors:

- Although monopolies may have the *resources* to undertake large and risky research projects, they have comparatively low *incentives* to undertake them, since any innovations they make will tend to cannibalise their existing monopoly franchise. Indeed, they may have the incentive to *not* introduce innovations that they may have already made in order to continue to 'milk' their existing monopoly position.
- The growth of the capital markets, particularly the market for venture capital, has meant that even small firms with limited resources but with good ideas can obtain financing for their projects reasonably easily. Thus, the lack of funds is no longer a serious constraint to small firms with innovative ideas.

## 9.1.4 Cartels: A Digression

Short of merger, companies that would like to monopolise a market could do so by forming cartels. A **cartel** is an organisation of companies formed for the purpose of coordinating their activities in order to increase the profitability of all the members. The most famous cartel these days is of course OPEC, the Organization of Petroleum Exporting Countries, formed in 1960 to coordinate the production levels and pricing decisions of some of the major oil producing and exporting countries. But there have been many other cartels. There is a diamond cartel centred around the De Beers Company, and historically, there were some major cartels (then called trusts) for oil and steel in the United States in the late 19th and early 20th centuries. It was as a response to these cartels that the United States enacted major anti trust (anti-cartel) legislation in the early 20th century, which has inspired similar legislation in many other countries, including India.

Why do governments want to curb or prevent the formation of cartels? To see this, we need to understand how a cartel would operate if it wanted to maximise the profits of its members. Put simply, the cartel would behave as a multi-plant monopoly. Each member of the cartel would produce a quantity such that its marginal cost of production was equal to the *MC* of every other member, and all these *MCs* would be set equal to the common marginal revenue in the market. We have already seen that this behaviour maximises the profit of a multi-plant monopoly, and so quite clearly it would maximise the joint profits of the members of the cartel. To all intents and purposes, the cartel would look like a monopoly, and so governments would want to curb cartels for the same reasons that they would want to curb monopolies.

There is one aspect of cartels because of which they do differ from monopolies. A multi-plant monopoly operates the plants for the good of the company as a whole, so enforcement of the policy to set all *MCs* equal is not an issue. However, a cartel's members are all independent decision-makers seeking to maximise their own individual profits. This creates a problem in enforcing any cartel agreement, since each member will have an incentive to cheat on its prescribed production target. This incentive is strongest for the smallest members of the cartel, who will be the most difficult to monitor and control.

To see this, let us look first at the cartel's profit-maximising decision a little more formally. The total profits of the cartel are given by

$$\pi = (q_i + \tilde{q}_i) \cdot p(q_i + \tilde{q}_i) - \sum_{i=1}^{n} C_i(q_i),$$

where $q_i$ is the output of the $i$th firm, $\tilde{q}_i$ is the total output of all firms other than the $i$th firm, $p(q_i + \tilde{q}_i)$ is the market price as a function of total output $p(Q)$ and $C_i(q_i)$ is the cost function of the $i$th firm.

To maximise the total profits of the cartel, the partial derivative of $\pi$ with respect to each $q_i$ will be set equal to zero:

$$\frac{\partial \pi}{\partial q_i} = p + (q_i + \tilde{q}_i) \cdot \frac{\partial p}{\partial Q} - \frac{\partial C_i}{\partial q_i} = 0,$$

which can be written as

$$p + q_i \cdot \frac{\partial p}{\partial Q} - \frac{\partial C_i}{\partial q_i} = -\tilde{q}_i \cdot \frac{\partial p}{\partial Q}. \tag{9.9}$$

Equation (9.9) is a set of first-order conditions, one for each member $i$ of the cartel.

Now the *i*th firm's own profit is given by

$$\pi_i = q_i \cdot p(q_i + \tilde{q}_i) - C_i(q_i)$$

and the derivative of this with respect to $q_i$ is

$$\frac{\partial \pi_i}{\partial q_i} = p + q_i \cdot \frac{\partial p}{\partial Q} - \frac{\partial C_i}{\partial q_i}. \tag{9.10}$$

This is the left-hand side of (9.9), and therefore we know that, at the cartel equilibrium, this derivative can be written as

$$\frac{\partial \pi_i}{\partial q_i} = -\tilde{q}_i \cdot \frac{\partial p}{\partial Q},$$

which is positive, since $\tilde{q}_i > 0$ and $\frac{\partial p}{\partial Q} < 0$. Thus, the *i*th firm's profit is positively related to $q_i$ at the cartel equilibrium: $\pi_i$ would rise if the firm cheated and raised its output level above what the cartel 'allocated' to it. Further, the smaller the member firm, the bigger would be $\tilde{q}_i$ and hence the derivative $\frac{\partial \pi_i}{\partial q_i}$. Thus, the smaller the firm, the greater is its incentive to cheat and raise its output. It is thought that one of the factors that led to Iraq's invasion of Kuwait in 1990 was that Kuwait, which had a share in total OPEC production of 8.7%,[1] was cheating on its OPEC quota and selling more than its share, thereby depressing prices for other members such as Iraq, whose share was 12.8%. Since the largest members of any cartel have the most to lose by the cheating of others, they are the ones who have to play the most significant role in policing the agreement. In OPEC, Saudi Arabia normally plays this role, frequently lowering its production level in order to accommodate the excess production of other countries. Without such behaviour on the part of the largest producers, every cartel is unstable and will tend to break down, as the discussion in this section has shown.

# 9.2 VARIATIONS TO THE BASIC MODEL: ALTERNATIVE PRICING STRATEGIES

**Task for this section:**

To look at various ways in which a monopoly (or any firm with market power) could increase its profits by using pricing strategies other than the standard one of simply charging a price per unit. These strategies include two-part pricing, and three different types of price discrimination.

[1] www.wtrg.com/opecshare.html, consulted 16 February 2012.

In the previous section, we have studied the basic monopoly model, in which the monopoly is assumed to face a simple demand curve and then maximises its profit by choosing a level of output (implying a choice of price also). In this section, we will look at variations to this basic model, in which the monopoly adopts more complex pricing strategies in order to further increase profits or to consolidate its position in some way. As in much of the previous section, the results of this section apply to any firm with some market power, not just a strict monopoly.

## 9.2.1 Two-Part Pricing

The basic monopoly model discussed in the previous section and illustrated in Figures 9.1 and 9.6 has the characteristic that the monopoly restricts output in comparison to the competitive solution. As a result, the firm is able to charge a higher price and make higher profits than competitive firms do. At the same time, consumers are left with some consumer's surplus (the area above the monopoly price $p_m$ and below the demand curve) and there is a deadweight loss due to the quantity distortion (the shaded areas in Figure 9.6). Might there be some way for the monopoly to capture these 'losses' or 'leakages'?

One way to do so is to charge a two-part price. The simplest sort of two-part price would be to charge each customer a fixed fee for 'entry' into the market and then an additional price for each unit of the good consumed. The first example of this sort of pricing strategy to be analysed by an economist was a theme park (Disneyland) where a separate charge is made for admission and then additional prices are paid for consumption within the park, such as food and, possibly, rides. (Not charging for rides is just setting the per unit price of a two-part price to zero.) Other examples of this sort of pricing strategy are cover charges at bars, followed by priced drinks, and telephone calling plans that charge a fixed monthly fee and then per call charges, perhaps after a fixed threshold of 'free' calls.[2]

In principle, the idea behind a two-part price is to enlarge the size of the total surplus in a market by charging a relatively low per unit price, but to then capture the bulk of this surplus through the fixed fee. We can use an idealised example to illustrate the principle. We will look at the basic model for this idealised case first, followed by an analysis of a two-part pricing scheme.

Suppose there is a good for which $n$ identical customers have identical demands. Say each person's demand curve is

$$q = a - p$$

and since there are $n$ such consumers the market demand is

$$Q = na - np.$$

[2] Examples such as razors and razor blades and printers and ink cartridges are sometimes given for this pricing strategy, but these are not examples of two-part prices at all.

The inverse of the market demand would then be

$$p = a - \frac{1}{n}Q.$$

If the monopoly's cost of production is a constant $c$ per unit of output, the equilibrium in the basic model would require $MR = MC$, which here would be

$$a - \frac{2}{n}Q_m = c.$$

Then the profit-maximising quantity will be

$$Q_m = \frac{n}{2}(a - c)$$

and the price will be

$$p_m = \frac{a + c}{2}.$$

The firm's profit will be

$$\pi = Q_m \cdot (p_m - c) = n\left[\frac{a - c}{2}\right]^2.$$

The profit-maximising equilibrium is depicted in panel (a) of Figure 9.8, where the firm's profit is given by the shaded area.

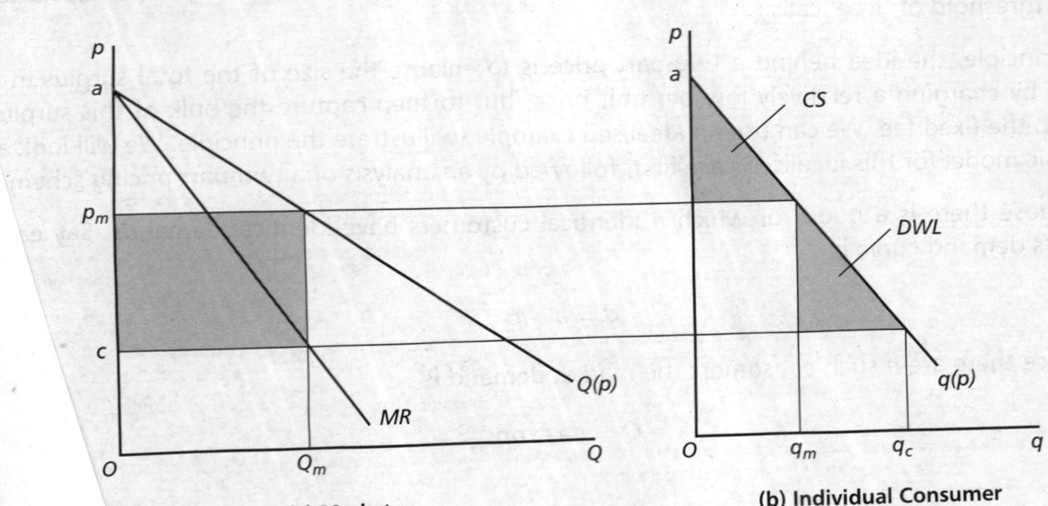


(a) Market

(b) Individual Consumer

**Figure 9.8** *Monopoly Equilibrium in the Basic Model*

Panel (b) of the figure shows the situation of the individual consumer. Each consumer faces the price $\frac{a+c}{2}$, and since the individual demand is $q = a - p$, each consumer will buy

$$q_m = \frac{a-c}{2}.$$

The consumer will enjoy a consumer's surplus of the upper shaded area in Figure 9.8(b), which can be calculated to be

$$CS = \frac{1}{2} \cdot \left(\frac{a-c}{2}\right) \cdot \left(\frac{a-c}{2}\right) = \frac{1}{2} \cdot \left(\frac{a-c}{2}\right)^2.$$

In addition, there will be a deadweight loss associated with each consumer which will equal the lower shaded area in panel (b) of Figure 9.8.

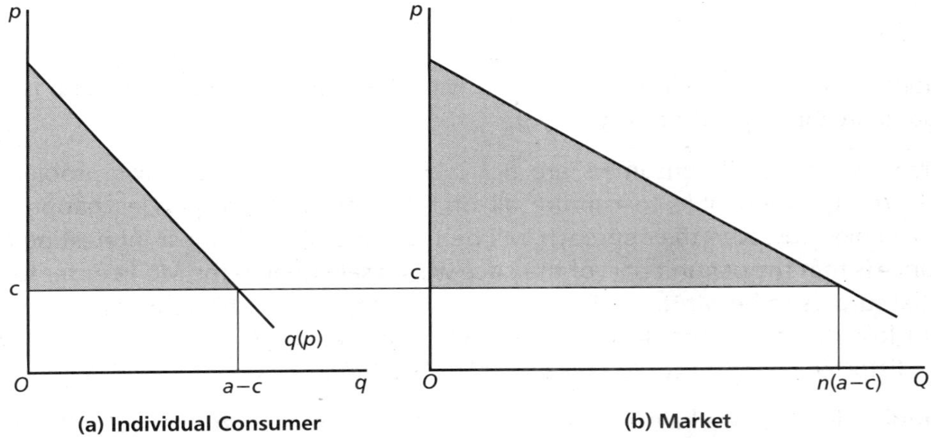


**Figure 9.9** *Capturing Consumers' Surplus through a Two-Part Price*

Now consider a two-part pricing scheme. Suppose the monopoly sells the good at a (second-part) price of $c$, which is its marginal cost. Each consumer would now buy $(a - c)$ units of the good and would enjoy a consumer's surplus equal to the shaded area in panel (a) of Figure 9.9. This can be shown to be

$$CS = \frac{1}{2}(a-c)^2.$$

But now suppose the monopoly charges each consumer a fixed fee (this would be the first part of the two-part price) of exactly this amount, $\frac{1}{2}(a-c)^2$, in order to be permitted access to this market. The consumer would just buy the good (he can be induced to do so if the fee is set $\epsilon$ below the fixed fee specified and $\epsilon$ can be made as small as desired) and so the monopoly would have captured all of the consumer's surplus. If we look at the situation in the market as a whole, as in panel (b) of Figure 9.9, we see that the monopoly's profit is the entire shaded area. All of what was previously profit, consumer's surplus and deadweight loss has been captured by the monopoly as profit under the two-part pricing scheme.

Formally, the two-part price would be a function that showed the total amount paid as a function of the quantity purchased:

$$P(q) = \frac{(a-c)^2}{2} + cq.$$

The first term on the right-hand side is the fixed fee and the second term is the per unit charge. Each consumer would buy $(a - c)$ units, so total sales would be $n(a - c)$. The second part of the price would cover all of the monopoly's costs and so the profit would be the fixed fee collected from each of the $n$ customers. Thus, profits are now

$$\pi = n \cdot \frac{(a-c)^2}{2},$$

which is double the profit the firm was earning with the basic pricing scheme, and is illustrated by the shaded area in panel (b) of Figure 9.9.

Of course, in reality, all consumers are not identical, so the monopoly's problem is more complex. It will be impossible to capture all of the consumer's surplus as happened in the idealised example. However, the approach will be the same. What is most interesting about the two-part price is that the per unit part of the price will be set equal to the *MC* in order to maximise the potential surplus to be captured through the fixed fee. This sharply reduces or eliminates the deadweight loss due to monopoly. If the per unit price is equal to *MC*, the quantity consumed will not be distorted from the competitive level, and so the deadweight loss disappears.

One complication that we have ignored is that, if the fixed fee is large enough, there could be an income effect due to the two-part tariff that could cause the demand curve to shift inward. For example, there may be some consumers whose level of consumption (and hence consumer's surplus) is relatively low, and they might decide to drop out of the market altogether rather than paying the fixed fee. We will discuss this issue in greater detail in the section on natural monopoly regulation, where the two-part pricing scheme will reappear.

### 9.2.2 First-Degree Price Discrimination

The two-part price attempts to capture more profit for the monopolist at the expense of the consumer and by recovering some or all of the deadweight loss normally associated with monopoly power. In the idealised example of the previous section, the firm captured *all* of the potential consumer's surplus and recovered *all* of any potential deadweight loss, earning the maximum possible profit. Another way it can do that is through first-degree or perfect price discrimination.

In **first-degree price discrimination**, a firm sells each successive unit of the good for the maximum consumer willingness-to-pay for that unit. We know that the height of the demand curve at any point represents the marginal value of that unit and thus the maximum willingness-to-pay for that unit by the consumer whose demand is being reflected at that point. So, if the height of the demand curve at $q = 1$ is $p_1$, that represents the highest willingness-to-pay for that first unit. Similarly, $p_2$ in Figure 9.10 would represent the highest willingness-to-pay for the second unit and so on.

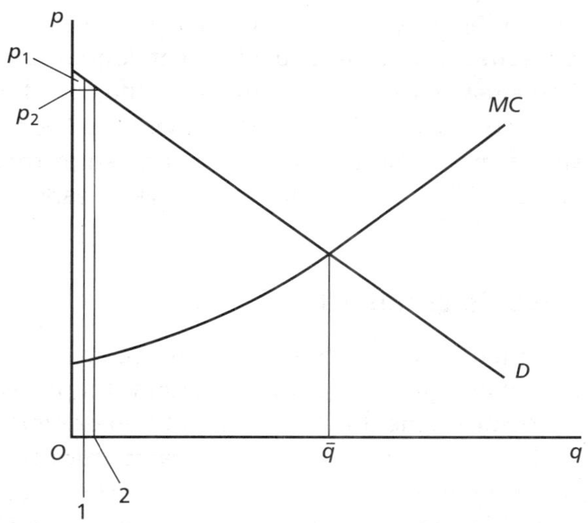


**Figure 9.10** *First-Degree Price Discrimination*

If the monopoly of Figure 9.10 practises first-degree price discrimination, it would sell the first unit for $p_1$, the second unit for $p_2$ and so on, until the point where the *MC* curve crosses the demand curve. As long as $p_i > MC_i$, the firm would find it profitable to sell additional units. But, once $p_i = MC_i$, further sales would incur losses. Thus, the firm in Figure 9.10 would sell $\overline{q}$ units, the quantity at which $p_i = MC_i$.

There are two important observations to make about the solution in the case of perfect price discrimination. The first is that the equilibrium is efficient in the sense that the perfectly competitive equilibrium is efficient: on the margin, price is equal to *MC* and so the quantity sold is the efficient one. It is not distorted the way it usually is under monopoly. The second is that the level of consumer's surplus has been driven down to zero. The firm has captured all the surplus! The firm's profits are at their absolute possible maximum.

Actually, implementing a scheme of perfect price discrimination is obviously difficult since it requires the firm to have a tremendous amount of information about the buyers' demand and willingness-to-pay. Nevertheless, one does occasionally see examples of firms at least attempting to practise this pricing scheme. One such example is the way in which new discoveries of rare coins are dispersed in the market. To illustrate, a few years ago, a hoard of approximately 200 gold coins of the Bactrian king Diodotus was found somewhere in Bihar. Up until that point, only about 10 or 15 gold coins of this king had ever been found and they commanded prices of around \$ 10,000–\$ 15,000 or more on the international rare coin market, the price varying with the condition of the coin. The dealer who acquired the new hoard did not announce the availability of 200 coins of this king. Rather, he offered one or two coins each to a variety of dealers and collectors, giving each the impression that he was being offered the only one or two of these coins available. Naturally, the initial prices paid were very high. Then, a year or so later, one or two coins at a time started appearing in major auction catalogues. Since many of the keenest and wealthiest collectors had already acquired specimens of the coin, the prices realised at these auctions were lower, in the region of \$ 3,000–\$ 5,000 depending upon condition. Over the next few years, first a trickle and then a flood of the coins appeared in the markets and the prices continued to tumble, to the \$ 1,000–\$ 3,000 range. This was clearly an example of attempted first-degree price discrimination.

### 9.2.3 Third-Degree Price Discrimination

The next variation to the basic model looks at a form of price discrimination that is far more feasible and far more prevalent than first-degree price discrimination. It applies in situations where the monopoly can somehow divide or segment the market into two or more mutually exclusive parts and then take advantage of differences in the demand characteristics of the different segments to increase profits by charging different prices. This is why this practice is called price discrimination, and **third-degree price discrimination** occurs when a firm charges different prices in different market segments. (Second-degree price discrimination will be examined in the next section.) In order for this strategy to work, it must be the case that re-sale from one of the market segments to the other is impossible or too expensive to be worthwhile. For example, a simple way in which price discrimination is practised is for firms to give discounts to students or senior citizens. Generally, such discounts are given for goods and services that are consumed on the spot and so re-sale becomes impossible. Examples include discounts on travel, restaurant meals, movie tickets and so on. Another important situation that lends itself to this kind of price discrimination is when different parts of the market are geographically separated. Prices in domestic and export markets can frequently be different.

How will the monopoly set prices if the market can be segmented in this way? Suppose there are two market segments characterised by different inverse demand curves $p = f_1(q_1)$ and $p = f_2(q_2)$. Cost depends only upon the firm's total output $Q = q_1 + q_2$. Then the firm's profit is the sum of revenue from the two markets minus cost:

$$\pi = R_1(q_1) + R_2(q_2) - C(Q)$$

which can be written in this case as

$$\pi = q_1 \cdot f_1(q_1) + q_2 \cdot f_2(q_2) - C(q_1 + q_2)$$

To maximise profits, the firm must set the partial derivatives of $\pi$ with respect to each of the quantities equal to zero:

$$\frac{\partial \pi}{\partial q_1} = MR_1 - MC = 0 \tag{9.11}$$

$$\frac{\partial \pi}{\partial q_2} = MR_2 - MC = 0. \tag{9.12}$$

The first-order conditions (9.11) and (9.12) can be combined and summarised as follows:

$$MR_1 = MR_2 = MC. \tag{9.13}$$

That is, to maximise profits, the firm must set the marginal revenue in each market equal to the (common) marginal cost, and hence equal to the *MR* in the other market. The result is generalisable to any number of markets; the *MR* in each should be set equal to the *MC*.

The intuition for this result is as follows. The *MR* in any market represents the increase in revenue gained from selling one more unit of output in that market. If the MRs in the two market segments are not equal, say if $MR_1 > MR_2$, the firm could unambiguously raise its profits by reducing sales in market 2 by one unit and increasing sales in market 1 by the same amount. Since total production has not changed, the total cost is unaffected. The reduced sales in market 2 would have lost the firm $MR_2$ in revenue, but this is counterbalanced by a gain in revenue in market 1 of $MR_1$. Since $MR_1 > MR_2$, there is a net gain in revenue, and since costs are unchanged, there is an increase in profits. This sort of adjustment in the disposition of sales would always raise profits as long as $MR_1 \neq MR_2$. Thus, setting MRs equal must be necessary for profit maximisation. Further, the MRs must be set equal to *MC*, as in the basic monopoly model. Note that there are not separate values of *MC* for the two markets, a common misconception of students. There is just one *MC*, as any additional production can be sold in either market. Each *MR* must be set equal to this single *MC*.

Coming back to the conditions in (9.13), if we simply apply the formula (9.2) for *MR*, we can write $MR_1 = MR_2$ as

$$p_1 \cdot \left\{1 + \frac{1}{\varepsilon_1}\right\} = p_2 \cdot \left\{1 + \frac{1}{\varepsilon_2}\right\},$$

where $\varepsilon_1$ and $\varepsilon_2$ are the elasticities of demand in markets 1 and 2, respectively. Since $\varepsilon_1$ and $\varepsilon_2$ are both negative, we might make the discussion more intuitive if we write this condition as

$$p_1 \cdot \left\{1 - \frac{1}{|\varepsilon_1|}\right\} = p_2 \cdot \left\{1 - \frac{1}{|\varepsilon_2|}\right\}. \tag{9.14}$$

Equation (9.14) implies that

$$|\varepsilon_1| > |\varepsilon_2| \rightarrow \frac{1}{|\varepsilon_1|} < \frac{1}{|\varepsilon_2|} \rightarrow \left\{1 - \frac{1}{|\varepsilon_1|}\right\} > \left\{1 - \frac{1}{|\varepsilon_2|}\right\} \rightarrow p_1 < p_2.$$

Thus, the price-discriminating firm will charge a higher price in the market with the less elastic demand. This result makes intuitive sense. A market with a less elastic demand is one that is easier to exploit and so the price there will be higher.

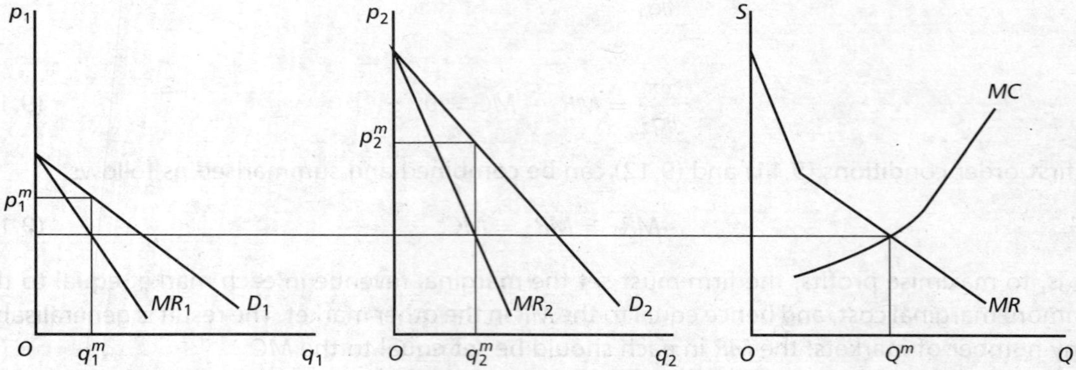


**Figure 9.11** *Third-Degree Price Discrimination*

Representing this result graphically requires a construction similar to the one we had for multi-plant monopoly. There, in order to ensure $MC_1 = MC_2$, we constructed a combined $MC$ curve by summing the individual $MC$ curves horizontally. Here, since we need to ensure $MR_1 = MR_2$, we construct a combined $MR$ curve by summing the individual $MR$ curves horizontally. The intersection of the firm $MC$ curve with this combined $MR$ curve yields the profit-maximising output level. In Figure 9.11, panels (a) and (b) represent the two market segments while panel (c) represents the whole firm. The line marked $MR$ in panel (c) is the combined $MR$, the horizontal summation of the two individual $MR$ curves in panels (a) and (b). The intersection of $MR$ with the firm's $MC$ in panel (c) yields the profit-maximising output level $Q^{\mathrm{m}}$. To see how this production is divided into sales in the two markets, we look for the points on $MR_1$ and $MR_2$ where the height is equal to the height of $MR$ and $MC$ at $Q^{\mathrm{m}}$ in panel (c). That is achieved by the long horizontal line connecting all three panels. We thereby find the levels of sales in the two markets, $q_1^{\mathrm{m}}$ and $q_2^{\mathrm{m}}$. Since $MR$ is the horizontal sum of the two individual $MR$ curves, it must be the case that

$$q_1^{\mathrm{m}} + q_2^{\mathrm{m}} = Q^{\mathrm{m}}.$$

Finally, the prices in the two markets are determined by looking at the heights of the demand curves at $q_1^{\mathrm{m}}$ and $q_2^{\mathrm{m}}$ respectively. In this way, we have fully characterised the price discrimination equilibrium.

### 9.2.4 Second-Degree Price Discrimination

In the previous section, we looked at third-degree price discrimination, a pricing technique whereby a firm can increase its profits by charging different prices to different market segments.

In order for this to be feasible, re-sale between market segments must be too expensive or impossible and, in addition, the firm must be able to identify the members of the different market segments. Students and senior citizens can be identified by checking their ID cards. It therefore becomes easy to price discriminate between them and regular customers. Price discrimination between consumers in different countries or regions can be implemented by virtue of the geographic separation between the different market segments. But what can a firm do if it is difficult to identify members of the different market segments? The essence of price discrimination is to try to charge high prices to customers with a relatively high willingness-to-pay and lower prices to customers with a low willingness-to-pay. How can a firm achieve this when it cannot identify these customers explicitly?

This is the task tackled by the pricing technique called **second-degree price discrimination**. In this form of price discrimination, the firm offers customers a menu of different price schedules in an attempt to get customers to self-select themselves into different groups based on their willingness-to-pay. In this way, it can extract more of the potential surplus for itself. The menu of price schedules has to be chosen in a manner suitable to the particular circumstances of the situation, and since the circumstances can vary considerably, there are a wide variety of ways in which second-degree price discrimination can be implemented.

One very simple form of second-degree price discrimination is the offering of different size packages of the same product. For example, cornflakes may be offered in packages of 300 g or 500 g and the per gram price turns out to be different; normally, the 500-g package would have the lower per gram price, but this need not always be true. Virtually, all consumer products come in such varying package sizes, and one might wonder what the point is. We shall see that it is a way to engage in second-degree price discrimination, using an idealised example to illustrate the technique.

Suppose there are two types of customers for spring water; let us call them low-demand types and high-demand types. For simplicity, let us assume that there are an equal number of the two types. Demand curves for one of each type of customer are drawn in Figure 9.12, with the low-demand type having the demand curve that cuts the horizontal axis at $Q_1$ and the high-demand type the demand curve that cuts the axis at $Q_2$. Again for simplicity, assume the *MC* of producing spring water is zero. Recalling the two-part pricing system discussed earlier, it is easy to see that the firm can capture the entire surplus from the low-demand customer by offering a package of size $Q_1$ and charging the price given by area A in Figure 9.12, the entire potential consumer's surplus.

Ideally, the firm would like to offer the high-demand customer a package of size $Q_2$ at price $(A + B + C)$, thereby capturing all of the high-demand customer's potential consumer's surplus as well. However, this is not feasible, because, if both sizes are on offer, the high-demand customer would opt for a package of size $Q_1$, since that would give her a surplus of B, while the package of size $Q_2$ would give her no surplus at all. Thus, it seems that the firm can collect a profit of A from both types of customer or a profit of $(A + B + C)$ from only the high-demand customer (by abandoning the size $Q_1$ altogether and leaving the low-demand customer unsupplied).

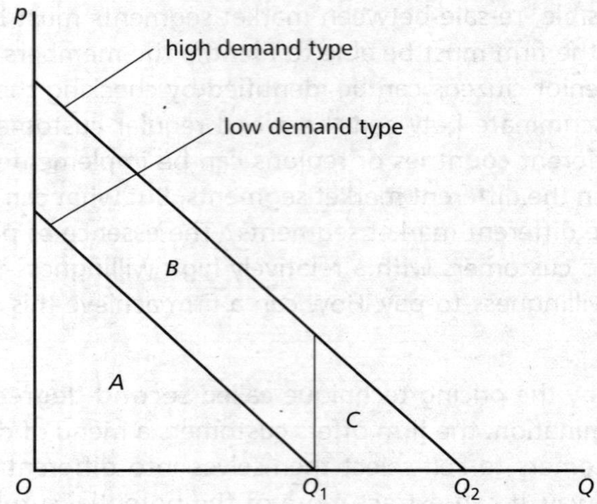


**Figure 9.12** *Second-Degree Price Discrimination*

Abandoning the low-demand customer may be the most profitable thing to do, but the firm can do better than getting A from both customers through second-degree price discrimination. It can offer packages of size $Q_2$ at a price not of $(A + B + C)$, which the high-demand customers would reject, but at a price of $(A + C)$. By buying this size, high-demand customers would still be getting a surplus of B, and the firm would be extracting $(A + C)$ from them rather than just A. So the pricing scheme would be to offer two sizes: $Q_1$ at a price of A, and $Q_2$ at a price of $(A + C)$. The customers would self-select into two different groups, and the firm's profit would be $(2A + C)$ per pair of customers. Note that the average price per unit would be $A/Q_1$ for the small size and $\frac{A+C}{Q_2}$ for the large size.

This is not the end of the story, as the firm can do even better. If it made the small package slightly less attractive to the high-demand customers, it could capture more of their surplus. Suppose, for example, that, instead of packets of size $Q_1$, it offered slightly smaller packages of size $Q_3$ in Figure 9.13. It would have to charge less for these packages, of course, and the reduction in price would have to be *D* from Figure 9.13, since this is the amount by which the low-demand customer's potential surplus has fallen because of the reduction in the size of the package. But they can charge the high-demand customers more for the $Q_2$ size packages. The high-demand customer's consumer's surplus from the small ($Q_3$ size) package is only $B'$; it is smaller than the previous surplus of B from the $Q_1$ packages by the area *E* in Figure 9.13. Therefore, the firm can charge them E more for the $Q_2$ size package. The firm loses *D* but gains E through this adjusted scheme. As long as *E* is large enough compared to *D* and the number of high-demand customers is large enough as compared to the number of low-demand customers, such adjustments would be worthwhile for the firm to make. If the number of low-demand customers and high-demand customers were equal, as we have been assuming, the optimal size of the small

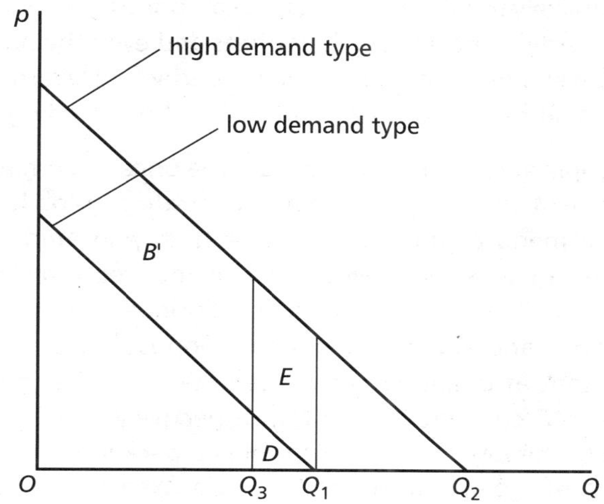


**Figure 9.13** *Capturing More Consumers' Surplus*

packages would be $Q_4$ in Figure 9.14 where the distance *d* is equal to the distance e in the figure. This is because *d* is the rate at which *D* (the loss in revenue) is growing as the package size is reduced and e is the rate at which *E* (the gain in being able to charge more for the large package) is growing. Profits will be maximised when the rate at which revenue is falling from an expansion in *D* is equal to the rate at which revenue is rising from an expansion of *E*, and that happens when $d = e$, as at $Q_4$.

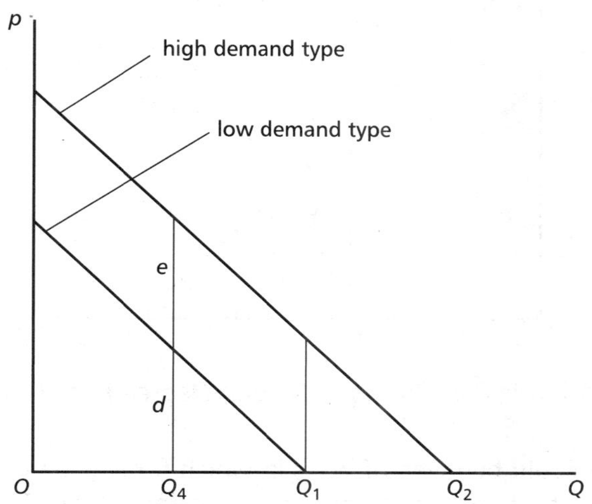


**Figure 9.14** *Optimal Separating Equilibrium*

Of course, demand is unlikely to fall neatly into two categories as in our example, so the problem of calculating the optimal sizes of packages, their prices and even the number of different sizes to offer is very complex and well-nigh impossible to solve perfectly. Nevertheless, the basic principles on which the solution should be based are as outlined in the preceding discussion.

A somewhat more complicated form of second-degree price discrimination is when a firm uses two-part prices to implement the price-discriminating strategy. Mobile telephone providers, for example, typically offer a menu of monthly plans with varying amounts of minutes and then varying rates of 'overages' or fees for services beyond the free threshold. Once again, we will use an idealised example to illustrate the principles. Suppose, once again, that there are two types of customers, low demand and high demand. Suppose the average and marginal cost of providing service is constant at $c$, and suppose the low-demand and high-demand customers' demand curves cross the $MC$ curve at $Q_1$ and $Q_2$, respectively (see Figure 9.15). The firm could then contemplate offering the low-demand customers a package with which they can consume up to $Q_1$ units at a price of $c$ per unit in addition to a fixed fee of $A$. The target package for high-demand customers would be a package offering up to $Q_2$ units at a price of $c$ in addition to a fixed fee of $(A + B + C)$, but of course this would be rejected in favour of the smaller package. So a feasible price-discriminating package would offer up to $Q_2$ units at a price of $c$ in addition to a fixed fee of $(A + C)$. In this way, the example starts to look like the one in the previous illustration. The optimal set of packages would involve a small package of size to be determined in the same way as package $Q_4$ in Figure 9.14 was determined.

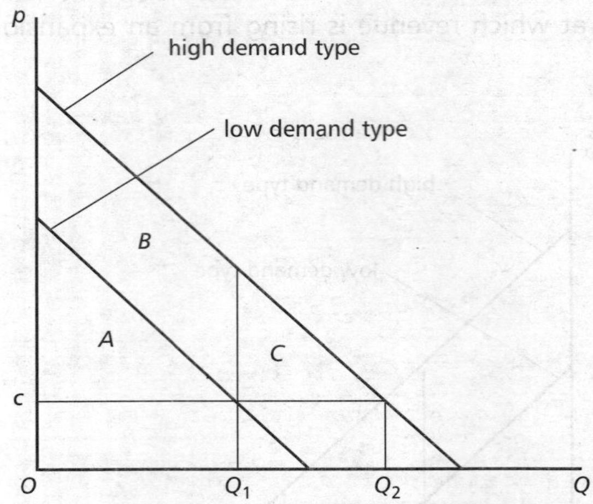


**Figure 9.15** *Two-Part Pricing in Second-Degree Price Discrimination*

Many more examples could be given of ways in which firms practice second-degree price discrimination. One important variant is where they do not offer packages of different sizes but rather packages of different qualities. Examples might include different classes of seats on airplane flights or different qualities of rooms in hotels, economy versus luxury cars, free versus paid greetings cards on internet sites and so on. The number of examples one could give is virtually endless.

If we treat quality as a continuous variable, the analysis of optimal pricing would be analogous to the previous analysis of package sizes, with a high-quality good being analogous to a large package size and a low-quality good to a small size. If, however, we treat quality as discrete, say as consisting of adding or subtracting features, the analysis would need to be modified, although it would be similar in spirit or concept.

For example, suppose a product can contain two features, *a* and *b*. Think of *a* as being the basic functionality of the product, such as the ability to transport people from one place to another (if the product is a car), while *b* might represent 'optional' features such as comfort or safety. Suppose low-demand customers have a willingness-to-pay for these features of $a_L$ and $b_L$, while high-demand customers are willing-to-pay $a_H$ and $b_H$. Naturally, $a_H > a_L$ and $b_H > b_L$. If the firm considered offering two 'models' of the product, one containing only feature *a* and the other containing both *a* and *b*, we can readily see that the price-discriminating prices will be $a_L$ for the 'basic model' and $(a_L + b_H)$ for the 'luxury model'. The firm cannot charge $(a_H + b_H)$ for the luxury model, since customers would then reject it in favour of the basic model as they would get higher surplus there. Therefore, the firm misses out on a potential surplus of $(a_H - a_L)$.

However, analogous to the idea of making a small package even smaller in order to extract more surplus from high-demand customers even while losing some surplus from low-demand customers, the firm could possibly lower the quality of the basic model in order to be able to charge much more for the luxury product. Suppose, for example, that they could offer the basic model in such a low quality, $a'$, that the willingness-to-pay by the high-demand customers for this low-quality version was only slightly higher than that of low-demand customers, that is, $(a'_H - a'_L)$ is small. Perhaps $a_L$ has not fallen much in response to the lowering of quality, but $a_H$ has fallen a lot. Now the firm can offer two models: a basic model $a'$ at price $a'_L$ and a luxury model containing *a* (not $a'$ ... this is the key to the exercise!) and *b* at price $[a_H + b_H - (a'_H - a'_L)]$. Under this scenario, the firm has lost $(a_L - a'_L)$ per low-demand customer but has gained $[(a_H - a'_H) - (a_L - a'_L)]$ from every high-demand customer. If $a_L > a'_L$ only slightly, while $a_H > a'_H$ by a lot, the firm would have gained through the altered scheme. Any cost saving $(c - c')$ from producing the lower quality $a'$ as opposed to *a* for the low-demand customers would be an added benefit to the firm.

Sometimes, if a lower-quality version $a'$ does not exist, a firm can literally manufacture such a low-quality version in order to implement a price-discrimination scheme. For example, Intel sold two versions of its 486 computer chip, one, with all of its functions intact, at a high price and another, with some of its functions disabled (not missing but actually disabled, making this version of the chip slightly more expensive to produce), at a lower price. Similarly, IBM sold two versions of its LaserPrinter E: a fast version at a high price and a slow version, produced by adding special controllers to the fast version to actually slow down the printing, making this version again more expensive to produce, at a low price. Such 'manufactured' low-quality versions of products have been given the name 'damaged goods' and the point is that firms will sometimes incur additional costs in order to produce damaged goods in order to implement a second-degree price discrimination scheme.

## 9.3 LIMIT (ENTRY-DETERRING) PRICING

**Task for this section:**

To look at what effect the threat of potential entry of other firms might have on the optimal strategy of an incumbent monoplist. After this section, you should know what a limit prices are, and have a good idea of the kinds of situations where they may arise.

In the previous sections, we have looked at the basic monopoly pricing model and then at various ways in which a monopoly (or really any firm with market power) might introduce more complex pricing strategies in order to increase profits over what is attainable under the basic model. We have implicitly taken the monopoly's position as sole seller in the market as given and unchallenged.

However, while a monopoly may indeed be the sole seller in a market at any given point in time, it may face the *threat* of entry from a rival or rivals. If this is the case, it may not always be the best policy to charge monopoly prices because the profitability the monopoly would enjoy might make entry an enticing proposition for rivals. Instead, the monopoly may find it in its long-run interest to charge **limit prices** or **entry-deterring prices**, prices that would limit or deter entry. In other words, it might make sense for the monopoly to charge prices that make entry unprofitable.

We will look at limit or entry-deterring prices in detail in the chapter on oligopoly, in the context of models of strategic competition, but in this section, we will look at two broad classes of models that shed light on limit prices.

### 9.3.1 Contestable Markets

One of the key factors that is surely going to influence the behaviour of a monopolist under threat of entry is how easy it is for rivals to enter the market. If entry is expensive, involving large sunk costs, and time-consuming, involving long lead times, a monopoly can probably behave as a profit-maximiser and simply wait to alter its behaviour as entry becomes imminent. If, however, rivals can enter quickly and at little cost, a monopoly may need to moderate its behaviour somewhat.

The **contestability** of a market refers to these entry conditions. A **perfectly contestable market** is one where rivals can enter instantaneously and costlessly. When we say 'costlessly', we mean that there are no *sunk costs* involved, sunk costs being costs that cannot be recovered. For example, if an airline company decides to start flying on a new route (i.e. enter the market consisting of that route), it must have an aircraft to fly on that route. If it can simply lease an airplane, or if it could re-sell an aircraft it purchased for the purpose at the same price as it paid (minus *actual* depreciation), we would say there are no sunk costs of entry. If the airline could start flying on that route at more or less a moment's notice, we would classify that market as perfectly contestable.

An important result for perfectly contestable markets is that an incumbent monopolist must set price equal to the potential entrant's marginal cost. The argument is that, if price is higher than this $MC$, and entry can take place costlessly and instantaneously, the entrant could engage in 'hit-and-run entry', entering and capturing the market for as long as it takes for the incumbent to respond. Indeed, the entrant could stay in the market and engage in competition long term as well. So to deter or limit entry, the monopoly must set $p = MC$ (of the rival) in order to make entry unprofitable. We will look at this result in more detail in the chapter on oligopoly since it is closely related to the model of Bertrand competition.

The theory of contestable markets, developed by William Baumol, Elizabeth Bailey and others played an important role in the deregulation of the airline industry in the United States in the 1980 and, by extension, in India in the 1990s. Until that time, most economists regarded the airline industry as characterised by significant barriers to entry, since setting up an airline involved buying a fleet of aircraft. It was therefore thought to be essential to regulate the industry. However, Baumol and others pointed out a new way to think about the industry. Rather than thinking of airline services as one large market, they suggested looking at the route on each city-pair (say, Boston–New York or Delhi–Mumbai) as a separate market. While there may be large barriers to entering the airline market as a whole, entering a particular route might be quite an easy and cheap thing to do for an airline that is already operational but is not flying on that particular route. Thus, even if there is only one airline flying on a particular route, it may be forced to charge a price quite close to the marginal cost if the route is contestable and it wishes to deter entry. Regulation of airline prices would then not be necessary.

Of course, it should be mentioned that another reason deregulation of the airline industry was possible was that the size of the market had expanded considerably. In the infancy of the industry, most routes could sustain only one operating airline (they were 'natural monopolies', a topic we discuss in the next section). As the number of passengers grew, it became increasingly viable for more than one airline to operate profitably on most routes and so the forces of competition could be allowed to rule.

## 9.3.2 The Price Leadership Model

Another model in which limit pricing behaviour on the part of a monopoly emerges naturally is called the price leadership model. This is not by design a monopoly model; rather, it is meant to model a situation in which a large, dominant firm is competing with a large number of small firms. It was originally developed in the 1960s as a way to think about the car market in the United States. At the time, General Motors (GM) was unquestioned as the market leader with well over

50% market share, and it was observed that the other car companies would wait to announce their new year models (and prices) until after GM had made its announcement. Thus, it was clear that GM was the 'leader' and the other companies were 'followers'. The model could be applied to many other situations. For example, in the Indian context, it might be used to study the effect of the entry of a large international retailer such as Walmart into the Indian multi-brand retail industry.

The model itself assumes a homogeneous product, being produced by a large, dominant firm and many small 'fringe' firms. The fringe firms are assumed to behave as price-takers, that is, as perfect competitors. Their behaviour is therefore characterised by a supply curve, derived the same way as any supply curve in a perfectly competitive market. The dominant firm is assumed to know this supply curve and therefore takes it into account in determining its optimal behaviour. To see how exactly it does this, we need to look at a more formal specification of the model.

Suppose $D(p)$ is the market demand curve, $S(p)$ is the supply curve of the competitive fringe and $q$ is the dominant firm's output.

Note that

$$q = D(p) - S(p).$$

Therefore,

$$\frac{dq}{dp} = \frac{dD}{dp} - \frac{dS}{dp} = \frac{dD}{dp} \cdot \frac{p}{D} \cdot \frac{D}{p} - \frac{dS}{dp} \cdot \frac{p}{S} \cdot \frac{S}{p}$$

which can be written as

$$\frac{dq}{dp} = \frac{1}{p} \cdot \{D \cdot \varepsilon_d - S \cdot \varepsilon_s\}, \tag{9.15}$$

where $\varepsilon_d$ and $\varepsilon_s$ are the elasticities of demand and supply, respectively. Inverting (9.15), we get

$$\frac{dp}{dq} = \frac{p}{D \cdot \varepsilon_d - S \cdot \varepsilon_s}. \tag{9.16}$$

The dominant firm's choice problem is to maximise its profit, $\pi_d$, which is given by

$$\pi_d = p \cdot q - C(q),$$

where $C(q)$ is the dominant firm's cost function. The first-order condition for profit maximisation is

$$\frac{d\pi_d}{dq} = p + q \cdot \frac{dp}{dq} - C'(q) = 0.$$

Substituting (9.16) in this and rearranging, we get

$$p + q \cdot \frac{p}{D \cdot \varepsilon_d - S \cdot \varepsilon_s} = C'(q),$$

which can be written as

$$p\left\{1+\frac{q}{D\cdot\varepsilon_d - S\cdot\varepsilon_s}\right\}=C'(q). \tag{9.17}$$

Equation (9.17) is the usual profit-maximising condition $MR = MC$. The effect of the competitive fringe is seen in the second term within the curly brackets. Had there been no competitive fringe, $S = 0$ and $q = D$ in equilibrium, so (9.17) would reduce to

$$p\left\{1+\frac{1}{\varepsilon_d}\right\}=C'(q),$$

which is the standard monopoly first-order condition. Thus, this model can be seen as a generalisation of the monopoly model that allows for the presence of a competitive fringe. But the presence of a competitive fringe does not automatically mean that the fringe firms will produce a positive quantity. Rather, the dominant firm might engage in limit pricing, thereby forcing the fringe to exit the market. It is now perhaps easiest to see this through a graphical analysis.

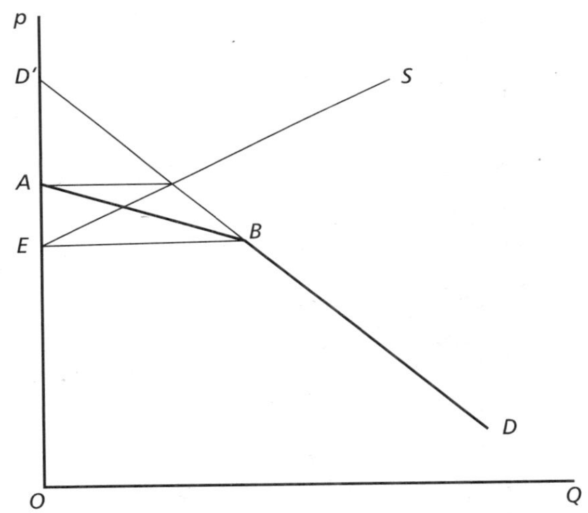


**Figure 9.16** *The Dominant Firm's Residual Demand Curve*

We start in Figure 9.16 with the market demand curve $D(p)$, represented by the line DD′ in the figure, and the fringe supply curve $S(p)$, represented by the line $ES$. By subtracting the fringe supply curve horizontally from the market demand curve, we get the dominant firm's residual demand curve, shown by the kinked line $ABD$ in the figure. This line shows the combinations of price $p$ and the dominant firm's output $q$ that would be consistent with equilibrium in the market. For example, if the price were higher than $OA$, the competitive fringe would be willing to supply more than would be demanded in the market, so such a price could not be an equilibrium price.

Thus, the dominant firm's residual demand is zero for prices above *OA*; it cannot sell anything at those prices. For prices at *OE* and below, the supply from the fringe would be zero, and so the dominant firm would have the whole market demand to itself. Thus, it would face the demand *BD*. Finally, for prices between *OA* and *OE*, the market demand would exceed the supply from the competitive fringe, and it is this 'excess demand' that would be the dominant firm's 'residual demand'. This is shown by the line *AB* in Figure 9.16. It is the horizontal difference between *DD*′ and *ES* and shows the quantity that the dominant firm could sell at each price between *OE* and *OA*. The full residual demand faced by the dominant firm is therefore *D*′*ABD*.

The next step is to see what the marginal revenue curve corresponding to this kinked residual demand curve looks like. We do this in Figure 9.17. *ABD* is once again the kinked residual demand curve. The *MR* curve corresponding to this is the double-kinked line *AFGH*. The double kink may come as a surprise and may not seem intuitive. One way to see this is that, if we look at the full market demand curve *DD*′, it is easy to see that *D*′*GH* is the *MR* curve corresponding to this demand curve. Since the segment *BD* belongs to this, it seems natural that the segment *GH* would be the corresponding *MR* curve. Further, if we look at the demand curve *AB*, it is clear that *AF* would be its *MR* curve. Thus, the *MR* curve for *ABD* has two segments: the segment *AF* corresponding to

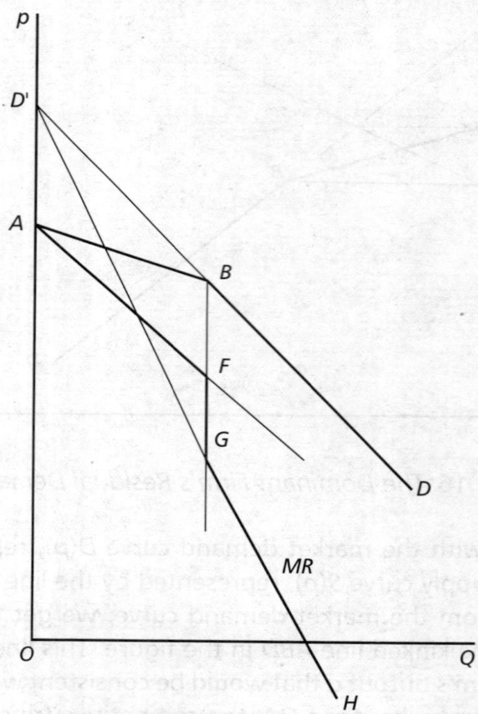


**Figure 9.17** *Marginal Revenue Curve for the Residual Demand Curve*

*AB* on the demand curve, and the segment *GH* corresponding to *BD* on the demand curve. The line segment *FG* is not really part of the *MR* curve, but it connects the two actual segments and we will see that it is convenient to think of it as being part of the *MR* curve.

Another way to think about the shape of the *MR* curve is to recall why *MR* lies below the demand curve in the first place. Remember that, for a monopoly, the demand curve is nothing but the average revenue (*AR*) curve. If it is falling, that is, downward-sloping, the *MR* must be lower than the *AR*. (If $MR > AR$, *AR* would have to be rising.) Now *MR* is below *AR* because the change in revenue from selling one more unit (the *MR*) is the price at which that unit can be sold (the *AR*) *minus* the lost revenue from having to lower the price for all the infra-marginal units. When the demand curve is kinked, as at *B* in Figure 9.17, the rate at which the firm has to lower price in order to sell one more unit suddenly drops, and so the *MR* also takes a sudden drop (the segment *FG*).

Having established the shape of the *MR* curve and, in particular, having noted that it has three different segments, we can look at the dominant firm's choice. There are three cases, depending upon which of the three segments of the *MR* curve is crossed by the dominant firm's *MC* curve. The three cases are illustrated in the three panels of Figure 9.18.

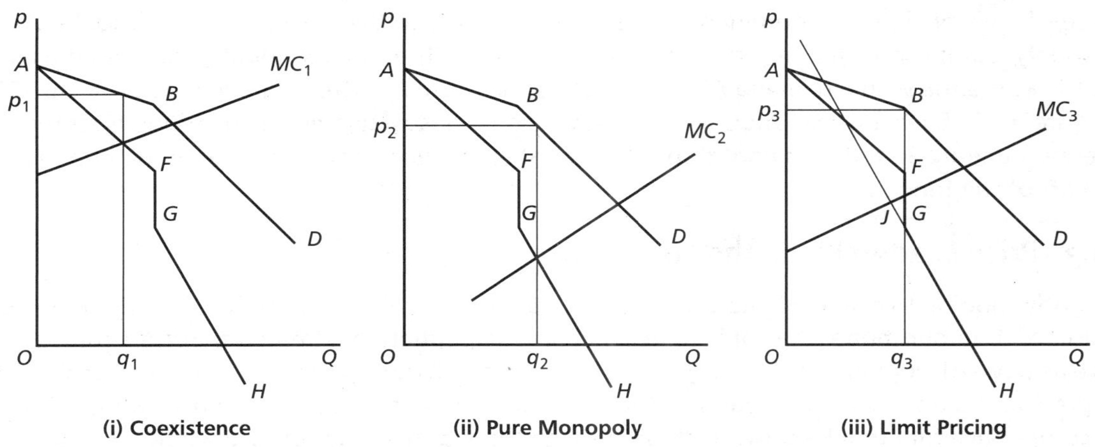


**Figure 9.18** *Three Possibilities for the Dominant Firm's Equilibrium*

**Case (i):** The dominant firm's *MC* curve cuts the *MR* curve in the segment *AF*. This is shown in panel (i) of Figure 9.18 and is the case we obtained in the algebraic derivation earlier. In this case, the dominant firm chooses to produce $q_1$ and the price, reading from the dominant firm's residual demand curve *ABD*, is $p_1$. Although the market demand curve is not shown in Figure 9.18 in order to keep the figure as uncluttered as possible, we can see from Figure 9.17 that, when the dominant firm is producing on the segment *AB*, the market demand is higher (along the segment *D′B* in Figure 9.17). The excess of market demand over what the dominant firm is producing will be supplied by the fringe firms. In Figure 9.16, we had seen how the residual demand curve was derived by subtracting the fringe supply curve from the market demand curve, so here the supply from the fringe firms will exactly match the 'excess' of the market demand over what the dominant firm is supplying. This equilibrium could be called the coexistence equilibrium, since the dominant firm and the fringe firms coexist in the market.

**Case (ii):** The dominant firm's *MC* curve cuts the *MR* curve in the segment *GH*. This outcome is illustrated in panel (ii) of Figure 9.18, and is nothing but the standard or pure monopoly solution. Here, the dominant firm's *MC* is so low that the monopoly profit-maximising price is below the price at which the competitive fringe is willing to supply anything to the market. Thus, the efficiency of the competitive firm drives all competitors out of the market. This solution can be called the pure monopoly solution.

**Case (iii):** The dominant firm's *MC* curve passes through the *MR* curve in the segment *FG*. As was noted earlier, this segment is not really part of the *MR* curve, which just has a gap between the segments *AF* and *GH*. Rather, we have a situation where *MR* is never equal to *MC*, but $MR > MC$ for $q < q_3$ and $MR < MC$ for $q > q_3$, so $q = q_3$ becomes the choice of quantity and $p_3$ then would be the price (see panel (iii) in Figure 9.18). The equilibrium is therefore at the kink *B*, which means the price is just at that level where supply from the competitive fringe falls to zero. This is therefore a case of limit pricing. The dominant firm is the only seller in the market, so that it looks like a monopoly, but it is not charging the pure monopoly price. The true monopoly equilibrium would be at J, where the whole demand *MR* curve meets the *MC* curve (this *MR* curve was the line *GD'* in Figure 9.17). Such a true monopoly solution would be unsustainable, as the fringe firms would enter production. So the dominant firm sets price at $p_3$, a price just low enough to deter entry on the part of the fringe firms.

## 9.3.3 Price Leadership in the Long Run

A slightly modified version of the price leadership model could be thought of as the long-run version of it. In our model of supply under perfect competition, we treated the short-run supply curve as upward-sloping and the long-run supply curve as flat, or perfectly elastic. The analysis of the previous section could be thought of as a short-run analysis, since we took the supply curve of the competitive fringe to be upward-sloping. So to think of the long run, we would need to take a fringe supply curve that is perfectly elastic. In Figure 9.19, we see what difference this makes to the equilibrium in the price leadership model.

We first need to see what is the shape of the dominant firm's residual demand curve. In the figure, AS is now the fringe supply curve, while *DD'* is the market demand curve as before. Clearly, the dominant firm cannot charge a price higher than *OA*, as the fringe firms' supply is perfectly elastic at that price. The residual demand curve for the dominant firm is therefore the kinked line *ABD*. The corresponding *MR* curve will then be a double-kinked line as before; here, however, it is the line *ABGH*, with the first segment *AB* coinciding with the demand curve, since it is flat in this region.

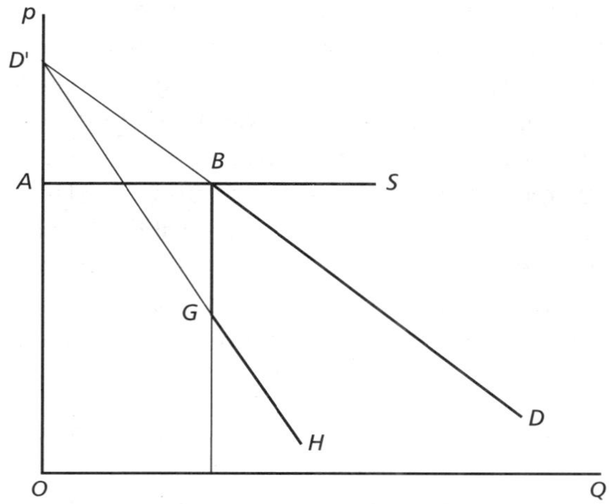


**Figure 9.19** *Price Leadership in the Long Run*

As before, we have three different possible solutions for the dominant firm's choice, depending upon the position of its *MC* curve:

**Case (i):** If the *MC* curve cuts *MR* in the segment *AB*, that point of intersection will determine the dominant firm's output and the price will be *OA*. This would be a coexistence equilibrium, since the fringe firms would be able to produce the difference between the market demand *AB* and what the dominant firm supplies.

**Case (ii):** If the dominant firm's *MC* cuts *MR* in the segment *GH*, we would once again have a pure monopoly solution, since the pure monopoly price would be below *OA*.

**Case (iii):** If the dominant firm's *MC* curve cuts *MR* in the segment *BG*, we would have a limit pricing solution, with the price at *OA* but the dominant firm monopolising the market and producing the quantity *AB*.

# 9.4 NATURAL MONOPOLY AND REGULATION

**Task for this section:**

To study the phenomenon of 'natural monopolies', situations where it makes sense from the social point of view to have only one supplier in the market. We will learn what potential problems might then arise and what can be done about those through regulation. A wide range of such problems, and the regulatory responses to them, are discussed.

A natural monopoly exists in a market when it is cheaper to produce any desired level of output with just one operating firm than with two or more firms each producing part of the desired output. In general, this implies that the average cost of a single firm is declining over the relevant range of output. If we draw on one graph the market demand curve *D* and the average cost curve of a single firm (*AC*), the *AC* curve would be downward-sloping up to the point where it cut the demand curve, as in Figure 9.20. If, for example, the desired output level is $Q_1$, one firm could produce that output at an average cost of $c_1$. However, if two identical firms each produced $Q_1/2$, yielding a total output of $Q_1$ as before, the average cost of this output would be $c_2$, which is higher than $c_1$. Thus, from the social point of view, it is desirable to have just one firm operating since resources are not wasted, and it is for this reason that the situation is called one of 'natural' monopoly.

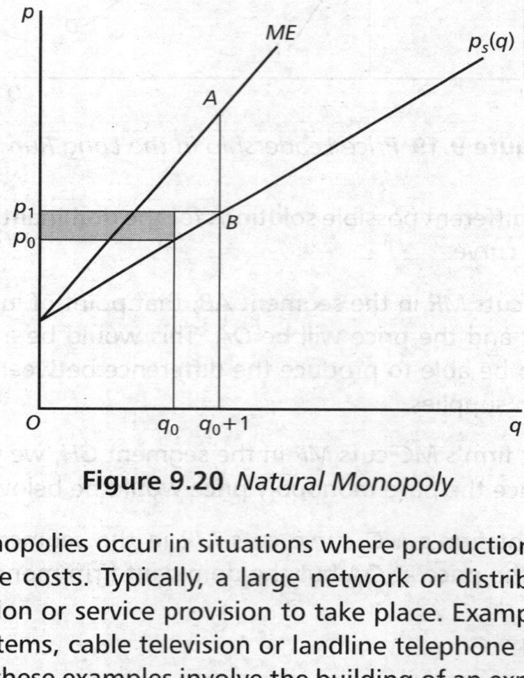


**Figure 9.20** *Natural Monopoly*

In general, natural monopolies occur in situations where production involves a large fixed cost and relatively low variable costs. Typically, a large network or distribution system needs to be built in order for production or service provision to take place. Examples include water, gas and electricity distribution systems, cable television or landline telephone networks, sewage disposal systems and so on. All of these examples involve the building of an expensive network of pipes or cables, along with low marginal costs of service provision to individual households or businesses.

It is important to remember that the definition of a natural monopoly looks at the shape of the *AC* curve *relative to the size of the market*. A market that is a natural monopoly at one point in time, relative to a particular market size, may cease to be a natural monopoly as the market size expands. A good example of this is the airline industry. Building an airline involves the building of an expensive fleet of aircraft, and when the market was small, it could not have sustained many airlines flying on each route. So the airline industry had the characteristics of a natural monopoly over much of the route network. But over time, as the market expanded dramatically, the natural monopoly aspect of it disappeared and this may have played a role in the deregulation of the airline industry. The telephone industry has ceased to be a natural monopoly also as new technology for wireless telephony and fast electronic switching between network systems has made competition much more feasible.

## 9.4.1 The Fundamental Pricing Problem in Natural Monopoly

We have already seen that there should be just one firm under natural monopoly. By the same token, if there are two or more firms operating in such a market, it is quite likely that one of the firms will drive the others out of business since, once one grows larger than the others, it will have a cost advantage and should be able to undercut the other firms' prices. However, if a single firm acquired a monopoly under such circumstances, either by competitive victory or by government directive, it is likely to behave in a manner undesirable from the social point of view. Specifically, a monopoly setting its price or output level to maximise its profit would produce where $MR = MC$, shown as $Q_m$ in Figure 9.21. However, the optimal level of output from the social point of view is where $p = MC$, shown as $Q_c$ in the figure, with the monopoly solution therefore involving the deadweight loss shown by the shaded area. Because $MC$ is very low and demand is typically high for such 'necessary' goods, the deadweight loss due to monopoly may be quite large. For this reason, most countries do not permit unfettered monopoly power in natural monopoly markets. There are two alternatives that are most widely used: government ownership and operation of natural monopolies, and government regulation of privately owned 'utilities' or other natural monopolies.

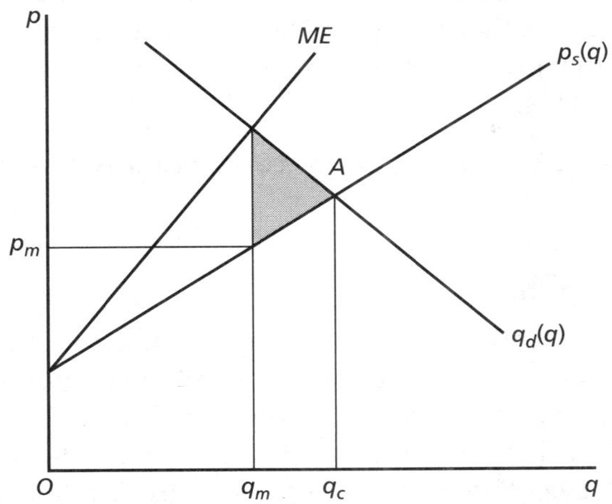


**Figure 9.21** *Deadweight Loss under Monopoly Pricing*

Traditionally, most countries, including India, chose the first option and operated public utilities as state-owned or public enterprises or as municipal corporations. The United States and some other countries, mostly in the Americas, had a mixed system, with companies such as water and sewage mostly municipally owned but electricity and telephone companies being private but regulated. However, this situation started to change in the 1980s, with many countries privatising or disinvesting some or all of their public utility companies. The primary reason for this change was the growing realisation that publicly owned utilities had a tendency to be very inefficient and that it was difficult to improve their efficiency as long as their ownership lay in the hands of the government.

The problems of how to optimally operate a publicly owned natural monopoly and of how to regulate a privately owned one are essentially the same. We need to understand what the optimal pricing regime would be. We look at this question in the next and succeeding sections.

### 9.4.2 Marginal Cost Pricing and the Deficit Problem

We have already seen that the optimal price under natural monopoly would set $p = MC$, as in perfect competition. However, there is a problem with this sort of pricing under natural monopoly. With average cost declining, it must be the case that $MC < AC$, as shown in the chapter on cost functions (see pp. 138–39 in Chapter 5). Therefore, with $p = MC$, we would have $p < AC$, as at $Q_c$ in Figure 9.21, and the firm would be operating at a loss. A private company under regulation would not tolerate such a situation and would rather go out of business instead. A publicly owned company could continue operating as long as it was subsidised by the treasury. Indeed, historically, many publicly owned companies in India and elsewhere did operate at huge losses and created considerable budgetary problems for the government. As we saw in our discussion on the effects of commodity taxes, raising tax revenues involves creating distortions and 'excess burdens' or deadweight losses in the markets that are taxed. Thus, in trying to prevent deadweight losses in a natural monopoly market, the government ends up creating deadweight losses in other markets, hardly a desirable state of affairs.

Thus, the problem of deficits under marginal cost pricing is a serious one and it is highly desirable to find a solution for it.

### 9.4.3 Average Cost Pricing

A simple solution would be to set price equal to average cost, that is, to look for the point where the demand curve cuts the *AC* curve and set quantity and price from this point. In Figure 9.22, this would result in a price equal to $p_a$ and a quantity produced of $Q_a$. The quantity distortion $(Q_c - Q_a)$ is now relatively small, but it is there and it involves the deadweight loss shown as the shaded area in Figure 9.22. Even though this deadweight loss is relatively small, it would still be desirable to find a solution that did not involve such a loss.

### 9.4.4 Two-Part Pricing

A close to perfect solution is to employ a two-part pricing regime , as was discussed in section 2. The difference from the profit-maximising scheme outlined earlier would be that the 'fixed fee' or

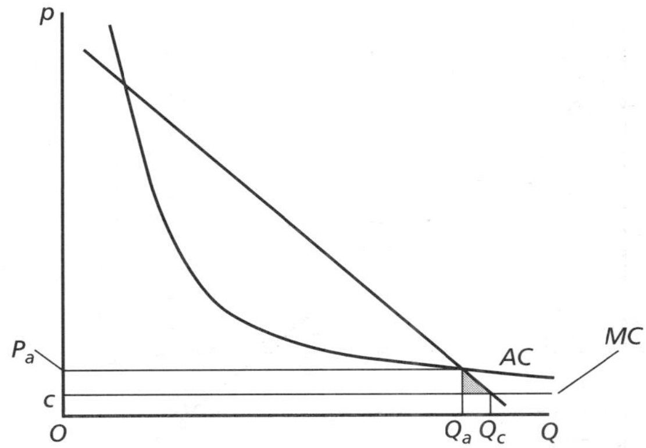


**Figure 9.22** *Average Cost Pricing*

first part of the price would be set not to maximise profits or capture as much of the consumer's surplus as possible, but rather to simply generate enough revenue to cover all of the fixed cost. The second part of the price would be set equal to *MC* so that the quantity choice of the consumers was at the optimal level and undistorted. If the *MC* curve is flat (i.e. marginal cost is constant), the second part of the price would exactly cover the variable costs, and so the first part would be set exactly to cover the fixed cost. If the *MC* curve is rising, then the second part of the price (= *MC*) would cover more than the variable costs, and then the first part of the price could be set lower than the level needed to cover all of fixed cost since a part of the fixed cost would have already been recovered in the second part of the price.

Figure 9.23 illustrates the solution. Here the *MC* curve has been drawn rising slowly and intersecting the demand curve at M. The second part of the two-part price would then be set at OL so that $p = MC$ on the margin. Consumers will then choose the quantity ON and the firm will collect LMNO in revenue from the second part of the price. In this example, that covers all of the variable costs (the area below the *MC* curve) plus some extra that would cover part of the fixed cost. Total cost is the area *ABNO* (average cost times quantity produced), and the difference between this and what is collected from the second part of the price is *ABML*. This is the amount of cost that must be covered by the first part of the price, which should therefore be set equal to ABML divided by the number of consumers. It is very important to note that the first part of the price is *not* equal to *BM* per unit of consumption. If it were set that way, it would be functionally indistinguishable from the second part of the price and the consumers' quantity choice would be distorted. They would choose the quantity where the line *AB* cuts the demand curve, since the height *AO* would effectively be the single price. For the two-part price to be effective, the first part of the price must be a *fixed fee* per consumer, and that is why it needs to be set equal to the ratio of the amount that needs to be collected from it (*ABML*) to the number of people who will pay it (the number of consumers).

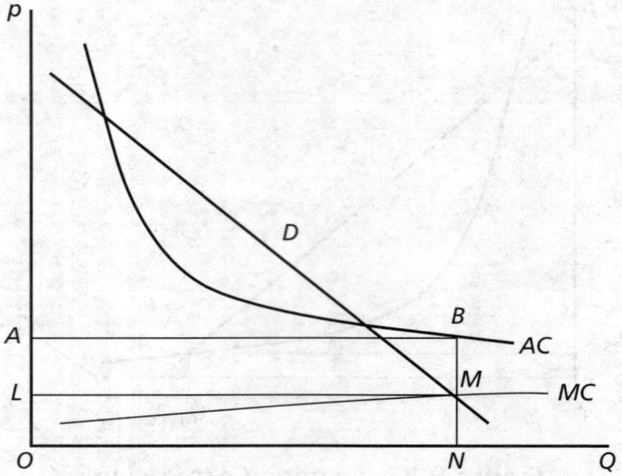


**Figure 9.23** *Two-Part Pricing*

The two-part price solution to the problem of natural monopoly pricing seems ideal in that the quantity choice is undistorted (so there is no deadweight loss) and the firm covers its costs (so there is no deficit problem). There is a potential problem, however, albeit probably a small one. If the fixed fee is in any sense 'large' even for a few consumers, the demand curve might shift inward due to the effect of the fixed fee on the net income of the consumers, and so there might be a small quantity distortion after all.

Let us consider the problem of an individual consumer, whose conventional demand curve *d* is shown in Figure 9.24. The second part of the price is *OL*, and the consumer's demand is *ON*. Absent any fixed fee, the consumer's surplus would be *ELM*. But, if there is a fixed fee, the

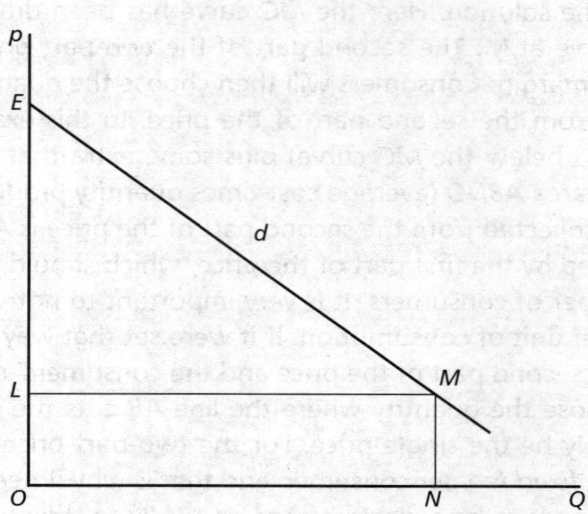


**Figure 9.24** *The Fixed Fee and Individual Demand*

consumer's disposable income net of the fixed fee would be lower, and it is conceivable that, if the fixed fee is 'large' for this consumer, her demand curve might shift to the left. In the extreme case, if the fixed fee is larger than the area *ELM*, the consumer would drop out of the market altogether and her demand would fall to zero (since she would have negative surplus from engaging in this market). If this happens, there would be a quantity distortion at the market level, since the *MC* of serving this customer is only *OL*. Problems of this kind are sometimes noticed for poor consumers whose level of consumption *ON* might be quite low. Regulators normally would require the regulated monopoly to serve such customers anyway, perhaps by waiving or sharply reducing the fixed fee for them.

### 9.4.5 The Multi-Product Firm and Ramsey Pricing

We have seen how the natural monopoly might not be able to adhere to the principle of setting price equal to marginal cost because of the problem of deficits. The solutions have been either to set price equal to average cost, or to use a two-part price in order to raise enough revenue to break even. But what if the firm produces multiple products? Since the costs of the firm will be partly specific to the products (say the raw materials) and partly common to all products (such as general administrative costs or the costs related to the factory building and grounds), we face a dilemma. How do we 'allocate' the common costs to the different products? This is the question addressed in this section. A simple example of a multi-product natural monopoly is a landline telephone network that offers multiple products such as voice calls, data communication, internet access and Yellow Pages. The problem was particularly topical at the time when local and long-distance calls were regarded as distinct products with quite different demand characteristics and it was not obvious what each one's 'share' of the common network costs should be.

In setting up the problem, we assume the firm offers two products whose demands are independent. The firm needs to decide how much of each product to produce, and hence how much to charge for each, in order to maximise social welfare, subject to a revenue constraint such as breaking even. We will measure social welfare in the usual way as the sum of consumers' and producers' surplus. If $(p_1, q_1)$ and $(p_2, q_2)$ represent the prices and quantities of the two products, the problem is to

$$\text{Maximise} \qquad W = V_1(p_1) + V_2(p_2) + p_1q_1 + p_2q_2 - C(q_1, q_2)$$

$$\text{subject to} \qquad p_1q_1 + p_2q_2 - C(q_1, q_2) = R.$$

Here $V_i$ represents the consumers' surplus in the $i$-th market, $C(q_1, q_2)$ represents the cost function, which is not separable in $q_1$ and $q_2$ so as to allow for common costs, and $R$ is the fixed revenue target. $R$ could be zero, so that the company just breaks even, or it could be some other number, positive or negative. A positive value of $R$ would indicate that the government has decided it must raise a certain amount of revenue from this firm (assuming it is a state-owned enterprise), while a negative value of $R$ would indicate government's willingness to subsidise the company up to the fixed amount $R$.

Before proceeding to the solution, we need to derive one preliminary result. Consider the consumer surplus $V(Q)$ in a market when the consumption level is $Q$, $V(Q)$. This is equal to the area below the demand curve up to the quantity $Q$ minus $p \cdot Q$, the expenditure on the good (see Figure 3.6). Therefore, letting $q$ be the variable of integration,

$$V(Q) = \int_0^Q p(q)\, dq - p(Q) \cdot Q.$$

The rate at which this changes as $Q$ changes is

$$\frac{dV}{dQ} = -Q \cdot p'(Q).$$

We will need this result in what follows.

To solve the problem, we set up the Lagrange function for the problem:

$$\mathcal{L} = V_1(p_1) + V_2(p_2) + p_1q_1 + p_2q_2 - C(q_1, q_2) - \lambda[p_1q_1 + p_2q_2 - C(q_1, q_2) - R]. \tag{9.18}$$

Then, using the result derived above on the rate at which consumer surplus changes, the first-order condition with respect to $q_1$ will be

$$\frac{\partial \mathcal{L}}{\partial q_1} = -q_1 \cdot \frac{dp_1}{dq_1} + q_1 \cdot \frac{dp_1}{dq_1} + p_1 - \frac{\partial C}{\partial q_1} - \lambda \left[ p_1 + q_1 \cdot \frac{dp_1}{dq_1} - \frac{\partial C}{\partial q_1} \right] = 0. \tag{9.19}$$

Note that

$$p_1 + q_1 \cdot \frac{dp_1}{dq_1} = p_1 + \frac{p_1}{\varepsilon_1},$$

where $\varepsilon_1$ is the elasticity of demand for product 1. Denoting $C_1' = \frac{\partial C}{\partial q_1}$, we can write 9.19 as

$$p_1 - C_1' = \lambda \left[ p_1 + \frac{p_1}{\varepsilon_1} - C_1' \right]$$

$$\text{or} \quad p_1 - C_1' = \lambda \left( p_1 - C_1' \right) + \frac{\lambda p_1}{\varepsilon_1},$$

which can be written as

$$\frac{p_1 - C_1'}{p_1} \cdot \varepsilon_1 = \frac{\lambda}{(1 - \lambda)}. \tag{9.20}$$

Similarly, differentiating (9.18) with respect to $q_2$, setting the derivative equal to zero, and simplifying, we would get

$$\frac{p_2 - C_2'}{p_2} \cdot \varepsilon_2 = \frac{\lambda}{(1 - \lambda)}. \tag{9.21}$$

Combining (9.20) and (9.21) , we can write

$$\frac{p_1 - C_1'}{p_1} \cdot \varepsilon_1 = \frac{p_2 - C_2'}{p_2} \cdot \varepsilon_2. \tag{9.22}$$

Equation (9.22) is the basic solution to the welfare maximisation problem, and the prices that emerge are called Ramsey prices. The main conclusion is that the prices of the the firm's products should be set in such a way that the proportional 'mark-up' $\frac{p_i - C_i'}{p_i}$ should be inversely proportional to the elasticity of demand, with the 'constant' of proportionality $\frac{\lambda}{1-\lambda}$ being constant across the goods.

This result is reminiscent of the 'inverse elasticity rule' for commodity taxes that we saw on page 194 and indeed the two problems are essentially the same. The problem of setting prices optimally within one firm is fundamentally the same problem as setting tax rates across commodities in such a way that welfare losses are minimised. Thus, it is not surprising that we get the same sort of inverse elasticity formula as the solution.

### 9.4.6 Peak-Load Pricing

Demand for certain types of goods or services tends to fluctuate during the course of a day or other time period such as a week. The classic example is the demand for electricity, which tends to peak in the evening hours, but other examples include the demand for highway use, which peaks during the commuter 'rush hours', the demand for airline seats, which peaks during the work week at the morning and evening hours, the demand for telephone service, which is higher during the day than at night, and so on. Traditionally, we might set the price of each of these goods and services and accept the fact that demand is high at certain times and low at other times. But can we do better?

What if we consider 'peak-load' or 'peak-period' or 'time of day' pricing? The idea is to think of the demands at peak periods and off-peak periods almost as separate goods and price them accordingly. In the previous section, we considered the case of the multi-product firm with common costs of production and derived the rule for Ramsey prices. But here perhaps we can make a more direct allocation of costs.

The basic observation to be made is that, when building the network or the factory that will produce this good, the capacity has to be set at a level sufficiently high to meet the peak-period demand. Ideally, consumption will be at or close to capacity during peak periods, while the off-peak periods will be characterised by excess capacity. Therefore, on the margin, the off-peak period price should simply be the marginal cost of production, while the peak-period price should capture both the variable and the fixed costs of production.

Figure 9.25 illustrates the basic approach. There are two demand curves in the figure, an off-peak demand curve and a peak-period demand curve. The marginal cost (*MC*) is taken to be constant and the same for both peak and off-peak consumption. If a simple average cost pricing rule were adopted, let us suppose the price would be $p_a$. Demand would then be $Q_a$ in the peak period and $Q_b$ in the off-peak period. Total revenue would be $p_a \cdot (Q_a + Q_b)$.

Now suppose we introduce a peak-load pricing scheme. The price in the off-peak period would be set equal to *MC* at $p_0$; demand in the off-peak period would then be $Q_0$ and revenue from this market segment would be $p_0 Q_0$. In the peak period, the price would be set at $p_p$ in such a way as to cover all the remaining variable costs and the whole fixed cost. In the case where *MC* is constant, this price would be *MC* plus the average fixed cost, calculated only over the peak-period demand.

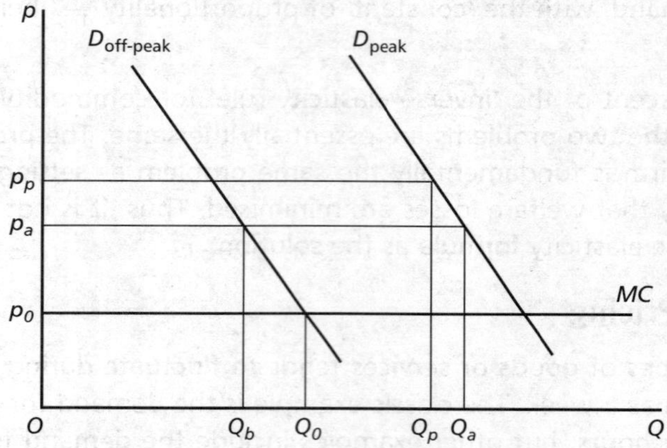


**Figure 9.25** *Peak-Load Pricing*

This pricing scheme has two significant benefits. First, it will 'shift' some demand from the peak period to the off-peak period. Notice how consumption in the peak period has fallen from $Q_a$ to $Q_p$, while consumption in the off-peak period has risen from $Q_b$ to $Q_0$. If electricity prices are higher at certain times, perhaps people will be a little more careful to turn off lights that are not needed and perhaps they will run their clothes washers or dryers at a time when rates are lower. Similarly, if tolls on a highway are higher during rush hour, perhaps some people will choose to time their commute to an off-peak period. Airlines use this kind of pricing to encourage people with flexible schedules to fly when there is less demand for seats. In this way, there is fuller capacity utilisation during off-peak periods.

The second significant benefit of the peak-load pricing scheme is that the firm need not build as much capacity. Whereas the simple average cost pricing scheme would have forced the firm to build a capacity of $Q_a$, the peak-load pricing system necessitates a capacity of only $Q_p$. Thus, the scheme would bring about significant savings in capacity costs.

### 9.4.7 Rate-of-Return Regulation and the Averch–Johnson Effect

Throughout our discussion on natural monopoly and its regulation, we have assumed that the regulators know the firm's *MC* and *AC*. As we know from our discussion of cost functions, economists include in costs the opportunity cost of all owned inputs. Thus, the firm's *MC* and *AC* are assumed to include the opportunity cost of all the capital of the firm, including the plant and equipment. In actual practice, however, the regulator would typically not know the opportunity cost of a firm's capital and therefore would have a difficult time trying to set price equal to *MC* or to calculate *AC* in order to determine the two-part prices needed.

Traditionally, regulators have tackled this problem by setting a target rate of return rather than prices. Essentially, this amounts to saying that they believe the target or allowed rate of return is the firm's opportunity cost of capital. In this way, they are able to carry out the regulation on the basis of the accounting data of the firm rather than having to delve into detailed data on its product markets and prices.

Setting a target rate of return, however, has an unintended consequence known as the Averch–Johnson effect, after the authors who first pointed it out. What Averch and Johnson argued was that it is unlikely that the target or allowed rate of return will be exactly equal to the firm's actual cost of capital, if for no other reason than that the cost of capital tends to fluctuate, sometimes considerably, with market conditions, while the allowed rate of return is likely to be set at some round number, such as 10% or 12%, for years at a time. The Averch–Johnson effect is the observation that rate-of-return regulation will give the firm's management distorted incentives when they make their investment plans. If the actual cost of capital is lower than the allowed rate of return, the firm would have an incentive to borrow heavily at the low rate and invest the money, since they will be allowed a higher rate of return in the regulatory regime. If it costs 9% to borrow money, and the allowed rate of return is 12%, the shareholders make a 3% profit on all that they invest, regardless of the actual rate of return on the investment. Thus, the firm may undertake investments that are not actually desirable if the correct discount rate were used. Conversely, if the rate at which the firm can borrow is higher than the allowed rate of return, the managers would shy away from borrowing and investing, even if it would be optimal for them to do so on economic grounds.

### 9.4.8 The Problem of X-Inefficiency in Regulated and State-Owned Monopolies

Somewhat similar to the problem of distorted investment incentives discussed in the Averch–Johnson effect is the problem of what Harvey Leibenstein called 'X-inefficiency'. In thinking about optimal pricing rules such as $p = MC$ for natural monopolies, we assume that the firm is operating on its cost function, which is the minimum cost at which any given output level can be produced. In other words, we assume that resources are being used efficiently. When a firm faces competition, it is forced to keep costs low because, if it did not, it would probably be forced out of business by more efficient firms. Therefore, a competitive firm is likely to be operating on or very close to its cost function. But a regulated or state-owned natural monopoly does not face competitive pressure to keep costs low and so it is quite possible, indeed likely, that it will use resources inefficiently. In other words, it will be 'X-inefficient'. Being efficient actually takes managerial effort, so, if there is no competitive pressure, it is quite likely that the firm's managers will prefer the 'easy life' and allow costs to escalate. This does not even hurt the shareholders of the firm as the regulators are going to allow all costs to be recovered.

Beyond the 'easy life', we could have a situation where the managers go out of their way to escalate costs because they may benefit directly from the increased costs. Such costs as fancy offices, corporate jets and large support staffs are probably quite unnecessary for the firm but provide utility to the managers. In the extreme case, managers may plunder the resources of the company for their direct personal enrichment. For all these reasons, regulated or state-owned natural monopolies may be quite inefficient. Rate-of-return regulation in no way dampens this tendency to be inefficient.

It was this realisation more than any other, that state-owned natural monopolies tend to be highly cost-inefficient, that led to the wave of privatisation or disinvestment of public enterprises that swept the world starting in the 1980s. Note that, since a private regulated natural monopoly will face the same incentive structure as a state-owned one, changing ownership from public to private is unlikely to make a significant difference to the X-inefficiency of the firm. Rather, it is the introduction of competition wherever possible that is likely to make the biggest difference. Of course, introducing competition is not a viable option in the case of true natural monopolies, so other solutions have been sought to address the problem in their case.

### 9.4.9 Price-Cap Regulation and Other Trends in Regulatory Policy

What can a regulator of a private natural monopoly do to encourage the firm to be X-efficient? This was the question the UK's telecom regulators faced as the UK was in the process of privatising the telephone monopoly British Telecom (BT) in the 1980s. The solution they came up with was price-cap regulation.

In price-cap regulation, the regulatory authority puts into place a regulatory regime for a period of time, say 3–5 years, during which it specifies a cap on the average rate of price increase it will permit for the company's products. Normally, this price cap takes the form (RPI-X), where RPI stands for the rate of product inflation, a measure of the average rate of inflation in the economy, and X stands for an adjustment factor to allow for differences in the rate of productivity change or rate of inflation in this sector as opposed to the rest of the economy. Initially, the regulators of BT specified (RPI-3)% as the regulatory regime for BT after its privatisation. Average prices of BT's products were permitted to grow at a rate 3% below the average rate of inflation in the economy. The figure of 3% was supposed to capture the fact that productivity in the telecommunications industry was increasing much more rapidly than productivity in the economy as a whole and therefore telecom prices should not be rising as fast as prices generally.

The main goal of this regulatory regime was actually to improve X-efficiency in BT. As a state-owned enterprise, BT had been thought to have been quite inefficient. By focusing on prices and removing the ceiling on the rate of return, the regulators theorised that BT's managers would now have full incentives to cut costs, since all cost savings would accrue to the firm in the form of increased profits.

While this theory seems plausible, there are in retrospect some problems with it. First, it is well known that the managers of a large firm do not necessarily follow the interests of the shareholders all the time and the problem of managerial agency (getting managers to do what the owners of the firm want them to do, a typical principal–agent problem) can be quite severe. This problem exists of course in private unregulated companies also, but the pressure of competition does exert some discipline on the managers, a pressure they do not face in a regulated environment. Second, even if managers act in the best interests of the shareholders, there is a powerful reason, which has come to be known as the 'ratchet effect', why they might not want to reduce costs as much as they are able to do. The reason is that they can rationally predict that, if they reduce costs much faster than the X factor the regulators specified in the regulatory regime, they would probably face a higher X factor when the next regulatory regime is implemented. A company facing (RPI-3)% for the first 3-year period that reduced costs at, say, 6% per year could well face (RPI-5)% in the next regulatory period. It might therefore be in the best long-term interests of the firm to hold cost reductions to only 3–4% (or even less, for that matter) in order to argue for a less stringent regulatory regime in the next regulatory period.

The upshot of this discussion is that it is difficult to induce X-efficiency in regulated natural monopolies. One more recent approach has been to use 'yardstick competition' among firms, a technique originally developed as a way to manage groups of state-owned enterprises. Say we need to regulate electricity distribution companies, which are natural monopolies. As a result, electricity distribution in any one region would be allocated to a monopoly, but we would take care to award these monopoly licenses to different companies in different regions. We could then look at the performance of the best-performing company among all the regional companies to guide the regulatory regime for all the companies. Thus, we use the best-performing company as a 'yardstick' against which to measure the performance of the other companies.

One last trend worth mentioning is the tendency to move away from regulation entirely and to try to rely on competition wherever possible and in unusual ways. One important aspect of this is that it has been realised that what we thought of as natural monopolies are not entirely natural monopolies at all. For example, 'the electricity industry' was thought of as a natural monopoly, but it is really only electricity *distribution* that is a natural monopoly. Electricity *production* can be decentralised and reliance placed on competitive forces. Further, thanks to new and reliable switching and metering technology, it is now clear that more than one company can operate on one network. Thus, there could be two or more telephone companies or even electricity distribution companies operating on one network of cables and wires. They can therefore be allowed to compete.

Even in a pure natural monopoly situation, the problem of X-inefficiency could cause competition to be superior to monopoly despite the presence of natural monopoly. The idea is illustrated in Figure 9.26. Suppose $AC_1$ is the average cost curve of a single firm when it is the only firm operating and therefore prone to X-inefficiency. Suppose $AC_2$ represents the average cost of each firm

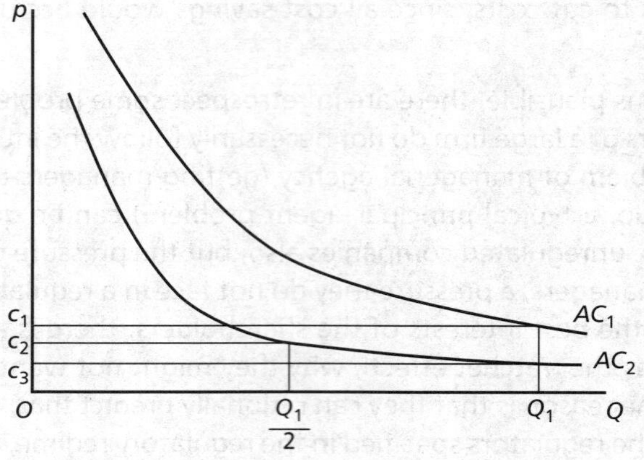


**Figure 9.26** *Natural Monopoly with and without Competition*

when there are two firms operating and competing, and therefore more likely to be X-efficient. That is why $AC_2$ is lower than $AC_1$. The industry still looks like a natural monopoly, with the *AC* curve declining throughout the relevant range of output. But now the average cost of producing the output level $Q_1$ with just one firm is $c_1$, while the average cost of producing the same output with two firms, each producing $Q_1/2$, is $c_2$, which is lower than $c_1$. Thus, even though the industry is a natural monopoly in theory, the presence of X-inefficiency in practice might result in a situation where it is better from the social point of view to have two firms rather than one.

In this situation, we might be able to dispense with regulation entirely and simply allow the firms to compete. Depending on the nature of that competition, we might get pricing that is acceptably close to MC pricing.[3] And we could use 'competition for the monopoly' to capture for the government a large proportion of any potential rents that companies might earn from monopoly positions. For example, by auctioning licenses to operate in industries with legal entry restrictions (spectrum bandwidth would be an example), government can capture a high proportion of potential future profits from the bidding companies.

Apart from the fact that competitive pressure forces firms to be more X-efficient, another important reason to avoid regulation is the phenomenon of 'regulatory capture'. It has been observed that frequently the regulators of an industry seem to start acting in the interests of the regulated firms rather than the public or social interest. This is because the regulators are frequently retired industry veterans and therefore focus more on the industry's point of view, with which they have been sympathetic throughout their careers. In any case, regulated firms spend large sums of money on lobbyists who seek to influence (or 'capture') the regulators,

[3] As we will see in the chapter on oligopoly, Bertrand competition results in MC pricing even with two firms.

and we cannot rule out the possibility of corruption playing a role also in the phenomenon of regulatory capture. From this point of view, reliance on market forces and competitive pressure may in the long run be the best form of policy intervention.

# 9.5 MONOPSONY

**Task for this section:**

To look at the behaviour of a market where there is only one buyer and to study how such a buyer can take advantage of the situation.

A **monopsony** is a market in which there is only one buyer and many sellers. Thus, monopsony is a situation that is the mirror image of monopoly, the difference being that the market power is on the demand side of the market rather than the supply side. Monopsony is normally presented in the context of labour markets, because it is thought that one of the best examples of monopsony is the market position of a large employer vis-à-vis the labour market in a small town with few alternative employment opportunities. But of course this is not the only possible example. Large firms such as Walmart have tremendous market power in their supply markets and probably use this power to extract favourable prices from their suppliers. Any large firm buying materials from small firms, such as the big car companies or electronics giants such as Apple, have a similar monopsonistic position. So it is useful to consider monopsony in a general context and see how a monopsony might behave in any type of market.

## 9.5.1 Basic Monopsony Model

We will consider a situation where there is one buyer, the monopsony, and a large number of price-taking sellers, whose behaviour therefore can be modelled simply by a competitive supply curve. The key insight into the behaviour of the monopsony is that it realises it faces an upward-sloping supply curve and will therefore take advantage of this fact. Much like the monopoly realises it faces a downward-sloping demand curve and therefore works with the marginal revenue curve it faces, the monopsony will work with the marginal expense ($ME$) curve, that is marginal to the supply curve it faces. Suppose $p_s(q)$ is the inverse supply curve that the monopsony faces for the good it wants to buy. Then its total expense on the good will be

$$E(q) = q \cdot p_s(q),$$

and so the rate at which its expense on the good is changing as it buys more of it, the marginal expense, will be given by

$$ME(q) = \frac{dE(q)}{dq} = p_s + q \cdot p_s'(q) = p_s \left\{ 1 + \frac{q}{p_s} \cdot p_s'(q) \right\}.$$

Thus, the marginal expense can be written in a form analogous to (9.2) for the marginal revenue:

$$ME = p_s \left\{ 1 + \frac{1}{\varepsilon_s} \right\}, \tag{9.23}$$

where $\varepsilon_s$ is the elasticity of supply of the good being bought. Since $p_s$ is a function of $q$, $ME$ is also a function of $q$ and will be upward-sloping such as $p_s(q)$. Further, because $\varepsilon_s > 0$, the expression in (9.23) that is within the curly brackets will be greater than zero and therefore $ME > p_s$, the marginal expense curve will be everywhere higher than the supply curve.

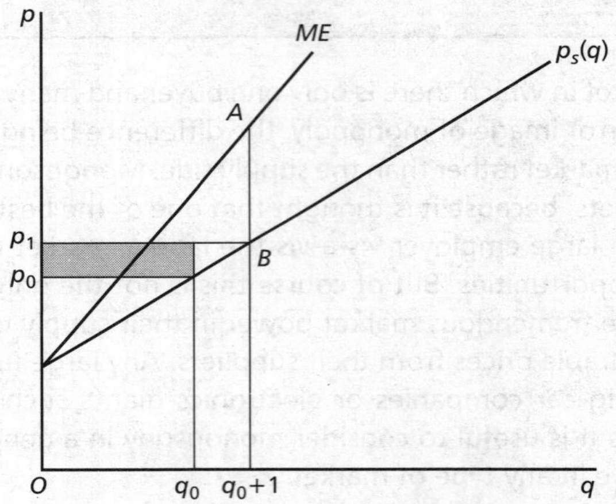


**Figure 9.27** *The Marginal Expense Curve Lies above the Supply Curve*

The situation is illustrated in Figure 9.27. The supply curve of the good is $p_s(q)$ and is upward-sloping. Suppose the monopsony would have to pay a price of $p_0$ to buy $q_0$ units of the good, while to buy $(q_0 + 1)$ units would require a price of $p_1$. Then the amount by which the monopsony's total expense has gone up (the marginal expense) is the price paid for it, $p_1$, *plus* the additional expense of $(p_1 - p_0) \cdot q_0$ on the first $q_0$ units of the good (the infra-marginal units) which also now have to be paid $p_1$ instead of $p_0$. The length of the line AB in the figure is equal to this additional expense on the infra-marginal units, which is shown as the shaded area (shown unrealistically large in order to make the diagram more readable). That is why $ME > p_s$.

Now let us consider the monopsony's optimal choice. The monopsony's demand curve can be viewed as its marginal benefit curve, as usual. For example, if the good in question is an input into the monopsony's production activity, the demand curve would be the marginal revenue product curve, as we saw in the chapter on labour markets. For the purposes of our example, we will assume this to be what the demand curve is. In that case, the area below the demand curve is the total revenue product. Then the monopsony's profit would be given by

$$\pi = \int_0^{q_m} p_d(q)dq - q_m \cdot p_s(q_m),$$

where $p_d(q)$ is the monopsony's inverse demand curve and $q_m$ is its choice of how much of the good to buy. Profit is maximised where

$$\frac{\partial \pi}{\partial q_m} = p_d(q_m) - p_s\left\{1 + \frac{1}{\varepsilon_s}\right\} = 0,$$

which can be written as

$$p_d(q_m) = p_s\left\{1 + \frac{1}{\varepsilon_s}\right\} \equiv ME. \tag{9.24}$$

Equation (9.24) says that the monopsony's profit (or, more generally, net surplus) will be maximised at the point where the demand price is equal to the marginal expense (ME), that is, where the demand curve cuts the ME curve. However, the price paid will *not* be the demand price; this equilibrium condition just determines the quantity to be purchased. The actual price paid will be the supply price at that quantity, that is, the lowest price needed to elicit supply of the chosen quantity. Unlike the competitive equilibrium, here $p_d \neq p_s$ and the price that will prevail is $p_s$.

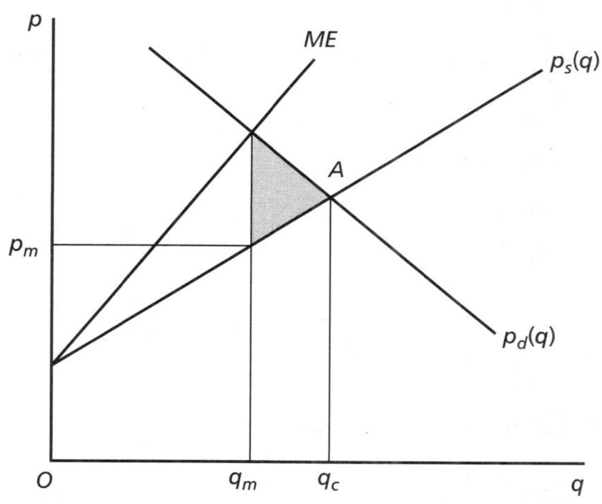


**Figure 9.28** *Monopsony Equilibrium*

Figure 9.28 illustrates the equilibrium. The monopsony's demand curve is its marginal benefit curve, so the optimum for it is at the intersection of the demand curve and the ME curve. This determines the quantity $q_m$. The price paid will be $p_m$, which is the height of the supply curve at $q = q_m$. If the market had been competitive, the equilibrium would have been at A where the demand and supply curves cross and so the quantity would have been $q_c$. This is the socially optimal quantity. Like a monopoly, a monopsony restricts the quantity traded in order to extract a more attractive price. There is a deadweight loss due to the quantity distortion and this is shown by the shaded area in Figure 9.28.

### 9.5.2 Alternative Pricing Strategies

Just like a monopolist, a monopsony could engage in various alternative pricing strategies in order to increase profit or surplus from the market where it has market power. For example, it could use **two-part pricing**. In order to be able to sell anything at all to the monopsony, sellers could be required to pay a 'fixed fee' such as a kickback on a sales order. Or it could engage in one of the various forms of **price discrimination**. We will illustrate by looking at the possibility of third-degree price discrimination because it shows that price discrimination such as wage discrimination on the basis of some observable characteristic such as race, caste or gender may simply be a manifestation of profit-maximising behaviour on the part of a monopsony.

Consider a labour market where workers can be separated according to an observable characteristic such as gender. We will take gender as the distinguishing characteristic, but the analysis could be generalised to other characteristics and also to markets other than labour markets. Suppose men and women are equally productive but that their supply characteristics are different. Suppose $p_1(q_1)$ and $p_2(q_2)$ are their supply curves. Then the monopsony's profit is

$$\pi = \int_0^{q_1^m+q_2^m} p_d(q_1+q_2)dq - q_1 \cdot p_1(q_1) - q_2 \cdot p_2(q_2).$$

Maximisation of the profit will require

$$\frac{\partial \pi}{\partial q_1} = p_d(q_1^m + q_2^m) - p_1\left\{1 + \frac{1}{\varepsilon_1}\right\} = 0$$

$$\frac{\partial \pi}{\partial q_2} = p_d(q_1^m + q_2^m) - p_2\left\{1 + \frac{1}{\varepsilon_2}\right\} = 0$$

and so the optimality condition for the monopsony is

$$p_1\left\{1 + \frac{1}{\varepsilon_1}\right\} = p_2\left\{1 + \frac{1}{\varepsilon_2}\right\} = p_d(q_1^m + q_2^m). \tag{9.25}$$

Equation (9.25) says that the monopsony must set the *ME*s of each class of worker equal and that these *ME*s must also equal the marginal benefit, given by the demand price. The similarity to the case of third-degree price discrimination is obvious, where $MR_1 = MR_2 = MC$ was the profit-maximising condition. Here we have $ME_1 = ME_2 = MB$, where MB is the marginal benefit or demand price. Like in the monopoly case, we can also derive a final result about this equilibrium, namely

$$\varepsilon_1 > \varepsilon_2 \quad \rightarrow \quad p_1 > p_2.$$

The supply source with the lower price elasticity of supply will suffer a lower price. This result is intuitive. A low supply elasticity can be exploited more, and so the price paid will be lower.

# 9.6 BILATERAL MONOPOLY

**Task for this section:**

To briefly examine situations in which there is only one buyer and only one seller in a market.

What if there was a market situation in which there was only one buyer and one seller? This kind of situation is called a **bilateral monopoly**. Situations of this kind are not common, but they can arise. For example, perhaps the monopsonistic hirer of labour in a small town faces a situation where the workers have formed a union, which thereby becomes the monopolist supplier of labour services. Another possible example is a situation where the government is the sole buyer of a weapons system for which there is only one potential supplier.

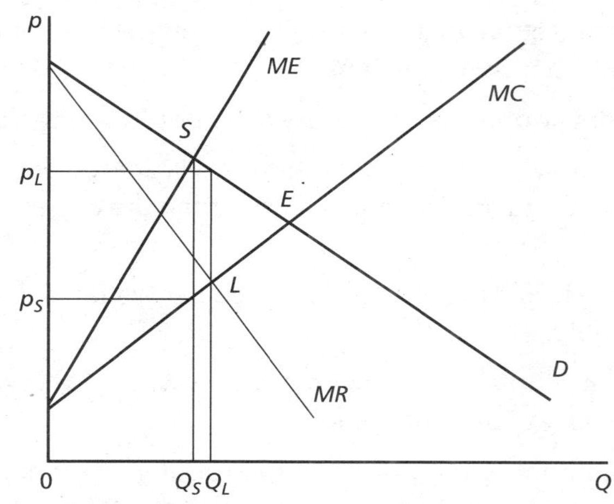


**Figure 9.29** *Possible Equilibria in Bilateral Monopoly*

In principle, the desired equilibria from each party's point of view is known from the standard monopoly and monopsony models. In Figure 9.29, *D* represents the buyer's marginal benefit curve, what would be the demand curve if the buyer were a price-taker. If the buyer is a firm and the product in question is an input in its production process, *D* would be the marginal revenue product of that input. The curve *MC* in the figure represents the seller's marginal cost curve, what would be the supply curve if the seller were a price-taker. If both parties were price-takers, the equilibrium would be at $E$.

However, if the parties are not price-takers, as we would expect, the equilibrium would not be at $E$. The seller would want the monopoly equilibrium at $L$, the normal monopoly equilibrium where $MC = MR$. The quantity and price would be $Q_L$ and $p_L$ in this equilibrium. The buyer, however, would want the monopsony equilibrium at $S$, where his marginal expense $ME$ is equal to his marginal benefit, represented by $D$. The quantity and price would be $Q_S$ and $p_S$ in this equilibrium. Clearly, both these equilibria cannot hold simultaneously and so no equilibrium can be established. The situation is one in which a bargaining process would ensue. The methods discussed in the next chapter on Game Theory would be applicable in such a situation.

## SUMMARY

In this chapter, we have considered the behaviour of markets characterised by market power, whether on the supply side (monopoly) or on the demand side (monopsony). We saw that the effect of market power is to restrict (and thereby distort) the quantity traded and alter the price to the advantage of the side of the market with power: a higher price under monopoly and a lower price under monopsony. The main points were as follows:

- The marginal revenue curve of a monopolist is downward-sloping, in contrast with a competitive firm's, which is constant.
- A monopoly will never operate on the inelastic portion of the demand curve.
- The monopoly profit-maximising condition is $MR = MC$, and this will result in a quantity that is lower and a price that is higher than the corresponding competitive market levels.
- The monopoly equilibrium results in lower social welfare; there is a deadweight loss due to monopoly.
- A monopoly with multiple plants will set $MC_1 = MC_2 = MR$, where $MC_1$ and $MC_2$ are the marginal costs of different plants.
- A cartel is an agreement among firms to monopolise a market. A cartel would, in principle, operate like a monopoly with multiple plants, but cartels are inherently unstable, as firms, particularly small ones, have an incentive to cheat on the cartel agreement.
- A monopoly can extract higher profits by using more complex pricing strategies than the simple one product, one price scheme; examples include two-part prices and various forms of price discrimination.

- A two-part price charges consumers a fixed fee (invariant to how much they buy) in addition to the usual price per unit charge; its purpose is to extract more surplus from the consumers.
- First-degree price discrimination is where a monopoly charges the maximum willingness-to-pay for each unit it sells; it thereby extracts all the consumer's surplus and the equilibrium is efficient.
- Third-degree price discrimination is where a firm charges different prices to different market segments, such as students or senior citizens, or to different geographic regions; the profit-maximising condition is $MR_1 = MR_2 = MC$, where $MR_1$ and $MR_2$ are the marginal revenues in the different market segments and $MC$ is the monopoly's marginal cost.
- Second-degree price discrimination is where the firm offers consumers a menu of different pricing schemes in an attempt to induce them to self-select into different groups; the goal is once again to extract more of the surplus from each group.
- Sometimes a monopoly may face the *threat* of entry; in such cases, it may not engage in its usual profit-maximising equilibrium, but may rather practice limit pricing, pricing designed to limit or deter entry.
- A contestable market is one where entry is relatively inexpensive and quick; in such a market, a monopoly may be forced to set price close to or at $MC$ in order to deter entry.
- Price leadership is a market in which a dominant firm competes with a large number of price-taking rivals; here, three types of equilibria are possible: coexistence, pure monopoly and limit pricing.
- A natural monopoly occurs when it is cheaper to produce all the desired output with just one firm rather than two or more; the main reason for this is that the average cost curve is downward-sloping throughout.
- The problem of a natural monopoly is that, if operated as a monopoly, it would charge high prices, restrict output and cause a significant loss in social welfare. The firm must therefore be operated in the public sector or, if private, be regulated.
- Theoretically, the optimal price for a natural monopoly, like for any market, is $p = MC$. However, this would result in the firm running at a loss and is therefore untenable in the long run.
- Setting $p = AC$ would solve the deficit problem, but results in a small deadweight loss.
- Two-part prices can be used to get marginal cost prices plus a solution to the deficit problem; thus, these prices are close to ideal.

- Ramsey prices are optimal prices for a multi-product firm; the efficiency rule involves charging higher prices for goods with lower elasticities of demand.
- Peak-load pricing is a pricing system that charges different prices for the same good or service at different points in time; higher prices are charged at times when demand is high and lower prices when demand is low. This system can be more efficient than one in which prices are invariant to demand conditions.
- In practice, regulation of natural monopoly has taken the form of setting a ceiling on the rate of return. The Averch–Johnson effect points out that, when the allowed rate of return is not equal to the actual cost of capital, the firm's investment incentives are distorted.
- Perhaps the greatest practical problem with state-owned or regulated natural monopolies is their tendency to be very cost-inefficient ('X-inefficient') because they do not face any competitive pressure.
- Price-cap regulation attempts to improve the X-efficiency of natural monopolies by capping their prices and allowing them to profit from cost reductions; however, the incentives to be X-efficient are muted.
- Attempting to use competition wherever possible and in creative ways may be the best solution to improve the efficiency of natural monopolies.
- A monopsony is a market with a single buyer and many price-taking sellers. A monopsony sets the demand price equal to the marginal expense to determine quantity and sets price equal to the supply price at that quantity; the quantity and price are both lower than the corresponding competitive levels.
- A monopsony is the mirror image of a monopoly, and many of the same results apply with suitable modification. For example, a monopsony can engage in price discrimination to different supply sources by setting $ME_1 = ME_2 = MB$.
- A bilateral monopoly is a situation with only one buyer and only one seller. Equilibrium is not easy to establish in such a situation, which would need to be analysed using the techniques of game theory, discussed in the next chapter.

## EXERCISES

1. The per plant cost function for producing widgets is

$$C(q) = 20 + 2q + 0.05q_2.$$

The market demand curve for widgets is

$$Q = \frac{160,000}{p^2}.$$

(a) What will be the long-run market price, the total quantity produced and the number of firms, if the widget industry is perfectly competitive? (*Assume that each firm can have only one plant.*)

(b) What will be the long-run market price, quantity produced and the number of plants, if the widget industry is a monopoly?

(c) How much is the deadweight loss due to monopoly?

2. A textile firm's marginal revenue product from labour is given by

$$MRP_L = 10 - \frac{L_d}{40},$$

where $L_d$ is the amount of labour it hires. The supply curve of labour faced by the firm is

$$L_s = 80w,$$

where $w$ is the hourly wage rate.

(a) How many workers will the firm hire and what wage will it pay if it acts as a price-taker in the labour market?

(b) How many workers will the firm hire and what wage will it pay if it realises its monopsony power in the labour market?

(c) Suppose government introduces a minimum wage of ₹4 per hour. What will now be your answers to (a) and (b)? Comment on the difference in the effects of minimum wage laws under perfect competition as opposed to monopsony.

3. The demand for widgets is given by

$$Q = 100 - p.$$

The cost of producing widgets is ₹10 per unit. The government imposes a ₹5 per unit excise tax on widgets. Calculate the deadweight loss of this tax in each of the following two cases:

(a) The widget industry is perfectly competitive.

(b) The widget industry is a monopoly.

Explain (preferably using a diagram) the relationship between your answers to (a) and (b) (i.e. explain why one is bigger than the other, or why they are the same size, as the case may be.)

4. Widget Corp. is the only producer of widgets in Smalliland. Its cost function for the production of widgets is

$$C(q) = \frac{q^2}{6},$$

where $q$ is the total number of widgets produced. Widget Corp. can sell widgets domestically (where it is the only seller) or internationally (where it is a perfect competitor). Trade restrictions prevent the import of widgets and the export of widgets by anyone other than Widget Corp. The domestic demand curve for widgets is

$$Q_h = 50 - p_h,$$

where $Q_h$ is the number of widgets transacted in the home market and $p_h$ is the price at home. The price at which Widget Corp. can export widgets is ₹10.

(a) Find how many widgets Widget Corp. would produce, how many it would sell at home and how many abroad and at what prices, in order to maximise profits.

(b) Suppose the Government of Smalliland imposed an excise tax of ₹5 per widget produced (whether to be sold at home or abroad). Answer the questions of part (a) under this scenario.

(c) Draw a single graph illustrating your solutions to (a) and (b).

5. The supply of beaver pelts for use in the production of beaver hats comes from many native beaver trappers whose supply curve is

$$Q_s = 2p_s - 100,$$

where $Q_s$ and $p_s$ are the quantity and price of untreated pelts, respectively. All the pelts are bought by the Beaverbrook Company, which then, at a cost of ₹10 per pelt, treats them and re-sells them to the beaver hat manufacturers whose demand for pelts is

$$Q_d = 210 - p_d,$$

where $Q_d$ and $p_d$ are the quantity and price of treated furs.

(a) How many pelts will Beaverbrook buy and re-sell and what will be the prices of untreated and treated pelts, if Beaverbrook maximises profits?

(b) What are the efficient levels of quantities and prices?

6. The American Fur Co. (AFC) sells fur hats at a price of ₹5 each. The production function for the hats is

$$q = 240x - 2x^2,$$

where $x$ is the number of fur skins used each period. The skins are supplied by the Trapper John Company (TJC), which hires Innuit hunters to hunt the animals. TJC pays the hunters ₹10 per day and the production function for the skins is

$$x = L^{\frac{1}{2}},$$

where $L$ is the number of man-days of hunting per period.

(a) If TJC acts as a monopolist and AFC acts as a price-taker, what will be the equilibrium price and quantity of skins traded?

(b) If instead TJC acts as a price-taker and AFC acts as a monopsonist, what will be the equilibrium price and quantity of skins traded?

(c) From the social point of view, what is the efficient number of skins that should be traded, and at what price?

7. National Widget (NW) is the only producer of widgets and the only hirer of widget-makers. The following are various functions of relevance:

$$Q_s = 2L \qquad \textit{widget production function}$$

$$Q_d = 100 - p \qquad \textit{demand curve for widgets}$$

$$L = \frac{w}{2} - 10 \qquad \textit{supply curve of widget-makers,}$$

where $p$ and $Q$ are the price and quantities of widgets, $L$ is the number of widget-makers hired and $w$ is the wage rate paid to them.

(a) Find the values of $p$, $Q$, $L$ and $w$ that will emerge if NW maximises profits.

(b) What are the socially desirable values of all of these variables? (*Hint: Think about the true opportunity cost of producing widgets.*)

8. The Jolly Roger Amusement Park Company (JRCo) has built an amusement park, and is now trying to decide on a pricing strategy. Their market research has shown that there are two types of potential customers – munchkins and smurfs. The demand curve of each munchkin is given by

$$q_m = 12 - p,$$

where $p$ is the price of rides. The demand curve of each smurf is

$$q_s = 8 - p.$$

There are 100 munchkins and 100 smurfs in JRCo's market area. The marginal cost of producing rides is zero.

(a) Assuming that JRCo cannot price discriminate, find the market demand curve for rides.

(b) What price for rides should JRCo set if it wishes to maximise its profits? How much profit will it make?

(c) Suppose now that JRCo is considering an alternative strategy, where it would simply charge customers a fixed admissions charge, and would then offer rides for free. Given that it cannot price discriminate, what admissions fee would JRCo set to maximise profits? How much profit will it make?

(d) Suppose a third strategy is under consideration, under which JRCo would offer different bundles of rides, each at a separate price. How many bundles should JRCo offer, what would be the number of rides in each and the prices of the bundles? How much profit will it make under this strategy?

9. There are 50 firms in the perfectly competitive widget industry, each with the cost function

$$C(q) = 0.5q^2 + 10q + 18,$$

where $q$ is the individual firm's output level of widgets.

(a) What is the short-run widget supply curve for each firm? What is the industry supply curve?

(b) Suppose the market demand curve for widgets is

$$Q_d = 3{,}600 - 150p,$$

where $p$ is the market price and $Q_d$ the market quantity demanded of widgets. What would be the short-run equilibrium price and quantity of widgets? How much would each firm produce?

(c) Assuming that the demand curve remains the same and that new firms can enter with the same cost function, what is the long-run competitive equilibrium for widgets? How many firms would operate in the industry?

(d) Suppose the widget industry were a monopoly, with 50 plants each with a cost function as above. How much would the monopoly produce and what price would it charge in the short run? How much would be produced in each plant?

(e) What would be the long-run monopoly equilibrium, assuming the monopoly could build as many plants as it liked, each with the same given cost function? How many plants would the monopolist operate?

10. The market demand for widgets is given by

$$Q_d = 160 - p,$$

where $p$ and $Q_d$ are the price and the market demand, respectively. The per-firm cost function for producing widgets is

$$C(q) = 50 + 50q^2,$$

where $q$ is the firm-level output.

(a) In the short run, there are 100 price-taking firms operating in the industry. Assuming that fractional quantities are acceptable, what will be the short-run equilibrium price and quantity of widgets? How much will each firm produce, and how much profit will each firm make?

(b) What will be the long-run equilibrium price and quantity of widgets? How much will each firm produce, and how many firms will operate in the industry?

(c) Suppose Tech Corp enters the industry with a new technology of production that allows it to produce widgets according to the cost function

$$C(q_T) = 100 + 10q_T + \frac{1}{2}q_T^2,$$

where $q_T$ is Tech Corp's output. Tech Corp behaves as a price leader and the rest of the firms continue to behave as price-takers. What will be the long-run equilibrium price and quantity of widgets now? How much will Tech Corp produce? How much will the fringe firms produce? How many fringe firms will operate in the industry?

(d) Has Tech Corp's entry reduced or improved social welfare? By how much?

11. Suppose a monopolist produces widgets at a constant average cost of ₹5 per unit. There are two distinct widget markets, characterised by the following demand curves:

$$Q_1 = 55 - p_1$$

$$Q_2 = 55 - 2p_2.$$

(a) If the monopolist can maintain separation between the two markets, what level of output will he produce and what price will he charge in each market, in order to maximise profits?

(b) What would your answer be if it costs demanders only ₹5 per unit to transport and re-sell widgets between markets?

12. The plant-level cost function to produce widgets is

$$C(q) = 5q^2 - 10q + 20,$$

where $q$ is the output level of the plant. Widgets are bought by two types of customers. Customers of type A have the aggregate demand curve

$$D_a = 200 - 10p_a,$$

where $D_a$ is the number of widgets they demand and $p_a$ is the price they face. Customers of type B have the aggregate demand curve

$$D_b = 250 - 5p_b.$$

(a) Suppose there are 90 widget producers, each with one plant, and the market for widgets is perfectly competitive. What will be the short-run equilibrium? State clearly the total level of widget production, the number of widgets produced by each firm, the number of widgets bought in each market and the price in each market.

(b) What will be the long-run equilibrium of the widget market?

(c) Suppose a monopolist acquires all widget producers and further entry of new producers is impossible. The monopolist can operate as many widget plants as he likes, each with the cost function given above. Suppose also that the monopolist is able to charge different prices to the two classes of customers and that re-sale between customer classes is impossible. How many widgets will the monopoly produce, how many will he sell in each market and what prices will he charge?

(d) Answer part (c) for the case where price discrimination is not possible.

13. The demand for oil is given by

$$Q_d = 10 - p,$$

where $p$ is the price and $Q_d$ is the market quantity demanded. The cost function for producing oil for each firm in the market is

$$C(q) = 6q,$$

where $q$ is the firm-level output.

(a) Suppose the oil market is perfectly competitive and in long-run equilibrium. What is the price of oil and the quantity sold in the market? How much is consumer surplus?

(b) The government decides the price of oil is too high and subsidises it by paying ₹2 per unit sold to the oil producers. What will the price be in long-run equilibrium now? How much does consumer surplus rise? What happens to profits? Is the increase in the sum of consumer surplus and profits larger or smaller than the cost to the government of paying the subsidies?

(c) Now suppose the oil industry is monopolised. Answer question (a) and (b) for this case.

14. Suppose a monopolist can sell electricity y in two markets, 1 and 2. The demand curves in the two markets are

$$p_1(y_1) = 3 - \frac{y_1}{2}$$

$$p_2(y_2) = 2 - \frac{y_2}{2},$$

where $y_i$ is the quantity and $p_i$ is the price in the market $i = 1, 2$. The monopolist's cost function is

$$C(y_1, y_2) = \frac{7}{3} + y_1 + y_2.$$

(a) What are the profit-maximising prices in each market and what are the corresponding demand elasticities at the profit-maximising price?

(b) What would happen to output if the monopolist is prohibited from charging different prices in the two markets?

(c) Argue whether the monopolist should have the right to charge different prices in the two markets.

CHAPTER

# 10 The Theory of Games

In looking at the supply side of markets, we looked first at markets where there were a very large number of sellers (perfect competition) so sellers were able to make their decisions just on the basis of the market price; they did not really have to think too much about what their competitors were doing. We then looked at monopoly, where the sole seller had no competition to worry about (although we did look briefly at situations where the monopolist did worry about the entry of *potential* competitors). Most real-world markets are characterised neither by perfect competition nor by monopoly, but by situations where the number of sellers may be quite small, at least in a local geographic area. In such situations, firms have to be very much aware of what their competitors are doing and how their competitors might respond to any decisions they make.

The Theory of Games, first proposed by John von Neumann and Oskar Morgenstern in 1944, is a theoretical approach to analysing situations like these. Although the analysis of economic behaviour in situations involving small numbers of competitors has been going on since at least the 19th century, the Theory of Games brought a new order to such analyses, incorporating within its domain many of the old approaches and concepts, but also providing new ways of thinking about these situations systematically. Particularly since the last quarter of the 20th century, game theory has become the primary approach taken by most economists to study a wide variety of strategic situations, situations where decision-makers try to take into account the behaviour of other decision-makers whose actions interact with their own in producing the outcomes experienced by everyone.

## 10.1 BASICS

**Task for this section:**

To introduce the basic terminology used in the theory of games.

A **game** is any strategic situation involving two or more decision-makers whose actions jointly determine the outcomes for all of them. Any game can be characterised by the following features and concepts:

- **Players**: The decision-makers in the game, following the practice in typical board and parlour games such as chess and checkers, are called players.
- **Actions**: At any point in the game, if a player makes a decision, it would be to 'play' an action. The action is his or her move at that point in the game.
- **Strategies**: A strategy is a complete description of all the possible actions that a player would take at all possible junctures of the game. Some games, such as chess, may be so complex and have such a large number of possible combinations of actions that it may be impossible to fully specify a strategy. However, for many games, it is possible to fully articulate all the possible situations that might arise and to specify all the actions that a player might make at each of those situations.
- **Pay-offs**: At the end of every game, all the players receive pay-offs. These may be monetary, such as profits or monetary winnings, non-monetary such as utility levels or simply outcomes such as winning and losing. The units in which the pay-offs are measured are the units of whatever the players care about, such as profits, money and utility. The goal of each player during the game is assumed to be maximisation (or minimisation) of her pay-off. When the pay-offs of all the players at every possible conclusion of a game add up to zero, the game is called a **zero-sum game**. Such games typically involve one player (the loser) paying the other player (the winner), so that the pay-offs net to zero.
- **Information and Beliefs**: It is important to be clear about what each player does or does not know at each point of the game and what beliefs players hold. **Games of complete information** are games in which each player knows all the possible strategies, pay-offs and objectives of each of the other players. **Games of incomplete information** are games in which players have different degrees of information, knowledge and beliefs about the game.
- **Stages**: Games can have just one stage or multiple stages. A single-stage game is one in which players can make only one move and they do so simultaneously, such as the games 'rock-paper-scissors' or 'matching pennies'. Such games are called **static games**. A multi-stage game is one which will typically have players making moves in sequence, as in chess. Such games are called **dynamic games**.
- **Repetitions**: Static games can be played just once, in which case they are called **one-shot games**, or they may be played repeatedly, in which case they are called **repeated games**. Real-life games of market competition may be modelled as repeated games or as dynamic games.
- **Equilibrium**: The game theorist's notion of a 'solution' to a game is to find its equilibrium, a situation where players are playing a combination of strategies such that no player has any incentive to change her strategy. There are different notions of equilibrium in games, and we will study some as we move forward.
- **Form**: Games are generally presented in one of two forms. **Normal form games** are presented in the form of a matrix (easier to do when there are only two players), while **extensive**

**form games** are presented in the form of a decision tree. We will see examples of both forms as we look at some actual games.

## 10.2 STATIC GAMES OF COMPLETE INFORMATION

**Task for this section:**

To study games where the players move simultaneously and share all the same information. Several well-known game types are discussed and the concept of Nash equilibrium with both pure and mixed strategies is introduced and analysed.

The simplest games are static one-shot games between two players who each are fully informed about all the details of the game. Such games are called static games of complete information. There are a number of classic examples of games of this kind that bring out various aspects of games and their solutions. We will look at a number of these classic example games.

### 10.2.1 The Prisoners' Dilemma

This is perhaps the most famous of all games, as it captures one of the most fundamental dilemmas of competition. If the two players in this game could cooperate, they would both do well. But they both have an incentive to cheat on any cooperative agreement, and, when they do cheat, they both end up worse off.

The traditional scenario of the game, the one that gives it its name, goes something like this. Two men committed a murder, after having broken into a house and stealing some valuables. The police have arrested them, separated them so they can no longer communicate with one another and have told each the following: We have proof that you stole the valuables and therefore know that we can have you both sentenced to 2 years in prison. We do not yet have proof that you committed the murder. Why don't you confess? If you do, and your partner doesn't, we will reward you by reducing your sentence to 1 year, and punish your partner by sentencing him to 20 years. If you don't confess, and your partner does, you will end up in jail for 20 years and he will be let off with just 1 year. Finally, if you both confess, we'll arrange to have you both sentenced to 10 years in prison.

The game is presented in its normal form in Figure 10.1. Each player has just two strategies: 'Confess' and 'Don't Confess'. In the normal form, the game is presented in the form of a matrix, with the strategies of one player, who we will call the 'row player', presented in the rows, and the strategies of the other player, the 'column player', presented in the columns. The cells of the matrix show the pay-offs if that particular pair of strategies is played, with the row player's pay-off listed first and the column player's pay-off listed second. The pay-offs in this example are the

| | | Column Player's Strategies | |
|---|---|---|---|
| | | Confess | Don't Confess |
| Row Player's Strategies | Confess | −10, −10 | −1, −20 |
| | Don't Confess | −20, −1 | −2, −2 |

**Figure 10.1** *The Prisoners' Dilemma Game*

number of years to which each player gets sentenced, and to indicate that these are 'bads' that the players would want to minimise, we have added minus signs to the pay-offs. To take one cell as an example, suppose the row player confesses (top row) and the column player does not confess (right column), the row player gets 1 year and the column player gets 20 years. Similarly for the other cells. In general, in a $2 \times 2$ matrix of this sort, the strategy of the row player presented in the top row (here, Confess) is called 'Top' (T), and the strategy presented in the bottom row (here, Don't Confess) is called 'Bottom' (B). Similarly, the column player's strategies are called 'Left' (L, here Confess) and 'Right' (R, here Don't Confess).

How will the players play this game? It turns out that, in all likelihood, they will both Confess. We can see why this is by considering the reasoning of the row player. He might think: I don't know what my partner is going to do, but let me think about what my best strategy would be depending upon what he does. Suppose he confesses. Then I'm better-off confessing, since I get only 10 years rather than 20. So, if he confesses, I should confess too. But what if he doesn't confess? Well, in that case, I'm better-off confessing again, since I'll get only 1 year rather than 2. So, no matter what he does, it's better for me to confess. The column player could go through the same process of reasoning and, as the problem is perfectly symmetric, would arrive at the same conclusion. Thus, both players would conclude that Confess is their best strategy, and both would end up with 10 years in jail.

Note that the pay-offs under this outcome (−10, −10) are the only set of pay-offs that the two players would unanimously agree is worse than another set of possible pay-offs: (−2, −2) if neither confesses. If both players could somehow agree to not confess, and somehow enforce this agreement, they would both be better-off. But any agreement to not confess is unlikely to stick. Suppose, for example, that, as the two are being bundled into the police van upon their arrest, Row says to Column: 'Look, they're going to play Prisoners' Dilemma on us. Let's agree to not confess!' And suppose Column agrees, and they swear to abide by the agreement. Once the two are separated, they each go through their thought process, realise they are unambiguously better-off if they confess, especially if there is a cache of money and jewellery hidden away that they can access once they are out of jail, and therefore they each have a powerful incentive to renege on their agreement. That could be one reason why criminal organisations such as the Mafia have the strong code of *omerta*, silence under all circumstances, the breaking of which is punishable by death. In effect, the organisation changes the pay-offs by making Confess a very expensive strategy and thereby helps enforce agreements to Don't Confess.

The Prisoners' Dilemma game is a rather special one in that both players have what are called **dominant strategies**, strategies that are the best choice no matter what the other player does. The strategy pair (Confess, Confess) is therefore a **dominant strategy equilibrium** and is considered a very robust outcome for the game were it to actually be played.

It is worth noting that Confess is the dominant strategy for each player, *even if they did not actually commit the murder*. Thus, this kind of pay-off structure can elicit false confessions for the police.

| | | Column Player's Strategies | |
|---|---|---|---|
| | | *L* | *R* |
| Row Player's Strategies | *T* | 5, 5 | 20, 0 |
| | *B* | 0, 20 | 10, 10 |

**Figure 10.2** *Pay-off Matrix for the Generic Prisoners' Dilemma Game*

A more generic version of the Prisoners' Dilemma game is presented in Figure 10.2. Here, the row player has the two strategies Top ($T$) and Bottom ($B$) and the column player has the two strategies Left ($L$) and Right ($R$). Pay-offs are now good, so each player wants to maximise his or her pay-off. Row's dominant strategy is $T$ and Column's is $L$, so ($T$, $L$) is the dominant strategy equilibrium. The pay-offs are (5, 5), even though this outcome is not Pareto efficient, since the outcome (10, 10) is Pareto superior to it.

The Prisoners' Dilemma game has been found to have many applications in many different fields, including biology, ecology, nuclear strategy, economics and so on. In economics, it is seen as a simple way to describe many competitive situations in which cooperation between competitors would be beneficial to them but difficult to implement. For example, suppose the two players in the game were rival firms trying to decide how much to spend on advertising. Suppose $T$ and $L$ represent high levels of advertising and $B$ and $R$ represent low levels of advertising. Suppose, with both firms engaging in low levels of advertising, each firm's profits would be 10, but with both firms engaging in high levels of advertising, each firm's profits would be 5, because advertising is expensive and each firm's advertising neutralises the other's. However, if one firm advertises a lot and the other advertises a little, suppose the pay-offs are 20 and 0, respectively, because the high advertiser can steal a lot of the low advertiser's customers. Thus the pay-off matrix in Figure 10.2 can represent this competitive situation. We can see that high advertising is the dominant strategy for each firm, resulting in the Pareto-inefficient outcome of (5, 5). High advertising becomes the dominant strategy because, if your rival advertises high, you must advertise high to protect your market share, while, if your rival advertises low, you want to advertise high in order to steal his customers and increase your market share. Thus, we have a classic Prisoners' Dilemma type of game situation.

### 10.2.2 Battle of the Sexes

The next game we will look at is called by the colourful title 'Battle of the Sexes'. This game describes a situation in which the players might agree that cooperation is desirable, but they differ on the nature of the cooperation they would like to see. The outcome could be a deadlock.

The story told to paint a picture for this game is that a couple are planning to go out for the evening. They love one another dearly and so they both agree they would like to go out together, but one, say Rohit (he will be the Row player), wants to go to a cricket match, while the other, say Chandrika (who will be the Column player), wants to go to the theatre. A typical pay-off matrix for this game might look like the one in Figure 10.3. It shows that Rohit and Chandrika would like to be together (the pay-offs at $(T, L)$ and $(B, R)$ are strictly greater than the others), but Rohit prefers they both go to the cricket match, while Chandrika prefers they both go to the theatre. If they go their separate ways, Rohit to the cricket and Chandrika to the theatre $(T, R)$, they are both worse off, while if they each go to the other's favourite event $(B, L)$, they are even more worse off.

| | | Chandrika's Strategies | |
|---|---|---|---|
| | | *L* Cricket | *R* Theatre |
| Rohit's Strategies | *T* Cricket | 3, 2 | 1, 1 |
| | *B* Theatre | 0, 0 | 2, 3 |

**Figure 10.3** *Pay-off Matrix for the Battle of the Sexes Game*

This game does not have a dominant strategy equilibrium. If Chandrika absolutely insists on going to the theatre, Rohit is better-off going to the theatre as well (rather than his separate way), while if Chandrika agrees to go to the theatre, Rohit would clearly prefer that. So Rohit's optimal strategy depends upon what Chandrika does; he does not have a dominant strategy. Similarly, Chandrika's optimal strategy depends upon what Rohit does, so she does not have a dominant strategy either.

We therefore need a different equilibrium concept for this game than we did for the Prisoners' Dilemma. The most widely used equilibrium concept in game theory is that of Nash equilibrium. The **Nash Equilibrium** of a game is a set of strategies, one for each player, such that each player's pay-off is optimised, conditional on the strategies of every other player. That is, conditional on what everyone else is doing, no player can improve his or her pay-off by changing their strategy.

The way to check if any set of strategies is a Nash equilibrium is to look to see if any player can improve their pay-off, holding all the other strategies fixed. In the present game, consider the strategy pair $(T, L)$, that is, where Rohit plays Top (goes to the cricket) and Chandrika plays Left (also goes to the cricket). The pay-offs are (3, 2). Rohit's only alternative is to play Bottom, and, if he did, with Chandrika continuing to play $L$, his pay-off would fall to 0. Thus, Rohit has no incentive to deviate from $(T, L)$. Chandrika's only alternative is to play Right, and her pay-off falls to 1 if she does that, so she has no incentive to deviate either. Thus, $(T, L)$ is a Nash equilibrium.

Let us look at $(T, R)$, where the pay-offs are (1, 1). Here, if Rohit changed his strategy to Bottom, his pay-off would go up to 2. So Rohit has an incentive to deviate from $(T, R)$, and that is enough for us to determine that $(T, R)$ is not a Nash equilibrium. In fact, even Chandrika has an incentive to deviate from $(T, R)$.

Let us look at $(B, L)$, where the pay-offs are (0, 0). Here, Chandrika could raise her pay-off to 3 by switching to $R$, and Rohit could raise his to 3 also by switching to $T$. Thus, $(B, L)$ is not a Nash equilibrium.

Finally, let us look at $(B, R)$, with pay-offs (2, 3). Here, neither player can improve by changing strategy, so $(B, R)$ is also a Nash equilibrium. Thus the Battle of the Sexes game has two Nash equilibria: $(T, L)$ and $(B, R)$.

There are two things that need to be said at this stage of the discussion. First, there is nothing in the structure of the game or in the method of solution that would help us determine which of these two Nash equilibria would actually be achieved. Each spouse could fight tooth and nail for 'their' equilibrium and the couple could end up at an impasse (many real-world couples do!). Second, there is nothing that guarantees that the outcome *will* be one of the Nash equilibria anyway. Although most authors presume that rationality will push players towards the Nash equilibria, there is actually no assurance that they will actually end up there.

The Battle of the Sexes game is illustrative of many problems. Where two agents attempt to negotiate anything, reaching some sort of agreement would be better for both, but each has a vested interest in a different equilibrium than the other. For example, in negotiations between the management of a firm and its labour union over a new labour contract, both might agree that they would want to avoid a strike or a lockout. Yet each may press for a cooperative equilibrium more favourable to their interests, the union for higher wages and shorter hours and management for the opposite. Thus, this situation is much like the Battle of the Sexes. Another example is where makers of products might try to agree on standards that make their products mutually compatible. Here experience seems to suggest that the impasse tends to win. IBM and Apple were unable to agree on a common operating system, Sony and the VHS consortium were unable to settle on a standard format for videotape and, in recent years, manufacturers of mobile phone handsets have failed to agree on a common system either.

### 10.2.3 Matching Pennies and Mixed Strategies

In the game Matching Pennies, each of the two players, say Rohan and Kalpana, puts a covered coin on the palm of their hand and then they simultaneously reveal the coins to one another. If the coins match (i.e. both are Heads or both are Tails), Kalpana pays Rohan. If the coins don't match (one is Heads and the other is Tails), Rohan pays Kalpana. The pay-off matrix is shown in Figure 10.4. Note that the pay-offs in each cell of the pay-off matrix of this game sum to zero; this is therefore an example of a **zero-sum game**.

| | | Kalpana's Strategies | |
|---|---|---|---|
| | | **Heads** | **Tails** |
| **Rohan's Strategies** | **Heads** | 1, −1 | −1, 1 |
| | **Tails** | −1, 1 | 1, −1 |

**Figure 10.4** *Pay-off Matrix for the Matching Pennies Game*

An examination of the four strategy pairs in this game reveals that none of them is a Nash equilibrium. Consider

- $(H, H)$: Kalpana would want to deviate.
- $(H, T)$: Rohan would want to deviate.

- $(T, H)$: Rohan would want to deviate.
- $(T, T)$: Kalpana would want to deviate.

Is there no equilibrium in this game?

A little thought reveals a rather obvious solution to this game. Each player could simply flip the coin, or place it randomly on their hand without looking. In that case, each player's expected pay-off is zero and neither can do any better by doing anything differently. So this would be an equilibrium. What we have here is a **mixed strategy Nash equilibrium**. There is no Nash equilibrium in pure strategies, that is, in either of the available strategies played with certainty, but there *is* an equilibrium in mixed strategies, where the players play the pure strategies with certain probabilities. In this mixed strategy equilibrium, each player is playing the pure strategies with probability 1/2.

The idea of just flipping the coins seemed intuitive, but it would be useful to have a systematic way of finding mixed strategy equilibria. The process goes as follows. Suppose Rohan is thinking of playing $H$ with probability $p$ and $T$ with probability $(1-p)$, and Kalpana is thinking of playing $H$ with probability $q$ and $T$ with probability $(1-q)$. Then Rohan's expected pay-off is

$$E\pi_R = p\left\{q \cdot 1 + (1-q)(-1)\right\} + (1-p)\left\{q(-1) + (1-q)\cdot 1\right\}$$

$$= p(q-1+q) + (1-p)(-q+1-q)$$

$$= p(2q-1) + (1-p)(1-2q).$$

Then, to choose $p$ so as to maximise $E\pi_R$, Rohan would set

$$\frac{\partial E\pi_R}{\partial p} = 2q - 1 - 1 + 2q = 0,$$

which yields the 'solution'

$$q = 1/2.$$

Note that $p$ has dropped out of this first-order condition! There is no particular value of $p$ at which $E\pi_R$ is maximised. However, we have found that, if $q = 1/2$, $\frac{\partial E\pi_R}{\partial p} = 0$, that is, $E\pi_R$ is invariant to changes in $p$.

A similar analysis for Kalpana will show that there is no particular value of $q$ where $E\pi_C$ is maximised, but, if $p = 1/2$, $E\pi_C$ will be invariant to changes in $q$. Thus, if Rohan plays $(H, T)$ with probabilities $(1/2,\ 1/2)$ and Kalpana plays $(H, T)$ with probabilities $(1/2,\ 1/2)$, neither player will have any incentive to change their decision. Thus, we have a Nash equilibrium in mixed strategies. It turns out that we can always find a Nash equilibrium of a game, if not in pure strategies, then in mixed strategies.

## 10.2.4 Mixed Strategies in the Battle of the Sexes Game

As another example of mixed strategies equilibria, we could look at the possibility of such an equilibrium in the Battle of the Sexes game. Recall the pay-off matrix from Figure 10.3. Suppose Rohit contemplates playing T and B with probabilities $p$ and $(1 - p)$, and Chandrika contemplates playing L and R with probabilities $q$ and $(1 - q)$. Then Rohit's expected pay-off would be

$$E\pi_R = p\{3q + 1 \cdot (1 - q)\} + (1 - p)\{0 \cdot q + 2 \cdot (1 - q)\}$$

$$= p(1 + 2q) + (1 - p)(2 - 2q).$$

To maximise $E\pi_R$, Rohit would set

$$\frac{\partial E\pi_R}{\partial p} = 1 + 2q - 2 + 2q = 0,$$

which yields the 'solution'

$$q = 1/4.$$

So if Chandrika plays $L$ and $R$ with probabilities 1/4 and 3/4, Rohit's expected pay-off will be invariant with changes in $p$. It can be shown that then $E\pi_R = 3/2$.

We can similarly write down Chandrika's expected pay-off:

$$E\pi_C = q\{2p + 0 \cdot (1 - p)\} + (1 - q)\{1 \cdot p + 3 \cdot (1 - p)\}$$

$$= q(2p) + (1 - q)(3 - 2p).$$

For maximisation,

$$\frac{\partial E\pi_C}{\partial q} = 2p - 3 + 2p = 0,$$

which simplifies to

$$p = 3/4.$$

So if Rohit plays $T$ and $B$ with probabilities 3/4 and 1/4, Chandrika's expected pay-off will be invariant to changes in $q$. Her expected pay-off will also be 3/2.

We therefore have a Nash equilibrium in mixed strategies for the Battle of the Sexes game, in which Rohit plays $T$ and $B$ with probabilities 3/4 and 1/4 and Chandrika plays $L$ and $R$ with probabilities 1/4 and 3/4.

# 10.3 SEQUENTIAL GAMES

**Task for this section:**

To study games where the players share all the same information but move sequentially. Two ways of looking at such games, as normal form or as extensive form games, are discussed and the concept of Subgame Perfect Equilibrium is introduced.

Most real-world games do not involve just one set of simultaneous-moves by all the players, but rather a sequence of moves, where one player moves first, the other responds and so on. Such games with multiple stages are called sequential or dynamic games.

We can illustrate these types of games by looking at a sequential version of the Battle of the Sexes game. Suppose the cricket match and the theatre are located in completely different parts of the city and Rohit and Chandrika are each at work and plan to meet at the location of their evening date. No matter where they decide to go, Rohit will have the longer drive and so he would have to leave work earlier than Chandrika, and will have first choice in deciding where to actually go. In this way, he decides where to go first and informs Chandrika where he is headed. At that point, she can choose to join Rohit where he is already going, or choose to go her separate way. However, she can announce to Rohit before he leaves work what her intentions are.

In this two-stage version of the game, since he moves first, Rohit still has just two strategies available to him: to go to the cricket match or to the theatre. But Chandrika is going to move later, so she is going to find herself at one of two different decision points. Rohit could have gone to the cricket match or to the theatre, and, for each of these possibilities, Chandrika has two possible actions she can take, to go to the cricket match or to the theatre. So Chandrika has four possible strategies:

1. If Rohit plays *T*, she plays *L*, and if Rohit plays *B*, she plays *L*. This strategy will be denoted *LL*, the first *L* denoting her response to his playing *T* and the second her response to his playing *B*.
2. If Rohit plays *T*, she plays *L*, and if Rohit plays *B*, she plays *R*. This strategy will be denoted *LR*.
3. If Rohit plays *B*, she plays *R*, and if Rohit plays *B*, she plays *L*. This strategy will be denoted *RL*.
4. If Rohit plays *B*, she plays *R*, and if Rohit plays *B*, she plays *R*. This strategy will be denoted *RR*.

The pay-off matrix for this game can then be written as in Figure 10.5. The pay-offs are obtained from the static version of the game whose pay-off matrix was in Figure 10.3. Here, for example, (*T*, *LL*) results in pay-offs of (3, 2) because *LL* means that Chandrika will play *L* if Rohit plays *T*, so we end up with the pay-off that (*T*, *L*) would have yielded in the static game. (*T*, *RL*) results in

| | | Chandrika's Strategies | | | |
|---|---|---|---|---|---|
| | | *LL* | *LR* | *RL* | *RR* |
| Rohit's Strategies | *T* | 3, 2 | 3, 2 | 1, 1 | 1, 1 |
| | *B* | 0, 0 | 2, 3 | 0, 0 | 2, 3 |

**Figure 10.5** *Normal Form of the Sequential Battle of the Sexes Game*

pay-offs of (1, 1) since *RL* means that Chandrika plays *R* if Rohit plays *T*, resulting in the outcome from (*T*, *R*) in the static game.

If we examine the pay-off matrix in Figure 10.5, we see that this game has three Nash equilibria in pure strategies: (*T*, *LL*), (*T*, *LR*) and (*B*, *RR*). Of these three equilibria, the first two are somewhat similar in that they both involve Chandrika playing *L* if Rohit plays *T*. Since that gives Rohit his most preferred option, he has no incentive to deviate from playing *T*. And since *L* is *ex post* Chandrika's best option if Rohit plays *T*, she has no incentive to deviate from either of her strategies either.

The interesting Nash equilibrium is (*B*, *RR*). If Chandrika manages to convince Rohit that she is going to play *R* no matter what he does (that is what *RR* implies, that she plays *R* whether he plays *T* or *B*), he can be induced to play *B*, since that is his best response to her playing *R*. That is why (*B*, *RR*) is a Nash equilibrium. The trouble with this equilibrium is that Chandrika's threat to play *R* no matter what Rohit does is not credible, because it is not in her best interest to play *R* if he plays *T*. In other words, she could threaten to go to the theatre (play *R*) no matter what he does, but once he has left his office and has been driving for 15 minutes towards the cricket match (by which time he would not be able to reach the theatre in time if he changes his destination), and if he now calls her and tells her he is already part of the way to the cricket match, it would no longer be rational for her to follow through on her threat. Thus, Rohit could call her bluff and simply play *T*, in which case Chandrika's best response would be to abandon her threat and play *L* anyway.

The preceding analysis calls into question the type of Nash equilibrium embodied in the strategy pair (*B*, *RR*) and suggests a new notion of equilibrium for multi-stage games. This is called **sub-game perfect equilibrium** (SPE) and is defined as a Nash equilibrium in which each player plays rationally at all stages of the game. In other words, it is an equilibrium that does not involve any non-credible threats. The Nash equilibrium (*B*, *RR*) is not an SPE because it involves Chandrika's threat to play *R* if Rohit plays *T*, a threat that is not credible, because it would not be rational for Chandrika to do so. Similarly, the Nash equilibrium (*T*, *LL*) is not an SPE because it involves a threat by Chandrika to play *L* if Rohit plays *B*, another threat that is not credible. The only SPE of this game is (*T*, *LR*) since *LR* involves Chandrika playing *L* if Rohit plays *T* (which is indeed her best response to *T*) and playing *R* if Rohit plays *B* (which is her best response again). Thus, (*T*, *LR*) is an SPE, and we have already shown that the other two Nash equilibria are not SPEs.

Having the first move gives Rohit the advantage in this game and the SPE gives him the outcome that he would have preferred from among the two previous Nash equilibria of the static version of the game. Chandrika's threat to play *R* no matter what Rohit does is really a bluff, and Rohit can call her bluff and simply play *T* in the knowledge that it would then be rational for her to abandon her threat and play *L*. But what if Chandrika could somehow pre-commit to carry out her 'irrational' threat? Perhaps she could then turn the game in her favour. For example, suppose they already have tickets to both events and new tickets are impossible to buy at this point. What if, before Rohit has left his office, Chandrika calls him on Skype and, in full view of him on the video feed, burns her ticket to the cricket match? She has now *pre-committed* to going to the theatre because she no longer has a ticket to the cricket match! In this case, her strategy *RR* does not involve a non-credible threat, because she has effectively eliminated the possibility of playing *L*. Thus the strategy pair (*B*, *RR*) is now an SPE and the outcome will be Chandrika's preferred one. A credible pre-commitment to an otherwise non-credible threat has turned the game to Chandrika's favour.

The foregoing analysis has analysed the game in its normal form, and this has yielded interesting insights into the way threats can be used in games.

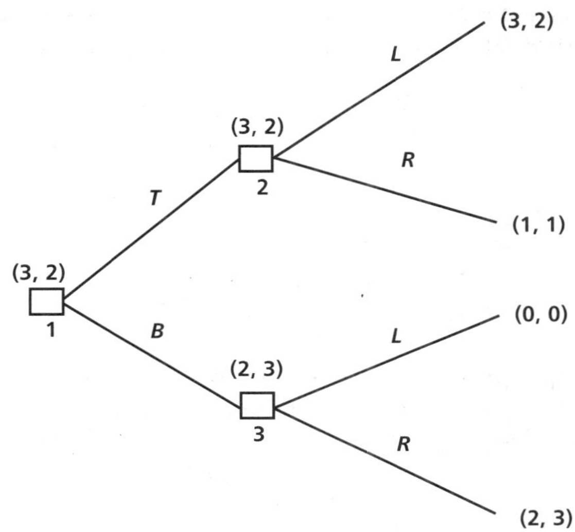


**Figure 10.6** *Extensive Form of the Sequential Battle of the Sexes Game*

Another way of analysing this game is by looking at it in **extensive form**, that is, in the form of a decision tree, and then solving it by backward induction. The extensive form of this game is presented in Figure 10.6. Rohit moves first and can select *T* or *B*, which are the two branches emanating from decision node 1. Chandrika moves second and can find herself either at decision node number 2 (if Rohit chose *T*) or decision node 3 (if Rohit chose *B*). At each of these nodes, Chandrika could choose *L* or *R*, so there are four possible outcomes, and the pay-offs for each are written at the ends of the respective branches of the tree.

The extensive form of the game is solved by backward induction. We ask (or, properly, Rohit asks) what Chandrika would do at each of the two decision nodes where she might find herself. At node 2, her best response to Rohit playing *T* would be to play *L*, since she would get a pay-off of 2 rather than 1 by playing *L*. Thus, Rohit can reason that, if he plays *T*, Chandrika will play *L* and the outcome will be (3, 2). Accordingly, we write (3, 2) as the pay-off above decision node 2. Similarly, we ask what Chandrika would do at node 3. Here, her best response to Rohit playing *B* is to play *R*, and so the outcome would be (2, 3). Therefore, Rohit can deduce that, if he plays B, Chandrika will play *R* and the outcome will be (2, 3). Rohit can now look at his options at decision node 1 and can see that if he plays *T*, the outcome will be (3, 2), and if he plays *B*, the outcome will be (2, 3). Rohit can therefore see that his better option is to choose *T*. Chandrika will then choose *L* and the pay-offs will be (3, 2). We therefore find the same outcome as we did with the SPE of the normal form game.

We could actually derive the SPE specifically from the extensive form of the game. Think of Chandrika's two decision nodes being the starting points of two 'sub-games', marked by the dotted lines outlined in Figure 10.7. We can then ask what her rational choice would be in each of these sub-games. We have already seen that her rational choice in the upper sub-game is to choose *L* in response to Rohit's choice of *T*, and in the lower sub-game is to choose *R* in response

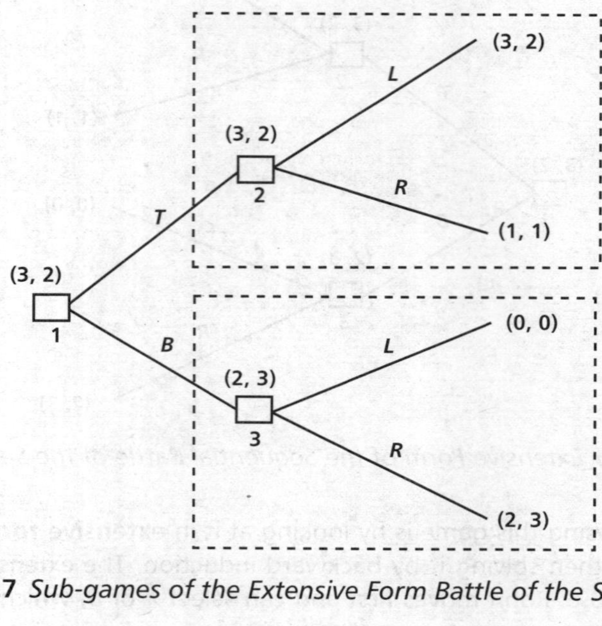


**Figure 10.7** *Sub-games of the Extensive Form Battle of the Sexes Game*

to Rohit's choice of *B*. Thus, her rational strategy is *LR*. We have also already seen that Rohit's choice in the 'sub-game' around decision node 1 is to choose *T*. Putting the two players' rational strategies together, we have the SPE as (*T*, *LR*).

## 10.4 REPEATED GAMES

**Task for this section:**

To discuss briefly how playing games repeatedly might change the outcomes we would expect.

We have looked at single-stage and multi-stage games, but have had the players play them just once. In most real-world situations, games are played not just once but repeatedly. For example, married couples do not have just one evening to plan, they have thousands. Firms that are competing with one another may find themselves in a Prisoners' Dilemma type of situation, but they know they will face the same situation again and again. What happens to the equilibrium outcome of the game when it is played repeatedly? Do the players keep playing the same strategies again and again, or do they change their behaviour once they realise they will face the same opponent again tomorrow? These are the questions economists try to answer when they look at repeated games.

In thinking of the repeated Battle of the Sexes, it is quite clear that a threat such as *RR* on the part of Chandrika, while being a non-credible threat in the one-shot game, may be a valid strategy in the repeated game. Imagine that Chandrika threatened to go to the theatre no matter what Rohit did, and suppose Rohit decided to 'call her bluff' and go to the cricket match. Chandrika could well want to follow through with her threat in order to establish a 'reputation', to convince Rohit that she does not make empty threats. Her hope would be that in future Rohit would be more likely to believe her threats and would therefore not call her bluffs. Of course, Rohit could also issue his own threats and could keep calling her bluffs, and the couple could end up warring with each other and finish in divorce court! But it is not clear what the equilibrium would be.

Let us focus on the repeated Prisoners' Dilemma, since that is the game that has been studied the most, both theoretically and experimentally. It turns out that the outcome is likely to depend upon whether the game is played a known finite number of times, or an infinite number of times (which can be closely modelled by looking at a game which is played an unknown but finite number of times). The question is, might players cooperate with each other more when the game is played repeatedly? Think of 'Confess' as being the non-cooperative, or 'defect', strategy in the game and think of 'Don't Confess' as being the cooperative strategy since it is mutually beneficial if both players play this strategy. Might repetition encourage players to not confess more often?

If the game is played a finite number of times, theory tells us that hope for cooperation unravels. Suppose the game is to be played five times. Then, before the fifth round, the situation would have reverted to the one-shot game. Both players will realise that cooperation is no longer beneficial and so both would defect. Looking forward before the fourth round, rational players would realise that defection is the rational strategy on the fifth round and would therefore see no benefit in cooperating in the fourth round. By this process, cooperation unravels as a viable strategy at any stage of the game, and so both players would defect, or play the non-cooperative strategy, at all times. In fact, this result has been shown to be generalisable to any game which has a unique Nash equilibrium in its static version. If the game is repeated a known finite number of times, the only SPE of the repeated game is the static Nash equilibrium at each stage of the game.

If the game is played an infinite number of times, or at least if there is no known end point for the game, it is possible that more cooperative behaviour might emerge. This is borne out by results of experiments in which players play the game for real money. It is found that cooperative behaviour frequently emerges in actual practice. And in a tournament of strategies playing against one another, the strategy that generated the highest cumulative pay-off and won the tournament was the 'Tit for Tat' strategy. This strategy simply plays whatever the opponent played on the previous round. If the opponent defected on the previous round, Tit for Tat defects, and if the opponent cooperated on the previous round, Tit for Tat cooperates.

## SUMMARY

In this chapter, we have looked at the Theory of Games, an approach to thinking about strategic behaviour in situations where multiple decision-makers interact and whose decisions mutually affect everyone. The basic points were as follows:

- The fundamental solution concept in games is of equilibrium. We studied several types of equilibria.
- A Dominant Strategy Equilibrium is one where every player in the game is playing a strategy that is their optimal one regardless of what other players play.
- A Nash Equilibrium is one where every player is playing their best response to what all other players are playing, that is, every player is playing their optimal strategy conditional on what every other player is playing.
- A Mixed Strategy is one where players play their (pure) strategies according to probabilities they choose. It is possible for Nash equilibrium to involve mixed strategies and in fact every static game has a mixed strategy Nash equilibrium.
- A Subgame Perfect Equilibrium is a solution concept for multi-stage games and is one where every player plays their optimal strategy at every stage of the game. In other words, an SPE involves no non-credible threats.

- **When games are played repeatedly for a known finite number of times, there is a tendency for the static game Nash equilibrium to be played at each repetition.**
- **However, when games are repeated an infinite (or an unknown finite) number of times, departures from static Nash equilibrium can occur and more cooperative behaviour tends to emerge.**

## EXERCISES

1. AIR, Inc. and RMS, Inc. are in competition. Each can follow one of two strategies, it can either cooperate, or compete. The pay-off matrix, showing profits in crores of rupees, looks like this:

| | | RMS Strategies | |
|---|---|---|---|
| | | **Cooperate** | **Compete** |
| **AIR Strategies** | **Cooperate** | **40, 30** | **10, 60** |
| | **Compete** | **80, 10** | **30, 20** |

   (a) Identify any Nash equilibria in pure strategies to this game. Explain your reasons.

   (b) Prove that there does not exist a Nash equilibrium in mixed strategies different from the pure strategy Nash equilibrium you found in (a). In one sentence, provide an intuitive reason for this result.

   (c) If AIR acquired RMS, it could coordinate the two firms' strategies. (Assume there are no other advantages or disadvantages to the merger.) What is the maximum amount AIR would be willing to pay for RMS? What is the minimum amount RMS would require to be willing to be acquired?

2. Consider the Battle of the Sexes game with the pay-off matrix below when played as a static game of full information (the husband is the row player and the wife is the column player). Suppose that the game changes to a dynamic game in which the husband moves first.

| | Left | Right |
|---|---|---|
| Top | 2, 1 | 0, 0 |
| Bottom | 0, 0 | 1, 2 |

   (a) Write down the normal form of the dynamic game and find any Nash equilibria of this game. Explain your reasons. Also find the SPE of this game, explaining your choice.

   (b) Now write down the extensive form of this dynamic game and find its solution.

3. Grand Corp. and Little Corp. are the only two producers of blodgets. Each can produce blodgets at a per unit cost of ₹4. Presently, Grand has an 80% market share. The two firms agree to form a cartel, and the agreement is that they will preserve market shares at 80% and 20% respectively, while trying to maximise joint profits. The demand curve for blodgets is

$$P = 44 - 4Q.$$

   (a) How much should each firm produce for the cartel agreement to be realised?

   (b) Suppose each of the firms is thinking about cheating on their cartel agreement by producing one unit more than the agreement had specified. They also know that their 'partner' may cheat in this way. Each firm therefore has two possible output levels: the output agreed upon [your answer to (a)], or an output level one unit higher than that. By suitable calculations, construct a pay-off matrix for the game the two firms find themselves playing.

   (c) By analysing the game, what would you predict the two firms to do? Comment briefly on this outcome as compared to the cartel outcome.

4. Consider a static game with the following pay-off matrix:

| | Left | Right |
|---|---|---|
| Top | 10, 5 | 5, 3 |
| Bottom | 5, 0 | 20, 2 |

   (a) Find all Nash equilibria in pure strategies for this game.

   (b) Find all Nash equilibria in mixed strategies for this game.

   (c) Write down the normal form for the dynamic version of this game in which the row player moves first.

   (d) Find all Nash equilibria in pure strategies for the dynamic game of part (c) and also find the SPE of that game.

CHAPTER

# 11 Market Structures between Competition and Monopoly

So far, we have looked at markets that are either perfectly competitive or monopolies, with brief digressions into contestable markets and markets with dominant 'price-leader' firms. Most real markets lie in between the extremes of monopoly and perfect competition. There is no single way in which all these 'intermediate' market forms can be characterised and analysed. Rather, economists have constructed many different types of models in an attempt to describe and analyse the different kinds of market behaviour they observe. In thinking about a real-world market that we might want to analyse, we might look to see which model of 'imperfect competition' or 'oligopoly' seems most applicable to that market. In this chapter, we will look at some of these market models that economists have constructed. This is an area in which much new research has been carried out since about 1990 and where microeconomics has changed the most over this period.

## 11.1 MONOPOLISTIC COMPETITION

**Task for this section:**

To study the model of monopolistic competition (also called imperfect competition) in which firms produce differentiated products but entry of firms producing close substitutes is possible and free. The short-run and long-run equilibria of the model are discussed.

There are many products that are unique and yet have close substitutes. Many consumer goods, particularly branded ones, are like this. The example often cited, perhaps because it has been quite intensively studied, is the ready-to-eat cereal industry, where products such as cornflakes, wheat flakes and muesli are produced and sold. Each brand and type of cereal is slightly different from all the others, in which sense it is a monopoly, and yet there are many other products that are close substitutes to it, making the 'monopoly' a rather empty one since it faces keen competition. Many consumer goods have this characteristic: soap, detergent, toothpaste, soft drinks, paper, pens, padlocks and so on; the list is virtually endless. The model of monopolistic competition, proposed independently in the 1930s by the American economist Edward Chamberlin and the British economist Joan Robinson (who called it 'imperfect competition'), is designed to describe this kind of market.

The model of monopolistic competition needs to include two key features characteristic of the situation described in the previous paragraph:

- Products are characterised by **product differentiation**, that is, goods that are essentially the same, or fulfil the same essential need, are nevertheless differentiated from one another either through small differences in their composition, design or features, or, if there is no substantive difference between them, through branding and advertising. In the latter case, the product differentiation may not be real, but only in the minds of consumers; what is important is that their demand behaviour responds to the perceived differences, specifically that the demand curve they face is downward-sloping. An example of this is brand name versus generic drugs that are chemically (and hence therapeutically) identical.
- Competition among products is sufficiently intense and entry is sufficiently free that no firm can make extra-normal profits in the long run.

Given these characteristics, we can describe the behaviour of firms operating in such a market. The important consequence of product differentiation is that firms will face downward-sloping demand curves. If we start with the flat, perfectly elastic demand curve faced by a perfectly competitive firm (producing an undifferentiated, homogenous product) and ask what is the effect of product differentiation, we see immediately that this must impart some slope to the demand curve. Once the product is distinguished from others along some dimension or the other, it will develop loyal customers for whom that particular dimension is important. Such customers would continue to demand the good even if its price went up and therefore the demand curve would no longer be flat but would have some downward slope to it.

What would equilibrium look like for such a firm? In the short run, if no entry and exit are possible, the equilibrium will look just like that of a monopoly, and we can refer back to Figure 9.1 on page 283 to review that. Simply put, the firm will set $MR = MC$ and thereby maximise its profits. If the firm chooses to behave strategically, it might set a limit price or try to pre-empt entry in some way, and we will consider such possibilities later in this chapter. However, in the standard Chamberlinian model of monopolistic competition, the firm is assumed to behave non-strategically in the short run.

The situation changes in the long run, however, and it is in the long run that the model displays its uniqueness. The simple monopoly solution cannot last in the long run, according to the model, because the second key feature in it is that entry is relatively free and firms cannot make extra-normal profits in the long run. The idea is simply that, as long as firms are making extra-normal profits in this market, other firms can enter the market with slightly differentiated products and, in this way, steal some of the incumbent firms' customers. It seems reasonable to suppose that entry of new firms will push any incumbent firm's demand curve to the left (i.e. reduce demand for each incumbent firm's product) and also make it more elastic. Further, as long as the incumbent firms are making extra-normal profits, further entry of differentiated products will take place until the profits of each incumbent firm are driven down to their 'normal' level. Yet, throughout this process, the fact that the products are differentiated means that each firm faces a downward-sloping demand curve.

How are zero profits compatible with a situation where all firms have downward-sloping demand curves and therefore have some monopoly power? Figure 11.1 illustrates the equilibrium. The key insight here is that entry will push each incumbent firm's demand curve to the left until it is tangent to the firm's *AC* curve. At this point of tangency, profits are maximised. Therefore, at this quantity, simultaneously $MC = MR$ and also extra-normal profits are zero, since $AC = AR$.

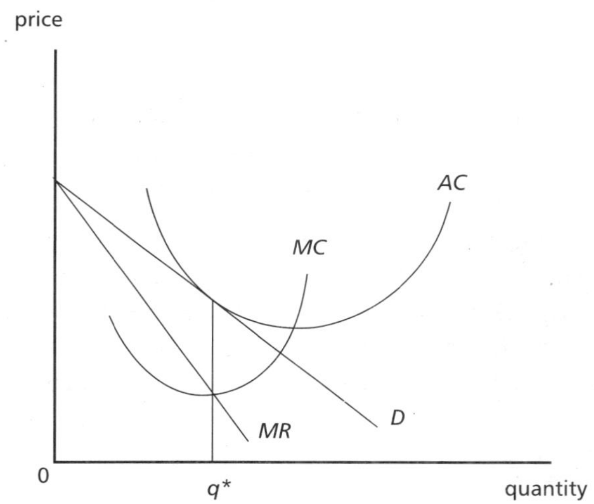


**Figure 11.1** *Equilibrium in Monopolistic Competition*

Why must $MC = MR$ at this quantity, $q^*$? One simple way to see that profits must be at a maximum at $q^*$ is to observe that, at all other values of $q$, $AC < AR$ (the *AC* curve lies below the demand curve), and therefore profits must be negative. At $q^*$, $AC = AR$, and profits are zero. Therefore, this is the profit maximum and *MC* must equal *MR* also, since $MC = MR$ is the condition for profit to be maximised.

To see this result more formally, note that, where *AC* is tangent to the demand curve, two conditions are satisfied:

$$AC = AR \tag{11.1}$$

$$\text{and } \frac{dAC}{dq} = \frac{dAR}{dq}. \tag{11.2}$$

Now

$$AC = \frac{C(q)}{q}.$$

Therefore,

$$\frac{dAC}{dq} = \frac{q.C'(q) - C(q)}{q^2} = \frac{1}{q}\{C'(q) - AC\}.$$

Similarly.

$$\frac{dAR}{dq} = \frac{1}{q}\{R'(q) - AR\}.$$

From (11.1) and (11.2), it then follows that

$$C'(q) = R'(q),$$

that is, that $MC = MR$ at the point where $AC$ and $AR$ are tangent to one another. We therefore have an equilibrium where firms are 'monopolistic' with downward-sloping demand curves, and yet make zero profits in the long run, as in perfect competition.

One particular aspect of the long-run equilibrium in monopolistic competition is known as Chamberlin's Excess Capacity Theorem. The equilibrium occurs at a point such as E in Figure 11.2, where quantity produced is $q^*$. One thing we can observe about this point is that $AC$ is still falling, and continues to do so until the quantity $q^c$ where $AC$ is at a minimum. In a sense, we might call $q^c$ the 'capacity' of the firm since $AC$ is minimised at this quantity. Since the equilibrium production

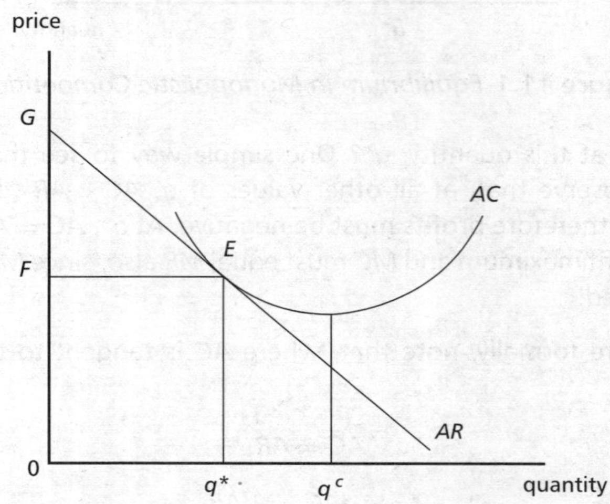


**Figure 11.2** *Excess Capacity in Monopolistic Competition Equilibrium*

level $q^*$ is less than $q^c$, there is a sense in which the firm has 'excess capacity'. To the extent that firms could reduce their average cost of production by expanding output, there is an inefficiency in the system.

Whether social welfare could be increased by reducing the number of firms is a difficult question to answer. Note that consumers enjoy a surplus equal to the area *EFG* in Figure 11.2 from this firm's output. They enjoy similar amounts of surplus from the output of other firms. If the number of firms were reduced, the surplus enjoyed by the consumers of the products produced by the firms which exited would be lost. Against this, the surplus from the output of the firms that remain, including consumers' and producers' surplus, would go up. So it seems that welfare might go up or down in response to a reduction in the number of firms.

There is also the question of who would decide which firms would leave or be prevented from entering if a control on the number of firms were implemented through a policy of industrial licensing such as India followed for many years and still does to some extent. It is quite possible that a regulatory agency charged with this task would make incorrect choices or, worse, be subject to corruption leading to quite bad choices. The 'license raj' that prevailed in India for many decades was strongly supported by incumbent firms who did not want their privileged position to be threatened. The process of 'excessive entry' in free markets, to the extent that it does happen, is an important part of the process by which the market system discovers the best products to fit the customers' needs most closely, and the best (or most efficient) firms to carry out production of those products. If there is some 'waste' in the system in the form of excess capacity, this may be a small price to pay for the benefits that accrue in the long run. This is a theme to which we will return later in this chapter.

## 11.2 THE COURNOT MODEL

**Task for this section:**

To study the Cournot model of oligopoly in which quantity-setting firms produce homogeneous products and move simultaneously. We see that the model is a generalisation of the perfect competition and monopoly models, which fall out as special cases of the Cournot model.

The Cournot model, first proposed by the French economist A. A. Cournot in the nineteenth century, is a model of an oligopolistic market, which is a market in which there are just a few sellers. This model has been popular among economists because both the model of perfect competition and the monopoly model fall out as special cases of this model. In that sense, it is a more general model that could be used to analyse any kind of market structure. Whether it is realistic as a model of oligopoly, however, is not entirely clear, as we shall see.

### 11.2.1 The Basic Model

The model has the following key distinguishing features:

- Firms in the market produce an undifferentiated, homogenous good. No firm's product can be distinguished from that of any other firm.
- The firms are quantity-setters; that is, they choose their output levels, and the market price is then determined to clear the market of the chosen aggregate output.
- Equilibrium in the market occurs when each firm has chosen an output level that maximises its profit, given the output levels of all the other firms. This is clearly the same equilibrium concept as we saw earlier in Nash equilibrium, and is often called Cournot–Nash equilibrium.

Based on these features, we can characterise the firms' choices and the equilibrium in this kind of oligopolistic market. Suppose there are $n$ firms, and let $q_i$ be the output of the $i$th firm, $\tilde{q}_i = \sum_{j \neq i} q_j$ be the sum of output of all firms other than $i$, $p(q_i + \tilde{q}_i)$ be the market price as a function of total output $Q = q_i + \tilde{q}_1$ and $C_i(q_i)$ be the cost function of the $i$th firm.

Then the $i$th firm's profit is

$$\pi_i = q_i \cdot p(q_i + \tilde{q}_1) - C_i(q_i).$$

To maximise profit, conditional on every other firm's output, the $i$th firm will set

$$\frac{\partial \pi_i}{\partial q_i} = p + q_i \frac{dp}{dQ} - C_i' = 0. \tag{11.3}$$

We can write this as

$$p + p \cdot \frac{q_i}{Q} \cdot \frac{dp}{dQ} \cdot \frac{Q}{p} - C_i' = 0$$

which can be written as

$$p\left(1 + \frac{\theta_i}{\epsilon_d}\right) = MC_i, \tag{11.4}$$

where $\theta_i = q_i/Q$ is the $i$th firm's market share. Since $\theta_i > 0$ and $\epsilon_d < 0$, (11.4) implies that $p > MC_i$; each firm in equilibrium will be producing at an output level short of where $p = MC$. Since there is (11.4) for each firm, there are $n$ such equations, which should in principle be sufficient to solve for the $n$ unknowns $q_1, q_2, \ldots, q_n$.

Equation (11.4) can be used to illustrate how the perfectly competitive and monopoly models fall out as special cases of the Cournot model. For perfect competition, $\theta_i$ would tend to zero, and so (11.4) would reduce to $p = MC$. For monopoly, however, $\theta_i = 1$ and so (11.4) would become

$$p\left(1 + \frac{1}{\epsilon_d}\right) = MC,$$

the standard monopoly equilibrium. The fact that Cournot spans the major models at either end of the market structure spectrum is certainly an attractive feature of the Cournot model.

### 11.2.2 Graphical Exposition of the Duopoly Case

To analyse the Cournot model graphically, we need to focus on the duopoly case, where there are just two firms. Now (11.4) for the first firm becomes

$$p(q_1 + q_2) \cdot \left(1 + \frac{\theta_1}{\epsilon_d}\right) = MC_1, \tag{11.5}$$

where $p$ has been rewritten so as to emphasise the fact that it is a function of total output. Equation (11.5), being firm 1's first-order condition for a profit maximum, implicitly defines $q_1$ as a function of $q_2$; for all possible values of $q_2$, it shows the value of $q_1$ that would maximise firm 1's profits. For this reason, (11.5) is called firm 1's **reaction function** or **best-response function**, since it shows firm 1's optimal reaction or best response to firm 2's output decision.

Since $p(Q)$ is the demand curve, $p'(Q) < 0$ and so the best-response function would also be downward-sloping. Figure 11.3 shows the generic shape of firm 1's best-response function. When $q_2 = 0$, (11.5) would reduce to

$$p(q_1) \cdot \left(1 + \frac{1}{\epsilon_d}\right) = MC_1$$

since $q_2 = 0$ would imply $\theta_1 = 1$. This is nothing but the monopoly level of output for firm 1, labelled $q_1^m$ in Figure 11.3. At the other extreme, the value of $q_2$ for which firm 1's best response would be to set $q_1 = 0$ must satisfy

$$p(q_2) = MC_1$$

since $q_1 = 0$ implies $\theta_1 = 0$. Thus, if $q_2$ were so high as to make $p = MC_1$, which would be the price at firm 1's competitive level of output, firm 1 would not find production profitable and so would set $q_1 = 0$. In Figure 11.3, this value of $q_2$ has been labelled $q_2^c$. It is like firm 2's competitive level of output, but using firm 1's $MC$.

By a similar process of reasoning, we can derive firm 2's best-response function and draw it on the same graph as firm 1's best-response function (see Figure 11.4). In the graph, firm 2's reaction function will be flatter, as its intercept on the vertical axis is $q_2^m < q_2^c$, and on the horizontal axis is $q_1^c > q_1^m$. The point where the two best-response functions intersect, labelled $C$ in the graph, represents the Cournot–Nash equilibrium, since at this point each firm is maximising its profit, conditional on the other firm's output level. Thus, $q_1^*$ and $q_2^*$ are the equilibrium output levels

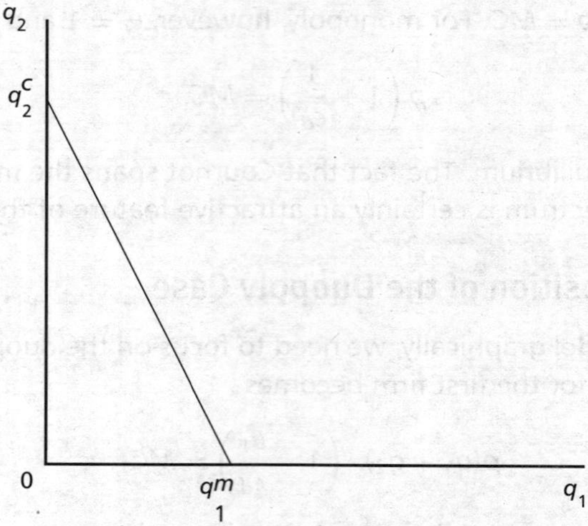


**Figure 11.3** *Firm 1's Best-Response Function*

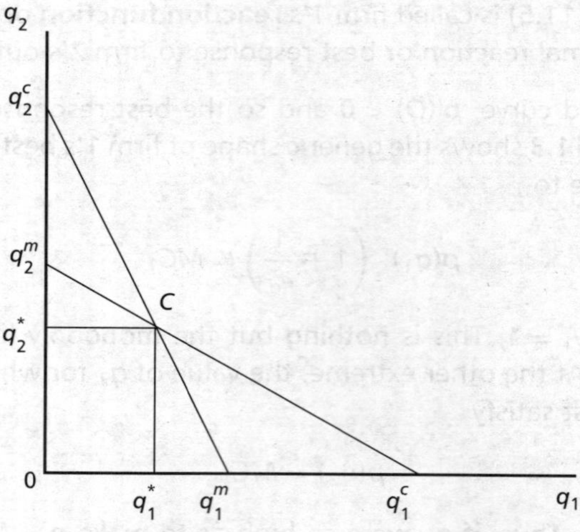


**Figure 11.4** *Cournot Equilibrium Where Best-Response Functions Intersect*

for the two firms. Note that these output levels are smaller than the respective monopoly output levels, but we cannot say much more than that without specifying the model more explicitly.

## 11.2.3 Reaching the Cournot Equilibrium: A Dynamic Process

There is nothing inherent in the model as specified so far that guarantees attainment of equilibrium at *C* or explains how it might be reached. In his original exposition, Cournot offered a simple dynamic process which would lead to the equilibrium. In this process, firm 1 is taken to move first, with $q_2 = 0$, and chooses a value of $q_1$ to maximise profits, assuming that $q_2$ will remain fixed. Firm 2 observes firm 1's output choice and then chooses $q_2$ as its best response to firm 1's choice, assuming firm 1 will keep its output fixed. Firm 1 then reassesses its choice and modifies it in light of what firm 2 has done. Each firm in turn chooses its best response to what the rival did in the previous step, assuming its rival's choice will remain fixed. The process continues back and forth until equilibrium is reached.

To see that this process leads to the Cournot equilibrium, note that firm 1 would start the process by choosing $q_1 = q_1^m$, which is its best response to $q_2 = 0$. Firm 2, looking at $q_1 = q_1^m$, would choose point A in Figure 11.5, which illustrates its best response to $q_1 = q_1^m$. Firm 1 will then choose point *B* and the process will continue until point *C* is reached.

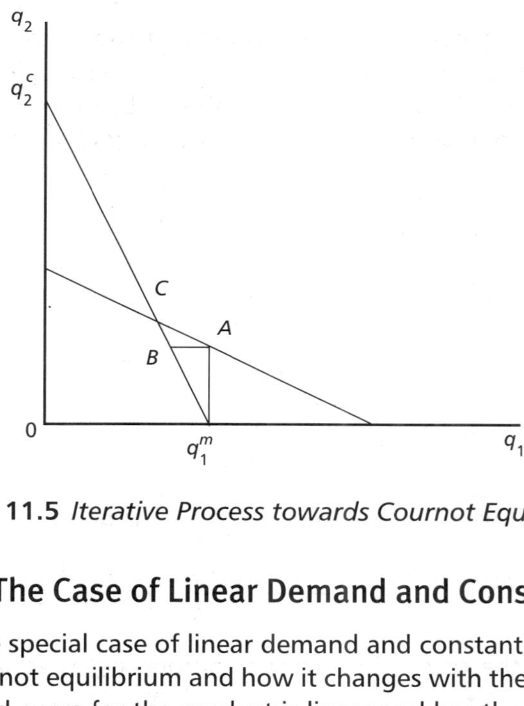


**Figure 11.5** *Iterative Process towards Cournot Equilibrium*

### 11.2.4 An Example: The Case of Linear Demand and Constant Costs

It is useful to consider the special case of linear demand and constant average costs to get a feel for the nature of the Cournot equilibrium and how it changes with the number of firms. Suppose therefore that the demand curve for the product is linear and has the form

$$p(Q) = a - bQ$$

and suppose there are *n* firms, each with constant average costs of production, *c*. If the firms behaved as price-takers, price would equal *MC*, that is $p = c$, and the level of total output, $Q_c$, would satisfy

$$c = a - bQ_c$$

which can be written as

$$Q_c = \frac{a-c}{b}. \tag{11.6}$$

In the Cournot model, the first firm's profit can be written as

$$\pi_1 = q_1 \cdot \{a - b(q_1 + \tilde{q}_1)\} - cq_1,$$

where $\tilde{q}_1$ is the output of all firms other than firm 1. Then the first-order condition for profit maximisation is

$$\frac{\partial \pi_1}{\partial q_1} = a - b(q_1 + \tilde{q}_1) - bq_1 - c = 0. \tag{11.7}$$

Equation (11.7) is firm 1's best-response function, showing the optimal $q_1$ as an implicit function of the sum of output from all other firms, $\tilde{q}_1$. We could write down the best-response functions of the other $(n-1)$ firms and then solve the system of $n$ equations simultaneously in order to find the equilibrium. However, we can take a short cut. Since the problem is symmetric across all the firms, it must be the case that in equilibrium all the firms' outputs will be equal. Therefore, in (11.7),

$$q_1 + \tilde{q}_1 = nq_1.$$

Therefore, (11.7) becomes

$$a - b(n+1)q_1 = c$$

and so

$$q_1 = \frac{a-c}{b(n+1)}. \tag{11.8}$$

Then total output of all $n$ firms, $Q_n$, which is equal to $nq_1$, is given by

$$Q_n = \frac{n}{n+1} \cdot \left(\frac{a-c}{b}\right). \tag{11.9}$$

Recalling from (11.6) that the competitive level of output, $Q_c$, is equal to $(a-c)/b$, (11.8) and (11.9) tell us that

$$q_i = \frac{1}{n+1} \cdot Q_c \quad \text{for all } i \tag{11.10}$$

and

$$Q_n = \frac{n}{n+1} \cdot Q_c. \tag{11.11}$$

Equation (11.11) is particularly useful as an illustration of what the Cournot equilibrium might look like. If $n = 1,\ Q = Q_c/2$, which we know to be the monopoly solution. Then we have

$$n = 2 \rightarrow Q = \frac{2}{3}Q_c$$

$$n = 3 \rightarrow Q = \frac{3}{4}Q_c$$

$$\vdots \quad \vdots \quad \vdots \quad \vdots$$

$$n \rightarrow \infty \rightarrow Q = Q_c.$$

So as the number of firms goes up, the total output in the market keeps rising but at a decreasing rate and, in the limit, goes to the competitive level of output as $n$ becomes very large.

This example also provides some insight into the welfare implications of Cournot equilibrium. Because $p > MC$ in the equilibrium, there is a deadweight loss associated with it, although this deadweight loss is not as great as it is under monopoly. Figure 11.6 illustrates the deadweight loss (the shaded area) under Cournot equilibrium. Since the quantity produced $Q_n$ is smaller than the optimal (or perfectly competitive) output level $Q_c$, the deadweight loss is the lost surplus over these foregone units of production and consumption, $(Q_c - Q_n)$. As the number of firms in the market goes up and the equilibrium level of output moves closer to $Q_c$, the deadweight loss decreases.

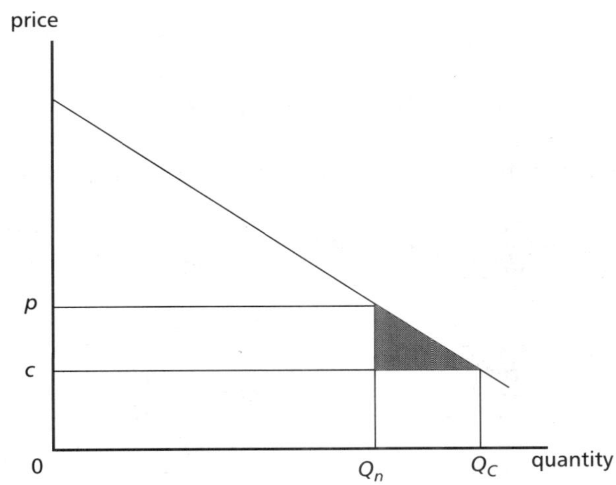


**Figure 11.6** *Welfare Loss in Cournot Equilibrium*

### 11.2.5 Free Entry in Long-Run Cournot Equilibrium

So far we have treated the number of firms in the Cournot model to be fixed, but there is no particular reason why this should be so in the long run. A long-run Cournot equilibrium with free entry (i.e. no sunk costs) would have to have each firm on its best-response function and, in addition, would have a restriction to determine the equilibrium number of firms, $n^e$. This restriction would say that, at the long-run symmetric equilibrium, firms would be making non-negative profits:

$$\pi_i^{n^e} \geqq 0$$

but, if another firm entered, the profit per firm would become negative:

$$\pi_i^{n^e+1} < 0.$$

If we treat $n^e$ as a continuous variable, we could say that the restriction would simply be

$$\pi_i^{n^e} = 0.$$

The question of interest is, will the level of entry be 'excessive' or 'insufficient'? In other words, would welfare be higher if we had fewer or more firms? It turns out that, in general, there is a tendency for there to be too many firms in free entry Cournot equilibrium.

We will measure welfare in the usual way as the sum of consumers' and producers' surplus. We will assume the equilibrium is symmetric, since in the long run, every firm will choose the best available technology. Welfare is then given by

$$W = V(p) + n\pi_i^n$$

which can be written as

$$W = V\left[p(nq)\right] + n\left[pq - C(q)\right].$$

If we differentiate welfare with respect to the number of firms, we obtain

$$\frac{dW}{dn} = -nq\left[q + n\frac{dq}{dn}\right] + \left[pq - C(q)\right] + n\left[p\frac{dq}{dn} + q\left\{q + n\frac{dq}{dn}\right\} - C'\frac{dq}{dn}\right]$$

which simplifies to

$$\frac{dW}{dn} = \left[pq - C(q)\right] + n(p - C')\frac{dq}{dn}.$$

At the free entry equilibrium,

$$\left[pq - C(q)\right] = 0,$$

that is, profit per firm is driven down to zero (remember we are treating $n$ as a continuous variable). Therefore,

$$\frac{dW}{dn}|_{n^e} = n(p - C')\frac{dq}{dn} < 0 \qquad (11.12)$$

since $n(p - C') > 0$ and $\frac{dq}{dn} < 0$. Thus, at the free entry Cournot equilibrium, welfare is declining with the number of firms; the level of entry is excessive. This result is moderated if we treat $n$ as a discrete variable (which we should). In that case, the number of firms under free entry may be optimal or excessive (but never sub optimal) as long as entry has taken place. The only exception to this result is the case where no firm at all may have entered and social welfare maximisation would have required one firm to enter.

We can illustrate the result on excessive entry with a simple numerical example. Consider the case of linear demand where the market demand curve is

$$p(Q) = 105 - Q$$

and suppose

$$C(q) = 25 + 5q,$$

that is, there is a fixed cost of 25 and $MC$ is a constant 5 per unit. We know from the analysis in the previous section that the output under perfect competition would be $Q_c = 100$ and the Cournot output per firm would be

$$q = \frac{100}{n+1}.$$

Total output would be

$$Q_n = \frac{n}{n+1}(100).$$

It is easy to show then that the free entry number of firms would be $n^e = 19$, since then

$$q = 5, \quad Q_n = 95, \quad p = 10$$

and so profit per firm would be

$$\pi = (p - c)q - 25 = 0.$$

Thus, the firms would be just making normal profits with $n = 19$. Welfare would then be given by the consumers' surplus

$$W_{19} = \frac{1}{2} \cdot 95 \cdot 95 = 4,512.5.$$

Now suppose we reduced the number of firms by 1. We want to see if welfare goes up or down, and the result in (11.12) says it should go up if we reduce the number of firms from the free entry equilibrium level. Now, if $n = 18$,

$$q = \frac{100}{19}, \quad Q = \frac{18}{19}(100) = 94.73684 \quad \text{and } p = (105 - Q) = 10.26316.$$

Now profits per firm are

$$\pi = (p - 5)q - 25 = 2.700831$$

and total profits are 18 times, that is, 48.61496. Consumers' surplus is now

$$CS = \frac{1}{2} \cdot (94.73684) \cdot (94.73684) = 4{,}487.535.$$

Total welfare is then the sum of $CS$ and total profits:

$$W_{18} = 4{,}487.535 + 48.61496 = 4{,}536.15.$$

Thus, welfare has gone up by 23.65 as a result of the reduction in the number of firms, as predicted by the result in (11.12).

Despite this result, it is difficult to argue for a policy of licensing to control entry into oligopolistic markets. As we discussed in the previous section on monopolistic competition, there may appear to be 'waste' in a market system in the form of excessive entry, but this is a narrow view of what is actually going on. Much like Nature experiments with various genetic mutations to see which mutations yield the greatest survival probability, the market system encourages experimentation by entrepreneurs to help discover what consumers really want and which products best satisfy people's needs. The vast majority of new firms actually fail within five years of their formation, and this may seem wasteful, but the ones that survive are truly the 'fittest' to serve the needs of customers.

## 11.3 THE STACKELBERG MODEL AND STRATEGIC BEHAVIOUR

**Task for this section:**

To study a modification of the Cournot model in which quantity-setting firms move sequentially. This induces strategic behaviour and confers an advantage to the firm that moves first. We see under what conditions the first mover might engage in limit pricing to deter entry and under what conditions it might accommodate entry.

One criticism that can be and has been levied on the Cournot model is that the firms are assumed to be very myopic. This comes home particularly clearly in the dynamic or iterative version we looked at in section 2.3. If firm 1 knows that firm 2 has the ability to respond to its choice in the first move of the game, why would it not take that into account instead of assuming that firm 2 will not respond and will leave its output at zero? Surely it would make some attempt to anticipate what its rival would do. The Stackelberg model attempts to address this problem. This is primarily a duopoly model and could be thought of as a duopoly version of the price leadership model discussed in the chapter on monopoly. In the Stackelberg model, one firm is assumed to be the leader and behaves strategically, while the other firm is the follower. It can be thought of as a two-stage game in which the leader plays first and the follower plays second.

### 11.3.1 The Best-Response Function Revisited

Before we can analyse the behaviour of firms in the Stackelberg model, we need to look again at the best-response functions we discussed in the course of the Cournot model. In drawing firm 1's best-response function in Figure 11.3, we calculated the end points, argued why it would be downward-sloping and then simply drew a generic line connecting the two end points. That is all we needed to do at the time. But in thinking about the Stackelberg model, we need to understand more clearly how the intervening points on the reaction function are found.

In the duopoly case, firm 1's profits can be written as

$$\pi_1 = q_1 \cdot p(q_1 + q_2) - C_1(q_1). \tag{11.13}$$

Here firm 1's profit is clearly seen as a function of the output levels $q_1$ and $q_2$ of the two firms. If we fix firm 1's profit level at, say, $\bar{\pi}_1$, (11.13) would trace out an iso-profit line, showing different combinations of $q_1$ and $q_2$ that yield the same level of profit for firm 1. Since we can fix $\bar{\pi}_1$ at many different levels, we can trace out a whole family of iso-profit lines. Figure 11.7 shows what this family of iso-profit lines for firm 1 might look like. The firm's profits are highest at the point on the horizontal axis where $q_1 = q_1^m$, which is firm 1's monopoly situation. The iso-profit lines that radiate around that point represent lower and lower profit levels as they move further and further from $q_1^m$. The one that is drawn furthest away in the figure represents a profit level of zero since $q_1 = 0$ at the point where this line meets the vertical axis. Clearly, when $q_1 = 0$, it must be the case that $\pi_1 = 0$.

To illustrate the shape of the iso-profit lines, consider the simple case where demand is linear:

$$p = a - bQ$$

and firms' average costs are constant at $c$. Then

$$\pi_1 = q_1 \cdot \{a - b(q_1 + q_2)\} - cq_1.$$

The typical iso-profit line then has the equation:

$$\bar{\pi}_1 = -bq_1^2 + (a - c)q_1 - bq_1q_2$$

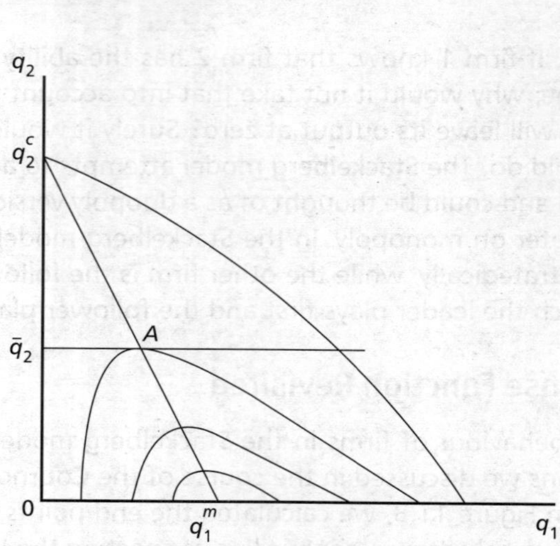


**Figure 11.7** *Iso-profit Lines and Firm 1's Best-Response Function*

which can be written as

$$q_2 = -q_1 + \frac{a-c}{b} - \frac{\bar{\pi}_1}{bq_1}.$$

Then

$$\frac{dq_2}{dq_1} = -1 + \frac{\bar{\pi}_1}{bq_1^2}.$$

Note that

$$\frac{dq_2}{dq_1} \lesseqgtr 0 \leftrightarrow q_1^2 \gtreqless \frac{\bar{\pi}_1}{b},$$

showing that it is upward-sloping for low values of $q_1$ and downward-sloping for high values of $q_1$. Further,

$$\frac{d^2q_2}{dq_1^2} = -\frac{\bar{\pi}_1}{bq_1^3} < 0,$$

showing that the iso-profit lines are concave, as shown in Figure 11.7.

If we choose a specific value of $q_2$, say $\bar{q}_2$, and ask what is firm 1's best response to this, we can answer the question by referring to the iso-profit lines. Clearly, firm 1 wants to choose a value of $q_1$ where its profits are maximised, given that $q_2 = \bar{q}_2$. This occurs at point *A* in the graph, where the horizontal line at $\bar{q}_2$ is tangent to an iso-profit line. All other points along $\bar{q}_2$ lie on iso-profit lines that represent lower profits, so profits must be maximised at *A*. The point *A* must therefore lie on firm 1's best-response function and we immediately see the following: all iso-profit lines must have a slope of zero at the points on the best-response function of firm 1. They must fall downwards towards the horizontal axis on either side of the best-response line.

Firm 2's iso-profit map and best-response function would be similar to those of firm 1, except that they would be oriented towards the vertical axis and radiate around the point where $q_1 = 0$ and $q_2 = q_2^m$. Figure 11.8 illustrates firm 2's iso-profit map.

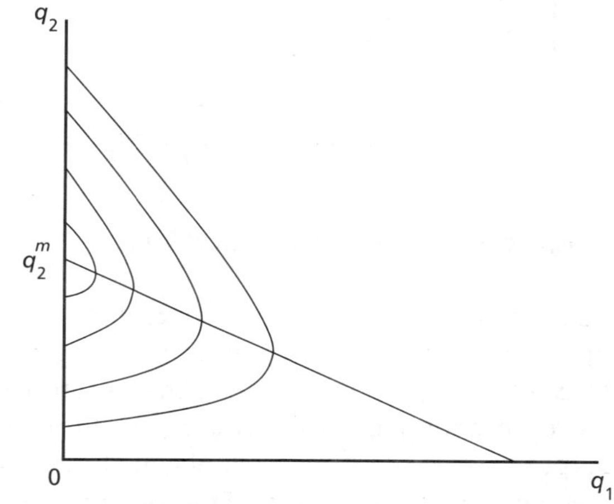


**Figure 11.8** *Firm 2's Iso-profit Lines and Best-Response Function*

## 11.3.2 The Stackelberg Model

We are now in a position to analyse the Stackelberg model. The model has the following key features:

- Firms produce a homogeneous, undifferentiated product, as in the Cournot model.
- Firms are quantity-setters; they choose the quantities of output to produce and then price is determined to clear the market.
- The game is played in two stages. One firm, the Stackelberg leader, moves first and plays the game strategically, by choosing an output level that maximises its profits given the best-response function of its rival. The other firm, the follower, plays passively in the second stage and simply chooses its best response to the output decision of the first firm.

Consider now the decision of the leader. Since it moves first, and knows that firm 2 will respond according to its best-response function, it will want to choose that point on firm 2's best-response function where its (firm 1's) profits are maximised. Since we now have firm 1's iso-profit map, we can see what its choice will be. Figure 11.9 plots the best-response functions of both firms.

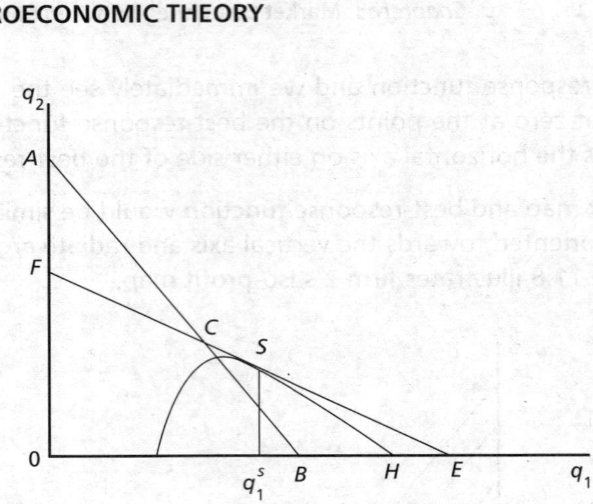


**Figure 11.9** *Stackelberg Equilibrium*

*AB* is firm 1's and *FE* is firm 2's best-response line. *C* represents the Cournot equilibrium. Now, if firm 1 plays as the Stackelberg leader, it will want to choose that point on *FE* where its profits are maximised. This will be at point *S*, where one of its iso-profit lines is tangent to *FE*. All other points on *FE* will lie on iso-profit lines representing lower levels of $\pi_1$, so firm 1's profits are maximised at *S*. It will therefore set its output level at $q_1^s$. Firm 2 will play its best response to $q_1^s$ and so we will have a subgame perfect equilibrium at *S*. This is the Stackelberg equilibrium.

Note that firm 1 is not on its best-response line at *S*. This is the sense in which it is playing the game strategically. While it is not maximising its profits conditional on firm 2's output decision (this is what it does on its best-response line), it is doing better, since it is taking into account firm 2's response to its decision. Therefore, it is maximising its profits conditional not on firm 2's current decision but on its best response. If firm 1 played its best response, and firm 2 reciprocated, the two firms would end up at *C*, the Cournot equilibrium. But firm 1 is on a higher iso-profit line at *S* than it would be on at *C*. Firm 2, however, has lower profits at *S* than it would have at *C* (try drawing its iso-profit lines through these two points to see this). Thus, firm 1 has a clear first-mover advantage in the Stackelberg model.

[Exercise: What would happen if firm 2 is the leader and firm 1 is the follower? What would be the outcome if both firms tried to play the leader's strategy?]

We could solve explicitly for the Stackelberg equilibrium if we specified the functions and parameters of the model. For example, suppose demand is linear:

$$p = a - bQ$$

and the firms have constant marginal costs $c_1$ and $c_2$. Since this is a two-stage game, we solve by backward induction, and so we solve firm 2's problem first. Firm 2's profit is

$$\pi_2 = q_2 \cdot \{a - b(q_1 + q_2)\} - c_2 q_2.$$

To maximise profits, firm 2's first-order condition is

$$\frac{\partial \pi_2}{\partial q_2} = a - b(q_1 + q_2) - bq_2 - c_2 = 0.$$

This can be simplified to

$$q_2 = \frac{a - c_2 - bq_1}{2b}. \tag{11.14}$$

Equation (11.14) is firm 2's best-response function, showing its optimal output as a function of firm 1's output.

Firm 1's profits are

$$\pi_1 = q_1 \cdot \{a - b(q_1 + q_2)\} - c_1 q_1. \tag{11.15}$$

The firm wants to maximise this, subject to (11.14) as a constraint. We can incorporate (11.14) into (11.15) by substitution:

$$\pi_1 = q_1 \cdot \left\{a - b\left(q_1 + \frac{a - c_2 - bq_1}{2b}\right)\right\} - c_1 q_1$$

which can be written as

$$\pi_1 = q_1 \cdot \left\{\frac{a}{2} - \frac{bq_1}{2} + \frac{c_2}{2}\right\} - c_1 q_1.$$

The first-order condition for a maximum is

$$\frac{d\pi_1}{dq_1} = \frac{a}{2} - \frac{bq_1}{2} + \frac{c_2}{2} - \frac{bq_1}{2} - c_1 = 0$$

which yields the solution

$$q_1^s = \frac{a + c_2 - 2c_1}{2b} \tag{11.16}$$

This is firm 1's output level in the Stackelberg equilibrium. If $c_1 = c_2 = c$, (11.16) reduces to

$$q_1^s = \frac{a - c}{2b} = q_1^m,$$

which is the monopoly output level for firm 1. So in this special case, the leader produces the monopoly output level in the Stackelberg equilibrium. But if $c_1 < c_2$,

$$q_1^s > q_1^m,$$

and the opposite is true if $c_1 > c_2$. This is the situation that has been illustrated in Figure 11.9, which shows that being able to move first in this model can yield higher profits even though firm

1 has higher costs. Finally, note that substituting (11.16) in (11.14) would yield firm 2's output level in the Stackelberg equilibrium:

$$q_2^s = \frac{a + 2c_1 - 3c_2}{4b}.$$

### 11.3.3 Entry Deterrence in the Stackelberg Model

In deriving the Stackelberg equilibrium in the previous section, we have taken as given that firm 2 will enter the market and play according to its best-response function. But what if firm 1 could engage in a further level of strategic play and deter firm 2's entry by making it unprofitable? Just as we saw in the chapter on monopoly that a monopoly firm might engage in limit pricing in order to deter entry, the Stackelberg leader may be able to do the same thing. In fact, the two situations are identical, the only difference being that here we are calling the market a duopoly even though firm 2 may not yet have entered although may be contemplating doing so. We would like to understand under what circumstances the Stackelberg leader can and would want to deter entry, and what the equilibrium would look like.

The first observation that needs to be made here is that, for entry deterrence to be possible, firm 2 would have to have a positive entry cost, a sunk cost that it cannot recover by exiting the market. If the annualised value of this sunk cost is *F*, then firm 2's annual profits in the Stackelberg equilibrium must be higher than *F* if it is to find entry profitable. If its profits are *F* or lower, it would choose not to enter.

Let us assume that firm 2's profits at *S* in Figure 11.9 (the Stackelberg equilibrium) are higher than *F*, so it would enter in this situation. If its profits at *S* had been lower than *F*, it would not have entered the market and then firm 1 would not need to do anything different to deter entry: entry would have been deterred automatically by its playing of the Stackelberg strategy. Note that, since firm 2's profits are lower at the Stackelberg equilibrium than at the Cournot equilibrium, it is possible that it would have entered if the game were Cournot rather than Stackelberg. In any case, we wish to focus here on the case where firm 2 would want to enter under the Stackelberg equilibrium, which requires its profit at *S* to be higher than *F*. What does firm 1 now have to do to deter entry?

Consider Figure 11.10. In this figure, we have drawn firm 2's best-response function, and superimposed on this firm 2's iso-profit line representing the profit level *F*. If firm 1 wants to deter firm 2's entry, it must set its output level equal to *OD*. Why? Because if $q_1 = OD$, firm 2's best response would be at point *G* (i.e. the point on its best-response function corresponding to $q_1 = OD$), and so its profits would be equal to *F*. Thus, entry would not be profitable for it and its entry would be deterred.

What would firm 1's profits be if it deterred entry? Since $q_1 = OD$ and $q_2 = 0$ (since firm 2's entry has been deterred), *D* must be the equilibrium point under entry deterrence. In that case, firm 1's profits would be given by its iso-profit line through point *D*. However, if it did not deter

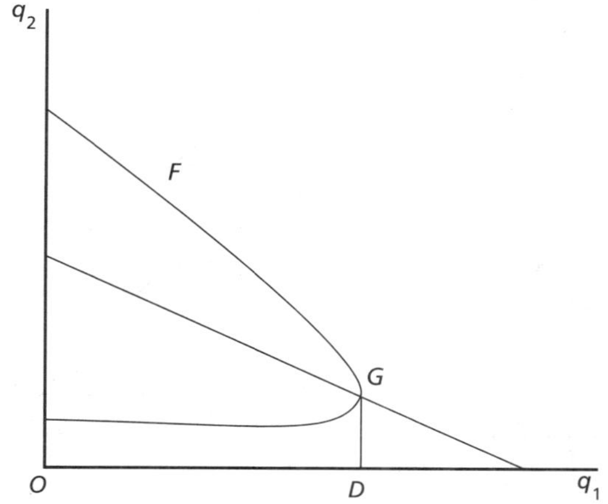


**Figure 11.10** *Entry-Deterring Output Level for Firm 1*

entry and played instead its Stackelberg strategy, equilibrium would be at the Stackelberg point *S* in Figure 11.9 and firm 1's profits would be given by its iso-profit line through *S*. If that iso-profit line meets the horizontal axis at *H* in Figure 11.9, we have a simple rule for entry deterrence: firm 1 should deter entry if point *D* in Figure 11.10 is to the left of point *H* in Figure 11.9 (since then *D* would be on a higher iso-profit line) and it should accommodate entry and choose the Stackelberg equilibrium if *H* is to the left of *D*. Figure 11.11 makes the comparison easy by putting both points on the same graph and illustrates the two possibilities. Panel (a) of the figure shows a situation where firm 1 would want to deter entry (since *H* and *S* are on a lower iso-profit line than *D*) and panel (b) shows a situation where it would accommodate entry (since now *D* represents lower profits). Note that, although the difference between the two situations in the graph has been drawn by changing the shape of firm 1's iso-profit line through *S*, this is not the only factor that could cause a difference; notably, if the sunk cost of entry *F* for firm 2 were lower, *G* and *D* would get pushed to the right and a situation like panel (b) could emerge.

There are a couple of things worth noting about the equilibria we have just discussed. First, note that entry deterrence is the chosen strategy when the entry cost *F* for firm 2 is sufficiently high. If *F* were sufficiently low, as in panel (b) of Figure 11.11, the level of output *OD* required for firm 1 to deter entry is so high as to cause profits to fall. In this case, firm 1 would choose to 'play soft' and accommodate entry. The notions of 'playing tough' and 'playing soft' are the second thing worth noting. Compared to the Cournot equilibrium, the Stackelberg equilibrium involves firm 1 'playing tough' by aggressively expanding its output to the level at *S* in order to force firm 2 to keep its output low. If *F* is high enough (as in panel (a) of Figure 11.11), firm 1 would play even tougher by expanding its output all the way to *OD* in order to deter firm 2's entry. But if *F* is low, firm 1 would 'play soft', not expanding its output beyond what it chose for the Stackelberg equilibrium. We will return to this theme later in the chapter.

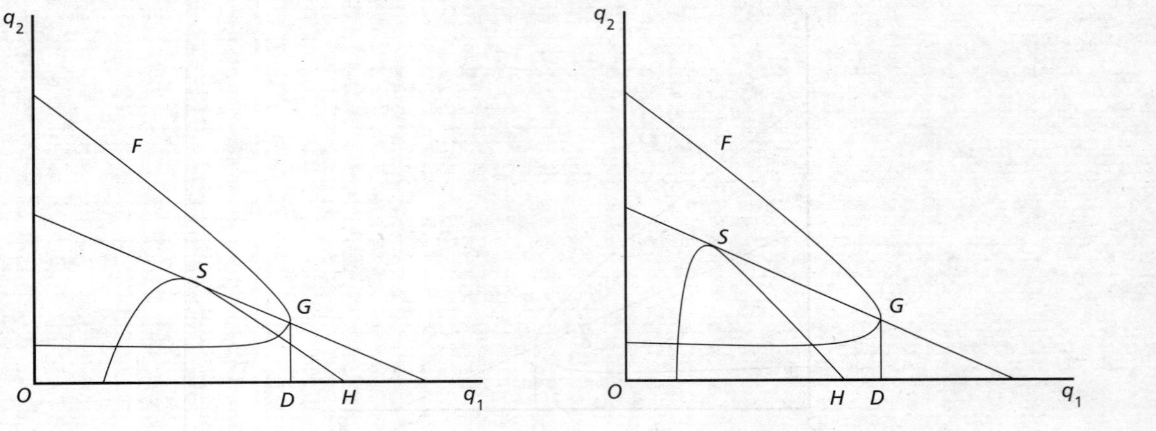


**Figure 11.11** *When to Deter and When to Accommodate Entry*

## 11.4 PRICE COMPETITION

**Task for this section:**

To study the nature of oligopolistic competition when firms producing homogeneous products set prices rather than quantities. We see under what conditions such firms behave just as quantity-setting firms would and under what conditions their behaviour would be quite different. In particular, we modify the model to allow firms to produce differentiated products (as in monopolistic competition) and study how this alters their competitive behaviour. A further modification allows firms to move sequentially. This induces strategic behaviour and, surprisingly, confers a disadvantage to the firm that moves first.

In the models discussed so far in this chapter, firms are assumed to choose quantities and prices then emerge in the market in order to ensure market clearing. But what if we assume that firms choose prices instead and then produce enough to satisfy the demand they face at the price they announced? In the monopoly model, this would make no difference, as can be shown quite readily. Normally, for the quantity-setting monopolist, we write profit as

$$\pi(q) = q \cdot p(q) - C(q)$$

and the first-order condition for a profit maximum is

$$\frac{d\pi}{dq} = p + q \cdot \frac{dp}{dq} - C'(q) = 0. \qquad (11.17)$$

If, instead, we assumed that the monopolist is a price-setter, we would take profit to be

$$\pi(p) = p \cdot q(p) - C\{q(p)\}$$

and the first-order condition for a profit maximum would be

$$\frac{d\pi}{dp} = q + p \cdot \frac{dq}{dp} - C'(q) \cdot \frac{dq}{dp} = 0,$$

which can be written as

$$\left[q \cdot \frac{dp}{dq} + p - C'(q)\right] \cdot \frac{dq}{dp} = 0. \tag{11.18}$$

Clearly, (11.18) yields the same solution as (11.17), so a price-setting monopolist ends up in the same equilibrium as a quantity-setting monopolist. But what about a price-setting oligopolist? This is the question taken up in the Bertrand model.

### 11.4.1 The Bertrand Model

This model, proposed originally by the French economist Joseph Bertrand in the late nineteenth century, analyses the behaviour of an oligopoly where firms set prices. It has the following key features:

- Firms produce a homogeneous, undifferentiated good.
- Firms set prices and then produce whatever quantity the market demands at the prices they have set.
- The firm with the lowest price always takes the entire market; any firm with a price higher than the lowest faces zero demand.
- If two or more firms have the lowest price, they share the market demand at that price equally.
- All firms have constant average and marginal costs.

Under these assumptions, the Bertrand model yields a startling result: if there are even two firms in the market, the Nash equilibrium will involve both firms setting $p = MC$, where the $MC$ in question is the marginal cost of the second-most efficient firm. If all firms have the same cost, which would be the natural assumption in the long run, all firms would set $p = MC$ and would share the market equally. If there is one firm whose $MC$ is lower than that of all other firms, that firm would get the entire market, with price equal to the second-lowest $MC$. Upon reflection, the result is perhaps not that startling, as we have seen it before in the context of contestable markets. Implicit in the assumptions underlying the model are that 'entry' into an otherwise monopolised market is free and instantaneous, thereby making the Bertrand model the same as a perfectly contestable market.

The model is best understood as a duopoly. Suppose there are two price-setting firms whose average costs are constant at $c_1$ and $c_2$, respectively. For convenience of discussion, let $c_1 < c_2$. Then the equilibrium will clearly occur where firm 1 announces a price of $c_2 - \epsilon$, where $\epsilon$ is arbitrarily small (which is why we just say price is equal to $c_2$), and takes the whole market. Firm 2 is unable to compete.

If, however, $c_1 = c_2 = c$, both firms can co exist in the market. Now the only equilibrium is where $p_1 = p_2 = c$ and the two firms share the market equally. Proving that this is the only equilibrium takes two steps:

**Step 1:** Observe that the equilibrium must involve $p_1 = p_2$. Suppose it did not, but instead involved $p_1 > p_2$. Then firm 2 could raise its profits by raising $p_2$ to $(p_1 - \epsilon)$, since this would give it more revenue without costing it any sales. Equally, firm 1, which has no profits in the trial equilibrium since it would have zero sales, could raise its profits by reducing $p_1$ to $p_2$. Thus, each firm would have an incentive to move its price towards the other's price; the trial equilibrium with $p_1 > p_2$ is not an equilibrium. A similar argument can be constructed if we start with a trial equilibrium where $p_1 < p_2$.

**Step 2:** Given that $p_1 = p_2$ in the equilibrium, we need to show that they must equal $c$. Suppose $p_1 = p_2 < c$. Then each firm would be making a loss and could reduce that loss to zero by raising its price. Therefore, this could not be an equilibrium. Alternatively, suppose $p_1 = p_2 > c$. Then each firm could raise its profit, conditional on the other firm's price, by lowering its price by $\epsilon$. In this way, it could corner the entire market (rather than getting just half of it) and its price would still be above $c$ so it would be making positive profits. Therefore, $p_1 = p_2 > c$ could not be an equilibrium either. The only equilibrium therefore is where $p_1 = p_2 = c$. Here, each firm is breaking even and neither firm has any incentive to change its price.

The model can clearly be extended to $n$ firms without any difficulty. If all firms have the same costs, they would all set price equal to that common marginal cost and share the market equally. If costs differ, only the firm or firms with the lowest $MC$ would operate. If there is more than one firm with the lowest cost, price would equal that lowest cost and the market would be shared between the low-cost producers. If there is only one firm with the lowest cost, it would be the sole producer and price would be $\epsilon$ below the second-lowest-cost firm's marginal cost.

### 11.4.2 Capacity Constraints in the Bertrand Model

One particularly strong assumption in the Bertrand model is that firms have the capacity to produce a quantity sufficient to satisfy the entire market demand at whatever price they might announce. An important part of the equilibrium argument involves the assertion that a firm could possibly undercut its rival's price and thereby expand its sales to the entire market. But building productive capacity is expensive, and since the final equilibrium typically involves firms sharing the market, each firm in this scenario would have a lot of idle capacity on its hands. This is unlikely to be something firms would actually tolerate. To properly understand the likely equilibrium, we need a more explicit treatment of the capacity decision.

Specifically, suppose the Bertrand game is played in two stages. At the first stage, firms make a decision on their capacity, which then remains fixed through stage two. In the second stage, firms engage in Bertrand competition. Since building capacity is time-consuming, this separation of a prior capacity decision from a later pricing decision seems reasonable. Somewhat surprisingly, it turns out that in this case the equilibrium will be the Cournot equilibrium.

To see why this is so, we solve the game using backward induction as before. Suppose there are two firms and they choose their capacities $\bar{q}_1$ and $\bar{q}_2$, respectively, in stage 1 of the game. What will be the equilibrium in stage 2? As before the argument proceeds in two steps:

**Step 1:** Observe that the equilibrium must involve $p_1 = p_2$, since, if the prices were different, each firm would have an incentive to move its price towards the other's price.

**Step 2:** Given that the prices are equal, the question is, at what level will they settle? The answer is that the prices will be such that the firms produce at full capacity, that is, $p_1 = p_2 = \bar{p}$, where $\bar{p}$ is the price at which demand is $(\bar{q}_1 + \bar{q}_2)$, as shown in Figure 11.12. Let us see why no other price could be an equilibrium. Consider a candidate price below $\bar{p}$. Now both firms will be producing at full capacity and there will be excess demand, so for each firm raising price to $\bar{p}$ would not cause any loss in sales while raising revenue. Therefore, each firm would want to raise its price. Now consider a candidate price above $\bar{p}$. In this case, firms would be sharing the market and each firm would have excess capacity. This could not be an equilibrium either, as each firm would have an incentive to lower its price slightly and expand their sales to full capacity. Therefore, the

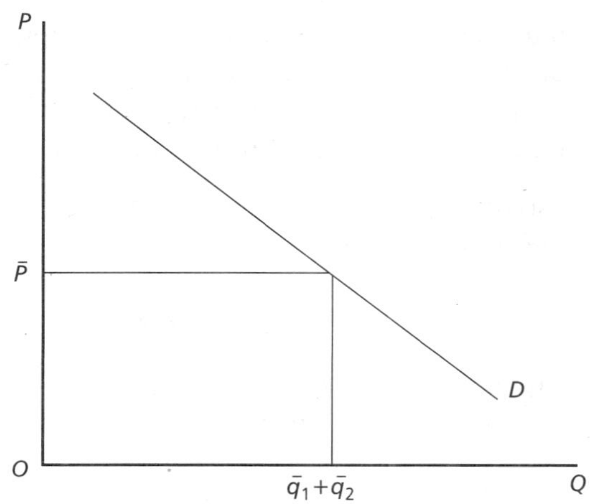


**Figure 11.12** *Bertrand Equilibrium with Capacity Constraints*

only equilibrium in the second stage of the game would be the one where $p_1 = p_2 = \bar{p}$ and each firm is producing at full capacity.

Now let us consider the first stage of the game and ask what capacity each firm would choose, given that, in the second stage of the game, they would produce at full capacity and set a price just sufficient to clear the market. It is easy to see that this game is identical to the single-stage Cournot game, and therefore the equilibrium is nothing but the Cournot–Nash equilibrium. Thus, the Cournot model can be seen as a short hand way of modelling this two-stage Bertrand game with capacity pre-commitment in the first stage.

### 11.4.3 Bertrand Competition with Increasing Marginal Cost

Another serious assumption and shortcoming of the Bertrand model is that each firm's average and marginal costs are constant. A natural extension is to ask what the model would say in situations where average and marginal costs are increasing. It turns out that, in this case, equilibrium may not always exist, partly because of difficulties with deciding what happens when demand at a particular price exceeds the quantity that a firm would ideally want to sell at that price. Further, if the equilibrium exists, it may not be unique. We can illustrate these issues with a simple numerical example.[1]

Suppose there are two firms in the market. Demand is linear and is given by the function

$$Q = 10 - p$$

and each firm's costs are given by

$$C_i(q_i) = \frac{1}{2}q_i^2$$

so that $MC_i = q_i$. Suppose that, if, say, $p_1 < p_2$, firm 1 must supply the entire demand at $p_1$, regardless of its marginal cost. Of course, in this situation, firm 2 would be selling nothing, since its price is higher than firm 1's. Then it can be shown that, in equilibrium, $p_1 = p_2 = p^*$, where $p^*$ is any price between 2 and 4.285. Thus, the equilibrium is not unique.

For example, consider the solution $p_1 = p_2 = 4$. In that case, $Q = 6$ and each firm's output is $q = 3$. Then the profit of each firm would be

$$\pi = (4 \times 3) - \frac{1}{2} \cdot 9 = 7.5.$$

Neither firm would want to raise its price, since it would lose all sales and profit would go to zero. But might one firm, say firm 1, want to reduce its price to, say, 3.99 in order to try to corner the

[1] Example taken from K. G. Dastidar: 'On the existence of pure strategy Bertrand equilibrium,' *Economic Theory*, 5, 1995, pp. 19–32.

entire market? If firm 1 did that, $q_2$ would fall to zero, while $q_1 = Q = 6.01$, and firm 1's profit would be

$$\pi_1 = (3.99) \cdot (6.01) - \frac{1}{2} \cdot (6.01)^2 = 5.92.$$

Thus, despite the big increase in sales, firm 1's profit actually falls, and so it would not want to deviate from the original price $p_1 = 4$. Thus, $p_1 = p_2 = 4$ is an equilibrium.

Similarly, we can show that $p_1 = p_2 = 3$ is also an equilibrium where each firm's profit is $\pi = 4.375$. Neither firm would want to deviate from this position. Raising price above 3 would cause sales and profits to go to zero and lowering price to, say, 2.99 would raise sales to 7.01 but cause profits to turn negative. Thus, neither firm has an incentive to change its price from 3.

In this way, all prices that yield the firms a non-negative profit would be equilibrium prices. In this particular example, it turns out that all prices between 2 and 4.285 satisfy this property and so all these prices can serve as equilibrium prices. The non-uniqueness of the price equilibrium of course makes the model much less appealing.

What is driving the existence of these equilibria is the requirement that each firm must supply the entire amount demanded at the price it announces. In the case where firm 1 reduced its price from the equilibrium price of 4 to the trial price of 3.99, it was forced by this assumption to produce and sell 6.01 units, even though the *MC* of all units above 3.99 was higher than the price of 3.99. If the firm could choose not to supply the entire demand, the equilibrium would unravel and no equilibrium would exist.

### 11.4.4 Bertrand Competition with Differentiated Products

Part of the reason why the Bertrand model seems to have problems is the sharp discontinuity caused by the fact that even a tiny difference in the prices of the firms leads to a radical difference in their market shares. The model assumes that if the firms' prices are equal, they share the market equally, but if one price is even $\epsilon$ lower than the other, the firm with the lower price gets the entire market and the other firm sells nothing at all. This is the logical consequence of the assumption that the products of the two firms are homogeneous. Why would anyone pay even $\epsilon$ more if the products of the two firms are indistinguishable? The way out of this dilemma is to abandon the assumption of homogeneous goods and instead allow the firms' products to be differentiated. In this case, small price changes would not lead to dramatic changes in market shares. This not only allows the model to be more tractable but is also more realistic for oligopolistic markets, where product differentiation is a key aspect of competitive behaviour.

We will focus on the duopoly case for simplicity and to permit graphical analysis. Suppose there are two firms producing differentiated products that are nevertheless close substitutes and therefore constitute a reasonable 'market'. Each firm faces a demand function which shows quantity demanded for that firm's product as a function of both firms' prices:

$$q_i = q_i(p_i, p_j), \qquad \text{with} \quad \frac{\partial q_i}{\partial p_i} < 0, \quad \frac{\partial q_i}{\partial p_j} > 0.$$

Since the goods are substitutes, the cross-partial derivatives $\frac{\partial q_i}{\partial p_j}$ are positive: if firm 2 raises its price, the demand for firm 1's product goes up.

In choosing its price, each firm will attempt to maximise its profit. Firm 1's profits are given by

$$\pi_1 = p_1 \cdot q_1(p_1, p_2) - c_1 q_1.$$

Then the first-order condition for a profit maximum would be

$$\frac{\partial \pi_1}{\partial p_1} = q_1 + p_1 \cdot \frac{\partial q_1}{\partial p_1}(p_1, p_2) - c_1 \cdot \frac{\partial q_1}{\partial p_1}(p_1, p_2) = 0. \tag{11.19}$$

Equation (11.19) describes firm 1's optimal price as an implicit function of firm 2's price, $p_2$. It is therefore a **best-response function**, much like we saw in our analysis of the Cournot model. To study the shape of this function, we use the implicit function theorem to find the derivative $\frac{dp_2}{dp_1}$ along this function:

$$\frac{dp_2}{dp_1} = -\frac{\partial^2 \pi_1 / \partial p_1^2}{\partial^2 \pi_1 / \partial p_1 \partial p_2}$$

which is

$$\frac{dp_2}{dp_1} = -\frac{\frac{\partial q_1}{\partial p_1} + \frac{\partial q_1}{\partial p_1} + (p_1 - c_1) \cdot \frac{\partial^2 q_1}{\partial p_1^2}}{\frac{\partial q_1}{\partial p_2} + (p_1 - c_1) \cdot \frac{\partial^2 q_1}{\partial p_1 \partial p_2}}.$$

If we take a first-order approximation to the demand function, so that we can ignore its second-order partial derivatives, this reduces to

$$\frac{dp_2}{dp_1} \approx -\frac{2\frac{\partial q_1}{\partial p_1}}{\frac{\partial q_1}{\partial p_2}} > 0. \tag{11.20}$$

Thus, firm 1's best-response function will be upward-sloping and it is so drawn in Figure 11.13, which plots $p_2$ on the vertical axis and $p_1$ on the horizontal axis. The best-response function is labelled $BR_1$. Also drawn on the graph are a few of firm 1's iso-profit lines, which show combinations of $p_1$ and $p_2$ that yield the same level of profit $\pi_1$ for firm 1. Here profits rise as we move to iso-profit lines that are higher in the graph, that is, $\pi_1^2 > \pi_1^1 > \pi_1^0$. The point $p_1^0$ on the horizontal axis represents firm 1's best response to $p_2 = 0$. If $p_2 = 0$, clearly firm 1's demand curve will be at its lowest possible level since its rival's price is so low. Figure 11.14 shows its choice, which is simply the 'monopoly' price given that its demand curve is $q_1(p_1, 0)$, that is, at the level where

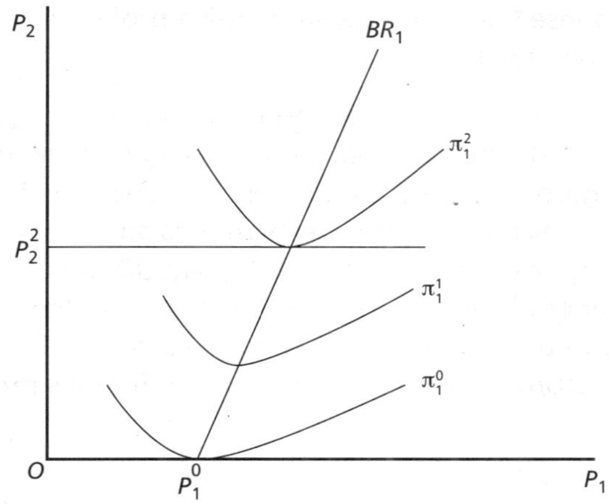


**Figure 11.13** *Firm 1's Best-Response Function*

$p_2 = 0$. As $p_2$ rises, firm 1's demand curve shifts to the right and it is able to charge higher prices. These higher best-response prices as $p_2$ rises are what are represented in the best-response line in Figure 11.13. As $p_2$ becomes very high, firm 1's demand curve shifts far to the right and it is able to charge very high prices and make large profits; this is what would happen as we move up the best-response line $BR_1$.

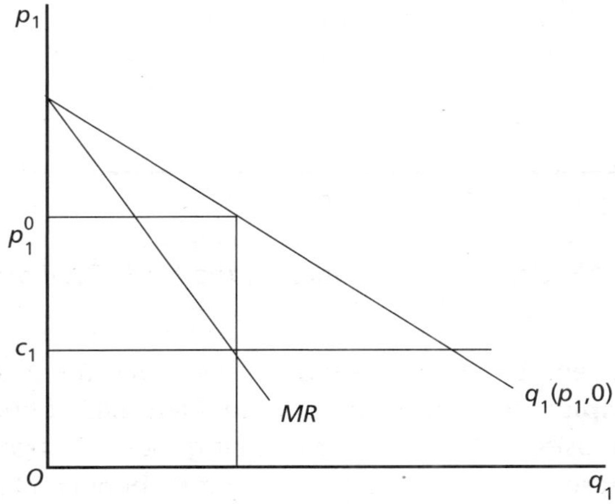


**Figure 11.14** *Optimal Price for Firm 1 if $p_2 = 0$*

As in the case of the best-response functions for the quantity-setting Cournot competitors, the iso-profit lines in Figure 11.13 will have the property that they will reach turning points (in this case, minimum points) along the best-response line. Then, for any given value of $p_2$, say $p_2^2$, the point on firm 1's best-response line will be where an iso-profit line has a slope of zero (and is tangent to the horizontal line at $p_2^2$).

In like manner, we can derive firm 2's best-response function, $BR_2$, and plot it on the same graph as $BR_1$ (see Figure 11.15). The Nash equilibrium will be at the intersection of the two *BR* lines, which is at *B* in the figure. What is most interesting about this Nash equilibrium is that the two prices move together. For example, if firm 2 experiences an increase in demand for its product for some reason, its best-response line will shift up to, say, $BR_2'$ and the Nash equilibrium would now be at *B*′. Here, *both* prices have gone up. The increase in demand allowed firm 2 to raise its prices, and the increase in $p_2$ allowed firm 1 to raise *its* prices. Thus, both prices move up in equilibrium; firm 1 benefits from the increased demand for firm 2's product.

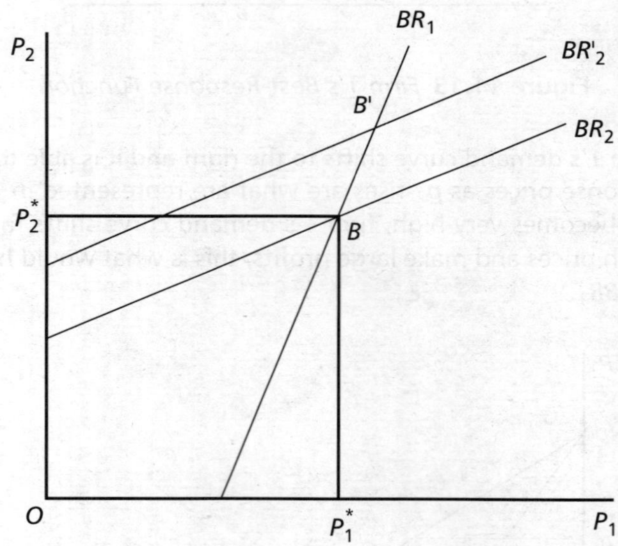


**Figure 11.15** *Comparative Statics on the Nash Equilibrium*

Because equilibrium prices tend to move in tandem, we say that the products of firms 1 and 2 in this case are **strategic complements.** In contrast, since quantities of two competing firms in a Cournot duopoly move in opposite directions, we say their goods are **strategic substitutes.** This distinction plays an important role in the nature of competition between firms when they engage in strategic behaviour.

### 11.4.5 Strategic Behaviour in the Bertrand Model

In the previous section, we analysed the Bertrand model with differentiated products, and examined the Nash equilibrium of this game. The Nash equilibrium of the Bertrand game, such as the Cournot–Nash equilibrium of the Cournot game, implies rather passive or myopic behaviour on the part of the firms, since in each case they are optimising on the assumption that their rival will not respond to any changes in their choice. One way to justify this approach is to assume the game the firms are playing is a simultaneous-move game. What if the firms move sequentially?

The two-stage version of the Cournot game yielded the Stackelberg model. In that model, one firm got to move first and therefore behaved more strategically by taking into account what its rival's best responses would be to its choices in the first stage of the game. We can similarly look at the Bertrand game and ask what would be the outcome in a two-stage version of the game in which, say, firm 1 got to move first.

Figure 11.16 illustrates the outcome. If firm 1 gets to move first, it will want to pick a point on firm 2's best-response function, $BR_2$, where its profits are maximised. This happens at point *A* in the figure, where an iso-profit line of firm 1 is tangent to $BR_2$. Since $BR_2$ is upward-sloping, this tangency must be to the right of $BR_1$, since the iso-profit lines are downward-sloping to the left of $BR_1$. Thus, the tangency is to the right of *B*, the original single-stage Bertrand equilibrium. Clearly, firm 1's profits are higher at *A* than at *B* since the iso-profit line through *A* lies above *B*.

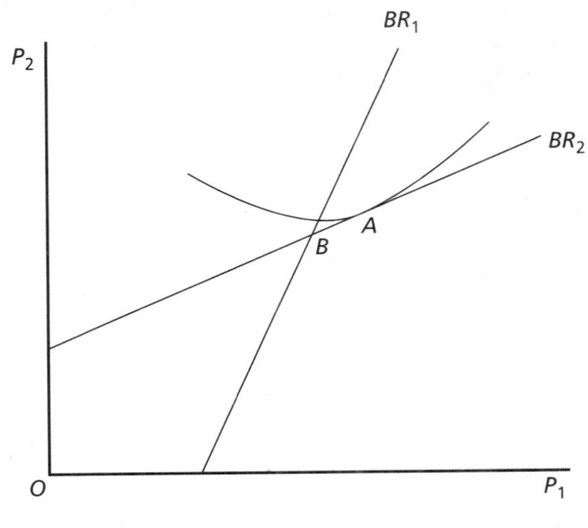


**Figure 11.16** *Firm 1's Optimum in the Two-Stage Bertrand Game*

An interesting aspect of this new equilibrium at *A* is that, while expectedly firm 1's profits have risen since it is now behaving strategically, firm 2's profits have also risen! Clearly, firm 2's profits have risen since its iso-profit line through *A* has a turning point at *A* and is therefore 'above' (i.e. to the right, in the graph) the iso-profit line through *B*. In sharp contrast to the Stackelberg model, where strategic behaviour by the first mover led to increased profits for the leader but reduced profits for the follower, strategic behaviour in the Bertrand model leads to increased profits for both firms. This result is a consequence of the fact that, under Bertrand price competition, the goods produced by the two firms are strategic complements, and this leads the first mover to 'play soft'. In the Stackelberg model, the goods produced by the two firms are strategic substitutes; in fact, they are perfect substitutes since they are indistinguishable from one another, and this led the first mover to 'play tough' as it adopted a more aggressive competitive posture and set quantity high.

Even more surprising than the fact that the follower's profits go up is the fact that the follower's profits go up by more than those of the first mover! Suppose the problem is perfectly symmetric in that the demand and cost functions of both firms are identical. Then the Bertrand equilibrium $B$ would lie on the 45° line (see Figure 11.17), with $p_1 = p_2$ and $\pi_1 = \pi_2$. Consider point $A$, the new strategic equilibrium in the two-stage Bertrand game. Suppose the profits of the two firms at $A$ are denoted $\pi_1^A$ and $\pi_2^A$. Now consider the point $A'$, which is the mirror image on $BR_1$ across the 45° line from $A$ on $BR_2$. Clearly, $\pi_1^{A'} = \pi_2^A$ and $\pi_2^{A'} = \pi_1^A$; since the two firms would have just swapped prices at $A'$ compared to $A$, they must have just swapped profits as well. Clearly, firm 1's profits are higher at $A'$ than they are at $A$, since $A'$ must lie on a higher iso-profit line. We can be sure this is true because $BR_2$ is flatter than the 45° line and therefore $p_1^A > p_2^A$. Thus, moving along $BR_1$, $A'$ must be above $A$ and $A$ itself is already above the point $C$ where the iso-profit line through $A$ crosses the 45°.line. Therefore, firm 1's profits are higher at $A'$ than they are at $A$, which means firm 2's profits are higher at $A$ than those of firm 1. The follower has benefited more from the strategic behaviour of firm 1 than firm 1 itself.

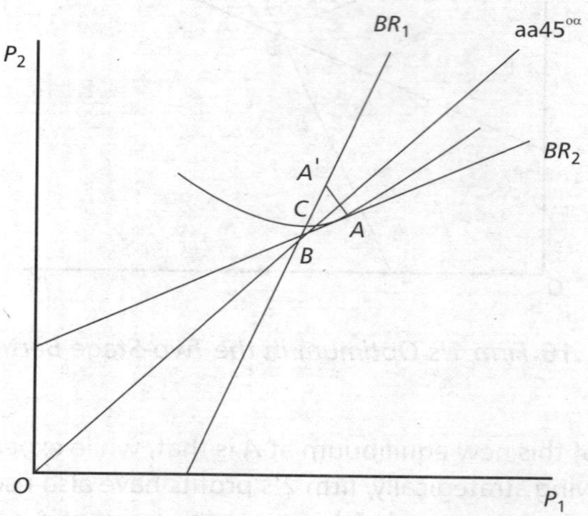


**Figure 11.17** *The Advantage of Moving Second*

## SUMMARY

In this chapter, we have looked at markets whose structure is neither perfectly competitive nor monopoly, but something in between. There are many models that have been proposed as ways to analyse such situations. The ones discussed, along with their main points, were as follows:

- Monopolistic Competition is a market form in which each firm has some monopoly power, gained primarily through product differentiation, but competition is also strong, because of free entry in the long run.
- In monopolistic competition, a firm can make extra-normal profits in the short run, but in the long run, profits are driven down by entry of other firms to the normal level.
- The Cournot model characterises a market in which a relatively small number of firms produce a homogeneous product and compete by setting quantities.
- Equilibrium in the Cournot model occurs when every firm has chosen an output level so as to maximise its profit conditional on the output levels of all other firms. This equilibrium concept is the same as that of Nash equilibrium and so this is sometimes called Cournot–Nash equilibrium.
- The Cournot equilibrium reduces to the monopoly equilibrium when the number of firms in competition is reduced to one, and reduces to the perfectly competitive equilibrium when the number of firms is allowed to become infinitely large. In this sense, the Cournot model provides a general model of which competition, oligopoly and monopoly are special cases.
- A major criticism of the Cournot model is that it assumes firms are myopic, in the sense that they do not allow for the possibility that their rivals might change their behaviour in response to changes they themselves might make.
- The Stackelberg model is one where a single firm becomes a 'leader' who takes into account the 'best responses' of its rivals, who remain myopic. This can be thought of as a two-stage version of the Cournot game and gives rise to an equilibrium in which the leader does better (in terms of profit) than it would as a follower.
- The Stackelberg model can be used to examine the possibility of a 'leader' using its first-mover advantage to deter entry. Conditions under which it is preferable to deter or accommodate entry can be derived.
- The Bertrand model is one where firms compete by setting prices rather than quantities.

- When Bertrand firms produce identical products, the equilibrium price will be the marginal cost of the second-most efficient firm.
- If firms in the homogeneous good Bertrand model must choose a capacity level before engaging in the price game (say because they have to build their plants), the resultant equilibrium will be the Cournot equilibrium.
- When Bertrand firms produce differentiated products, their prices can be different from marginal cost.
- In the two-stage version of the differentiated product Bertrand game, both the first and the second mover gain, but the follower gains more!

## EXERCISES

1. The market demand for gadgets is given by

$$Q = 25{,}000 - 1{,}000P.$$

The cost of producing gadgets is ₹10 each. However, there exists the possibility that, for an investment of ₹60,000 (*think of this as the annual cost of the investment*), it would be possible to reduce the cost of production to ₹5.

(a) Suppose the only firm in the gadget industry is Incumbent, Ltd. Would Incumbent undertake the investment? Would it be socially desirable for Incumbent to undertake the investment?

(b) What is the maximum amount Incumbent would pay to cut its cost of production to ₹5?

(c) Suppose instead that, although the gadget industry is initially a monopoly, it is a potential entrant, Rival, Ltd., that has the possibility of discovering a way to produce gadgets at ₹5 each. If it entered, Rival could engage in price competition with Incumbent (i.e. a lower price would capture all the market). Would Rival do the investment and enter? Would it be socially desirable for Rival to enter?

(d) Suppose Rival has spent the ₹60,000 and has discovered the low-cost technology. How much would Incumbent be willing to pay to take over Rival? Compare this answer to your answer to (b) and comment briefly.

2. Polaroid Corp. has a patent (and hence a monopoly) on the production of instant cameras. The demand for such cameras is

$$Q = 25{,}000 - 1{,}000P.$$

Polaroid can produce them at a cost of ₹5 each.

(a) How many cameras will Polaroid produce, what price will it charge and how much profit will it make, if it maximises profits?

(b) Camera Research Corp. (CRC) has developed and patented a new way to take instant pictures that consumers find a perfect substitute for Polaroid's cameras. It costs ₹10 per unit to produce the CRC camera. CRC offers this technology to Kodak, a competitor of Polaroid. Assuming Kodak and Polaroid would compete as a Cournot duopoly, what would be the new equilibrium price of cameras, and how much profit would Polaroid and Kodak make?

(c) What is the maximum amount CRC could hope to charge Kodak for an exclusive license to produce its camera? What is the maximum Polaroid might be willing to pay for this same exclusive license? Write a one-sentence comment comparing your two answers in this part of the problem.

3. Suppose a monopoly with a constant average cost of ₹3 faces the following demand curve for its product:

$$Q = \frac{360}{P^2}.$$

(a) If the firm wants to maximise profits, how much will it produce? What price will it charge?

(b) Suppose the firm is nationalised, and its management is instructed to maximise social welfare. How much will now be produced, and what price will be charged?

(c) What is the deadweight loss associated with the monopoly solution in part (a) as compared to part (b)?

(d) Suppose a second firm, identical to the first, enters the industry. What is the Cournot equilibrium of the industry now?

4. The market demand for roller skates is given by

$$Q_d = 500 - \frac{1}{2}p.$$

There are only two producers of roller skates: the Select company, whose cost of production is ₹100 per pair, and the Exclusive company, whose cost of production is ₹200 per pair. The products of the two companies, despite the difference in cost of production, are identical and sell for exactly the same price.

(a) What would be the equilibrium price of roller skates and the production levels of each firm, if the firms behaved as Cournot competitors?

(b) What would be the equilibrium price of roller skates and the production levels of each firm, if both firms instead assumed that their rival would always match any change they made in their production level?

(c) What would be the equilibrium price of roller skates and the production levels of each firm, if Select played as a Stackelberg leader and Exclusive as a follower?

5. The demand for gadgets is given by

$$Q_d = 300 - p.$$

Acme Corp. is the only producer of gadgets. Acme's cost function is

$$C(q_a) = 60q_a.$$

(a) How many gadgets will Acme produce and what price will it charge, if it wants to maximise its profits? How much profit will it make?

(b) Now suppose Bingo Corp. enters the gadget industry, with exactly the same cost function as Acme, and the two firms engage in Cournot competition. How many gadgets will each firm make, what will be the price of gadgets and how much profit will each firm make, in the Cournot–Nash equilibrium?

(c) Suppose Acme and Bingo decide to collude. How many gadgets will each firm make, what will be the price of gadgets and how much profit will each firm make, in the cartel equilibrium?

(d) Finally, suppose Acme abides by the collusion agreement, but Bingo decides to cheat. Under this scenario, how many gadgets will each firm make, what will be the price of gadgets and how much profit will each firm make?

6. Able Widget Co. is the only producer of widgets, which it can produce at a cost of ₹2 per widget. The demand for widgets is

$$W = 14 - p,$$

where $p$ is the price of widgets.

(a) How many widgets would Able produce, what would be the price and how much profit would Able make, if it maximised its profit?

(b) Now suppose Baker Widget Co. can enter the widget market by spending ₹4 in entry cost. Once it enters, Baker would also be able to produce widgets at a cost of ₹2 per widget, and Able and Baker would engage in Cournot (quantity-setting) competition. How much would each firm produce, what would be the price and how much profit would each firm make in the Cournot equilibrium?

(c) Suppose, before Baker entered, Able could pre-commit to producing any output level. What output level would it select if it wished to maximise its profit? How much would each firm produce, what would be the price and how much profit would each firm make in this scenario?

7. There are two firms in the gadget industry. Firm 1 can produce gadgets at a constant per unit cost of ₹20, while firm 2 can produce them at zero cost. The demand curve for gadgets is

$$P = 100 - Q,$$

where $P$ and $Q$ are the price and total quantity of gadgets.

(a) Suppose the firms are Cournot competitors. Find each firm's reaction function. Then solve the reaction functions to find each firm's output level, the price in the market and each firm's profits.

(b) Suppose instead that firm 2 is a Stackelberg leader. Find each firm's output, the market price and each firm's profits under this assumption.

(c) What is the net welfare difference between the Stackelberg and Cournot solutions?

8. There are two firms competing in the market for widgets. The demand curve for widgets is

$$Q = 30 - 2P,$$

where $Q$ and $P$ are, respectively, the market quantity and price of widgets. There is no threat of entry. Firm 1 produces widgets at a constant average cost of ₹6 per widget, and firm 2 produces widgets at a constant average cost of ₹9 per widget.

(a) Suppose the firms are Cournot competitors. Find how many widgets each frim will produce, the market price of widgets and the total profits of each firm in the Cournot equilibrium.

(b) Suppose the firms agreed to form a cartel. How many widgets would each firm produce under the cartel equilibrium? What would be the market price and the total profits of each firm under this solution?

(c) How much would each firm be willing to pay to buy the other? What is the minimum each firm would require in order to be purchased?

9. The demand for widgets is

$$Q = 10 - 0.2P,$$

where $P$ is the price of widgets. Acme Widget Corp's cost function for producing widgets is

$$C_A(q_A) = 20 + 10q_A,$$

while Best Widget Corp's cost function for producing widgets is

$$C_B(q_B) = 10 + 12q_B.$$

(a) Suppose both firms have entered the industry. What is the joint profit-maximising output level? How much will each firm produce?

(b) What would be the joint profit-maximising output level of each firm if entry has not already taken place?

(c) Suppose entry has taken place and collusion is illegal. How much will each firm produce now, assuming that they compete according to the Cournot model? How much profit does each firm make?

(d) Suppose that, although collusion is illegal, mergers are not. How much would Acme be willing to pay to take over Best? How much would Best be willing to pay to take over Acme?

10. The demand for widgets is

$$Q_d = 100 - p,$$

where $p$ is the price of widgets. There are two firms in the industry: Acme Widget Corp and Best Widget Corp. They each have the following cost function for producing widgets:

$$C_i(q_i) = 10q_i + \frac{1}{2}q_i^2,$$

where $q_i$ is the level of output of firm $i$.

(a) Suppose the firms behave as price-taking perfect competitors. What will be the short-run equilibrium price and quantity produced of widgets? How much will each firm produce?

(b) Suppose the firms agree to collude and maximise their joint profits. Now what will be the short-run equilibrium price and quantity produced of widgets? How much will each firm produce?

(c) Who gains and who loses as a result of this collusion? Calculate the respective gains and losses.

(d) How much better-off or worse off is society as a whole as a result of this collusion? Draw a graph that illustrates as clearly as possible the net change in social welfare.

11. Suppose there are two firms, AppleOrchard and BeeHoney. Denote by $x_A$ AppleOrchard's level of production and by $x_B$ BeeHoney's level of production. AppleOrchard's profit function is

$$\pi_A = 2\sqrt{x_A} + 2\sqrt{x_B} - x_A,$$

and BeeHoney's profit function is

$$\pi_B = 2\sqrt{x_B} - x_B.$$

(a) Find the levels of production $x_A^*$ and $x_B^*$ which maximise the joint profits of the two firms.

(b) Consider a game where AppleOrchard and BeeHoney simultaneously and independently choose their individual levels of production. Find the equilibrium levels of production $x_A^e$ and $x_B^e$.

(c) Consider the following government subsidy scheme: AppleOrchard gets paid $s_A$ per unit of its level of production $x_A$, while BeeHoney gets paid $s_B$ per unit of its level of production $x_B$. Find the subsidy rates $s_A$ and $s_B$ which achieve the levels of production $x_A^*$ and $x_B^*$ (which maximise the joint profits of the two firms) in the game where the firms simultaneously and independently choose their individual levels of production.

(d) Suppose the government wants to finance the subsidy scheme in part (c) without bringing in any outside funds. Let $T_A$ be a lump-sum tax paid by AppleOrchard, and $T_B$ be a lump-sum tax paid by BeeHoney. Find lump-sum taxes $T_A$ and $T_B$ required to finance the above subsidy scheme.

12. Toyota and Honda offer warranties on their cars. Let $w_T$ represent the number of years on a Toyota warranty and $w_H$ the number of years on a Honda warranty. For each firm $i$, the cost of the warranty is

$$C_i = 2000w_i.$$

The revenue for each firm is

$$R_i = \frac{32{,}000w_i}{w_T + w_H} \quad \text{for} \quad w_T, w_H > 0.$$

(a) If the firms set warranties simultaneously, what is the Cournot–Nash equilibrium in warranties? How much profit does each firm make?

(b) Suppose Honda decides to set its warranty first, that is, to behave as a Stackelberg leader? What will be the equilibrium in warranties now?

(c) If Toyota and Honda decide to collude on setting warranties, what warranties would they set?

13. There are two firms in a market for widgets. The market demand for widgets is

$$Q_d(p) = 10 - p.$$

Each firm's cost function for producing widgets is

$$C_i(q_i) = 2q_i \quad \text{for} \quad i = 1, 2.$$

(a) Suppose first that the firms hold the Cournot assumption and simultaneously decide how many widgets to produce. What are the firms' strategy sets? What is the equilibrium number of widgets that will be produced?

(b) Suppose instead that the two firms decide to collude. What will be the equilibrium quantity and price in this case?

(c) Suppose finally that instead of the firms simultaneously choosing how many widgets to produce, Firm 1 now gets to make its production decision before Firm 2. Once Firm 1 has made its decision, it cannot be changed. Firm 2 then has the opportunity to observe Firm 1's output before making its own production decision. What are the firm's strategy sets in this case? What is the equilibrium number of widgets that will be produced?

(d) Calculate the profits for both firms in the three scenarios (a, b and c) above. Briefly explain any differences in the two firms' profits you might have found in the three scenarios.

CHAPTER

12

# Externalities and Public Goods

In this chapter, we will look at two more broad areas where markets seem to fail to deliver an efficient allocation of resources: externalities and public goods. One of the key topics in modern microeconomic theory is the theory of externalities. In a world where many believe that economic activity is leading to large changes in global climate, with possibly serious repercussions for billions of people, understanding the theory of externalities and the relevant policy interventions has become an important part of the economist's tool kit. And public goods, as we will see, comprise a wide range of goods and services typically provided by the government because of the inability of markets to properly deliver them.

## 12.1 EXTERNALITIES

**Task for this section:**

To study the problem of externalities, in which economic transactions affect those who are not parties to the transactions themselves. We see how this creates welfare losses to society and study policy interventions to correct it, including price-type policies such as taxes or effluent fees and quantity-type policies such as standards and emission limits. The Coase Theorem, an alternative way of looking at externalities emphasising the role of property rights and transactions costs, is discussed. Finally, we look at common property externalities.

An **externality** occurs when economic activity affects economic agents who are not involved directly in that activity. We saw one simple example of an externality when we discussed the market supply curve. If a firm buys more of an input, it is putting some upward pressure on the price of that input and is therefore negatively affecting all other firms that buy that input. Normally, if the firm is small, this effect is also small and we can safely ignore it. But if the firm is not small, or if many small firms are simultaneously trying to buy more of the input, the cumulative effect might become substantial.

Of course, there are many other examples. We can classify externalities into at least four broad classes:

- consumer to consumer
- firm to consumer
- consumer to firm
- firm to firm

Within each of these types of externalities, we could have positive externalities (where the agent who experiences the externality is better-off as a result) and negative externalities (where the agent is worse off as a result).

Consider first consumer-to-consumer externalities. Someone who plays very loud music, or fails to keep his house and yard neat and clean, is negatively affecting his neighbours. However, somebody who plants beautiful flowering trees and bushes in front of her house creates a positive externality for her neighbours and even people who just pass by. Each driver commuting to work is imposing a small negative externality on every other driver on the road. When there are a small number of drivers on the road, this effect is negligible, but when the number of drivers on the road becomes large, the cumulative effect of the congestion externality can become quite large. Similar congestion externalities can occur in many other situations. When consumers increase their use of electricity, they increase the chance of a brown-out or a power failure for all consumers. When many users are actively using the internet, the speed of access for everyone slows down. A similar degradation in the quality of the signal can occur in cable systems. Overcrowding at national parks and other tourist sites reduces the pleasure everyone gets from visiting those places. So congestion externalities are a major class of consumer-to-consumer externalities.

Of course, there is another major class of consumer-to-consumer negative externality: the pollution caused by our consumption behaviour. Every time we drive a car, we add carbon to the atmosphere and contribute to global warming. The use of simple wood or coal fires for cooking or to provide heat is also a major source of carbon pollution. Indeed, *all* our consumption behaviour has some environmental impact. The question is, which behaviours have a large impact? The use of aerosol cans, for example, was a major contributor to the depletion of the ozone layer in the atmosphere. This is one area in which concerted worldwide action has had a very beneficial impact on controlling this source of environmental damage.

Examples of firm-to-consumer externalities are easy to find, as some of these constitute major policy issues of our time. The environmental impact of manufacturing activity is huge in many areas. Sulphur pollution, primarily from the burning of coal in electric power plants, creates the problem of acid rain. Carbon pollution is now clearly known to be a major factor in global warming, and there are many examples of chemical pollution having damaged water supplies and other food sources to the point of causing major health problems.

Positive firm-to-consumer externalities are not as obvious, but they do exist. When a business decides to locate its operations in a particular city, it is creating positive externalities for the households in that area. This is one of the reasons why city administrators are often so keen to see professional sports teams locate in their cities, and why the state of Gujarat in India so quickly and readily facilitated the move from West Bengal of a new car factory to produce the Tata Nano.

Consumer-to-firm externalities are relatively hard to find. One example is the congestion externality imposed by highway drivers on firms that provide transportation services, such as bus or trucking companies. And, of course, to the extent that global warming affects everyone, any consumer activity that adds to the carbon problem does impose external effects on a variety of firms.

Finally, as far as firm-to-firm externalities are concerned, a classic example of a positive externality is the one created for owners of fruit orchards by producers of honey. Since fruit blossoms need to be pollinated for the fruit to set, having plenty of honeybees around helps to ensure a large fruit crop. We will return to this example later in this chapter. An example of a negative firm-to-firm externality is the reduction in fish catch for fishing companies, caused by overfishing on the part of all fishermen and fishing companies.

The fundamental problem with externalities is that they are typically not mediated by any market. When people make economic decisions, they are normally guided by their own self-interest. They weigh the costs and benefits to themselves and make decisions in order to maximise their net benefits. We have seen how, under certain conditions, such self-interested behaviour can have very beneficial effects, notably that the allocation of resources in the economy is led to Pareto efficiency. But the first optimality theorem of welfare economics is predicated on the assumption that there are no externalities. With externalities present, the result no longer holds, as we will see in the next section, where the problem and possible policy solutions are discussed.

### 12.1.1 The Allocation Problem under Externalities

We will focus on a firm-created negative externality in order to set out the principles of the problem and its solution. The starting point for the analysis is the basic competitive market (Figure 12.1). Suppose $p(Q)$ and $S(Q)$ represent the inverse demand and supply curves for the final output $Q$, and suppose $(Q_0, p_0)$ at point A represents the quantity–price equilibrium under perfect competition. In the absence of any externalities, this equilibrium represents a Pareto-efficient solution to the allocation problem in this market. The curve $p(Q)$ can be interpreted as the social marginal benefit (*SMB*) curve and $S(Q)$ can be interpreted as the social marginal cost (*SMC*) curve; their intersection is the point at which the *SMB* and *SMC* are equalised.

Now suppose the production of this commodity results in the discharge of pollutants into the environment. The curve $S(Q)$ is no longer the *SMC* of production; it is only the private marginal cost of production. The *SMC* curve would lie above the curve $S(Q)$, say at *SMC*, where the vertical distance between $S(Q)$ and *SMC* is equal to the marginal external cost (*MEC*). This is a measure

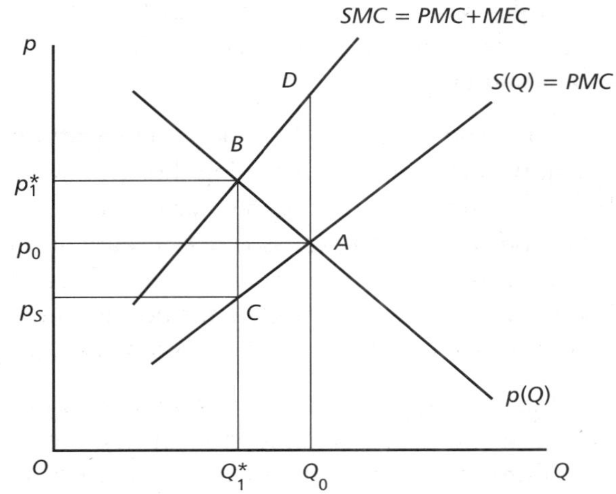


**Figure 12.1** *Negative Externality in a Competitive Market*

of the social cost of the pollution created in the course of the production of this good. Now the market optimum has shifted to point *B*, where the *SMC* curve intersects with *p*(*Q*), although the competitive outcome remains at *A*. Since we are interpreting *p*(*Q*) to be the *SMB* curve, point *B* represents the intersection of *SMC* and *SMB*, and is therefore the social optimum. Under the competitive outcome, production is $Q_0$, but we would like to see production at $Q_1^*$. Thus, the competitive solution leads to over production of the good.

The competitive equilibrium is not efficient in this case. The welfare loss due to this overproduction is given by the area of the triangle *ABD*. For each unit of production beyond the optimum of $Q_1^*$, there is a loss equal to the amount by which the *SMC* exceeds the *SMB p(Q)*. Adding up these losses for all the units of output between $Q_1^*$ and $Q_0$ gives us the area *ABD*.

### 12.1.2 The Pigouvian Tax

How can we attain the efficient solution at *B*? One way would be to use **quantity restrictions**, specifically to order firms not to produce more than $Q_1^*$. The problem with this approach is that we would need to decide how much each individual firm in the market should reduce its output. We could simply order the same proportionate reduction for each firm. That is, we could order all firms to produce a fraction $Q_1^*/Q_0$ of what they produced in the initial equilibrium. But would this be the optimal pattern of reduction? It does not seem likely. The optimal pattern of reduction would require a situation where the marginal costs of all the firms are equalised. The problem for the policy-maker is similar to that of a multi-plant monopoly, in that production of a desired quantity needs to be carried out in the most efficient way. In the case of multi-plant monopoly, we saw that the solution is to equalise the *MC* of each plant with that of every other plant in order to ensure that production of the desired quantity was distributed efficiently among its plants. In the same way, we would want the production of $Q_1^*$ to be distributed among firms in such a way that the *MC's* of all the firms are equalised. It is unlikely that this would occur exactly by ordering an equal proportional reduction in output.

An alternative approach, first proposed by the Cambridge University economist A. C. Pigou, is to use **price restrictions**. The Pigouvian method for attaining the optimum is to impose a commodity tax equal to the size of the *MEC* (= the distance BC in Figure 12.1), in order to force the quantity level down to $Q_1^*$ . We know that commodity taxes cause a reduction in the output produced, and that is what is being sought here. The price to buyers would rise to $p_1^*$ , while the net price received by sellers would be $p_S$. Since all firms would be facing the same price, the distribution of output across firms will automatically be optimised as each firm sets net price equal to their *MC*.

Apart from ensuring the efficient allocation of production among firms, the Pigouvian tax has another important benefit. As we saw in our discussion of commodity taxes, raising revenue to meet government expenditures normally involves the creation of distortions, and hence of deadweight losses, in the markets where taxes are imposed. This is a necessary evil, as revenues do have to be raised in order to meet government's expenditure needs. But the Pigouvian tax raises revenue without creating any distortions or deadweight losses; in fact, the Pigouvian tax *corrects* an existing distortion (the misallocation in the presence of externalities) and improves welfare by eliminating the deadweight loss caused by the competitive solution in the face of externalities. The tax causes welfare to rise by the area *ABD* in the figure. For both these reasons, most economists would prefer the Pigouvian tax to the use of quantity restrictions.

### 12.1.3 The Possibility of Abatement and Effluent Fees

The Pigouvian tax is levied on the final output (say, electricity) in order to try to address the problems caused by polluting emissions from the production process. An alternative, more direct approach to solving the problem of a negative externality caused by a production process, would be to try to reduce the quantity of the pollutant itself. For example, when it was realised that the sulphur generated by burning coal interacted with water vapour in the atmosphere to create sulphuric acid (thereby creating acid rain), one method employed to correct the problem was to try to 'scrub' the exhaust gases produced during coal combustion and thereby reduce the amount of sulphur entering the atmosphere, capturing some of it instead at the plant site itself. Thus, the level of pollution was abated directly instead of indirectly through the reduction of final output; this is a solution superior to the one where the level of final output is reduced. In what follows, we will look at how to decide the optimal level of abatement and why this mode of intervention is better than the intervention in the market for the final product.

We start by looking at the 'market' for emissions or abatement. Of course, there is not truly a market for emissions or abatement until government intervention forces the creation of such a market, but it is convenient to think of the problem in this way. Figure 12.2 illustrates the approach. There are two panels in the figure, one for emissions and one for abatement, and

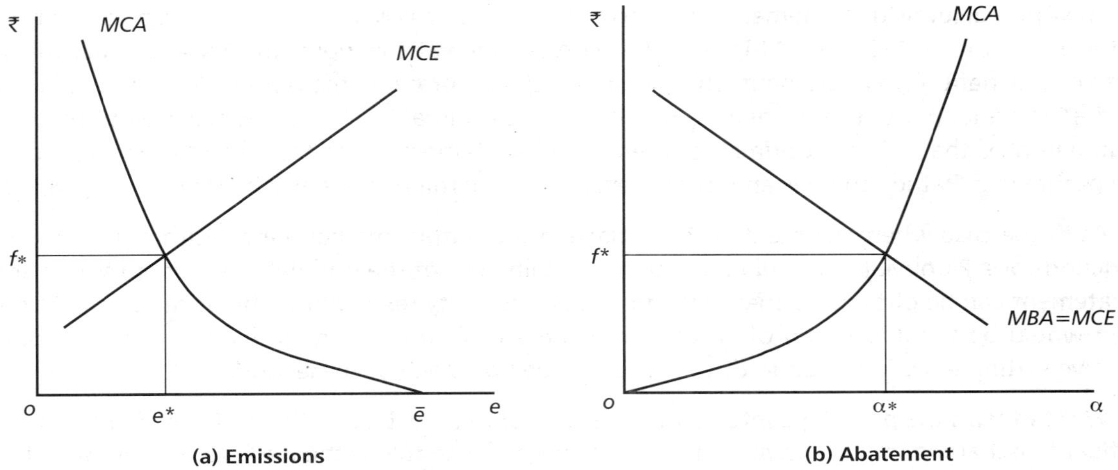


**Figure 12.2** *Optimal Abatement of Emissions*

they are mirror images of one another, since abatement is simply a reduction in emissions. The curve labelled *MCE* represents the marginal cost of emissions. Note that, although there is a close connection between the two curves, this *MCE* is not the same as *MEC*, the vertical distance between *S*(*Q*) and *SMC* in Figure 12.1, because the units of analysis are different. The horizontal axis in Figure 12.1 represented the quantity of the final output, while the same axis in Figure 12.2 represents the level of emissions or of abatement of the pollutant. Thus, the *MCE* in panel (a) of the figure here is the marginal damage cost of emissions as a function of the level of emissions, while the *MEC* implicit in Figure 12.1 was the *MEC* of emissions as a function of the level of final output. But this is the only difference between them; the two curves are conveying the same information. If there was exactly one unit of the emission produced with each unit of output, the two curves would be identical. In the mirror image of panel (b), *MCE* becomes the marginal benefit of abatement (MBA), since the benefit of abatement of emissions is the prevention of the damage that the emissions would cause if they were discharged into the environment. Moving to the curve *MCA* in Figure 12.2, this represents the marginal cost of abating or reducing emissions. In panel (b), this curve is drawn normally, while in panel (a), it is drawn in mirror image, since increasing abatement is a reduction in emissions. The point $\bar{e}$ represents the level of emissions that would occur absent any abatement. For purposes of the analysis, this level is treated as fixed, even though in reality it could be a choice variable of the firms. The curve *MCA* then shows the marginal cost of abating or reducing the level of emissions being discharged into the environment, and in panel (a), we are reading the level of abatement from right to left, starting at the point $\bar{e}$. In panel (b), the curve is seen in the shape we would expect, with the level of abatement rising as we move to the right and the *MCA* curve, the marginal cost of abatement, showing a convex shape to reflect the difficulty of removing literally *all* of any substance from the discharge.

The optimal levels of abatement and emissions are then easily seen in this context to be at the intersection of the *MCE* (or *MBA*) and *MCA* curves, since at this point the MCA is equal to the marginal benefit from abatement. Thus, $e^*$ in panel (a) represents the optimal level of emissions, and $a^*$ in panel (b), which is equal to $(\bar{e} - e^*)$, is the optimal level of abatement. Note that the figure implies that it is not optimal to attempt full abatement, since the cost of doing so would be prohibitive. Rather, there is an optimal level where marginal costs and benefits are equalised.

As in the case where intervention took place in the output market, where either quantity restrictions or a Pigouvian tax could be imposed, attainment of the optimal levels of emissions and abatement can be obtained either through price or quantity restrictions. The price-type intervention would be the imposition of an effluent charge of $f^*$ and the quantity intervention would involve setting emissions standards at $e^*$. Let us see how each of these work.

We start with the price-type intervention. This would simply be an effluent fee of $f^*$ per unit of effluent discharged into the environment. Faced with having to pay the fee for any pollutants they discharge, firms will look for ways to avoid paying the fee. The only way to do that is by abating the pollution before discharge, and firms would find it profitable to abate the emissions as long as the MCA was lower than the effluent charge. Therefore, abatement would be at the efficient level, $a^*$ in Figure 12.2(b) and emissions would also be at the efficient level, $e^*$ in Figure 12.2(a). Further, government would collect effluent fees equal to the area of the rectangle $e^*f^*$ in panel (a) of the figure, revenue which has the advantage, such as the Pigouvian tax, of being raised while correcting the distortion.

We turn now to emissions standards. This seems like a straightforward solution, since it simply involves mandating a maximum amount of emissions that would be allowed, but implementing it has the same problems that the quantity intervention in the output market had. Specifically, there is the issue of how the mandated maximum amount of emissions are to be distributed among the producing firms. Since mandating a maximum amount of emissions is tantamount to requiring firms to engage in abatement activity, here to the extent of $a^*$, we could equally well ask how the abatement required should be distributed among firms. From the point of view of efficiency, the answer is quite straightforward: firms should abate emissions in such a way that the MCAs are equalised across firms. The argument is the same as before, and the same as the argument for the multi-plant monopoly. If MCAs are not equalised, overall costs could be reduced by increasing abatement in the firms where the *MC* of abatement is low and decreasing abatement by an equal amount in firms where the *MC* of abatement is high. Only when marginal costs are equalised across firms will the total cost of abatement be minimised. But how can this be achieved? The policy-maker would need to have detailed information on firms' costs of abatement in order to mandate the different levels of emission or abatement on each firm. This seems like a cumbersome and indeed an administratively impossible task to accomplish.

One way out is to issue pollution vouchers to the firms and to allow firms to trade these vouchers. If we have decided on a total acceptable level of emissions $e^*$, we can distribute pollution vouchers, giving firms the right to pollute up to specific levels, that add up to $e^*$. How these are distributed is not important. They could be distributed equally to all firms, or in proportion to the different firms' contributions to total production of pollution $\bar{e}$, or in any other manner. What is important is that the vouchers be made tradable, that is, firms' should be allowed to transfer vouchers among one another in exchange for monetary payments. If the market for vouchers is competitive, this will lead to an efficient allocation of vouchers and of abatement activity.

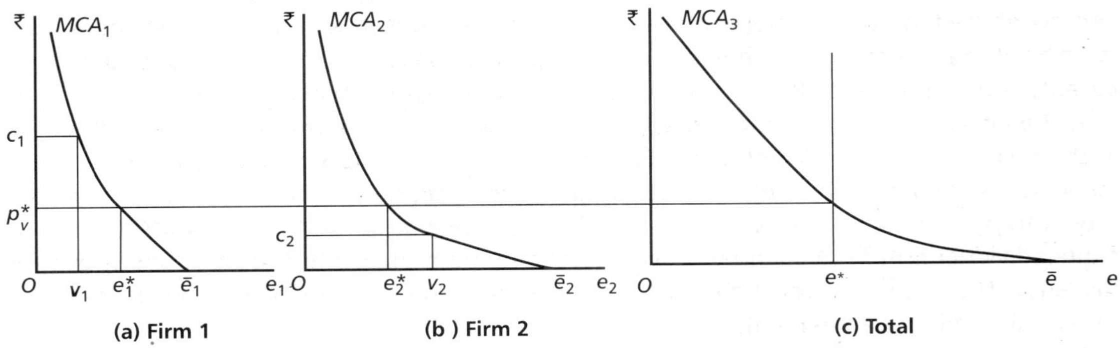


**Figure 12.3** *Optimal Allocation of Abatement across Firms*

Let us see why by looking at Figure 12.3. For simplicity, we have assumed there are just two firms. In the graph, the horizontal axis in each panel measures the level of emissions, firm 1's in panel (a), firm 2's in panel (b) and the total in panel (c). Before any abatement, firm 1 is generating $\bar{e}_1$ emissions in panel (a) and firm 2 is generating $\bar{e}_2$ in panel (b), for a total of $\bar{e}$ in panel (c), which is the same $\bar{e}$ as in panel (a) of Figure 12.2. With the respective emissions levels as the 'origin', the MCA curves (*MCA*) are drawn for each firm, in mirror image (going from right to left), as is the total *MCA*, which is just the horizontal summation of the two individual *MCA* curves. Again, this combined *MCA* is intended to be the same as the *MCA* in Figure 12.2(a). We have just broken it down into its component parts here, assuming there are only two firms. Now suppose e* is the optimal level of emissions, determined as in Figure 12.2 and shown here in panel (c). Government is going to distribute vouchers adding up to e*, giving firms permission to discharge emissions up to the amounts of the vouchers they hold. The question is how these vouchers should be allocated. Suppose the government gives firm 1 vouchers to emit $v_1$ emissions and firm 2 vouchers for $v_2$ units of emissions, respectively. These quantities of vouchers must add up to the optimal level of emissions, e*, so $v_1 + v_2 = e^*$. If no vouchers are traded, firm 1 can emit $v_1$ units of emissions and must clean up or abate the remainder of their effluent, $(\bar{e}_1 - v_1)$. Similarly, firm 2 can emit $v_2$ units of emissions and must clean up or abate the remainder, $(\bar{e}_2 - v_2)$. As drawn, this is not an efficient allocation of abatement, as firm 1's MCA is $c_1$ and firm 2's is $c_2$. Since $c_1$ and $c_2$ are so different, it is clear the allocation is not efficient.

What if the vouchers are tradable? The key insight is that the mirror images of the *MCA* curves (i.e. the curves drawn in Figure 12.3) are nothing but the demand curves for vouchers! Why is that? Look at panel (a) in the figure. If the price of vouchers were $c_1$, firm 1 would be content with the vouchers they had, so their demand for vouchers would be $v_1$. If the price of vouchers were $p_v^*$, firm 1 would want to have $e_1^*$ vouchers, so that it could pay just $p_v^*$ per unit and discharge emissions into the environment, instead of having to abate the emissions. It would have to abate only $(\bar{e}_1 - e_1^*)$ units, the ones where its MCA was lower than the price of vouchers. Thus, $MCA_1$ is firm 1's demand for vouchers, $MCA_2$ is firm 2's demand for vouchers and $MCA$ is the aggregate demand for vouchers. We know that e* in panel (c) is the total supply of vouchers, since vouchers were distributed in order to hold total emissions to this level. Therefore, the price of vouchers would be at the intersection of demand and supply, which is labelled $p_v^*$, and this price of vouchers guarantees the efficient distribution of abatement. Firm 1 would buy $(e_1^* - v_1)$ vouchers, so that it could emit $e_1^*$ units of effluent and abate only $(\bar{e}_1 - e_1^*)$ units, and firm 2 would sell $(v_2 - e_2^*)$ vouchers, since the price it is getting for them is greater than its MCA up to $e_2^*$. Thus, firm 2 would emit $e_2^*$ units and abate $(\bar{e}_2 - e_2^*)$ units. Both firms are abating up to the point where their MCA is equal to $p_v^*$, and hence the $MCA$'s are equal across firms. Note that, because $MCA$ is the sum of the individual firm $MCA$'s, and $v_1 + v_2 = e^*$, the number of vouchers being bought by firm 1 must equal the number of vouchers being sold by firm 2. Thus, the tradable vouchers result in an efficient allocation of abatement.

So both price- and quantity-type interventions work to get the optimal level of emissions and abatement. Note that the standards approach works by mimicking the price approach; the tradable vouchers result in a price of vouchers which are equal to the optimal effluent fee. It is worth noting also that the precondition for the tradable vouchers to work correctly is that the market for vouchers be perfectly competitive. If the market is not competitive, the price of vouchers will not necessarily equal the optimal effluent fee, and the allocation would then not be efficient. Aside from this issue, the arguments for and against the two approaches are the same as for the Pigouvian tax versus quantity restrictions. The main argument in favour of effluent charges is that government receives the revenue. Of course, this end could be achieved in the voucher system also, if government sold or even auctioned the vouchers. The benefit of auctioning the vouchers would be that there would be no need for trading between firms later; the auction would automatically result in an efficient allocation of the vouchers.

It is worth pointing out that some authors label effluent fees also as Pigouvian taxes, although Pigou himself never spoke of effluent charges. This causes needless confusion, as clearly the two types of intervention are quite distinct from one another. Here, therefore, they are being called by different names. Pigouvian taxes will refer only to taxes on final output, intended to reduce the level of output in an attempt to ameliorate the problem of a negative externality. Effluent fees will refer to charges levied on polluting discharges into the environment, intended to encourage abatement of these pollutants at the source.

### 12.1.4 Relationship between Effluent Fees and Pigouvian Taxes

We have seen that the problem of a negative externality can be corrected through Pigouvian taxes in the output market or through effluent fees on emissions. Intuitively, it seems that the latter option would be the better one, since it is tackling the problem head-on by taxing (or controlling) the level of pollution directly rather than indirectly by trying to change the output levels of the final products. But it is worth seeing this explicitly and to see the relationship between intervention on emissions versus intervention in the output market. We will look at this first algebraically and then graphically.

We begin by writing down a simple model of a competitive market without externalities. Let $p(Q)$ and $S(Q)$ represent the inverse demand and supply curves in the commodity market. For convenience, think of the suppliers as a single price-taking firm. The inverse supply curve is then nothing but the firm's marginal cost curve and its integral is the firm's cost curve. One way to think about optimality in a competitive market is to maximise surplus, $W$:

$$W = CS(Q) + pQ - C(Q), \tag{12.1}$$

where $CS(Q)$ represents consumer surplus as a function of the quantity $Q$. Now, letting $q$ be the variable of integration,

$$CS(Q) = \int_0^Q p(q)dq - p(Q) \cdot Q \tag{12.2}$$

and therefore

$$\frac{dCS(Q)}{dQ} = -Qp'(Q). \tag{12.3}$$

Differentiating (12.1), and using (12.3), we then have

$$\frac{dW}{dQ} = -Qp'(Q) + Qp'(Q) + p(Q) - C'(Q) = 0 \tag{12.4}$$

for a welfare maximum. This simplifies to the familiar condition that price must equal marginal cost:

$$p(Q) = C'(Q). \tag{12.5}$$

Now let us introduce a negative externality. Suppose the production process in this industry leads to the creation of a toxic substance according to the 'effluent production function':

$$e = e(Q), \qquad \text{with } e'(Q) > 0, \tag{12.6}$$

where e represents the quantity of effluent produced. It may not be unreasonable to think of the function $e(Q)$ as linear, in which case $e'(Q)$ is constant. Emission of this substance causes damage to the environment according to the convex damage function:

$$D = D[e(Q)], \qquad \text{with } D'(e) > 0,\ D''(e) > 0. \tag{12.7}$$

Social surplus is now

$$W = CS(Q) + pQ - C(Q) - D[e(Q)] \quad (12.8)$$

and the social optimum can be found by differentiating (12.8) and setting it equal to zero:

$$\frac{dW}{dQ} = -Qp'(Q) + Qp'(Q) + p(Q) - C'(Q) - D'[e(Q)] \cdot e'(Q) = 0. \quad (12.9)$$

This reduces to

$$p(Q) = C'(Q) + D'[e(Q)] \cdot e'(Q). \quad (12.10)$$

This condition is the familiar one that says the optimal level of output occurs where the price is equal to the marginal social cost of production. The first term on the right-hand side of (12.10) is the private marginal cost of production and the second term is nothing but the *MEC* of production. This second term has been given some greater structure here through the recognition that production of the pollutant is a side-product of the production process for the final product, and damage to the environment is caused by the level of pollutants emitted. This recognition is crucial to understanding the relationship between Pigouvian taxes and effluent fees, as will become clear as we consider the level of optimal abatement. Before turning to that, we should note that the optimal Pigouvian tax would simply be equal to the *MEC* of production, the second term on the right-hand side of (12.10):

$$t^* = D'[e(Q)] \cdot e'(Q). \quad (12.11)$$

Turning now to the possibility of abating the effluent, suppose the representative firm could abate, at a cost of $A$, an amount $a$ of the effluent before emitting it into the environment, according to an abatement cost function:

$$A = A(a), \qquad \text{with } A'(a) > 0,\ A''(a) > 0. \quad (12.12)$$

Presumably, this function would be convex. Further, if the abatement level is $a$, the environmental cost to society of the emissions will be

$$D = D[e(Q) - a] \quad (12.13)$$

since now only $e(Q) - a$ of the effluent is emitted into the environment. Social surplus is now

$$W = CS(Q) + pQ - C(Q) - D[e(Q) - a] - A(a) \quad (12.14)$$

and the social problem is to maximise this by suitable choice of $Q$ and $a$. The first-order conditions for this maximisation are

$$\frac{\partial W}{\partial Q} = -Qp'(Q) + Qp'(Q) + p(Q) - C'(Q) - D'[e(Q) - a] \cdot e'(Q) = 0 \quad (12.15)$$

and

$$\frac{\partial W}{\partial a} = D'[e(Q) - a] - A'(a) = 0. \qquad (12.16)$$

Equation (12.15) reduces to

$$p(Q) = C'(Q) + D'[e(Q) - a] \cdot e'(Q) \qquad (12.17)$$

which is similar to (12.10) except that the marginal damages are now evaluated at the net emission level $[e(Q) - a]$ rather than simply $e(Q)$ in order to allow for the abatement level. Equation (12.17) is the condition for the optimal output level, which is at the point where price is equal to the marginal social cost. Note that this optimal output level is not the same as the output level absent abatement that we saw in (12.10), since here the quantum of emissions is lower by the amount of abatement $a$. Thus, the optimal output level is now higher. Simultaneously, (12.16) specifies the optimal level of abatement, which is at the point where the MCA $A'(a)$ is equal to the MBA, which is simply the marginal damage averted $D'[e(Q) - a]$.

To attain the optimal levels of output and abatement, we need to set an effluent fee according to (12.16) equal to the MCA at the optimum:

$$f^* = D'[e(Q^*) - a^*], \qquad (12.18)$$

where the asterisks represent the optimal levels of the respective variables. Substituting this in (12.17), we get the condition for the optimal output level:

$$p(Q) = C'(Q) + f^* e'(Q). \qquad (12.19)$$

This is precisely the level of output that firms will choose if faced with the effluent fee $f^*$. To see this, we treat the producers of the final output as a single price-taking firm. The firm's problem will be to choose $Q$ and $a$ in order to maximise profits:

$$\pi = pQ - C(Q) - A(a) - f^*[e(Q) - a]. \qquad (12.20)$$

Its first-order conditions for this maximisation will be

$$\frac{\partial \pi}{\partial Q} = p - C'(Q) - f^* e'(Q) \qquad (12.21)$$

and

$$\frac{\partial \pi}{\partial a} = -A'(a) + f^* = 0. \qquad (12.22)$$

Taking into account (12.18), we easily see that (12.21) and (12.22) are precisely the same as the social optimality conditions (12.19) and (12.16), respectively. Thus, the setting of the optimal effluent fee leads the price-taking firms to choose the level of output and the level of abatement optimally (Table 12.1).

Let us see how we can illustrate what is happening here with a graphical approach. Essentially, if we look back at Figure 12.1, the availability and use of abatement technology shifts the *SMC* curve down. Figure 12.4 reproduces Figure 12.1, except that it adds the new *SMC* curve. Here the curve labelled $SMC_1$ is the same as the *SMC* curve from Figure 12.1, while the dotted line labelled $SMC_e$ is the new *SMC* curve with abatement. Why is this lower? The reason is because the MCE is lower.

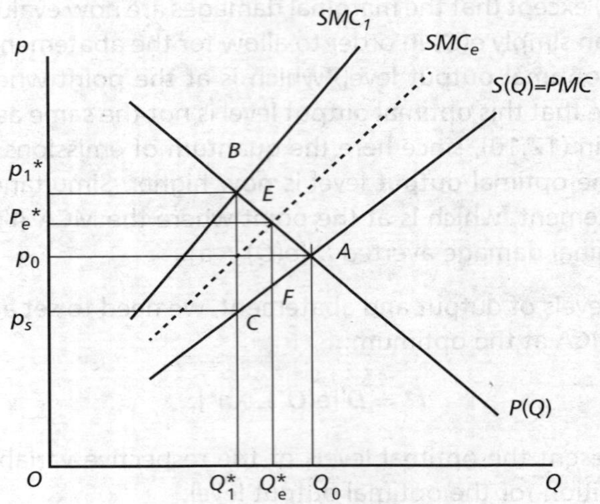


**Figure 12.4** *The Effect of Optimal Abatement on the Output Market*

In Figure 12.2(a), we had seen the *MCE*. This showed the marginal damage caused by emissions, and, when multiplied by $e'(Q)$ to convert it to output units, it gave us the *MEC*, which was the gap between the supply curve $S(Q)$ and the *SMC*. Once abatement is possible, this will everywhere be lower, since some of the units of effluent produced will be abated (at relatively low cost) instead of being emitted into the environment. Let us look at Table 12.1 to see why this is so. Suppose panel (a) shows the marginal damage *MDC* caused by the first 10 units of emissions discharged into the environment. If there is no abatement, this would also be the *MEC* of those emissions. Now suppose abatement is possible, and the marginal cost of abating up to 10 units is given in panel (b). Assuming abatement is carried out optimally, what will now be the *MEC* of any effluents produced? The first two units of effluent will be emitted into the environment, as the *MDC* is below the *MCA*. But now the next unit of effluent would cause 1.25 worth of damage but only costs 1 to clean up, so it will be abated and the marginal social cost of this unit is only 1. The next two units produced will be emitted, at a marginal social cost of 1.25 and 1.75, respectively, but then another unit will be abated at a cost of 2. In this way, the last column in panel (c) shows the *MEC* given optimal abatement, and we can see it is lower than the *MDC* in the second column of panel (a), which was the *MEC* before abatement.

**Table 12.1** *Numerical Example to Illustrate Optimal Abatement*

| Units of Emission | *MCD* |
|---|---|
| 1 | 0.25 |
| 2 | 0.75 |
| 3 | 1.25 |
| 4 | 1.75 |
| 5 | 2.25 |
| 6 | 2.75 |
| 7 | 3.25 |
| 8 | 3.75 |
| 9 | 4.25 |
| 10 | 4.75 |

**Panel (a)**

| Units of Abatement | *MCA* |
|---|---|
| 1 | 1 |
| 2 | 2 |
| 3 | 3 |
| 4 | 4 |
| 5 | 5 |
| 6 | 6 |
| 7 | 7 |
| 8 | 8 |
| 9 | 9 |
| 10 | 10 |

**Panel (b)**

| Units of Effluent | Emit or Discharge | *MEC* |
|---|---|---|
| 1 | Emit | 0.25 |
| 2 | Emit | 0.75 |
| 3 | Abate | 1 |
| 4 | Emit | 1.25 |
| 5 | Emit | 1.75 |
| 6 | Abate | 2 |
| 7 | Emit | 2.25 |
| 8 | Emit | 2.75 |
| 9 | Abate | 3 |
| 10 | Emit | 3.25 |

**Panel (c)**

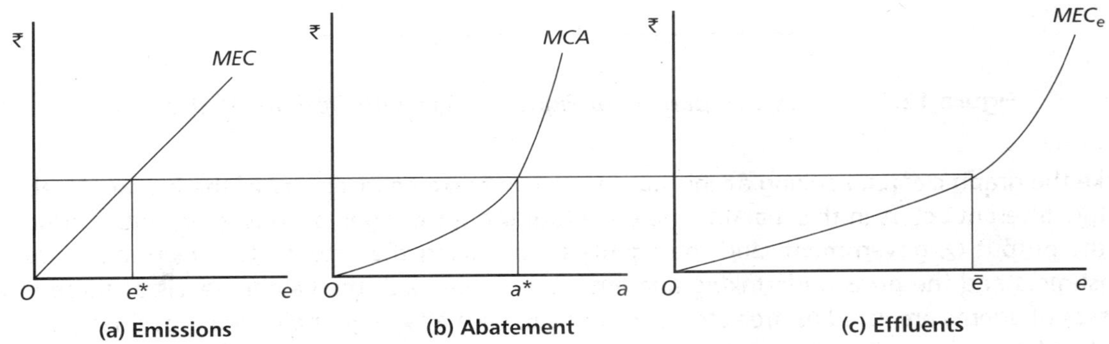


**Figure 12.5** *A Different Way to Look at Optimal Abatement*

If we were to express the same argument graphically, we could do so as in Figure 12.5. In panel (a), we have the original *MEC* curve, showing the marginal damage caused by emissions. Since there is no abatement, all effluents produced are discharged into the environment. In panel (b), we have the MCA, and in panel (c), we have the new *MEC* curve, $MEC_e$, which is the horizontal sum of the two curves in panels (a) and (b). If abatement is carried out efficiently, *MEC* will equal *MCA* and that is why $MEC_e$ is the resultant MCE. Obviously, this is below the *MEC* curve in panel (a) and that is why the curve $SMC_e$ is below the curve $SMC_1$ in Figure 12.4.

We can now look at Figure 12.4 and compare the outcomes under optimal abatement and under the Pigouvian tax. We see first of all that optimal abatement functions like an effective Pigouvian tax, as it drives a wedge between the price paid by buyers and the net price received by sellers. But where the Pigouvian tax was given by *BC* in the figure, the effective Pigouvian tax under optimal abatement is only *EF*. Thus, optimal abatement results in less of a deviation from the competitive output level; output is at $Q_e^*$ under optimal abatement as compared to $Q_1^*$ under the Pigouvian tax. To see the different welfare implications of the two interventions, look at Figure 12.6, which is just Figure 12.4 again, with the shapes of the curves exaggerated in order to

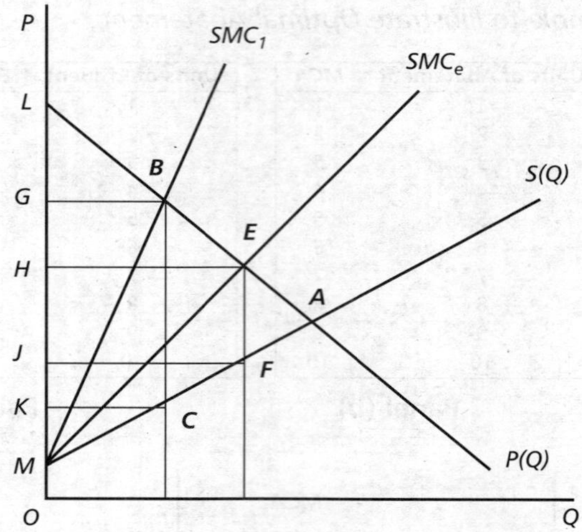


**Figure 12.6** *Welfare Comparison of Pigouvian Tax with Optimal Abatement*

make the graph clearer. Looking at this figure, we can make an inventory of the welfare levels of all the different actors in this market. There are four groups of agents: consumers and producers of the output *Q*, government, and the agents experiencing the externality, which may include consumers and the firms undertaking abatement. In Table 12.2, the welfare levels of these four classes of agents are listed as areas from Figure12.6, with a '+' sign indicating a positive welfare level and a '−' sign indicating a welfare loss. The last row of the table shows the net welfare level, and we see that, under the Pigouvian tax, the level is at +LBM, while under optimal abatement, it is +LEM. Thus, welfare is higher under optimal abatement by the area BEM in Figure 12.6.

**Table 12.2** *Welfare Effects of Pigouvian Tax versus Effluent Fee*

| | Pigouvian Tax | Effluent Fee |
|---|---|---|
| Consumers | +LBG | +LEH |
| Producers | +MCK | +MFJ |
| Government | +GBCK | +HEFJ |
| Externality | −MCB | −MFE |
| Net | +LBM | +LEM |

Since the level of output (and hence effluent produced) is higher under optimal abatement, the question arises whether it might be possible that the total level of emissions actually emitted into the environment might be higher, despite the abatement. In other words, could it be the case that the amount of effluent abated is smaller than the increased production of effluent due to the output increase? The answer to this is no. A simple way to see this is to note that the *MEC* at the optimum is smaller under optimal abatement; *EF* in Figure 12.6 is smaller than *BC*. That means we are lower down on the *MEC* curve (say in Figure 12.5), which shows that the level of actual emissions must be lower.

### 12.1.5 Positive Externalities

It is worth pointing out that there is a 'problem' with positive externalities also. If some activity generates positive externalities, the equilibrium level of such an activity in competitive equilibrium will be too low; that is, there will be too little of the activity. For example, consider the simple activity of keeping one's front yard looking clean and beautiful. Perhaps it is a matter of planting nice flowering trees and shrubs that would be seen and enjoyed by neighbours and other passers-by. If the cost of these plantings is $c$ per unit (see Figure 12.7) and the demand is $D$, we would expect to see $Q_c$ of this activity in equilibrium. Now the demand curve is normally taken to be the *SMB* curve, if the benefits from this consumption accrue only to the buyer, and then $Q_c$ is the optimal level of this activity. But if some external benefits accrue to neighbours, the *SMB* is higher than the demand curve (say at *SMB* in the figure) and in that case the optimal level of the activity would be $Q^*$. Thus, normal competitive equilibrium would result in too little of the activity being undertaken. The Pigouvian solution to this problem would be to introduce a subsidy to lower the price to $p^*$. The amount of the subsidy would be the marginal external benefit at the optimum. In the figure, the amount of the subsidy would have to be $(c - p*)$.

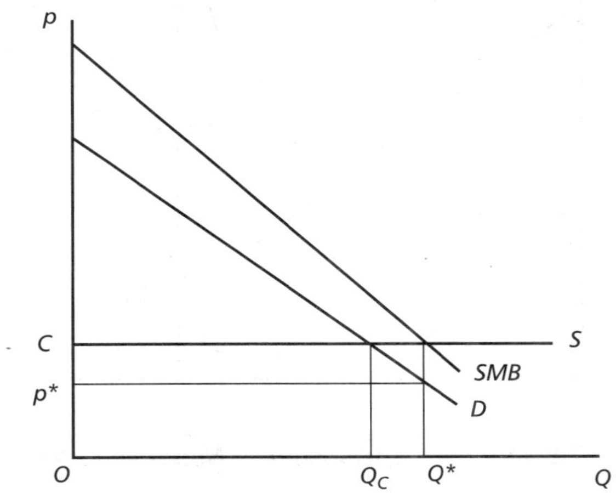


**Figure 12.7** *Misallocation due to a Positive Externality*

### 12.1.6 The Coase Theorem

In an influential 1960 paper,[1] University of Chicago professor Ronald Coase cast an entirely new light on the problem of externalities. He emphasised that the problem of externalities could be

[1] R. H. Coase: 'The Problem of Social Cost', *Journal of Law and Economics*, Vol. 3 (Oct. 1960), pp. 1–44

boiled down to one of lack of markets, and the lack of markets in turn could be explained by one or both of two things: lack of well-defined property rights, and transactions costs. These ideas can perhaps best be elaborated if we take a specific example.

Consider a fishing company that operates on a lake. It has been operating there for years and has a stable catch every year. Now a chemical company starts operations at a factory on the shores of the lake; its operations involve discharging factory waste into the lake. The fishing company notices a decline in their catch. Here is a classic negative externality problem: the chemical company is creating a negative externality for the fishing company, whose profits decline as a result. What is the solution? We have seen what needs to be done in Figure 12.2(b), reproduced here as Figure 12.8. The horizontal axis measures quantities of emissions and abatement, and the initial level of emissions is $\bar{e}$. If *MBA* measures the marginal benefit of abatement, which in this case would be the marginal increases in the fishing company's profits, and *MCA* measures the marginal cost of abatement borne by the chemical company, the optimal level of abatement would be $a^*$. We know we could get to this optimal level of abatement if we imposed an effluent charge of $f^*$ or set pollution standards limiting the amount of pollution to $(\bar{e} - a^*)$.

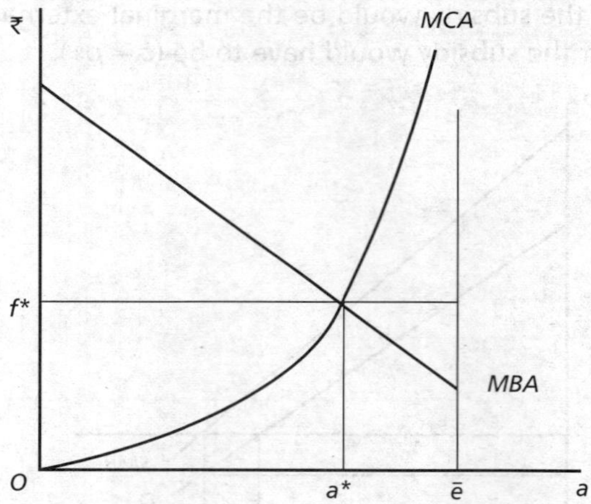


**Figure 12.8** *Optimal Response to a Negative Externality*

Now let us look at Coase's analysis of the situation. Suppose the fishing company owns the lake and therefore has the right and ability to enforce no dumping of wastes into its waters. If it orders the chemical company to stop discharging any pollutants into the lake, the chemical company will have to incur the cost of abating the entire $\bar{e}$ amount of emissions, which amounts to the whole area below the *MCA* curve between the origin O and $\bar{e}$. The fishing company would get back all of its lost profits, which will amount to the area below the *MBA* curve between O and $\bar{e}$. This situation is not efficient, since the chemical company is having to bear all of the abatement costs between $a^*$ and $\bar{e}$ (we know abatement up to $a^*$ is optimal), but the benefit of this abatement to the fishing company is only the area below the *MBA* curve between $a^*$ and $\bar{e}$. So, if negotiation is costless, the chemical company could approach the fishing company and offer to pay them for the right to discharge a certain amount of effluent into the lake. If the two parties agree in principle, and negotiate in good faith, Coase argued that they would agree to allow discharges of exactly $(\bar{e} - a^*)$, since the total surplus is maximised in that case. How the surplus is allocated between the two firms depends upon the bargaining skills of the two parties, although it seems that the fishing company would be able to garner most of the surplus, since it has the property rights in the lake.

However, suppose the ownership of the lake rested in the hands of the chemical company and therefore they were free to discharge all the effluent into the lake. The fishing company would now be forced to approach the chemical company and offer to pay them to abate some of the effluent. Again, Coase argued, the amount of clean-up they would agree on is exactly $a^*$, since surplus is maximised at that point. The distribution of the surplus would now be skewed towards the chemical company, since it had the property rights, but the allocation would be the same as in the case where the fishing company had the property rights in the lake.

Coase's observations on externalities have come to be called the Coase Theorem. Simply put, it says that the problem of externalities disappears if property rights are clearly defined and there are no transactions costs. It emphasises that the disposition of the property rights is immaterial to the achievement of efficiency, although it naturally makes a difference in the distribution of surplus between the concerned parties.

The Coase Theorem seems to suggest that the problem of externalities is not as severe as we might have thought, that if we could only assign property rights clearly and reduce or eliminate transactions costs, we could address the problem. However, this is not so in practice. One problem with the applicability of the theorem is that many of the cases where externalities are particularly important, such as with environmental pollution, are precisely situations where the property rights are diffuse (who owns the atmosphere?), particularly internationally. The transactions costs of trying to reach international agreements on carbon pollution, for example, have proven to be particularly high. Further, the Coase Theorem applies only in special cases such as the example we have considered, of two firms who care only about their respective profit levels and therefore evaluate the externality problem along only a single dimension. If the externality were evaluated within a multi dimensional framework, the conditions over which the Coase Theorem would apply would be highly restricted. An example would perhaps help elaborate. [2]

Suppose two roommates are trying to settle on the level at which one of them can play his stereo. Madan, the music-lover, loves to blare music loudly, while his room mate Qazi, the

[2] This example was suggested by one in the book by Hal Varian: *Intermediate Microeconomics: A Modern Approach.*

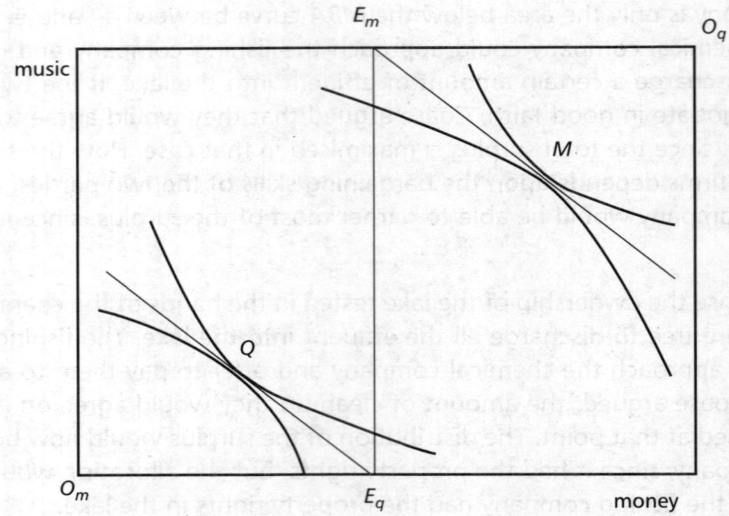


**Figure 12.9** *How Different Distributions of Property Rights could lead to Different Optimal Solutions*

quiet-lover, would rather have the music off. So we have a negative externality problem, which they are trying to resolve through Coase-like negotiations and side payments. Let us draw an Edgeworth box to analyse the situation (see Figure 12.9). On one axis, the dimension of the box represents the total amount of money the two students have. On the vertical axis, we measure the loudness of the music, with the volume going up as we move higher on the graph. $O_m$ is Madan's origin. For him, money and the volume of the music are both goods and so he has the normal-shaped indifference curves over these two goods. $O_q$ is Qazi's origin. He also likes money, but for him the volume of music is a 'bad'. Measured from his origin, however, as we move down the graph, the volume of music is falling, so this is a good, and therefore his indifference curves also have the normal shape from his origin.

Now let us consider the agreement they might reach under alternative scenarios on property rights. If Madan gets the property rights, the effective endowment point is $E_m$, where Madan has his money and plays his music at maximum volume, while Qazi has his money and has to suffer the loud music. If they negotiate on perhaps Qazi paying Madan to turn down the volume, they might settle on a point such as $M$, which is efficient and a Pareto improvement over $E_m$. If, instead, Qazi has the property rights, the effective endowment point is $E_q$, where each student has his money and the music is turned off (volume is at zero). Negotiations now would lead to an allocation such as $Q$, where Madan pays Qazi to allow him to play the music softly in exchange for an appropriate payment. Thus we see that, whereas efficiency is reached in either case, the allocation of property rights makes a significant difference in *which* efficient allocation results.

Technically, the case where the Coase Theorem would work is one where the preferences are quasi-linear, in which case they would be horizontally parallel and therefore there would be just one level of music volume that would be efficient. This condition is automatically satisfied with regard to firm-to-firm externalities, since the firms are assumed to care only about their profits and do not have independent preferences over the level of pollution. Effectively, their 'indifference curves' are vertical straight lines, and therefore the efficient allocation is one where the amount of money (or surplus) is maximised.

There is another important reason why the Coase Theorem does not seem to apply in most cases of externality that we observe in the economy: in cases where the Coase Theorem would apply, *the externality problem would have already been resolved through markets, negotiation or merger*. Let us think back to our example of the chemical and fishing company negotiating over pollution in the lake. One simple solution that we did not mention is for the two firms to simply merge. Each firm would have the incentive to acquire the other and thereby internalise the externality. Once the two firms are one, the maximisation of profits will automatically lead to the efficient level of abatement, and any costs of negotiation can be avoided. Thus, we would expect many potential situations of externality would have been resolved or averted through merger.

Short of merger, in situations where the property rights can be clearly defined and transactions costs are low or zero, markets should emerge to address the externality problem. A good example of this is the classic example of a positive externality that was mentioned earlier: the externality created by beekeepers for the owners of fruit orchards. In fact, this problem has been addressed quite effectively in the United States through the emergence of a market for 'bee services'. Beekeepers mount their hives on trucks and start in the extreme south of the United States as the fruit orchards come into bloom. If an orchard owner contracts their service, they park their truck next to the orchard and release their bees. After pollination is over, they drive a little further north, and in this manner make their way further and further north, keeping pace with the blossoming of the fruit trees and renting out their bees. Thus, we have a market solution to the externality problem.

### 12.1.7 Common Property Externalities

Whenever a firm competes in a market, it creates a negative externality for all its competitors by reducing their profitability. However, we do not regard such an externality as a bad thing, because competition helps to force firms to be more efficient, and consumers benefit from this improved efficiency and the effect of competition on prices. However, there is a class of activities where the externalities created by a firm on others engaging in the same activity *is* considered to be a problem, and this problem has come to be called 'The Tragedy of the Commons'. The problem arises when firms are competing over a resource that is in limited supply and over which no individual firm has property rights.

The term 'Tragedy of the Commons' comes from an early example of this sort of problem. Many towns in the United States have public parks called commons. Originally, these commons were intended to serve poor people who did not own their own pastures to be able to graze their animals, or for travellers passing through the town to be able to graze their horses. However, it turned out that even property owners in town, people who did have their own pastures, would frequently allow their animals to graze on the common land, and would graze their animals on their own land only when the grazing on the common land got too poor. Further, there would be a tendency for lots of poor people to keep animals since they could graze them for free on the commons. The net result was that, although private pasture land was carefully husbanded, with flocks or herds optimised for the available land, the common would be over grazed and would consequently tend to be in poor condition. This was the tragedy.

The root problem here is that there is a limited resource, the common pasture, which is a common property. No one owns the grass on the land until someone's animals eat it; once that happens, the owner of the animal has effectively appropriated that grass. The fact that there is now less grass available for others is not a part of the animal owner's calculation; the negative externality created by using the common property resource is ignored. As a result, too much of the externality-creating activity is carried out.

There are many examples of this sort of negative externality. Two prime examples in today's international economic environment are fishing and whaling. Since fish or whales swimming in the world's oceans are nobody's property until they are caught, they are common property, and the tragedy of the commons applies here also. Too many fish and whales are caught compared to what is socially desirable, and the result is that many species are being driven to extinction. India is staring at a potentially huge problem with its groundwater resources. The aquifers that lie underground are nobody's property until the water is extracted and used for irrigation, so once again there is a tendency for too much water to be pumped out. A similar situation exists on oilfields where multiple leases may have been given out on land above the field, and so each owner tries to pump out as much oil as possible before the other lease holders do. Undiscovered knowledge is also a common property resource, with the first one to discover a new cancer drug, for example, standing to make substantial profits. The result is frenetic research activity in an attempt to 'win the patent race'.

Analysis of the common property externality is relatively straightforward. Consider the decision the potential owner of a fishing boat must make. Suppose it costs $c$ to operate a boat for a year. The potential boat owner will find it profitable to operate a boat if the returns from operating the boat are at least $c$. Now suppose the returns from operating a boat depend upon how many boats there are on the fishing grounds. If these returns did not depend upon the number of boats, there would be no externality problem; this was perhaps the case a few hundred years ago when the pressure on fishing grounds was not that great. In Figure 12.10, where we are measuring the number of boats operating on the fishing ground on the horizontal axis and returns and costs on the vertical axis, we have drawn a downward-sloping average product (AP) curve, which embodies the assumption that the average catch per fish declines as the number of boats increases. Since the decision on whether or not to operate a boat depends upon whether or not the returns are greater than the cost, the equilibrium number of boats on the grounds will be $n_c$, where the AP per boat is equal to the cost of operating a boat, $c$.

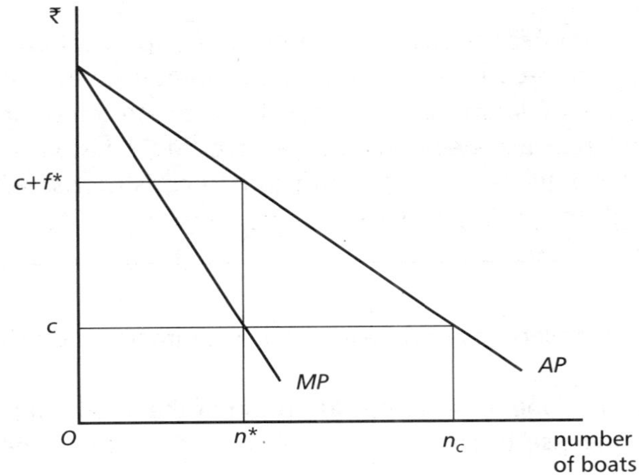


**Figure 12.10** *A Fishery as a Common Property Externality*

If we ask what is the number of boats at which the total surplus is maximised, we see that it will not be at $n_c$, but rather at $n^*$, where the *marginal* product per boat is equal to the cost of operating a boat. If $F(n)$ represents the production function of fish, as a function of the number of boats, surplus would be

$$S = F(n) - cn$$

and surplus would be maximised where

$$\frac{dS}{dn} = F'(n) - c = 0,$$

which is where $MP_n = c$. Thus, free entry results in too much entry. A simple 'Pigouvian' way to get to the optimum would be to impose a license fee on the boats. The optimal license fee, $f^*$, would be such that the total cost of running a boat (inclusive of the fee) would equal the AP per boat at $n^*$. In other words,

$$c + f^* = \frac{F(n^*)}{n}$$

$$\text{or} \qquad f^* = \frac{F(n^*)}{n} - c.$$

## 12.2 PUBLIC GOODS

**Task for this section:**

To study the problem of public goods, goods which are non-rival and non-excludable. We see how the property of non-excludability makes the emergence of a market impossible and how the problem of non-rivalry makes it difficult to calculate the optimal level of provision of the good. For these reasons, decisions on the level of provision are made through the political system, but we find that it is very difficult to construct sensible rules for making those decisions through the voting process.

Public goods are goods or services that have two key characteristics; they are:

- Non-rival, meaning that one person's consumption of the good does not reduce the amount available for someone else to consume; all people can consume them equally at the same time.
- Non-excludable, meaning no one can be prevented from consuming the good once it has been produced and made available to anyone.

A pure public good has both these characteristics in full measure, while a pure private good has neither to any extent at all. Mixed goods have one or the other of these characteristics, perhaps in full or part.

The classic example of a pure public good is national defence. Everyone in the country is being protected simultaneously, so it is non-rival. And no one can be excluded from that protection, so it is non-excludable. Broadcast radio and television are also pure public goods, since one person's tuning in does not preclude someone else from tuning in, and, once the signal has been cast into the ether, no one can be excluded from tuning in. Cable television, however, is a mixed good: it is non-rival, at least at most times of the day, but it is excludable. The slight rivalness may arise at peak demand periods when the quality of the signal may degrade slightly with heavy use. All the examples we discussed in the context of congestion externalities are mixed goods of this kind. Free roads, for example, are pure public goods most of the time, but at peak demand periods, they become somewhat rival due to the congestion externalities. A toll road, being excludable, becomes a mixed good. A well-functioning legal system is also a pure public good, but once it starts functioning in the interests of select people, it becomes somewhat excludable, and when it becomes highly congested, it becomes somewhat rival. Many of the goods and services provided by the government are public goods, but the fact that they are provided by the government is not what makes them that. For example, government-funded school lunches are not a public good; they are pure private goods that happen to be provided by the government. But, as we shall see, markets do a poor job of providing public goods, which is why the state frequently needs to step in to provide them.

### 12.2.1 The Allocation Problem with Public Goods

The essential reason why markets do a poor job in providing public goods stems from the fact that they are non-excludable, which makes it difficult if not impossible to get people to pay for them. In the United States, National Public Radio and the TV network run by the Public Broadcast Corporation are examples of public goods that are provided privately, being funded largely by donations and grants. So these are examples of private non-market provision of public goods. Most commercial radio and television companies worldwide obtain funding through advertising and so these are examples of market-based private provision, although the revenue model is quite different from the normal one of getting revenue from sales to consumers. In any case, these examples of private provision of public goods are hard to find, and even here it is not the normal market process at work.

At the same time, as the non-excludability of public goods makes it difficult for markets to function in their case, the non-rivalness of public goods raises anew the question of what is the optimal level of provision? With private goods, we take someone's willingness-to-pay for the good as a measure of its value to them; in other words, we take an individual's demand curve to be the private marginal benefit curve. In aggregating individual demand curves to the market demand curve, we add horizontally, which is basically a way of ordering all the marginal benefits people derive from the good from highest to lowest. It is like asking, who values the first unit of this good the most? How about the second unit? The third? And so on. Since the good is rival, only one person can consume each unit of the good and the market demand curve ranks the valuations people have for the good from highest to lowest. This market demand curve is then nothing but the *SMB* curve, since it shows the marginal benefit consumers get from consuming the good. Then we compare this marginal social benefit curve with the marginal cost of producing the good, and see that the optimal level of provision is at the point where the marginal benefit and marginal cost curve intersect. All units where the value to a consumer is greater than the marginal cost should be produced and no unit which costs more to produce than it is worth to someone should be made.

With a public good, however, the construction of the marginal social benefit curve needs to be done in a different way. While the marginal social benefit from the first unit of a private good was simply the highest that anyone was willing to pay for it, the marginal social benefit of the first unit of a public good is the *sum* of everyone's marginal valuation of it. If Aruna and Bala are the only two people in society, and the first unit of a private good is worth ₹15 to Aruna and ₹13 to Bala, we would say the marginal social benefit from the first unit of the good is ₹15. But if the good is a public good, the marginal social benefit from the first unit is ₹28, because both Aruna and Bala will get to enjoy the benefit of the first unit simultaneously (it is non-rival, remember). Similarly, the marginal social value of the second unit of the public good is the sum of the individual marginal benefits from the second unit for everyone. In this way, we see that the marginal social benefit curve for a public good (think, demand curve) is the *vertical* summation of all the individual marginal benefit curves (think, demand curves), as demonstrated in Figure 12.11. (The reason these are not really demand curves is that demand curves pre suppose markets and markets do not exist for public goods because of their non-excludability.) In the figure, we see Aruna's and Bala's marginal benefit curves and then the *SMB* curve is their vertical summation.

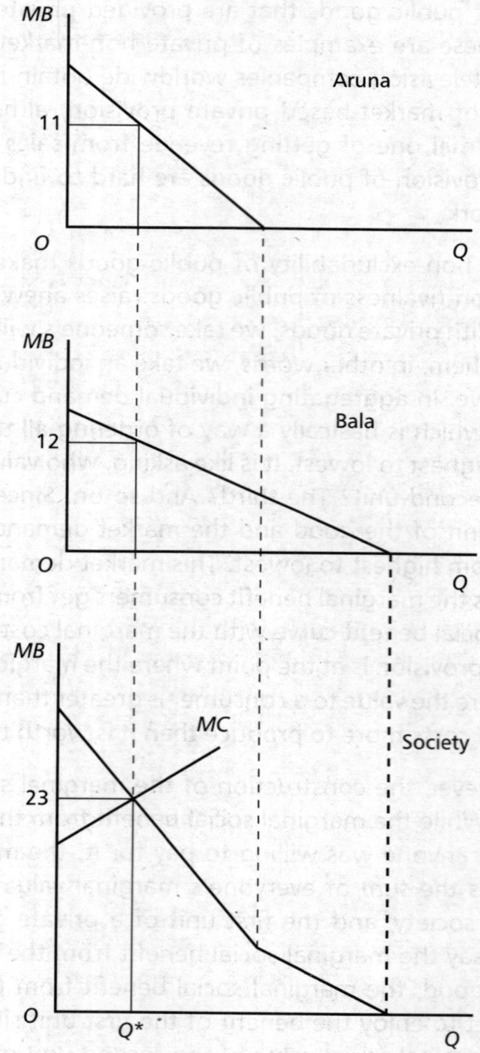


**Figure 12.11** *Optimal Provision of a Public Good: Partial Equilibrium Approach*

The optimal level of provision of the public good would then be at the point where the marginal cost of producing the good intersects the marginal social benefit curve. In the figure, this quantity is marked $Q^*$. All consumers get to consume the good at that level and enjoy their respective benefits from this level of provision.

Although this partial equilibrium approach is sufficient to get across the main point about the optimal provision of a public good, a general equilibrium approach is needed to understand more fully the nature of equilibrium in the presence of public goods. We can capture all the essential elements of the problem in a two-person, two-good model. Suppose there are two individuals, indexed 1 and 2, who each consume two goods, a private good $x$ and a public good $g$. Their utility functions are

$$u^1 = u^1(x_1, g) \qquad \text{and} \qquad u^2 = u^2(x_2, g).$$

Note that, while the quantities of the private good $x$ are indexed according to the amount of the good each individual consumes, the amount of the public good $g$ is common to both, as both will simultaneously consume all of the public good that is provided. The production possibilities for the economy can be summarised in an implicit production technology

$$F(x_1 + x_2, g) = 0.$$

The allocation problem is to maximise the level of utility for one individual (say person 1) given any arbitrarily chosen utility level for the other and the production technology, that is to

$$\text{Maximise} \quad u^1(x_1, g)$$

$$\text{subject to} \quad u^2(x_2, g) = \bar{u}$$

$$\text{and} \quad F(x_1 + x_2, g) = 0.$$

Before proceeding to the solution of this problem, we will transform it slightly. Let $x = x_1 + x_2$, so that $x_2 = x - x_1$. Substituting these into the previous statement of the problem, we can rewrite it as

$$\text{Maximise} \quad u^1(x_1, g)$$

$$\text{subject to} \quad u^2(x - x_1, g) = \bar{u} \qquad \text{and} \qquad F(x, g) = 0.$$

The choice variables in the problem are now $x$, $x_1$ and $g$. Write down the Lagrange function

$$\mathcal{L} = u^1(x_1, g) + \lambda[u^2(x - x_1, g) - \bar{u}] + \mu[F(x, g)],$$

where $\lambda$ and $\mu$ are Lagrange multipliers. The first-order conditions for a solution are

$$\frac{\partial \mathcal{L}}{\partial g} = u_g^1 + \lambda u_g^2 + \mu F_g = 0$$

$$\frac{\partial \mathcal{L}}{\partial x_1} = u_x^1 - \lambda u_x^2 = 0$$

$$\frac{\partial \mathcal{L}}{\partial x} = \lambda u_x^2 + \mu F_x = 0,$$

where $u_g^1 = \frac{\partial u^1}{\partial g}$, $u_g^2 = \frac{\partial u^2}{\partial g}$, $u_x^1 = \frac{\partial u^1}{\partial x_1}$ and $u_x^2 = \frac{\partial u^2}{\partial x_2}$. These three first-order conditions can be rewritten as

$$u_g^1 + \lambda u_g^2 = -\mu F_g \tag{12.23}$$

$$u_x^1 = \lambda u_x^2 \tag{12.24}$$

$$\lambda u_x^2 = -\mu F_x. \tag{12.25}$$

Dividing (12.23) by (12.25), using (12.24) to substitute, we get

$$\frac{u_g^1}{u_x^1} + \frac{u_g^2}{u_x^2} = \frac{F_g}{F_x}. \tag{12.26}$$

Equation (12.26) says that the efficiency condition in the presence of a public good is that the *sum* of the marginal rates of substitution (MRS) must equal the marginal rate of transformation (MRT). Note that the two terms on the left-hand side of (12.26) are the MRSs between the two goods for the two individuals respectively, while the right-hand side is the MRT, the slope of the production possibilities frontier (PPF). The efficiency condition when both goods were private was that the MRS for each individual had to equal the MRT (and hence each other), but here it is the *sum* of the MRSs that must equal the *MRT*. The partial equilibrium way of describing this contrast is that, for private goods, each person's marginal benefit must equal the marginal cost (and hence everybody else's marginal benefit), but, for a public good, the *sum* of individual marginal benefits must equal the marginal cost.

The general equilibrium result can also be seen graphically. In Figure 12.12, panel (a) starts with a *ppf* between the private good $x$ and the public good $g$. The curve $\bar{u}$ represents the indifference curve for an arbitrarily chosen utility level for individual 2. Given the particular $\bar{u}$, the curve $S$ represents the consumption possibilities frontier for individual 1. $S$ is the vertical difference between the *ppf* and the curve $\bar{u}$. Clearly, the level of the public good must be between $g_1$ and $g_2$, since $\bar{u}$ lies above the *ppf* for values of $g$ outside this range and hence $\bar{u}$ would be unattainable. Given a level of the public good within the feasible range, the amount of good $x$ that individual 1 would be able to consume would be the amount of $x$ that would be produced minus the amount of $x$ needed to ensure individual 2 is on $\bar{u}$. For example, if the level of production of the public good was $g^*$ in panel (b) of the figure, production would be at point $C$ on the *ppf*, individual 2 would have to be at point $B$ so her utility reaches the requisite level and so the amount of $x$ available to individual 1 would be the difference between $C$ and $B$, which is the height of $A$ in the figure. The curve $S$ is derived in this way and shows how much $x$ individual 1 could get for different levels of $g$.

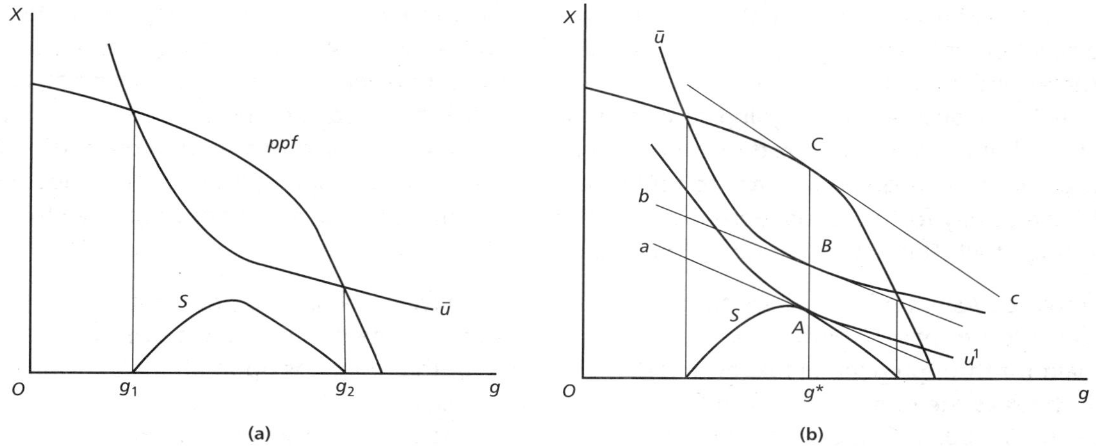


**Figure 12.12** *Optimal Provision of a Public Good: General Equilibrium Approach*

Now let us turn to the determination of the optimal level of $g$. If $S$ represents the set of consumption possibilities for individual 1, and we want to maximise his utility, we must look for a point on $S$ where one of his indifference curves is tangent to $S$. In panel (b) of Figure 12.12, we have drawn such an indifference curve: the curve labelled $u^1$ is an indifference curve for individual 1 which is tangent to $S$ at $A$. This is the highest utility individual 1 can achieve given the production constraint and given the utility level $\bar{u}$ for individual 2. But now notice something about this point $A$. Since $S$ is the vertical difference between the *ppf* and the indifference curve $\bar{u}$, the slope of $S$ at $A$ must be the difference between the slope of the *ppf* at $C$ and the slope of $\bar{u}$ at $B$. But the slope of $S$ at $A$ is equal to the slope of $u^1$ at $A$, which is individual 1's *MRS* at $A$. Further, the slope of $\bar{u}$ at $B$ is individual 2's *MRS* between $x$ and $g$. And the slope of the *ppf* at $C$ is the *MRT*. Thus, we have a graphical demonstration of the result in (12.26) that, for efficiency with a public good, we must have the sum of MRSs equal to the MRT.

## 12.2.2 The Free Rider Problem and Demand Revelation

Having established the optimal level of provision for a public good, let us now turn to the problem of how we implement this. Let us suppose the government has decided to provide a public good, but it needs to find out its value for people in order to determine the optimal level of provision. How does it get this information? With private goods, people's demand behaviour reveals how much they value different goods. They have to reveal how much a good is worth to them because, if they do not they will have to do without the good. But with public goods, since they are non-excludable, people are going to hope that others will pay for and provide the good, and they can 'free ride' on this behaviour from others.

Let us be more specific. Let us even ignore the question of the level of provision by assuming that a particular public good has to be provided at one and only one level, and the question we face is: should it be provided? We want to find out how much it is worth to people in order to decide whether the cost of providing it is justified. Now suppose Ashok values this public good to the extent of ₹5,000 and a government survey asks him to reveal how much it is worth to him. Before Ashok answers, he is going to want to know how the good is going to be paid for. If he believes that he might be asked to contribute what he says it is worth to him, or a proportion of that amount, he is going to want to understate the value in the hope that he can free ride and not have to pay for the good. Perhaps he can report a value of zero, so he does not have to pay anything at all. This is the free rider problem.

However, Ashok might believe that what he says will have no bearing on how much he might be called on to pay. For example, suppose he knows that, if the public good is provided, it will be paid for through general tax revenues and his share of that depends upon his income and not what he says the good is worth to him. Suppose Ashok calculates that his share of the cost will come to ₹7,500. In that case, he would be a net loser if the good is provided, he would not want to see it provided, and therefore he has the incentive to announce that his value is very low, maybe even negative. Alternatively, if he calculates that his share of the cost will come out to ₹1,000, he would be a net gainer if the good is provided, he would like to see it provided and therefore he has the incentive to overstate his value in order to improve the chances that the good will indeed be provided. So in neither case does Ashok have the incentive to truthfully reveal his value of the good. This is the problem of demand revelation.

Economists have been trying for over a century to come up with a mechanism to induce people to reveal truthfully their demand for public goods, but as yet no practical solution has been found. Two solutions that do work in principle are the mechanisms of Groves and Clarke. They can be illustrated by means of a simple example, outlined in Table 12.3. Suppose there are three individuals in society, Aruna, Bala, and Chetan, and suppose their net valuations of a public good (after taking into account what they will be called on to pay if the public good is provided) are given in the 'Values' column. We see that the sum of the values is positive and so this public good should be provided. But can we find out what people's true values are?

**Table 12.3** *Transfers under the Groves and Clarke Solutions: An Example*

| | Values | Groves Payments | Clarke Tax |
|---|---|---|---|
| Aruna | −195 | +200 | 0 |
| Bala | −200 | +205 | 0 |
| Chetan | +400 | −395 | −395 |
| Net | +5 | | |

The Groves mechanism calls for each person to receive a payment, if the public good is provided, equal to the sum of everybody else's valuations. If this sum is negative, the person has to pay that amount. In our example, Aruna would receive a payment, if the public good is provided, of ₹200, since this is the sum of Chetan's and Bala's valuations (assume for now that they will reveal their true valuations, as we shall see is optimal for them to do). Bala would receive ₹205 and Chetan would be charged ₹395. Note that each person's net pay-off will now be +5 if the public good is provided. Thus, each person's interests have been aligned with the social interest. Consider Aruna's decision on what to report as her value. If she reports a number such as −205 (i.e. exaggerates how much the good will hurt her), the net social value will become negative and the good will not be provided. Aruna would then lose her net surplus of +5. However, if she under-reports her values, say be saying it is −185, this will not change the social decision, so she has no incentive to do so. Thus, Aruna has an incentive to report her value truthfully. A similar argument holds for Bala. Chetan also has an incentive to report his value truthfully. If he overstates his value, it will not make any difference, while if he understates his value, he runs the risk of reversing the decision and thereby losing his surplus of +5. So each person has an incentive to report their value truthfully. The reason is that their pay-offs have been aligned with the net social benefit, and the only time reporting their value untruthfully makes any difference is to change the decision from the one they prefer. The main problem with the Groves mechanism, of course, is the very large side payments that it calls for, making it totally impractical.

The Clarke mechanism, proposed independently and actually slightly earlier than the Groves one, adopts essentially the same approach but focuses only on the 'pivotal' voters. As in the Groves mechanism, we add up the reported values of all individuals other than the one whose situation is being evaluated, but we charge them a tax, the Clarke tax, only if their valuation would reverse the decision. For example, the sum of values other than Aruna's is +200, which would suggest providing the public good; her value would not reverse this decision, so she is not regarded a pivotal voter and is not charged the Clarke tax. Similarly, Bala's −200 would not reverse the +205 being bid by everyone else and so Bala is not charged a tax either. With Chetan, however, the sum of everyone else's valuation would be −395 and the public good would not be provided. Chetan's 'bid' of +400 would reverse that decision, so he is charged a tax of 395. However, Chetan has no incentive to distort his valuation, for the same reasons as under the Groves mechanism. Similarly, Aruna and Bala have no incentive to distort their values either, since the only time it would make a difference would be if they reversed the decision, and that would make them pivotal and liable for the Clarke tax. For example, if Aruna announced her value to be −205, the public good would not be provided and this may seem good as her pay-off from it was −195. However, she would now be pivotal and would be liable for a Clarke tax of 200. Note that, in the Clarke mechanism, nobody ever receives a payment, there are only taxes equal to the absolute value of the sum of everyone else's bids. So Aruna would pay 200, which is worse than the −195 pay-off she gets from the public good's implementation.

Although the Clarke tax works in theory, it also involves potentially large side payments. In addition, it is administratively very cumbersome, as it involves calculating the sum of everybody else's valuations for each of the voters in society. Further, the money that is collected in Clarke taxes should not, in theory, be used by government in any way since that would upset the careful balance of the incentive calculations. It is not clear what should be done with it. Finally, the mechanism is sufficiently complex that it is unlikely many voters would understand it and therefore their bids may be somewhat random anyway. So at this stage, we do not have a way to practically elicit people's truthful revelation of their valuation of public goods.

### 12.2.3 Voting

As a practical matter, decisions about the level of public goods provision get decided in the political arena through voting, at least in democratic countries. The normal rule used is majority voting, but this has problems too. The 'paradox of voting' is a very old mathematical problem, sometimes named after the French mathematician Condorcet. Suppose there are three individuals in society, say Aruna, Bala and Chetan again, and they are trying to decide between three different alternatives. To give the problem the flavour of a public goods problem, suppose the decision concerns the level of spending on education and the three alternatives are high spending, medium spending and low spending. If the symbol $\succ$ signifies a preference and the three alternatives are labelled $H$, $M$ and $L$, suppose the preferences of the three individuals are as follows:

Aruna: $L \succ M \succ H$

Bala: $M \succ H \succ L$

Chetan: $H \succ L \succ M$.

If we now use majority voting to try to decide between these three alternatives, we get a voting cycle or an intransitivity. Consider the following pairwise comparisons:

choosing between $L$ and $M$: $L$ would win 2–1,

choosing between $M$ and $H$: $M$ would win 2–1 and

choosing between $H$ and $L$: $H$ would win 2–1.

After finding the social preferences $L \succ M$ and $M \succ H$, we would have expected $L \succ H$ by transitivity, but we get $H \succ L$. This is the paradox; which of the three options should society choose?

This kind of situation is subject to manipulation and it points to the advantage one would have if one could set the agenda or decide on voting procedures. For example, to try to choose between three alternatives, we might use a pairwise elimination method: take a vote between two of the options and then vote the winner against the third option. In this kind of procedure, any of the three options could win, depending on the order of the voting:

first $L$ vs. $M \rightarrow L$ wins, then $L$ vs. $H \rightarrow H$ wins,

first $M$ vs. $H \rightarrow M$ wins, then $M$ vs. $L \rightarrow L$ wins and

first $L$ vs. $H \rightarrow H$ wins, then $H$ vs. $M \rightarrow M$ wins.

So whoever controls the voting procedure can control the outcome. That is why the Speaker of the House is so powerful in any parliamentary system, since he or she exercises considerable influence on the procedures of the legislative body.

Scholars have been trying for centuries to try to design a voting mechanism that did not have such problems, and have consistently failed to do so. Eventually, the search was put to rest when Kenneth Arrow proved an amazing result: that it was impossible to find any social decision-making procedure that satisfied a set of reasonable conditions. Instead of trying to design a decision rule, Arrow asked the question: what are the minimal conditions we would want any decision rule to satisfy. He chose four 'axioms' and showed that they were mutually incompatible. Arrow's axioms were:

- the rule should be an **ordering**, that is, it should be **complete** (be able to choose between all possible pairs of alternatives, and be able to aggregate all possible individual preference patterns), and **transitive** (be free of all voting cycles such as the Condorcet paradox),
- it should satisfy the **Pareto criterion**, that if all individuals prefer *A* to *B*, then so should society (or, a weaker condition: if at least one person prefers *A* to *B*, and no one prefers *B* to *A*, then society should prefer *A* to *B*),
- it should satisfy the **Independence of Irrelevant Alternatives** axiom, that the choice between *A* and *B* should not depend on people's preferences over a third, irrelevant alternative *C* (this is to avoid manipulation of the outcome through the introduction of irrelevant alternatives) and
- it should be **Non-dictatorial**, that is, no one person's preferences should automatically be the social choice.

Arrow proved that no social decision rule could satisfy all four of these axioms. Since they all appear to be so reasonable, and so minimal, the upshot is rather pessimistic: that democracies are fated to be riven by dissension and fundamental incompatibilities.

Many authors have tried to weaken Arrow's conditions to find a set of conditions under which a consistent social decision rule could be designed and most of these attempts have not yielded much of great interest. One result in this vein, however, is interesting. It can be shown that, if voting is being conducted on choices where the preferences of all voters are single-peaked, then majority voting gives consistent results and the results can be called the median voter rule. This rule simply says that the social choice coincides with the preference of the median voter.

Let us first explain the notion of single-peaked preferences. If we go back to the preferences of our three voters, Aruna, Bala and Chetan, over the three alternatives of low, medium or high spending on education, and arrange them on a chart such as Figure 12.13, we can see that the preference patterns seem fundamentally at odds. Think of the patterns made in the chart as looking like mountains with peaks. We see that, while Aruna has one 'peak' at *L*, and Bala has one peak at *M*, Chetan has two peaks, one at *H* and the other at *L*, with a 'valley' in between. Thus, these preferences are not single-peaked, and this is what gives rise to the voting cycle. It is

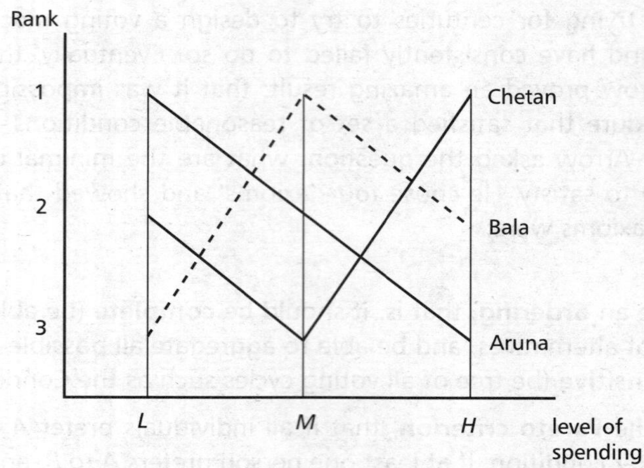


**Figure 12.13** *A Non-Single-Peaked Preference Pattern*

worth pointing out that the non-single-peakedness is not an artefact of where we have positioned the three alternatives. For example, if we moved $L$ to the middle and put $M$ over at left, Bala's preference pattern would have two peaks, and if we put $H$ in the middle, Aruna's would have two peaks. Thus, there is a deep incompatibility in these preferences.

It might be tempting to argue that single-peakedness is a reasonable condition, that the preferences as specified do not make sense. While Aruna seems perfectly reasonable, with a preference going from low to medium to high spending (perhaps her children have already finished school and therefore she gets no benefit from spending on education), and similarly Bala seems to care a little about education but not so much as to be willing to pay a lot for it, Chetan's preferences may seem bizarre, in that his best option is high spending but then his second choice switches dramatically to low spending. Wouldn't it be more reasonable if his second choice were $M$? If that were the case, the preference pattern would be single-peaked. There is certainly something to be said for this argument, but here is a scenario under which Chetan's preferences might make sense. Suppose he cares a lot about education and that is why he would prefer to see high spending. But he cares so much that, if the spending level is not high, he plans to take his children out of the government schools and send them to expensive private schools instead. In that case, he would rather not have to pay for even a medium level of spending since he would be getting no benefit from it, and so his second choice is low spending. Thus we see that, while single-peakedness may seem like a reasonable condition, it might easily be violated.

Nevertheless, the median voter rule gives some comfort that, in some situations, majority voting can yield consistent choices. And this rule helps explain why political parties tend to coalesce in the 'middle' of the viewpoint spectrum. Consider the problem faced by two ice cream sellers trying to decide where to locate their stands on a beach. Hotelling showed that the equilibrium would be for them to locate right next to one another in the middle of the beach. In the same way, we see

(a) How many fishermen will choose to fish on each lake and what will be the total catch?

(b) What is the efficient allocation of fishermen between the two lakes? How much would be the total catch in this case?

(c) Suppose the government could charge a license fee for each fisherman on each lake. What license fee should the government set in order to achieve the efficient solution?

2. National Lead Co. (NLC), a monopoly public enterprise, produces lead at a cost of ₹5 per unit. Demand for lead is given by

$$Q = 25{,}000 - 1{,}000p.$$

(a) How much lead should NLC produce, and what price should it charge, to maximise welfare?

(b) Suppose environmentalists discover that that for each unit of lead it produces, NLC also produces one unit of a toxic waste (W) that causes a total damage given by

$$D = \frac{W^2}{8{,}000},$$

where $W$ is the amount of waste discharged. What would be your answer to part (a) given this additional information?

(c) Suppose that NLC now discovers that it could eliminate waste at a cost of

$$C = \frac{A^2}{2{,}000},$$

where $A$ is the amount of waste abated. Answer again the questions in part (a).

3. Vacation Resort is a popular spot for people to spend sunny days. All the people who go there are identical in that they like secluded resorts better than crowded ones. The benefit that each person receives from visiting the resort therefore depends (negatively) on the number of visitors the resort has, according to the function

$$B = 20 - \frac{n}{200},$$

where $n$ is the number of visitors at the resort, and $B$ is a measure (in rupees) of the benefit each person receives.

(a) If the resort charges an entrance fee of ₹6 per visitor, how many visitors will there be in equilibrium?

(b) What is the socially optimal entrance fee to set, assuming that the cost of providing resort access is zero? Explain clearly.

4. Chem-Clean Corp. (CCC) produces 10 tons of toxic waste in its production process. It presently does no clean-up and makes profits of ₹100 per period. It could abate its wastes at a cost of

$$C = a^2,$$

where $a$ is the amount abated, in tons.

(a) Suppose the government levies a ₹14 effluent charge on CCC. How much of its wastes would it abate? What would its profits be now?

(b) Suppose instead that the government offers CCC a subsidy of ₹14 per ton of effluent abated. Now how much waste would CCC abate? What would be its profits now?

(c) Under what circumstances would either policy in (a) or (b) be optimal? Which of the two policies would you prefer? Explain why.

5. The demand for blodgets is given by

$$Q_d = 50{,}000 - 1{,}000P,$$

and the supply by

$$Q_s = 2{,}000P - 10{,}000.$$

The production of blodgets involves the simultaneous production of gunk, a toxic by-product. Two units of gunk are produced for each blodget produced. When discharged into the environment, each unit of gunk causes ₹3 worth of environmental damage.

(a) How many blodgets should be produced, and what price should be charged for them, in order to maximise welfare?

(b) What will be the equilibrium number of blodgets produced, and what will be the price, if the blodget market is perfectly competitive and is unregulated? What is the deadweight loss to society of this equilibrium, compared to the efficient one of part (a)?

(c) What would be the Pigouvian tax that would force the competitive market to the efficient solution? Identify the winners and losers from this tax and calculate the extent of their gains and losses.

(d) Suppose that it is possible for blodget producers to clean up the gunk before it is discharged into the environment at a cost of

$$A = \frac{a^2}{20{,}000},$$

where $a$ is the amount of gunk abated. What is now the efficient level of production of blodgets, and how much gunk should be abated? What is the gain in welfare, if any, in this solution as compared to the solution in part (c)?

6. The total daily catch of fish in Lake Bass is given by

$$Q = 200n - n^2,$$

where $n$ is the number of boats fishing in the lake on any given day, and $Q$ is the quantity measured in barrels. Fish sell for ₹100 per barrel. It costs ₹1,000 per day to operate a boat in the lake.

(a) What will be the equilibrium number of boats fishing in the lake? How many barrels of fish will be caught?

(b) What is the socially efficient number of boats? What would be the total fish catch then?

(c) Devise a simple tax or subsidy scheme that would cause the efficient outcome to emerge in an otherwise competitive market. What would be the net effect of this scheme on government's budget?

7. There are 80 firms in the widget industry. Of these, 40 are of type $A$, whose cost functions are

$$C_A(q_A) = \frac{1}{2}q_A^2,$$

where $C_A$ is the total cost of a firm of type $A$ and $q_A$ is its output level. The other 40 firms are of type $B$, whose cost functions are

$$C_B(q_B) = \frac{2}{5}q_B^2.$$

The firms behave as price-takers. The demand for widgets is

$$Q_d = 900 - 90p,$$

where $p$ is the price of widgets.

(a) Find the supply curve of widgets and the equilibrium price and quantity of widgets. How many widgets do firms of each type produce? What is the profit per firm of each type?

(b) Suppose that the production of widgets releases carbon into the atmosphere. It has been estimated that each widget produced releases 1 unit of carbon and each unit of carbon causes ₹1 worth of environmental damage. What is the socially efficient level of widget production? How should this be divided up between firms of type $A$ and type $B$?

(c) Suppose firms could reduce the amount of carbon they release if they undertook abatement activities. The abatement costs for type $A$ and type $B$ firms are respectively

$$y_A = \frac{1}{4}x_A^2 \quad \text{and} \quad y_B = \frac{1}{5}x_B^2,$$

where $y_i$ for $i = A, B$ are the abatement costs for a type $i$ firm and $x_i$ for $i = A, B$ are the amounts of carbon abated. What are the efficient levels of abatement for each type of firm? What level of carbon tax should be imposed in order to induce the efficient level of production of widgets and carbon abatement?

# ANSWERS TO CHAPTER-END EXERCISES

## CHAPTER 2: THEORY OF CONSUMER BEHAVIOUR

1. (a) $G = \frac{2I}{5p_g}, \quad M = \frac{3I}{5p_M}.$
   (b) $M = 10, \quad G = 40.$
   (c) $M = 10, \quad G = 80.$

2. $X = \frac{I}{p_x + p_y}$

3. True.

4. See Chapter.

5. (a) $x = \frac{I - p_x}{2p_x}, \quad y = \frac{I + p_x}{2p_y}.$
   (b) $x = 2, \quad y = 6.$
   (c) $\epsilon_x = -1.25.$

6. (a) $A = \frac{I + 10p_A}{2p_A}, \quad B = \frac{I - 10p_A}{2p_B}.$
   (b) $\epsilon_A = -\frac{I}{I + 10p_A}, \quad \epsilon_{AB} = 0.$
   (c) $\eta_A = \frac{I}{I + 10p_A} < 1$, so A is a necessity.

7. (a) $F = 80, \quad C = 100.$
   (b) 75.44.

8. (a) $x = 15, \quad y = 15.$
   (b) $x = 22, \quad y = 8.$
   (c) Without quota: $x = 15, \quad y = 20$. With quota: $x = 24, \quad y = 8.$
   (d) A quota $q$ of $y = 10$.

## CHAPTER 3: APPLICATIONS OF CONSUMER THEORY

1. (a) He is better off in year 2, since bundle 1 is available.
   (b) Inconsistent.
   (c) $PI_P = 100, PI_L = 109.$

2. (a) $Y = \begin{cases} \dfrac{I}{p_y} & \text{if} \quad p_y < 2p_x \\ 0 & \text{if} \quad p_y > 2p_x \end{cases}$

(b) $Y^h = \begin{cases} \dfrac{U - 10}{2} & \text{if} \quad p_y < 2p_x \\ 0 & \text{if} \quad p_y > 2p_x \end{cases}$

3. (a) $-20.79$.

(b) $-23.39$.

4. (a) $C = \dfrac{I}{2p_c}, \quad S = \dfrac{I}{2p_s}$.

(b) $C = 5, \quad S = 2$.

(c) $\Delta I = 1$.

5. $X = \dfrac{3I}{4p_x}, \quad X^h = \left(\dfrac{3p_y}{p_x}\right)^{\frac{1}{4}} U.$

$\epsilon_x = -1, \quad \eta_x = 1, \quad \alpha_x = 0.75, \quad \epsilon_x^h = -0.25,$ so $\epsilon_x = \epsilon_x^h - \alpha_x \eta_x$.

6. (a) $F = 25, \quad C = 75$.

(b) $F = 0, \quad C = 100$.

(c) Both $\Delta W_{CV}$ and $\Delta W_{EV}$ equal 75.48.

7. (a) $X = 200, \quad Y = 100$.

(b) $X = 200, \quad Y = 60$.

(c) 358.66.

8. (a) $U(x, y) = 0.75x + 2y$.

(b) $x = \begin{cases} \dfrac{I}{p_x} & \text{if} \quad p_x < \dfrac{3}{8}p_y \\ 0 & \text{if} \quad p_x > \dfrac{3}{8}p_y \end{cases}$

(c) $x^h = \begin{cases} \dfrac{4U}{3} & \text{if} \quad p_x < \dfrac{3}{8}p_y \\ 0 & \text{if} \quad p_x > \dfrac{3}{8}p_y \end{cases}$

9. (a) $U(W, R) = W + R$.

$W = \begin{cases} \dfrac{I}{p_w} & \text{if } \dfrac{p_w}{p_r} < 1 \\ 0 & \text{if } \dfrac{p_w}{p_r} > 1 \end{cases}$ and $R = \begin{cases} 0 & \text{if } \dfrac{p_w}{p_r} < 1 \\ \dfrac{I}{p_r} & \text{if } \dfrac{p_w}{p_r} > 1 \end{cases}$

(b) $W = 25, R = 0$.

(c) $W = 0, R = 50, \quad \triangle W_{EV} = 100.$

(d) Cost = 150. Direct payment of 100 would be cheaper.

10. (a) $X = \dfrac{p_y I}{p_x(p_x + p_y)}$ and $Y = \dfrac{p_x I}{p_y(p_x + p_y)}$.

(b) $X = 80, Y = 5.$

(c) $X^h = \left(\dfrac{p_y}{p_x + p_y} \cdot u\right)^2.$

11. Cannot say because $C(q_2, p_1) > 100$ and $C(q_1, p_2) > 170$.

12. (a) $X = 50, Y = 50.$

(b) $X = 50, Y = 40.$

(c) $CV = 48.12.$

(d) $EV = -41.47.$

13. (a) $x = \dfrac{I - p_x}{2p_x}$ and $y = \dfrac{I + p_x}{2p_y}$.

(b) $x^h = \sqrt{\dfrac{Up_y}{p_x}} - 1$ and $y^h = \sqrt{\dfrac{Up_x}{p_y}}$.

(c) 9.16.

14. (a) $A = \dfrac{I}{3p_A}$.

(b) $A = 8, B = 32.$

(c) $A^h = e^{\dfrac{U + 2ln(p_b) - 2ln(2p_a)}{3}}$.

(d) Yes, bananas are normal.

15. (a)

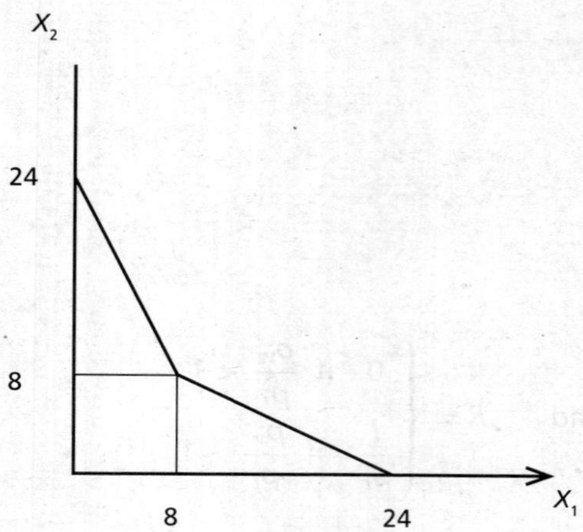

(b) $MRS = \frac{1}{2}, \quad I = 96.$

(c) $(x_1^*, x_2^*) = (12, 12).$

(d) $(x_1^{**}, x_2^{**}) = (24, 0)$, Substitution effect $= -12$, Income effect $= 0$.

(e) $$x_1^h = \begin{cases} 24 & \text{if} \quad p_1 < 2 \\ 8 & \text{if} \quad 2 < p_1 < 8 \\ 0 & \text{if} \quad p_1 > 8 \end{cases}$$

16. (a) $F_0 = 25, C_0 = 10.$

(b) $F_1 = 20, C_1 = 10$. Substitution effect $= -2.64$, Income effect $= -2.36$.

(c) 11.80.

# CHAPTER 4: EXTENSIONS OF CONSUMER THEORY

1. (a) 12 hours, Income = ₹480.

(b) Both substitution effect and income effect cause him to work less.

(c) 4.5 hours, Income = ₹390.

2. (a) $A = \frac{1}{2}A_0, \quad B = \frac{p_a A_0}{2p_b}.$

(b) $\epsilon_a = 0, \epsilon_{ab} = 0, \epsilon_b = -1, \epsilon_{ba} = 1.$

3. (a) $L^s(w) = 12.$

(b) 12.

(c) $L^s(w) = 12 - \frac{5}{w}$, 11.5 hours.

4. $L^s(w) = \frac{a}{a+b}(24).$

5. Fewer hours. Yes, she would accept it.

# CHAPTER 5: PRODUCTION, COST AND SUPPLY

1. (a) $q = 10.$

(b) $p = 10$. Number of firms = 3,000.

(c) $q = 5, \quad p = 30, \quad n = 2{,}000.$

2. (a) $q^s = \frac{1}{2}p.\ p^* = 4, Q^* = 24.$

(b) $p^* = 2, Q^* = 26$. Number of firms = 26.

3. (a) L-shaped isoquants.

   (b) $$C_{SR} = \begin{cases} 20r + \frac{w}{2}q & \text{for} \quad q \leq 20 \\ \infty & \text{for} \quad q > 20 \end{cases}$$

   $$q^s(p) = \begin{cases} 20 & \text{for} \quad p \geq \frac{w}{2} \\ 0 & \text{for} \quad p < \frac{w}{2} \end{cases}$$

   (c) $C_{LR} = \left(\frac{w}{2} + r\right) q$.

   See Figure 5.19.

4. (a) $C_{LR} = \frac{1}{2}q$.

   (b) $$C_{SR} = \begin{cases} 10 + \frac{3}{10}q & \text{for} \quad q \leq 50 \\ \infty & \text{for} \quad q > 50 \end{cases}$$

   (c) See Figure 5.19.

5. (a) $C_{LR} = 2(\sqrt{r})q$.

   (b) $\bar{K}$ is optimal at $q = \sqrt{r}\bar{K}$.

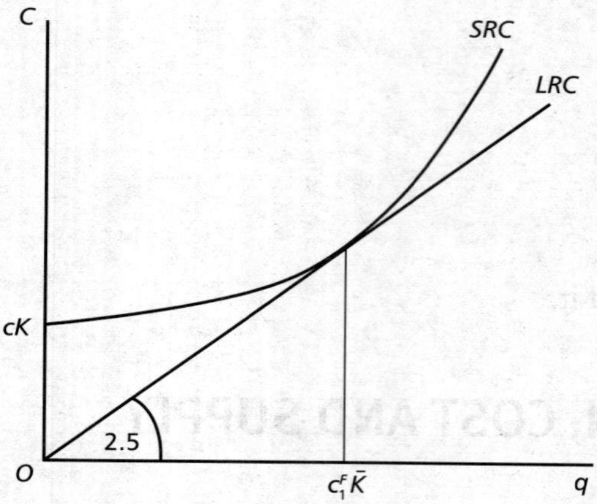


6. (a) Constant returns to scale.

   (b) $L^d = \left(1 + \sqrt{\frac{r}{w}}\right) q$ and $K^d = \left(1 + \sqrt{\frac{w}{r}}\right) q$.

(c) Yes, because otherwise $q = 0$.

7. (a) $C_{LR}(q, w, r) = (r + 4w)q^2$.

(b) $C_{SR}(q, w, r, \bar{K}) = \begin{cases} 100r + 4wq^2 & \text{for} \quad q \leq 10 \\ \infty & \text{for} \quad q > 10 \end{cases}$.

$$AC(q, w, r, \bar{K}) = \begin{cases} \dfrac{100r}{q} + 4wq & \text{for} \quad q \leq 10 \\ \infty & \text{for} \quad q > 10 \end{cases}$$

$$MC(q, w, r, \bar{K}) = \begin{cases} 8wq & \text{for} \quad q \leq 10 \\ \infty & \text{for} \quad q > 10 \end{cases}$$

(c)

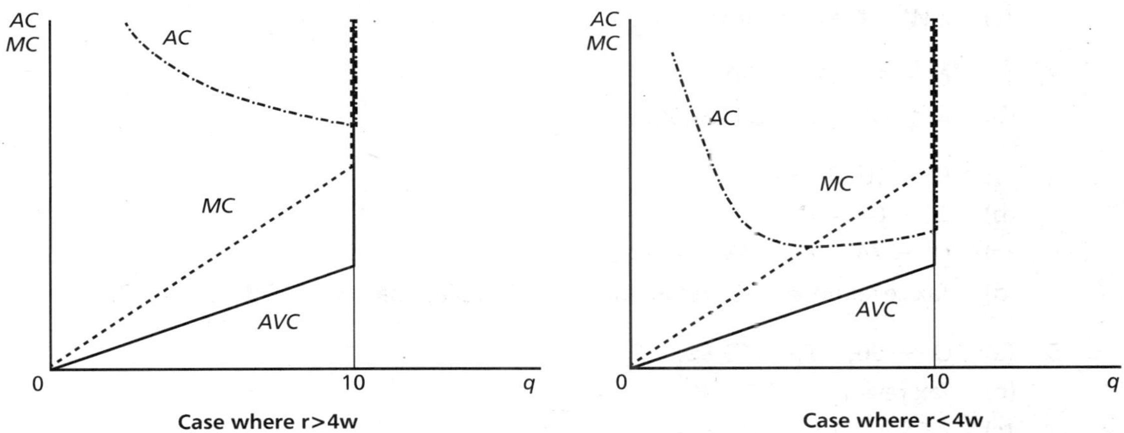


(d) $q_s = \begin{cases} \dfrac{p}{8w} & \text{for } p \leq 80w \\ 10 & \text{for } p > 80w \end{cases}$

10 units.

8. (a) Downward-sloping straight line. $MRTS = \dfrac{2}{3}$.

(b) Decreasing returns to scale.

(c) $C_{SR}(q, K_0) = \begin{cases} 3K_0 & \text{for} \quad q \leq (2K_0)^{\frac{1}{2}} \\ 2q^2 - K_0 & \text{for} \quad q \geq (2K_0)^{\frac{1}{2}} \end{cases}$

(d) $C_{LR}(q) = \frac{3}{2}q^2$.

# CHAPTER 6: MARKETS IN PARTIAL EQUILIBRIUM

1. (a) $w^* = 10,\ L^* = 800$.
   (b) $L^* = 761.5,\ w^* = 10.84$.
   (c) $w_t = 9.76, w_c = 11.93$. Burden greater on firms as demand is less elastic than supply.

2. (a) $Q^* =$ ₹9 million, $p_d^* = 120, p_s^* = 90$.
   (b) $p_{\text{coupon}} = p_d - p_s = 30$.
   (c) $\triangle W =$ ₹890 million.

3. (a) $p^* = 10,\ Q^* = 100$.
   (b) No. $\triangle W = 343.85 < 400$.

4. (a) $P^* = 10, Q^* = 80$.
   (b) $Q_s = 6P - 4$.
   (c) $Q^* = 74, \quad P_d = 13, \quad P_s = 9$.
   (d) Tax revenue = 296, Buyers pay = 222, Sellers pay = 74, DW loss = 12.

5. (a) $Q^* = 96, \quad P_d = 10.80, \quad P_s = 9.80$.
   (b) Tax revenue = 96.
   (c) $\triangle CS = -78.4,\ \triangle PS = -19.6$, Excess burden = 2.

6. (a) $Q_s = p$.
   (b) $p^* = 3, Q^* = 3, q^* = 0.3$.
   (c) $Q^* = 2.5, p_d^* = 3.5, p_s^* = 2.5$.

7. (a) $p^* = 20, Q^* = 3{,}000$.
   (b) $p^* = 10, Q_d^* = 4{,}000, Q_s^* = 1{,}500$, Imports* = 2,500.
   (c) $p^{**} = 15, Q_d^{**} = 3{,}500, Q_s^{**} = 2{,}250$, Imports** = 1,250
   (d) $\triangle W = -3, 125$.

8. (a) $w^* = 4, L^* = 40$.
   (b) $L^* = 30$. $\Delta W$ is indeterminate in the range $-10 \leq \Delta W \leq -70$ because it depends upon how the scarce jobs are rationed.
   $\Delta W_{\text{employers}} = -35, \quad -35 \leq \Delta W_{\text{workers}} \leq 25$.
   (c) $w^* = 4.50, L^* = 45$.
   $\Delta W_{\text{employers}} = 21.25$.
   $\Delta W_{\text{workers}} = 21.25$.
   $\Delta W_{\text{taxpayers}} = -45$.
   Net $\Delta W = 2.50$.

9. (a) $C(q) = 2q^2$.
   (b) $p_1 = 8, q_1 = 2,\ K_1 = 4$.
   (c) $C_{SR}(q) = 4 + \frac{1}{4}q^4$.
   (d) $p_2 = 64, q_2 = 4$.
   (e) $p_3 = (256)^{0.6} \approx 27.858, q_3 \approx 6.9644$.

# CHAPTER 7: GENERAL EQUILIBRIUM AND WELFARE ECONOMICS

1. (a) $W = 2{,}000 - \frac{G^2}{20}$.
   (b) $G^* = 123.6,\ W^* = 1{,}236, p_G = 12.36$.
   (c) Production: $G_p^* = 100,\ W_p^* = 1{,}500$.
   Consumption: $G_c^* = 125, W_c^* = 1{,}250$.

2. (a) $\frac{p_x}{p_y} = 1$.
   (b) $X_s = 14, Y_s = 6; X_j = 10, Y_j = 10$.
   (c) $L_X = 12, L_Y = 8$.

3. (a) $C = 18 - 2F^2, \quad MRT = 4F$.
   (b) $L_c^* = 6,\ L_f^* = 3$.
   (c) $MRT = MRS = 4\sqrt{3}, \left(\frac{p_f}{p_c}\right)^* = 4\sqrt{3}$.

4. (a) $\left(\frac{p_x}{p_y}\right)^* = \frac{3}{2}$.
   (b) $x_s^* = 6, y_s^* = 21; x_j^* = 10, y_j^* = 15; \quad$ Production: $x^* = 16, y^* = 36$.

5. (a) $C = 800 - 4B$.
   (b) $B^* = 100,\ C^* = 400,\ w^* = 4, p_c^* = 1, p_b^* = 4$.

6. $w^* = ₹5,\ L_b = 2{,}000,\ L_c = 8{,}000.$

(a)

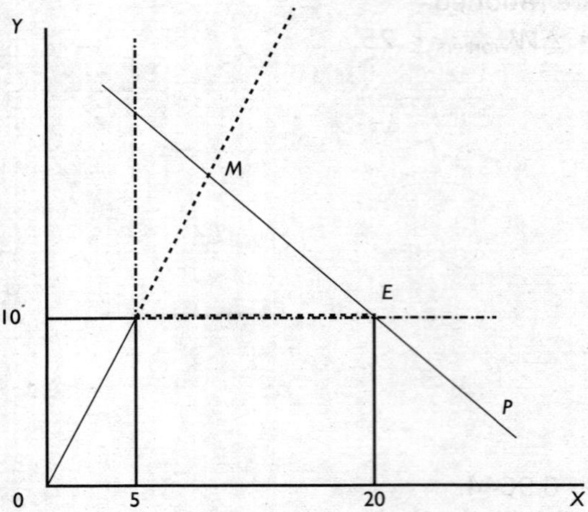


(b)

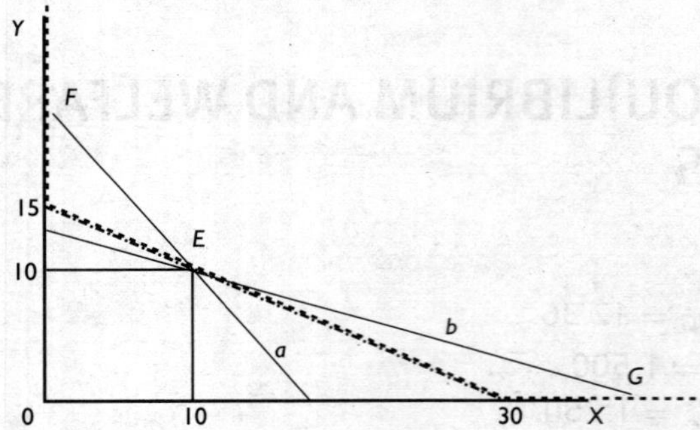


(c) $\left(\frac{p_x}{p_y}\right)^* = \frac{1}{2}$. Ashok will sell 12 units of $X$ and buy 6 units of $Y$; Beena the opposite.

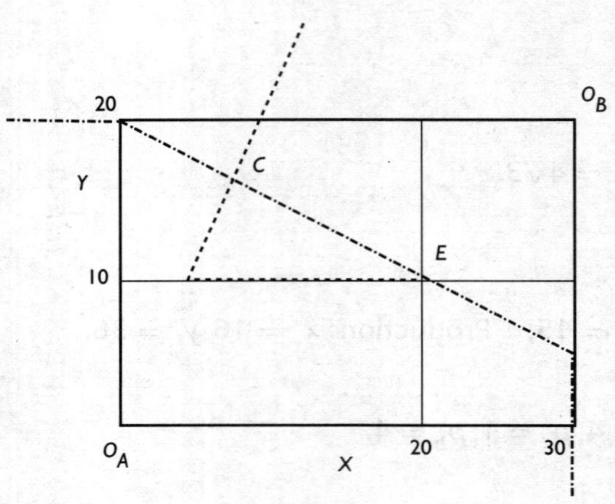

7. (a) $x_j = \dfrac{8p_x}{p_x + 2p_y}$ and $y_j = \dfrac{16p_x}{p_x + 2p_y}$.

$x_b = \dfrac{6p_y}{p_x}$ and $y_b = 6$.

(b) $\left(\dfrac{p_x}{p_y}\right)^* = \dfrac{6}{5}$; $x_j^* = 3, y_j^* = 6$; $x_b^* = 5, y_b^* = 6$.

(c) $\left(\dfrac{p_x}{p_y}\right)^* = 1$; $x_j^* = 4, y_j^* = 8$; $x_b^* = 4, y_b^* = 4$. Jai is better off now, with $U_j = 8 > 6$.

(d) No, because competitive equilibrium is Pareto efficient.

8. (a) Tangency points; see Figure 7.3.

(b) $\left(\dfrac{p_x}{p_y}\right)^* = 2$; $x_A^* = \dfrac{5}{4}, y_A^* = \dfrac{5}{2}$; $x_B^* = \dfrac{15}{4}, y_B^* = \dfrac{15}{2}$.

9. (a) The Pareto efficient allocations have $x_B = y_B$ and $x_B, y_B \leq 10$. The Pareto improving allocations have $x_B = y_B$ and $5 < x_B, y_B \leq 10$. The contract curve is the set of Pareto efficient allocations.

(b) $\left(\dfrac{p_x}{p_y}\right)^* = 1$; $x_A^* = 12.5, y_A^* = 2.5$; $x_B^* = 7.5, y_B^* = 7.5$.

10. (a)

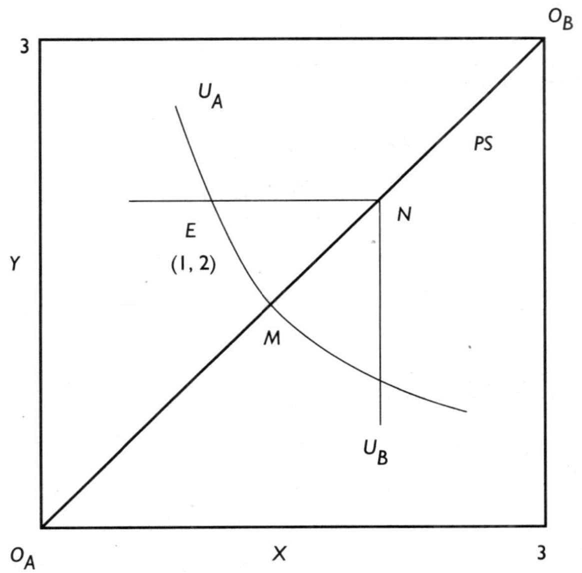


(b) Pareto improvements are on the line segment $MN$ where $A$'s allocations are at $M$: $(\sqrt{2}, \sqrt{2})$, and at $N$: $(2, 2)$.

(c) $\left(\frac{p_x}{p_y}\right)^* = 1; \quad x_A^* = 1.5, y_A^* = 1.5; \quad x_B^* = 1.5, y_B^* = 1.5.$

# CHAPTER 8: UNCERTAINTY AND INFORMATION

1. (a) 2.50.
   (b) 2.40.
   (c) (a) is bigger because of risk aversion.
   (d) 0.10.
2. (a) 9.184.
   (b) 250. Yes, he will buy it.
   (c) 260.
   (d) 300. No, he will not buy it, his expected utility is higher without insurance: 9.184 > 9.18.
3. (a) 25.
   (b) No.
   (c) 475.
4. (a) Yes. $EU_{\text{project}} = 102.4 > 100 = EU_{\text{no project}}$.
   (b) No. $EU_{\text{project}} = 9.6 < 10 = EU_{\text{no project}}$.
   (c) With $U(y) = y$, Yes: $EU_{\text{survey}} = 111.2 > 102.4 = EU_{\text{no survey}}$.
   With $U(y) = \sqrt{y}$, Yes: $EU_{\text{survey}} = 10.228 > 10 = EU_{\text{no survey}}$.
   (d) $x$ is the solution to

$$0.8(100 - x)^{\frac{1}{2}} + 0.2(100 - x - 36 + 192)^{\frac{1}{2}} = 10.$$

   Solving: $x = 24.39$.
5. (a) Corn. $EU_{\text{corn}} = 137.066 > 136.603 = EU_{\text{wheat}}$.
   (b) Yes. $EU_{\text{mixed}} = 137.296$.
   (c) 38.1% wheat, 61.9% corn.
6. (a) −20.
   (b) Yes. $EU_{\text{well}} = 6.598 > 6.425 = EU_{\text{no well}}$.
7. (a) $E_{\text{wet}}(Y) = 82, E_{\text{dry}}(Y) = 65$.
   (b) He is indifferent. $EU_{\text{wheat}} = 8.5 = EU_{\text{rice}}$.
   (c) 49.65%.
   (d) He will plant rice and buy insurance. $EU_{\text{rice}} = 8.63 > 8.56 = EU_{\text{mixed crop}}$.

8. (a) Option (iii) as $EU_{iii} = 620.20 > EU_{ii} = 616.36 > EU_{i} = 512.35$.
   (b) Fair premium = 135,000. Max WTP = 167,500.

9. (a) $W_{fire} = 60{,}000 + (1 - \pi)x, \quad W_{no\ fire} = 100{,}000 - \pi x$.
   (b) 0.10.
   (c) Full insurance (40,000). $EU_{insured} = 11.47$.
   (d) Zero insurance. $EU = 11.46$.

# CHAPTER 9: MONOPOLY AND MARKET POWER

1. (a) $p_{LR} = 4, Q_{LR} = 10{,}000$, number of firms = 500.
   (b) $p_m = 8, Q_m = 2{,}500$, number of plants = 125.
   (c) $DW\ Loss = 10{,}000$.

2. (a) $L_c = 266.67, w_c = 3.33$.
   (b) $L_m = 200, w_m = 2.5$.
   (c) In both cases, $w = 4,\ L = 240$. So employment will fall in the competitive case but rise in the monopsony case.

3. (a) $DWL_c = 12.5$.
   (b) $DWL_m = 115.625$.
   (c) DWL is much higher under monopoly because output is already restricyed and $p > MC$.

4. (a) $q^* = 30, Q_h^* = 20, p_h = 30, Q_x = 10, p_x = 10$.
   (b) $q^* = 19.286, Q_h^* = 19.286, p_h = 30.714, Q_x = 0, p_x = 10$

5. (a) 50 pelts. $p_{untreated} = 75, p_{treated} = 160$.
   (b) 100 pelts. $p^*_{untreated} = 100, p^*_{treated} = 110$.

6. (a) $x_1 = 20, p_1 = 800$.
   (b) $x_2 = 20, p_2 = 400$.
   (c) $x^* = 30, p^* = 600$.

7. (a) $p_m = 70, Q_m = 30, L_m = 15, w_m = 50$.
   (b) $p^* = 40, Q^* = 60, L^* = 30, w^* = 80$.

8. (a) $Q = 2{,}000 - 200p$.
   (b) $p_m = 5, \pi_m = 5{,}000$.
   (c) $F_f = 72, \pi_f = 7{,}200$.
   (d) Two bundles: 4 rides at 24, and 12 rides at 56. $\pi^* = 8{,}000$.

9. (a) $q^s = p - 10. \quad Q^s = 50p - 500$.
   (b) $p_{SR} = 20.5, Q_{SR} = 525, q_{SR} = 10.5$.

(c) $p_{LR} = 16, Q_{LR} = 1{,}200, q_{LR} = 6, n_{LR} = 200.$
(d) $p_{mSR} = 21.2, Q_{mSR} = 420, q_{mSR} = 8.4.$
(e) $p_{mLR} = 20, Q_{mLR} = 600, q_{mLR} = 6, n_{LR} = 100.$

10. (a) $p_{SR} = 80, Q_{SR} = 80, q_{SR} = 0.8, \pi_{SR} = -18$ (or $+32$ if fixed cost is ignored).
(b) $p_{LR} = 100, Q_{LR} = 60, q_{LR} = 1, n_{LR} = 60.$
(c) $p_T = 100,\ Q_T = 60, q_T = 60, q_{\text{fringe}} = 0, n_{\text{fringe}} = 0.$
(d) $\Delta W = +3{,}500.$

11. (a) $p_1 = 30,\ Q_1 = 25, p_2 = 16.25,\ Q_2 = 22.5.$
(b) $p_1' = 24.17,\ Q_1' = 30.83, p_2' = 19.17,\ Q_2' = 16.67.$

12. (a) $Q_{SR} = 225, q_{SR} = 2.5,\ Q_{aSR} = 50,\ Q_{bSR} = 175, p_{aSR} = p_{bSR} = 15.$
(b) $Q_{LR} = 300, q_{LR} = 2,\ Q_{aLR} = 100,\ Q_{bLR} = 200, p_{aLR} = p_{bLR} = 10, n = 150.$
(c) $Q_m = 150, q_m = 2,\ Q_{am} = 50,\ Q_{bm} = 100, p_{am} = 15, p_{bm} = 30, n = 75.$
(d) $Q_m' = 150, q_m' = 2,\ Q_{am}' = 0,\ Q_{bm}' = 150, p_{am}' = p_{bm}' = 20, n' = 75.$

13. (a) $p^* = 6,\ Q^* = 4,\ CS = 8.$
(b) $p_s = 4, \Delta CS = 10, \Delta\pi = 0,$ Subsidy $= 12 > \Delta CS + \Delta\pi.$
(c) Part (a): $p_m = 8, Q_m = 2,$ CS $= 2.$
Part (b): $p_{ms} = 7, \Delta CS_m = 2.5, \Delta\pi_m = 5,$ Subsidy$_m = 6 < \Delta CS_m + \Delta\pi_m.$

14. (a) $p_1^* = 2, p_2^* = 1.5, \epsilon_1 = -2, \epsilon_2 = -3.$
(b) Output goes to zero as the firm would shut down.
(c) Yes, because otherwise it would make losses and shut down.

# CHAPTER 10: THE THEORY OF GAMES

1. (a) (compete, compete) is the only NE.
(b) Because 'compete' is a dominant strategy for both players.
(c) AIR's max = 60. RMS's min = 20.

2. (a) NE: (T,LL),(T,LR),(B,RR).
(b) SPE: (T,LR).

3. (a) $q_G = 4, q_L = 1.$

(b)

| | | $q_L$ | |
|---|---|---|---|
| | | 1 | 2 |
| $q_G$ | 4 | 80,20 | 64,32 |
| | 5 | 80,16 | 60,24 |

(c) $q_G = 4, q_L = 2$ are both dominant strategies.

4. (a) NE: (T,L),(B,R).

(b) Mixed Strategy Equilibrium: $\left(T : \frac{1}{2} \text{ and } B : \frac{1}{2}, L : \frac{3}{4} \text{ and } R : \frac{1}{4}\right)$.

(c)

| | LL | LR | RL | RR |
|---|---|---|---|---|
| T | 10,5 | 10,5 | 5,3 | 5,3 |
| B | 5,0 | 20,2 | 5,0 | 20,2 |

(d) NE: (T,LL),(B,LR),(B,RR).
SPE: (B,LR).

# CHAPTER 11: MARKET STRUCTURES BETWEEN COMPETITION AND MONOPOLY

1. (a) No, because $\Delta\pi_I = 43{,}750 < 60{,}000$. Yes, because $\Delta W_I = 65{,}625 > 60{,}000$.

(b) Max WTP $= \Delta\pi_I = 43{,}750$.

(c) Rival would enter because $\pi_R = 75{,}000 > 60{,}000$. Yes, it s socially desirable because $\Delta W_R = 103{,}125 > 60{,}000$.

(d) Incumbent's Max WTP $= \pi_I = 100{,}000$, because the alternative now is to be driven out of business.

2. (a) $Q = 10{,}000, p = 15, \pi = 100{,}000$.

(b) $p_c = \frac{40}{3}, \pi_P = \frac{625{,}000}{9}, \pi_K = \frac{100{,}000}{9}$.

(c) CRC could ask up to $\frac{100{,}000}{9}$. Polaroid would pay $\frac{275{,}000}{9}$, which is more, because it would like to preserve its monopoly.

3. (a) $Q_m = 10, p_m = 6$.

(b) $Q^* = 40, p^* = 3$.

(c) $\Delta W = -30$ ($-45$ if linearity is assumed).

(d) $Q_c = 22.5, p_c = 4, q_1 = q_2 = 11.25$.

4. (a) $p_c = \frac{1{,}300}{3}, q_s = \frac{500}{3}, q_e = \frac{350}{3}$.

(b) $p_2 = 575, q_{s2} = \frac{950}{8}, q_{e2} = 93.75$.

(c) $p_3 = 350, q_{s3} = 250, q_{e3} = 75$.

5. (a) $q_a = 120, p_a = 180, \pi_a = 14{,}400$.

(b) $q_{a2} = q_{b2} = 80, p_2 = 140, \pi_a = \pi_b = 6{,}400$.

(c) $q_{a3} = q_{b3} = 60, p_3 = 180, \pi_a = \pi_b = 7{,}200.$

(d) $q_{a4} = 60, q_{b4} = 90, p_4 = 150, \pi_a = 5{,}400, \pi_b = 8{,}100.$

6. (a) $q_a = 8, p_a = 6, \pi_a = 36.$

(b) $q_{a2} = q_{b2} = 4, p_2 = 6, \pi_a = 16, \pi_b = 12.$

(c) Entry-deterring: $q_{a3} = 8, q_{b3} = 0, p_3 = 6, \pi_a = 32, \pi_b = 0.$

7. (a) $q_1 = 40 - \frac{1}{2}q_2$ and $q_2 = 50 - \frac{1}{2}q_1.$

$q_1^* = 20, q_2^* = 40, p^* = 40, \pi_1^* = 400, \pi_2^* = 1{,}600.$

(b) $q_1^{**} = 10, q_2^{**} = 60, p^{**} = 30, \pi_1^{**} = 100, \pi_2^{**} = 1{,}800.$

(c) $\Delta W = +550.$

8. (a) $q_1^* = 8, q_2^* = 2, p^* = 10, \pi_1^* = 32, \pi_2^* = 2.$

(b) $q_1^{**} = 9, q_2^{**} = 0, p^{**} = 10.5, \pi_1^{**} = 40.5, \pi_2^{**} = 0.$

(c) Firm 1 would pay 8.5 for firm 2 and would require 32 to be bought out. Firm 2 would pay 38.5 for firm 1 and would require 2 to be bought out.

9. (a) $Q^* = 4, q_A^* = 4, q_B^* = 0.$

(b) $q_A^{**} = 0, q_B^{**} = 3.8.$

(c) $q_A^C = 2.8, q_B^C = 2.4, \pi_A^C = 19.2, \pi_B^C = 18.8.$

(d) Acme would pay 30.8 to take over Best. Best would pay 31.2 to take over Acme.

10. (a) $p^* = 40,\ Q^* = 60, q_i^* = 30.$

(b) $p^C = 64,\ Q^C = 36, q_i^C = 18.$

(c) $\Delta CS = -1{,}152, \Delta\pi = +720.$

(d) $\Delta W = -432.$

11. (a) $x_A^* = 1, x_B^* = 4.$

(b) $x_A^e = 1, x_B^e = 1.$

(c) $s_A = 0, s_B = \frac{1}{2}.$

(d) Any $T_A, T_B$ such that $T_A + T_B = 2.$

12. (a) $w_T^C = 4, w_H^C = 4, \pi_T^C = 8{,}000, \pi_H^C = 8{,}000.$

(b) Same solution as in (a).

(c) $w_T^* = 0, w_H^* = 0.$

13. (a) $Q^C = \frac{16}{3}.$

(b) $Q^* = 4, p^* = 6.$

(c) $Q^S = 6, p^S = 4.$

(d) $\pi_1^C = \pi_2^C = \frac{64}{9}; \pi_1^* = \pi_2^* = 8; \pi_1^S = 8, \pi_2^S = 4.$

# CHAPTER 12: EXTERNALITIES AND PUBLIC GOODS

1. (a) $L_x^c = 10, L_y^c = 10, Q^c = 100.$
   (b) $L_x^* = 5, L_y^* = 15, Q^* = 112.5.$
   (c) $F_x^* = 2.5, F_y^* = 0.$
2. (a) $Q^* = 20{,}000, p^* = 5.$
   (b) $Q^e = 16{,}000, p^e = 9.$
   (c) $Q^a = \frac{100{,}000}{6}, p^a = \frac{50}{6}.$
3. (a) $n^e = 2{,}800.$
   (b) $F^* = 10.$
4. (a) $a_1 = 7, \pi_1 = 9.$
   (b) $a_2 = 7, \pi_2 = 149.$
   (c) Either is optimal if marginal damage is 14. (a) is preferable because it raises revenue.
5. (a) $Q^* = 26{,}000, p^* = 24.$
   (b) $Q^c = 30{,}000, p^c = 20, DWL = 12{,}000.$
   (c) $t^* = 6.$ $\Delta CS = -112{,}000, \Delta PS = -56{,}000,$ Tax Revenue $=$ $+156{,}000,$ Environment $= +24{,}000.$
   (d) $Q^a = 26{,}000, a^a = 30{,}000, \Delta W = 45{,}000.$
6. (a) $n^e = 190, Q^e = 1{,}900.$
   (b) $n^* = 95, Q^* = 9{,}975.$
   (c) Charge licence fee of 9,500. Budgetary impact $= +902{,}500.$
7. (a) $Q^s = 90p, p^c = 5, Q^c = 450, q_A^c = 5, q_B^c = \frac{24}{5}, \pi_A^c = \frac{25}{2}, \pi_B^c = \frac{125}{8}.$
   (b) $Q^* = 405, q_A^* = \frac{9}{2}, q_B^* = \frac{45}{8}.$
   (c) $x_A^a = 2, x_B^a = \frac{5}{2}, t^a = 1.$

# INDEX